SECOND EDITION

Improving the Teaching
of Reading

EMERALD V. DECHANT
President and Professor of Education
Marymount College of Kansas
Salina, Kansas

PRENTICE-HALL, INC. Englewood Cliffs, New Jersey

To my wife, Deloris,
and to our children, Randy, Lori, and Pami

© 1970, 1964 by Prentice-Hall, Inc., Englewood Cliffs, New Jersey

13–453415–8

Library of Congress Catalog Card Number: 78–102932

Current printing (last digit):
10 9 8 7 6 5 4

PRINTED IN THE UNITED STATES OF AMERICA

Prentice-Hall International, Inc., London
Prentice-Hall of Australia, Pty. Ltd., Sydney
Prentice-Hall of Canada, Ltd., Toronto
Prentice-Hall of India Private Limited, New Delhi
Prentice-Hall of Japan, Inc., Tokyo

Contents

Introducing the Pupil to Reading: The experience chart, Basal reading materials, Preprimers, primers, and first readers. *Teaching Reading:* Picture reading, Association of sound with the whole word, Use of the verbal context, Learning the names of the letters, The manuscript formation of the letter, Association of sound with the beginning consonant and medial vowel letter. *Group vs. Individualized Instruction:* Ability grouping, Individualized reading, The need for eclecticism in classroom organization. *The Primary Program. The Intermediate Reading Program. Rate Skills:* Tachistoscopes, Accelerating devices, Reading-related machines, Skimming and scanning, Evaluation of machine programs. *Readability. Efficiency in Reading:* Type sizes, Kinds of type, Leading, Illumination, Color and contrast. *Summary. Questions for Discussion.*

Terminology. The Phonetic Consistency of Our Language. Linguistic Systems of Teaching Reading. The Order of Priority in Sounds. The Sequence of Phonic Skills. The Beginning Consonant: Teaching the beginning consonant; The letters B, C, D, G, H, J, M, N, P, T, W; The letters F, L, R, and S; The letters K and Q; The letters V, X, Y, Z; The soft sounds of C and G. *Teaching the Short Vowel. Teaching the End Consonant. Teaching Structural Analysis Skills:* Teaching S, Teaching the compounds, Teaching -ing, The past tense with ed, Prefixes and suffixes, The possessive case and contractions. *Summary. Questions for Discussion.*

Teaching the Beginning Consonant Blends. Teaching the Ending Consonant Blends. The Speech Consonants—ch, sh, th, wh, gh, ph: The diagraph ch, The diagraphs sh and th, The diagraphs wh, gh, ph. *The Long Vowels:* The principle of variability, The principle of position, The principle of silentness. *The Diphthongs:* Au and Aw, Oi and Oy, The combination Oo. *Other Vowel Combinations:* The combination Ei (Ey), The combination Ie, The combination Ou, The combination Ow, The combinations Ew, Ue, Ui. *Teaching the Long Vowels. The Effect of R on a Preceding Vowel. The Effect of W on A. Syllabication:* Rule I, Rule II, Exceptions and observations. *Accentuation. Silent Letters. Multisyllabic Words. Common Sight Words. Summary. Questions for Discussion.*

Part V ADVANCING THE PUPIL'S READING SKILLS

Problems in Developing Meaning. Conceptualization: The percept, Perceptual schematism, Contextual perception, Perception of difference, Abstract concept, Categorization. *Generalization. Techniques for Teaching Meaning:* Study and analysis of the context, Synonyms and antonyms, Qualifying words, Overworked words and phrases, Homonyms, Roots, prefixes, and suffixes, Compound words, Figurative and idiomatic expressions, Developing skill in using punctuation marks as clues to meaning, Study of dictionary, text glossaries, and word lists,

Study of word origins and change, Study of technical vocabularies. *A Summary of Techniques for Improving Vocabulary. Summary. Questions for Discussion.*

13   Advancing the Pupil's Comprehension Skills   400

Comprehension Skills. Developing Comprehension Skills: Word meaning, Phrase meaning, Sentence meaning, Paragraph meaning, Reading the context, Reading for the main idea, Reading for details, Reading for the organization, Reading for evaluation (critical reading), Reading for learning. *Reading Maps, Charts, and Graphs:* Reading maps, Reading graphs, Reading tables, Reading charts. *Comprehension in a Specific Content Area:* Literature, Social studies, Mathematics, Science. *Summary. Questions for Discussion.*

Part VI   DIAGNOSTIC TEACHING OF READING

14   Diagnosis and Remediation   450

Definition of Diagnosis. Principles of Diagnosis: Steps in diagnosis. *Step 1—The Screening Process:* The nature of retardation, Reading potential, Reading achievement. *Step 2—Diagnostic Testing:* Personal data sheet, Learning and behavior checklist, Formal or informal inventory, Oral reading tests, Diagnostic reading tests, The symptomatology of reading disability, The developmental reading program, The teacher's task. *Step 3—A Detailed Investigation of Causality. Step 4—Remediation:* Decisions required of the teacher, Principles of remediation, Systematic instruction in the basic reading skills, Organizing for corrective and remedial reading. *Meeting Individual Needs:* The slow learner, The disadvantaged reader, The gifted learner. *Remedial Methods:* Monroe method, Fernald method, The united phonics methods, The color phonics system, The progressive choice reading method, Gillingham method. *Evaluating Remedial Instruction. Summary. Questions for Discussion.*

Part VII   THEORY AND PRACTICE IN TEACHING

15   Understanding the Reading-Learning Process   516

Teaching. The Determinants of Reading Success: Individual variables, Task variables, Method variables, Institutional variables. *Stimulus-Response Theories of Learning—An Overview. Field Theories—An Overview:* Emphasis on cognitive processes, Emphasis on purposive behavior, Emphasis on learning as an organizational process, Emphasis on the contemporary experience, Emphasis of wholes rather than parts. *Thorndike's Connectionism:* The law of readiness, The law of exercise, Motivation and learning, The law of effect, The law of belongingness, summary. *Guthrie's Contiguous Association:* The behaviorism of Watson, Pavlov's classical conditioning, The law of contiguity. *Skinner's Operant Conditioning. Hull's Habit Theory:* Reaction potential, Effective reaction potential, Momentary reaction potential. *Field Theory:* The perceptual process, Going beyond the sensory data, The central intermediary, The role of experience and organization, Perceptions and the reading process. *The Field Concept:* Characteristics of the perceptual field, Observations and inferences, Differentiation. *Kurt Lewin and Edward Tolman. S–R and Field Theories Compared. Summary and Conclusion. Questions for Discussion.*

READING—AN OVERVIEW

part

The Latins had a phrase, *"tot capita, tot sententiae,"* that perhaps best describes our predicament when we seek to define reading. There are just about as many descriptions or definitions of reading as there are "reading experts." Let us then reserve our definition of reading until later and list here eight characteristics of reading:

1. *Reading is a sensory process*

    Reading requires the use of the senses, especially vision. The reader must react visually to the graphic symbols. The symbols themselves must be legible, the eyes must see clearly and singly, and the light must be adequate. The good reader must also *hear* the sounds in words. The pupil needs to be able to make proper associations between the spoken sound and the graphic symbol.

2. *Reading is a perceptual process*

    Reading occurs when meaning is brought to graphic stimuli. It is a progressive apprehension of the meanings and ideas represented by a sequence of words. It includes seeing the word, recognition of the word, awareness of the word's meaning, and relating the word to its context. This is perception in its fullest sense.

3. *Reading is a response*

    Reading is a system of responses made to some graphic stimuli. These include the vocal and/or subvocal muscular responses made at the sight of the word, the eye movements during reading, physical adaptations to the reading act such as postural changes, the critical and evaluative responses to what is being read, the emotional involvement of the reader, and meaningful reactions to the words.

4. *Reading is a learned response*

Reading is a response that must be learned by the child and is under control of the mechanisms of motivation and reinforcement. Reading is a perceptual process, but it is also an associative process. It involves the *learned* association of the spoken with the written word. The same laws of learning that govern all other learned processes govern the child's learning to read.

5. *Reading is a developmental task*

Developmental tasks have one basic characteristic: the child's readiness for them depends on the child's general development. There is a most teachable moment for beginning reading and for each of the specific skills in reading. The child's level of achievement in reading depends on his over-all growth and development.

6. *Reading can be an interest and a motive*

Reading may become an interest or a goal in its own right. It then may motivate other activity.

7. *Reading is a learning process*

Reading may become one of the chief media for learning. The child can use reading to acquire knowledge and to change his own attitudes, ideals, and aspirations. Genuine reading involves integration and promotes the development of the reader. As Aldous Huxley points out, "Every man who knows how to read has it in his power to magnify himself, to multiply the ways in which he exists, to make his life full, significant and interesting."

8. *Reading is a language process*

Reading is a process of putting the reader in contact and communication with ideas. It is the culminating act of the communicative and language process, initiated by the thoughts of the writer and expressed through the symbols on the printed page. Communication from writer to reader occurs only if the reader can take meaning to the printed page. Without the reader, communication via the printed page is impossible.

Part One consists of two chapters. Chapter 1, the "Introduction," identifies the general goals of reading and the specific goals of this book. Chapter 2, entitled "The Nature of the Reading Process," deals primarily with the sensory and perceptual nature of the reading process. It emphasizes that reading is:

> . . . a perfect interaction between ocular functions and interpretive factors. The reader coordinates his eyes as he moves them along the lines of print in a left-to-right fashion, stopping to perceive words or word-parts which he continuously adds up into thought units. He interprets what he reads in light of his background, associates it with past experience, and projects beyond it in terms of ideas, judgments, applications, and conclusions.[1]

[1] Stanford E. Taylor, Helen Frackenpohl, and James L. Pettee, *Grade Level Norms for the Components of the Fundamental Reading Skill* (Huntington, New York: Educational Developmental Laboratories, Inc.), Bulletin No. 3, 1960, p. 1. Reprinted by permission.

Introduction

In this introduction we should like to identify the general goals of reading instruction and the particular goals of this book. Goals of teaching reading have changed constantly through the years, and being able to identify them seems to be a first essential for an effective reading program.

In 1927 Young (19, pp. 1–2), for example, included the following among the objectives of reading instruction: increase in vocabulary, eye span, and comprehension; promotion of the desire to read many books; development of rhythmic eye movements; reduction of regressions and fixations; rapid reading of easy material; intense concentration for short periods; and elimination of vocalization.

In all fairness we must admit that some of these goals have never been fully attained. For example, we have not yet developed a permanent interest in reading in many pupils. There also is still room for much improvement in reading achievement generally. Perhaps 25 per cent of high school and college students are not reading up to their ability. An even larger percentage of students may not be reading at grade level (17), and the most seriously retarded youngsters in reading frequently are those with high intelligence.

But as significant as these inadequacies is the fact that Young's statement of goals is inadequate today. Our reading goals have been broadened and our emphasis has shifted.

Smith (14) has outlined reading development over the last fifty or sixty years. Her analysis will help us to identify this broadening and shifting of goals.

The 1910–1920 decade initiated the trend away from the centuries-old emphasis on the physiology of reading and on oral reading. Reading was viewed more from a psychological perspective. The advantages of silent reading were emphasized particularly in studies by Buswell and Judd (3, 10). In 1917 Thorndike (16) had already clearly delineated the differences between simply saying the words to oneself as one read and understanding what was being read. He compared the reading of a paragraph to the process of solving a problem.

The 1920–1930 decade continued the emphasis on silent reading and comprehension and stressed individual differences and remedial reading. With increased emphasis on individual differences came a greater demand for psychological testing and statistical and experimental methods were applied to the analysis of the child's behavior.

The emphasis away from oral reading and toward silent reading was perhaps too great. In fact, in the 1950's, some schools were severely criticized (perhaps rightfully so) because they had abandoned formal instructions in oral reading (18). Oral reading was taught, but it never again occupied the same eminent place as prior to the 1920's.

Gates' *The Improvement of Reading* (7) developed a trend in diagnosis and remediation. Reading retardation was viewed as a complex process explainable only by a group or syndrome of related causes or factors.

The 1930–1940 period was not noted for its innovations. It was rather a period of consolidation. The concept of reading readiness became more intrenched and broadened. Thus, readiness was extended to include readiness for high school, college, and adult reading. More attention was focused on remedial reading and on reading materials. The quantity of books and supplementary reading materials increased tremendously.

In 1940 much of the world was at war. With it came the stark reality that many youths could not read sufficiently well to understand simple Army literature. Reading was taught to these men.

The 1940's also were accompanied by emphasis on reading in the content areas.

In the early 1950's the trend which began in the 1940's continued. There was perhaps a greater realization by all the teachers that they had a responsibility in reading.

Then in 1957 with the launching of the Russian satellite came a new era in reading. Suddenly, national shortcomings were attributed to so-called classroom failures, especially reading failures. Public education became the whipping boy for loss of pride on the international scene.

Unfortunately, the cause so readily found by so many was rarely the true cause and the solutions advanced for educational inadequacies in general, and reading in particular, if indeed there were any, were frequently neither realistic nor satisfactory. Little has been gained by going back to the "good old days." The words of Will Rogers come to mind: "Things ain't what they used to be, and probably never was."

Crowded classrooms and teacher shortages are no less causes of educational inadequacies than is teacher ineffectiveness, and yet, teachers and teaching methods bore the brunt of public attack.

Criticism is essential to success in education. Some criticism stimulates action, arouses interest, squelches apathy, and restores balance. Unfortunately, not all criticism directed at the schools and at teachers of reading has been of this kind. Teachers of reading were forced to contend with the nagging, carping type of criticism that like a perpetual hailstorm unleashes an unmerciful beating. This type quite frequently either stifles all growth and development or leads to meagre growth in an atmosphere of bitterness and discontent.[1]

Teachers always have had to bear the brunt of criticism for inadequacies in reading instruction. Cribbin (5)[2] has so ably described the teacher's plight that we quote him directly. He writes:

All the king's horses
And all the king's men
Couldn't put Humpty Dumpty
Together again.

But had they been teachers,
The critics and screechers
Would have demanded with ire
That he be made whole and entire.

Although some few teachers may indeed take off in September, cover a predetermined amount of material, and land in June only to find that one by one students have been lost, the greatest number of teachers are doing an excellent job.

Although some few teachers have found a scapegoat for their own inadequacy (It is not uncommon for such a teacher to say: "The child is a product of his environment"; "He never had a chance"; "He is emotionally disturbed"; "His parents are culturally backward"; "Teachers aren't paid enough"; or "Parents aren't strict enough with their children"), the average teacher neither has sought scapegoats nor has he given up the ideals of his profession. He has maintained that precarious inner balance required in teaching. He believes in an ideal goal, but is

---

[1] For a discussion of these misuses of criticism see Hanson (8).

[2] Reprinted from the October, 1959 issue of *Education,* by permission of the publishers, The Bobbs-Merrill Co., Indianapolis, Indiana.

compassionate toward those who miss the mark; he respects excellence, even glories in it, but at the same time respects struggle and understands failure (4, p. 78).

The 1957 furor, as we look back upon it, probably had a good effect. Reading may have come of age in the last decade. In the 1960's, the emphasis in reading was on specialization. The profession became more concerned with the respective roles of the classroom teacher, the reading specialist, and the reading consultant. Federal programs allowed for greater emphasis on correction and remediation. Teachers themselves became increasingly concerned with the prevention of reading disability. A clear distinction was drawn between the retarded reader, the slow learner, the reluctant reader, and the disadvantaged reader. State departments in increasing numbers began to issue reading certificates. Teachers wanted to know what the basic ingredients of good diagnostic procedure are, how to become a better observer of the symptoms of reading disability, and how to hook symptoms to their proper cause. There was a proliferation of methods of teaching reading. Linguistics and its significance in reading was studied and analyzed.

In October 1964 Congress passed the Economic Opportunity Act, out of which developed Project Head Start. In the same year, the Cooperative Research Program in First and Second Grade Reading Instruction, which resulted in a series of coordinated studies and which was a major undertaking of the U.S. Office of Education, was initiated.

In 1966, the U.S. Office of Education established the Educational Resources Information Center (ERIC). This nationwide retrieval center makes available information derived from the accelerated programs in research and development. It collects, stores, reduces, retrieves, disseminates, and analyzes information. The ERIC Clearinghouse on Retrieval of Information and Evaluation on Reading (ERIC/CRIER) is located at Indiana University. It is responsible for acquiring research reports, materials, and information on all aspects of reading behavior, with special emphasis on physiology, psychology, sociology, and the teaching of reading. It includes reports on the development and evaluation of instructional materials, curricula, tests and measurements, preparation of reading teachers and specialists, methodology at all levels, the role of libraries and other agencies in fostering and guiding reading, and diagnostic and remedial services in schools and clinic settings.

The year 1968 marked the beginning of the *Journal of Learning Disabilities,* a multidisciplinary journal dealing with learning disabilities. The diagnostic forces of the professional world began to pool their resources to cope with learning and reading problems, asking: "Why has this child a learning disability?" and "What can be done to remove it?"

The 1960's saw a merger of hardware and software distributors, with hardware distributors buying major book publishing companies (CBS–Holt, Rinehart and Winston; Litton Industries–American Book Company; Raytheon–D. C. Heath).

The computerized age came into its own. We began speaking of and engaging in computer-assisted instruction. Increasing focus was on electronic innovations in education, on computer systems, computer programs, and computer-based instructional strategies.

The question arises, "Can we summarize our reading goals?" Perhaps our goals today are best described as the goals of a developmental reading program whose basic aims are:

1. The developmental program coordinates reading with the pupil's other communicative experiences.

2. The developmental program is a continuous program extending through the elementary and secondary grades and college. It provides instruction and guidance in basic reading skills, both silent and oral, in content-area reading, in study skills, and in recreational-reading.

3. The developmental program is a flexible program that is adjusted at each level of advancement to the wide variations in pupil characteristics, abilities, and reading needs. Readiness for reading as a concept is applied at all age and grade levels.

4. The developmental program has a stimulating classroom setting in which attitudes and interests favorable to the development of habitual reading are developed effectively.

5. The developmental program provides plentiful reading materials, basal readers, experience charts, films, film readers, etc. that cover a wide range of difficulty and interest.

6. The developmental program provides for continuous measurement and evaluation of the effectiveness of the program as a whole and of its more specific aspects.

7. The developmental program provides for continuous identification and immediate remediation of deficiencies and difficulties encountered by any pupil.

8. The developmental program includes differentiated instruction to meet the needs of each child, but it does not ignore the commonality of needs, interests, and abilities among children.

9. The developmental program looks upon reading as a perceptual process rather than as a subject. Reading is taught on all levels in all subject areas by all teachers.

10. The developmental program emphasizes reading for understanding, thinking, and learning and aims to develop critical skills and flexibility in comprehension and rate in accordance

with the pupil's abilities and purposes and the difficulty levels of the materials.

11. The developmental program allows each pupil to progress at his own success rate to his maximum capacity.

12. The developmental program seeks to develop reading maturity. A mature reader reads all kinds of materials. He perceives words quickly and accurately and reacts with correct meaning. He reads both for information and recreation. He gets personal satisfaction from reading. He is a skillful, self-reliant reader who enriches his understandings and satisfactions throughout his life by reading.

13. The developmental program, based on sequential instruction in the basic skills and upon the need for differentiated instruction, gives appropriate emphasis to the sight and phonic methods and to group and individualized instruction.

Certainly, these goals are formidable. How to achieve these goals and how best to proceed so as to help us come closer to their attainment is difficult to outline.

In this book we hope to describe the nature of the reading process and then to deal with this process in the various stages of reading development. Thus, much emphasis will be given to reading readiness, to the problems associated with "learning to read," to "reading for learning," and to "correction and remediation in learning."

Since we feel that the teaching of reading functions best when it is one phase of the total communicative process, the book will emphasize the early language experiences of the child. It will attempt to relate the psychology of reading to the everyday problems facing the teacher in the classroom. It will emphasize phonics instruction more than most books because it is our firm conviction that children early need to learn a code that is useful in identifying words.

A study by Aaron (1), involving 293 students[3] enrolled in an introductory reading course, suggests that many teachers and prospective teachers need to acquire in college even the most basic phonic generalizations. 213 students, or 73 per cent, got less than forty items of a sixty-item phonic test correct. The mean score of correct answers was 34. Teachers with experience generally scored better than those without experience, but teachers at the primary level did not score better than teachers at other grade levels. Spache and Baggett's study (15) essentially corroborated these findings, but their experienced teachers had no greater knowledge of syllabication principles than did the inexperienced

---

[3] The composition of the group was: 189 without teaching experience; 42 with 1–5 years of experience; 24 with 6–10 years; and 38 with 10 or more years experience.

teachers. The teachers answered correctly 75 per cent of the phonics, 91 per cent of the syllabication, and 68 per cent of the syllabication rules test questions. The junior and senior high school teachers were significantly poorer in knowledge of phonics.

The items on Aaron's test measured ability in dealing with:

1. Vowels in open syllables;
2. Vowels in closed syllables;
3. Silent e preceded by a long vowel (mete);
4. Long vowel before a silent second vowel (boat);
5. C before e, i, or y;
6. G before e, i, or y;
7. Vowels followed by r; and
8. The vowel a followed by l.

Ramsey (12), after studying reading manuals to determine what phonic skills the teacher of reading needed, developed a test to measure the teacher's competencies in these. He then administered the *Test of Word Recognition Skills* to 236 students from five teacher-education colleges. All of the students were planning to become elementary teachers and had not yet taken the first course in methods of teaching reading.

The students knew their consonant sounds, but were weak in vowels, in the differences between short and long vowels, in diphthongs, and in verbalizing principles or rules governing phonic and letter relationships.

Austin and her associates (2) also found that many classroom teachers are not adequately prepared to teach the skills required for successful reading.

It is practically impossible to discuss in detail within a few hundred pages all the phases of a complete reading program, and this book does not propose to do so. Rather, we have concentrated on the answers to a few basic questions: *What is reading?* (Chapters 2 and 5); *Who is the learner* or *whom must we teach?* (Chapters 3 and 4); *What is to be learned* or *what must we teach?* (Chapter 6, 7, 10, 11, 12, and 14); *How does the pupil learn to read?* (Chapters 8 and 9); and *What can the teacher do when the pupil fails to learn to read?* (Chapter 14).

The final chapter of the book seeks to place the teaching of reading in its proper theoretical context.

In attempting to answer these questions, we have divided the book into the following seven parts:

Part I   READING—AN OVERVIEW
          Chapter 1   Introduction
          Chapter 2   The Nature of the Reading Process

This book is concerned with reading method and the actual teaching of reading. Thus, the book is written first and foremost for the practitioner or the *teacher in-service*. Therefore our first concern has been the problems of the teacher *in the classroom*. Nevertheless, we hope that the book will be of genuine value to the remedial teacher, the reading specialist, and the reading supervisor. We hope that it meets the needs of those students preparing to become teachers, and we also hope that administrators and state department personnel will find it helpful in obtaining a better understanding of the reading process.

This revision of our 1964 edition differs from the first edition in that:

1. It discusses in detail the question of prekindergarten-kindergarten reading instruction.
2. It has added a major section on visual screening tests.
3. It has expanded the sections dealing with auditory factors in reading, with listening, with problems of articulation as they relate to reading, and with language generally. It has added a section on the philosophy and sociology of reading and discusses the implications of generative and transformational grammar on reading instruction.
4. While adhering to its basic philosophy of eclecticism in reading method, it discusses ITA, David's Ten-vowel Modification Model, the Diacritical Marking System, Words in Color,

Linguistic Approaches, Programmed Approaches, Language-experience Approach, Textfilm Reading Program, Delacato Approach, and such remedial approaches as the Monroe Method, Fernald Method, Unified Phonics Method, Color Phonics System, Progressive Choice Reading Method, and the Gillingham Method.

5. It has incorporated the basic facts of linguistics and deals in depth with the fact that there is a one-to-one relationship between the spoken word and the printed symbol, even though the spelling irregularities are many.

6. It reaffirms the position taken in 1964 that the pupil must learn a coding system either on his own or through formal instruction which permits him to deal successfully with new and strange words.

7. It discusses the value of the basal readers in the total reading program.

8. It takes another look at grouping within the classroom.

9. It discusses the question of rate instruction in the school and reevaluates the concept of readability, especially in the light of computerized and close-technique research.

10. It substantially modified Chapter 10, "Introducing the Pupil to Linguistic Phonics," and Chapter 11, "Advancing the Child's Phonic Skills," to incorporate the best of linguistic knowledge.

11. It has added a new chapter, entitled "Diagnosis and Remediation." While putting special emphasis on prevention, it leads the reader step by step through diagnostic procedure, showing him how to determine whether a pupil is a retarded reader or not, how to identify reading potential and actual achievement, what tests to use, how to evaluate test results, how to administer a reading inventory, both informal and formal, how to use oral reading tests in diagnosis, how to use diagnostic tests, and how to identify the causes of reading disability. It concludes with a compilation of proven remedial and psycho-therapeutic principles, techniques, and methods.

12. It lists and discusses causes of reading disability, and in addition seeks to develop in the reading teacher a modus operandi, a savoir faire, in identifying the specific cause in a given reading disability case. It thus shows the teacher how to tie together symptom and cause. It takes the position that those factors that are associated with good achievement in reading, if absent, may become causes of reading deficiency.

13. The revision offers differential programs for the retarded reader, the slow learner, the reluctant reader, the disadvan-

taged reader, the severely emotionally-disturbed retarded reader, and the dyslexiac.

14. It supplies the teacher with an up-to-date list of reading materials, including basal readers, materials designed to develop comprehension and word-recognition skills, audiovisual materials, mechanical devices, and programmed materials.

15. It incorporates the findings of some 300 1964–1968 studies, books, and literature. Exercises, lists of materials, and tests have similarly been updated.

We have made every attempt in Chapter 15 and throughout the book to relate psychological theory and research to practice. Sometimes the results are rather frustrating, but this should not keep us either from theorizing and engaging in research or from making applications.

Psychology does not consist of a catalogue of education how-to-do-its telling the teacher how to teach, the administrator how to administer, and the parent how to be a parent. It would be fine if it had attained this degree of refinement, but there are no ready-made cures available for educational ills.

Psychology, in a sense, may even make the answers come less easily, but this should not discourage the teacher. It is worthwhile to work a little harder at a solution if the solution tends to be correct. Frequently, those who have the quickest answers are in error. Psychology should help the teacher to avoid making errors because it opens up for him more alternatives of action. Before acting, he will consider more possibilities. The average layman would have little difficulty in deciding whether to retain or not to retain a pupil. The trained teacher may find it not as easy, but he may make fewer errors.

There are few questions in education that have clear-cut answers. Furthermore, there is no automatic, one-to-one relationship between theory and practice or application. The theorist, even the learning theorist, cannot replace the educator. The theorist offers advice, gives direction, and prevents errors, but in the final analysis the educational programs "must emerge from the distillation of theoretical principles with practical know-how" (11). William James, writing in 1899, pointed out that:

> . . . you make a great, a very great mistake, if you think that psychology, being the science of the mind's laws, is something from which you can deduce definite programmes and schemes and methods of instruction for immediate schoolroom use. Psychology is a science, and teaching is an art; and sciences never generate arts directly out of themselves. An intermediary inventive mind must make the application, by using its originality.

The science of logic never made a man reason rightly and the science of ethics . . . never made a man behave rightly. The most such sciences can do is to help us catch ourselves up and check ourselves, if we start to reason or to behave wrongly; and to criticize ourselves more articulately after we have made mistakes. . . . Everywhere teaching must agree with psychology, but need not necessarily be the only kind of teaching that would so agree; for many diverse methods of teaching may equally well agree with psychological laws. . . .

But, if the use of psychological principles thus be negative rather than positive, it does not follow that it may not be of great use, all the same. It certainly narrows the path for experiments and trials. We know in advance, if we are psychologists, that certain methods will be wrong, so our psychology saves us from mistakes. It makes us, moreover, more clear as to what we are about (9, pp. 7–11).

Nevertheless, if psychology is to have a significant effect upon teaching procedures and techniques, theory and practice must be tied up in a very definite way. We simply can't be an "ammunition wagon" loaded with knowledge which we don't know how to use; we must be a rifle (13, p. 281).

The transition from what we know as individuals to what we do is always a great leap. Perhaps an even greater transition exists between what researchers, as a group, have learned and the individual teacher's practices in the classroom. Durrell (6) notes that the challenge facing teachers today is the improvement of classroom practice in the light of present knowledge. This is particularly true in reading where research has been above the ordinary.

These are genuine problems facing the profession. Is there a solution to them? Durrell suggests that perhaps the greatest needs are for an improvement in teacher education, both preservice and in-service, and for the production of new instructional materials. We hope that this book will in some small way contribute to the first of these needs.

The Nature of
the Reading Process

In the introduction to Part I of this book, we viewed eight different aspects of reading. We also suggested that there are about as many definitions of reading as there are reading experts.

Nevertheless, it is possible to categorize reading definitions into three types: (*1*) those that equate reading with interpretation of experience generally; (*2*) those that equate reading with interpretation of graphic symbols; and (*3*) combinations of types *1* and *2*. The first is a broader definition and encompasses the second. The only basic difference between type *1* and type *2* is in the nature of the stimulus.

In type *1* we might speak of reading pictures, reading faces, and reading the weather. We read a squeaking door, a clap of thunder, and a barking dog. The golfer reads the putting greens, the meteorologist reads the weather, the detective reads clues, the geologist reads rocks, the astronomer reads stars, and the doctor reads the symptoms of illness. A mother reads the cries of her children. Some cries call for immediate action; to other cries she may simply react with "Everything is still O.K."

The definition of reading that has come out of the Claremont Reading Conference fits this first category. In the eleventh Claremont Conference, Dr. Spencer wrote: "In the broadest sense, reading is the process of interpreting sense stimuli. . . . Reading is performed whenever one experiences sensory stimulation." (32) Benjamin Franklin in *Poor Richard's Almanac* had such a definition in mind when he wrote: "Read much, but not too many books."

Perhaps in our reading readiness program, in which we emphasize experience with the concrete object, in which we stress visual and auditory discrimination and in which we require children to read pictures and conversation, we are closest to the meaning of reading implied in the first type of definition.

However, most definitions of reading given in professional textbooks are of the second type. Deboer and Dallmann (11) define reading as "an activity which involves the comprehension and interpretation of ideas symbolized by the written or printed page." Bond and Tinker point out that "reading involves the recognition of printed or written symbols which serve as stimuli for the recall of meanings built up through the reader's past experience." (3) Harris says that reading may be defined as "the act of responding appropriately to printed symbols." (17) Gibson (14) says that reading "is receiving communication; it is making discriminative responses to graphic symbols; it is decoding graphic symbols to speech; and it is getting meaning from the printed page."

A team of experts, under the sponsorship of the U.S. Office of Education, tentatively defined reading as "a term used to refer to an interaction by which meaning encoded in visual stimuli by an author becomes meaning in the mind of the reader." Communication always involves encoding (the transmitting process) and decoding (the receiving process).

Let us take a look at what these two types of definitions mean to the teacher of reading.

READING AS INTERPRETATION OF EXPERIENCE

What are some of the implications for the teacher of a definition of reading which equates reading with the interpretation of experience generally?

One implication of this definition is that teachers of reading must become experts in reading children. The teacher of reading must understand children. He needs to identify personal differences in children, for these differences make for achievement differences between pupils.

A second implication is that the teacher needs to become expert in reading the symptoms of reading success and reading disability. One of the lessons we have learned the hard way in combating cancer is that many people die from the disease because someone either ignored the symptoms or did not read them correctly. Children likewise become reading disability cases because someone ignored or did not read the symptoms of reading disability correctly.

A third implication is that the teacher needs to become expert in reading the causes of reading disability. Smith and Carrigan (30) note:

Clinicians are like a small group standing beside a river full of drowning people. The victims are being swept seaward by the current of time. The clinicians can pull out a few, but the rest are lost. Few of the group are willing to go upstream to find out how the victims get into the river in the first place.[1]

The teacher needs to know how the disabled reader falls into the river of reading disability. To do this, he needs to be able to read the causes of reading disability. It is not enough to know the symptoms; they have to be hooked up with the proper cause. Only in this way are prevention and remediation of reading disability possible.

What are the implications of this type of definition for the reader? The pupil must be a reader of experience before he can become a reader of graphic symbols, but he cannot do this without having read experience—without having those experiences that give the symbol meaning.

READING AS INTERPRETATION OF GRAPHIC SYMBOLS

Let's turn now to the second type of definition of reading, which equates reading with the interpretation of graphic symbols. It implies that the reader must be able to identify the word and be able to associate appropriate meaning with it. Reading requires identification and comprehension.

Reading is far more than recognition of the graphic symbols. It is much more than the mere ability to pronounce the words on the printed page; it is even more than the gaining of meaning from printed materials. The reader is stimulated by the writer's words, but in turn vests these words with his own meaning. "Reading typically is the bringing of meaning *to* rather than the gaining of meaning *from* the printed page (31, p. 22)."[2] Horn (20) points out that the author

. . . does not really convey ideas to the reader; he merely stimulates him to construct them out of his own experience. If the concept is . . . new to the reader, its construction more nearly approaches problem solving than simple association.[3]

[1] D. E. P. Smith and Patricia Carrigan. *The Nature of Reading Disability* (Harcourt, Brace and World, Inc., New York, 1959), p. 6. Reprinted by permission.
[2] Henry P. Smith and Emerald V. Dechant, *Psychology in Teaching Reading* (Prentice-Hall, Inc., 1961), p. 22. Reprinted by permission.
[3] Ernest Horn, *Methods of Instruction in the Social Studies* (New York: Charles Scribner's Sons, 1937). Reprinted by permission.

And yet, it is not enough to put our own stamp of meaning on the words. Langman (22, p. 19) notes that to read is to comprehend the meaning of visually presented word sequences; that the reader must follow the thought of the *writer* (22, p. 23). Thus, the reader may and even must gain meaning from the printed page. This occurs when the writer's symbols stimulate the reader to combine or reconstruct his own experiences in a novel way.

Word-calling without understanding is not reading. Reading always involves the arousal of meaning in response to symbols, and sometimes it is necessary to select one specific meaning from numerous possible meanings (6, p. 8).

In speech and writing, this latter aspect becomes especially important. The writer may want to stimulate the reader to arrive at a very particular meaning. Thus, instead of using the general word "little" he may choose any of the following: small, minute, microscopic, puny, tiny, petty, dwarfed, stunted, diminutive, Liliputian, short, or miniature. The reader must be able to appreciate the particular nuances of meaning if he is to interpret the message correctly.

Gray (16), discussing the dimensions of the reading process, suggested that these include recognition, understanding, reaction, and integration. Shaw (28) noted that reading is the process of seeing or perceiving independent items, of observing and assimilating their interrelationships, and of integrating or grouping them into main ideas. Thorndike (38, p. 331) suggests that the reading of a paragraph involves the same sort of organization and analysis as does thinking. It includes learning, reflection, judgment, analysis, synthesis, problem-solving behavior, selection, inference, organization, comparison of data, determination of relationships, and critical evaluation of what is being read (13). It includes attention, association, abstraction, generalization, comprehension, concentration, and deduction. Hildreth (19, p. 72) pointed out:

> Reading requires inference, weighing the relative importance of ideas and meanings, and seeing the relationships among them; it is a process of forming tentative judgments, then verifying and checking guesses. To solve the problems in a passage the reader must be continuously in an alert, anticipatory frame of mind, suspending judgment, correcting and confirming his guesses as he goes along.[4]

Obviously, reading of graphic symbols involves a twofold process. There are the mechanical processes involved in bringing the stimuli to the brain, and there are the mental processes involved in interpreting the

---

[4] Gertrude Hildreth, *Teaching Reading* (New York: Holt, Rinehart and Winston, Inc., 1958). Reprinted by permission.

stimuli after they get to the brain. When the light rays from the printed page hit the retinal cells of the eyes, signals are sent along the optic nerve to the visual centers of the brain. This is not yet reading. The mind must function in the process, the signals must be interpreted, and the reader must give significance to what he reads. He must bring *meaning* to the graphic symbol. Meaning depends to a great degree upon the reader's ability to recreate those experiences for which the symbol stands. The critical element in reading often is not what is on the page, but, rather, what the graphic symbol signifies to the reader (31). *Reading thus is the process of giving the significance intended by the writer to the graphic symbols by relating them to one's own fund of experience.*

READING—A SENSORY PROCESS

Reading begins as a sensory process. Reading is a visual process and a word-identification process. Sensation is the first occurrence in all perception. The reader reacts visually (in the case of Braille, kinesthetically) to the graphic symbols. He must visually identify and recognize upon subsequent occasions the language symbol.

Visual Readiness

The child must have acquired certain visual skills before he is ready for reading. He must be able to focus at distances of 20 inches or less. He must have acquired some skill in depth perception and in binocular coordination. He must be able to center and to change fixation at will. And he must see clearly, singly, and for sustained periods.

Children are born farsighted. At birth, the eye is only about one-third of its adult size. This prevents adequate focus of the image of near objects on the retina. As the eyeball lengthens, farsightedness decreases, and the child can adapt to the demands of near vision. Children generally achieve 20/20 vision at about five or six years of age. Unfortunately almost immediately deterioration sets in, and by seventeen nearly 40 per cent cannot demonstrate 20/20 acuity in both right and left eyes (23). Figure 2-1 illustrates the relationship of near and far vision to reading.

The Eye Movements in Reading

Much of our knowledge of how the eyes react during reading has come from the early work of Javal, Buswell, and Dearborn. In reading the eyes do not make a continuous sweep across the page. They move in quick, short, staccadic movements with pauses interspersed. Eye movements are

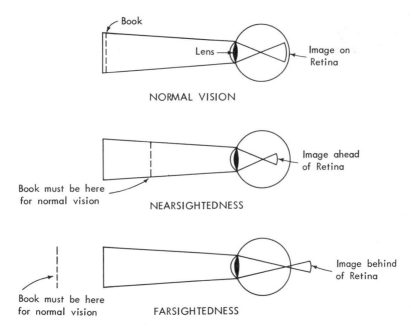

NORMAL VISION

NEARSIGHTEDNESS

FARSIGHTEDNESS

Figure 2-1. Vision and Reading

characterized by fixations, interfixation movements, regressions or refixations, and return sweeps. The time elements in reading are two: fixation time and movement time.

A *fixation*[5] is the stop that the eye makes so that it can react to the graphic stimuli. It is the pause for reading. During fixations the intake process is suspended and the inner process of reading occurs. The length (in terms of words) and frequency of the fixation vary with the difficulty of the reading material, with the reader's facility in word recognition, with his vocabulary level, with his familiarity with the content, with his purpose, with his ability to assimilate ideas, and with the format of the printed page. For example, the more difficult the reading matter, the longer and more frequent the fixations tend to be. The length may vary from as much as .22 seconds for reading easy material to .32 seconds for reading objective test items (42).

The length of the pause includes both seeing and thinking time. The reader must have time to see and to process the visual stimuli. Fixation time accounts for about 92 to 94 per cent of the reading time; *interfixa-*

---

[5] Photographs of eye movements record the approximate center of the field of vision (40). This "fixation field" is usually termed the point of fixation. When "fixating" on this point, the reader normally sees and recognizes also a part of the peripheral visual field.

tion eye movements take from .01 to about .023 second (42) and account for about only 6 to 8 per cent of the reading time.

Buswell (7, p. 26) found that the average child in grade one made between 15.5 and 18.6 fixations per 3½-inch (21-pica) line. The average college student made only 5.9 fixations on a line of similar length. Other studies (33, 43, p. 133) indicate that the average college student makes about eight fixations per 4-inch (24-pica) line. And Taylor (36) reports that the average first grader makes about 224 fixations per 100 words; the average college student, about 90.

To understand the role that the fixation pause plays in reading it is necessary to familiarize ourselves with three terms, namely, visual field, perception span, and recognition span. The visual field generally consists of an horizontal arc of about 180 degrees and a vertical arc of about 60 degrees. It includes peripheral and foveal vision (spot of clearest vision) as well as depth in vision.

The perception span or the visual span is the amount (usually in terms of numbers, letters, or words) that is *seen* in a single fixation. This is measured by a tachistoscopic exposure and usually is larger than the amount seen in a single fixation in normal reading.

The recognition span is the amount that is *seen and organized* during a single fixation. It is the number of words that are recognized and understood during a single fixation. The size of the recognition span is obtained by dividing the number of words read by the number of fixations made while reading.

Thought-unit reading sometimes is wrongly identified with the concept of phrase seeing or with the suggestion that it is possible or even common to read three or four words per fixation (36, p. 17). Even though a child reads in thought units, he rarely comprehends more than one word per fixation.

A study in which the writer played a small role points this out rather forcefully. Taylor, Frackenpohl, and Pettee (36), using the Reading Eye Camera, analyzed the eye characteristics of 12,143 subjects from grades one through college. The subjects were of average socioeconomic status, and 90 per cent attended public schools. They resided in 19 different states. They read selections that were at their grade level of difficulty. Whenever the pupil's comprehension score was 60 per cent or below, he was given a new selection to read and was tested again. Table 2-1 (36, p. 12) reports the findings.

The findings of a previous study by Taylor (34) of the eye movements of 5000 pupils were similar.

The data in Table 2-1 certainly should lead us to reevaluate our previous assumptions. In these studies not even one student read three words per fixation. Thought units, then, must consist of a series of fixations (36, p. 17).

TABLE 2-1* Averages for Measurable Components of the Fundamental Reading Skill

Grade†	1	2	3	4	5	6	7	8	9	10	11	12	Col.
Fixations (incl. regressions) per 100 words	224	174	155	139	129	120	114	109	105	101	96	94	90
Regressions per 100 words	52	40	35	31	28	25	23	21	20	19	18	17	15
Average span of recognition (in words)	.45	.57	.65	.72	.78	.83	.88	.92	.95	.99	1.04	1.06	1.11
Average duration of fixation (in seconds)	.33	.30	.28	.27	.27	.27	.27	.27	.27	.26	.26	.25	.24
Rate with comprehension (in words per minute)	80	115	138	158	173	185	195	204	214	224	237	250	280

MALE

Grade†	1	2	3	4	5	6	7	8	9	10	11	12	Col.
Fixations (incl. regressions) per 100 words	230	178	158	143	133	123	116	111	106	102	97	94	90
Regressions per 100 words	54	42	37	32	29	26	24	22	20	19	18	17	15
Rate with comprehension (in words per minute)	75	108	132	152	168	180	190	200	210	220	234	248	280

FEMALE

Grade†	1	2	3	4	5	6	7	8	9	10	11	12	Col.
Fixations (incl. regressions) per 100 words	218	170	152	135	125	117	112	107	103	100	95	93	90
Regressions per 100 words	50	38	33	30	27	24	22	20	19	18	17	16	15
Rate with comprehension (in words per minute)	85	122	146	164	178	190	200	208	218	228	240	252	280

* Stanford E. Taylor, Helen Frackenpohl, and James L. Pettee, Grade Level Norms for the Components of the Fundamental Reading Skill (Huntington, New York: Educational Developmental Laboratories, Inc., 1960), Bulletin No. 3, p. 12. Reprinted by permission.

† First grade averages are those of pupils capable of reading silently material of 1.8 difficulty with at least 70 per cent comprehension. Above grade one, averages are those of students at midyear reading silently material of midyear difficulty with at least 70 per cent comprehension.

A *regression* is a reverse movement. It is a return to a previously fixed letter, syllable, word, or phrase for a refixation. It is a fixation in a right-to-left direction on the eye-movement photograph (12, p. 17). Eye deficiencies that have prevented accurate sensation, inadequate directional attack, and improper coordination between vergence (permitting single vision) and focus (permitting clear vision) are frequent causes of regression (12, p. 17). Sometimes the reader regresses out of habit. Such a pupil lacks confidence and feels the need for constant rereading.

Regressions are not necessarily bad. Most of them may well be means by which the child corrects himself and learns (15). Regressions occur when the flow of thought is interrupted or when perceptions are recognized as inaccurate (2). Eye movements frequently over- or under-reach the limits of the reader's recognition span. Regressions for verification, for phrase analysis, and for reexamination of a previous sentence seem especially useful. The flow of thought may be broken in numerous ways, such as by failing to comprehend the basic meaning of a word, by failing to comprehend the meaning suggested by the context, or by failing to interrelate the meanings of all the words.

The number of regressions made per hundred words varies from reader to reader. The average first grader makes about 52; the average ninth grader about 20; and the average college student about 15. For averages for the other grades see Table 2-1.

Upon completing a line the reader makes a *return sweep* to the beginning of the next line. The return sweep takes from 40 to 54 milliseconds (42). If the next line is missed entirely or if the eye lands on a point before or after the first word of the new line, the reader must locate the proper place and a refixation is required.

Figure 2-2 illustrates the various components of the movements of the eye as recorded by the eye movement camera.

Developmental Aspects of Eye Movement

Eye-movement skills develop rapidly during the first four grades, but after this relatively little improvement occurs. A slight improvement may occur between grades six and ten, after which a leveling process occurs (1, pp. 105–106).

Oculomotor behavior has come to be regarded primarily as a symptom of the underlying perceptual and assimilative processes. There is an interaction and an interdependence between the oculomotor activity and the central processes (37). Eye movements do not cause but merely reflect efficient or poor reading performance. Generally, as the difficulty of the material increases and as the reader takes greater pains to read well, the pauses become more frequent and grow longer (41). The difficulty of the material rather than the nature of the subject matter is the crucial element.

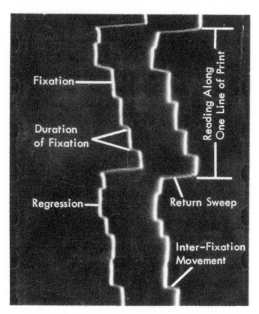

Figure 2-2. Eye-movement Photograph*

The immature reader generally does not vary his eye movements with the difficulty of the reading matter or with a change of purpose. The good reader, on the other hand, is distinguished from the poor reader by his better word recognition, word analysis, and comprehension, and these frequently are reflected in more efficient eye movements. Thus, eye movement patterns reflect the efficiency of the central processes of comprehension (42) and are generally symptomatic of the level of reading maturity the child has achieved. The poor reader makes extra fixations and regressions because he doesn't understand, and he needs training to improve word recognition and comprehension rather than eye movement.

Under certain conditions both good and poor readers show irregularities in their eye movement. And, although eye-movement surveys indicate that a great number of children have not developed the habit of perceiving materials in a left-to-right progression, while making a minimum number of fixations and regressions (35, p. 32), one must always remember that most of these surveys involve situations that are somewhat atypical. The pupil's eye movements might be different in normal reading.

* From Bulletin No. P-248 (Huntington, New York: Educational Developmental Laboratories, Inc.). Reprinted by permission.

The Eye-voice and Eye-memory Spans

Thought-unit reading, as noted previously, is not the same as interpreting an eyeful of print at a time. Because of this distinction, we speak of the eye-memory span in silent reading and the eye-voice span in oral reading.

The eye-memory span is the distance the eyes have traveled ahead of the point at which interpretation occurs. The eye-voice span is the distance the eyes have moved ahead of the point at which the pronunciation occurs. The mature reader has a wide eye-memory span and a wide eye-voice span. He does not commit himself to an interpretation until he has read a sufficient amount of material. He delays his interpretation of the visual intake until he has perceived enough material to grasp a thought unit (19, p. 75). He keeps in mind a sufficient amount of context so as to make the best interpretation. We find a similar span in listening. The good listener listens for meaning and for thought units, rather than for one word at a time.

Generally in silent reading the mature reader has a span of from fifteen to twenty letters. In oral reading it is slightly less. Rate improvement depends, to a great extent, on the shortening of the fixation pauses and on the lengthening of the eye-memory and eye-voice spans (19, p. 81).

Auditory Readiness

Auditory factors are also significant for reading achievement. The good reader can discriminate between the many sounds that form words. Unless he can do this, he will not be able to make the proper associations between the spoken sound and the graphic symbol.

The most natural way of teaching reading is still to go through the spoken word. Thus we say to the child: "Look at this word. This word says (spells) cat." The spoken word is the familiar stimulus, the written word is the novel stimulus. Gradually, with repeated associations between the written and the spoken word, the child brings to the written word the same meanings that he previously attached to the spoken word.

Some children experience much difficulty in associating with the written word the meaning that has been associated with the spoken word. Many of these difficulties stem from failure to properly identify the written word. Some may not see the word distinctly and correctly. Some may even fail to look at the word. They do not really identify the word; they learn rather that the word *cat* is on the flash card with the broken corner. Thus reading should always be a "look while you say" activity. The kinaesthetic, tracing, or writing method of teaching word identification may be effective precisely because it forces the child to pay close attention to the word and thus to make a proper association.

Other children are handicapped because they are not able to discriminate between the various phonetic elements of words, do not hear and do not speak the sound correctly, and thus will confuse words. No child learns to pronounce distinctions which he does not hear. The resultant confusion leads to an inability to associate the sound with the appropriate printed symbol.

READING—A PERCEPTUAL PROCESS

Reading, however, is more than a sensory process. It is more than a skill to be learned through practice; it also is a conceptual and thinking process. Conceptual thought is required to react with meaning to the word, the sentence, and the paragraph. Reading and thinking are inseparable processes when the printed word provides the stimulus for thought (29).

Perception refers to the interpretation of everything that we sense. We give meaning to what we see, hear, taste, smell, and touch. At a very elemental level, such as when the perceiver sees a black dot on a white background, sensation may dominate perception and the percept may have few characteristics not found in the stimulus. At a more complex level, the sensation is clothed with the perceiver's wealth of past experience and values, and the percept reflects the biological and environmental characteristics of the perceiver.

Thus, although reading begins with sensation and the subsequent recognition of the printed symbol, the critical element in the reading act is the meaningful response rather than the recognition of the symbol. Perception must include the arousal of meaning. To understand the meaning of a word the reader needs to have some awareness of the experiences that the word stands for. Beginning readers sometimes become so engrossed with the mechanical aspects of reading, with word identification and pronunciation, that they fail to understand the need for comprehension.

Reading, which requires interpretation of what is read, occurs only when the reader understands what he is reading (8). Korzybski notes that reading is the reconstruction of the events behind the symbols. And Semelmeyer (27) points out that reading should bear the same relationship to experiences or events that a map bears to the territory which it is supposed to represent.

Since the symbol has no meaning of its own, perception must go beyond the sensory data. It must, and does, involve information that is not present to the senses. The reader does not see the object, person, or experience of which the author writes. His eyes are in contact with a word, in fact with the light rays that are reflected by the word, and so it is impossible for him to see meaning. And yet, the child takes meaning to the word. He has learned the meaning of the word with the same mental operations that he used to learn the meaning of a squeaking door, a clap of thunder, a barking dog, or a square room (25). His reactions to the printed word are determined by the experiences that he has had with those objects or events for which the symbol stands. This is what we mean by perception.[6] Perception is a consciousness or awareness of the experiences evoked by a symbol.

Specific and Generic Meaning

Individuals differ in their ability to react to symbols, and their interpretations have varying degrees of accuracy. They think of words in their general or specific sense (10, p. 120). Aphasics, individuals who have lost the ability to react to and handle abstract symbols, do not react with a general meaning. A "bear" indicates not a class of bears but one specific bear in their experience. Young children and frequently poor readers are like aphasics in their reactions to symbols.

Lukina (24) reports that a one-year-old child associated the word "ribbon" with the ribbons on her bonnet but not with the ribbon from which dangled a celluloid parrot. The same child applied the word cup to a small pink cup with white spots, but not to a larger white cup.

Jan Tausch (21), studying 170 children in the fourth to the seventh grade, found that good readers were characterized by abstract thinking and that poor readers demonstrated concreteness in behavior. The relationship is more significant in the upper grades, suggesting perhaps that reading comprehension at the upper grade levels is more abstract in nature. Other studies show that intelligence is more closely related to reading comprehension at the upper grade levels than at the lower levels. Thus intelligence may become a more important determinant of reading success as the abstractness of the materials read increases.

Specific reactions to symbols also are observable with older children. They find abstract words especially difficult and identify them with specific experiences: "Beauty is when you comb your hair neatly." "Sportsmanship is when you do not kick somebody." Children easily give meaning to *a book, a building, a car,* but not to the more complex concepts represented by the words beauty, democracy, and truth.

Another example may be taken from reading itself. Pupils frequently make substitutions when they read. The good reader tends to

---

[6] Hebb (18, p. 179) defines perception as those mediating processes to which sensation gives rise. Quite commonly, these mediating processes are labelled thought, cognition, or ideation, and they serve as a link between the sensory input and the organism's response (19, p. 48).

substitute words that harmonize with the context. The poor reader, on the other hand, substitutes words that do not fit the context. He may not have had sufficient experience to bring the appropriate meaning to the printed page, and communication between writer and reader does not occur. He cannot see the relationships between the various words and the various ideas communicated.

Generally, the writer and the reader communicate only if they are capable of assigning some common meaning to a symbol. This means that they must have had some commonality of experience. And usually they must be able to make a generic response to their experience.[7] Thus, Bruner (5, p. 125)[8] notes: "If perceptual experience is ever had raw, that is, free of categorical identity, it is doomed to be a gem serene, locked in the silence of private experience."

With experience the person makes the word generic in meaning. He abstracts, forms concepts, learns to associate these concepts with printed symbols, and identifies the word with a category or a class of objects. When perception is on an abstract level, when the reader associates a concept with a word, then, indeed, perception is a kind of summing up of the meanings of numerous sensory impingements (25). The reader then is capable of bringing sufficient meaning to the printed page to permit him to obtain from the page an approximation of the experience that the writer is trying to convey. The reader attains an understanding of the writer's experience and hence his perceptions. Only then is communication via reading taking place.

And yet, the perception of a word is rarely completely congruent with the meaning intended by the writer. Furthermore, concept-environment concordance is rarely completely present. Verbal symbols at best are inadequate substitutes for direct experience. There is no direct connection between symbol and referend, the datum, object, or event.

The Development of Meaning

Since the good reader may well be differentiated from the poor reader by his inability to take the appropriate meaning to the page, the reading teacher is concerned about the development of meaning and concepts. We know that children can learn to conceptualize. Depth and variety of experience perhaps are most significant. And the broader the concept, the more abstract it is, the greater is the amount of experience needed for its formation.

Not all concepts, however, can be taught through direct experience,

[7] One cannot infer, however, that all words represent class concepts. The words, *yes, no, in, whether,* and *or,* for example, do not refer to classes of things.

[8] Jerome E. Brunner, "On Perceptual Readiness," *Psychological Review,* 64 (March 1957) 123–152.

nor do children come to school prepared to handle all concepts. Children go through stages as they learn to interpret words. Concrete and specific concepts probably are developed first. They often relate an object to its function: a bat is used to hit a ball.

The child gradually engages in more complex thinking. The concept of time in sequence and the concepts of latitude, sphericity, date line, zone, altitude, or longitude, for example, generally do not develop before grades six or seven. Cause and effect relations rarely are understood before the age of nine, and many social concepts escape children until they are twelve or thirteen.

Even though experience is a major determinant of meaning, other factors are important. The culture in which one lives surely is an important determinant of what a word will mean. We also know that each perceptual experience has its emotional matrix. In this sense reading involves feeling. The affective state of the reader may distort, color, or alter meaning to such an extent that communication becomes impossible. Some things forever escape our comprehension because we cannot accept them emotionally.

These elements—culture, experience, affective factors, and our own perception of them—combine to make our interpretations of a word a very personalistic experience. The fact that our reactions are organismic, that they involve our whole being, makes it almost impossible to communicate perfectly. Our interpretations and our meanings are truly our own.

ORAL READING

Even though the major emphasis in reading today is on silent reading, children need to become good oral readers. Pupils benefit educationally by reading aloud prose, poetry, or drama. There are many benefits in choral reading—oral reading by a group. It leads to better appreciation of literature and to improved pronunciation, phrasing, interpretation, rhythm, and flexibility.

Oral reading also has social values. It provides enjoyment in a social group, helps the child to substantiate answers challenged by others in a group, lets him share content to which all do not have access, and is useful in making reports and announcements, and presenting other information to a group.

Oral reading has diagnostic values. It is helpful in testing for fluency and accuracy in reading. Since reading requires the association of a printed form with an oral equivalent, it would seem only logical that oral reading would be used to emphasize this relationship.

But most important perhaps is that oral reading teaches the pupil that writing is a record of the oral language, although an incomplete record to be sure (4). The intonation pattern cannot be fully represented by writing. The tone of voice (the paralanguage) and the gestured bodily movements (the kinesics) are only crudely represented by underlined words, exclamation points, or word choice (sauntered, gesticulated). The pupil right from the beginning should read aloud the whole sentence. This develops an awareness of the intonation pattern and is probably the best preventer of word-by-word reading.

Oral reading requires all the sensory and perceptual skills required in silent reading, such as visual discrimination, rhythmic progression along a line of print, and the ability to take to the word those experiences that the writer, by his peculiar choice and arrangement of words, hoped to call to the reader's attention. Oral reading also requires skills beyond those needed in silent reading.

Habits of oral reading usually are quite different from those in silent reading. The child who exercises great care in his oral reading may pass over the difficult words in silent reading. In oral reading there are generally more fixations, more regressions, and longer pauses. Oral reading generally is slower than silent reading. In oral reading, reading rate is limited by pronunciation; in silent reading, it is limited only by the ability to grasp meaning. Oral reading calls for interpreting to others; silent reading only to oneself. Oral reading demands skills in voice, tempo, and gesture and in sensing the mood and feeling intended by the author. And, there are some differences in neural pathways in oral and silent reading (Figure 2-3).

Oral reading, like silent reading, consists of a complex of skills. The basic reading skills are discussed at length in Chapter 9. Let us confine ourselves then for the moment to those specific skills required for proficiency in oral reading. The good oral reader:

1. Interprets the author's meaning accurately.
2. Transmits correctly the author's meaning to the listener.
3. Makes a proper interpretation of the author's feelings and moods.
4. Reads in meaningful thought units.
5. Is accurate and clear in articulation, enunciation, and pronunciation.
6. Gives an accurate translation of the writer's punctuation marks into pauses, stops, etc.
7. Is fluent and smooth in reading, keeping the eye well ahead of the voice.
8. Has suitable quality and volume of voice.

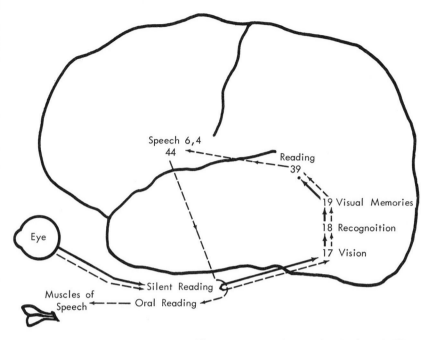

Speech 6,4
44
Reading
39
19 Visual Memories
18 Recognoition
17 Vision
Eye
Muscles of
Speech
Silent Reading
Oral Reading

Figure 2-3.   Pathways in Oral and Silent Reading*

9.   Has suitable pitch.
10.   Has unlabored speech.
11.   Avoids labored precision in reading aloud.
12.   Has appropriate rate.
13.   Has proper posture.
14.   Looks at the audience at frequent intervals.
15.   Holds the attention of the audience.

The good oral reader must get the author's meaning, sense his moods, and must be able to convey the author's meaning and mood to others. He must recognize words instantly, using good phrasing, pronunciation, and proper voice inflection. He needs to adapt his voice to the room and must have auditory and visual contact with the audience. He should be poised and confident, and must assume the proper posture. He must keep his eyes well ahead of his voice, must enunciate clearly, must pronounce correctly, and must hold the attention of the audience. The good oral reader cannot be many other things. He cannot, for example, be a

* Thomas H. Eames, "Visual Handicaps to Reading," *Journal of Education,* 141, February, 1959, p. 35. Reproduced by permission of the Journal of Education, Boston University Press.

word caller, jerkily attacking one word at a time in a high-pitched mono-tone and giving little consideration to meaning (9).

Thus, oral reading rarely should be done without previous silent reading. In the primary grades, particularly, where pupils have not yet developed an adequate sight vocabulary and adequate recognition skills, pupils should not be allowed to read their stories to the class without previous silent reading. From the beginning stress should be on natural-ness of tone. The teacher should encourage this by asking the pupil to read the sentence in the manner that he would speak it, since the best model for oral reading is speech. Passages frequently should be read to the pupil to give him a feeling for conversational tone.

The teacher also needs to pay particular attention to the child's articulation, enunciation, and pronunciation. The emphasis should be on simple rhymes and stories using the sounds needed at the child's specific stage of development. Pronunciation should be corrected tactfully, with-out embarrassing the child. Mispronounced words should be practiced as parts of a sentence.

The pupil also must learn appropriate pitch, quality, and volume of voice. Voice factors are important for the listener. Listening is more or less difficult depending on the voice qualities of the reader. Rhymes re-quiring the child to change moods, to interpret sounds of animals, and to interpret various human voices promote voice proficiency. The pupil needs to be given the opportunity to read to a single child, to a group, and to engage in choral reading.

The most essential vocal skills are phrasing and smoothness. The reader must be able to keep his eyes well ahead of his voice so he can organize and group the words, giving them the proper inflections. This means that the child should read simple materials without too many new words. Generally, materials written by the child himself which are based on the vocabulary that he knows are most effective. Many errors of com-munication are the result of faulty phrasing or grouping of words. Gen-erally, phrasing will be appropriate if the child understands what he is reading. Sentences should be broken into meaningful phrases and clauses. Only if the reader understands what he reads can he convey a meaning-ful message.

The teacher can check upon the child's proficiency here by asking the pupil to read two or three lines aloud and then stopping him. The pupil then is to say aloud additional words that he read silently, but that he has not yet read aloud. A narrow eye-voice span indicates that the pupil needs help in looking ahead.

The oral reader also must learn to emphasize words properly. He does this by giving the word more stress, by elongating the pronunciation, or by saying it with a higher pitch.

A technique with a lot of possibilities in developing oral reading skills has been developed by Wilson (45). His pupils' oral reading was taped, and the pupils then listened to their own reading in the language laboratory. Each lesson concentrated on a specific oral reading skill. The pupil analyzed his reading, reread the story orally, and then compared the two readings. Testing seemed to indicate that significant improvement occurred as a result of the program.

Botel (4) suggests additional techniques:

1. Make sure that written-down speech is a record of clear, complete sentences.
2. Record pupil speech, as in experience charts, and teach pupils to read the materials as they were spoken in the first place.
3. Provide choral speaking and reading opportunities.
4. Encourage dramatizations.
5. Make sure that silent reading precedes oral reading and that oral reading is fluent.
6. Let pupils see how a shift of stress in a sentence alters the meaning of the sentence.

SUMMARY

In this chapter we have looked at two different types of definitions of reading and have concluded that a pupil does not become a good reader of graphic symbols without becoming a reader of experience. In addition, we examined reading as a sensory and a perceptual process. As a sensory process reading is dependent on certain *visual* skills. The eyes must have matured to the point where they can react to printed symbols. They must be able to distinguish one printed form from another. They must focus on minute stimuli, and they must progress from left to right and from one line to the next. Reading is dependent also on certain *auditory* skills. The reader must be able to discriminate between the many sounds that form words.

Reading also is a *perceptual* process. The reading act is complete only after the child has interpreted the printed symbol by bringing meaning to it. Meaning itself is dependent on experience, culture, the emotional state of the reader, and the reader's ability to reconstruct his experiences. Meaning is complete only when the reader has developed the ability to pick out the key words, and to relate words and sentences to one another.

Finally, the importance of oral reading was outlined. Oral reading has educational, social, and diagnostic values. Since fluency in oral reading seems to be just as much of a basic reading skill as is silent reading, the reading program must make provision for the development of those skills required for successful oral reading.

QUESTIONS FOR DISCUSSION

1. Discuss the implications of Gray's description of the reading process on the teaching of reading.
2. What are the implications of the general findings of the study by Taylor, Frackenpohl, and Pettee?
3. Is it desirable to develop the eye movements of the reader? In your answer discuss the relationship between eye movements and the central processes of comprehension.
4. Reading is said to be a thinking process. Find four reading passages that illustrate the thinking processes of analysis-synthesis, problem solving, inference, and organization.
5. Discuss the various levels of definitions of reading.
6. Why in the definition of reading is it necessary to include the words: "giving the significance *intended by the writer* to the graphic symbols"?
7. Reading in this chapter is described as "the bringing of meaning *to* the printed page." What are the implications of this for the beginning reader, the slow learner and/or reader, for rate improvement training, and for reading in the content areas?
8. What is the relationship between degrees of comprehension and experiential background?
9. Discriminate between thought-unit reading and the suggestion that the child should learn to read two or three words per fixation. Does a fixation constitute a thought unit? What are the implications of recent findings in this area as regards to the development of the child's memory and retention span?
10. Compare a child's development of a percept of "chair" with his perception of the word "cat."
11. Discuss the following statements:
    a. "Reading should bear the same relationship to experiences or events that a map bears to territory which it is supposed to represent."
    b. "Perception is a kind of summing up of the meanings of numerous sensory impingements."
    c. Reading is the development or creative construction of meaning in response to external stimuli, usually written words.
    d. The greater the number of concepts that the reader has fixed through words, the better will be his understanding of what he reads. Comprehension, or the apprehension of meaning, is a direct function of

(1) the number of words the person knows and (2) the number of meanings that he associates with each word.

e. Facility in conceptualization is a function of previous experience in concept formation. The progression in concept formation is from simple to complex; from diffuse to differentiated; from egocentric to objective; from specific to general; and from inconsistent to consistent.

f. The number of meanings associated with a word is a function of the number of experiences. Words may suggest multiple meanings. The number of meanings actually suggested depends on the number of experiences the reader has associated with the word.

g. The number of different meanings of a word is related positively to the frequency of word usage. "It has been discovered that the number of different cultural meanings (m) of a word tends to be directly proportional to the square root of the relative frequency (F) of its occurrence, i.e.,

$$m = F^{\frac{1}{2}}$$

This was found by plotting logarithmically the average number of different meanings (as ascertained by a previously made *semantic* count) of the 20,000 most frequently occurring words (as ascertained by previously made *frequency* counts) against the logarithm of the respective frequency-rank of the words (36, p. 74)." [9]

h. The specific meaning elicited by a word is a function of the context in which it occurs.

i. Perception of new words and the recognition of words that have been seen before occur more readily when these words are accompanied by familiar rather than by unfamiliar words.

j. The validity of the reader's perception is its predictive value in action. The meaning of tractor that may be aroused by the word "caterpillar" may be adequate in one response situation; in another situation such a response to the word would not be validated in action. The word might then more appropriately suggest the concept larva. The perceiver calls upon his previous experience and assumes that the perception that was most probable in the past is the most probable now. He decides on the meaning that has the best predictive value, on the basis of his previous experience, for interpreting what is read. When he finds that he is wrong, he changes his interpretation, even though the retinal image does not change.

k. The reliability of the initial perception of a word decreases as the number of meanings that may be associated with the word increases. A six-year-old child's perception of a word tends to be more reliable

[9] Joshua Whatmough, *Language: A Modern Synthesis* (New York: St. Martin's Press, Inc., 1956). Reprinted by permission of the publisher.

if the printed word suggests only one meaning than if it can suggest ten different meanings.

l. Perceptual veridicality or concept-environment concordance is a function of experience. The fact that the poor reader substitutes words that do not fit contextually is explainable by his lack of the experiences that are necessary for veridicality. The reader perceives whatever represents for him the most likely prognosis for action based upon his experience. The good reader's prognosis generally is better than that of the poor reader.

THE NATURE
OF THE LEARNER

part **II**

In our introduction to Part I, we pointed out that it is possible to view reading from many angles. In Chapter 2 we emphasized the sensory and perceptual nature of the reading process. The emphasis was on the *nature* of the reading process. In Part II our emphasis is upon the *learner*. Reading is a *response* made by a learner. Reading must be learned by a learner. It is interrelated with the learner's total growth and development. Children show vast differences in physical, intellectual, social, and emotional development. They have different backgrounds, experiences, and interests, and they have received different instruction.

Chapters 3 and 4 attempt to identify the pupil who learns to read well and the child who frequently ends in failure. They are designed to help the teacher to become a better reader of the symptoms and causes of reading disability, to study the correlates of reading achievement and proficiency, to study the child to see if there are any inhibitory factors to making the response for successful reading, and to help the teacher to remediate deficiencies that exist. They are designed to help the teacher to understand children in general, children on the level on which he is teaching, and the individual child in the classroom. We are interested in answering *why* certain children have more difficulty than do others.

The causes of behavior are multiple, complex, and interrelated. The child is a product of both heredity and environment, and generally it is impossible to differentiate the particular role of each. Nevertheless, certain principles of behavior, growth, and development can be stated:

1. The development of each child is caused. In general, there is a reason why the child either achieves or fails to achieve in reading.
2. The causes of development are multiple and complex. Achievement in reading and retardation in reading must be viewed as complex processes explainable only by a group of related causes or factors.
3. Development is a continuous process: What happens at one stage of development influences subsequent stages. Each stage of a child's development is an outgrowth of an earlier age, not simply an addition to it. This principle suggests the need for careful planning of the reading program. It has important implications for the teaching program. Too much of a delay or too early an introduction of reading teaching may both be harmful.
4. Development and growth generally are orderly and gradual. All children go through the same genetic and developmental sequences. Children usually learn to walk only after learning to stand. They learn to speak only after a certain amount of experience in listening. However, some children may skip one of the intermediate steps or, because of structural defects, the order may be altered. Thus, a child may learn to read before learning to speak.
5. Growth sequences generally are sufficiently lawful to permit the teacher to develop norms for the average child. These norms, however, must not become standards by which individual pupils are rated. It is no more ridiculous to have children of one class wear shoes of the same size than to expect them to achieve equally. Group norms must be used to appraise the progress of individuals, not to restrict their progress.
6. Children usually develop as a unified whole. Children's physical, social, emotional, and intellectual growth generally is unified. The growth curves for any given child in each of these areas usually are high, average, or low. Thus, the relative rates of growth tend to remain constant from childhood to adulthood. However, not all aspects of growth proceed along an even front. After having learned a few words, the child may not learn another word for a long time. During this period of apparent language stagnation, the child may be progressing along another front.
7. There are wide variations in growth and development. Not all children reach a plateau or make a spurt at the same time. Each child's growth is unique. He is different in some degree from any other child. The rate of growth and the ceiling of potential levels of achievement vary considerably, even though the devel-

opmental sequence is fairly constant. Sex differences in growth and development are particularly noticeable.

These principles have important implications for the teaching of reading. Development in reading closely parallels and is an expression of the forces of human development generally. Indeed, if teachers could truly divorce achievement in reading from other aspects of growing up, they might be able to produce a standardized product (1).

Unfortunately, this is not possible. The child reads with his biology and his geography, with his nature and his nurture. He is a product of the interaction of these two forces, and these forces are accountable for the vast differences between children. No two children develop to the same point at the same time in any given characteristic. Growth and development are variable and so is achievement in reading.

There is for each child a most *teachable* moment for learning to read and for the learning of every subsequent reading skill. This teachable moment depends on many factors. Thus, the following two chapters attempt to identify those aspects about pupils that have a major bearing on their readiness for and achievement in reading. Chapter 3 will emphasize the experiential, intellectual, and physical aspects.

The Learner

chapter 3

Reading is a developmental task. It is a task that the child must perform in order to satisfy his own needs, so that he may satisfy the demands made upon him by society and so that he may be better prepared to handle subsequent developmental tasks. As with other developmental tasks, success in reading is determined by the child's state of progress in other areas of development and in turn this success affects the child's development in these areas.

There are both biological and environmental determinants of readiness for and achievement in reading. Among the more important factors are the child's intellectual, physical, social, and emotional development, his general proficiency in language, and his sensory equipment. Success in reading also depends on the child's proficiency in auditory and visual discrimination. It is assured by a wide background of personal experience, by a genuine interest in reading, and by an adequate instructional program. The pupil, if he is to learn, must perceive the learning situation as meeting his needs. He also must have had adequate preparation so he can profit from the present learning experience.

These factors are inextricably interrelated. Obviously, no one single factor determines a child's success. It is rarely a single factor that explains reading disability. It is the pattern, the complex of correlates, with which we must be concerned. The child must have a certain degree of readiness in each of the areas, because each in its own way may contribute to reading disability or prevent future growth. It is illogical to expect to produce a successful reader by promoting growth and development in a few specifics while ignoring others. The teacher must examine the composite of interacting factors, and on the basis of them must identify each pupil's *overall* readiness for reading.

Nevertheless, some factors contribute more to achievement than do others. They are relatively more important than others; they have a higher weight value in the correlate pattern. A pupil might be ready for reading in all areas except motivation. This factor alone may keep the pupil from learning. If the pupil does not want to read, no reading will occur.

Let us now examine more closely each of the factors that make for achievement or lack of achievement in reading.

EXPERIENTIAL BACKGROUND

Experience is the basis for all educational development. Concepts develop from experience, and their richness and scope are in direct proportion to the richness and scope of the individual's experience. The most important reason for the difference between the adult's concepts and those of the child is the differential in experience and knowledge. Frequently the significant reason for differences in reading achievement is the differential in experience.

Most studies have shown that children from homes that provide a rich background of experience generally are ready to attack the printed page (60a). Children who have had experience with books and magazines and who have opportunities to make trips, to go to summer camp, to hear good language, to be read to, and to attend a nursery school tend to develop an interest in and generally are proficient in reading. Their potential for concepts and meaning is greater than that of children who lack this background. They are ready to bring meaning *to* the printed page.

Although high socioeconomic status is not a completely accurate indicator of reading achievement, it generally goes hand in hand with broadness of experience and with language facility (80). This broadness of experience and the added language facility result in superior readiness for reading by equipping the child with the tools for meaningful reaction to the printed page. The symbols on the page are empty unless the reader endows them with meaning. For this the pupil needs the appropriate experience.

Schools today are geared to children from middle- and upper-class socioeconomic homes. Unfortunately, this does not raise the status of less privileged children. These children usually have lower IQ's, are less proficient in language, leave school at an earlier age, have more adjustment problems, and are less interested in school. Their self-concept is usually low, and thus they frequently do not aspire to high levels of achievement. They are wise in the ways of the street but are often not interested in cultural opportunities in the world about them. Their cultural horizons rarely extend beyond the city alleys, and, because of this, they cannot bring meaningful concepts to the symbols on the printed page.

The duty of teachers seems clear. If the child comes from an environment that does not stimulate experiential and perceptual growth, the school must provide the preparatory experiences. There is a special need to supply children from the lower socioeconomic groups with stimulating nursery school and kindergarten experiences, with neighborhood reading centers, and with bookmobiles. Unfortunately, such experiences and opportunities are most available to children in the higher economic groups.

Of even greater significance in teaching culturally deprived children is the realization that their reading achievement scores frequently are low because the reading materials in school present experiences alien to their own. As one teacher put it, these children read stories about "Saturday Night on Madison Street," but either can't or won't read "Dick and Jane." They find little material in the "Dick and Jane" stories that is familiar to them. When they work with stories and other materials, prepared by themselves or by the teacher, which use vocabulary words familiar to their own experiences, their interest is stimulated and they begin to make progress. The value of teacher-prepared or pupil-prepared materials is readily apparent.

Readiness programs generally have proved valuable. They are especially successful with children who are handicapped by a foreign language background, with children from lower socioeconomic classes, and with dull-normal or underprivileged children. However, some children, although from the upper socioeconomic group, have led an extremely sheltered life. Servants take care of them, and they have little contact with other children. These may need as much experiential stimulation as do children from lower socioeconomic homes.

Generally, the lower the intelligence, the longer should be the reading readiness program. However, the highly intelligent child is not necessarily more ready for reading than is the less intelligent. He knows how to sound out words, but he frequently needs experience to give meaning to his verbalizations.

When there is no kindergarten program, the first-grade teacher should not hurry children into formal reading instruction. Some children have a real need for the readiness program. The teacher cannot overlook the wide diversity in experience between the country child and the city child; between the youngster whose family lives in a slum and the child who comes from a wealthy home. And he must remember that each child's reactions to the printed page are limited by his environment.

Some children, because they come to school able to read, actually may be harmed by a readiness program. Not all children get the needed experiential background in school. Probably most five- and six-year-old children are ready to handle the demands for meaning that are made in first-grade materials.

The following statements summarize the importance of experience for reading achievement:

1. Experience is one factor that accounts for differences in reading achievement, and lack of experience may be a cause of reading disability.

2. Experience and maturation are the basis of all educational development. To predict behavior both the person and the environment must be considered as a constellation of interdependent factors.

3. Differences in learning ability of children are related to their biological potentials, but also to the environmental opportunities. Some children become reading disability cases because the environment does not call forth their potential.

4. It is impossible to predict the learning of the pupil without knowing the structure of his social environment, the types of behavior that are rewarded, and the types of rewards that are provided.

5. The child from the middle-class home has an advantage because his home contains "a hidden curriculum" (38) which permits him to deal appropriately with first school experiences.

MATURATIONAL DEVELOPMENT

Even though we began this chapter by emphasizing experience, the pupil's achievement depends as much on maturation as on experience. Baller and Charles (3, p. 22) note that "Maturation is an unfolding or 'ripening' of potentials that an individual possesses by virtue of his being a member of a given species and by virtue, more specifically, of his biological inheritance from a particular heritage." [1]

We generally assume that the child receives his biological inheritance through maturation, while he acquires his social inheritance through learning. Maturation, however, is a prerequisite to much learning, and environment and experience are prerequisite to maturation.

[1] Warren R. Baller and Don C. Charles, *The Psychology of Human Growth and Development* (New York: Holt, Rinehart and Winston, Inc., 1961). Reprinted by permission.

The pupil's achievement is certainly affected by inadequacies and delays in maturation or in development of the physical-physiological functions. There is a difference between maturational delays and developmental delays (6). Developmental delays are delays in progress in which the experiential factors play a predominant role; in maturational delays, physical-physiological factors are of primary importance.

Belmont (6) notes that the stage as well as the rate of physical maturation influence and probably are influenced by the nature of the child's experience. And Harris (37, p. 3) writes: "Without maturation the child cannot learn; without experience he has nothing to learn."

Belmont adds that just as it is very difficult for a seven-month-old child to establish voluntary control over bowel function for biological reasons (the nerve pathways necessary for this function are not yet completely myelinated, and, hence, are not voluntarily operational) so there are varying degrees of biological maturational preparedness to undertake learning.

Maturational changes usually are orderly and sequential. Wide variations of environmental conditions seem to have little effect on maturation. The nervous system develops regularly according to its own intrinsic pattern. There thus seems to be very little benefit in rushing the maturation process. For example, we don't teach the child to swing a bat before he is capable of lifting a bat. The child learns to talk only after he is old enough. Practice needs to wait for maturation.

However, teaching and other environmental stimulations are not useless. Children need appropriate environmental stimulation if maturational development is to progress at an appropriate rate. In many instances the child has inadequacies in his experiential background. The teacher cannot overemphasize either maturation- or experience-learning. Too much emphasis on maturation may lead to useless postponing of what could be learned; too much emphasis on learning or experience may lead to futile attempts at teaching that for which the child is not ready. Nevertheless, instruction must march slightly ahead of development. "It must be aimed not so much at the ripe as at the ripening function (76, p. 104)."

In summary:

1. The pupil develops reading skills most readily if they are built upon the natural foundation of maturational development.
2. Children should not be forced into readiness for either beginning reading or for any subsequent reading skill before maturational development is adequate.
3. In *Walden* Thoreau noted: "If a man does not keep pace with his companions, perhaps it is because he hears a different

drummer. Let him step to the music which he hears, however measured or far away."

4. The child whose difficulty is basically maturational, who is a slow developer, may *best* be helped by being given the opportunity to catch up (6).

INTELLECTUAL DEVELOPMENT

Experience and maturation alone do not guarantee success in reading. The child needs certain intellectual skills. He must perceive likenesses and differences, must be able to remember word forms, and must possess certain thinking skills. He must have developed an appropriate memory and attention span. He must be able to tell stories in proper sequence, to interpret pictures, to associate symbols or language with pictures, objects and facts, to anticipate what may happen in a story or poem, to express his thoughts in his own words, and to think on an abstract level. He must be able to give identity and meaning to objects, events, and symbols. He must be able to categorize or to associate the particular object or experience with the appropriate class or category.

Intellectual development is a function of both biology and environment. Biology sets the limits to the child's mental development, and how close the child comes to attaining his potential depends upon the environment and the use that he makes of that environment. It depends also upon other factors, among which are opportunity, challenge, desire, nutrition, rest, self-discipline, aggressiveness, and the need to achieve. Thus, biology provides the potential and the environment converts it into abilities. "Native ability" actually is the potential to become able; ability is realized potential.

Intelligence always has been difficult to define. Surely one of the reasons for this is the removal of intelligence from the realm of time. A child's potential for intellectual activity at the moment of conception may not be the same as his potential at birth or indeed at any given moment of life.

At conception the child possesses what might be described as native intellectual endowment. Biology has set a limit at that time to the child's intellectual capacity. In a later portion of this chapter we discuss the human brain. The brain is biologically determined and the "mind," "intellect," "cognition," or "perception" must operate through this brain. In a very real sense, man's potential for intellectual behavior is completely dependent upon the proper functioning of the brain.

Aphasia is an instance of improper brain functioning. As a result of cerebral injury, the aphasic is unable to deal with symbols. He can think only on a concrete or specific level. He cannot think abstractly, he cannot categorize, and he is unable to think of the individual object as a member of a class. He cannot, for example, see that a polar bear and a brown bear are bears. These have an individuality for him that does not allow for categorization.

If brain injury can so limit human thought, biology can do likewise. Inadequacy in the genes is a very real cause of inadequate brain development. Nervoid idiocy, amaurotic idiocy, gargoylism (grotesque bone structure), phenylpyruvic idiocy, and primary microcephaly, to mention a few, are caused by gene disturbances. Feeblemindness frequently occurs when the mother's Rh factor is positive and that of the child is negative. When the mother's blood and the child's blood are combined, the embryo does not get a sufficient amount of oxygen, the brain is injured, and mental deterioration results.

Intelligence in this sense is the

> . . . functional manifestation of the integrity of the central nervous system. The idea implies that the degree of intelligence manifested by an individual bears a relationship to the structural and functional state of his brain. Damage or failure of development or better than average development of a part of it is likely to produce corresponding variations in the capacity to perform the functions affected by the part (27, p. 16).[2]

Intelligence can be viewed in another way. At the moment of birth the child has an intellectual potential that has been limited and defined by biology but now also is conditioned by environment. The child's intrauterine existence may have been favorable, or it may have been unfavorable for the realization of the child's full intellectual potential at the moment of conception.

Experiments with salamanders and squids have produced marked structural changes during embryonic development. The normally two-eyed squid has been changed to a one-eyed organism. In other experiments it was possible to condition the human fetus and some, for example, have intimated that left-handedness may be an example of prenatal conditioning.

Experience has shown repeatedly that the brain, and hence the intellectual functioning of the child, may be damaged by infection, by birth trauma, by toxic agents, or by endocrine disorders. It may be damaged

---

[2] Thomas H. Eames, "Some Neural and Glandular Bases of Learning," *Journal of Education,* 142 (April 1960). Reprinted by permission of the Journal of Education, Boston University Press.

by pressure upon the fetus, by faulty position of the fetus, by temperature changes, by overexposure to X rays, by premature separation from the placenta, by umbilical-cord complications, by an overdosage of the mother with drugs, by delayed breathing of the infant, or by forceps delivery. Barbiturates may produce asphyxiation in the fetus. The mother also can pass diseases on to the child that interfere with normal brain development. Some common ones are: smallpox, German measles, scarlet fever, syphilis, and tuberculosis.

Finally, intelligence may be viewed as the child's present functioning level. This is essentially what scholastic aptitude tests measure. However, if the child's environment or experience is defective, it frequently happens that a measure of the pupil's present functioning level is not a good indicator of his true potential. It is not uncommon to have a pupil obtain scores like the following on a group intelligence test: linguistic IQ—85; quantitative IQ—115; and total IQ—100. The linguistic score and the total score probably are the best predictors of the child's present scholastic functioning level. Scholastic functioning depends most on the child's ability to deal with symbols, and the linguistic score measures this ability. The quantitative score may be closer to the pupil's true potential. The chances are that a pupil with such discrepancies between linguistic and quantitative scores is from a poor cultural environment, has a reading problem, and/or is bilingual. If the causative factor is removed, it is not uncommon to find that the IQ score of such a pupil will rise from fifteen to twenty points.

The teacher essentially is an environmentalist. Even though he cannot add to the child's basic capacity, he can do much to encourage the child to develop his potential. The child commonly has a much greater mental capacity than he is willing to use. As teachers, our task is to challenge the existent capacity of the pupil rather than to try to add increments to his native endowment.

In the light of the above discussion the biological-environmental [3] controversy seems to be a pseudoconflict. The relative contribution of biology, for example, depends on the trait under consideration, upon the individual possessing the trait, and upon the environment. Thus, in some environments, the principal cause of reading inadequacy may be biological in origin; in others, where there is inadequate teaching, it may be environmental. Anastasi and Foley (2, p. 11) point out that most hereditary-or-environmental discussions are actually concerned with structural or functional factors. Teachers are more concerned with the following: "Is reading failure caused by structural or functional conditions?" For a more complete dicussion, see the heading "Wordblindness" in this chapter.

[3] We prefer the term biological-environmental to hereditary-environmental.

Mental Age

For years intelligence was thought to be a unitary factor. Today, few adhere to this point of view. Some persons are spatially or artistically intelligent; others are numerically or verbally intelligent. Some are better able to discover underlying principles; others have a remarkable memory. As educators, we are most interested perhaps in the pupil's scholastic aptitude. This is essentially a combination of verbal and numerical intelligence and is usually expressed as a mental age or an intelligence quotient.

Mental age (MA) refers to the level of mental development that the person has attained. It is the pupil's score on an intelligence test expressed in age units, or put another way, it is the average age of the individuals who attained that score in the standardization process (72, pp. 216–217).

Thus the average five-year-old child has a mental age of five; the average child of ten, a mental age of ten; and the average youth of fifteen, a mental age of fifteen. But because it generally has been accepted that beyond the age of fifteen or sixteen the mean scores on intelligence tests no longer increase significantly, the average youth of eighteen or twenty will still have a mental age of but fifteen or sixteen.[4]

The Intelligence Quotient

Another term, the intelligence quotient (IQ) refers to the *rate of mental development*. We all remember the simple formula: Distance equals Rate multiplied by Time $(D = R \times T)$.

We may use an analogous formula in thinking about mental age and IQ: thus, $MA = IQ \times CA$. In the formula MA refers to the distance that the pupil has traveled mentally; the IQ refers to the rate at which he has been going; and the CA refers to the length of time that he has been at it.

If we think of an IQ of 120 as meaning that the person has advanced at the rate of 1.2 years mentally for each year of chronological life (up to the age of fifteen or sixteen), and of an IQ of 80 as meaning that he has advanced 0.8 of a year mentally for each year of chronological life, the formula $(MA = IQ \times CA)$ is easy to understand and to use. A ten-year-old boy with an IQ of 120 has a mental age of twelve $(MA = IQ \times CA$—$1.2 \times 10)$. Another ten-year-old with an IQ of 80 has a mental age of 8 $(MA = IQ \times CA$—$0.8 \times 10)$. The first boy has attained the

---

[4] Actually, the scores cease to increase at the *average* age of fifteen or sixteen years, and thus for some they do not increase at an earlier age and for others they increase even at a later age.

mental level of the average twelve-year-old; the second, the mental level of the average eight-year-old.

There are four statements that we can make about the IQ:

1. IQ is the rate of mental development.
2. $IQ = \dfrac{MA}{CA} \times 100.$
3. An IQ of 120 means that the individual has developed 1.2 years mentally for each year of chronological life.
4. An IQ of a given magnitude also describes the percentage of children in the general population that possess that IQ.

Let us give some consideration to this last point. IQ also may be defined in terms of a relative position among a defined group of persons. An IQ tells how much above or below the average an individual is when comparing himself with persons of his own age. It measures the person's ability relative to persons of his own age group.

Studies have shown that the IQ is normally distributed. We plot this distribution on what we call a normal curve. The curve is merely a graph showing on the baseline some type of score, and the height of the curve at any given point indicates the number of cases that fall at that point. The curve shows the distribution of IQ's and the percentage of persons that have a given IQ.

Educational Implications

The IQ certainly is not an adequate criterion for reading readiness or achievement. However, it is significant in that it puts a ceiling upon individual achievement. Individuals with an IQ below 25 have little chance of learning to read; those with an IQ below 50 will experience difficulty with abstract materials; and those with IQ's between 50 and 70 rarely will be able to read above a fourth-grade level.

The IQ also is an important long-range predictor of the child's performance. The child with a 150 IQ who is only six years old may not be as efficient a reader as the child with a 100 IQ who is ten years old. With time, however, the chances are that he will reach a higher level of reading proficiency.

Mental age, generally, is a much better indicator of reading readiness and achievement than is IQ, especially at the early levels. To be able to read, many skills are necessary that come only with age.

Correlations between intelligence and reading ability generally vary from about .35 in the first grades to about .65 in the sixth grade (9, p. 42). Cohen and Glass (17) found no significant relationship between IQ scores and reading ability in first grade; in the fourth grade, IQ and reading ability were significantly related. These findings are significant. They imply that intelligence is a more important determinant of reading success in the later grades than in the earlier grades. In the later grades, reading scores are an expression of proficiency in content-area reading. Content-area reading generally requires greater use of those skills that we associate with intellectual activity.

Even though the correlations between intelligence and reading achievement are high, they are not perfect. Intelligence is not the sole, nor necessarily the best, indicator of reading readiness or achievement. High intelligence does not guarantee success in reading. Research indicates that the great majority of poor readers have IQ's between 80 and 110 (79, p. 228) and that frequently the most severely retarded readers in relation to their mental age have IQ's of 130 or more.

The question arises: When is the child ready for reading? There is evidence against hurrying the child too much as well as evidence against delaying instruction.

Through the years a mental age of six and one-half has been generally accepted as the optimal age for beginning reading. Research, however, provides little support for choosing a specific mental age as a criterion. The facts are that many children with a mental age of six and one-half do not succeed in reading and many other children learn to read who have not attained a mental age of six.

Durkin (20,21,22,23,) in various and continuous studies of early and nonearly readers, found significantly higher achievement among the early readers. She reports that even after six years of instruction in reading, the early readers, as a group, were better achievers than their classmates of the same mental age who did not begin to read until the first grade (23). The I.Q.'s of the early readers ranged from 82 to 170.

The children who early learned to read manifested an interest in learning to print either simultaneously or prior to developing an interest in reading. They eagerly responded to their word-filled world. These "pencil and paper kids" moved from scribbling and drawing to copying objects and letters of the alphabet, to questions about spelling, to ability to read. They wanted to see their name in print and used small blackboards. They were curious, conscientious, persistent, self-reliant, and became intensely interested in projects (making a calendar) for long periods of time. Their attention spans were decidedly not short, and their memories and concentration were good. They had parents or siblings who read to them. Their mothers played a key role in encouraging early achievement.

Sutton (73) reports that children who read early tend to be girls, have siblings and parents who read to them, come from upper-socioeconomic homes, have parents who are interested in school affairs and educational progress, are interested in words, are conscientious and self-reliant, have good memories and know how to concentrate, can name most of the letters of the alphabet, and have fathers who engage in mental rather than manual work. Plessas and Oaks (64) found that early readers were taught to read by their parents or siblings; their reading was not simply a chance happening.

Brzeinski and others (13,14), in a five-year follow-up study of 4,000 Denver school children who began to read in kindergarten, noted that there was a definite advantage in the early instruction, that it did not affect visual acuity, and that it did not lead to school maladjustment, nor to a dislike for reading. Mood (58), however, raised questions about the research design of the Denver study, about the methods of reporting, about the different attrition rates of the experimental and control groups, and about the failure to deal adequately with the Hawthorne effect.

There is little doubt that three-, four-, and five-year-olds can be taught to read. The important question is: "Is this desirable? It would appear that children who are *ready* for an early start in reading may not suffer adverse effects when taught; they, in fact, seem to profit from activities which stimulate their interest in reading (45).

Mason and Prater (53) found that introducing the teaching of reading in the kindergarten tended to increase negative social behavior among the boys, and the teacher felt that the learning was hard work and a much slower process than with first graders. In another article (52), Mason and Prater reviewed the research and concluded that:

1. Younger children make less progress than older ones of the same intelligence when they are exposed to the same program.
2. The best age for beginning reading is dependent upon the materials used, the size of the class, the pacing of the program, and teacher expectancies.

If the reading materials are suited to their level, if they are interesting, and if the teaching method is adapted to their intellectual maturity, children may learn to read at mental ages considerably below six and one-half. It appears that the younger the pupils, the lower should be the teacher-pupil ratio. A teacher needs to work more closely with younger children.

Instruction must march slightly ahead of maturation but it might be better to err by going too slowly than by going too fast. Rousseau (p. 83) [5] put it aptly when he wrote:

[5] Jacques Rousseau, *Émile* (New York: Appleton-Century-Crofts, Inc., 1899).

> I would much rather he (Émile) would never know how to read than to buy this knowledge at the price of all that can make it useful. Of what use would reading be to him after he had been disgusted with it forever?

It may be good to introduce formal reading instruction to *some* three-, four-, or five-year-old children, but *en masse* introduction to children may cripple the spirits of some children. It seems important that we allow the child to enjoy and to live his childhood. Tomorrow's problems can wait. Indeed, for the best development of the child, they must wait.

It would seem that if teachers of reading are expert in teaching children, they will not push children beyond their maturational level. The timing of instruction is especially important in preventing reading disability. Reading disability too often is caused by starting the child in a reading program before he is ready for it. Such a child cannot handle the day-by-day learning tasks and finds himself farther and farther behind as the time goes by. He becomes frustrated and develops antipathy toward reading. He actually learns *not to read*. This is quite different and far more serious than not learning to read. Bond and Tinker (10, p. 140) note that:

> Reading disability is frequently caused by starting a child in a standard reading program before he has acquired the readiness which will assure success in classroom reading activities. Due to his lack of experience, verbal facility, intellectual or emotional maturity, or a combination of these, he is unable to achieve enough of the learnings day by day to handle satisfactorily what is coming next. He gets farther and farther behind as time goes on. Inability to cope with the assignments produces frustration which leads to feelings of inadequacy, inferiority, insecurity, and perhaps even rebellion. Such a child is likely to develop an attitude of indifference to reading. He may even come to hate reading and all persons and activities connected with reading activities.[6]

Another caution seems indicated. It may be dangerous to emphasize one phase of education at the expense of another. Although we can teach very young children to read and to type, we agree with Bugelski (15, p. 59) that "Typing is not a substitute for geography, nor is reading a substitute for tying one's shoes."

[6] Guy L. Bond and Miles A. Tinker, *Reading Difficulties: Their Diagnosis and Correction* (New York: Appleton-Century-Crofts, Inc., 1967). Reprinted with permission.

It would be a serious indictment of us as teachers if children became reading disability cases because we introduced them to reading too early or because we pushed them beyond their level of endurance. As Bond and Tinker (10, p. 15) point out:

> In general, the writers believe that most disability cases are made rather than born that way. Reading disabilities are sometimes the result of predisposing conditions within the child that are unrecognized, but for the most part they are brought about by factors in the child's environment at home, at play, and in school.[7]

McCormick (55) cautions that happiness is a child learning to read, but security is allowing him to do it when he is ready.

PHYSICAL DEVELOPMENT

We have discussed three determinants of the child's achievement in reading. Let us look at another group of related conditions which, for want of a better term, we shall refer to as physical factors.

The child is both physical and physiological. Functions such as vision, hearing, and thought are possible only through the organs of the body, the eye, the ear, or brain. If the organ is defective, the function is likely to be impaired. This may, especially in the case of vision, hearing, and thought, lead to serious reading difficulties. In general, good health is conducive to good reading, and poor health is often associated with reading deficiency.

PHYSICAL HEALTH

Reading is an act, a performance, or a response that the reader makes to the printed page. Unfortunately, certain factors may prohibit making the response. Glandular dysfunction (27,26, pp. 23–32), hemoglobin variation,[8] vitamin deficiencies, nerve disorders, nutritional and circulatory problems, heart conditions, infected tonsils, poor teeth, rickets, asthma, allergies, tuberculosis, rheumatic fever, or prolonged illness can lower reading achievement and postpone or prevent reading readiness.

[7] Guy L. Bond and Miles A. Tinker, *Reading Difficulties: Their Diagnosis and Correction.* (New York: Appleton-Century-Crofts, Inc., 1967). Reprinted with permission.

[8] Low hemoglobin content is associated with the diminution of acuity in vision and hearing and with impaired writing performance.

Eames (28) points out that tumefaction of the pituitary gland may lead to a reduction in eye span and consequently to an increase in the number of fixations. Hypothyroid conditions may prevent normal fixation on what is being read and thus lead to daydreaming, poor attention, slow word recognition, and general fatigue. Diabetes mellitus is associated with visual defects, confusions, excessive regressions, and loss of place.

However, Schiffman (66) states that there is no known relationship between errors of biochemical functioning and any *specific* reading syndrome.

The eating habits of our children are related to a child's overall functioning and also may be a direct cause of poor learning. Far too often the elementary school child either does not eat at all or gulps down a few bites to satisfy his mother.

The teacher must be cautious in interpreting the relationship that these factors seemingly have to reading deficiency. Generally, physical inadequacies are contributory factors rather than factors causing reading problems. Illness keeps the child from school and causes him to miss important phases of instruction. Any physical inadequacy makes it difficult to become enthusiastic about learning and may result in lowered vitality, in depletion of energy, in slower physical development, and hence in mental retardation. Physical inadequacies cause the child to center attention on them and away from learning. The child with a smashed finger, a broken hand, a headache, or poor eyesight may be unable to concentrate on a learning task. The malnourished child does not have the energy to be an effective learner.

Sometimes a lowering of the child's basic vitality is closely related to the functions required for successful reading. The basal metabolic rate, *BMR,* for example, affects the convergence of the eyes.[9] If the rate is low, the child may not be able to aim his eyes properly in binocular vision, and thus may frequently regress, omit words, lose his place, and become fatigued. And, fatigue makes it difficult to become interested in a reading task. Attention suffers and comprehension is usually lowered. As nervous tension builds up, the pupil becomes disinterested, disgusted, and may even turn from reading completely.

VISUAL ADEQUACY

We already have spoken of the child's need for visual proficiency. Studies also indicate that children often may not be visually ready for reading

[9] The basal metabolic rate is lowered by endocrine deficiencies. These also seem to be a factor in the inability to focus and in strabismus.

before the age of eight (65, p. 91). The eye becomes structurally complete about that time. At six, the eyes frequently are too farsighted to see clearly and with ease objects as small as a word. The image of near objects does not focus adequately on the retina. Thus, the visual age of the learner may be an important determinant of the child's "organismic age," and we may have to give consideration to it in the planning of the pupil's reading program.

The ability to focus the eyes correctly during reading is part of the wider problem of motor coordination. For efficient reading the child must learn to coordinate the eyes, to move them along a line of print, and to make appropriate return sweeps. He must see clearly and distinctly both near and far, must be able to change focus and to fuse the impressions of each eye into a single image, and must have visual memory for what he has seen. He must be able to sustain visual concentration, must have good hand-eye coordination, and must be able to perceive accurately size and distance relationships (65, p. 91).

Even after children have become visually ready, numerous visual defects may occur. It is difficult to evaluate the specific effect of the various visual disturbances. The eyes can make amazing accommodations so words may be seen clearly. With the proper motivation the pupil may learn despite visual handicaps. He can ignore a distortion from one eye if he sees clearly with the other or if he adjusts his reading position to compensate. He may suppress the vision in one eye or alternate from one eye to another. The result is monocular vision. Generally, however, for effective vision the child must be able to use his eyes in unison.

Visual Acuity

Visual acuity does not seem to have the significance for reading achievement that some other visual factors have. First: Reading is a near-point task. One could fail the visual acuity test at 20 feet but possess good visual acuity at 16 inches. Second: To read the average book, one needs only 20/60 visual acuity.[10] Nevertheless, acuity is important. Each child should probably have at least 20/30 acuity at far point.

The emmetropic or normal eye sees with 100 per cent of acuity only a very small portion of the visual field, perhaps no more than four or five letters (32). Figure 3-1 shows this and indicates that the words and letters either to the right or left of this point are seen with ever decreasing clarity.

---

[10] Snellen's formula is $V = d/D$. V represents visual acuity; d is the distance at which the person is reading the letters; and D is the distance at which the person should be reading. Thus 20/60 means that the person sees at 20 feet what he should see at 60 feet. A 20/20 notation means that the pupil has 100 per cent visual efficiency at far point; 20/200 means 20 per cent visual efficiency.

Refractive errors are due to damage to, disease of, or weakness in the lens or other portion of one or both eyes. Generally refractive errors can be corrected by glasses. Glasses, however, do not increase the sensitivity of the eyes. They help the eye to focus and lower eye strain but frequently fail to provide normal vision.

Myopia or nearsightedness is perhaps the most common among the refractive errors. The myopic eye is too long, with the result that the light rays come into focus in front of the retina instead of on the retina. This forces the pupil to hold the book closer than the normal 16 inches or so. Distant vision generally is blurred. Usually concave lenses are prescribed for myopic conditions.

A work shop sponsored by an advisory group to the National Institute of Neurological Diseases and Blindness held in Washington in 1966, commenting on the etiology of myopia, noted that the evidence points strongly to genetic factors as significant but noted that there may also be considerable environmental influence. Restricting the visual field to close objects induced myopia in monkeys. Among honor students in college, who do significantly more reading than the average college population, the incidence of myopia is 66 per cent.

Eberl (29) believes that the child may become myopic through premature attempts to adapt his eyes to the demands of close vision. Perhaps even more important, she concludes that the child who cannot adjust through becoming myopic may avoid reading (and other near-point tasks) and turn to what for him are more pleasant activities.

Kosinski (48) suggests that myopia is symptomatic of a general weakness of connective tissue, which manifests itself also in hernias and varicose veins. The sweep in reading from the end of one line to the beginning of the next leads to congestion and pressure on the posterior role of the eye, causing it to become myopic. Mills (56) believes that hurried and excessive use of peripheral vision may be the causal factor.

Hyperopia or hypermetropia generally is known as farsightedness. Where the myopic eye is too long, the hyperopic eye is too short. In this case, the image falls behind the retina. To remedy this condition, convex lenses are prescribed. In testing for farsightedness, if the child reads the 20/20 test line with +2.00 diopter lenses, he should be referred.

Another type of refractive error, *astigmatism,* is the inability to bring the light rays to a single focal point. Vision is blurred and distorted. The underlying cause is an uneven curvature of the front or cornea of the eye. The cornea is spoon-shaped rather than spherical. Unless the distorted image is corrected by the use of cylindrical lens, the child fatigues easily and usually dislikes close work or prolonged distant vision. Astigmatism is a major cause of ocular asthenopia or eyestrain (66a).

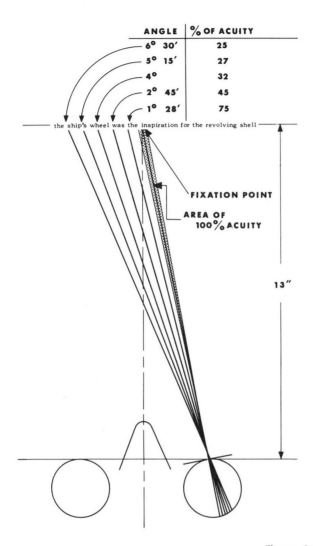

ANGLE	% OF ACUITY
6° 30'	25
5° 15'	27
4°	32
2° 45'	45
1° 28'	75

the ship's wheel was the inspiration for the revolving shell

FIXATION POINT

AREA OF
100% ACUITY

13"

Figure 3-1.   Visual Acuity*

Headaches are common, similar letters and words are confused, and the pupil experiences difficulty in sustained reading.

Coleman's study (18) indicates that it is not enough to evaluate children's refractive errors. This will identify only about 20 per cent of the children with problems. Furthermore, 30 per cent of the children with more serious visual-perceptual disturbances and deficits will readily pass routine refractive evaluations.

* Stanford E. Taylor, *Speed Reading vs. Improved Reading Efficiency* (Educational Developmental Laboratories, 1962), p. 11. Reproduced by permission.

The binocular difficulties have the commonality of giving the child a double image. Either the two eyes do not aim correctly or they give conflicting reports. When the ocular maladjustments are minor, the individual may compensate for them. If the maladjustments are major, the child may see two of everything or the two images may be so badly blurred that he sees neither image clearly. Somehow he needs to suppress one stimulus. When he can suppress it only partially or only temporarily, he is likely to lose his place, to omit words, or to regress.

Strabismus or muscular imbalance stems from an incoordination of the muscles that move the eyeball. The eyes actually are aiming in different directions. One eye aims too far outward, too far inward, or in a different vertical plane from the other eye. A severe case of strabismus may result in double vision; a less severe case, in a general blurring of the image.

Each of the eyes has six muscles that must function together if the eye is to aim correctly. This is made somewhat more difficult because the eyes are set in a movable base, the head.

There are three types of strabismus or heterophoria. When the deviation is outward, it is called exophoria (wall eyes); when it is inward, esophoria (crossed eyes); and when one eye focuses higher than the other, it is called hyperphoria. Hyperphoria may lead to jumping of lines or misplacement of a word to a line above or below.

Even a moderate amount of heterophoria or tendency of the eye to deviate results in fatigue. As the reader tires, his eyes tend to deviate even farther. Attempts to counteract this increase fatigue. A vicious circle is set up. The pupil becomes inattentive and irritable, loses his place, omits, and regresses. This incoordination is sometimes corrected by cutting some of the eye muscles.

Some research indicates that myopic children with phoric conditions read about as well as do children without phoria, but that children with phorias at far point have poorer reading skills.

Two additional binocular defects are *lack of fusion* and *aniseikonia*. To see clearly, the lenses of the two eyes must be in focus. The images must fuse correctly, thus giving one mental picture.

The light patterns focused on the retina generate nerve impulses that travel via the optic nerve and the visual pathways to the visual centers of the brain. On the way, the impulses from the nasal side of each eye cross, thus joining the impulses from the temporal side of the opposite eye. Each cerebral hemisphere thus receives impulses from both eyes. These impulses are then blended into one picture (8).

An inability to fuse correctly is manifested by mixing of letters and words, inability to follow lines across a page, loss of place, and by slowness in reading.

Aniseikonia occurs whenever there is a difference in size or shape between the two ocular images. As a result fusion is difficult and the reader may become tense, experience fatigue, and have headaches.

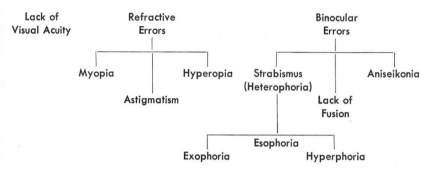

Figure 3-2.   Visual Deficiencies

Figure 3-2 illustrates the various visual defects that are present among school children. Naturally, there are other visual defects, but the incidence of these is not as great.

Symptoms of Eye Disturbances

The teacher of reading cannot be satisfied with a general knowledge of eye defects. He needs to know the individual pupil's eye condition well enough to answer a number of specific questions (71, p. 163): Does the pupil need special reading materials? When should he wear his glasses? Does he require special lighting? Can he read for prolonged periods of time?

The teacher frequently must seek help from a specialist. Perhaps the teacher's chief responsibility here is to be familiar with the symptoms of eye defects. A knowledge of these will help him to detect visual problems before they have become visual defects. He should be able to identify functional problems before they have become structural problems.

Bing (8) groups symptoms into: (1) avoidance symptoms, such as in the case of the child who shuns reading tasks; (2) behavior symptoms such as squinting, fatigue, or excessive blinking; and (3) complaints such as dizziness, blurring, or double vision.

The symptoms of visual difficulty are many. Knox (47, p. 98) categorized ninety-four symptoms and from these selected thirty that optometrists and ophthalmologists felt were significant. These are:

1. Inflammation, reddening, or thickening of the lids and watering of the eyes
2. Assumes poor sitting position
3. Attempts to brush away blur
4. Blinks eyes often
5. Changes distance at which book is held
6. Deviation in one eye
7. Drooping of upper lid
8. Excessive head movement while reading
9. Facial contortions: scowls, puckers forehead, squints, etc.
10. Forward thrusting of head
11. Rubs eyes often
12. Shuts or covers one eye while reading
13. Tilts head
14. Very restless or nervous
15. Alignment in penmanship unsatisfactory
16. Apparently guesses words from quick recognition of parts of words
17. Avoids as much close work as possible
18. Confuses letters such as o and a, e and c, n and m, etc.
19. Holds book far from face while reading
20. Holds book close to face while reading
21. Holds body tense while looking at distant objects
22. Is inattentive in reading lesson
23. Is inattentive during a group lesson on a chart, map, or blackboard
24. Makes errors when copying from board or works slowly while copying from the board
25. Reads smoothly and accurately at first, then jerkily and with errors
26. Skips words or lines while reading orally
27. Has tendency to reverse in reading, spelling, or arithmetic
28. Has tendency to lose place in reading
29. Is tense during close work
30. Tires quickly upon beginning to read or to do other close work[11]

Certainly the teacher should know these danger signs and look for them. Early detection of a child's visual difficulty may depend upon his

[11] Gertrude E. Knox, "Classroom Symptoms of Visual Difficulty," Clinical Studies in Reading: II, *Supplementary Educational Monographs*, No. 77 (Chicago: The University of Chicago Press, 1937. Reprinted by permission.

For another listing of symptoms of visual difficulty see: Samuel M. Diskan, "Eye Problems in Children," *Postgraduate Medicine*, 34 (August, 1963), 168–178.

alertness. The child's achievement in school generally is related to good vision. Good vision will mean more comfortable reading, and the child that sees well tends to develop favorable attitudes toward reading.

It must be recognized that many of these symptoms are common during colds, and other illnesses, but any persistence of these complaints indicates the need for an eye examination.

Teachers frequently are appalled by the poor concentration of some of their students. Unfortunately, in this instance "poor concentration" is not a good term. The pupil usually can concentrate, but it is on only one idea at a time. His attempt to maintain single vision or to clear blurred vision may prevent concentration on the mental task at hand. His cortical powers are directed entirely to the maintenance of basic visual skills (24). This same need for conscious control of the ocular factors may keep the child from reading as rapidly as he might.

Educational Implications

Eye defects of one sort or another are rather common. These defects increase throughout the grades and may play an important role in reading inadequacy. Good readers in the elementary grades generally have fewer visual defects than have poor readers. In high school and college— possibly because by high school many of those with poor vision have left school, and those who remain have adapted their scholastic approach to their reading deficiencies—there are few indications of visual differences between good and poor readers.

Generally, the incidence of myopia does not distinguish the good reader from the poor reader. In fact, myopia may be associated with better than normal progress. Although hyperopia seems to occur somewhat more frequently among poor readers (25, p. 7), the evidence certainly is not definitive. However, Foote, former director of the National Society for the Prevention of Blindness, suggests that 10 to 15 per cent of first graders are so farsighted that they are unable to use their eyes in deciphering print without developing headaches, fatigue, or nervousness. There also is a lack of agreement concerning the effect that astigmatism has on reading. It may be a handicap to successful reading when the learner has a severe case.

Failure of the eyes to coordinate, as in strabismus and in lack of fusion, and failure of the eyes to give images of the same size seem to have more serious impact on reading development. When the deviations are vertical, as when one eye focuses higher (hyperphoria), the reader frequently loses his place and fixates at a point either below or above the line on which he should be reading. He frequently complains of not understanding what he is reading. This condition appears to occur with equal frequency among both good and poor readers. When the deviations are lateral in nature, the convergence may be insufficient as in exophoria, or excessive as in cross eyes (esophoria). The former condition seems to occur more frequently among poor readers than does any other heterophoric condition. It leads to omissions, regressions, and loss of place.

Difficulties with fusion and aniseikonia also seem to be more common among poor readers than among good readers. Taylor (74) reports that a survey of some 2000 children with academic difficulties showed that 95 per cent of these lacked sufficient coordination and had difficulties with fusion. They failed to show the 13 to 19 diopters of convergence required to direct the eyes toward a single fixation point at 13 inches of reading distance while maintaining appropriate divergence or eye balance. Figure 3-3 illustrates the relationships involved.

Taylor adds that deficiencies in binocular control lead to inadequate word perception and the consumption of an excessive amount of

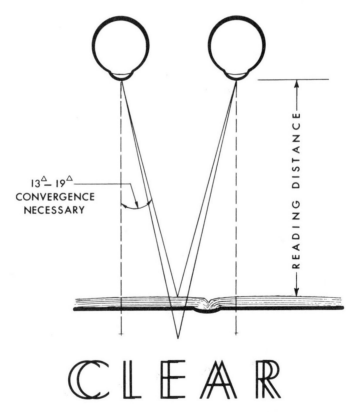

Figure 3-3.   Binocular Control *

* Stanford E. Taylor, *Speed Reading vs. Improved Reading Efficiency* (Educational Developmental Laboratories, 1962), p. 9. Reproduced by permission.

energy in maintaining single vision. The pupil will fatigue easily, experience distraction, poor comprehension, constant moving of the head, and difficulties in concentration.

Any interpretation of the relationship between visual defects and reading must consider the likelihood of multiple causation. Some children are more sensitive to visual problems than are others. Some are able to perform well in short test periods and thus escape detection through the usual methods. In fact, some eye defects may not yet have been identified. We know far too little about the syndromes or patterns of reading defects generally. Eye defects frequently may be but one of a number of factors contributing to a reading deficiency. The simple fact is that some children with defective vision become good readers and that others without any visual difficulty do not learn to read. However, this does not indicate that good vision is unimportant to reading. Eye defects are a handicap to both good and poor readers.

Eames (25, pp. 30–31) lists the following ways of helping children with visual difficulties:

1. Control the glare in the classroom by eliminating highly polished, glass-topped, or highly reflective surfaces.
2. While teaching do not stand directly in front of the light source.
3. Shield light sources so the light doesn't shine directly into children's eyes.
4. Arrange pupils in the classroom so that the light comes over the left shoulder of right-handed children and over the right shoulder of left-handed children.
5. Write on the blackboard in large letters at or slightly above the level of the children's eyes.
6. Use large-size materials—heavily printed charts and maps, large sheets of paper, sight-saving texts.
7. Seat children either near or away from the light depending on the nature of their visual difficulty: albinos prefer subdued illumination, amblyopic (dimmed vision) pupils prefer to sit near the window.
8. Provide pupils with ample rest periods.
9. Use only black and white materials with color blind pupils.
10. Do not try to change the eyedness of the pupil.[12]

Finally, teachers should learn to use various visual screening tests.

[12] Thomas H. Eames, "Visual Handicaps to Reading," *Journal of Education*, 141 (February, 1959), 1–36. Paraphrased and reprinted by permission of the Journal of Education, Boston University Press.

Visual Screening Tests

In the past, the Snellen Chart test was the acceptable screening test. It consists of rows of letters or *E*'s in varied positions. The pupil being examined stands twenty feet from the chart and names progressively smaller letters. The test identifies nearsightedness and measures visual acuity at a distance of twenty feet, but it fails to detect astigmatism and farsightedness. Since nearsightedness frequently is associated with good reading rather than with poor reading, the test is not too helpful in reading diagnosis.

Here are some tests commonly used in visual screening:

1. *A O Sight Screener* [American Optical Company, Kansas City, Missouri]. The A O Sight Screener is a portable vision screening instrument designed for rapid appraisal of seven visual functions. The Sight Screener utilizes polarized light, which permits a check of binocular vision without the need of prism lenses at the important near point. In addition, monocular acuity is measured in such a way that the subject is unaware of which eye is being checked.

   The visual functions checked are:
   a. Simultaneous binocular vision—to determine if the subject is using both eyes together, or is suppressing the image of one eye.
   b. Visual acuity of both right and left eye.
   c. Visual acuity of both eyes together.
   d. Stereopsis—ability to judge depth binocularly.
   e. Vertical phoria—the degree of neuromuscular imbalance in the vertical plane (amount of hyperphoria).
   f. Lateral phoria—the degree of neuromuscular imbalance in the horizontal plane (amount of esophoria or exophoria).
   The screening procedure consists of rotating one control knob to 14 numbered positions and recording the subject's responses. Because of this simplicity, little time is needed for operator training.

2. *Atlantic City Eye Test* [Freund Brothers, 1514 Pacific Avenue, Atlantic City, New Jersey]. This is an individual test usable in grades one and above. The test is designed to detect defective visual acuity, excessive farsightedness, and abnormal eye muscle balance. The test is compact and portable and requires no technical knowledge to administer.

3. *Keystone Visual Survey Telebinocular* [Keystone View Company]. This test uses stereoscopic slides to detect near and far-point fusion difficulties, visual acuity difficulties, muscular im-

balance, binocular efficiency, depth perception, nearsightedness, and farsightedness.

Available also is a Visual-survey Short Test, a Preschool Test, Tests of Binocular Skill (tests binocular impediments that interfere with reading), a Plus-lens (for Hyperopia), Ready-to-read Tests (these test fusion, vertical posture, lateral posture, and usable vision of each eye at near point), and a Periometer (ascertains the side vision of the subject).

4. *Massachusetts Eye Test* [Welch-Allyn Inc., Skaneateles Falls, New York or American Optical Company, 62 Mechanic, Southbridge, Massachusetts]. This test contains a visual acuity test for distance, a plus-sphere lens test for hyperopia, and Maddox-red test lenses for vertical heterophoria testing at distance and for horizontal heterophoria testing at distance and at near.

5. *Master Ortho-Rater Visual Efficiency Test* [Bausch and Lomb, Rochester, New York]. This test uses stereoscopic slides to detect difficulties of visual acuity, binocular coordination, and depth perception. The test may be given in five minutes.

The test provides tests for vertical and lateral phorias, acuity for both right and left eyes, stereopsis, and color. Ortho-Rater scores are recorded on an easy-to-use card. When these cards are placed underneath the transparent standard, it is immediately evident if the person tested has adequate, below-standard, or seriously lowered vision.

A Perimeter Attachment is available for the Master Ortho-Rater. It provides a simplified technique for measuring lateral visual fields. A clearly marked dial indicates the degrees of side vision.

6. *New York School Vision Tester* [Bausch and Lomb, Inc., Rochester, New York]. This test, usable at kindergarten level and above, measures acuity at far point and phoria at near or far point. It requires about two minutes for administration. It is an adaptation of the Ortho-Rater, except that the slides are different.

The test measures acuity, farsightedness, and muscular balance. It has easily manipulated Snellen tests of the well-known Massachusetts type. The child being tested does not have to read letters. The test distances of 20 feet and 13 inches are produced optically, thus eliminating the need for a twenty-foot testing aisle.

7. *Prism Reader* [Educational Developmental Laboratories, Huntington, New York (McGraw-Hill Publishing Company)]. This instrument requires the eyes of the reader to diverge and converge to maintain binocular vision while reading.

Normal binocular vision requires the individual to coordinate the vergence function, which enables him to maintain single vision, with the focus mechanism, which enables him to see clearly. The eyes thus must perform two acts simultaneously: posture themselves so as to produce a single image and accommodate so that they can produce a clear image.

The test permits the examiner to determine whether or not the individual will be able to maintain comfortable, single binocular vision under all conditions of seeing and accept whatever lenses may be required.

8. *Reading Eye Camera* [Educational Developmental Laboratories, Huntington, New York (McGraw-Hill Publishing Company)]. This camera measures the pupil's ability to use his eyes in reading.

After an oral pretest, the individual reads a test selection appropriate for his level of achievement. While he reads, small beads of light are reflected from his eyes and photographed onto a moving film. When he has finished, identifying initials are flashed onto the film. After a comprehension check, the filmed record is analyzed, and the reader's performance is compared with national norms derived from a study of 12,000 cases.

In addition to the standard test selections, an eye-movement photography version of the Reading Versatility Test is available. This test is used in measuring the reader's ability to adjust his approach while reading for varied purposes.

9. *Spache Binocular Vision Test* [Keystone View Company, Meadville, Pennsylvania]. This test measures eye preference in reading. It is usable at first grade level and above and requires a stereoscope to administer. Three levels are available: nonreaders and grade one, grade one and one-half to two, and grade three and above.

The test tells whether the pupil reads more with one eye than with the other and whether heterophoria or lack of good fusion at near point interferes with binocularity in the act of reading.

10. *T/O Vision Testers* [Titmus Optical Company, Inc., Petersburg, Virginia]. These tests for ages 3 to adult measure acuity and vertical and lateral phoria (near and far) on the lower levels. On the seventh grade and above level they measure acuity, stereopsis, color discrimination, vertical phoria, and lateral phoria. These tests can be given at 20 foot approximations. Acuity and vertical and lateral phoria can be tested at reading distance. A perimeter attachment identifies individuals with restricted visual fields. A Plus-lens attachment quickly identifies excessively farsighted children.

Two simple tests which the teacher can use are the *Point of Convergence Test* and the *Muscle Balance and Suppression Test* (12). The *Point of Convergence Test* is administered by holding a penlight or pencil in front of the pupil. The examiner gradually moves the pencil horizontally toward the pupil's nose until the student sees two pencils. The near point of convergence is the distance in inches from that point on to the eye. Normal near-point convergence is from one to three inches. In the *Muscle Balance and Suppression Test,* a two or three foot string is held by the pupil. One end of the string is held against the bridge of the nose by the index finger, being careful so as not to block the line of sight of either eye. A knot is then tied in the string 16 inches away from the eyes. The student is instructed to look at the knot. Normally, he will see the two strings touching each other at the knot, making a V shape. If the two strings seem to cross in front of the knot, the condition is esophoria; if they cross behind the knot, it is exophoria. Orthophoria or normal muscular balance is present if the strings cross at the knot. If only one string is seen, the child is suppressing one eye. If one string is higher than the other, the condition is termed hyperophoria (12).

Since the vision tests suggested in this chapter are for screening purposes and frequently lack somewhat in reliability, in doubtful cases the child's welfare is better served if the teacher errs in referring him to the specialist than if he errs in not referring him.

AUDITORY ADEQUACY

Auditory adequacy includes hearing, listening, and comprehension; it encompasses auditory acuity, auditory discrimination, auditory blending, and auditory comprehension (51, 77).

Hearing is "the process by which sound waves are received, modified, and relayed along the nervous system by the ear" (42). It is our prime concern in this section. Listening and comprehension of sound will be discussed at length in Chapter 5.

Auditory acuity is the recognition of discrete units of sound (77). Auditory discrimination is the ability to discriminate between the sounds or phonemes of a language. We discuss it fully in Chapter 7. Auditory blending is the ability to reproduce a word by synthesizing its component parts (16, p. 113). Finally, hearing is not complete until the hearer can comprehend and interpret what he has heard.

Sound waves are described as wave frequencies rather than wave lengths. Wave frequency is equivalent to the number of complete waves that pass a given point per second and is reported in cycles per second, or hertz (hz). Amplitude refers to the height of the wave. High frequencies give high pitch, and low frequencies result in low pitch. By increasing the amplitude, a low pitch becomes lower and a high pitch gets higher. Intensity of the sound is expressed in decibels. The human ear is sensitive to frequencies ranging from 20 to 20,000 hz.

Normal acuity is variously defined. Some believe that a hearing loss of as little as six decibels puts one in the hard-of-hearing group; others would put the cut-off point at 15 or more decibels. Because of this difference in definition, writers have reported percentages of hearing deficiencies ranging from 3 to 20 per cent. Generally, it is estimated to be about 5 per cent (54).

Types of Auditory Deficiency

There are two kinds of auditory deficiency: intensity deafness and tone deafness. A tone deaf person cannot discriminate between pitches. Intensity deafness is of three types. Central deafness is caused by damage to the auditory areas of the brain or by a neurotic conversion reaction (hysteria). A conductive loss stems from an impairment in the conductive process in the middle ear. Either the eardrum is punctured or there is a malfunction of the three small ossicles or bones in the middle ear. This reduces the person's hearing ability, affecting the loudness with which a person hears speech, but if the loudness of the sound is increased, he hears and understands. A person with a conductive loss can hear his own voice through bone conduction. Thus, the voices of others sound much softer than his own. To compensate, he frequently speaks softly so his voice conforms to the voices of others around him.

Nerve loss stems from an impairment of the auditory nerve and affects clarity and intelligibility of speech. A person with such a loss hears the speech of others, but may not understand what he hears. The high-tone nerve loss prevents him from hearing and distinguishing certain speech sounds, especially such sounds as *f, v, s, z, sh, zh, th, t, d, b, k,* and *g.* Articulation generally is affected. The pupil may speak too loudly or may develop monotony in his voice. He shows signs of frequently

Figure 3-4

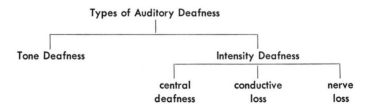

misunderstanding the teacher. The pupil may be thought of as mentally retarded. Figure 3-4 categorizes the various types of auditory deficiency.

Causes and Symptoms of Hearing Deficiencies

In more than 75 per cent of the cases of deafness, German measles, erythroblastosis fetalis, meningitis, bilateral ear infection, fluid in the middle ear, obstructions in the ear canal, or a family history of deafness can be identified. In the remaining cases, the chief symptom is the inability to speak at the customary age.

Here are behaviors that may be indicative of hearing problems:

1. The pupil is inattentive during lectures in the classroom.
2. The pupil turns the head toward the speaker, cups the hands behind the ears, or tends to favor one ear.
3. The pupil complains of ringing or buzzing in the ears.
4. The pupil listens with a tense facial or blank expression.
5. The pupil confuses words with similar sounds.
6. The pupil hears the speech of others, but may not understand what he hears.
7. The pupil has special difficulty with the sounds f, v, s, z, sh, zh, th, t, d, p, g, k, and b.
8. The pupil speaks in a monotone or the pitch is unnatural.
9. The pupil fails to respond to phonic instruction.
10. The pupil's pronunciation is faulty.
11. The pupil breathes through the mouth.

Tests of Hearing

The hearing of every child showing any of the above symptoms should be tested. Bond and Tinker (10, p. 113) suggest a number of methods for doing this. A loud ticking watch may be used as a simple test. Normally a child can hear the ticking up to a distance of about 48 inches. Anything below 20 inches probably indicates hearing deficiency. For a more accurate test an audiometer may be used. Audiometers produce sounds of different frequency and intensity levels for the purpose of measuring auditory sensitivity. They permit the audiologist to obtain an audiogram of an individual's hearing in terms of frequency and intensity.

The audiometer used in testing should provide for both air-conduction and bone-conduction testing and for introducing masking tones. There are two general types of audiometers: discrete frequency, providing tones in half- or full-octave steps; and sweep frequency, providing a continuous variation of frequencies. Hearing loss usually is measured in five-decibel steps. Some audiometers are similar to a portable phonograph with several connected telephone receivers that permit individual testing or the simultaneous testing of as many as ten children. For group testing with such an instrument, children must be able to write numbers, although in individual testing a teacher could record a child's answers.

A technique, called VASC (Verbal Auditory Screen for Children), permits easy testing of pre-school children (30). VASC may be administered by housewives and consists of a picture chart, a modified tape recorder, and two sets of earphones. The tape uses words of two syllables rather than abstract tones. The tape plays automatically going from loud to soft, starting at 51 decibels. Children point to the pictures as they hear the words in their earphones. Each ear is tested separately. If the child can't get two of the last three words at 15 decibels, he is tested again. If he is still unable to do so, he is referred. The total testing time is about five minutes. The package of test materials including tape recorder costs $375.00.

Educational Implications

O'Connor and Streng (62) divide the hard of hearing into four groups. Those with an average loss of 20 decibels or less in the better ear require no special treatment, although it would be wise to seat them advantageously in the classroom. Children in the 25 to 55 decibel loss group may need speech training, and those with a loss of 35 decibels may need a hearing aid. A third group with losses ranging from 55 to 75 decibels usually cannot learn to speak without aid. The individuals in this group are considered educationally deaf. A fourth group consists of those who are suffering more than a 75 decibel loss. Members of this group cannot learn speech through sounds, and ordinarily the public school is unable to meet their needs. They require special treatment. Children with a 40 decibel loss across the speech range will have particular difficulty with *ch, f, k, s, sh, th,* and *z.*

Loss of hearing can aggravate a reading deficiency. Studies generally have indicated that the ability to discriminate speech sounds is important for speech and reading development. Without it, children cannot isolate the separate sounds in words and thus find phonics training incomprehensible. However, in seeking to understand the relationship between auditory deficiencies and reading disability, we again must remember that causes often are complex rather than simple, multiple rather than single. Auditory factors may be especially important when there is a severe hearing loss, when the specific hearing loss involves high-tone deafness, or when instruction puts a premium on auditory factors. The exclusive use of the phonic method with a child who has suffered a hearing loss may prevent achievement in reading.

The child will be at a disadvantage if the teacher fails to distinguish between mistakes in reading and differences in pronunciation (49). The pupil, who reads "I write wif a pin," has read correctly, but may not have spoken the way the teacher would speak. Admonishing this child for poor reading may only hurt him. In fact, the child may not be able to hear the difference between *with* and *wif* or *pen* and *pin,* even under the most favorable of instructional procedures.

Retardation occurs much more frequently among children with defective hearing than among children with normal hearing. When the hearing defect is unilateral, achievement is not so adversely affected as when the hearing defects are bilateral. Deaf children are handicapped educationally much more than are the hard of hearing. Even low-level perception of sounds allows for most of those experiences that are essential to normal development in speech and language. Generally, as hearing loss increases, reading achievement becomes poorer.

The teacher cannot be satisfied, however, with the mere detection of auditory deficiencies. He cannot do much about improving the child's auditory acuity. A hearing aid is much simpler. He can do much in developing the pupil's auditory discrimination skills. He must train the child in the awareness of sound, in making gross discriminations such as between the sounds of a bell and a horn, in making discriminations among simple speech patterns such as differences between vowels, and in the finer discriminations necessary for speech (19, p. 284). The latter involves the ability to distinguish the phonetic elements within words. Silvaroli and Wheelock (67) report that auditory discrimination training helped children to discriminate more effectively among 33 basic speech sounds. Auditory discrimination and its development will be taken up again in more detail in Chapter 7.

NEURAL ADEQUACY AND READING

The brain controls the rest of the body by sending commands, as it were, through a network of eighty-six major nerves that expand into thousands of smaller nerves. The nerves spread from the brain through the brain stem down the spinal cord. The nerves may be likened to miles of telephone wire; the brain, to a central switchboard. The impulses travel through the neural network, transmitting sensory data and messages.

Obviously, brain activity is much more complex than a telephone switchboard connection. In the neurons, through a combination of glucose and oxygen, an electrical charge builds up. At a certain level of buildup it discharges, becoming the nerve impulse that moves from neuron to neuron. It is a combination of these impulses or tiny bursts of electrical energy that we record on electroencephalographs and that result in thoughts and actions. The transmission of the impulse from one neuron to another is chemically controlled. It is not the impulse itself but a resulting chemical, acetylcholine, that stimulates a muscle and makes it move.

The mysteries of brain activity are many. The reticular formation in the brain stem seems to make it possible for us to pay attention or to ignore the multitude of stimuli that bombard us. The thalamus plays a role in the perception of pain. Rage and fear are produced when the amygdala is stimulated. Destruction of the amygdala leads to extreme nymphomania in the female cat and to satyrism in the male. Electrical stimulation at the proper spot can cause a cat to purr contentedly when hurt or to become panicky at the sight of a mouse. The usually fierce rhesus monkey will permit itself to be petted when stimulated at the caudate nucleus.

Projection and Association Areas

Research by Gall, Dax, Broca, Jackson, Head, Wernicke, Goldstein, Halstead, Sherrington, and the Penfields and recent experiments with electrical stimulations of the brain have given us much information concerning the projection areas of the brain.[13] Figure 3-5 shows the auditory, visual, motor, somesthetic, and olfactory areas. Two fissures, the central and the Sylvian fissure, separate the brain into lobes. That part lying in front of the central and Sylvian fissure is known as the frontal lobe. The sense organs are connected with their special projection areas in the cortex, and the essential sensory processes occur there. An injury to the visual projection area, for example, may cause blindness.

The functions of the brain, however, are not restricted to the projection areas. More than three-fourths of the brain consists of association areas. The associations between the various sensory and motor areas are the result of learning.

When the child touches a burning match, a sharp signal of pain is received in the projection area. He avoids a burning match later, not because of the pain, but because he associates the pain with the sight of fire. To be meaningful, the experience of the present must be related to the experiences of the past. This occurs in the association areas. There

---

[13] Experimentation with animals tends to support Lashley's theory of equipotentiality. The rat, for example, does not seem to use any specific area of the brain for learning. Experiments with humans, however, supports Nielsen's thesis of cerebral localization. Thus, we speak of Exner's writing center, Wernicke's learning center, and Broca's speaking center. Pinpoint localization of brain functions is rarely possible. It is quite possible that injury to the same area in two different brains would produce different symptoms (78, p. 472). In fact, some suggest that intellectual functions are functions of the brain as a whole. Ketchum (46) says that the concept of a direct function-to-location relationship is outmoded.

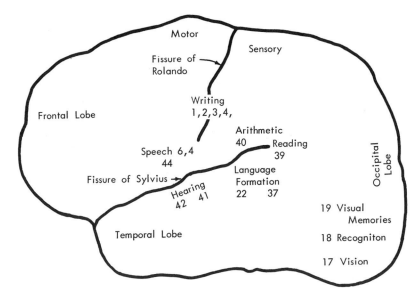

Figure 3-5.   The Brain*

the sensory and motor areas are united into the countless hookups and the "memory" of the past is preserved (33).

The impulses that travel through the neural network may be blocked by injuries along the neural path or by damage to the brain itself. Eames (28) notes that interferences with the frontal-occipital fasciculus affects auditory memory and creates difficulties in the learning of phonics. Other interferences in the association areas affect eye movement and eye span.

The visual projection area is surrounded by an association area known as the parastriate cortex. A second association area, known as the peristriate cortex, surrounds the parastriate cortex. If the parastriate cortex is injured, the person cannot recognize or identify what he sees. If the peristriate cortex is injured, the person may be able to recognize what he sees, but he cannot recall the appearance of objects when they are not in view.

The nerve impulse travels from the retina along the optic nerve to visual area 17 in the occipital lobe. This area is concerned with seeing without recognition. In areas 18 and 19 recognition and visual memory occur. There the words are recognized as words. In area 39, the angular

* Thomas H. Eames, "Visual Handicaps to Reading," Journal of Education, 141 (February 1959), p. 35. Reproduced by permission of the Journal of Education, Boston University Press.

gyrus, the meaning of the word is comprehended. Eames (25, p. 4) notes that

> This part of the brain has to do with the *interpretation of symbols* (letters, words, syllables) and combines the functions of *recognition and visual memory* for word forms. It is well known in neurology that a lesion here will interfere with the ability to read.[14]

In the part of the brain lying between the hearing and reading areas, roughly areas 22 and 37, the association of sounds and visual symbols occurs. Thus, since reading is commonly an association of a visual symbol with an auditory symbol, this part is of major importance in reading and is called the language-formation area. Injury here results in the inability to name one's concepts.

Neurological disorders affect perhaps twenty million persons in the United States (60, p. 4). One in sixteen babies suffers some neurological injury; approximately 200,000 persons die yearly from strokes, and another million are disabled;[15] some eight million have brain or spinal cord diseases; about six million have hearing problems; a half million have Parkinson's disease; glaucoma, cataracts, and other blinding diseases claim a half million; and another half million suffer from cerebral palsy (60, p. 5).

Wordblindness

The term wordblindness traditionally has meant the inability to remember word forms. We use it here to mean any condition, whether permanent or temporary, that makes it impossible for the pupil to read. The condition may be either structural or functional in nature. It is called alexia if it is accompanied by structural defects of an environmental nature in the cerebrum and dyslexia in all other instances.

It is impossible to distinguish between the two forms of wordblindness on the basis of symptoms alone. Jensen (44) uses the term "reading disability" to designate cases manifesting organic injury and the term "reading inability" to designate cases manifesting functional difficulties. If the disturbance is of functional origin, perhaps only reading is affected;

---

[14] Thomas H. Eames, "Visual Handicaps to Reading," *Journal of Education,* 141 (February 1959) 1–36. Reprinted by permission of the Journal of Education, Boston University Press.

[15] Strokes are generally divided into five kinds (60, p. 12): (1) hemorrhage, (2) thrombosis or blood clotting, (3) embolism or blocking of a blood vessel by a floating blood clot, (4) compression resulting from pressures such as a tumor, and (5) spasm or the closing or tightening of the walls of the artery.

if the disturbance is structural, the pupil's perceptual functioning is generally affected and difficulties will show up in areas other than reading.

Structural defects may either be the result of brain injury or they may have been biologically determined. The brain may suffer injury, or it may not develop adequately. Microcephaly, mongoloidism, epilepsy, and mental retardation are symptoms of inadequate development.

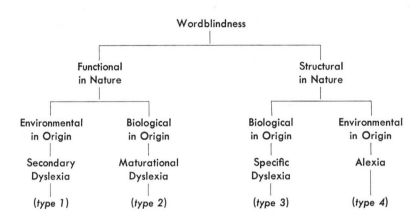

Figure 3-6

Injuries to the brain are numerous. Cerebral tumors, infections, and changes accompanying old age may damage brain tissues. Tumors crowd brain tissues and restrict the metabolism of the nerve cells. Encephalitis and paresis are infections that damage brain tissue. Pick's disease, Alzheimer's disease, and arteriosclerosis are degenerative diseases that result in impaired functioning.

Finally, the brain may be damaged by certain metabolic disorders and toxins. Disordered chemistry may have serious effects on brain functioning. Enzyme, vitamin, and hormone deficiencies may lead to metabolic disturbances. Pellagra, for example, is caused by a vitamin deficiency. Cretinism is the result of an endocrine disturbance. Toxic conditions resulting from excessive intake of lead, alcohol, carbon monoxide, or opium and high fever and lack of oxygen also may damage brain tissue. A lack of oxygen, for even a few seconds, may lead to irreparable damage of brain cells. Increasing or decreasing significantly the sugar content of the blood may result in coma.

Aphasia is a form of injury frequently caused by stroke and is especially significant for reading. It may lead to a loss of speech but always results in a disturbance of the thought processes.

The aphasic or brain-injured child (61) is hyperactive. He flits from one activity to another without apparent purpose or meaning. His behavior is compulsive, and the condition may be associated with difficulties in perception, memory, attention, and social control. Frequently, he is destructive.

A mild brain damage (61), frequently undetected, is associated with difficulties in reading (alexia), writing, and arithmetic. The child finds abstract thinking difficult and has poor coordination and concentration. His speech is rapid and mumbled and hence unintelligible. He can count to twenty or recite the alphabet but cannot tell what number comes after eight or what letter comes after *c*. He reverses the letters in writing, omits letters, and spells as though English were a completely phonetic language. The writing is cramped and angular. The letters vary in size and slant.

The brain-injured child frequently has not developed dominance. He switches from one hand to the other and confuses left with right. He perseverates, repeating activities again and again.

Hirsch (40) suggests that generalized language disturbances frequently run in families and that they are associated with disturbances in body image, poor motor and visuo-motor patterning, inadequate figure-ground discriminations, and hyperactivity. Clumsiness in manipulation of small muscle groups (as in writing) is rather common. The execution in writing is jerky and arrhythmic. Hirsch notes that frequently the jerkiness in writing is accompanied by jerky, stumbling, and explosive speech (cluttering). The writing looks as the speech sounds. Drawings of the human form are immature and distorted. The limbs are out of proportion, incorrectly placed, or perhaps omitted. Finally, because of inadequate figure-ground discrimination, children with general language disabilities hear speech as an undifferentiated noise and see words on the printed page as an undifferentiated design. On more advanced levels (ten to fourteen years) these children will usually have difficulty in organizing what they read or study. In explaining the language-disturbance syndrome, Hirsch suggests that the underlying cause may be delayed or disorganized maturation of the neural system.

Harris (36) notes that in reading disability cases exhibiting neurological defects the whole-part relationship is inadequate. Parts (letters) are seen as discrete units rather than as parts of a whole, and wholes (words) are seen as undifferentiated wholes. He also points out that frequently there is a figure-ground disturbance. The figure (word) does not have clear boundaries. The problem seems to become more acute when the figure is discontinuous or when the contrast with the ground is minimal. Harris raises the question whether word perception might be improved if the letters were continuous or if they were in a different color, perhaps red.

Harris also notes that laterality and directional orientation are usually delayed. Reading cases with a structural inadequacy frequently reverse in reading and writing (directional confusion).

Hinshelwood (39, p. 53) points out that any condition that reduces the number of cortical cells within the angular (area 39) and supramarginal (area 40) gyri of the left side of the cortex or that interferes with the supply of the blood to that area lowers the functional activity of that part of the brain, and will be accompanied by a diminished retention of the visual images of letters and words.

He (39, p. 102) felt that treatment for structural wordblindness consists in developing: (*1*) a visual memory for the letters of the alphabet; (*2*) an auditory memory for words by having the child spell aloud the word letter by letter; and (*3*) a visual memory for words.

Severely handicapped readers, however, need not always have suffered structural defects. For example, such conditions as inadequate instruction, emotional disturbances, lack of interest, or social incompetency may terminate in a reading problem.

Cerebral Dominance

A condition thought to be dependent on the development of the brain is cerebral dominance. This implies that one cerebral hemisphere is more important in behavior or functionally more efficient than the other. The left hemisphere commonly is the language hemisphere and for most individuals, since most of us are right-handed, it also is the dominant hemisphere.[16]

There are, however, exceptions to this general rule. Some persons are left-handed (right dominance), some are ambidextrous with neither hemisphere being dominant (lack of dominance), and in others the dominance changes from activity to activity. The latter is termed crossed dominance and is seen in individuals exhibiting left-eyedness and right-handedness. Do these conditions hinder reading proficiency?

Orton (63) suggested that in learning to read the pupil develops memory traces for words both in the dominant (left for the average individual) and the nondominant (right) hemisphere, but that those in the nondominant hemisphere normally are mirror images of the former and thus are suppressed.[17] He adds that if cerebral dominance is well devel-

[16] Speech musculature is served by both hemispheres simultaneously. It is a bilateral function, permitting recovery of articulation following unilateral injury or excision (46). The young child can tolerate damage to the language hemisphere because the function can be transferred to the other hemisphere. In older children such damage will lead to aphasic disorders.

[17] Injury to the nondominant hemisphere usually does not lead to reading difficulties. Lindsley (50) found that the percentage of alpha waves out of phase between the cerebral hemispheres is greater among the ambidextrous than among those consistently right sided, thus substantiating Orton's theory of hemispheric conflict.

oped by the time reading begins, reading proficiency is not affected. If, however, no special dominance is developed or if the engrams or memory traces in the right hemisphere (left dominance) become active, reading difficulties occur, and the child will read once with a left and then with a right orientation.

In cases of lack of dominance (as in the ambidextrous person), the engrams of each hemisphere are equally dominant, and the reader may become confused and indecisive in his reading. He sometimes reads in a left-to-right direction and at other times reverses the direction. Letters and words are reversed because the pupil sometimes uses the mirror images developed in the nondominant hemisphere.

Although Orton did not concern himself with the left-handed individual,[18] similar difficulties may arise. The left-handed person has a natural tendency to move from right to left in attacking words. And if he follows this natural tendency in reading, he will see little difference between the printed words and their mirror images. This results in reversals of words and word forms.

Unfortunately, it is not at all clear that reversals, confusion in orientation, and reading disability are related to lack of or left cerebral dominance.

Ketchum (46) states that Orton's views are no longer tenable. He suggests that difficulties in directional stability may arise from inefficiencies within the nonverbal hemisphere itself.

Dominance is not an either-or proposition; rather it is a matter of degree. To some degree everyone is two-handed, the embryo is completely symmetrical, and the development of a dominant hand is a gradual process. Ananiev (69, p. 31), in an investigation of the dominant eye, dominant ear, and dominant hand, also found that a different member may be preferred for a different function.

However, poor readers, especially those showing up in reading clinics, generally show a greater frequency of undeveloped dominance. Harris (34, p. 254), for example, reports a high proportion of reading disability cases develop preference for one hand later than the age of nine. In a later study (35) he suggests that if tests are sufficiently discriminative, genuine relationships between reading disability and laterality are found.

Silver and Hagin (68), in an intensive study of 18 subjects over a period of years, concluded that the persistence of anomalies of laterality, even when maturation in perceptual areas has occurred, suggests that

---

[18] In an eight-year study of handedness involving some 92,000 pupils in grades one through six, Enstrom (31) found that the percentage of pupils writing with the left hand was 11.1. The percentage for boys was 12.5; for girls, 9.7. These percentages, higher than those reported in previous studies, were generally constant from grade to grade and suggest that fewer teachers are changing the handedness of the pupil.

for some children "reading disability may be a basic biologic defect resulting from the failure to establish clear-cut cerebral dominance."

Alexander and Money (1) believe that defective direction sense and defective space-form perception may explain some cases of reading retardation, but the presence of these defects alone is not sufficient to cause retardation. The defect may be explained in some children by a maturation lag or developmental defect in direction sense and in space-form perception (57). The authors developed the *Road Map Test,* which is an outline map of several city blocks, to measure direction sense. The pupil is required to follow a route and to report whether he turns to the left or to the right at each corner. It was found that right-left spatial orientation normally becomes established between 11 and 14, but dyslexic boys of age 11–14 made significantly more errors than did the standardization group.

Muehl (59) found that left lateral subjects made more left and right recognition errors than consistent right lateral subjects, suggesting that left laterality might be associated with unique patterns of visual or perceptual behavior.

The research data are far from being definitive. Cohen and Glass (17) found significant relationships between knowledge of left- and right-hand dominance and reading ability in the first grade, but not so in the fourth grade. Those first-grade pupils who knew the difference between left and right and who had a dominant hand tended to be the better readers. Crossed dominance (right-handed left-eyed or vice versa) was found not to be related to reading ability. The data indicated that it might be better to be left-handed than to be mixed. The authors suggest that in the first grade it may be worthwhile to develop techniques for firmly establishing hand dominance and directional certainty.

Stephens et al. (70) found no relationship between crossed eye-hand preferences and reading readiness; Balow (4,5) reported that hand preference and eye preference, either singly or in interaction, or knowledge of right or left were not significantly associated with readiness or with reading achievement; Belmont and Brick (7) reported that retarded readers were not differentiated from normal readers by mixed dominance; and Tinker (75) concluded from her study that laterality is not a factor in reading disability. Most studies like that of Cohen and Glass show that hand preference becomes better established with age.

In summary:

1. Learning occurs in an organism, and whatever affects the nervous system of the organism may affect learning. Lack of neurological organization may be a key factor in reading difficulty.
2. The more we know about nerve excitation and brain function-

ing, the better we will understand the pupil's ease or difficulty of learning.

3.   We may have two types of learners: those who have had appropriate neural development for learning and those who have not.

4.   Since nerve impulses are tiny bursts of electrical energy brought about by chemical changes, it may well be that some learning deficiencies reflect subtle chemical changes (69a).

SUMMARY

This chapter has examined four broad factors that account for some of the differences in reading achievement: experiential background, maturational development, intellectual development, and physical developmnt. A knowledge of these factors alone is not enough to provide adequately for the pupil's reading needs. However, few of us would deny their importance.

This chapter should have cautioned us in the interpretation of reading failures. *Not all children can learn to read with ease.* Some children want to learn but attain little success. They are motivated; they are not lazy or indifferent. For some of these learning to read is difficult because they are handicapped intellectually, experientially, physically, or physiologically.

Teaching reading would be rather simple if the teacher knew exactly how to bring forth the desired responses from the pupil. Unfortunately, the same stimulus or teaching will elicit different reactions from different pupils and even from the same pupil at different times. Some explanations for variability in behavior have been stated in this chapter. In the following chapter we shall examine additional reasons why pupils are different and why they will behave differently in the classroom.

QUESTIONS FOR DISCUSSION

1.   State five basic principles of growth and development and point out how they apply in the teaching of reading.

2.   Is it possible to raise all children's reading proficiency to the same level? Why?

3.   Explain: "Many of the unexplained failures in reading may be the result of the child's failure to have a satisfactory relationship with the mother."

4.   What is the advantage of a broad experiential background in reading?

5.   What is the value of reading readiness programs?

6.   Discuss the reasons for identifying, at least in a general way, the pupil's intellectual capacity and discuss the implications of this for the pupil's reading achievement.

7.   If it is recommended that the pupil have a mental age of six for beginning reading and if intelligence test scores indicate that a given child's IQ is approximately 120, at what age would he be mentally ready for beginning reading? Are there any other considerations before actually beginning the teaching of reading?

8.   Discuss the reasons for and against delaying reading instructions.

9.   If children's intellectual aptitude scores range from 80 IQ to 120 IQ in grade 4, what are the implications for class instruction? In your answer discuss the use of basal readers, multi-level materials, grouping, and individualized reading approach.

10. What are some factors that must be carefully evaluated before one initiates a program of teaching five-year-old children to read?

11. Discuss visual adequacy and its implications for the developmental reading program.

12. Make an evaluation of the various visual screening tests.

13. Discuss the relationship between neural functioning and achievement in reading.

14. Elaborate on the statement: "Not all children can learn to read with ease."

15. Discuss the following:

a. Development in reading closely parallels and is an expression of the forces of human development generally.

b. Experience is related positively to reading readiness up to a certain point; beyond this point there are diminishing returns. (Moderate television viewing may aid readiness; excessive viewing may hinder readiness.)

c. Intelligence test scores are not as significant for determining readiness for learning to read as for predicting achievement in reading in later grades.

d. Mental age is not as significant for determining readiness for beginning reading as is ability in visual and auditory discrimination, but achievement in reading is a more direct function of intelligence than of auditory or visual discrimination.

e. The poor reader is distinguished from the good reader by: (1) his inability to perceive the relationship to one another of the details within the total word shape or (2) his inability to perceive parts and details, in which case he perceives unanalyzable wholes. He is weak in the ability to analyze the visual and auditory structures of words and in the ability to synthesize phonetic units to form whole words.

f. The greater the amount of energy the reader must expend in reading (because of physical inadequacies, for example), the less he tends to read.

g. The mind (perceptual and cognitive processes), not sight, is the limiting factor in rate of recognition.

h. The more similar the symbols, the greater the tendency to reverse.

The Learner (continued)

Reading is a complex process. It is a composite of many skills, habits, and attitudes. The good reader possesses these qualities. To acquire them one needs a certain amount of readiness or proficiency in many related areas.

Chapter 3 emphasized the need for a wide background of experience, for adequate maturation, for adequacy in intellectual growth, for physical health, for visual and auditory adequacy, and for freedom from neurological defects. These are necessary conditions, but they do not assure success in reading. It is illogical to expect to produce a successful reader by promoting growth and development in only certain specifics. The teacher of reading must give consideration to all aspects of development.

Educators frequently overlook the child's *wholeness*. They have dealt separately with his intelligence, his physique, his emotions, and his social skills. Each expert sees the child in light of his own biases and his own discipline. Each fragments the child and each is a piece worker. Someone has suggested that if a child were to appear in the midst of a group of educational psychologists he would be a stranger to them. We sometimes forget that all aspects of the child's development are interrelated and that the child usually advances on an even front in all areas. And yet, it is easier to discuss the pupil's development by dissecting him as it were. Let us then continue to examine those factors about all pupils that have a bearing on their achievement in reading.

To help children both to develop adequate personalities and to become successful readers the teacher of reading needs to understand the facts, principles, and symptoms of social and emotional development of the child. He must be able to interpret pupil behavior. He must know how a child's social and emotional reactions influence his reading and how reading failure or success influences his emotional and social development.

Educators long have debated what the goals of the elementary school program are or should be. On one thing all are agreed. The child is the focal point of this program. In essence, educators believe that good education generally (and reading instruction in particular) should enhance the personal and social adjustment of the pupil.

Emotions are an important aspect of human development. Without emotional behavior life would be dull and personalities would be flat and uninteresting. Few individuals would achieve, for none could feel the joy of success or long for the esteem of others.

However, sometimes emotional development is maladjustive. Thus, studies show that the incidence of maladjustment among poor readers is greater than among good readers. It is not always easy to establish whether personality maladjustment is the cause, the effect, or a concomitant circumstance. Frequently it is impossible to tell whether emotional and/or social maladjustment causes reading failure, or whether reading failure causes maladjustment. Some studies have failed to find a positive correlation between reading failure and personality maladjustment. Not all emotionally disturbed pupils are poor readers, nor are all poor readers emotionally disturbed.

All children have physiological needs. They need water, food, sleep, and warmth to maintain their physical well-being. They also have psychological needs. They need to feel secure. They long for affection and for the friendship of others. They want the respect of others and go to extremes to win the esteem of their pals. The self image of the learner is so obviously a significant determinant of learning that sometimes it does not receive the attention that it deserves.

The child needs to perceive the law and order in the universe. He needs to learn to trust people. He needs to assert his own autonomy, to try out his initiative, and to accomplish. He needs to feel successful. He must know that he has done a good job, and that he is realizing his potentialities. His personality constantly seeks self-realization and self-actualization (41, p. 290).

The Early Development of Children

By the age of six the average child has already become a rather well-structured individual. He has learned to walk, can control his bowels and bladder, can dress and undress, and can feed himself. He ties his shoes, bathes, and brushes his teeth. He lives an orderly life, eating three times a day and sleeping a desirable number of hours.

He has become a member of his family. He identifies with his brothers and sisters and with his father and mother.

He is curious. He wants to know. He has developed his senses and communicates in sentences. He discriminates, generalizes, and makes judgments. He generally accepts society's rules and can discriminate between right and wrong.

He wants things for himself, is egocentric, and has unbounded faith in rules. "It's not fair" are common words for the six-year-old. He tags along with the "gang" and by seven or eight would rather be with them than his family, but is still somewhat of an outsider looking in.

In the middle years of childhood the development started at an earlier age is continued. Social interest is developing. White (51) notes that three- and four-year-old children prefer to be with one or two companions. They do not like big crowds. By age seven children align themselves into groups, but these flounder without adult guidance. At nine the first unsupervised activities occur and it is common for one child to praise the accomplishments of another. Prior to that there are many criticisms of others and few compliments. Eleven- and twelve-year-old children are able to see others as they see themselves. They have some idea of why the other person does whatever he is doing. Friendship takes on new meaning. It is not mere interest in what another can do for the giver of friendship. Friendship is sought for its own sake. The person is concerned with doing something for the well-being of another.

Sex roles become rather clearly differentiated by age nine. The boy would not be caught crying (and so he develops an ulcer later in life). He will not be a sissy or a crybaby, nor will his father let him be. The girl has no such inhibitions. She is dainty and sweet but cries freely.

Jersild (29, p. 861) has summarized the developmental patterns that characterize the transition from infancy to maturity. Children generally develop:

1. From helplessness to self-help with consequent reduction of frustration and fear.
2. From dependence on others to self-reliance.
3. From living in the immediate present to wider grasp of the past and future.

4. From parent-centered to peer-centered to a wide-ranging social interest.

5. From all-or-none emotional reactions to control over one's emotional responses.

6. From self-centered egotism toward satisfaction in sharing and giving.

7. From low frustration tolerance toward ability to endure tension and to function effectively despite anxiety.

8. From emotional attachment to parents to interest in the same sex during middle childhood to heterosexual responsiveness and love in adolescence and maturity.[1]

Personal Adjustment and Reading Achievement

Even though developmental sequences are fairly uniform, the behavior differences among children are numerous. Some are egocentric and preoccupied with themselves. They are shy and timid and recoil from social interaction. Others plunge into social interaction with reckless abandon. They are alert and sensitive and reach out for the experiences around them. Some like to fight; others will never fight. Some lie and steal; some daydream or work too much. Some pay attention; others ignore everyone around them. Some are easily discouraged; others constantly show off in class. Some are unhappy, moody and quick-tempered; others are quiet and contented just to be left alone. Some are cool and indifferent to reading, avoid it completely, and may actually learn to hate it. Others love to read and can't wait to tell another what they have read.

How can the teacher deal with these children? What has he learned from the normal development of children that can help him to plan for the proper personal development of the pupil? How can he deal with the anxious child, with the daydreamer, and with the exuberant one? How can he individualize the reading program so that it will meet each child's needs? How can he satisfy the child's basic psychological needs? How can he satisfy the child's need for accomplishment, for success, for self-realization?

There are no easy answers to these questions. Children vary in their behavior for many reasons, and to adjust the school program to meet the needs of each is practically an impossible task. There seems no ready solution to reading difficulties. Reading failure will perhaps always be with us. Failure of any kind makes the satisfaction of the child's needs rather difficult. It prohibits the actualization of his potentialities. It threatens especially self-esteem and the child's esteem in the eyes of

---

[1] Reprinted with permission from Arthur T. Jersild, "Emotional Development," *Manual of Child Psychology*, ed. by Leonard Carmichael (John Wiley and Sons, Inc., 1954).

others, thus thwarting both emotional and social adjustment. Failure in reading is a continuing block to normal development. For the poor reader, self-esteem and self-actualization rarely become a reality.

Reading is a developmental task. It is a task that the pupil must perform in order to satisfy his own needs and so that he may satisfy the demands made upon him by society. There is no adequate compensation for success in reading. In the academic work of today's school a child cannot succeed partially. He either succeeds or he doesn't, and without success in reading, success in almost any other area becomes an improbability, if not an impossibility.

Poor reading ability threatens social acceptance and thus leads to feelings of inadequacy. The pupil is subjected to bad publicity as it were. The poor reader is a child who has compared unfavorably with his peers. He has competed but has failed to meet competition. Such a child is humiliated and hurt. He becomes a social reject in his own mind and in the minds of others. He feels ashamed. He may become shy and withdrawn. He is thought to be "stupid," and even his parents may show discouragement and dissatisfaction with him, for their egos have suffered. Their child has not measured up to *their* expectations.

It is not difficult to see why the poor reader, rejected by others and lacking the self-confidence that comes with success, should be tense, antagonistic, self-conscious, nervous, inattentive, defensive, discouraged, irritable, fearful, frustrated, defiant, indifferent, restless, and hypercritical. Unable to achieve recognition through success in reading, he may stutter, be truant, join gangs, and engage in destructive activity. He may show evidence of a psychological tic, of psychosomatic conditions, or of enuresis; he may bite his nails and suck his thumb.

Bettelheim (3, p. 392) notes that the poor student who fears failure, even if he does his best, frequently will protect himself by *deciding not to learn*. He convinces himself that he wants to fail rather than that he can't succeed. He begins to feel that he could do rather well if he wished. Bettelheim adds that this is an insidious process. The more the pupil falls behind academically, the more his pretense of adequacy is threatened and the more pronounced becomes his deviant behavior. The fourth grader might defy the teacher; by the eighth grade he defies police and society.

Schiffman (40) believes that many retarded readers, especially on the secondary level, have such a negative level of aspiration and such a low self-estimation that they can't succeed. This lack of achievement motivation is often encouraged by parents and teachers. In a study of 84 functional junior high slow learners, Schiffman found that 78 per cent had average intelligence scores on either the Verbal or Performance scales of the WISC and 39 per cent had average scores on both, but teachers felt that only 7 per cent and the pupils themselves and their parents felt that only 14 per cent had average ability.

Children learn to behave in ways that they consider appropriate to themselves. What is considered appropriate often depends upon the expectations of the significant people about them (4,5). It is in his interaction with significant others that the pupil develops an image of himself as a learner. In the classroom, the child often learns only that which he believes significant others in his life expect him to learn. If others think him to be a poor reader or a poor learner, he tends to be one.

Research tends to indicate that most children come to school with rather well-adjusted personalities. Personal maladjustment seems more frequently to be an effect of rather than a cause of reading failure. However, in some cases, personal maladjustment seems to precipitate problems with reading. Educational malfunctions, most commonly those of reading, frequently signify emotional problems.

Harris (22) suggests that painful emotional events during early efforts at reading may turn the young learner against reading. The young reader may also at times transfer feelings of resistance from his mother to the teacher, or from his eating to his reading. A pupil may seek gang approval by not learning to read. Finally, he may exert so much energy in repressing hostile impulses that he has little left for intellectual effort.

There are numerous other factors of an emotional nature that may hinder success in learning generally. Difficulties in adjusting to a new environment make it impossible for the child to expend the energies needed for learning. Poor parent-child relationships, sibling rivalry, unfair comparisons with a neighborhood prodigy, lack of encouragement from the home, and negative attitudes of parents to learning in general may lead to failure.

The child may be afraid that he is "no good" and thus is sure that he cannot learn to read. Reading makes such a child feel "bad inside." Another child may be afraid of making mistakes. He doesn't want to be wrong because at home he has learned that it is "bad" to be wrong. A third child may look upon success in reading as a sign of growing up, and this is the last thing he wants to do.

Children literally punish themselves by not learning to read. They feel a deep sense of guilt and atone for it by receiving the reprimands that accompany failure. Others use failure as a way of punishing the adult.

Figure 4-1

1	2	3	4
Serious reading difficulty	→ Pupil receives remedial instruction	→ No noticeable sign of improvement	→ A new method (X) is attempted →

	5	6	7	8
	No positive results	→ Try method Y →	No positive results	→ Solution may be in removing emotional inhibitions

They demonstrate their independence by refusing to read. Their attitude is: "I'll show you."

A frontal attack on the reading problem of a pupil who is emotionally disturbed may have little effect. The situation might be visualized as in Figure 4-1.

In this situation, remediation begins with an attack on the emotional factors that prohibit the child from making the responses required for successful learning to read. Eisenberg (16) notes:

> No single pattern of psychopathology is characteristic: among the more common patterns are anxiety states that preclude attention to academic tasks, preoccupation with fantasy such that the child is psychologically absent from class, passive-aggressive syndromes in which resistance to parental coercion is subtly executed by a hapless failure to learn, low self-esteem based upon identification with an inadequate parent, and schizophrenic thought pathology in which letters and words become invested with idiosyncratic meanings. Reading failure is a final common pathway for the expression of a multiplicity of antecedent disruptions in learning.
>
> At the same time, it must be recognized that the reading difficulty is in itself a potent source of emotional distress. Embarrassed by fumbling recitations before his peers, cajoled, implored, or bullied by his parents and his teachers to do what he cannot, the retarded reader is first disturbed and finally despondent about himself. His ineptness in reading penalizes him in all subjects and leads to his misidentification as a dullard. With class exercises conducted in what for him is a foreign language, he turns to other diversions, only to be chastised for disruptive behavior. However begun, the psychiatric disturbances and the reading disability are mutually reinforcing in the absence of effective intervention. For such children, psychiatric treatment may be necessary before response to remedial techniques can be expected.[2]

Great care, however, must be taken that the emotional symptoms which result from reading failure are not immediately advanced as the cause of the reading problem. The first assumption that should be made is that the emotional disturbances are the result, rather than the cause of reading failure. One of the really great rationalizations in the classroom for doing nothing or giving up is that the child is emotionally disturbed.

In cases of severe emotional disturbance, a thorough study of the

---

[2] Leon Eisenberg, "Epidemiology of Reading Retardation," in *The Disabled Reader,* John Money (Baltimore: The Johns Hopkins Press, 1966), pp. 3–19. Reprinted by permission.

pupil's physical, mental, social, and emotional development is needed, an investigation which is not usually possible by one person alone. Psychiatrist, psychologist, teacher, social worker, pediatrician, neurologist, and others need to cooperate in resolving the emotionally disturbed pupil's learning and emotional disorders.

The teacher must be slow in attributing the reading difficulties of even one child to emotional and/or social problems. Poor readers do not have an identifiable personality. Poor readers may be adjusted or maladjusted; they may run the gamut of personal deviation. There is no one-to-one relationship between type of adjustment difficulty and type of reading retardation.

The relationship between reading disability and emotional and social maladjustment frequently is circular in nature. Early reading failure leads to maladjustment and personal maladjustment in turn prevents further growth in reading. It is quite conceivable that in certain cases reading failure and personal maladjustment have their own distinct causes. Generally, if the reading failure is emotional in nature, the child will have difficulties in other academic areas also. If the emotional problem was caused by failure in reading, the emotional difficulty is reduced when the child learns to read.

Holmes (26) points out that in discussing reading and personality difficulties with children and their parents phrases such as "reading diagnosis and treatment" are often more acceptable than "personality maladjustment and therapy."

In dealing with the severely emotionally disturbed pupil who is also a reading disability case, therapy and remedial reading often must be combined. The greater the intensity of the emotional problem, the greater tends to be the need for both therapy and individual instruction. Various therapeutic techniques, play therapy, group interview therapy, and individual interview therapy, have been used successfully.

Therapy removes pressures and tension and clears the way for attentive concentration on the reading material. In most cases it removes a fear of reading and allows the child to develop attitudes favorable to reading.

In summary:

1. Emotions are reactions to environmental stimuli that also motivate behavior.
2. Some types of emotion facilitate learning and some hinder or prevent learning.
3. The relationship between maladjustment and learning to read might be any of the following:
   a. Maladjustment causes reading failure.
   b. Reading failure causes maladjustment.

c.   Maladjustment and reading failure have a common cause.
d.   Maladjustment and reading failure have each their own distinct cause.
e.   The relationship often is circular: maladjustment causes reading failure and the reading failure in turn increases the maladjustment or reading failure causes the maladjustment which in turn increases reading failure.

MOTIVATIONAL READINESS

Readiness for and achievement in reading are dependent also on the pupil's motivational readiness. Lack of interest is an important cause of poor reading. To achieve in reading the child must want to learn.

Children generally come to school wanting to learn to read. The reading teacher must foster this interest and expand it. He must locate those children who are not motivated to read. He must know how to further the interest of the child who wants to read. He also must be concerned with the type of reading materials that will encourage extensive reading and that will raise the child's general level of reading interests and tastes.

The Nature of Interest

Interests are defined as positive attitudes toward objects or classes of objects to which we are attracted (17, p. 213). Ryans (39, p. 312) says that interests are learned responses which predispose the organism to certain lines of activity and which facilitate attention. Getzels (20) defines interest as a disposition which impels an individual to seek out particular objects, activities, understanding, skills, or goals for attention. Cummins and Fagin (9) suggest that interest is an emotional involvement of like or dislike which is associated with attention to some object. Interest is the set of attending; the tendency to give selective attention to something.

Interests arise through the interaction of our basic needs and the means we use to satisfy them. The child who is interested in reading is usually the child for whom reading satisfies the basic needs of self-esteem, esteem of others, curiosity, or the need for success and personal adequacy. Interests are the active forces that direct our attention to activities or objects. They determine whether the child will read, how much he will read, and in what area he will read. The average child is actively seeking new experiences. His reaction to the world about him is selective. He chooses what he wants to experience and usually rejects those elements in which he is not interested.

As teachers, we are concerned with two phases of interest. First, the interest of the child somehow must be captured if he is to learn to read, and second, we must help the child to make reading an habitual activity.

> As a person learns to read, reading enters his mental make-up as a permanent mode of behavior. . . . Henceforth he uses reading as a means of enjoyment and as a means of studying and thinking. To the extent that he can read with ease, reading is a major factor in the control of his behavior. He will often arrange his daily schedule of work and play in order to provide time for reading. He will make sacrifices in order to provide himself with books to read. He will turn to reading as a means of discovering new interests and of losing himself for a time from the actualities of the external world. It is at this point that we see the employment of advanced spontaneous attention. No longer is reading an end on the outside that conflicts with other tendencies. It is now a dominating interest that is within (50, pp. 57–58).[3]

Indeed, it is at this point that reading acquires a motivational force of its own.

Our prime concern is that pupils do read (48a). A reader is not a pupil who *can* read; he is a pupil who *does* read (43). The kindergarten teacher, especially, is more interested in fostering interest in reading than in developing specific reading skills, but even the primary teacher should not be so busy teaching reading skills that she neglects to develop readers (7). Although children come to school with an attitude favorable to reading, this attitude is not necessarily self-perpetuating. As children learn how to read, they must be directed to materials that appeal to their basic needs. By observing what a child reads, we may see what his special interests are. We then can provide him with reading materials appropriate not only to his intelligence and age but also to those broader interests that stem from his basic needs.

Children's Reading Interests

Bettelheim (3, pp. 386–388) notes that if teachers want to promote an interest in reading, they must let children read materials that are realistic. He points out that it is difficult to find children's stories that describe differences between parents or between parent and child; stories in which mother is not always willing to go for walks or to play with the child;

---

[3] H. G. Wheat, *Foundations of School Learning* (New York: Alfred A. Knopf, Inc., 1955). Reprinted by permission.

stories in which children do not love the newborn baby; and yet, these are reality. The pupil reads *"run, run"* in the book, but must sit quietly at his desk. Thus, the reading program is built around pleasant experiences and may create unrealistic images of life and encourage reading that is pointless to the child.

Generally children prefer fictional materials to informational materials and prose to poetry. Their preferences for reading content show great variations and are influenced most by their age, sex, and intelligence. Girls read more than boys and before the age of eight or nine prefer the same content as boys. Interest in reading reaches a peak during the junior high years and then declines sharply.

Primary children like fairy tales, animal stories, nature stories, humorous tales, adventure stories, comics, and how-to-do-it books. Boys show special interest in animal stories; girls like stories with child characters.

Children in the intermediate grades are interested in adventure stories, animal stories, fantasies, in stories about family life, famous people, and children; they are interested in sports, humor, and in stories dealing with machines, personal problems, physical science, and social studies (54). Boys generally are most interested in real-life adventure; girls prefer fantasy stories and those dealing with school, home, and personal problems. Comics become especially popular during this period.

In the junior high years boys prefer comic books, animal stories, western stories, adventure, fiction, humor, and biography; girls prefer fiction, comic books, animal stories, biography, and western stories.

On the high school level girls prefer romance, society, and fashion, but also read adventure, science, and mystery stories; boys like sports, adventure, mystery, action, exploration, travel, science, mechanics, and politics. Humorous books and books on hobby pursuits also are popular during this period.

We already have mentioned that intelligence is a major factor in determining what children will read. Generally, the areas of interest of more intelligent children are on a slightly higher level than are those of less intelligent children. Children with high IQ's read books that are more difficult and more adult. Intelligent boys (IQ 130 or more) read mystery stories, biographies, history, historical fiction, comics, scientific materials, sports, humor, and westerns; girls of above average intelligence read historical fiction, modern novels, biographies, mystery stories, teenage books, sports, animal stories, science, history, and books treating social problems (1).

The teacher must understand children's interests, but this is not enough. He must have more than a knowledge of the interests of children in general. He can never be certain that each child in his classroom has the same interests as does the "average" child. He must know the interests of each pupil and how these interests can be modified and developed.

Various inventories have been developed for finding out what interests a child may have. Interest blanks or inventories are found in Harris (23, pp. 479, 482–483); Witty (52, pp. 302–307); Dolch (12, pp. 444–446), Witty, Kopel, and Coomer (53); and Thorpe, Meyers and Sea (46).

Developing Interests

It is often said that "Appreciation should be caught, not taught," but, as Duffy (13) notes, the evidence seems to indicate that children cannot catch it by themselves. They need help, especially from teachers.

Children develop interests through learning, conscious or unconscious emulation, and identification. The child readily identifies with parents or individuals who take their place. He generally accepts their values and develops their interests. If the teacher is sincerely interested in reading, the child tends to incorporate this interest.

The development of interests is a lure and a ladder activity (10). The pupil must be lured to new interests through the ladder of suitable materials. The teacher must introduce the pupil to the appropriate reading materials in a way that motivates the student to action. The parent may help by providing a stimulating environment. Magazines, books, and story telling lure the child to reading. Television programs broaden present interests, increase vocabularies, encourage further reading, and generally help children to understand their environment.

The use of television to actually teach reading is open to serious debate. As Durrell (14) points out, a book can be selected that closely fits the needs of a particular child, but television requires "all noses turned toward Mecca" at the same time. He suggests that television might be useful if for every two children there were one television set equipped with push buttons whereby the child might call forth the lesson needed and with other mechanisms that would reinforce correct performance and discourage incorrect performance. The greatest use for television perhaps is still for "enriching the intake of ideas" (14).

The root of the reading difficulties of a given pupil often is the mental attitude of the pupil. He may not like school and he may like reading less. In such a case, there may be no genuine disability. The pupil is disinterested and therefore has not developed competency.

Motivation flows from interest. Without interest there is usually no will to do, no drive to learn. Without motivation, the pupil simply will not develop into a mature reader.

The solution to the reluctant reader's problem begins then with a change of attitude. The pupil will not be an adequate reader until he wants to read. How do you get him to read? The teacher can promote interest in reading in numerous ways besides those already mentioned:

1. Read to children.

2. Develop charts to be placed on the reading table containing pupil-made jokes, riddles, statements, and stories. Other charts may contain famous sayings, a poem, or a list of words.

3. Provide a wide selection of easy reading materials—materials which pupils *may* read, not *must* read. As Murphy (33) notes, when we say to children, "you must read this," we may be creating nonreaders. The pupil should not feel depraved because he doesn't like, "As You Like It."

4. Guide each pupil to books he can read independently. While interest in a book is a powerful motivational factor, interest alone is not enough to make a difficult book easy to read (13).

5. Help each child to find materials of appropriate content and difficulty. Do not emphasize literary content only. Generally, the content should provide adventure, action, humor, romance (for girls), and surprise. The stories should be about children and heroes and about people with whom the reader can identify. The teacher should take special interest in the pupil's independent reading.

6. Use book exhibits, book fairs, book advertisements, periodicals, and bulletins to stimulate interest in reading. Provide books to fit children's immediate interests.

7. Give children an opportunity to share their reading experiences through book reports, panels, or round-table discussions. Permit pupils to discuss the author, plot, theme, setting, and style.

8. Develop a book club or hobby club. Choose a "Book of the Week." Devote an assembly to a particular author or invite a favorite author to school.

9. Introduce children to the reading topic by illustrating the content with T.V., films, recordings, and other audiovisual aids. Give an introduction to the book to create interest. Whet their curiosity.

10. Provide class time for library reading.

11. Let children read more than one version of a biography.

12. Stay in the background. The pupil's recommendation of a book carries more weight than the recommendations of ten teachers.

13. Recommend the sports page, magazines, or even the comics to children who do not read.

14. Let the pupil keep a record of his own progress, of the books that he has read, of the books that he would like to read, and of the movies he has seen that are based on books. There is nothing so discouraging as a teacher who is concerned more with errors than with successes. The teacher should be an exciter rather than an examiner or tester.

15. Help the pupil to look upon himself as a reader. "Self-concept is closely related to reading success, and it is doubtful if a child who does not see himself as a reader will ever possess the reading habit" (13, p. 255).

16. Have reading materials parallel the pupil's interests. The teacher needs to identify the pupil's interest and to introduce the pupil to books dealing with topics of special interest to him. Anita E. Dunn, Mabel E. Jackman, and J. Roy Newton in *Fare for the Reluctant Reader* (Albany: Argus-Greenwood, Inc., 1964) provide an annotated bibliography for children in grades seven through twelve. The books are listed alphabetically by author under categories that represent these teen-age interests: adventure, sports, love, careers, tips for teens, and mystery. Other book lists are the following:

   a. Adams, Ruth. *Books to Encourage the Reluctant Reader.* Scholastic Book Services, Englewood Cliffs, New Jersey.
   b. Bush, Bernice. *Fare for the Reluctant Reader: Books, Magazines, and Audio-Visual Aids for the Slow Learner in Grades 7–10.* New York State University, Albany, 1964.
   c. Martin, Marvin. "Fifty Books They Can't Resist." *Elementary English*, 39 (May, 1962) 415–416. (for sixth graders)
   d. *Books for Reluctant Readers,* Doubleday and Company, Inc., Garden City, New York. This annotated book samples English Classics, poetry, music, science, social studies, teen-age interests, and novels. Each book is accompanied by a designation of interest level and of reading level.

Here are some low vocabulary–high interest materials.

   a. *Basic Vocabulary Series.* Garrard Press.
   b. *Cowboy Sam Series.* Benefic Press.
   c. *Everyreader Series.* Webster Publishing Company.
   d. *Folklore of the World Series.* Garrard Press.
   e. *The Frontiers of America Books.* Children's Press, Inc.
   f. *High Interest Easy-to-read Books.* Follett-Publishing Company.
   g. *Jim Forest Readers.* Harr Wagner Publishing Company.
   h. *Gateways to Reading Treasures.* Laidlaw Brothers.
   i. *Junior Everyreader Series.* Webster Publishing Company.

    j. *Morgan Bay Mystery Series.* Harr Wagner Publishing Company.

    k. *Pleasure Reading Series.* Garrard Press.

    l. *Reading Caravan Series.* D. C. Heath and Company.

    m. *Reading Incentive Series.* Webster Division, McGraw-Hill Book Company.

    n. *Reading-motivated Series.* Harr Wagner Publishing Company.

    o. *Stories for Teenagers.* Globe Book Company.

    p. *Target Series.* Mafex Associates.

    q. *Teen-age Tales.* D. C. Heath and Company.

    r. *Webster's New Practice Readers.* Webster Publishing Company.

The teacher cannot ignore the interests of children, nor can he always feed the pupil only what he likes. He must stimulate the child to acquire tastes and to increase the variety of his interest. Harris (23, p. 491) makes a pertinent observation:

> Children do not develop discrimination by being allowed contact only with superior reading matter; on the contrary, it is often found that the brightest children and most voracious readers read much that is of a trashy nature, as well as much that is good. Taste develops through comparison and contrast, not from ignorance.[4]

Developing Reading Tastes

It is frequently an observation that many children do not read, that the quality of what some read is inadequate, and that schools are not developing a permanent interest in reading in many pupils.

The teacher can remedy this situation. First: He must use his understanding of the pupil to help the pupil choose books that will lead him to a higher level of appreciation. It is not enough to know that the book does not positively "harm" the child. The teacher must encourage the pupil to read books that make a positive contribution to his cultural, social, and ethical development. Second: He must be well acquainted with the books that he recommends to the pupil. When he suggests a book to a child, he must have the conviction that the content and the style will motivate him to read it. Third: He must know the specific interests of each child. If he is to help the pupil to develop reading tastes, he must consider the pupil's interest patterns, his voluntary reading, the availability of materials, and the time that he has for leisure reading. He must also

---

[4] Albert J. Harris, *How To Increase Reading Ability* (Longmans, Greene and Company, 1956). Reprinted with permission, David McKay Company, Inc.

know the level of the pupil's reading abilities. He cannot nurture pupil interest with books too difficult to be read easily.

An Observation

Where there is behavior, there is motivation. Human beings generally act to satisfy physiological and psychological needs. The child normally learns to read to satisfy his need for self-esteem. When reading is thus associated with need-satisfaction, reading becomes a meaningful activity. Repetition of this activity leads to the development of a lasting interest in reading *per se*. At this stage reading becomes a habit motive and may motivate other activity. The child will then seek a reading activity (for interest directs attention) and, to the degree that reading challenges his mind, he will have acquired the major by-product of interest. He will be able to concentrate.

SEX AND READINESS

Teachers have always been concerned with differences in achievement among boys and girls. One of the more obvious differences is in readiness for and achievement in reading. Girls as a group achieve better than boys in reading. They learn to read earlier, and fewer of them are significantly retarded in reading. They generally seem to perform better than boys in English usage, spelling, and handwriting.

Girls and boys exhibit differences also in other areas. For example, the incidence of stuttering, defects in color vision, and brain damage is substantially greater among boys. Boys also tend to lisp and lall more.[5] Girls tend to be better than boys in auditory (15) and visual discrimination. The incidence of left-handedness, ambidexterity, and high frequency hearing loss is greater among boys.

Numerous attempts have been made to explain the differences in reading achievement. In general, the explanations have emphasized either hereditary or environmental factors. It has been suggested that girls have an inherited language advantage or that they reach maturity about a year and a half earlier than boys. Bentzen (2) advances the hypothesis that the boy's problems stem from the stresses put on his immature organism by a society which fails to make appropriate provisions for the biological age differential between boys and girls. Since the attainment of a skill or neuromuscular maturation seems to depend upon the myelination of the motor and association tracts, myelination may be completed earlier in girls than boys.

---

[5] The laller substitutes an easier sound for a more difficult one. For example, instead of pronouncing robin as robin, he makes it "lobbin" or "wobbin."

Some writers suggest that today's schools are more fitted to the needs of girls. Most of the teachers are women and they may adjust more easily to girls than to boys. Furthermore, teaching methods frequently may be more suited to the needs of girls than to those of boys. Studies also indicate that girls are promoted on lower standards and that both men and women teachers tend to overrate the achievement of girls and to underrate the achievement of boys. A study by Davis and Slobodian (11), however, indicated that teachers showed no differences in verbal behavior toward boys and girls. They report that teachers did not call on girls with greater frequency, did not direct more negative comments toward boys, and did not treat boy responses differently during reading instruction. Apparently, on the basis of this study, differential teacher behavior is not a significant cause of sex differences in reading achievement.

The expectations of society require boys and girls to play distinctly different roles. Girls are supposed to be good, feminine, and to achieve in school. On the other hand, boys are expected to be active and to excel in sports rather than in books. Girls, in addition, before coming to school engage in numerous activities that may better prepare them for reading. In their weaving, sewing, and doll playing they have more opportunity to develop near vision and motor coordination (23, p. 27). Girls use reading more frequently for recreation than do boys. Reading materials generally are more in accordance with the interests of girls.

Certainly, not all reading disability cases are referred to the reading clinic. And of those who are referred not all of them may be referred for reading disability alone. It is quite possible that boys more frequently than girls tend to manifest their reading problems through aggressive tendencies, and as a result more of them are referred to the clinic. The reading problems of well-behaved girls may go undetected, or may be taken care of in the classroom (47, p. 114).

Studies generally have found that intelligence is more variable among boys than among girls. It may be that the reading ability of boys also is more variable, giving rise to a larger number of boys who are poor readers (47, p. 112).

A comparative study (37) of reading in Germany and the United States reveals that the mean reading scores of fourth- and sixth-grade German boys exceed those of German girls and that the variability of scores is greater among the girls than among the boys. These findings are just the reverse of those in this country and suggest that sex differences may best be explained by cultural and environmental factors. It is interesting to note that the teaching staffs in Germany, even in elementary school, are predominantly male.

That there are sex differences in readiness and reading achievement in favor of the girls in this country can hardly be questioned. There also are vast differences among boys themselves and, many six-year-old boys are more mature than the average six-year-old girl. What educational implications do these differences have? Two educational recommendations have been based on these differences. Some have suggested that boys begin first grade later than girls; other have suggested that separate mental age norms be devised for girls and boys.

In an attempt to evaluate these recommendations Clark (8) investigated sex differences in mental ability and achievement. His study is particularly significant because: (1) eight measures of mental ability and six measures of achievement were used; (2) the study involved third, fifth, and eighth grades; (3) he used a nationwide sample; (4) he used statistical controls in his analysis of differences in mental ability between boys and girls, so that the effects of variations in age were eliminated; (5) in his analysis of achievement differences between girls and boys the effects of variations in both age and mental ability were controlled.

The data indicated that intelligence as measured by the *California Test of Mental Maturity* is independent of sex. No significant differences were found between the sexes in reading vocabulary, reading comprehension, and arithmetic reasoning. In mechanics of English, however, the fifth- and eighth-grade girls did better than the boys. In spelling, the girls had better scores at all three grade levels. Thus, even when differences that are attributable to age and mental age are held constant, the girls still excelled in spelling and English mechanics.

Clark concludes that: (1) Sex differences in intelligence are nonexistent; (2) Since there were no differences in arithmetic and reading, the differences that are so noticeable in actual classroom conditions are attributable to environmental factors such as interest; (3) Girls have a definite advantage in English and spelling; and (4) Since a great variability in ability and achievement exists at all grade levels, educational decisions must give first consideration to the individuality of each pupil.

Educational provisions must ultimately be for the individual pupil. It is not enough to know what is best for the group. It is not enough to know what type of reading program would benefit most boys or girls. The teacher must prescribe for the individual boy and girl, and as soon as he attempts this, he realizes that differences between boys and girls and between one boy and another—differences other than sex—play a significant role in reading achievement.

INSTRUCTIONAL INADEQUACIES

The instructional inadequacies sometimes evident in the teaching of reading are variables of achievement that need to be evaluated. The child's readiness for reading and the level of achievement that he will attain in reading depend on his background of experience, his intellectual, physical, emotional, and social development, *and the instructional program he receives.* For some instructional programs, the child may not be ready until the age of seven; for others, he may be ready at the age of five.

Poor teaching may be a cause of reading disability or of lack of achievement in reading. Poor teaching is no less a handicap than is poor vision. It may even be true that reading disability cases are sometimes not understood because we have not looked in the right place. It is considerably easier to suggest multiple causality than to admit that our instruction has been inadequate (45, p. 120). It is easier to seek the cause of reading disability in lack of experience or emotional upset than to take a hard look at the instructional program.

Instruction may be inadequate because it is not adapted to the individual child, because it is unsystematic, because the teacher does not emphasize the basic skills, or because the teacher uses a single method exclusively.

One of the most potent factors in preventing reading disability is to provide systematic instruction in the basic skills. Pupils from the beginning need to get meaning from the printed page. They need to acquire a sight vocabulary and ways to independently identify words. They need to learn to avoid word calling, guessing at unknown words, or substituting words. They need to develop appropriate rate skills. They need practice in both silent and oral reading. Their reading needs to become smooth and rhythmical.

Inadequacy of Instructional Materials

Inadequacy of instructional materials is almost as serious as inadequacy in instruction. The classroom must be equipped with a variety of books and materials. For example, the kindergarten classroom must contain readiness workbooks, picture books, picture dictionaries, phonic games, preprimers, and primers. The teacher needs a hand printing set, oak tag, charts, labels, and signs. He should have at his disposal recordings, film strips, films, a radio, opaque projectors, and a television set. The classroom should be equipped with easels, paint brushes, finger paints, sandboxes, aprons, clay, oilcloth covers, cutting tools, blocks, beads, puzzles, and other concrete materials to broaden children's experiences.

Teaching Methods

The teaching technique also must be appropriate to the child and to the nature of what is taught. The child must be given a firm foundation in fundamentals. Efficient work habits must be encouraged from the start.

The reading readiness of each child must be determined. Drill on words out of context, on speed, and on word analysis should not be overemphasized, but it cannot be ignored. Reading for meaning must be stressed, but not to the exclusion of word identification and recognition.

The beginning reading teacher needs to be aware of numerous fallacies concerning reading methods. The following are some pertinent examples:

1. Learning the letters of the alphabet is a handicap to successful learning of reading (45, p. 70).

2. Learning to read and reading by a mature individual are the same process and involve the same factors. Because the letter is not the meaningful unit of perception in reading, it therefore cannot be the initial step in learning to read (45, pp. 70–73).

3. With the right method *every* child can learn to read. And, there is but *one* right method of teaching reading (45, p. ix, p. 36, pp. 93–98).

4. Every phonically-trained child necessarily is a word-caller. Indeed the child of very low IQ may become a word-caller because it is easier for him to learn to pronounce words than to learn and remember word meanings (45, pp. 101–102).

5. The reading readiness program exists *only* because present methods of teaching reading are so slow and so unsuccessful that we must justify our delaying of formal reading instruction until the child can be more successful with it. And it protects the teacher when certain children make no progress through the first grade (45, pp. 103–104).

6. Whenever our "favorite" method doesn't work, it must have been taught improperly.

7. The phonics approach interferes with the child's ability to take meaning to and from the printed page and keeps him from thinking with the material (45, p. 111).

8. Phonics is best taught incidentally. It should be introduced only after the child has learned a certain number of words by sight to help him to read words with which he has difficulty (45, p. 114).

9. The phonics approach is wrong because phonically-trained children do not read as rapidly nor as fluently as analytically-trained children. This may be true of beginning readers, but does drilling children to handle very rapidly a small, controlled vocabulary in grade one necessarily guarantee that they will be able to handle longer and less-controlled vocabularies in the sixth grade?

10. The whole-word method is completely visual, and the phonic method is completely auditory (25).
11. Drill in phonics will cause children to dislike reading.
12. Children learning to read by the sight method will develop a permanent interest in reading.
13. The developmental reading program prohibits children from exploring and broadening their interests. (The individualized reading program is thought to allow children this opportunity.)
14. The so-called "contextual reader" is the best reader. As Nelson (34) points out, the boy who reads "war" for the word "battle" because it makes sense in the sentence is not necessarily a better reader than the pupil who reads "bottle." The former simply guessed at the word; the latter was actually closer to identifying the word even though he confused the *a* with the *o*.

    There is a difference between reading and understanding. The pupil who substitutes "war" for "battle" has not identified the linguistic form (38), and reading always is an identification of linguistic form plus association of meaning with the form.
15. Practice alone will help the pupil to improve. Some proponents of the individualized approach seem to be falling into this error. Their admonition to the pupil at times sounds like this: "Mary, you are not ready to read to me yet. Go and practice some more."
16. The controlled vocabulary in the basal series is more insipid than the vocabulary used in phonic materials.
17. English is not a phonetic language or reading methods are not linguistic in nature.
18. Linguistics is synonymous with synthetic phonics.
19. A code emphasis in beginning reading is universally successful; it is totally without reading failures.
20. Linguists universally consider reading merely as a matter of recognizing words.

Incidence of Reading Retardation

This list of fallacies is just an example of the erroneous ideas existent in reading today. Teachers cannot close their eyes to the fact that some present-day practices are based on them. They cannot ignore this situation because there are still far too many children who are not learning to read as well as they might.

In the city of New York, for example, 4000 seventh graders were retained in 1958 because they were reading at or below fourth grade level (44, p. 5). Foster (18) reports that in the Phoenix, Arizona high schools, out of 1106 entering freshman tested, 21.4 per cent had a reading ability of fifth grade or lower and 34 per cent could not read at the seventh grade level.

Unfortunately, the problem is not entirely the teacher's fault. Some 25 per cent of the teacher-training institutions do not require special preparation in reading and only nine state certification agencies require elementary teachers to have completed a course in reading (42).

Other Factors

Reading disability is also related to numerous other factors that we might group under the general heading of institutional variables. The school environment is an important determinant of learning. Is the school achievement-oriented? Is the school environment unnatural? Children by nature have a need to behave aggressively, but in school may be confined almost completely to their chairs.

The books says, "Run, run, run," but the child must sit, sit, sit. Children by nature have a need to be active, but the emphasis in school may be to require them to be passive listeners. The type of control exercised in the classroom, the nature of the instructional materials, the library facilities, the expectations that the administration and staff have of the pupil, teacher shortages, grading practices, grouping practices, type of classroom organization, the types of measurement and evaluation, and the size of the instructional unit have a direct bearing on the rate of reading disability in a given school. It is obvious that the child must normally have reached a more advanced developmental stage to succeed in reading in a class of 36 pupils than in a class of 12 or 13 pupils (30, p. 27). Frymier (19) found that first graders in small classes achieved at a significantly higher level than pupils in larger classes. A class of 36 or more was considered a "large" class; one of fewer than 30 was a "small" class.

SUMMARY

In Chapters 3 and 4 we have examined numerous factors that have a bearing on the pupil's readiness for achievement in reading. The teacher cannot ignore them. To help the child most he must have a clear understanding of each factor.

It is impossible for the teacher to remember all these data about each child without some way for simplifying them. Thus, reading texts generally have presented a readiness chart, on the basis of which the teacher can rate the child's readiness for reading. Table 4-1 is based on the data discussed in this and the previous chapter and may well be considered a summary of them.

TABLE 4-1   The Nature of the Learner: Reading Readiness Chart

| Name.. Sex .... |
| Age in years............................. and months .... |
| IQ .... MA .... Reading Readiness Score |

Estimates of the Child's Development	1 2 3 4 5 *

1. Background of Previous Experience
   a. Has attended kindergarten†
   b. Has a foreign language background
   c. Is from a low-level socioeconomic home
   d. Is intellectually dull-normal

2. General Mental Development
   a. Perceives likeness and differences
   b. Remembers word forms
   c. Has appropriate memory and attention span
   d. Thinks clearly and in sequence
   e. Can express his thoughts in his own words
   f. Associates symbols with pictures, objects, or facts
   g. Sees the relationship of the part to the whole
   h. Can think on an abstract level

3. General Language Development
   a. Has appropriate vocabulary for his age
   b. Enunciates clearly
   c. Articulates clearly
   d. Pronounces words accurately
   e. Expresses himself clearly to others
   f. Is sensitive to sentence structure
   g. Talks in simple sentences
   h. Understands that what can be said also can be written

4. General Physical and Physiological Development
   a. Has sufficient visual acuity
   b. Manifests refractive errors: myopia, hyperopia, astigmatism
   c. His eyes aim in different directions
   d. His eyes are not in focus
   e. The visual images are different in shape and size

* We have used the same rating system as Gray (21, p. 126) for the six major headings: Namely 1 = well below average; 2 = below average; 3 = average; 4 = above average; and 5 = well above average. These ratings are dependent on the answers made to the subdivisions of each major grouping.
† The answers to the subdivisions should be *yes* or *no* answers.

(continued p. 106)

TABLE 4-1 (*continued*)

Estimates of the Child's Development	1 2 3 4 5 *

    f. Has a conductive hearing loss
    g. Has a high tone hearing loss
    h. Has good health
    i. Has suffered a neurological injury
    j. Has clearly developed dominance
    k. Has clearly developed eye-preference
    l. Makes reversals in speech, reading, and/or writing
    m. Has been converted from left- to right-handedness

5. Motivational, Emotional, and Social Development
    a. Is interested in learning to read
    b. Is interested in books
    c. Is interested in interpreting pictures and printed symbols
    d. Is curious about the shapes of words
    e. Works well with a group
    f. Is responsive to instruction
    g. Has a feeling of adequacy and belonging
    h. Has learned to help himself
    i. Has developed some tolerance for failure
    j. Exhibits a normal amount of self-confidence
    k. Tends to withdraw from the situation
    l. Is acceptant of authority
    m. Is normally communicative in the classroom
    n. Is usually attentive

6. Educational Development
    a. Can concentrate on or attend to learning activities
    b. Can follow directions
    c. Instructional materials are adequate
    d. Has had training in efficient work habits
    e. Has attended regularly
    f. Has changed schools

7. Mode of Learning
    a. Learns easier when he can see it in print
    b. Learns easier when he hears it
    c. Learns easier when he can write or use his hands

The teacher of reading must know his subject matter. The task variables, the things to be learned, are important determinants of reading success. The teacher must promote the development of word recognition and meaning skills.

However, this is not enough. He also must understand the individual variables. He must understand the nature of the learner. This has been the import of the last two chapters. The child's development in reading is dependent upon all the other interrelated aspects of his total development. Each child's development is different and so is his achievement in reading. Only by knowing each pupil can the teacher base his educational decisions on a psychology of individual differences.

The following anecdote will help to illustrate this point. A little boy was sitting on the floor and was trying to assemble a jigsaw puzzle. As his father passed him, the father noticed his plight and informed him that he would be back shortly to help him. When he returned, the amazed father saw that the puzzle had been completed.

"How did you get it?," he inquired. To which his son replied: "Daddy, I looked at the box and I saw what it was supposed to be. It was a picture of a boy surrounded by the world. I first got the boy and when I got him right the rest was easy."

So it is in reading. If we get the boy right, the rest of the teaching tasks fall imperceptibly into place. Good education must begin with a knowledge of the child.

The child's "wholeness" is very significant. A child is not really like a jigsaw puzzle that we can put together, piece by piece. The resultant mosaic may differ appreciably from the original youngster (40).

QUESTIONS FOR DISCUSSION

1. What is the parent's role in the socialization of the infant?
2. What is the teacher's role in socializing the pupil?
3. What are some of the defense mechanisms used by the child to protect himself from reading failure?
4. Discuss five significant activities through which the teacher can develop an interest in reading.
5. Explain the interrelationship of motives, needs, meaning, interest, habit, and concentration.
6. Explain the concept "wholeness" or the meaning of such phrases as "The whole child goes to school" or "The whole child reads."
7. In two parallel columns list conditions under which reading failure leads to personal maladjustment and when personal maladjustment leads to reading failure.
8. What are the arguments for presenting real life situations in children's reading materials? What arguments may be advanced against presenting them?
9. Study, analyze, and evaluate one recognized interest inventory. What place does it have in the reading program?
10. Discuss the implications of five fallacies in reading upon the instructional program in the school.
11. Discuss the following statements:
    a. The tendency to read is a function of habit strength, of drive (motiva-

tion), of the stimulus, of incentive motivation (reinforcement), and of delay reinforcement.

b. The more reading the child does, the greater is the tendency to engage in additional reading. Genuine interest in reading is developed through actual reading.

c. The more reading satisfies personal motives, the greater is the tendency to read.

d. The more interesting, reading becomes and thus the closer it comes to being a motive in its own right, the greater is the tendency to read.

e. The effective tendency to read is equal to the total tendency to read minus the inhibitory factors that tend to block performance. Among the inhibitory factors are health, fatigue, amount of energy needed for reading, and the number of unreinforced reading experiences.

f. The greater the amount of energy the reader must expend in reading, the less he tends to read. (The more difficult the materials, the quicker the student becomes fatigued.)

g. The more frequently reading is unrewarded, the less the student tends to read. (The student who reads but does not understand tends to lose his interest in reading.)

h. There is variability in an organism's tendency to respond through reading.

i. Motivation is a decreasing function of massed practice. (Massed practice tends to lead to fatigue.)

j. Socioeconomic status is more closely related to a child's general interest in reading than to a child's interest in a specific reading theme or content.

DEVELOPING READINESS
FOR READING

part III

Part III attempts to outline a program for developing reading readiness. It is not enough for the teacher to know what promotes or hinders reading readiness; he must know how to develop it.

Chapter 5, entitled, "Reading—A Language Experience" and Chapter 6, entitled, "Developing Language Readiness," lay the foundation for subsequent chapters. They are concerned with the nature of communication, with the meaning of language, with the significance of language and communication for the reading process generally and for reading readiness specifically, and with development of language readiness. The general assumption underlying the chapters is this: the first step in introducing the child to reading is to provide him with an adequate development in listening and speaking.

Chapters 3 and 4 emphasized the physical-psychological development of the child. Chapters 5 and 6 give primary consideration to the child's language development.

Reading instruction is more than psychological guidance. Sociological, neurological, physical, and psychological conditions do indeed produce many reading problems, but the misunderstanding of the relationship between the printed and spoken language may lead to many more.

In our language, reading requires the child to see mentally the oral counterparts of the printed symbols. Only after he has done this does he respond with meaning to the symbol. Reading and understanding are distinct processes even though reading always includes understanding. Reading is a *linguistic* process and is best taught as a communication and language skill. The child should learn that what he can think he can speak; what he can say, he or others can write or have written; and what is written, can be read.

Chapter 7, entitled, "Developing Reading Readiness," identifies the specific factors needed for successful beginning reading and provides techniques for developing them. It provides techniques for improving concept formation, auditory discrimination, visual discrimination, and left-to-right progression. It also takes up the learning of the alphabet and the use of readiness tests.

Reading—
a Language Experience

chapter 5

In the introduction to this book we suggested that the teaching of reading functions best when it is one phase of the total communicative process. In introducing Chapters 1 and 2 we noted that reading is language and it is communication. The next two chapters will concern themselves with the significance of the child's early language experiences upon his achievement in reading.

The teacher of reading needs to understand communication and language for the following reasons:

1. The child's proficiency in the communication and language skills, both speaking and listening, is the best indicator of the child's readiness for beginning reading. In fact, intelligence test scores may basically represent past opportunities for language experience.

2. The teacher himself cannot understand the reading process without understanding communication and oral language development.

3. The more alike the patterns of language structure in the reading material are to the patterns of language structure used in speaking, the better the pupil's comprehension tends to be (53).

Communication is the heart of the language arts. Without communication listening or reading cannot occur. Reading takes place only when the child shares the ideas that the communicator intends to convey.

THE NATURE OF HUMAN COMMUNICATION

Communication is a sensory-motor process. It includes the motor reactions of the signmaker—the speaker or writer, and the reception of the sign by the listener or reader (60, p. 166). In communication the organism is affected by an external event and reacts to it. The motor actions are principally two: natural signs and conventional symbols. The distress cries of children, the sex calls of the animal world, the emotional reactions of humans, our tears, cries, and groans, and our blushing, shivering, and yawning, are natural signs. Words and numbers are conventional symbols. They are conventional because they have no meaning of their own.

We have used the words, conventional symbols, deliberately. A sign in our estimation has a direct relation to its object or referent. If some balmy afternoon you look out of the window and see water dripping from the trees, you infer that it is raining. The water is a sign of the rain (70, p. 19). The word "water," on the other hand, does not have a direct connection with rain. The person may use it and rain need not fall. It is interesting to note that aphasics cannot do this. One such patient, when asked to repeat "The snow is black," immediately replied: "No, the snow is white." He could repeat the statement only after being assured that it need not be true to be assertable. For the aphasic the symbol generally must have a direct relation to its referent.

Except for the fact that we have conventionally agreed among ourselves that the word "rain" should be used when the vapor in the atmosphere condenses and falls in watery form, we might use the word "flour." However, if we want to communicate with others we must abide by their conventions.

Since the word does not have any meaning of its own, meaning must come from another source. Generally we get meaning through experience. Communication depends upon a certain commonality of experience between the signmaker and the observer. For communication to take place the symbol must call forth a similar response from the giver and the recipient of the communication. Unfortunately, this frequently is not the case. Porter (49) points out that

> Each human being represents a different tangle of motivations, attitudes and needs; each represents literally billions of varied experiences which have been assimilated and ordered in ways that are constantly undergoing change. Each attempt at communication, at understanding or being understood, bears the mark of this prodigious personal context. No word or gesture can ever mean *precisely* the same thing to any two individuals; the closer they can come to

using similar meanings, the more effective the communication between them will be.[1]

Perfect communication is rare. Not only are our experiences usually
different (and hence also our meanings, ideas, and concepts), but frequently we are not familiar with all the ways of expressing meaning. We
are not completely familiar with the speaker's or writer's specific modes
of expression. Finally, words create only a symbolic representation in
the mind—never exact reality.

Communication always involves two elements: (*1*) those ideas or
experiences that we wish to communicate and (*2*) the signs or symbols
that we use to convey these ideas or experiences. Thus, communication
is not necessarily only a human characteristic. The worker ant that with
its antennae strokes the head or the abdomen of another ant in order to
gain entrance is communicating. The bee that engages in a dance to
inform a fellow worker of the distance and the direction of a new supply
of food is communicating. The cluck of the hen that sends her chicks
scurrying is also communication (13, p. 4). Even a traffic light or a temperature control system can communicate (26, p. 267). To communicate is
not necessarily human; to use the most highly developed system of communication, to use speech, is necessarily human.

In summary, communication is a sensory-motor process involving the
use of signs. In human communication, these signs are symbols or words
and they receive their meaning from and through experience. In every
sense of the word reading is the culminating act of the communicative
process, initiated by the thoughts and the signs or symbols put on the
printed page by the writer.

THE MEANING OF LANGUAGE

Language has been variously defined. Soffietti[2] notes that language refers
to "the systemized set of vocal habits by means of which the members of
a human society interact in terms of their culture." Sapir (55) suggests that
language is a purely human method of communication through a system
of voluntarily produced symbols.

Writers generally have pointed out that language, the ability to use

[1] William E. Porter, "Mass Communication and Education," *The National Elementary Principal*, 37 (February 1958) 12–16. Reprinted by permission of the Department of Elementary School Principals, National Education Association.

[2] James P. Soffietti, "Why Children Fail to Read: A Linguistic Analysis," *Harvard
Educational Review*, 25 (Spring 1955) 63–84. Reprinted by permission of the Graduate
School of Education, Harvard University.

systemized verbal symbolism, puts man on a unique plane. Frisina (25, p. 11) notes that the acquisition of verbal symbolism is a unique human characteristic. Cassirer (12, p. 44) defines man as *"animal symbolicum."* Von Humboldt wrote that man is man only because of language; perhaps, it might be more correct to say that man had to be human to invent language. Without man, there is no language (51, pp. 6–7).

Langer (40, p. 83) notes that

> Language is . . . the most momentous and at the same time the most mysterious product of the human mind. Between the clearest animal call of love or warning or anger, and a man's least, trivial word, there lies a whole day of Creation—or in modern phrase, a whole chapter of evolution.[3]

Man, like the animal, can communicate through taste, touch, and smell, and through grunts and groans, but he also can learn to communicate through language or verbal symbolism. He alone has the ability to name his concepts. Bees use signs, but only man knows that the signs he uses are signs. Maritain thus notes that language is the use of a sign in a way that involves "the knowledge or awareness of the relation of signification (43, p. 90)."

The Characteristics of Language

Definitions of language generally emphasize the following six characteristics of language:

1. Language is a human attribute.
2. Language is acquired behavior.
3. Language is verbal symbolic behavior. Language primarily is oral in nature. Indeed, some cultures have not developed a written language.
4. Language is systematic behavior (70, p. 20). The speaker cannot alter indiscriminately the sequence of the words. He does not say: "The man fat in sat can."
5. Language generally is reflexive behavior. After the child has acquired language, language tends to become almost completely reflexive behavior. Like the man who walks home and doesn't know how he got there, in our use of language we

---

[3] Susanne K. Langer, *Philosophy in a New Key* (New York: Mentor Books, New American Library, 1948). Originally published by the Harvard University Press. Reprinted by permission.

proceed quite automatically even though the mind is occupied in thought (64).

6. Language has individual and social significance.

The Philosophy and Sociology of Reading (19, pp. 9–20)

The philosophy and sociology of reading have received increased emphasis in journal articles and are related to points three and six above. The first problem of a philosophy of reading, or more generally of a philosophy of language, deals with that meaningfulness which is utilized in communication. The linguistic philosopher concerns himself with linguistic significance. He grapples with the "individuality of things and the generality of language."

Are words just words, "cries of the forest corrupted and complicated by anthropoid apes" (Anatole France), or do they mirror the world, bear meaning, and act as a medium of communication?

Western man has always accorded language or the word a high evaluation. He believes that language is about something. Unless words express reality, we are just bantering about words. Whatmough notes:

> . . . If the deliberate fault of postulating a direct connection between symbol and referend is committed, or if this is done innocently by the unsophisticated, it gives rise to the dangerous illusion that by manipulating the symbols it is possible to manipulate the referends . . . Another danger is to exclude the referend. Here we have the vicious practice of verbalism, of moving repeatedly from symbol to cerebral construct and back again, of responding entirely to one's own verbal response (70, pp. 178–179).[4]

Even the Chinese philosopher Hsun Tzu noted that "Names have been fixed to denote realities. . . ." They have a content "determined by an identity of reaction in man . . . to the same things, to the same stimuli." (1, p. 13) The identity of reaction by various humans undergirds all human certainties. "The word, thus laden with the experience of the ages, becomes an entity which is neither [wholly] equivocal nor ambiguous and on which rest social and moral relations between men." (1, p. 13)[5]

A sociology of reading makes sense only if the words on the printed

---

[4] Joshua Whatmough, *Language: A Modern Synthesis* (New York: St. Martin's Press, 1956). Reprinted by permission.

[5] Ruth N. Anshen, "Language as Idea," in Ruth N. Anshen (ed.), *Language: An Inquiry Into Its Meaning and Function* (New York: Harper & Row, Publishers, Inc., 1957). Reprinted with permission.

page convey meaning. If the words did not communicate, we would not use language as the major vehicle of interaction with others, and we would not be concerned with the effects that reading has on the reader.

Language has a social utility (70). It is the basis for group communication and living. Without it, we should have difficulty sharing our ideas. We use language to influence others, and by it others influence us. Since society propagates itself through education, language becomes essential to the development and propagation of a civilization and culture. Through it we transmit to our children the accumulated knowledge of the past. Man, destined for social interaction, needs communication, and while he may use other forms of communicating, his social interaction is essentially linguistic (41, p. 188).

Language and writing exist for the *social* manifestation of thought. Language arose when man attempted to communicate his thoughts. Language thus arose from the needs of humanity and the nature of man. Man's use of words to express his thought and concepts is *natural* and derives from man's peculiar propensities. Words are *conventional* only in as far as *this* particular word signifies *this* particular concept.

Language needs a social context and must have social effects. Language grew and continues to grow in and through society. A word that has a private definition does not communicate, but instead represents a perceptual experience in the raw and is "doomed to be a gem serene, locked in the silence of private experience." (8)

Dewey noted that "Language . . . is the medium in which culture exists and through which it is transmitted." (22, p. 20) In other places he noted that men without language would be subhuman animals. He felt that words come into existence through cooperative action for a common purpose. Because man is an *animal sociale* and because man sought to accomplish social tasks, it became necessary to develop symbols.

The social role of language is illustrated in other ways. The mastery of speech is a prerequisite to full participation in society. Through language the child acquires beliefs and attitudes. Speech initiates the child into a community and provides a feeling of belonging. Language, for example, is a sign of the social solidarity of those who speak it—of the family, the club, the union, or the gang. When we say of a person that "he talks like us" we mean "he is one of us."

What we have said about language applies with equal force to writing and reading. Reading is a language process. Man interacts with his fellow man through speech and writing, through listening and *reading*. Listening is the other half of talking, and reading is the other half of writing. A culture becomes a civilization only when it possesses a written language and when there are *readers* of the history of that culture (28).

When writing and reading became a means of communication and of recording and encoding facts, a sociology of reading was born. We became concerned with who reads *what* and *why*. We became concerned with the ways and means by which reading might promote individual welfare and social progress. An immediate interest developed in such questions as: motives for reading; amount and kind of material read by members of different social classes; levels of difficulty of reading materials; and social effects of reading.

As a result of various inquiries into these questions, the social role of reading became unmistakably clear. It has been adequately demonstrated that reading is both a social and a socialization process. Reading quite frequently is done in a social group and always involves some degree of social interaction between the writer and the reader. Furthermore, in our society, unless a child can read, he does not perceive himself to be an "enfranchised" member of the group or society.

Let us briefly allude to just a few interrelationships with which a sociology of reading might deal.

1. *Reading is an indispensable means of communication in a civilized society.*
2. *Reading materials, the amount and the types of material read, the motives for reading, the levels of difficulty of reading materials, and the skill with which one reads are to a great degree socially determined.*

The initial motivator of reading is probably the child's attempt to duplicate what a sibling or a parent is doing. Thus the foundation of reading is imitation, a social learning process (75). A child does not perceive himself as an accepted member of society unless he has learned to read. Reading in this sense is a self-defining process (75).

We have found that the amount and kinds of reading are different in different sections of the country, among various occupational groups, and among individuals of various socioeconomic groups. In fact, Barton (3) found in a survey of 1200 teachers that the most important single factor in reading in school is socioeconomic class. When he divided classrooms according to the socioeconomic status of the pupil's parents (using a combination of income and occupation), he found that reading retardation rises steadily through the first six grades for working-class children and especially for the lower-skilled. Worley and Story (74) found that the language facility of first-grade children from low socioeconomic groups was over a year below that of children from high socioeconomic status.

The evidence shows that Negro children do not read as well as white children on an average, not because of an absence of symbolic activity, but because the Negro, especially from lower socioeconomic groups, has a different cultural base in which the language is different from that of the middle-class white person.

3.   *The language and the meanings that are ascribed to spoken and printed materials are determined partially by the social context.*

The evidence shows that culture affects language, and language in turn affects culture and thought habits. Whorf (71) has demonstrated that where a culture and a language have developed together, there are significant interrelationships between the general aspects of the grammar and the characteristics of the culture as a whole. The social organization and prevailing modes of thought in a society leave their imprint on language. Social selection gradually determines which phones becomes phonemes, what the vocabulary of the language shall be, and what the sentence structure shall look like.

Vocabulary differences are related to the environment. Eskimo languages have thirty words for different kinds of snow; we have only one; the Aztecs use the same word for cold, ice, and snow (71, p. 6). The Paiute, a desert people, have a language that permits detailed description of topological features, a necessity in a country where complex directions are needed for the location of water holes.

The changes are not confined simply to the vocabulary or grammatical differences. The language itself, the words and the idioms, frequently become encrusted with historic and cultural meaning. The word "crusade," for example, in our culture means "a crusading spirit" or an enthusiasm such as might be manifested in a "crusade for freedom." Translated into German, its becomes *Kreuzzug* and is identified with the Holy Wars of the Middle Ages. The word "compromise" since World War II has come to mean "an unsatisfactory and possibly cheapening outcome which pleases nobody" (1, p. 127); in recent years, it seems to be changing again. The simple fact is that "every society meets a new idea with its own concepts, its own tacit, fundamental way of seeing things." (40, p. 6)

4.   *The vocabulary and ideas acquired through reading may give rise to vital social and personal changes.*

We have evidence, although indirect, which suggests that the world itself appears different to a person using one vocabulary rather than another. Vocabulary influences a person's perceptions. A Chinese Aristotle probably would not have been able to formulate the system of ideas that a Greek Aristotle did. Vocabulary tells what features of the environment to pay attention to. The language of the people is a key to the concepts shared by members of a given culture, and changes in language reflect a change in concepts. "Language is indispensable not only for the construction of the world of thought but also for the construction of the world of perception, both of which constitute the ultimate nexus of an intelligible communion, spiritual and moral, between man and man." (1)[6]

Our experience tends to indicate that reading does in fact affect the social understandings, interests, attitudes, beliefs, judgments, morals, and behavior of the reader. Words mold men's thinking, direct action, and permit us to share genius. Speech, writing, listening, and reading are prerequisites to full participation in society.

Language also has significance for the individual. Whether justly or unjustly, others judge us by our language. Language is considered to be an index of intelligence, culture, and personality (46, p. 4). It is a tool that may be put to many uses. We use language to learn, to retain, to recall, to transmit information, and to control our environment. Through it we symbolize and order our concepts of the universe. Kraus (39) notes that words are symbols of reality and permit us to manipulate knowledge concerning reality. Sapir (56) adds that *"Language is primarily a vocal actualization of the tendency to see reality, symbolically."* Language allows us to speak of things not in sight and to project into the future. Language also allows us to hold on to reality, to fix it in experience, and to make it available when needed (40, pp. 109–110).

The word makes concepts usable. No better illustration of this can be had than the water-pump experience of Helen Keller (38, pp. 23–24).

> We walked down the path to the well-house, attracted by the fragrance of the honeysuckle with which it was covered. Someone was drawing water and my teacher placed my hand under the spout. As the cool stream gushed over one hand she spelled into the other the word *water*, first slowly, then rapidly. I stood still, my whole attention fixed upon the motions of her fingers. Suddenly I felt a misty consciousness as of something forgotten—a thrill of returning thought; and somehow the mystery of language was revealed to me. I knew then that "w-a-t-e-r-" meant the wonderful cool something that was flowing over my hand. That living word awakened my soul, gave it light, hope, joy, set it free! . . . I left the well-house eager to learn. Everything had a name, and each name gave birth to a new thought.

In the above incident Helen Keller became aware of the representational function of symbols. The endless job of associating each symbol with a specific object was now over. She had learned that a word can be used to signify and to order the events, ideas, and meanings of the world about her.

A child early learns to use language to manipulate his environment.

[6] Ruth N. Anshen, "Language as Idea," in Ruth N. Anshen (ed.), *Language: An Inquiry Into Its Meaning and Function* (New York: Harper & Row, Publishers, Inc., 1957). Reprinted with permission.

At first, he makes speech responses to get the esteem and recognition of others. Speech brings him social approval and usually gets him the food or water that he craves (60, p. 173). Gradually, other less direct incentives become sufficient, and indeed the drive to speak eventually becomes self-sustaining.

Reading can and often does serve as a tool for personal growth and adjustment, and we use the term *bibliotherapy* to describe this process. Reading frequently helps the reader to overcome insecurity based on his relations with his peers or with his family. It may help him to deal with failures. It may help him to accept himself for what he is, to obtain insights into his own problems, and to evaluate his own strengths and weaknesses.

The Role of Language in Thinking

As skills in language develop, language serves an increasingly significant role in thinking. Adults are prone to tell youngsters to "shut up," to "be quiet," or to "keep still." Fortunately, they don't succeed too well. The child

> . . . continues to "drip" speech, just as a leaky faucet puts forth a continuous spatter. This is not rank disobedience, as it might appear at first glance. Rather, the child's inner thinking and mental imagery are so closely associated with the vocal expression that he finds it difficult to separate them (61, p. 4).[7]

The child talks to himself as he tries to understand the mechanisms of the toy plane in front of him. The little girl carries on a full conversation with her doll in the course of a few minutes. What the adult only thinks, the child both thinks and speaks.

Adults are not different in this respect from children. Much of our thinking actually includes "talking to ourselves." When put on the spot as it were, the adult will speak to himself in anticipation of what he is going to say. All of us can remember the time when we were summoned to the principal's office or when we asked a girl for the first date. The words we were going to say were spoken many times first to ourselves.

Language and thinking are similar also in that they require the same basic processes. The ability to abstract, to conceptualize, and to form categories is a common requirement both for highest level language and thought. In fact it may be argued that language and thought are the same process. The Greek word *logos* is the symbol for both reason and speech.

---

[7] Charles Van Riper and Katharine G. Butler, *Speech in the Elementary Classroom* (New York: Harper & Row, Publishers, Inc., 1955). Reprinted by permission.

Kant (60, p. 183) wrote: "To think is to speak to oneself." Watson (67) referred to thought as "subvocal use of language." DeLaguna notes that "If an animal cannot express its thoughts in language, that is because it has no thoughts to express; for thoughts which are not formulated are something less than thoughts." (20) And Langer (40, p. 103) writes: "In language we have the free, accomplished use of symbolism, the record of articulate conceptual thinking; without language there seems to be nothing like explicit thought whatever." [8]

Implicit speech seems to accompany thinking as well as reading. Jacobson (36) suggests that the muscles controlling the eyes contract during imagination as though the individual were looking at the object. When the subject imagines that he is performing a muscular act, a contraction occurs in those muscle fibers that normally participate in carrying out the act. When the person thinks, the muscles of the tongue or upper lip vibrate as if he were saying the words. Edfeldt (23), studying the electromyographic records[9] of university students and adults, found that all engaged in silent speech while reading. Good readers engaged in less silent speech than poor readers, and the more difficult the material, the more silent speech occurred. This, of course, does not mean that reading without silent speech is impossible. It simply means that in these experiments silent speech was always present. It would seem that recommendations to the effect that training to remove silent speech be discontinued are somewhat premature. Reading may begin with almost total dependence upon speech; it perhaps can be freed from this dependence.

There is little doubt that a certain amount of vocal behavior and lip and tongue movement accompany many thought processes. Experiments show that students preparing for an examination actually become hoarse after four hours of intensive study. Hebb (31, pp. 59–60) suggests that some verbal behavior may play a vital role in problem solving. Intensive thought is much more than a simple intracranial process. He (31, p. 60) adds, however, that sentence construction shows that thought and speech are not entirely the same process. Thought processes run well ahead of our articulations. Van Riper and Butler (61, p. 100) note that "Just as there is an eye-voice span in oral reading, so, too, there is a similar scanning process preceding utterance. Our minds keep looking ahead of our mouths, scanning our memory drums for the words which will be needed." [10] We know that aphasics, although unable to speak,

[8] Susanne K. Langer, *Philosophy in a New Key* (New York: Mentor Books, New American Library, 1948). Originally published by the Harvard University Press. Reprinted by permission.

[9] In this process surface and needle electrodes pick up electrical potentials from the contracting muscles.

[10] Charles Van Riper and Katharine C. Butler, *Speech in the Elementary Classroom* (New York: Harper & Row, Publishers, Inc., 1955). Reprinted by permission.

do think and do learn to read. However, it is much more difficult for them to do so. It seems also that deaf mutes "think" and "read" with their fingers and their hands.

Up to this point we have emphasized the following points:

1. We have discussed the nature of communication and have found that *reading is communication*. Communication involves the transmission of meaning and this occurs in the reading process. Without the communication of meaning there is no reading.

2. We have examined the nature of language or communication through verbal symbols and have found that reading meets all the criteria of language, albeit, a written language. *Reading is a linguistic process.*

3. In examining the nature of language we found that it has many of the characteristics of thought. This brings us to another generalization. Reading is language; language involves thought; and *reading is a thinking process.*

The implications for the teaching of reading are many:

1. There is little point in teaching a child to read until he can use sentence language in conversation.

2. It is unsafe for the reading text to run any considerable distance ahead of the child's own oral language expression; otherwise he is virtually trying to learn a foreign language and valuable instructional time is lost.

3. Language training should accompany reading instruction every step of the way. A linguistic background for reading lessons should be continuously built at each stage of growth.

4. Every reading lesson should be an extension of language and a means of developing the child's linguistic skill.

5. The child's comprehension of speech and his oral use of language should be checked frequently. Appraisal of the linguistic competency of all slow learners and language handicapped children should be a part of the diagnostic and remedial program.

6. More oral work should be provided in teaching beginners and handicapped pupils.

7. Some of the effort expended in teaching slow learners by dint of drills and devices might better be expended in working on development in oral language and comprehension. [We classify slow learners on the basis of their intelligence test scores, but group tests of intelligence may be nothing more than measures of a child's language opportunity or deprivation (44).]

8. More attention should be paid to aural comprehension as a pre-requisite for beginning reading. Language work should include ample experience in listening with full comprehension (32, pp. 61–62).[11]

LEARNING TO LISTEN

We would like to emphasize the last point in the above statement taken from Hildreth. She suggests that there is a genuine need for the development of aural comprehension or listening. She implies that this will have an important effect on the development of competency in reading. It surely has an effect on pupil learning and achievement (72). The listener, not the speaker, is the prime director of the learning process.

Some writers use the term auding to refer to the "gross process of listening to, recognizing, and interpreting spoken symbols." (35) Auding thus includes hearing, which we discussed in Chapter 3, listening, and cognizing or comprehension of these sequences.

Communication among humans is usually through spoken symbols. However, communication may involve expression as through speaking and writing[12] or reception and comprehension as through listening or reading. (5) Listening is the first language art that the child develops, and so the remainder of this chapter will be devoted to its development. Chapter 6 will take up the development of proficiency in speech.

Listening, if it is to be learned at all, must be taught early in life. Carhart (16, p. 279) points out that

> *The capacity for mastering new sound discriminations diminishes with age.* It is common knowledge that a child will learn to speak fluently the language he hears, regardless of his race or nationality. By contrast, when an adult learns a new language, he finds that he has what native speakers call a "foreign accent." The fault is partly that he has fixed his habits of speech, and partly that he has fixed his habits of listening. The latter interests us here. What happens is that he does not notice subtle differences in the phonetic elements and cadences of the two languages. He "hears" the elements in the new language as though they were identical with those of his native tongue. When he talks, he puts the old patterns in the new language.

[11] Gertrude Hildreth, *Teaching Reading* (New York: Holt, Rinehart and Winston, Inc., 1958). Reprinted by permission.

[12] Written words do not have a direct connection with the *object* or *event*. They are only symbols of speech. They are symbols of symbols, much as a check is a symbol of money, which itself is merely a symbol of purchasing power (46, p. 24). Spoken words are primary symbols; written words are secondary symbols.

Unless he is taught to notice the subtle differences, he may go through life without even realizing that they exist.[13]

Unfortunately too many children are hearing but are not listening. They are apprehending and perhaps even taking notice of sound without understanding or interpreting that sound.

Ross (52) found that good listeners rated higher than poor listeners on intelligence, reading, socioeconomic status, and achievement, but not on a hearing test. Obviously listening is more than hearing. Two listeners, even with the same hearing acuity, often receive widely different messages from the same sound.

It may also well be that children from lower socioeconomic homes are at a distinct disadvantage in learning to read because they have spoken and heard language patterns that interfere with the comprehension of both oral and written materials (21). In support of this is the study by Clark and Richards (14). They found a significant deficiency in auditory discrimination in economically disadvantaged preschool children.

Listening is as much a thinking activity as is reading. Only by associating experiences with symbols can the pupil arrive at meaning. Listening occurs only when the pupil organizes and remembers what is heard. The major goal of all communication, including listening, is understanding or comprehension, and this is a central process involving thinking.

Pupils frequently complain of not being able to pay attention and to concentrate. The fact is that some pupils bring much more potential to the listening situation than others but leave with much less learning. They have a greater listening wattage, but may not be in focus with the speaker. They did not come prepared to listen. They are concentrating, but perhaps they are not concentrating on the task at hand. Listening ability also may be limited by lack of listening vocabulary, by misinterpretation of the speaker's words, or by inability to translate the speaker's words into the proper experiential content.

Although listening is the first language art, it has been the most neglected of the language arts. Children come to school "to learn to read and to write," but rarely do they express an interest in learning to speak or listen (15). For some strange reason it has been assumed that each child develops into a proficient listener without the benefit of formal instruction. If he can hear, it is assumed that he can and will listen. Thus teachers still may encourage the pupil "to listen" without helping him to improve his specific listening skills.

[13] Hallowell Davis and S. Richard Silverman (eds.), *Hearing and Deafness: A Guide for Laymen* (New York: Holt, Rinehart and Winston, Inc., 1947, 1960). Reprinted by permission.

It is also commonly assumed that children profit equally from listening (52). Teachers who wouldn't dream of asking all children in a class to read the same books often ignore the differences in listening ability. We test for differences in reading potential and achievement, but few elementary schools use similar measures of listening proficiency.

In the past, listening played a much greater role in the learning process than did reading. For ages communication was by word of mouth. The cultural heritage was passed from generation to generation in poem, story, and song. However, with the advent of printing, the emphasis passed to reading of the printed material. As significant was the trend from oral reading to silent reading.

Today, with radio, television, and improved means of transportation, oral communication (and hence listening) is receiving much greater emphasis. And, thus it should be. Listening allows the pupil to hear speeches and group discussions, to enjoy the theater and music, to enjoy assembly and club programs, to get the most out of radio and television programs, and to be successful on the job. Listening is beneficial in every school setting including the gymnasium, the shop, the science classroom, and music room.

In evaluating their programs, schools have found that the child is required to listen for a substantial amount of time in the average school day. For example, teachers give many of their classroom directions orally. They make oral assignments. They describe procedures orally. They constantly use verbal means for motivating children.

There are other reasons for improving the listening skills of children. Skill in listening is closely related to proficiency in many academic areas. Some children are better listeners than readers. For children in the lower grades, for children who are poor readers, and perhaps for boys generally (42), listening is the most important means for achievement.

Reading is not learning. It is only one of the media for learning, and for some children it is an inferior medium. In fact, up to about the fifth grade (mental age of ten) children generally learn more and remember better through listening than through reading. Many (42) found that sixth-grade pupils comprehended more by reading than by listening. Generally, the lower the reading ability and the lower the scholastic aptitude, the greater is the advantage of listening over reading. Since, however, reading allows the pupil to go back and reread, reading becomes more effective as the difficulty of the material increases.

Listening ability also is basic to the learning of reading. Coefficients of correlation between scores on listening and reading tests vary from .27 to .80 (68,6,24,54). Does this mean that improvement in listening will make for improvement in reading? Hollingsworth (34) reviewed the literature on this point and concluded that listening does indeed have a positive effect on reading achievement. Listening and reading have basic similarities. Both involve the reception of ideas from others. Reading demands sight and comprehension; listening calls for hearing and comprehension.

1. Listening provides the vocabulary and the sentence structure that serve as a foundation for reading. Reading success depends upon the child's aural-oral experience with words. In a very real sense the child reads with his ears, mentally pronouncing the words to himself.

2. Listening and reading utilize similar verbal factors, but they also encompass factors unique to each skill (54).

3. Without the ability to hear and interpret sounds, the child cannot learn phonics.

4. Ability to listen to and provide an ending for a story is a good indicator of readiness for reading.

5. Words most easily read are those that have been heard and spoken.

6. Listening ability (if scores on a listening comprehension test are higher than the scores on a reading comprehension test) is an indicator of the pupil's potential ceiling in reading ability.

The child learns language by ear. The vocabulary and skills in language structure that he brings to school were learned first through listening. In fact, if it were not for these learnings the child would not, or at least only rarely, learn to read (48, pp. 44–45). The teacher of reading should take advantage of these previous learnings. He should help the child to associate the visual symbols with the sounds previously learned. If the child has not learned to listen, he must be taught.

Listening Proficiency

There are varying degrees of ability in listening and these abilities develop sequentially (69). Perhaps the first level in listening development is auditory acuity. Unless the ear can react to sound waves and transmit them along the nervous system, all other listening skills are doomed. Listening, however, goes beyond the mere recognition of sounds. Adequate hearing is only the first step in listening. The second level is aural assimilation and interpretation (7,11) of the nerve stimuli. The listener must understand what has been said. A third level of listening proficiency is retention. The good listener can retain the various sounds. On the basis of his memory traces for sounds he can alter his speech production to fit the pattern of sounds which he has held in mind.

Ross (52) lists the basic skills of listening as the following:

1. Learning to recognize differences in phonemes.
2. Learning to recognize morphemes.
3. Learning to recognize the role of word arrangement in spoken language.
4. Learning to interpret sentences modified by intonation.
5. Learning to recognize the role that pitch plays in speech.

Let us examine some of the skills required for interpretative listening. The listener must:

1. Identify the speaker's purpose.
2. Develop empathy with the speaker.
3. Use context clues to understand.
4. Anticipate what is being said.
5. Listen for the main ideas.
6. Listen for the details.
7. Follow oral directions.
8. Remember a sequence of details.
9. Draw inferences and conclusions.
10. Mentally summarize what has been said.
11. Listen to and interpret idiomatic speech.
12. Weigh and evaluate the speaker's evidence.
13. Listen between the lines.
14. Distinguish fact from fiction.
15. Distinguish essential and relevant material from unessential and irrelevant material.
16. Identify transitional elements.
17. Listen in terms of past experience.
18. Listen for relationships.
19. Listen to connotative and denotative speech.
20. Analyze critically what is being said.
21. Listen appreciatively, creatively, and critically.

Children need training in these skills, and studies (24) indicate that they can be developed. Some children do not possess even a minimal degree of proficiency in listening. Some cannot detect sounds, and some cannot give meaning to what they have heard because they cannot relate it to their past experiences. Some cannot use the speaker's gestures, pitch, stress, and intonation as comprehension clues. Some cannot perceive the relationships that exist between the facts and ideas that were spoken. Some cannot discover the implications of what was said and some cannot follow directions or sequences in a story.

We do not mean to imply that every pupil in the first grade must possess all these skills or that even one child possesses all of them. However, for the sake of completeness we have listed even the more advanced skills, and later in discussing the development of listening skills we will suggest techniques applicable at various stages during the elementary school years. Since reading readiness is a concept applicable at all stages of development, and since teachers at all levels must concern themselves with the pupil's readiness for various reading tasks, teachers need to know whether the child's listening proficiency is keeping pace. If he doesn't listen well, he may not be able to read well. If his listening skills are more developed than his reading skills, it is an indication that he can become a better reader.

Children are not equally ready for listening. In fact, not all of them need the same degree of listening proficiency, and not all of them will reach the same levels of listening proficiency. The teacher must begin with lower levels of listening skill and gradually lead the pupil to higher levels.

Developing the Listening Skill

The listening skill must be consciously fostered in the school. The alert teacher plays a major role here. He provides an adequate physical environment. He sees to it that children have visual as well as auditory contact with one another. He adjusts listening time to fit the child, since young children have short attention and memory spans. He discovers children with hearing defects and adjusts learning tasks to fit their needs.

The teacher promotes the listening habit mostly by being a good listener himself and by providing the proper psychological climate for listening. He has high regard for what the child says. He helps the child to select content suitable to the experiences and interests of the group. He helps to formulate a purpose for listening. He encourages the child to listen for new words and ideas and personally provides the opportunities for listening. He introduces new words, reads good literature, and points out sound differences and similarities in words.

Listening can be taught through story telling, conversation, dramatization, singing of songs, reading of poems, and reading or speaking of rhymes. Children should be encouraged to engage in "show and tell" exercises, in debates, quiz shows, and discussions. They ought to discuss topics informally, ask questions, make plans, give reports, follow directions, criticize, and evaluate what others have said. Each of these activities creates multiple opportunities for listening by other pupils. The phonograph, radio, television, tape recorder, piano, telephone, and band instruments are particularly useful in developing the listening skill.

The last ten years have witnessed the development of listening centers in classrooms all over the country. Such centers include an autoinstructional device consisting of a tape recorder or record player, a number of earphones, and response sheets which are filled in by the pupil. Horrworth (35) notes that it has been her experience that the use of the listening center equipment does little to improve empathic listening, reactive listening, projective listening, or interpretive listening; these are best developed in face-to-face situations.

Recent literature (63) is replete with techniques for teaching the listening skill. We will enumerate only some of these, and in each instance will try to point out the implication that the exercise will have in the teaching of reading.

1. With eyes closed the child learns to make gross discriminations, for example, between a tap of a ruler, a knock on the door, a clap of the hands, or a footstep. This is the first step in developing the child's auditory discrimination skill and is necessary for proficiency in phonics.

2. The teacher demonstrates how to make a simple toy. He gives the directions orally and then asks the pupils to construct a similar toy. He asks some child to repeat the directions and checks the activity of each child to see that the desired directions are followed. This activity teaches the ability to follow a thought sequence, a skill needed for successful reading comprehension.

3. When teaching the discrimination between right and left, the teacher gives the directions orally, such as: "Raise your left hand"; "Put your right foot forward." This exercise, besides developing comprehension, also prepares the pupil for the left-to-right activity in reading by teaching the discrimination between right and left.

4. The pupils listen for the main idea of a paragraph, story, poem, or talk (10). This prepares them for reading for main ideas.

5. The teacher reads a poem or short story to the class and asks the pupils to submit a title for the poem or story (45, p. 215). This is another exercise in reading for main ideas.

6. The teacher administers tests orally (45, p. 213). This exercise teaches following of directions, comprehension, and critical listening. Critical listening will prepare the pupil for critical reading later.

7. The teacher starts a whispered message around the room from child to child and the last child repeats it aloud (45, p. 214). In this activity the emphasis is on accuracy in relaying the

message from one to another. This exercise perhaps best emphasizes the need for accuracy in communication and interpretation.

8. Pupils prepare short talks on a favorite topic. Other pupils in the class should be ready to state the organization of the talk. This exercise teaches the skill of listening to and reading for the organization.

9. The teacher reads a short paragraph containing a sentence or two that are not in harmony with the context. He may read materials that omit evidence, that are based on a false premise, or that are not logically organized. The pupil may be asked to discriminate between fact and fiction. He should learn to detect propaganda in advertising, in newspaper accounts, and in essays, and he should learn to listen for implied meanings. Later it is hoped he will apply these critical skills in reading.

10. Pupils listen to two different broadcasts or recording on the same news content, one giving a factual report, and the other giving an analysis. Pupils should analyze the two reports, studying the vocabulary used and looking for indications of distortion (45, p. 218). This exercise again teaches critical listening, and the techniques learned should be useful in critical reading.

11. The teacher requires pupils to respond to the first announcement of directions (45, pp. 214–215). If the pupil asks the teacher to repeat, it may be profitable to ask the pupil to do this. Many times the pupil has developed a habit of "not listening" the first time. Students frequently develop the habit of not reading carefully the first time. This exercise may help to develop proper habits in this area.

12. The teacher uses the tape recorder to record the child's speech and then gives the child an opportunity to hear himself. The teacher should guide him in "what to listen for." Later, before beginning reading, the pupil should identify his purposes for reading.

13. The pupil learns to listen for "language signals" such as: "first," "there are several ways," "furthermore," "several suggestions are," or "on the other hand" (37). In reading, he needs to look for similar language signals.

These exercises teach listening and develop many of the skills previously listed. In general they prepare the pupil for the recognition and comprehension tasks that he will meet in reading.

PROFICIENCY IN SPEECH AND READING READINESS

Thus far this chapter has concerned itself with three aspects: (1) the nature of human communication or language; (2) the importance of language in thought; and (3) the significance of listening proficiency and how it might be developed. In the section that follows we will review the early speech development of the child and outline its importance for reading readiness and achievement.

The child begins to vocalize almost immediately after birth. Generally, these vocalizations are global reactions, involving the entire bodily mechanism. There is no awareness or purpose in these responses. They arise as a column of air is expelled from the lungs. The process is reflexive in nature, and the air passes between vocal folds tense enough to produce sound. The child's first use of the physical apparatus necessary for speech occurs at birth when he takes in breath and emits the birth cry.

At this stage there are no speech organs as such. The child's grunts, gurgles, coos, snorts, cries, and hiccoughs are primarily associated with the nonlinguistic function of the organs. The child frequently is merely breathing, swallowing, or hiccoughing. He has not really begun to use the organs for speech. By exercising the physiological functions, he is conditioning the muscles for their nonspeech functions.

The child soon becomes aware of the sounds that he is making. He enjoys vocal play and in his cooing and gurgling produces a greater number and variety of sounds than are found in any given language.[14] Some children may be able to produce a *wh, ch,* or *l* sound at this time, but unfortunately are unable to use it correctly in words for another two or three years.

The third stage occurs at about nine or ten months of age and is called lalling. The laller produces a slurred kind of half intelligible speech because he has not learned to move the tongue independently of the jaw. At this time the child repeats *heard* sounds or sound combinations (4, p. 20). Referred to as echolalia, the child actually echos the sounds that he or others produce. A circulatory process is now set up. The child produces a sound (oral) and hears it (aural). The first oral-aural association is being developed. At this stage, through imitation, the child may learn new groupings of sounds, but he doesn't learn new sounds (59, p. 55). He repeats sounds which he already uses spontaneously.

Between twelve and eighteen months the child produces his first

[14] Speech sounds of any kind are called phones; speech sounds that are used in the language are called phonemes. Consequently, all phonemes are phones, but not all phones are phonemes.

words. These frequently are quite redundant (ma-ma, da-da, bye-bye, ba-ba) and represent a complete thought unit. Thus, "ba-ba" may mean "Give me the bottle." However, the speech is undifferentiated. "Da-da" may mean anyone that looks like daddy. The word cannot be differentiated because the child's perceptions of what a daddy is are not differentiated. With experience his perceptions become more discriminative and so does his usage of words.

Readiness programs have not paid sufficient emphasis to the difficulties that the child has in coping with language as a means of transmitting a message to another (58). The initial language experiences of children are not necessarily communicative. The child uses language to understand his environment and to express or "think aloud" his experiences. In monologue he orders the universe. His language is not the orderly and sequential language that he meets in the printed text.

The child next learns that the name of an object stands for a class of things. He identifies similar objects and groups them under one word. The child is not actually abstracting. He identifies similarities in objects, but is not yet capable of seeing their differences. Children during this period feel that they know the whole of reality. They do not discriminate between the object and the word that stands for the object. To them, the word is both perception and reality.

Finally, the child learns to develop concepts and uses words to communicate his concepts. The word now is a symbol in its true sense.

Experience has shown that the child must have reached a certain amount of oral language maturity before beginning reading. The reading teacher is interested in the "speech age" of the child. He must know how many phonemes the child uses consistently and how frequently the pupil substitutes because of an inability to use a certain sound. Consonant sounds generally develop in a definite order. Hildreth (32, p. 52) suggests that by the age of seven the average child articulates correctly the consonants and consonant blends 90 per cent of the time.

Poole (47) studied 140 pre-school children over a period of three years and found that the rate of development in articulation is similar among boys and girls between the ages of two and one-half and five and one-half. After this girls develop more rapidly and attain the same degree of proficiency by six and one-half that boys attain only at seven and one-half. Poole also found that there is a regular progression in articulation development. Table 5-1 summarizes her findings and indicates at what age certain sounds had been mastered by the 140 children in her group. Probably the reason that children learn to make the *b, p, m, w, d, t, n, g, k, ng,* and *y* sounds so early is that feeding exercises the tongue muscles required to make these sounds.

The *z* and *s* sounds are listed twice because after the age of five when dentition causes a spacing between the teeth they become distorted

TABLE 5-1   Ages When Children Normally Have Mastered the
Consonant Sounds (41; 9)

Ages	Consonants
3.5	b, p, m, w, h
4.5	d, t, n, g, k, ng, y
5.5	f, v, z, s
6.5	sh, zh, l, th,*
8.0	z, s, r, wh,
	ch, j

* *Th* as in thin or then.

in a lisp. This lisp disappears when normal dentition is reestablished.

Although serious deviation from normal speech development is not too frequent among first graders, Davis (17) indicates that quite commonly children have difficulty with *zh, sh, l, th, z, s, r,* and *wh.* Van Riper and Butler (61, p. 64) point out that most articulatory errors made by children involve *r, s, l, k, sh, th, ch,* and *f* and that the average child does not attain complete mastery of *s, l, r,* and *th* or their blends until the age of eight years (62). For example, it is not uncommon to hear a first or second grader speak in this manner:

> This is the boat that my gwandfathe' sent me fo' my bufday. . . .
> The postman bwought it just befo' we went to the lake on Satu'day.
> It will weally sail! One time when I wasn't watching it, it sailed wight
> unde' the wope to the deep pa't of the lake and my fathe' had to
> swim out fast and get it. It wides waves too. The moto' boats on the
> lake made some waves, but my boat didn't tu'n ova (33, p. 24).[15]

The sounding errors in the above are chiefly: *r, th,* and *l.* Many children show even more serious deficiencies in language structure. They cannot formulate sentences or turn ideas into words.

Undoubtedly many pupils who are deficient in reading actually are deficient in general language ability (9). Warfel (65) suggests that the initial step in reading instruction should relate what is in the ear and on the tongue to what is to be put into the eye. He (66) believes that good reading initially must be accompanied by vocal sounds. He adds that only after much experience is the child able to change marks into meaning without putting them first in the ear and on the tongue. Davis

[15] Mary Peebles Hinman, "The Teacher and the Specialist," *NEA Journal,* 49 (November 1960) 24–25. Reprinted by permission.

(17) adds that the earliest reading materials should contain a minimum of late-developing sounds and a minimum of words in which a single spelling combination indicates a number of different sounds. Van Riper (62) notes that the speech pathologist shudders when he scans primers, because they are filled with late maturing sounds. " 'Look' and 'see' and 'say' and 'run, Sally, run' probably fix and perpetuate consonant errors which otherwise would be outgrown."

Harris (30, p. 38) notes that the major aspects of language that are significant for reading readiness are: the child's vocabulary, mastery of sentence structure, and clarity of pronunciation. These skills are learned through listening and speaking.

Artley (2, pp. 325–326) has outlined the language areas in which the child needs special preparation before beginning to read. He suggests that the readiness teaching should include the following:

1. Developing awareness of oral words as language units. For example, "Gimmethe" is three separate words.
2. Enriching oral vocabulary.
3. Strengthening meaning associations.
4. Formulating sentences.
5. Organizing ideas into language units.
6. Using narrative expressions.
7. Improving articulation.
8. Developing sensitivity to inflectional variants.
9. Developing awareness of sentence structure.[16]

Not all children have equal proficiency in these areas. The slow learner generally has a difficult time interpreting speech and expressing himself. Children from lower socioeconomic levels and from home environments in which English is perhaps secondary to another language do not develop the vocabulary and the accuracy in pronunciation and sentence construction that is found among children with more favorable surroundings.

Oral language readiness basically means the following: the ability to speak without abnormal hesitation; to articulate and enunciate clearly; to pronounce words correctly; to associate words with experiences; to talk in simple sentences; to tell a simple story; and to think and speak sequentially. Above everything else, in learning to read, the child must perceive the relationships between the spoken and the written language. He must learn that what can be said also can be written (57).

[16] A. Sterl Artley, "Oral Language Growth and Reading Ability," *Elementary School Journal*, 53 (February 1953) 321–328, copyright 1953 by The University of Chicago Press. Reprinted by permission.

SUMMARY

This chapter has been concerned chiefly with the influence that listening and speaking proficiency have on readiness for and achievement in reading. In addition, some time was devoted to the discussion of listening and to the proposal of techniques for developing the listening skill.

In general, the chapter suggests that reading success depends upon the child's aural-oral experience with words (73). Training in listening develops auditory discrimination which in turn serves as a basis for phonetic analysis in reading. Listening and speaking provide the vocabulary and the sentence patterns for reading. The instruction in grammar, usage, and composition, occurring either directly or indirectly in learning to listen and to speak, is also beneficial in learning to read. Finally, words and sentences most easily read are those that have been heard and spoken. *The language is the same in all the language arts: only the media for communication are different* (50, p. 15).

QUESTIONS FOR DISCUSSION

1. Why must the teacher understand the communication process?
2. What is the meaning of (a) communication, (b) language, (c) sign, (d) symbol?
3. Why is communication rarely perfect?
4. Illustrate how the experience of Helen Keller at the well demonstrates that words make concepts usable.
5. Criticize Kant's statement: "To think is to speak to oneself."
6. Discuss some of the skills that are required for interpretative listening.
7. Identify five criteria of an effective listener.
8. List some bad listening habits and illustrate how they might be overcome.
9. What are the implications of the study by Poole, especially of the statement that the earliest reading materials should contain a minimum of late-developing sounds and a minimum of words in which a single spelling combination indicates a number of different sounds?
10. What language skills are significant for reading readiness? Include in your answer a discussion of recommendations by Warfel, Harris, and Artley.
11. Criticize Watson's statement that thought is the "subvocal use of language."
12. What are the implications for the teaching of reading in the studies that suggest that thought is accompanied by a certain amount of vocal behavior?

13. Discuss:
    a. The younger the child, the more vocal expression is tied to the child's thinking.
    b. Listening tends to result in better delayed recall than does reading.
    c. When listening ability is low, reading ability tends to be low.
    d. When listening ability is high, it is impossible to predict reading ability.
    e. When reading ability is low, it is impossible to predict the level of listening ability.
    f. When reading ability is high, listening ability may be high or low.
    g. Listening generally is more effective than reading as a learning device with children who suffer from deficiencies in near-point vision or who are below the chronological age of eight.

Developing
Language Readiness

chapter 6

Chapter 5 established the importance of oral language for beginning reading, and it identified the specific language or speech skills that the child needs before he can successfully undertake the reading task. In this chapter we are concerned with the nature and structure of the English language and with the actual development of language skills, especially those required for accurate reproduction of the sounds of the language.

The chapter may contain little that the average classroom teacher associates with the developmental reading program. This cannot and should not mean that it is unimportant. The teacher must know the sound system and the basic principles of language structure. Furthermore, in the self-contained classroom the teacher is daily a diagnostician and correctionist of the child's language difficulties. We cannot refer all children to the specialist, and on the other hand, we cannot simply ignore a child's defect. There is only one alternative. The teacher must be prepared to detect and correct language defects, especially those that have a bearing on the pupil's achievement in the other language arts areas.

The reading teacher is as interested in the development of good speech as is the speech correctionist. He is a teacher of language and communication skills. He knows that development in reading closely parallels development in speech. He realizes that if the child has not acquired the needed language facility before entering school, the child must be given the opportunity to do so in school.

THE PHONOLOGY OF LANGUAGE

Speech improvement is

> . . . more than tongue exercises, memorization, vocal phonics, artic-
> ulation drills, and activities. It is more than instruction in the im-
> provement of voice quality, pitch, and intensity. It is more than
> training in the ebb and flow of speech rhythms. Indeed, it is more
> than the sum total of all these parts. Speech improvement should
> go far beyond the mechanics of speech drills into the area of meaning-
> ful language. One of the most important aims might well be to help
> the children to verbalize their thoughts—to be able to "think on
> their feet" efficiently and adequately (38, pp. 2–3).[1]

Nevertheless, mechanics are important. Success frequently is dependent upon a command of the particulars of the language. A major concern
is that children learn to *articulate* all the vowels and the consonants
without distortion, omission, substitution, addition, or transposition.
Children must be taught to *enunciate* all syllables clearly. They must be
taught to *pronounce* accurately. They must give the total visual form its
proper sound and must accent the appropriate syllable or syllables. *Children generally must learn the alphabet of sound before they can be
taught the alphabet of letters.*

A student of language, and hence the teacher of reading, must familiarize himself with phonemics or the discrimination and production
of sound. He must have an elementary knowledge of the physiology of
speech (26). He must know how to analyze words for their specific sounds.
To teach language without this information is target practice in the dark.

Isolation of sounds is necessary for two reasons: (*1*) it frequently is
impossible to teach a sound without first isolating it, and (*2*) the teacher
cannot detect errors if he cannot isolate the specific sounds. Good speech
correction today proceeds on the principle that the isolation of the specific sounds in words is both desirable and necessary for retraining of
speech production.

Basically two kinds of sound are produced by the human speech
mechanism. Phones are sounds that have not become a part of the language. Young children always produce a far greater number of sounds
than they later use in the production of speech. Phonemes are sounds that

---

[1] Charles Van Riper and Katharine Butler, *Speech in the Elementary Classroom*
(New York: Harper & Row, Publishers, Inc., 1955). Reprinted by permission.

are a part of the language. The English language uses about forty significant phonemes or combinations thereof.

The phoneme has one prime purpose in language. It individualizes human utterances. The phoneme is the smallest unit of language which can differentiate one utterance from another (9, p. 9). For example, the sentences "Tom, will you wash these carrots?" and "Tom, will you wash those carrots?" are completely alike except for one phoneme. A single letter representing a simple sound changes completely the meaning of the following sentences "A stitch in time saves none" or "There's no business like shoe business." "The phonological system of language is therefore not so much a 'set of sounds' as it is a *network of differences between sounds* (11, p. 24)." [2] The child must learn these differences in speech and later their counterparts in writing. The good reader is one who does know these differences.

The Speech Mechanism[3]

Speech consists of the sound waves that are emitted by the human vocal mechanism. These sound waves strike the ear of another and elicit meaning from the recipient. Speech is a circular process. It is completed only when the sound waves (stimulus) elicit a response in a listener, that is, when they stir up meanings in another.

In most communication, and hence language, there is the *intention* to communicate something, the *intention* is then translated or *encoded* into symbols or words, and the necessary sounds are emitted. This latter process is termed *phonation*. The receiver of the communication in turn must hear the sounds (audition), must translate them (decoding), and must comprehend them (2, pp. 2–4).

Here we are not particularly concerned with how the speaker converts his idea, thought, or concept into sound waves nor how the recipient interprets them. We are interested in understanding the physiological process of speech.

To produce speech the lungs, windpipe, glottis (adam's apple), mouth, teeth, lips, and even the nose may be used. The lungs set the air into motion. The glottis contains the vocal cords. And the mouth contains the soft and hard palate and the tongue (29, pp. 73–74). The lips are used in producing *b, f, j, m, ch, p, sh, zh, v, w, wh;* the teeth are used in producing *f, s, v, th, z;* the tongue is used in producing *d, g, k, l, n, ng, r, t, y, ch, j, sh, th, zh;* the hard palate is used in producing *ch, d, l, j, n, t;* and the soft palate is used in producing *g, k, m, n, ng.*

---

[2] Reprinted with permission of the Macmillan Company from *A Course in Modern Linguistics* by Charles F. Hockett. Copyright 1958 by the Macmillan Company.

[3] For a full description see Hockett (14, pp. 63–68).

The Vowels

Children quite early learn to articulate the short and long vowels. The production of the vowels begins with a muscular contraction of the lungs which forces a steady unobstructed air stream through the trachea, larynx, and pharynx to the outside. Vowels are thus called unobstructed sounds. Webster's Dictionary describes a vowel as "a speech sound in the articulation of which the oral part of the breath channel is not blocked and is not narrowed enough to cause audible friction." Sometimes the air passes through the oral cavities to the outside; sometimes it passes through the nasal cavities.

The larynx contains the vocal cords. In normal respiration the cords are widely separated at the back side. This produces unvoiced sounds. When the cords are almost closed, forcing the air through the narrow opening sets the cords into vibration and produces a voiced sound. Vowels are voiced sounds.

The size and shape of the mouth and the position of the lips and tongue determine what vowel will be produced. Three tongue parts (front, middle, and back), seven tongue heights, and two lip positions are identifiable. For example, the sounds *i* (bit), *e* (bet), *e* (the), *a* (bat), *a* (bar), *ea* (beat), *ai* (bait), *ay* (bay), *y* (by), *i* (bite) are produced by spreading or flattening the lips. The sounds *oo* (book), *a* (ball), *oo* (boot), and *oa* (boat) are produced by rounding the lips. The *oy* (boy) or *oi* (loin) sound begins with rounded lips, but ends with flattened lips. The *ou* (thou) sound is just the reverse (11, p. 77). In Table 6-1 we have listed the vowels of the English language and the possible spellings of each.

The Consonants

Consonants are produced by obstructing the air stream much as a stricture in a hose obstructs the passage of water. Whenever the constriction in the breath channel is complete and is followed by a sudden release of the air, as in *p, b, t, d, k,* and *g,* the consonant is called a plosive consonant. The soft palate is raised so the air does not pass through the nose.

Three of these consonants, *p, t,* and *k,* are unvoiced sounds; *b, d,* and *g,* since their production requires the vibration of the vocal cords, are voiced sounds. When the production of the sound involves the use of the lips, as in *p* and *b,* the sounds are labials. When sound production involves the use of the teeth or gum ridges, as in *t* and *d,* the sounds are dental. When the production of the sound involves the use of the soft palate, as in *k* and *g,* the sounds are called gutturals (velars).

TABLE 6-1   Common Vowel Sounds and Variant Spellings*

Symbol	Key Word+	Variant Spellings
a	hat	plaid, ask, chaff.
ā	late	pain, day, break, veil, obey, gauge, eh, ay, chaotic, melee.
ä	far	hearth, sergeant, memoir.
e (ə)	care	there, bear, chair, prayer, heir, e'er.
e	pet	heifer, leopard, friend, Aetna, feather, bury, any, said, says, Thames.
ē	be	feet, beam, deceive, people, key, Caesar, machine, police, field, quay, Phoebe, mete, create, fiasco.
(ə)r	ever	liar, elixir, actor, augur, pressure, glamour, zephyr.
i	bit	sieve, pretty, been, women, busy, build, hymnal, money, cottage, guinea, coffee, carriage, lyric.
ə	(unstressed short i)	separate, senate, always, mischief, circuit, foreign, forfeit, surface, mountain.
ī	ice	vie, rye, height, eye, aisle, aye, sky, buy, choir.
ä	not (short o sound)	was, hough.
ȯ	off	broth, cost, across, cough, loft.
	all	talk, haul, awe, Utah, Arkansas, law.
ȯ(ə) or ō(ə)	orb	orb, board, sword, court, borne, coarse, before, door, swarm, fought, memoir.
ō	old	oh, roam, foe, shoulder, grow, owe, sew, yeoman, beau, hautboy, brooch, soul, obey.
ə	sun (short u sound)	come, nation, blood, double, does, twopence.
ə	canoe	banana, collect.
ə	fern	bird, urn, work, hurt, heard, journal, myrrh.
u̇	pull	wolf, Worcester, should, wood, foot, endure.
ü	use	unite, ewe, dew, beauty, feud, queue, lieu, cue, suit, yule.
	rude	brew, do, two, who, tomb, canoe, maneuver, blue, food, group, fruit, proof.
au̇	out	cow.
ȯi	soil	boil, oyster.

* Authorities disagree on the articulation of the vowels and consequently also on the number of different vowels. Vowel symbols used by permission. From Webster's Seventh New Collegiate Dictionary © 1969 by G. & C. Merriam Company, Publishers of the Merriam-Webster Dictionaries.

D is produced by pressing the tip of the tongue against the upper teeth ridge and by blowing down the tongue while starting the voice at the same time. The production of *d* is thus accompanied by a vocal-band vibration. The sound of *t* begins like *d*, but the blowing is so rapid that the breath escapes with an explosive result.

The *t* sound is an unvoiced dental plosive. It is made by obstructing the air stream and is followed by a sudden release of air. The soft palate is raised so the air does not pass through the nose. There is no vibration of the vocal cords in making the *t* sound, and it therefore is called an unvoiced sound. It is called a dental because in making the sound the tongue touches the upper gum ridge and then is quickly released, freeing a puff of air.

B is produced by closing the lips tightly and holding the teeth slightly apart. The lips are blown apart with a voiced breath. The *p* is made like the *b,* but there is no voicing.

G is produced with the lips and teeth slightly separated. The back of the tongue is raised against the back roof of the mouth. The tip of the tongue is kept behind the lower front teeth and the tongue is blown down suddenly with a voiced breath. *K* is made like *g* except that the slight explosion is voiceless.

The fricative or spirant consonants, *f, v, th,*[4] *s, z, sh, zh, j,* and *ch* are formed by partially closing the air passage. These sounds can be prolonged indefinitely and usually are accompanied by friction. To produce the labiodental fricatives, the unvoiced *f* and the voiced *v,* the upper teeth are in contact with the lower lip. Breath is forced out as the teeth and lip touch. When the sound is voiced, it is a *v*; when it is unvoiced, it is an *f.*

The production of both the voiced and unvoiced dental fricative *th* requires contact between the tip of the tongue and the back of the upper front teeth. The teeth and lips are slightly apart.

To produce the unvoiced *s* the air stream is allowed to pass through a narrow opening between the tip of the tongue and the gums. The front teeth are closed, and the entire tongue is raised and grooved along the midline. The tip of the tongue is placed about a quarter of an inch behind the upper teeth. The soft palate is raised. The *s* sounds like air going out of a tire. The voiced *z* requires a slightly larger opening and the teeth are separated.

The unvoiced *sh,* as in ship, is produced much like the *s,* but the air stream is forced over a broader surface than for the *s.* The tongue is raised and drawn back, the lips are rounded, and the soft palate is raised. The *zh* is the same sound as the *sh* except that it is voiced.

The unvoiced *ch* is produced by making the *t* sound and quickly exploding it into a *sh* sound. The tip of the tongue touches the upper gum ridge and then is quickly released, freeing a puff of air and producing a *t* sound. This then is quickly changed to the *sh* sound. The

---

[4] *Th* as in then (voiced) and in thin (unvoiced). The unvoiced *th* occurs, for example, in birth, booth, breath, broth, cloth, both, death, depth, doth, earth, faith, fourth, length, mouth, north, and path. The voiced *th* occurs in than, that, their, these, they, therefore, those, thus, bathe, breathe, clothe, scathe, smooth, sooth, with, although, brother, either, father, other, and gather.

j sound is voiced and made by raising the front part of the tongue toward the teeth ridge and hard palate. The sounds *ch* and *j* (which is produced like *ch*) sometimes are called plosives. More correctly, they are affricates in that they begin as plosives and end as fricatives.

The nasals or linguals, *m*, *n*, and *ng*, are formed by completely closing the mouth and allowing the air to escape through the nasal cavities. The soft palate is lowered and each sound is voiced. Closed lips prevent the air from passing through the mouth in the production of *m*. The teeth are slightly apart and a humming sound is sent through the nose. For *n* the tip of the tongue is pressed against the gums. The tongue is not dropped and the mouth is not closed until the sound has been made. For *ng*, the tongue is raised against the soft palate. The tongue is kept in this position until a voiced sound is sent through the nose.

The semivowels or glides, *y*, *hw*, *w*, *l*,[5] *r*,[5] and *h*, are produced by a gliding movement of the tongue or lips from one place to another. They are produced when the vocal organs are getting ready to produce another sound. The passage from the vocal cords to the outside is partially blocked. The voiced *r* before a vowel as in rabbit or train is produced by raising the tip of the tongue toward the gum ridge without actual contact. The teeth are slightly separated and a curl is formed down the middle of the tongue.

The voiced *l* is produced by elevating the tip of the tongue toward the upper gum ridge. Contact is made, and the air passes over the sides of the tongue. The soft palate is raised for making both sounds. Some describe the *l* sound as the "peanut butter sound." As the sound is made, it feels as though one were wiping peanut butter from the roof of the mouth.

The *hw* is produced like a *w* without vocal cord vibration. It is an unvoiced fricative. To produce the voiced *w* the lips are rounded and an opening is left for the air to emerge from the mouth. The tip of the tongue is raised back of the lower teeth. In teaching the sound, the teacher might ask the child to blow out a lighted candle while saying "while" or "what." The *w* is like a vowel in that it is pronounced in a vowel position and like a consonant in that it is pronounced with audible friction. *H* generally is an unvoiced sound; *y* is a voiced sound.

Like the *w*, the *y* has the position of a vowel but the friction of a consonant. The front tip of the tongue is raised nearly to the hard palate behind the upper teeth. The side of the tongue touches the side of the teeth, and the teeth and lips are slightly apart. *H* should be sounded with a vowel. When *h* occurs between vowels it may be a voiced

---

[5] *L* and *r* at the end of a word, as in water and panel, are not glides.

sound. The vowel determines the position of the tongue and lips. The air is blown outwards, and the tongue is behind the lower teeth. In Table 6-2 we have listed the various consonant sounds in the language.

TABLE 6-2   The Consonant Sounds of the Language

| Plosives | | Fricatives | | Nasals | Semivowels | |
Voiced	Unvoiced	Voiced	Unvoiced	Voiced	Voiced	Unvoiced
b	p	th	th	m	r	h
d	t	v	f	n	l	hw
g	k	z (azure)	s	ng	y	
		zh (rouge)	sh		w	
		j	ch			

LANGUAGE STRUCTURE

Language consists of phonemes, morphemes, words, and utterances. Phonemes already have been described. A morpheme is the smallest linguistic unit in our language that has meaning. It has lexical meaning if it has a meaning of its own (for example, prefixes and suffixes), and it has relational meaning if it has a grammatical meaning. For example, in the sentence, "She insists on it," the *in* in insists has lexical meaning. It has meaning wherever it occurs; the *s* at the end of the word has no meaning of itself. It has meaning only to the extent that it makes the verb a third person singular. It is said to have relational meaning. The *s* may take on a relational meaning also when it changes a noun from the singular to the plural or when it denotes the possessive case.

Words are the smallest linguistic units that have meaning and that can stand alone in a sentence. The study of how words are constructed is called morphology. An utterance is a series of words that are spoken at one time. The manner in which words are grouped into utterances is called syntax. And syntax and morphology compose the grammar of a language. Figure 6-1 illustrates the relationships existing between the various factors.

Grammar[6] has only one basic function: to make our utterances clearer. It is an aid to the expression and interpretation of meaning.

---

[6] For an outline of generative grammar, see F. Allan Briggs, "Implications of Structure in Language," *Junior College and Adult Reading Programs,* National Reading Conference, Milwaukee, 1967, 225–235.

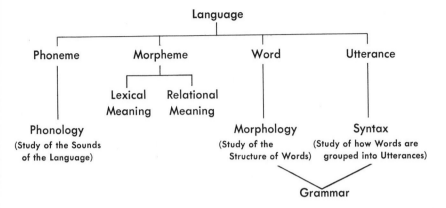

Figure 6-1. **The Components of Language**

Morphology, for example, allows us to introduce minute changes into the word to bring out a special meaning. The various uses of *s* given above are examples of this. Syntax permits us to group words to suggest certain nuances of meaning. For example, the same words might be grouped in this way to suggest various meanings: "The weak girl is playing a game of tennis," or "The girl is playing a weak game of tennis"; "The boy sat in a chair with a broken arm," or "The boy with a broken arm sat in a chair"; "The lion in the cage roared at the man," or "The lion roared at the man in the cage." The formal distinction between *runs* as a verb and *runs* as a noun (He runs home. The runs on the bank were many.) is syntactic in nature (12). The reader must first recognize the distinction in arrangement before he can perceive the distinction in meaning. An adjective can be given a noun meaning by syntax: "The *best* is not good enough for him." To read the word "lead," the reader must know whether it is a noun or a verb (30).

Punctuation in writing and pauses in speech are not so much an aid to writing and speaking as they are to reading and listening. The writer knows what the sentences mean; he does not need grammatical aids to get the meaning.

In addition to phonemes, morphemes, and words there are certain characteristics about the utterance that add to and develop meaning. The loudness of the voice changes or certain words are stressed more than others. We give a heavy, medium, light, or weak stress. The pitch is either low, normal, high, or extra high. High pitch is often associated with heavier stress. In speaking, utterances are combined by what are termed "plus junctures"; they are ended by "terminal junctures." (21) The plus junctures separate words; the terminal junctures are usually accompanied by falls or rises in pitch, and differentiate one phrase unit from another or one type of sentence from another. The declarative sentence has a slight drop in pitch at the end. Phrasing depends on the placement of the junctures.

Words do not give meaning to sentences; rather, words receive their meaning from the sentence or the verbal context of which they are a part. The pupil who has become a word reader has fallen into the error of not "reading" the phrase unit that gives meaning to the word. The word must be looked upon merely as *one* element in a series of elements that constitute a sentence. The sentence circumscribes the word, giving it the distinct meaning intended by the speaker or writer. The word "run" means many things dependent upon its usage in the sentence. Its meaning depends also upon the structure of the sentence.

Lloyd (21) notes that reading instruction should begin with familiar materials, materials that represent the child's speech. In this way the child learns that what he says can be written and read. The implications for beginning with experience charts in teaching reading are obvious.

The broader implications of a linguistic approach to reading seem to be (18):

1. Children should learn to read the language they already speak.
2. Efficient reading means an awareness of the spoken language structures represented by the graphic language.

Perhaps we have too long ignored the meaning-bearing language patterns. We may not have paid enough attention to the child's need to perceive language structures as wholes for *total comprehension* (18). Teachers of reading may need to become more familiar with the structure of the language.[7]

Thus far we have concerned ourselves with the individual sounds of the language—the consonants and vowels, with the teaching of the accurate production of the individual sounds or phonemes, the accurate pronunciation and articulation of the sounds of total words, and with language structure.

What are the implications of all this for reading? If the pupil cannot sound the individual phoneme, he probably will not be a good oral reader. He will have difficulty with phonics. He also may have difficulty in transmitting meaning.

The child's proficiency in reading, and certainly his word identification and recognition skill, is dependent upon his ability to articulate, enunciate, and pronounce the sounds met in his language.

Furthermore, genuine reading proficiency may mean the ability to read language structure. The best reader may be one mentally aware of the stresses, elongations of words, changes of pitch and intonation, and rhythms of the sentences that he reads. If he reads what was spoken the

[7] For a fuller discussion of the linguistic position see Chapter 10.

way the writer would like it to have been said, true communication of meaning may be possible. As Buswell (3, p. 114) notes:

> The first goal is to enable the child to derive meaning from the printed verbal symbols at the same level of functional efficiency that he has already attained in getting meanings from spoken words. The child has learned to interpret speech at functional level before entering school. The first obligation of the reading class is to produce this same efficiency with respect to the visual perception of print. There is no substitute for this ability; this is a first obligation.[8]

What is the school's role in teaching language structure and usage? Many five- and six-year-old children (and indeed two-year-olds) know the mechanics of grammar in a practical way. They can form sentences or utterances, handle subjects and predicates, and punctuate their spoken sentences by pauses and inflections. Without the benefit of formal instruction, they apply the rules of grammar in their speech. One doesn't have to be a linguist to use language effectively (5). In fact, it is not even necessary to be a linguist to use grammar correctly. After all, grammar is merely a summary, synopsis, a history, as it were, of the verbal habits of the speakers of the language. Today we do not approve of "he don't." Tomorrow it may be correct.

Students of language have always questioned the value of formal grammar instruction on the speech of pupils. Ervin and Miller (8) point out that by the age of four most children have learned the fundamental structural features of their language. Kean and Yamamoto (17) found that children have an adequate and usable grammar system by the time they get to school and that they use syntax cues to work out the meanings of new words. Carroll (4) suggests that after the age of six there is relatively little in the grammar or syntax of the language that the average child needs to learn. Joos (14) believes that it is not normal to learn grammar after the age of eight. Studies (5,31) also indicate that there is little, if any, value in formal instruction before the child has developed a certain amount of grammatical correctness in his everyday speech. In fact, it is doubtful that sentence analysis, parsing, and diagramming have any place in the elementary school. Grammar is the professional tool of the linguist, editor, and copyreader but hardly of the elementary pupil (36, p. 358). Grammar supports usage at the point when the child can grasp a generalization and apply it accurately to particulars (25, p. 224). The early grades generally lay the foundation for grammar, but principles, generalizations, and definitions are left for the junior high and high school years (37, p. 230).

[8] Guy T. Buswell, "The Process of Reading," *The Reading Teacher,* 13 (December 1959) 108–114. Reprinted with permission of the International Reading Association.

Thus, our teaching of grammar must be inductive. We must begin with the particular and gradually develop a principle. We must concentrate on actual errors made by children, not on hypothetical errors. We must motivate the child to want to develop acceptable speech and to acquire the formal standards of speech, writing, and usage of the school. We stress correctness in expression rather than the elimination of errors.

Authorities generally recommend that the elementary-school child should not be interrupted while speaking even if his usage is incorrect. Correction by other children may be especially harmful to the child. It may rob him of the confidence that he has developed with much difficulty. Goodman (10) found that prompting children or correcting them when they read orally seems to be undesirable and unnecessary since the child uses language cues to correct himself.

The emphasis of instruction should be on those errors that distinguish the child's speech from those of others in his milieu, that occur most frequently, or that impede communication. Pooley (25, p. 180) lists some of the common errors that should be overcome in the elementary school: They are: *ain't* or *hain't*; hair *are*; *a* orange; have *ate*; he *begun*; was *broke*; he *brung*; *climb* (short i); *clumb*; he *come*; have *did*; he, she, it *don't*; I *drunk*; *didn't, hadn't* ought; was *froze*; he *give*; I *got* for *I've got*; my brother, *he*; *her, him,* and *me* went; *hisself*; there *is, was* four; *knowed, growed*; *learn* me a song; *leave* me go; *me* and Mary went; haven't *no,* haven't *nothing*; he *run*; have *saw*; I *says*; he *seen*; *them* books; *their*selves; *this here*; *that there*; *us* boys went; we, you, they *was*; with *we* girls; have *went*; have *wrote*; and it is *yourn, hern, ourn, theirn.*

In another article (27) Pooley lists in sequential order the usages that should be developed or eliminated by the pupil as he progresses through the grades. The program should provide for:

1. The elimination of all baby talk and "cute" expressions.
2. The correct use of *I, me, he, him, she, her, they, them.* (Exception, *it's me.*)
3. The correct uses of *is, are, was, were* with respect to number and tense.
4. Correct past tenses of common irregular verbs such as *saw, gave, took, brought, bought, stuck.*
5. Correct use of past participles of the same verbs and similar verbs after auxiliaries.
6. Elimination of the double negative: We *don't* have *no* apples, etc.
7. Elimination of analogical forms: *Ain't, hisn, hern, ourn, theirselves,* etc.
8. Correct use of possessive pronouns: *My, mine, his, hers, theirs, ours.*

9. Mastery of the distinction between *its,* possessive pronoun, and *it's,* it is.
10. Placement of *have* or its reduction to *'ve* between I and a past participle.
11. Elimination of *them* as a demonstrative pronoun.
12. Elimination of *this here* and *that there.*
13. Mastery of use of *a* and *an* as articles.
14. Correct use of personal pronouns in compound constructions: as subject *Mary and I,* as object *Mary and me,* as object of preposition *to Mary and me.*
15. The use of *we* before an appositional noun when subject, *us* when object.
16. Correct number agreement with the phrases *there is, there are, there was, there were.*
17. Elimination of *he don't, she don't, it don't.*
18. Elimination of *learn* for *teach, leave* for *let.*
19. Elimination of pleonastic subjects: *my brother he; my mother she; that fellow he.*
20. Proper agreement in number with antecedent pronouns *one* and *anyone, everyone, each, no one.* With *everybody* and *none* some tolerance of number seems acceptable now.
21. The use of *who* and *whom* as reference to persons. (But note, *Who did he give it to?* is tolerated in all but very formal situations, in which *To whom did he give it?* is preferable.)
22. Accurate use of *said* in reporting the words of a speaker in the past.
23. Correction of *lay down* to *lie down.*
24. The distinction between *good* as adjective and *well* as adverb; e.g., *He spoke well.*
25. Elimination from writing of *can't hardly, all the farther* (for *as far as*) and *Where is he (she, it) at?* [9]

In correcting errors it is wise to work on a few errors at a time. Children in the primary grades may develop their own grammars by listing the errors they are prone to make and by noting the correct usage.

ERRORS IN SPEECH

The remainder of this chapter is devoted to a description of speech defects, to their causes, and their remediation. In most reading courses this

[9] Robert C. Pooley, "What is Correct English Usage?" *NEA Journal* 49 (December, 1960) 17–20. Reprinted with permission.

is not covered. However, children with reading problems frequently also have speech problems. And these affect their performance in oral reading and in the learning of phonics and reading. The child is at a disadvantage in learning to read because he cannot associate sound with its appropriate letter or word. It may be that some children will not learn to read well until they have corrected their speech difficulties.

There is adequate evidence that poor readers often have articulatory defects. Sonenberg and Glass (34), in a study of forty children between the ages of seven and sixteen who were remedial readers, found that only two of these children were free from articulatory errors, and 47 per cent had difficulty with auditory discrimination. They point out that most of those who had difficulties in auditory discrimination often made the following sound substitutions: *k-g, b-d, p-d, t-k, w-wh, m-s, f-t, d-t, t-l, t*-unvoiced *th,* f-unvoiced *th, p-m, p-g,* and *f-v,* substitutions which also frequently show up as reading reversals. It may be that problems of articulation, auditory discrimination, and reversals are basically one and the same problem.

Many children do not develop normal speech patterns. Even a very conservative estimate suggests that approximately one and one-half million children between the ages of five and seventeen have speech defects. These chiefly are disorders of articulation, but include disorders of voice, disorders of rhythm (stuttering and cluttering), cleft palate and cleft lip speech, cerebral palsied speech, and aphasic speech.

Articulatory Defects

Articulatory defects are by far the most common. They are speech deficiencies characterized by the imperfect production of phonetic elements and are accompanied by distortions, additions, substitutions, or omissions of certain speech sounds. Lisping is an example of a speech distortion. Cleft palate speech, delayed speech, and speech characterized by foreign dialects are classified as articulatory defects.

The average child of eight years of age is able to articulate 90 to 95 per cent of the sounds needed in speech. Some children, however, engage in baby talk, indistinct speech, tongue twisting, or lisping. These defects may confuse the child because the words sound one way when he says them and another way when he hears them spoken by someone else. This frequently leads to faulty word recognition and comprehension in reading. In Table 6-3 we have listed some common articulatory errors.

Errors of articulation may result from faulty sound discrimination, missing or misarranged teeth, a high or narrow hard palate, a sluggish or too large tongue, cleft palate, cleft lip, retarded speech development, or cerebral palsy (13, p. 7). Occasionally articulatory defects may be symptomatic of personal or emotional problems. Frustration with early attempts at speech may hinder normal development. Parental pampering, parental encouragement of baby talk, or inadequate speech standards in the home may lead children to develop carelessness in speech.

Children also frequently do not use the speech equipment that they possess. Many errors in articulation stem from lazy and indolent jaws, lips, tongue, or soft palate. The child drops end consonants, especially *t, d,* and *ng;* frequently changes *t* to *d* as dudy for duty; and uses contractions such as *woncha, lemme,* and *gimme* (29, p. 26). To overcome this, children should be encouraged to dramatize stories requiring them to yawn, whisper, or shout. They should overemphasize lip movements

TABLE 6-3   Common Articulatory Errors

1. Addition of speech sounds—"athelete" for athlete, "chimaney" for chimney.
2. Distortion of speech sounds—"Shister" for sister. This occurs in lateral lisps when the air escapes over the sides of the tongue.
3. Omission of speech sounds—"baw" for ball, "kool" for school, "tink" for think, "wat" for what, "sining" for singing.
4. Substitution of speech sounds—"fumb" for thumb, "wawipop" or "jajipop" for lollypop, "tap" for cap, "dive" for give, "wed" or "jed" for red, "doe" for go, "twy" for try, "choe" for shoe, "toap" for soap, "thoap" for soap, "shoap" for soap, "wery" for very, "ketch" for catch, "fink" for think, "jike" for like, "kin" for can, "bat" for bad, "bak" for bag, "tite" for kite.
5. Transposition of speech sound—"aks" for ask.
6. Slurring of speech sounds—not giving enough duration to the sound.
7. Delayed speech—inappropriate for the child's age level.
8. Foreign or regional dialect or accent—"thoid" for third.

and should engage in choral reading and speaking. Tongue twisters such as "Peter Piper picked a peck of pickled peppers" are especially helpful.

Delayed speech is associated with multiple factors. Lesions in the dominant hemisphere, shifts in handedness, confused hand preference, impaired hearing, mental subnormality, paralysis, or lack of speech stimulation in the home are commonly associated with it. Parents may delay the child's speech development by inadvertently punishing his early speech production. Intense shock, fright, or shame associated with the production of speech may keep the child from making further attempts. Sometimes the child is allowed to form a relationship with his parents and siblings that does away with the need for speech. Twins are said to be at a disadvantage in speech production because they get along with each other and understand each other so well that they frequently are not motivated to learn to speak.

Teaching the child with delayed speech generally consists of three phases (33). The teacher helps him to develop concepts by teaching him that objects or activities have names. The pupil must learn that ideas and objects are related, but that they are not the same. The pupil must be taught simple sounds. Usually, the speech pathologist finds it more efficient to begin with the syllable or single sound. Isolation of the individual sound makes transfer more effective. Van Riper (39) notes that "When an error is hidden within a word within a phrase within a sentence within a conversation, the child is unable to recognize it." However, with some pupils it is possible to begin with simple words. Finally, the pupil must learn that language is used to symbolize simple experiences. He is taught his own name, the names of his closest friends, and the names of common objects and activities in his environment.

The most common instance of articulation defects or dyslalia is characterized by the absence of any known pathology (22). It is a functional defect, and it decreases with age. This articulatory defect is usually overcome without therapy as the child matures. This led Morrency, Wepman, and Weiner to conclude that the children in their study spoke appropriately for their age, but they were simply at the lower end of the normal distribution. They showed a delay in growth necessary for accurate articulation and thus had a developmental speech inaccuracy. Many of these children had poorly developed auditory discrimination skills which normally mature at about age eight. The researchers believe that instances of developmental lag should not be considered defective in articulation, but merely accepted as being slower than their peers in acquiring the accuracy of adult speech. They suggest that the errors made have their roots in maturational factors.

Lisping is an example of distorted speech. It is of two kinds: *frontal* as when *th* is substituted for *s,* or *lateral.* Frontal lisping occurs when the child, while attempting to make the *s* sound, allows the tongue to protrude between the teeth. Lateral lisping occurs when the child makes the *s, sh,* and *ch* sounds inaccurately by allowing the air to pass over the sides of the tongue. Lisping also may be due to faulty occlusion between the upper and lower teeth, to loss of the front teeth, to hearing defects, or to malformation of teeth or jaws. To overcome the habit the child must close his teeth tightly, and the tongue must remain inside the mouth. The air is then blown through the teeth.

Children with *foreign language backgrounds* frequently have difficulty with *j, l, r, w, wh, ch,* and *th.* They substitute an unvoiced sound for a voiced sound at the end of a word. Thus hand, band, and land become "hant," "bant," "lant." A French child falters commonly on *th, wh,* and *ch;* the German child stumbles on *wh, th, j,* and short *u;* the Hebrew child says *sink* for *sing, lem* for *lame,* and *vot* for *what* (37, p. 244). These children must be encouraged to imitate good speech. The informal contacts that these children have with other children may well be the best speech therapy. Choral speaking and choral reading also are effective.

These children commonly have communication problems. Usually their vocabulary is inadequate. They cannot express their ideas because they do not know the appropriate words. They often lack the experiential background needed for communication in American schools. A program of correction must attack these inadequacies by broadening the child's experiences and by enlarging his vocabulary.

In general, the teacher must be concerned with accurate production both of the individual phoneme and of the word. Although not all children need training in these skills, the teacher must be prepared to handle articulatory problems when they appear.

A good program for teaching the phoneme is outlined by Van Riper and Butler (38) and would seem to include the following elements:

1. The teacher identifies each sound with a sound in the child's environment. (S is described as sounding like air going out of a tire, like the sound of a whistling teakettle, or like the hissing sound coming from an oxygen tank.)

2. The teacher gives the sound a name. (S is known as the "whistling teakettle sound," ch is the "choo-choo train sound," and z is the "buzzing bee sound"; B may be the "bubbling sound"; M is the "cow sound"; T is the "ticking watch sound"; G is the "angry dog sound"; U may be the "hooting-owl sound"; and ou may be the "crying baby sound" or the "ouch sound."

3. The teacher identifies the sound with a picture.

4. The teacher develops the placement of sound in the mouth. (Not all children need to have training on this last point.)

Most writers on speech improvement are more concerned with the production of the whole word than the production of the individual phoneme. Eastman (6) for example, developed speech improvement activities around the "game" idea.[10] The following techniques seem especially useful:

1. *Grocery Store Technique:* Children bring cartons, boxes, cans, and bottles, and set up their own toy grocery. Using toy money,

[10] The ultimate criterion is not whether the pupils are enjoying the game, but rather whether they are learning. The activity must be speech-centered. The game should be more than a mere game (16). Too often games are merely for amusement. Often word games are filled with new and strange words rather than with the words that the child is presently encountering in his text. If the game is to be effective, the child must understand the purpose of the game.

the child with *s* trouble buys items that have *s* in their names, such as salt, soap, soup, mustard, or salad dressing. To be able to buy the item the child must articulate the word correctly.

2. *Circle Technique:* A circle on the blackboard is divided into a number of sections. Each section contains one or more difficult words. With eyes closed, the child points at the circle saying: "Round and round I go, and when I stop, I stop here." He opens his eyes and attempts to pronounce the word or words on which his pointer landed. Correct pronunciation of the words in the block gives the pupil a point and another turn. A simple wheel with a pointer may be a more suitable device.

3. *The Grab Bag Technique:* Objects with the sound in their name to be exercised are placed into a bag. In the *th bag,* for example, are a clothespin, birthday card, feather, thimble, a piece of leather, or a mouth organ.

4. *The Question Technique:* Questions may be asked that call for answers requiring the speaking of the sound to be learned. For example, in teaching the *s* sound, the following questions are appropriate:
   1. "The number after six is⸺." (seven)
   2. "The grocer put the potatoes in a⸺." (sack)
   3. "He washed his dirty hands with⸺." (soap)
   4. "Cotton is not hard but is⸺." (soft)
   5. "After Friday comes⸺." (Saturday)

Does speech therapy help? Sonenberg and Glass (34) found that retarded readers who received both reading and speech instruction showed more reading improvement than those who received only the reading instruction. There seems little doubt that poor articulation and poor auditory discrimination are deterrents to reading achievement. Sonenberg and Glass recommend that teachers isolate the letters that often are reversed and develop an ear discrimination for them.

Voice Disorders

Voice disorders of one kind or another are common among children. These frequently are functional in nature. They have arisen from habits that with proper guidance may be changed. The pitch[11] may be too high, too low, or a monotone; the volume is either too soft or too loud;[12] and

[11] Pitch represents the number of vibrations or cycles per second as recorded on the oscillogram.

[12] The loudness of voice depends on the intensity as measured by the physical energy caused by the vibrating column of air (1, p. 194).

the quality may be too nasal, too hoarse, too breathy, too husky, too metallic, or too muffled.

Pronovost (28, p. 111) points out that the child must develop five vocal skills. These are:

1. A pleasing voice quality
2. Adequate volume
3. Variety in duration of words
4. Appropriate phrasing and smoothness
5. Variety of pitch[13]

A pleasant voice is free from nasality, huskiness, monotony, harshness, or breathiness and is characterized by freedom from vocal tension. Children develop vocal tension when they speak too loudly or at a too high pitch. In other cases vocal tension is a sign of emotional problems. The teacher develops vocal ease by overemphasizing the contrasts in voice quality, especially the contrasts of extreme tension or exaggerated relaxation.

To be an effective speaker the pupil also must use adequate volume. Volume naturally is dependent upon the situation. However, when the voice is too loud or too soft, the child's hearing should be checked. A soft voice, when there are no physical complications, may be symptomatic of insecurity; a loud voice may indicate aggressiveness.

The child must learn to prolong words to the required length. Some words are spoken quickly and some more slowly. The meaning that we expect words to convey frequently depends on how much emphasis is given to certain words by prolongating or shortening the vocal response.

The pupil must learn to join the words or the sounds, making up phrases into an orderly time sequence. Phrases generally are separated by pauses.

Finally, the student must develop an appropriate pitch.

Variety of pitch occurs as inflections and pitch shift. An inflection is a gliding change of pitch during a word, such as is heard in a cheery "hello." A shift is a quick change of pitch from one word to another. In the phrase, "come here!" the pitch will shift upward between the two words if the word "here" is emphasized (28, p. 141).[14]

[13] Wilbert Pronovost, *The Teaching of Speaking and Listening*, © 1959, Longmans, Green and Company. Reprinted by permission, David McKay Company, Inc.

[14] Wilbert Pronovost, *The Teaching of Speaking and Listening*, © 1959, Longmans, Green and Company. Reprinted by permission, David McKay Company, Inc.

Pitch often is associated with the accent or stress that is put on words of two or more syllables. The accent or stress helps to keep words apart, for example, in'valid and inval'id. It also helps to distinguish between questions, exclamations, and statements. This we call sentence stress or intonation. Intonation is the melody pattern of a language, and each language has its own characteristic pattern. For example, the declarative sentence in our speech has a downward intonation. The question has an upward intonation.

Voice disorders will most directly affect the pupil's oral reading. However, from a linguistic point of view, a much more serious defect is present. If the child cannot phrase properly, if his emphasis on words is wrong, if the pitch and intonation are improper, the child probably will not read with *full meaning* the sentence or total language structure.

Disorders of Rhythm

The third major group of speech disorders consists of disorders of rhythm. The two major disorders here are stuttering and cluttering. Stuttering is relatively common. It is hesitant speech accompanied by muscle spasms of the throat and diaphragm and results in an inability to produce voiced sounds. Emery (7) says that stuttering consists of abnormal nonfluencies in speech that are accompanied by prolongation and repetition of sounds and words, by excessive pauses, and by partial or complete blockages of speech. The stutterer may repeat the initial letter as "b-b-b-bat," or he may repeat the first word in a group of words, as for example, "my-my-my bat."

Today stuttering is viewed as an *intermittent* activity that sometimes characterizes the speech of a person (19). A person is not a stutterer 100 per cent of the time. Stuttering generally is identified between the ages of two and four, at which time the symptoms are not greatly different from the repetitious speech of normal children.

Psychologists have offered a variety of explanations for stuttering. Among these are deviations in the shape, size, and length of the palate or tongue, dental irregularities, overshot or undershot jaw, motor retardation, reversal of cortical dominance, cerebral lesions, feelings of inferiority, and fear of speaking. It may be caused by hurry, competition, excitement, fear of rebuke, and by the need to communicate something unpleasant. At this stage it is in its simpler form. In the more advanced forms the child develops a fear of sounds, words, and speaking.

Generally, the theories on the etiology of stuttering are grouped in this way:

1. those which stress that stuttering is caused by an unconscious wish or need to stutter

2. those which suggest that the neuromuscular activity required for smooth speech breaks down under emotional or constitutional stress
3. those which suggest that stuttering results from a conscious attempt to avoid stuttering and that the listener-speaker relationship is a vital element.

Karlin (15), for example, suggests that it may be due to delayed myelinization of the cortical association areas involved in speech. Lindsley (20) reports that the alpha rhythm of stutterers is out of phase in both hemispheres[15] and indicates that there is more unilateral blockage[16] when the individual is speaking than when he is silent. Wendell Johnson suggests that stuttering may develop because of parental disapproval of "normal nonfluency." He points out that the average child of five to eight is nonfluent approximately sixty times in every 1000 spoken words. Naylor (23) suggests that the stutterer, afraid of stumbling over a word, stops his forward movement and repeats. Too much regression in reading may be a similar difficulty. Vernon (40, p. 99) states that speech defects may be more common among completely left-handed individuals because such children have been under pressure to change from the left to the right hand. Rotter (32) suggests that pampering predisposes the would-be stutterer to use stuttering as a rationalization for failure. He believes that stuttering is a speech disorder in a person who perceives his speech as being different from that of others and as being a handicap to him.

In less severe forms of stuttering the child should be encouraged to speak when he is fluent, and his speech needs may be controlled when he is stuttering. Many children at this stage are not even aware of their difficulty, and certainly they should not be made aware of it if it can be avoided. In more advanced stages children are aware of their handicap. The teacher commonly controls all situations that would bring ridicule upon the pupil. Nevertheless, the pupil should be brought to face the problem frankly while he is developing confidence in handling speaking situations.

It seems unwise to interrupt the child, to tell him to speak more slowly, to say the word for him, or to criticize him. Even to praise him for fluent speech may only increase his fear of speech. It indicates disapproval of nonfluency. The teacher should accept him for what he says rather than for how he says it. He must teach him that stuttering is not something that the person *is;* it is something that the person *does* (23, p. 36).

[15] This means that the peaks of the waves from each hemisphere as recorded on the encephalographs do not coincide.

[16] Unilateral blocking is the absence of alpha waves on one side of the head. The rhythm on the opposite side is observable (20).

The average stutterer does not have merely a mechanical speech problem. He needs parents' and teachers' understanding. Teachers must stress his assets rather than his liabilities. They set goals for him that are attainable. They do not force him to engage in a situation, such as reading aloud, which is too stressful for him. They attempt to restore his self-confidence. The stutterer needs to feel enough security so that he can stutter without self-devaluation. In fact, if he is ever to overcome stuttering, he must do it *while stuttering* (23, p. 36). He must learn to accept that to stutter is permissible.

Cluttering

Cluttering is rapid speech characterized by slurring, omission, and distortion of words. The speech runs together, the sounds and syllables are slurred, the speed is excessive, and the flow of words is irregular (7). The speech is jerky, stumbling, and explosive, and is characterized by an erratic rhythm. The clutterer does not coordinate his thinking with his speech. Cluttering may be caused by insecurity or by fear of being interrupted. The pupil should be encouraged to slow down. He races his motor, but his motor was not designed for racing. The pupil may be aided in slowing down by a prolongation of the vowel and the consonant sounds.

Cleft Palate and Cleft Lip

Cleft palate speech includes excessive nasality in addition to articulatory defects. A child with this condition may have particular difficulty in producing the sounds for the letters *f, v, s,* and *z,* and less difficulty with *p, b, t, d, k,* and *g.*

Cleft palate and speech disorders accompanying cerebral palsy have specific organic bases. Cleft palate and cleft lip speech consists of

> . . . imperfections in voice, articulation and fluency or rate. In cleft palate the structures which normally form the roof of the mouth have failed to join properly. As a result, air passes too freely between the oral and nasal chambers. Moreover, the action of the tongue and the throat muscles is influenced in ways that affect speech. The speech tends to be nasalized and the articulation is affected. There is difficulty in building up breath pressure for the sounds of *p, b, t, d, k,* and *g,* often with a resulting plosive character of the nasal emission of air. Other sounds, too, particularly those of *s* and *sh,* are commonly distorted.
>
> The cleft may be slight or extensive. Although it may affect only the hard palate, it sometimes extends through the gum ridge at the front of the mouth and the lip may also be divided. In some cases

the cleft extends back to the soft palate and velum; the soft palate may be short, divided, or absent (13, pp. 9, 10).[17]

Perhaps as many as 60 to 65 per cent of the children with cleft palate also have poor auditory discrimination (22).

Cerebral Palsied Speech

The speech of the cerebral palsied child is labored, slow, and jerky. The voice is monotonous and not too well controlled. The sounds are not articulated correctly. Because of impaired muscle coordination the speech is distorted (13, p. 11).

Aphasic Speech

Aphasia is a defect in the central nervous system that may be accompanied by inadequacies in language expression and/or understanding. When the condition occurs in children, it is termed oligophasia.

Receptive oligophasia is a disturbance in auditory perception of sound. Expressive or motor oligophasia is a disturbance in recognizing and forming phonemic patterns and translating them into speech. And central oligophasia is a disturbance of symbolization. In this instance words cannot be used to deal with ideas and concepts (35, p. 110). We still speak of a writing disturbance as agraphia and of an aphasic reading disturbance as alexia.

Generally, the oligophasic child is taught to speak through a phonetic approach. The child must learn the sounds one at a time. He must become familiar with the articulatory position of each sound. Gradually he must combine the separate sounds to form a complete word.

Teaching the oligophasic or brain injured child to read has its own problems. He has a tendency to confuse similar letters, *b-d, p-q, m-n, m-w, b-p, n-u* and similar words, *there-their*. He does not organize the letters of words in their proper sequence, and thus makes frequent reversal errors, *tap-pat, was-saw*. He has difficulty with short vowels and with similar-sounding consonants, *s-z, p-b, f-v*. Sometimes he cannot isolate the sounds in words. He cannot sound the initial sound in a word, its end sound, or characteristic vowel sound. The oligophasic tends to transpose letters and syllables in words. Thus, *animal* becomes *aminal*. Finally, the brain injured child frequently cannot blend sounds into

[17] Wendell Johnson, *Children with Speech and Hearing Impairment,* Department of Health, Education, and Welfare Bulletin 5 (Washington, D.C.: Government Printing Office, 1959). Reprinted by permission.

words. If the *bl* in *blend* is separated by the teacher from the *end,* the pupil cannot unite the two parts to form a whole. How to help such a pupil is discussed in Chapter 14.

SUMMARY

In this chapter we have examined the phonological system of language and language structure, and have offered some suggestions for the development of accurate reproduction of both the individual phoneme and the word. We discussed the major speech defects and suggested procedures for dealing with them. This chapter in a sense concludes our survey of the various factors related to reading readiness and achievement.

Chapters 3 and 4 were concerned chiefly with the characteristics that the child brings to school. We delved into the significance of the child's intellectual, physical, physiological, emotional, and social development. In Chapter 4 we commented briefly on the importance of the instructional program. In Chapter 5 we related listening and speaking proficiency to reading achievement and suggested means for improving the child's listening skill.

The justification for Chapters 5 and 6 is the same as for any of the other chapters. The reading teacher must possess any and all knowledge that will improve his teaching, and that will lead to better reading by the pupil. The better the speech, the more successful a reader the child tends to be. The more readily the teacher can detect and correct the child's speech difficulties, the more successful his teaching of reading should be.

Disabilities of speech and of reading parallel each other. They both appear to be produced by multiple rather than by single causes.

QUESTIONS FOR DISCUSSION

1. Take one basic language sound and discuss how you might isolate it for the child, and how you would initiate and maintain a program of instruction that will eventually lead to its mastery by the pupil.
2. Illustrate by example the argument that the word receives its complete meaning only from the structure of the sentence in which it is embedded.
3. Identify the five most common misuses of grammar in your classroom, and discuss ways of helping the pupil to correct his mistakes.
4. What is meant by speech improvement? Why is it important that the pupil be able to speak words fluently before he reads them?

5. What is the purpose of the phonological system of a language?
6. Describe the physiology of vowel production.
7. Describe the physiology of five different consonant sounds.
8. How might a short talk be used to improve the child's skill in the mechanics of speech as well as in the communication of content?
9. Categorize the various errors in speech.
10. How are errors in speech related to reading proficiency?
11. Discuss:
    a. The phonological system of a language is a network of differences between sounds.
    b. Speech defects tend to be positively associated with faulty word recognition, with poorer comprehension, and with poorer reading achievement.
    c. The emotional reaction to the speech defects may have a greater effect on achievement than the defect itself.

Developing
Reading Readiness

Reading readiness has been defined as the developmental stage at which constitutional and environmental factors have prepared the child for reading instruction. Chapters 3 and 4 discussed the myriad of factors, both constitutional and environmental, that may interfere with the child's readiness for and achievement in reading. Chapters 5 and 6 discussed the importance of listening and oral language for reading readiness and achievement.

Reading readiness also may be described as the teachable moment for reading. The reading teacher realizes that it is not enough to know the factors that promote or prohibit adequate reading performance. He must examine the composite of factors and on the basis of them must identify each pupil's specific readiness for reading. The reading program must be individualized for each pupil.

Perhaps it would be valuable to enumerate the significant principles of readiness. Educational psychologists list the following:

1. Children generally become ready for specific learning tasks at different ages.
2. The child develops skills most readily if they are built upon the natural foundation of maturational development. Children put most effort into tasks that are neither too difficult nor too easy, that are within their "range of challenge"—that are possible for them but not necessarily easy.
3. Children should not be forced into readiness training before maturational development is adequate. Such premature train-

ing may lead to no improvement, to only temporary improvement, or to actual harm. Premature training may destroy the child's natural enthusiasm for a given activity and it is doubtful that drill and exercises will ever be a substitute for maturation.

4. Generally, the more mature the child is, the less training is needed to develop a given proficiency.

5. The teacher can promote the child's readiness by providing for gaps in his experience.

Let us repeat a few ideas from Chapter 3 about maturation or genetically determined growth. Too frequently it is confused with learning or environmentally induced growth. Maturation and learning are distinct concepts even though it commonly is impossible to identify the influence of each in any given learning situation.

Maturational changes usually are orderly and sequential. Wide variations of environmental conditions have little effect on maturation. Thus, the nervous system develops regularly according to its own intrinsic pattern. In learning to walk, the child goes through the following stages: he learns to raise his chin and chest, to roll, to sit, to stand with help, to crawl, to pull himself up, to walk when led by another, to stand alone, and to walk alone. Even during this first year of life, however, individual differences are existent.

Because of this orderly and sequential change, there is very little benefit in rushing the maturational process. Postponing the reading process until the child is older often seems less wasteful of teacher time and pupil effort and does not handicap the pupil later. Olson's concept of "pacing" suggests that it is an error to expect more from the child than he is capable of giving.

Readiness programs, however, are not thereby useless. Children need appropriate environmental stimulation if maturational development is to progress at an appropriate rate. In many instances the child has inadequacies in his experiential background, and the child benefits greatly from readiness experiences.

Readiness may refer to an intrinsic state of the organism, but also to the extrinsic acculturation of the organism (5). The latter is often referred to as building readiness, but some note that readiness comes with age, not with special drills or practice. It may be that both concepts have meaning in that a pupil is more or less ready dependent upon the method and materials used in teaching and that building readiness comes to mean such things as removing blocks to learning and filling gaps of experience.

Spache (42) found that an intensified readiness program was of significant value to black pupils. In another study (38), kindergarten children who were introduced to a formal readiness program complete with workbooks performed better than did children who were taught informally without the benefit of workbooks. And Bruner notes: "Readiness . . . is a function not so much of maturation as it is of our intentions and our skill in translating ideas into the language and concepts of the age level we are teaching." (8)

Pestalozzi in 1802 said it very beautifully when he wrote:

> **To instruct man is nothing more than to help nature develop in its own way, and the art of instruction depends primarily on harmonizing our messages, and the demands we make upon the child, with his powers at the moment.**

Although the average age for reading readiness has dropped in the last generation, very few average or above average five- and six-year-old children are ready in every respect for formal reading instruction. In one way or another almost every child can be helped to become more ready for instruction.

Reading readiness usually does not come at the same age for the sharecropper's child as for the college teacher's son, but even the professor's son may not be fully ready. In this chapter we are concerned particularly with those readiness elements that can be and usually are developed through classroom instruction.

It is not easy to list in sequence the major skills and attitudes that must be developed in the kindergarten and early first grade. However, research and experience indicate that for success in reading the child either should possess, or should develop in school, certain minimum levels of proficiency in a number of areas. The teacher of reading cannot forget that some children come to school perhaps fully prepared for reading. A readiness program for these children may be only harmful.

The first requisite for beginning reading is an interest in reading. Children generally come to school wanting to learn to read. When they have discovered that what can be said also can be written, they show an even greater interest. The most frequently repeated phrase during the readiness period is: "What does it say?" Unfortunately, this interest in reading is not necessarily self-perpetuating. The teacher must actively foster it by making available picture books on various topics. He must ask children to bring books to school and share them with other children. He must read stories to children. He must let children dictate simple experience charts. He must keep the bulletin board full of short readable messages. The objects in the room should be labelled.

After the child's interest has been obtained, major teaching tasks remain. The readiness skills that often must be developed through classroom instruction include the following:

1. Training in concept formation
2. Training in auditory discrimination
3. Training in visual discrimination
4. Knowledge of the alphabet
5. Training in left-to-right progression and in reading on a line
6. Acquisition of a sight vocabulary
7. Ability to associate meanings with printed symbols
8. Independence in working out the pronunciation of words

Figure 7-1 illustrates the various facets of the readiness program.

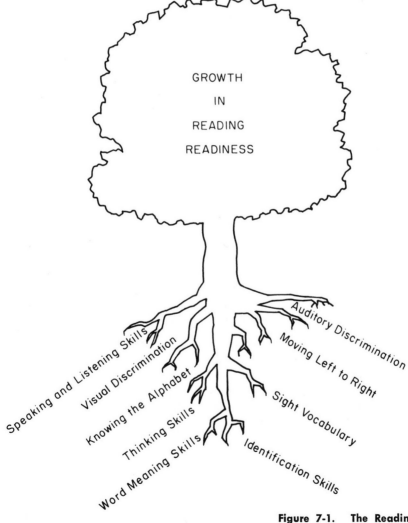

Figure 7-1.   The Readiness Tree

A good readiness program is directed toward the development of proficiency in these areas. The pupil must develop proficiency in each area in the day to day activities in the classroom. In this chapter we have suggested means for developing five of the eight skills. The development of sight vocabulary, the development of independence in word identification, and the development of skill in word interpretation are left for later chapters.

THE DEVELOPMENT OF CONCEPTS

Chapter 2 emphasized the importance of conceptual experience for successful reading. It was suggested that:

1. Children learn to conceptualize.
2. Depth and variety of experience are necessary for conceptual development.

In Chapter 12 conceptualization is described as a process involving the following stages of development:

1. Actual experience with the concrete object, person, or event.
2. Accurate discrimination of essential and nonessential characteristics in objects.
3. The formation of the concept.
4. The formation of categories—grouping the individual experiences into classes.

In Chapter 12 it also is suggested that the development of concepts may be encouraged through a series of activities. There we are concerned with the teaching of meaning beyond the primary level. Let us confine ourselves here to those activities that help the kindergarten and/or first-grade teacher to develop the conceptual readiness required by pupils on that level.

The following activities seem especially appropriate:

1. Give the child an opportunity to deal with the concrete object.
2. Label objects in the classroom.
3. Use pictures and art activities to expand the child's concepts.
4. Encourage conversation and storytelling.
5. Use description, riddle, rhyme, and puzzle games.
6. Use audio-visual aids.
7. Use dramatization, marionette and puppet shows, pageants and operettas.
8. Teach the pupil to construct and use picture dictionaries.
9. Use oral and written directions.

10. Teach the skills of classification and categorization.
11. Emphasize thought-initiating experiences.

Let us discuss each of these eleven activities.

Experience with the Concrete Object

A natural activity in the kindergarten is to have children bring toys and objects to school and tell about them. This "bring-and-tell" activity, besides being language training, is interesting to the children and extends their meanings.

Demonstrations, models, exhibits, and dioramas also serve to expand children's meanings and vocabulary. The child's experiences may be broadened by models of weapons, homes, and vehicles, and by bird and geological specimens. He may learn to construct a play house, a play town, a toy store, an airplane, or a fire engine. Science activities, such as collecting shells and rocks or caring for an aquarium, develop and clarify children's concepts of the real world that is symbolized by words. Children may discuss the seasons and the weather. They may care for plants and study about vegetables and flowers.

They learn the meaning of pint, quart, and gallon by handling and seeing such containers. A measuring cup may be used to develop meaning for half, fourth, or third. The height of the door, the weight of a bag of potatoes, or a foot rule are simple referents useful in teaching measurement concepts.

Concepts develop most easily through sense impressions. Visitation, for example, of farms, food markets, factories, trains, museums, circuses, newspaper plants, creameries, planetariums, zoos, fire departments, bakeries, airplanes, post offices, school buildings, libraries, and stores provide experience backgrounds for many words. Preparatory activities should familiarize the pupils with the objects that they will have an opportunity to see. The pupils need to know what to look for. After the trip the pupils need exercises in association of the experience and the symbol. They may draw pictures of what they saw or they may develop an experience chart about their trip.

In developing meanings, the teacher also should make use of the child's sense of touch, taste, smell, and hearing. The kindergarten child likes to handle objects. Nails, bolts, washers, screws, ball bearings, pliers, files, screw drivers, and hammers fascinate him. The teacher may blindfold the child and ask him to identify by touch—fur, bark, screen, soft flannel-like leaves, satin, sandpaper, and thistles (30).

The young learner likes to make sounds and to discriminate sounds made in the world about him. He finds the broadening of his meanings through the sense of smell a most delightful activity. He may never have identified a specific smell with paint, varnish, ink, oil, soap, fingernail polish, shoe polish, gas, or ether.

An interesting game is "My Nose Tells Me." A blindfolded pupil is asked to identify foods or objects by smell. Apples, onions, vinegar, paint, leather, bananas, oranges, or pepper may be used.

On more advanced levels the child should hear and "see" the meaning of words like stealthily, drowsy, steaming, or smoking.

In developing meaning for words the teacher usually proceeds from the concrete to the abstract. The word "pear" can refer to an individual pear or to a group of pears. In the latter case it has a class meaning. The child develops this meaning for pear *through experiencing all kinds of pears.* He observes differences in pears, but also notes their basic similarity.

Labelling

Labelling of objects in the classroom begins in the kindergarten. For example, labels are put on the desks, chairs, doors, windows, and pictures. The child's name is put on his kindergarten rug. Children develop scrapbooks with labelled pictures. In the upper grades teachers find labelling to be a useful way for teaching technical vocabularies. Pupils provide labels for collections of insects, leaves, rocks, shells, woods, and snakes. They label both the materials and the apparatuses used in class.

Signs and directions are additional means for teaching the child to associate meanings with printed symbols. Signs, such as, "Put milk bottles here," "Stop," "Go," and "Grocery Store," are effective teaching devices.

Learning to Read Pictures

Children frequently are introduced to the meaning of a word through the use of pictures. Children's books commonly have pictures accompanying the reading. The pictures are clues to the story, and the text often merely represents the conversation of one of the persons identified in the picture. Children should be encouraged to observe what is happening in the picture, to figure out what has happened before and what will happen next, and to decide what the characters in the pictures might be saying (28). The teacher says: "Open your book to page one. Look at the picture. What has happened? What is going to happen? What is Jack saying?"

Picture storybooks offer almost all children the opportunities for experiencing meaning. They both confirm and extend children's experiences. The teacher says: "Look at this picture. This is a camel. Camels live in a desert. They can go seven days without water."

Pictures give clues to the meaning of a story. By relating pictures to one another the child is preparing himself to follow a sequence of thought units in a sentence or a series of sentences in a paragraph (21, p. 127).

Pictures may be used to teach the multiple meanings of words, to develop meanings for prepositions, to understand the meanings of opposites, and to develop an understanding of sequential thought. The exercises in Figures 7-2, 7-3, and 7-4 are illustrative.

Figure 7-2.   Multiple Meanings of Words*

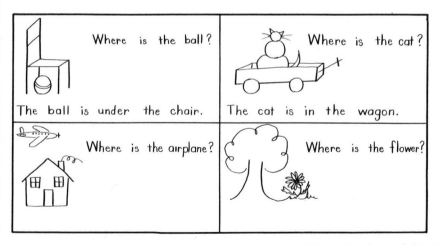

Figure 7-3.   Meanings of Prepositions†

* From *Thinking Skills,* Level 2, Continental Press, Inc., 1958, Elizabethtown, Pa. Plate 6. Reproduced by permission.

† From Mary E. Platts, Sister Rose Marguerite, and Esther Schumaker, *Spice* (Stevensville, Michigan: Educational Service, Inc., 1960) p. 79. Reproduced by permission.

Figure 7-4. **Understanding Opposites***

The meaning of the words *up* and *down,* for example, can be illustrated by a simple drawing of ascending and descending stairs. The child draws a red circle around the boy going up the stairs and a blue circle around the boy coming down the stairs. Art exercises also are effective for illustrating processes and for demonstrating the steps required in making something.

Pictures also may be used to teach word identification and word recognition skills. In the exercise in Figure 7-5 the pupil reads the sen-

Figure 7-5. **Meaning: Picture Stories†**

*From *Thinking Skills,* Level 1, Continental Press, Inc., 1958, Elizabethtown, Pa. Plate 4. Reproduced by permission.

†From Mary E. Platts, Sister Rose Marguerite, and Esther Shumaker, *Spice* (Stevensville, Michigan: Educational Service, Inc., 1960) p. 12. Reproduced by permission.

tences and uses the pictures above the line of print as clues to the incomplete words. He then writes the correct letter in the blank.

Conversation and Storytelling

In actively constructing sentences, stories, and experience charts,[1] children enlarge their vocabulary and increase the number of usable concepts while at the same time removing misconceptions and inadequacies in meaning. Let us suppose, for example, that the word "potato" appears in a sentence. The teacher may ask: "What kind of potatoes have you seen?" "Where are potatoes generally grown?" Children need a lot of experience with words, and letting them speak is one way of helping them to get this experience.

Numerous language activities can be planned for the child. We already have alluded to the "bring-and-tell" activity. The child also may tell a story about a picture, he may describe his own art, he may tell of his experiences the previous evening or on the way to school, he may select a title for a picture, or he may play word games. He may be asked to describe the normal activities of an animal, or he may be required to tell the sequence of events in a story that was read to him.

Description, Riddle, and Rhyme Games

In description games one side of the card contains a description and the other contains the correct word. The child hears the description and then is asked to identify what has been described. In another version of this exercise the pupil is given three words from which he selects the one that identifies what has been described.

Riddles are of two kinds: Who am I? and What am I? The following riddles are illustrative:

I'm the king of the beasts.
When I roar they all fear
They hurry to hide
When I'm sneaking near

My coat is red, my tail is bushy:
I'm sly and shrewd and cunning.

I trot for miles across the fields
And never tire of running

I'm a desert beast,
I won't run dry:
I carry a seven-day
Water supply

[1] Durrell (16, p. 220) points out that experience charts are too whimsical in their choice of vocabulary. He recommends that the teacher modify the oral suggestions of children so as to keep the vocabulary within the limits of the child's experience.

When you're asleep. I'm wide
awake,
I see the best at night.
The farmer likes me 'round the
barn
To catch the mice in sight,

I scamper up and down the
trees—

Busy all the day.
I gather nuts for winter's food
And put them all away,

I carry my young
in a pouch so furry.
I hop and I jump
When I'm in a hurry[2] (15).

Rhymes are useful in developing meaningful listening. Thus:

Johnny jumped over the wall
Only to have a terrible. . . .
(fall)

Audio-visual Aids

We have already spoken of pictures and their usefulness in teaching
meaning. Slides, filmstrips, television, radio, and disk and tape recordings
bring into the classroom numerous experiences that might never be had
first hand. Certain words, for example, satellite, rocket, pyramid, buffalo,
raccoon, porcupine, bellows, caboose, andirons, bronco, cactus, coyote,
catacomb, penguin, chariot, cathedral, and knight, become real only when
illustrated visually. In the upper elementary grades, charts, maps, diagrams, and graphs are especially useful for teaching relationships. The
sizes of animals—"How tall is a cow?", "Is a cow twice as tall as a horse?"
—can be illustrated through the use of comparative graphs.

Film readers appear to have special values. Not only can the child
see and hear while using the film, but he can then read the same words
and content in a correlated reader.

Educational Developmental Laboratories, Huntington, New York,[3]
provides a series of readiness and preprimer film materials that should
prove beneficial in the teaching of kindergarten and first-grade children.
The readiness set is designed to develop the ability to recognize gross
forms, to expand common experiences, to teach categorization, to develop
visual and auditory discrimination, and to quicken the child's ability to
see relationships. The preprimer set is designed to develop recognition of
letters, to teach discrimination of capital and lower case letters, to teach

---

[2] *Dot-to-Dot Zoo* (Akron, Ohio: The Saalfield Publishing Company). Reprinted
by permission of the Saalfield Publishing Company.

[3] For information on other sets of film readers see Chapter 14 in the section,
"Audio-Visual Materials."

initial sounds, to differentiate word forms, to develop the child's ability to associate pictures with print, and to develop ability in basic comprehension.

Dramatization, Marionette and Puppet Shows, Pageants, and Operettas

Acting out the activity frequently is the best way to teach the meaning of words like *hop* and *skip*. It is equally effective in teaching prepositions such as *into, upon, below, above, behind, through, around,* or *before;* in teaching such action words as *snail-like, trippingly, hesitantly, haltingly, nervously, clumsily, quickly, safely, quietly;* and in teaching feeling words such as *mourning, apathy, elation, anger, disgust,* and *fear.* Sometimes a dramatic bit is useful in teaching the meaning of abstract terms such as *love, courage, cooperation,* and *appreciation.*

Drama also may be used to relive trips, to learn safety rules and social manners, and to learn to interpret music.

Constructing and Using Picture Dictionaries

Children early construct their own dictionaries. Each new word they meet is included in the dictionary and is accompanied by a picture. The dictionary starts out as 26 pages, each page having the same capital and lower case letter. When the child has mastered manuscript writing, a description may accompany each word. Action words are accompanied by action pictures. Words like *here, there, wherefore, therefore,* and *why* must be explained by using them in sentences.

There also are many commercialized picture dictionaries on the market today. These are especially helpful in developing meanings for a word and in developing alphabetizing skills. Some of the common picture dictionaries are:

1. Clemens, Elizabeth, *Pixie Dictionary.* [New York: Holt, Rinehart, and Winston.]
2. Courtis, Stuart, and Watters, Garnette, *Illustrated Golden Dictionary.* [New York: Golden Press Educational Division.]
3. MacBean, Dilla W., *Picture Book Dictionary.* [Chicago: Children's Press, Inc.]
4. O'Donnell, Mabel, and Townes, Willmina, *Words I Like to Read and Write.* [New York: Harper & Row, Publishers.]
5. Parke, Margaret B., *Young Reader's Color-Picture Dictionary for Reading, Writing, and Spelling.* [New York: Grosset and Dunlap.]
6. Reed, Mary and Oswald, Edith, *My First Golden Dictionary.* [New York: Golden Press Educational Division.]

Use of Oral and Written Directions

As has already been mentioned, teachers help to develop word meanings by posting directions on the bulletin board or on the blackboard. They also may ask children to carry out certain actions. "Get your colors, Lori," "Pass the napkins, Pami." are examples of spoken directions.

Two games, the "Do This" and the "Yes and No" game are suitable activities. Each game requires a set of cards. One set gives directions and the other ask questions. The child selects a card, reads it aloud, and carries out the desired directions or answers the question. "Do This" cards contain statements like the following: "Stand up and then sit down," "Stand up and point to the left," "Point to the sky," "Clap your hands," or "Give the number that follows five." "Yes and No" cards contain statements like the following: "Can a dog fly?," "Can birds sing?," "Are cats bigger than lambs?," or "Are there boys in our class?" If the responses to the directions and questions show that the child does not possess the concept involved, the card is put on the bottom of the pack. If the response is adequate, the child keeps the card. The child with the most cards wins the game.

Fitting Objects and Words into Categories

In reading, the child is constantly required to think of an individual object as a member of a class. He has to think in categories. Initially the exercises used to teach this skill are pictorial in nature. The following are examples of such exercises:

Classifying Objects to Wear*   Classifying Furniture   Classifying Birds
                                 and Machines†   and Insects†

Figure 7-6

* From *Independent Activities*, Level 1, Continental Press, Inc., 1958, Elizabethtown, Pa. Plate 23. Reproduced by permission.
† From *Thinking Skills*, Level 1, Continental Press, Inc., 1958, Elizabethtown, Pa. Plates 2 and 3. Reproduced by permission.

Another activity requires the more advanced learner to place words into appropriate categories. In one column is a list of words; opposite the list are certain categories under which the words may be appropriately grouped.

Words		Categories	
Turkey	Pumpkin pie	Christmas	Thanksgiving
Mistletoe	Tree		
Bell	Cranberry sauce		
Santa Claus			

Other headings for the category columns, for example, may be: things that float, things that are mineral, things that are vegetable, things to eat, things to make, things that move, things to wear, things that are found in the country, things that are found in the city, things that grow under the ground, things that fly, things that walk, things that grow, things that run, things that crawl, or things that have wheels.

The child may be asked to sort articles into the following three categories: things found in a grocery store, things found in a hardware store, and things found in a clothing store. He may group objects according to color. Words that might be appropriately used here are: apple, avocado, beet, bread, butter, carrot, cherry, chocolate, corn, egg, milk, peach, pear, pea, orange, potato, grass, snow, squirrel, strawberry, tomato, and watermelon.

Generally three classifications, such as things to eat, things to wear, and things that run, are adequate. There is almost no limit to the number of categories that one can identify.

Additional Thought-initiating Activities

Numerous activities not classifiable under the broad categories suggested above promote the development of concepts necessary for beginning reading. One of these concepts is the meaning of symbols. The child must learn that the word stands for an idea or concept and thus for the real thing. Without this knowledge the child will always be merely a wordcaller.

Getting Ready to Read (29) emphasizes the importance of using the child's knowledge of thousands of spoken words in introducing the child to reading. The pupil has meaning for these words but cannot decipher their printed form. He needs to associate sound with form.

McKee and Harrison (29) note:

How does the child who is learning to read make the correct associations between strange printed forms and familiar spoken forms? It is not uncommon for teachers to tell children what each strange word is. But, as you know, this procedure cannot go on for an unlimited time if the child is to become an independent reader in the sense that, without help from anyone, he can automatically think of the familiar spoken word for which the strange printed form stands. Sooner or later he must gain control of an economical and effective technique—simply a key to the printed code—which he can use to stimulate himself to think quickly the familiar spoken word.[4]

McKee and Harrison go on to point out that the key consists of using together the context and the beginning consonant sound of the word to identify the specific word required. An exercise such as the following teaches this skill.

The teacher reads aloud a series of sentences omitting the final word. The pupil may be told that the words should begin with a specific sound such as *b*. Sample sentences are:

1. I went swimming in a ———— (brook)
2. In the birdhouse I saw a ———— (bird)
3. I use a bat to hit a ———— (ball)
4. I can drive a ———— (bike) [5]

In these exercises the pupil uses the first consonant of the word to help him to arrive at the correct word. Later in actual reading this skill will be useful in identifying words. He will think of a spoken word that fits both the context and the initial letter.

The exercises in Figures 7-7 through 7-12 are illustrative of additional ways for developing conceptual thinking.

Training in Auditory Discrimination

Auditory discrimination is the ability to discriminate between the sounds or phonemes of a language. It is evident that this skill is essential to successful achievement in reading. If the child cannot *hear* sounds correctly, he normally cannot learn to *speak* them correctly. A child cannot pronounce distinctions that he cannot hear (14, p. 302). Furthermore, if he confuses or distorts sounds in speech, it frequently is impossible for him to associate the correct sound with the visual symbol. Thus, inade-

---

[4] Paul McKee and M. Lucile Harrison, *Getting Ready to Read* (Boston: Houghton Mifflin Company, 1962). Reprinted by permission.

[5] Consult *Getting Ready to Read* for numerous similar exercises.

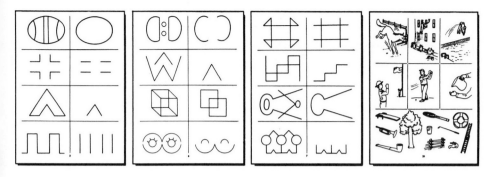

Figure 7-7. Supply the Missing Details*

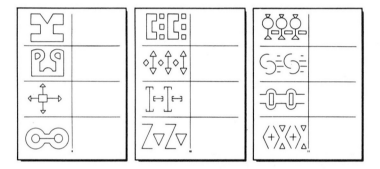

Figure 7-8. Copy the Design or Pattern*

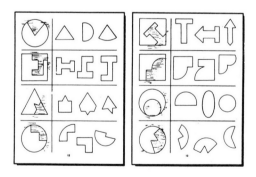

Figure 7-9. Identify the Missing Part*

* These illustrations are from *Independent Activities,* Level 1, Continental Press, Inc., 1958, Elizabethtown, Pa. Plates 5, 6, 7, 9, 10, 11, 12, 13. Reproduced by permission.

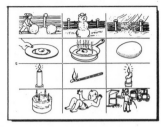

Figure 7-10.   Which Happens First*

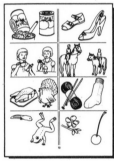

Figure 7-11.   Arrange the Ideas in Order*

Figure 7-12.   Detect the Absurdities*

quate auditory discrimination leads to improper speech and ultimately to an incorrect association of sound and printed symbol.

The learner must discriminate the phonetic elements that make up a word. He must make appropriate associations between the spoken and

---

* These illustrations are from *Independent Activities*, Level 1 and Level 2, and from *Thinking Skills*, Level 1 and 2, Continental Press, Inc., 1958, Elizabethtown, Pa. Reproduced by permission.

the written word. He gradually needs to realize that words that sound alike frequently look alike.

Studies (31,43) show that approximately 20 per cent of the normal speaking population has poor auditory discrimination.

The ability to make auditory discriminations is greatly lessened by high frequency hearing losses. Berry and Eisenson (6, p. 448) point out that the high frequency sounds, *f, v, s, z, sh, zh, th, t, d, p, b, k,* and *g,* determine the intelligibility of what is said. If these sounds are not heard correctly interpretation of what is said becomes more difficult.

Unfortunately, many other children who have not suffered a high frequency hearing loss are unable to discriminate the sounds necessary for accurate speech. Cole (11, p. 282), for example, notes that the average six-year-old is unable to distinguish consistently between the sounds of *g* and *k, m* and *n,* and *p* and *b.* This makes it more difficult to learn to read. Children must learn that words consist of sounds, that the same sound may occur in more than one word, and that one word generally has different sounds than another word.

Other writers have identified additional advantages of successful auditory and visual discrimination. Cordts (13) for example, notes that unless the child learns to differentiate between sounds in words, the foundation for phonics is inadequate. And Durrell and Murphy (18) report that training in auditory discrimination increases general reading achievement. They note that the child who learns to read easily is usually one who notices the distinct sounds in spoken words.

The facts (43) concerning auditory discrimination are these:

1. Children have varying degrees of ability in auditory discrimination.
2. The maturation of the auditory discriminatory skill is gradual and rarely is fully developed before the age of eight.
3. Poor auditory discrimination is related positively to inaccuracies in articulation and pronunciation and/or to poor achievement in reading.
4. The relationship between auditory discrimination and intelligence is essentially negative.
5. As auditory discrimination matures, the learner becomes capable of producing more and more of the sounds of the language. The child gradually learns to fashion his own speech after the speech that he hears.
6. Auditory discrimination can be developed through instruction (40).

Some writers (31) suggest that children whose auditory discrimination is slow in developing might be separately grouped for reading. Groupings based on the pupil's best way of learning or by modality ability might facilitate the task of teaching and enhance learning. Certainly it would appear that a child with a developmental delay in articulation because of slowness in auditory discrimination development might benefit from an emphasis on visual learning until he can correct his own articulation errors as he matures.

The following techniques may prove helpful in teaching auditory discrimination. The child should be tested on each of these exercises. But we drill him only on those aspects that he has not mastered. Some of these exercises are proper only after the child has begun to read.

1. Check gross discriminations for sounds: for example, the voices of specific children; taps on the desk, the radiator, or a bell; songs of a bird, the call of a cow, the chirping of a grasshopper, the neigh of a horse; the various sounds of a rhythm band. Each instrument may be associated with a physical activity, such as skipping, laughing, clapping of the hands, or tiptoeing.

2. List the names of children beginning with the same sound. Ask children to give other words *beginning* with the same sound.

3. Have children note similarities or differences in the initial consonants of pairs of words: for example, the similarities in *can* and *cat* and the differences in *cat* and *bat*.

   Picture exercises are especially beneficial here. The child is shown three pictures, the first of which may be that of a bell. Of the other two pictures, the name of only one begins with *b*. The teacher asks the pupil to pick out the one that begins with the same sound as *bell* and to draw a line to it.

4. Provide the pupils with three pictures and ask them to pick out the two pictures whose names begin with the same sound. Figure 7-13 (9) illustrates the technique.

   The objects in Figure 7-13, reading across the rows of boxes, are: box, gum, bed; nest, duck, needle; moon, monkey, dog; pillow, muff, pie; top, table, horse; lamp, letter, pig; ring, jug, rabbit; cake, pear, cane; feather, fan, leaf; door, watch, doll; goat, gate, boat; wagon, ball, wall; sock, lock, saw; house, mouse, hat. In the margin are: sun, valentine, vase; jack-in-the-box, telephone, jump rope. The child is asked to discover the two pictures whose names begin with the same sound.

5. After demonstrating the *b* sound, for example, ask pupils to provide words with *b* that answer questions like the following:
   a. What do you use to hit a ball?
   b. In what do you sleep?
   c. What word do you use when you want to say that something is large?

This exercise teaches the child to use both contextual and auditory clues to identify the correct word.

6. After demonstrating a given sound, for example, *f*, present the pupils with a mimeographed page of pictures. Ask them to put a line through the objects whose names do not begin with an *f*. The page may contain pictures of a hat, fox, foot, box, cat, hammer, finger, fan, and file.

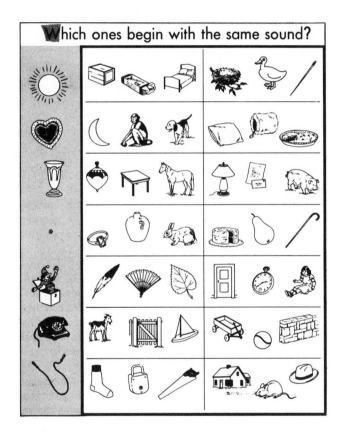

Figure 7-13 *

7. Explain the meaning of rhyme and illustrate it by providing words that actually rhyme, such as am, ham, jam, Pam, ram or at, hat, mat, Pat, cat, rat, fat.
8. Read simple verses to children and ask them to note the simi-

* *Bulletin Board Lessons for First Graders or Important Phonetic Skills* (Chicago: Scott, Foresman and Company, 1958). Reproduced by permission.

lar-sounding words at the end of each line. Ask them to identify the words that rhyme with a given word, as for example,
"stick." Common rhymes are: "Hickory, Dickory, Dock," "Jack
Be Nimble," and "Wee Willie Winkie."

9. Ask children to provide rhymes for simple words such as cat,
bet, lit, lot, but. The game "Quiz Panel" [6] is quite adaptable
to this task. The teacher selects a panel of four pupils who sit
in the front of the room. He pronounces a word and individual
members of the panel must provide a rhyming word. When
the panel member misses, he is replaced by another member
of the class. A variant form of this exercise asks the child to do
picture reading. The child is shown three pictures, the first of
which is a bat. Of the other two pictures, only one rhymes with
bat. The teacher asks him to pick out the one that rhymes with
bat.

10. Suggest three words, two of which rhyme. Ask children to pick
out the word that does not rhyme with the other two words.
Two small booklets, entitled *Rhyming,* are available from
Continental Press, Inc., for teaching rhyming skills. The booklets contain 24 lessons.

11. Ask children to note similarities and differences in final consonants of pairs of words.

12. Have children listen for and give words beginning or ending
with the same consonant blend or speech consonant. The
order should be: beginning consonant blend, final consonant
blend, initial speech consonant, and final speech consonant.

13. Have children listen for and give monosyllabic words containing the same short vowel.

14. Have children listen for and give monosyllabic words containing the same long vowel.

15. Have children listen for and give words of two or more syllables.

16. Have children read a printed word and then from three pictures have them select those two whose names rhyme with the
printed word (9). Figure 7-14 illustrates this exercise. The objects in Figure 7-14 are: cuff, muff, ball; leaf, clown, crown;
tree, cup, bee; moon, coat, goat; star, jar, bell; pan, pipe, fan;
bed, sled, bib; sun, saw, gun; hook, boat, book; snake, cake,
nest.

17. Have children associate consonant sounds with the appro-

[6] Mary E. Platts, Sister Rose Marguerite, and Esther Shumaker, *Spice* (Stevensville, Michigan: Educational Service, Inc., 1960) p. 143.

priate visual symbol. In Figure 7-15 (9) the child identifies each picture, says its name, and then locates that picture whose name begins with the same sound as symbolized by the letter at the top of each box. The pictures in Figure 7-15 are: dish, fish; hen, pen; barn, yarn; nest, vest; lock, sock; mouse, house;

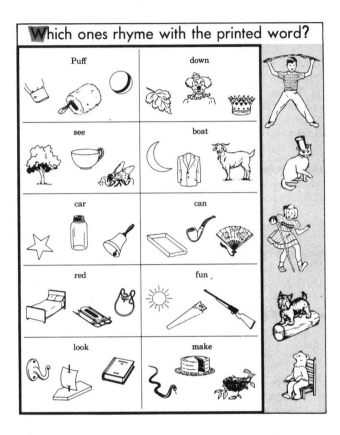

Figure 7-14 *

kitten, mitten; goat, coat; tacks, jacks; ball, wall; gun, sun; corn, horn; fan, pan; top, mop; cake, rake; tire, fire; bat, hat; and coat, boat. The same exercise may be used with final consonants, beginning and ending consonant blends and speech consonants, and with short and long vowels.

* *Bulletin Board Lessons for First Graders on Important Phonetic Skills* (Chicago: Scott, Foresman and Company, 1958). Reproduced by permission.

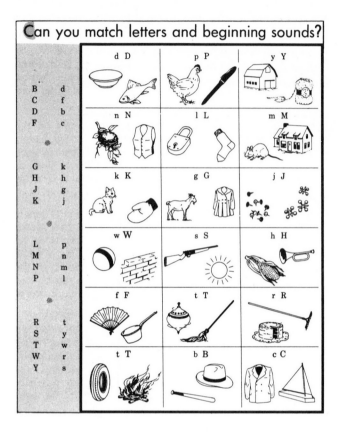

Figure 7-15 *

TRAINING IN VISUAL DISCRIMINATION

Surely one of the most important skills needed for reading is the ability to visually analyze and synthesize printed words. The pupil must be able to sort out and to distinguish differences between visual stimuli (20). He must be able to note similarities and differences in the form of objects, pictures, geometric figures, and words. Generally children have learned to discriminate between gross figures and objects. They see the differences between a cat and a dog and between circles, triangles, and squares. They also have learned something about words. Long before they come to school they have identified signs such as "Phillips 66," "Stop," "Wichita," or "Kansas." They have noted that some words are long and others short,

* *Bulletin Board Lessons for First Graders on Important Phonetic Skills* (Chicago: Scott, Foresman and Company, 1958). Reproduced by permission.

that some have ascending letters and others have descending letters, and that some words look alike and that others look different.

Unfortunately, it is not always possible to know whether the pupil has used the correct process in identifying a word. Unless he has identified the word through some peculiarity of the word itself, he may not have learned or at least has learned incorrectly. Children frequently learn to identify a word by a simple association process. Perhaps the word "Stop" is "Stop" only when it is seen at the end of a block and appears on an octagonal-shaped figure. The word "Bob" is "Bob" only when it appears on that card with the dirt splotch in the bottom left-hand corner.

Thus the question arises, "What should the teacher emphasize in visual discrimination training? Ever since there has been concern with identifying the factors that were indicative of both reading readiness and achievement, visual discrimination has been accorded a primary position. Gradually, concern focused on those specific visual discrimination tasks that are most predictive of reading readiness. Researchers identified the importance of visual discrimination of letters (15) or words. Some emphasized shape matching (36) or the ability to keep a figure in mind against distraction (19).

A series of studies at Boston University (17) suggests that most children are able to match one capital letter with another capital letter and one lower case letter with another. It was found that the matching of nonword forms and pictures had little benefit on letter or word perception. The learning in the former did not seem to transfer to performance on the latter.

Shea (39) found that the ability to discriminate visually between words was a significant indicator of reading readiness when the sight method of instruction was used.

Muehl and King's experiment (32) tends to indicate that visual discrimination training from the beginning should be with word and letter stimuli. Matching of animal pictures or geometric forms does not seem to have transfer value to word discrimination.

Barrett (3) found that being able to discriminate, recognize, and name letters and numbers was the best single predictor, but pattern copying and word matching were strongly related to first-grade reading achievement. However, other factors (auditory discrimination, language facility, story sense, etc.) still contributed as much or more to the prediction of first-grade reading.

In a later study Barrett (4) found that recognition of letters had the highest relationship with beginning reading achievement; discrimination of beginning sounds had the next highest relationship, but ending sounds in words, shape completion, ability to copy a sentence, and discrimination of vowel sounds in words were also positively related.

Wheelock and Silvaroli (44) found a significant difference in visual discrimination ability among kindergarten children from high and low socioeconomic groups, and their study indicated that the ability to make instant responses of recognition to the capital letters can be taught. The children from the lower extreme of the socioeconomic continuum seemed to profit most from the training.

Reading requires the ability to distinguish each word from every other word. The pupil must be relatively more skilled in noting the differences among words than in noting the similarities.

One cannot infer that all matching is useless. Some children may not have learned this simple step. The teacher uses a matching exercise as a diagnostic device. When the pupil has not developed adequately in this regard he should stress matching of objects, signs, and words. He starts teaching at the level the child has attained. The child must learn matching to the extent that he consistently responds to *b* as *b* or to *was* as *was*.

Certain other principles should guide the teacher in his teaching of visual discrimination. He must be careful not to overdrill on any one skill. If the pupil can do a specific exercise with ease, it is imperative that with him he work on a higher-level skill. There perhaps is no quicker way to destroy interest in learning to read than to force the pupil to engage in a readiness activity that he already has mastered.

The teacher also needs to develop some sequence in teaching the letters. He must begin with simple forms and proceed to more difficult ones. Some letters are readily distinguishable, for example, *x* and *b*. Others are not so readily distinguished. Children have a tendency to confuse *b* and *d, p* and *b, p* and *d, p* and *q, u* and *n, m* and *w, o* and *e, o* and *c, e* and *c,* and *g* and *b*. These letters profitably might be introduced at different times to minimize interference.

In recent years there has been an emphasis on the use of colored symbols to differentiate the phonemes of the language. Jones (25) found that color was a definite aid to visual perception among kindergarten children.

Finally, in visual discrimination exercises, the emphasis is not on reading. We do not specifically teach the pupil to associate a printed word with a spoken word or with an object or experience. The pupil must note differences in words. He should be able to verbalize the differences in words. He should be able to verbalize the difference in the initial letter, the final letter, or in the general form of the words. We expect to teach him "what to look for," so he may identify words as distinct units of language.

A desirable sequence of exercises in visual discrimination has not been identified. In many instances it has not been possible to develop exercises that are distinct from tests of intelligence. The following exercises are merely suggestive of some activities that may be used to develop discrimination between words, syllables, and letters:

1. Check on the pupil's discrimination of gross form; pictures, objects and geometric figures; differences in color; or ability to fit the pieces of a puzzle. The child may have to learn the blues or the reds in sweaters, dresses, and trousers worn by his classmates. He may learn to distinguish various shades of green in nature. And he may learn to mix colors so as to produce various shades (30).

   Children should learn to trace a design, to visualize spatial relationships, and to think and reason spatially; they must develop eye-hand coordination and visual motor skills. It is believed by many that reversals are errors in visual and spatial location.

   Four small books, *Visual Discrimination,* Level 1 and Level 3, and *Visual-Motor Skills,* Level 1 and Level 2, are available from Continental Press, Inc. Each booklet contains 24 lessons and teaches visual motor and spatial skills.

2. Present each pupil with a copy of his name. Let him note the differences and similiarities between his name and that of some of his classmates.

   An exercise of this type teaches gross discrimination in word forms. Exercises similar to the following teach the same skill.

   Encircle the Word That Is Different

cat—cry—cat	boy—bed—bed	car—her—car
day—yes—yes	fly—bee—fly	and—why—and

   Put a Line Under the Two Words That Are Alike

yes—yes	see—fell	mat—met
cat—bat	saw—saw	rat—bat
on—no	fan—pan	in—on

3. Provide each pupil with a mimeographed page of letters and/ or monosyllabic words that are arranged in columns by pairs. Let him encircle those pairs that are different.

   An exercise of this type teaches gross discrimination in letters. The following exercises call for the same type of skill.

   Encircle the Letter That Is Different

s s k	m l m	p p b
h y h	n m n	s s a
b b d	r r z	n n v

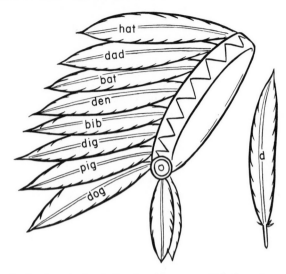

Color the feathers in the Indian headdress on which there is a word
that begins with the same letter as the letter in the feather on the right.

Draw a Line Between the Two Letters That Are Alike

| b a | k t | v t | s s | r h |
| c b | t l | h t | a z | b b |

*Draw a Line from Each Word to the Letter That
Is the Same as the Letter That Begins the Word*

bat ___ b		bib	t
hat	p	hen	h
map	t	mop	n
net	h	nut	h
pan	m	pet	m
top	n	tub	b

4. Present three words and let the pupil select the word that is
   repeated more than once in the sequence: for example, can,
   pan, can. By increasing the number of words to five the task is
   made more difficult.

5. Present three words and let the pupil select the two words
   that have the same beginning consonant, the same ending
   consonant, or the same two-letter beginning or ending consonant.

6. Present three words and let the pupil select the two words
   that have the same vowel.

7. Present three words and let the pupil select the two polysyllabic words. One of the words should be monosyllabic.

DEVELOPING A KNOWLEDGE OF THE ALPHABET

Studies (1,27,33) suggest that a knowledge of the names of the letters of the alphabet may be one of the best predictors of a child's readiness for reading. They also indicate that the ability to write the letters dictated and to identify the letters named are important indicators of first-grade reading achievement (3).

We can only surmise what the reason for his finding might be, but a child who has associated a name with a letter already has learned basic reading skills. He has associated some meaning with a printed symbol and he has learned to discriminate it visually from other forms.

Whereas the studies do not indicate that the pupil should be able to name all the letters or that he should know them in alphabetical order, this knowledge is not without value. Eventually, the pupil will find it necessary to file his words, to locate them, and to use the picture dictionary.

The names of both capital and small letters should be taught first, but from the start the pupil should realize that each letter both has a name and represents a sound. Some children will have learned to identify letters and to name them by the time they enter kindergarten. Others will have to be taught in school.

The following techniques may prove helpful in teaching the names and sounds of the letters:

1. Let each child become familiar with the specific letters used in his name. Point out the similarities and differences among the letters and tell him that these marks are called letters. Some pupils will learn to differentiate capital and lower case letters at this level.

2. Tell the child that the little marks or letters in his name have names. Begin teaching of names with a few letters at a time.

3. Identify each letter with a key word: *b* with bee; *c* with cat; *s* with sun. Teach the pupil that each letter also has a sound.

4. Let each child trace the specific letters being studied. After some practice ask him to reproduce it from memory. The name of the letter should be said while he is tracing the letter.

5. Expose the pupil to ABC books, letter cards, and picture dictionaries. Demonstrate that the reason that the sounds at the beginning and end of words are alike is because they have the same letter at the beginning or at the end.

6. Teach the pupil that the same name is given to two different manuscript or printed forms, the capital and the lower case letter. An exercise, like the one shown in Figure 7-16, that re-

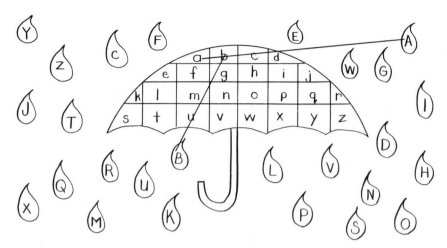

Figure 7-16 *

quires the pupil to draw a line between the capital letter and the appropriate lower case letter teaches this skill.

7. Let the pupil arrange the letter cards in alphabetical order, beginning with a few letters at a time.
8. Ask the pupil to locate or arrange words in an alphabetical list.

TRAINING IN LEFT-TO-RIGHT PROGRESSION

Reading is a left-to-right activity. This is a new concept for young children. They have not been taught to observe directions in their everyday perceptions. A dog looks like a dog whether the eye movement is from left to right or from right to left. Unfortunately, in reading a word this is not so. The letters, s-a-w, read from left to right say *saw*, but read from right to left say *was*. Thus, one of the first requirements in learning to read is the learning of new habits of perception. The child must perceive from left to right.

The term commonly used to indicate that the child is making the wrong directional attack on words is reversing.

There are two major points of view as to the origin of reversals. One represented by Orton (34) suggests that reversals result from lack of

* Mary E. Platts, Sister Rose Marguerite, and Esther Shumaker, *Spice* (Stevensville, Michigan: Educational Service, Inc., 1960) p. 97. Reproduced by permission.

cerebral dominance and are prime factors in reading disability. Another point of view suggests that reversals are a universal phenomenon and do not necessarily cause poor reading. Spache (41) suggests that they indicate an unfamiliarity with the symbols that the child is trying to learn. Studies also indicate that reversals may be caused by lack of maturation, visual defects, the habit of perceiving objects from right to left, overemphasizing the final sounds of words by concentrating on word families, and the exclusive use of the configuration method. If a word is taught to the child as a Gestalt or as a total configuration, the child has no need to differentiate between right and left. The word will be the same and he can "read" it if he remembers its sounds and meaning.

During the early school years reversals have been considered to be normal phenomena. Unfortunately, this assumption may have hindered progress in working with the difficulties. Reversals certainly become a serious problem in reading when they continue beyond the second or third grade. After those years children who reverse generally do not make normal progress in reading.

Reversals are of various kinds. Children may reverse certain letters, such as *b* for *d* or *p* for *q*. They may read an entire word backward, such as "was" for "saw." Or they may alter the position of certain letters in words, such as "aminal" for "animal." We thus speak of static reversals, kinetic reversals, and instances of transposition.

The elimination of reversals in reading is not easy. No one method has proved completely effective. In the following exercises we have attempted to suggest some that are suitable both for prereaders and for children at higher levels.

1. Teach children the meaning of left and right by showing them the difference between their right and their left hand or by playing the game "Simon Says." Here the child receives an oral direction sometimes with and sometimes without the words, "Simon Says." When the direction is not preceded by these words and the child carries out the direction, the child is out of the game. The teacher's directions should emphasize distinctions between right and left as: "Put your right foot forward." "Raise your left hand."

   Teachers in the Napa, California kindergarten project (12) have found that when children are taught the *b* and *p* with the letters which circle to the right (*B, P, J, p, b, h, m, n, r*) and when *d* and *q* are taught with letters which circle to the left (*c, a, d, q, e, f*) that reversals have been almost completely eliminated. Part of the pupil's problem is the discovery of what the critical dimensions of difference are such as "curve left," "curve right," and "obliqueness." (26)

2. Ask the child to draw an arrow pointing to the right under the first letter of a word.

3. In arranging a series of pictures into a narrative sequence the child should be required to follow a left-to-right sequence.

4. Point out to pupils that the left side of a word is the beginning of that word and that the right side is the end of that word.

5. Use mechanical devices such as the *Controlled Reader* to demonstrate the reading sequence. This particular machine permits thought units to appear in a left-to-right sequence.

6. In referring to a line of print, to a caption under a picture, or to written directions on the bulletin board, sweep the hand from left to right while indicating that in reading this is the required direction.

7. Demonstrate to children how meaning is distorted when the word is read from right to left. "Jim was in the barn" is quite different from "Jim saw in the barn." Some success may be obtained by teaching the child what a reversal is, how it is made, and what the results look like.

8. Let children engage in left-to-right tracing exercises. Initially these are finger tracing exercises; crayolas and pencils may be used later. These exercises also develop skill in staying on a line or in making an accurate return sweep. The child may trace a line, numbers, words, and strokes, or he may draw geometric figures in left-to-right progression. The "reading" of the calendar also is helpful in developing the left-to-right skill.

9. In demonstrating left-to-right progression in monosyllabic words, put each letter in a block and number the blocks in a left-to-right direction.

10. Require the pupil to write only one word on a line. The first letter is placed at the extreme left edge of the paper.

11. Require the pupil to cover the word with a card and move it slowly to the right, thus exposing one letter at a time in a left-to-right progression. The same process may be followed in reading an entire line of print.

12. Let the pupil engage in choral reading, provide alphabetizing and dictionary exercises, and let him use the typewriter.

13. Demonstrate to children that by changing the *d* to *b* in the word *dad* it becomes *bad*. Children should learn that words are pronounced in a left-to-right direction and that this is done by beginning with the first letter. Ask them to form other words from a list of given words by changing the first letter.

14. Let the pupil trace a word written in manuscript or cursive script. As he traces the word, he should speak out each part of the word. Some authorities suggest that there must be finger contact while tracing; others, that there should be pencil contact. The child continues this until he can reproduce the form from memory. He should have met the word in a reading context, and eventually files the word in an alphabetical file. Another method has the child write the word as the teacher speaks the sounds of the word in a left to right progression.

15. After the child has learned to read and can handle the alphabet, the teacher may want to check the pupil on a list of words similar to the one below. Each word, if reversed, will make a different word.

nab	net	pit	mad	tug	pal
bat	pin	top	den	gum	ram
bin	bun	bad	dog	wed	rap
but	on	bag	nod	won	rat
pan	Pam	Mac	dot	bus	saw
mat	tap	cod	bud	gas	

READINESS MATERIALS

Each of the basal reading series has a reading readiness program. *Getting Ready to Read* (Houghton Mifflin Company, Boston, 1962) is an example of such a program. In six units the pupil is taught how to use the spoken context, to distinguish letter forms from one another, to listen for beginning sounds, to associate letter sounds and forms, to use spoken context and letter-sound associations, and to use spoken context and the first letter in a printed word.

The *Getting Ready to Read* program is accompanied by letter cards, objects to illustrate and teach the sounds, containers to hold the objects, Letto Cards (a form of letter bingo), picture and key cards, and a pocket chart. Each lesson is carefully developed for the teacher. The *Teacher's Manual* tells the teacher how to prepare the lesson, how to develop it, and how to provide for individual differences.

In addition to the readiness materials that accompany the basal reading series, there have been developed books, games, audio-visual aids, readers, and other supplementary materials that are designed to help the pupil through the *preparatory* stage of reading. They are designed to develop the pupil's discrimination skills, his ability to follow a story sequence, to associate meaning with pictures and words, to see relationships, to sense likenesses and differences, and to identify a printed symbol.

Let us then suggest some supplementary readiness materials that may be useful during the preparatory reading period.[7]

1. *ABC Preprimer* [Hayes School Publishing Company]. This revised duplicating edition includes a color dictionary and stresses similarity in words and objects.

2. *Adventures in Reading Readiness Workbook* [Noble & Noble, Publishers, Inc.]. This workbook for kindergarten and first grade includes drill in phonics and emphasizes a vocabulary of one hundred basic words.

3. *Beckley-Cardy Reading Readiness Materials* [Beckley-Cardy Company].
    a. *Reading Readiness Picture Cards,* Sets 1, 2, & 3.
    b. *Ideal Reading Charts*
        1. *Reading Readiness Charts*
        2. *Initial and Final Consonant Charts*
        3. *Blends and Digraphs Charts*
        4. *Vowel Charts*
    c. *Ideal Magic Card Sets*
    d. *Primary Reading Cards*
    e. *Alphabet Flash Cards*

4. *Color ABC* [The Platt & Munk Co., Inc.]. This book has 26 full-page color pictures to illustrate both capital and lower case letters.

5. *Continental Press Reading Readiness Program* [Continental Press, Inc.]. This program consists of 12 titles covering rhyming, visual motor skills, visual discrimination, beginning sounds, independent activities, and thinking skills. All materials are sold in liquid-duplicator form so they can be reproduced for classroom use.

6. *Fun With Tom and Betty* [Ginn & Company]. This reading readiness book is accompanied by a record with songs for the reading readiness program.

7. *Getting Reading to Read* [Highlights Inc.]. This handbook helps youngsters to develop left-to-right movement, to identify shapes and symbols, to follow directions, and to think.

8. *Getting Ready to Read Workbook* [E. M. Hale & Company].

9. *Let's Learn to Read* [Steck-Vaughn Company]. This readiness workbook introduces the pupil to the necessary skills for success-

---

[7] You may want to consult: Lawrence W. Carrillo, *Informal Reading-readiness Experiences* (San Francisco: Chandler Publishing Company, 1964); also, Allen Berger, "Reading Readiness: A Bibliography," *Elementary English,* 45 (February, 1968) 184–189.

ful reading. It develops orientational and directional awareness, proficiency in oral language, visual and auditory discrimination, and ability to follow directions.

10. *Let's See* [Webster Publishing Company]. This book offers a
readiness program in word analysis for grade one.

11. *Match-Me* [Benton Review Publishing Company]. This is a readiness game on the kindergarten and preprimer level that requires
the child to match pictures.

12. *McCormick-Mathers Puzzle Series* [McCormick-Mathers Publishing Company]. This series of *New Puzzle Pages* and *My Puzzle
Books* for kindergarten through grade two develops visual discrimination, word attack skills, phonics, sight vocabulary, and
comprehension.

13. *On the Way to Reading* [Webster Publishing Company]. This
book uses rhymes as a means of recognizing words and puts
special emphasis on consonant and vowel sounds.

14. *Our Book* [Allyn and Bacon, Inc.]. *Our Book* offers a prereadi-
ness program developing correct eye movement, visual-auditory
discrimination, and oral expression. It is a huge book that can
stand alone with three ledges on each page. Children place
objects on the ledges in a left-to-right order.

15. *Pick-N Say-It Kit* [O'Connor Remedial Services]. This kit consists
of ten charts, forty flash cards, and nineteen color and number
sheets. It develops readiness for number words, color words,
and other simple nouns, and teaches left-to-right orientation and
visual discrimination. It is especially useful with slow learners
and handicapped children.

16. *Picture Readiness Game* [Garrard Press]. This consists of six
lotto cards with six pictures on each card designed to develop
attention and the perception of details.

17. *Rhymes for Children* [Expression Company]. This is only one
of a great number of speech and readiness aids offered by this
company. Other titles include *Jack-in-the-Box, Galloping Sounds,
Games and Jingles for Speech Development, Speech Drills for
Children in Form of Play, The First Steps in Speech Training,
Let's Play Hide and Seek* (training in *f, v, sh, th, l, s, z, r, th, ch,
j, s,* and *z*), *Sounds for Little Folks, The Child's Book of Speech
Sounds, Sound Ladder Game, Speech-O—A Phonetic Game,*
and *Sound and Articulation Card Game.*

18. *See-Quees* [Judy Company]. These are silk-screened materials
on heavy board telling in picture form such common stories as
"Three Pigs," "Goldilocks" and "Gingerbread Boy." Another
series develops the sequential skill through natural phenomena
and action stories. A third series is devoted to nursery rhymes.

All are designed to promote reading readiness and develop skill in story-telling, problem solving, and left-to-right movement. They are suitable for ages four to eight.

19. *Sullivan Reading Readiness Materials* [Behavioral Research Laboratories, Palo Alto, California]. One set of these materials consists of a four-book readiness program designed to prepare the pupil for the Sullivan Remedial Reading Program. The materials employ programming principles and use a synthetic phonics approach.

Another set consists of six Giant Books, designed to teach directions, colors, the alphabet, and simple reading and spelling. The set includes six teacher's manuals, two alphabet strips, and a wooden easel.

20. *Self-Help Reading Series* [Educational Publishing Corporation]. This series consists of:
    a. *Self-Help Wall Charts* (to teach new words to beginners)
    b. Book 1: *Reading Readiness*
    c. Book 2: *First Steps in Reading* (this book is on the preprimer and primer levels).
    d. Book 3: *On the Way in Reading* (first-grade level).

21. *Work and Play with Words* [Schmitt, Hall and McCreary Company]. This is a preparatory book for the preprimer and teaches the pupil that printed and written words are symbols of ideas and that such symbols talk.

THE USE OF READINESS TESTS

Observation of children and recording these observations on Readiness Inventories are a good means for identifying the child who is ready for reading. Teachers have for years made use of informal techniques to gauge a child's readiness and have been rather successful in their efforts. In this chapter, however, we have discussed six aspects of reading readiness that may be more easily and more accurately determined through standardized tests.

How good are reading readiness tests? Studies (37,46) indicate that they predict the general reading achievement of a total group of readers rather well, but the tests are probably not able to predict with sufficient accuracy the reading achievement of individual pupils. A good score on a reading readiness test does not necessarily mean that the pupil is ready for reading. There is, furthermore, no evidence to suggest that readiness test scores should be used as standards that the pupil must attain. It also appears that reading readiness tests should not be used alone to group children for reading instruction. Barrett (2) found that certain subtests

in readiness tests, such as letter and word matching, seem to be most related to reading growth. Bagford (1) reported that the subtest, "Giving
the Names of Letters," on the *Harrison-Stroud Reading Readiness Profiles* was most closely associated with the vocabulary score on *Iowa Tests
of Basic Skills*. He also found that readiness test scores were as significantly related to success in reading in grades four through six as to success in grade one.

Other studies reported by Weintraub (45) indicate that the number
subtests are more predictive of reading achievement than are other tests.
Bremer (7) points out that perhaps the greatest value of readiness tests
is in the diagnosis of the pupil's deficiencies. They indicate areas of
strength and weakness and help the teacher in making adequate provisions for individual needs. They help in the planning of children's learning experiences. They should increase the teacher's efficiency in teaching.

The following readiness tests seem especially useful:

1. *American School Reading Readiness Test* [Bobbs-Merrill Com-
    pany, Indianapolis 6, Indiana]. This group test measures: pic-
    ture vocabulary, discrimination of forms, letter form recognition,
    letter combination recognition, word matching, following direc-
    tions, and memory for designs.

2. *Binion-Beck Reading Readiness Test* [Acorn Publishing Company,
    Long Island, New York]. This readiness test requires the pupil
    to observe and note details. It consists of four subtests con-
    taining a large variety of picture recognition items, likenesses
    and differences items, motor control items, picture interpretation
    items, coordination items, visual discrimination items, sustained
    attention items, etc.

3. *Diagnostic Reading Tests: Reading Readiness Booklet* [Mountain
    Home, North Carolina]. This group test measures the child's
    ability to grasp relationships, his skill in eye-hand and motor
    coordination, his visual and auditory discrimination, and his
    vocabulary.

4. *Gates-MacGinitie Reading Readiness Test* [Bureau of Publica-
    tions, Teachers College, Columbia University, New York]. This
    test, for use at the end of kindergarten or the beginning of grade
    one, consists of seven subtests: listening comprehension, auditory
    discrimination, visual discrimination, following directions, letter
    recognition, visual-motor coordination, and auditory blending.
    An eighth subtest, word recognition, is included for simple iden-
    tification of those children who already have some reading skill.
    It is recommended that administration of the test be divided into
    four separate parts over a two-day period. It takes about one-
    half hour to administer each part of the test.

5. *Harrison-Stroud Reading Readiness Profiles* [Houghton Mifflin Company, Boston, Massachusetts]. This test is designed for kindergarten–first grade and measures the ability to use symbols, to make visual discriminations, to use the context, to make auditory discriminations, to use the context and auditory clues, and to give the names of letters.

6. *Lee-Clark Reading Readiness Test* [California Test Bureau, Los Angeles, California]. This group test measures the ability to note similarities and differences in letter forms; it measures the child's vocabulary and concepts; and it tests the ability to match letters with letters and words with words.

7. *Maturity Level for School Entrance and Reading Readiness* [American Guidance Service, Inc., Minneapolis 14, Minnesota]. This test helps to identify children mature enough to enter first grade, having readiness in reading regardless of high or low chronological age. It is a revision of the School Readiness Inventory. It yields a Maturity Level score and a Reading Readiness Score.

8. *The Metropolitan Readiness Test* [Harcourt, Brace and World, Inc., New York, New York]. This group test contains measures of (1) word meaning (the child selects from four pictures the one that is a picture of the word used by the examiner); (2) sentence meaning (the child must comprehend a sentence); (3) information (child picks the picture that depicts what the tester is describing); (4) matching (the child must select from four pictures one that matches with a sample picture); (5) numbers (various knowledge about numbers is tested) and (6) copying (this measures visual perception, motor control, and the tendency toward spatial reversal). A supplementary test requires the child to draw a man. It measures perceptual maturity and motor control.

9. *Monroe Reading Aptitude Test* [Houghton Mifflin Company, Boston, Massachusetts]. This test, part group and part individual, is designed to analyze five elements required for successful reading: visual discrimination, auditory discrimination, motor control, oral speed and articulation, and language.

10. *Murphy-Durrell Diagnostic Reading Analysis* [Harcourt, Brace and World, New York, New York]. This instrument tests for identifying separate sounds in spoken words, identifying capital and lower case letters named by the examiner, and recognizing sight words one hour after they have been taught. It thus measures auditory and visual discrimination and learning rate.

11. *Perceptual Forms Test* [Winter Haven Lions Research Foundation, Inc., Winter Haven, Florida]. This test measures visual development either in groups or individually.

12. *Reading Readiness Test* [Steck-Vaughn Company, Austin, Texas]. The test has ten parts: differentiation of letters; differentiation of pairs of letters; differentiation of words; differentiation of phrases; differentiation of pictures and designs; recognition of words; recognition of patterns; familiarity with names of objects; functions of objects; and interpretation of spoken sentences.

13. *Scholastic Reading Readiness Test* [Scholastic Testing Service, Inc., Bensenville, Illinois]. This test measures knowledge and understanding of facts, visual discrimination, and sound-symbol association.

14. *Steinbach Test of Reading Readiness* [Scholastic Testing Service, Inc., Bensenville, Illinois]. This test measures letter identification, word identification, ability to follow direction, and ability to relate words and pictures.

A program, called KELP (Kindergarten Evaluation of Learning Potential) and available from McGraw-Hill Book Company, offers another way of evaluating learning potential. It includes measures of auditory perception, visual discrimination, language skills, number concepts, physical adeptness, and social interaction.

SUMMARY

Although the various readiness skills have been discussed separately in this chapter, they must be developed simultaneously. The child should advance in each on a somewhat even front. Each day the teacher needs to help the pupil to grow in conceptual thinking, in auditory discrimination, in visual discrimination, in his knowledge of the alphabet, and in his ability to deal with reading as a left-to-right activity. The teacher begins with each child at the level that he has attained in *each* of these skills. And each of the readiness tasks is further developed in the first and second grade.

The child needs to learn that words stand for the real thing—that they have meaning. He needs to learn to use the context to identify the word, and he needs to use the spoken context *and the beginning sound* of a word to identify the word that makes sense in the sentence.

Readiness workbooks, offered as a part of the various basal series, provide numerous exercises for the development of these skills. In this chapter we have suggested numerous other manuals and materials useful in developing reading readiness.

Readiness exercises are valuable only in as far as they make it possible for the pupil to acquire a reading skill with greater ease. The teacher constantly needs to explore the "transfer value" of the readiness materials. He must constantly evaluate the usefulness of these materials.

QUESTIONS FOR DISCUSSION

1. Define reading readiness.
2. Discuss how a field trip to a fire station might help a child to develop conceptual thinking and thereby improve his readiness for reading.
3. What is the purpose of picture storybooks and picture dictionaries in the readiness program?
4. Examine one of the reading readiness manuals, especially one of those offered by a basal reading series, and list the skills in which the series gives practice. Prepare yourself in the teaching of one of these skills and present it in class.
5. What are the stages of development in conceptualization?
6. What factors in reading readiness are most amenable to training?
7. Discuss five activities that are useful in teaching conceptualization.
8. What do we know about the development of auditory discriminatory skills?
9. Discuss five activities that teach auditory discrimination.
10. What is the value of teaching matching of objects, pictures, and letters to beginning readers?
11. Is there any identifiable sequence in teaching visual discriminatory skills, especially of the letters of the alphabet, and is it desirable to follow the sequence?
12. Explain the origin of reversals and suggest activities for remediation.
13. Examine, administer, and evaluate one of the readiness tests suggested at the end of the chapter.
14. Discuss:
    a. Reading readiness is the teachable moment for each of the reading skills.
    b. The poor reader is distinguished from the good reader (1) by his inability to perceive the relationship to one another of the details within the total word shape, or (2) by his inability to perceive parts and details, in which case he perceives unanalyzable wholes. He is weak in the ability to analyze the visual and auditory structures of words, and in the ability to synthesize phonetic units to form whole words.
    c. Knowledge of the names of the letters of the alphabet shows a higher relation to achievement in reading than does mental age.

d. The names of the letters should be taught before the sounds of the letters are introduced.

e. Reversals after the third grade tend to be associated with poor reading. This is true whether they are interpreted as symptoms of left or crossed dominance or a spatial disorganization and figure ground disturbances.

f. The more similar the symbols, the greater is the tendency to reverse.

g. Retarded readers before the age of nine tend to have greater difficulty in distinguishing right from left than do unselected children.

h. Retarded readers and young children have excessive difficulty with the order and orientation of shapes, especially words.

LEARNING TO READ

part **IV**

Part IV of this book is composed of four chapters. It is the heart of the book in that it is devoted primarily to the problems of teaching the child to read. Chapter 8 is perhaps the most significant chapter. It attempts to delineate the process of word identification and discusses the associative nature of learning to read. It presents principles and guidelines for a reading method.

Chapters 9 through 11 attempt to apply the principles formulated in Chapter 8. Chapter 9 is a general overview of the total elementary program. It discusses the actual process of teaching reading, the pros and cons of various types of grouping within the classroom, and the skills that need to be developed during the primary and intermediate grades.

Chapters 10 and 11 put special emphasis on linguistic phonics. These chapters flow from the conviction that the learner must develop a general coding system and that it is the coding system that fosters independence and self-direction in the identification and recognition process. Phonics training may help the child to develop such a system.

Identification
and Association

Meaning is an absolute prerequisite in reading. Even so, it is only one aspect of the reading process. Reading cannot occur unless the pupil can identify and recognize the printed symbol. The pupil cannot read unless he can associate the appropriate meaning with the appropriate symbol.

This chapter consequently concerns itself with two elements: (*1*) the identification of the printed symbol, and (*2*) the association of meaning with the symbol.

First, let us examine how the child learns to associate meaning with the appropriate symbol. Logically, identification of the symbol comes before the association of meaning with it. However, the latter phase is more easily discussed and is much less controversial than is reading method.

READING AS AN ASSOCIATIVE PROCESS

Learning almost universally involves an association of the unknown with the known. To understand this process it is well to acquaint ourselves with the "classical conditioning" experiment.

Before we do this let us make a few observations. Association of meaning with a symbol and "reading" are quite different from the identification of a symbol. The ability to cognize symbolic units, to *identify or recognize words,* is not predictable by the IQ. The IQ best predicts the pupil's ability to take meaning to the symbolic unit, to cognize semantic units, or to excel in verbal comprehension (38).

"What is the basic word identification skill?" Many answers to this question reflect a confusion of this question with the following: "What is the basic reading skill?" The answer to the latter question is a twofold answer, involving both the identification of the symbol and the association of meaning with it; the answer to the first question merely concerns itself with the discrimination of one word from another word.

Is the acquisition of meaning a basic reading skill? Association of meaning with a symbol is one of the basic reading skills. The acquisition of meaning, discussed in Chapter 12, is not. The definition of reading suggests this distinction. Reading is the process of giving the significance intended by the writer to graphic symbols by *relating* them to our previous fund of experience. This definition stresses the importance of relating meaning as obtained through experience with the symbol. The teaching or development of meaning, then, is a distinct process. It is prerequisite for reading, but is not reading.

Meaning can be associated with the printed word only by associating the word with an experience, whether real or vicarious, or by associating it with another symbol (spoken word) that has meaning for the child. For most children this is a natural process. Teachers do not really provide the child with a method in making the association but only with the opportunity to do so (48, p. 7).

Meaning thus is a concept that has been standardized or that is shared by members of a speech community or society, and a word merely represents or stands for this concept (11).

Classical Conditioning

Pavlov (59) found that a dog salivated immediately when food was placed in its mouth. This he termed the unconditioned reflex. In a simple experiment, a tone was sounded (conditioned stimulus) and the dog then was presented with a plate of powdered food (unconditioned stimulus). Initially the tone did not arouse a salivary response, but after frequent associations between the tone and the food, the sound alone caused the dog to salivate. The dog had become conditioned to the tone.

Conditioning, then, is a term used ". . . to denote the behavioral fact that a stimulus inadequate for some response could become adequate by virtue of being combined one or more times with a stimulus adequate for the response. . . ." (63, p. 173).[1]

As we examine how a child learns to speak and to read, we see a

[1] Gregory Razran, "A Note on the Use of the Terms Conditioning and Reinforcement," *American Psychologist*, 10 (April 1955) 173–74. Reprinted by permission of the American Psychological Association.

striking similarity between these processes and the classical conditioning experiments. Certainly, both presuppose an association process. Reading is the linking of written or printed symbols with experience, just as the salivary response was the result of associating the tone with the food.

Association and Learning to Speak

Let us examine more closely the process of learning to speak. One theory (54) assumes that the baby at a very early age engages in reflexive and instinctive babbling. The child produces all kinds of vocalizations. By chance or trial and error he may enunciate the syllable *da*. An adult in speaking the syllable *da* causes the child again to "hear" and to speak the particular sound. The adult by imitating the baby eventually gets control of the baby's vocal responses and gets the baby to imitate adult speech. Gradually, the child will combine two syllables, such as *da* and *all,* to product the word doll. The adult then shows the child a doll and says the word doll. At this point an association between an experience (meaning) and the symbol *da* occurs. Eventually, the sight of the doll alone elicits the syllable *da* and the meaning of doll. The process is now complete. The child has associated meaning with a spoken symbol. He has learned to speak. Children frequently have associated meaning with the spoken word or the printed word long before they can speak or read. Word comprehension is not the same as word production.

Another theory (54, 55, p. 72), sometimes referred to as the *babble-luck* theory and originated by Thorndike, suggests that if the infant is fortunate enough to produce a sound similar to an actual word used in the language, and if an adult hears and rewards this sound, the child will tend to repeat that sound. Unfortunately, this theory assumes that all speech development begins with the child. The child must first make the appropriate sound. In reality, children learn to sound many words that they have *heard* others speak.

Not fully satisfied with either of the aforementioned theories, Mowrer (54, 55, p. 71) suggests that children learn to speak those words that have taken on a secondary reinforcing quality. If the mother, while supplying the child's wants, speaks certain words, the words occur in a "good and pleasant" context and the child will imitate that sound. He will repeat it whenever he wants to make a "situation without mother" more like the "situation with mother." Since words, however, also bring social approval, the satisfaction of one's wants, and control over others, words soon are repeated for other reasons.

Each theory allows for an association between the experience (object) and a symbol. In this way meaning is made real, and speech—the communication of meaning—becomes possible.

Association and Learning to Read

Learning to read is a further extension of the speech process. Generally, the child already has developed most of the meanings that he encounters in his early reading experiences. He also has associated these meanings or experiences with an aural-oral symbol. Teaching this child to read then means that the teacher must get him to identify the visual symbol and to associate with it the meaning that he already has associated with a spoken symbol. The child must associate the spoken and written word a sufficient number of times so that he comes to react to the written word with the same meaning that he previously took to the spoken word.

Rarely in English is meaning associated with the written symbol prior to associating it with the spoken symbol. The English language has an alphabet that represents sounds which in turn symbolize meanings. Chinese is an ideographic language in which the written symbols convey meaning directly.

Thus, in learning to read, the spoken word is the familiar stimulus; the written word is the novel stimulus. Gradually, with repeated associa-

TABLE 8-1   Comparison of Classical Conditioning and Learning to Speak and to Read

Pavlov's experiment	Meat Powder (US)	Salivation (UR)
	Sounding of tuning fork (CS)	Salivation (CR)
Learning to speak	The Object (US)	Meaning (UR)
	Spoken word (CS)	Meaning (CR)
Learning to read	Spoken word (US)	Meaning (UR)
	Written word (CS)	Meaning (CR)

Legend: US—unconditioned stimulus; CS—conditioned stimulus; UR—unconditioned response; CR—conditioned response

tions between the written and the spoken word, the child brings to the written word the same meanings that he previously attached to the spoken word. Through association, meaning becomes attached to the written word (67, p. 58).

Association of the spoken and the written word seems necessary in learning to read. In Chapter 2 we identified two basic facts: (*1*) reading is a sensory process; and (*2*) reading is a perceptual process. Here we have stressed that reading also is an associative process.

Whether learning to read always or ever involves conditioning is another consideration. Conditioning has difficulty with such facts as our cognitive experiences—thinking, insight, or understanding. Even though we know that a stimulus will tend to evoke the same response in the future, if the response has repeatedly occurred in temporal contiguity with a stimulus and has caused a reduction of a need (47, pp. 731–732), conditioning cannot explain the understanding of relationships between objects or of relationships between relations. Conditioning, furthermore, is based upon neurological and physiological conditioning. This may be cut short in human learning.

Table 8-1 illustrates the striking similarity between classical conditioning and the processes of learning to speak and to read.

Implications for Teaching Reading

Some children may experience much difficulty in associating meaning with the written word. Many of these difficulties stem from failure to properly identify the word. Some may not see the word distinctly and correctly. Some may even fail to look at the word. Thus, reading should always be a "look while you say" activity. The tracing or writing method of teaching the word is effective precisely because it forces the child to pay close attention to the word and thus to make a proper association.

Children also learn to identify a word by rather intangible properties of the word. Thus, they identify the word by a certain splotch on the paper on which the word is printed. They look at the word *house* and preceptually read *horse*.

The following incident illustrates the statement above. A certain major had a dog that reacted with joy and excitement whenever his master was ready to go out for a walk. One day the major, pretending to go out, put on his hat, got his cane, and made ready for his walk. To his surprise the dog just sat in his corner. After investigation it was found that the major had not checked, as he usually did, whether the drawer containing his valuables was locked.

The rattling of the drawer was the stimulus that to the dog meant that the master was ready to venture out of the house. For some children the stimulus for the printed word may be just as inconsequential and just as erroneous. We constantly must check on the validity of the child's perceptions. Only if his perception is valid, can the child make the proper association between meaning and the word.

Other errors in association of meaning with the word result from inadequacies in meaning. The child simply has not had the experiences necessary to develop meaning.

Finally, the association process itself may break down. Generally, the child needs more than one association between stimulus and meaning. The child needs to see the word in many and varied situations. Varied practice extends and refines meaning; repetitive practice makes the association habitual. Practice must be varied so that the child's perceptions and meanings for a word come closer to the meaning intended by the writer and practice must be repetitive so as to increase proficiency in meaningful response.

METHODS OF WORD IDENTIFICATION

Now let us examine how the child learns to identify the printed word, how he discriminates it from every other word, and how he recognizes it upon seeing it again in a different context. Identification is the initial acquaintance with a word, recognition is a subsequent acquaintance. The child then "recognizes" the word form as one that he previously identified and that he now knows. They are not the same process and the means of identifying a word may be completely different from those of recognition.

The history of the teaching of reading is replete with the various methods used to help the child to identify and recognize the printed symbol. These methods have been labelled the synthetic, analytic, or analytic-synthetic methods.

Synthetic Methods

Methods that begin with word elements, with letters (Alphabet Method), with sounds (Synthetic Phonic Method), or with syllables (Syllable Method) are called synthetic methods. They are so called because the letters, sounds, and syllables must be combined (synthesized) to form words.

The Alphabet Method　　The earliest formal attempt in teaching reading used the alphabet method, in which each word was spelled out. The New England Primer in 1690 and the Webster American Spelling Book in 1793 were based on the ABC method. The pupil first was taught to recognize the letters and gradually proceeded toward the word.

Recent studies show that a knowledge of the letter names is a good indicator of success in learning to read. The pupil who has learned to associate a name with a letter has already learned a basic reading skill. He has learned how to discriminate one visual form from another (an A is different from a B), and he has associated a sound and consequently a name and meaning with that symbol.

The Synthetic Phonic Method　　The second synthetic method to be used by teachers was the phonic method. It was originated by Ickelsamer in 1534 and was introduced to America in 1782 by Noah Webster. The alphabet method starts with the name of the letter; the phonic method, on the other hand, starts with the phonetic sound of the letter.

The Syllable Method   The third synthetic method is the syllable method. Here syllables are combined to form words. It is used, for example, in African languages like the Sudanese Dinka. Since structural analysis is based on syllable analysis, a syllable approach is an essential aspect of today's reading program.

Analytic Methods

Historically, the analytic methods of teaching reading are three: the word method, the phrase method, and the sentence method. They are called analytic methods because they begin with the word, phrase, or sentence, and these larger units then are broken down into their basic elements.

The Word Method   The word method is the most common analytic method in use today. It was introduced in Europe in 1648 by Comenius in his book, *The Orbis Pictus,* and was proposed in the United States in 1828 by Samuel Worcester.

It frequently is termed the sight or configuration method, but often in error. Various sense avenues may be used in teaching the word method. There is a method of teaching reading that begins with the total word, but whose emphasis is on sound, or phonics. It is termed analytical phonics. Another word method emphasizes the kinaesthetic sense avenues and is termed the Kinaesthetic Method. This method is most frequently associated with the name of Fernald (26). It has been very successful with remedial readers. However, it has not been used often enough as a regular part of the developmental reading program.

Spearman (69) points out that touch discrimination is a valuable technique, especially in the preschool and kindergarten years, but notes that it degenerates after age seven because of the increasing thickness of the skin.

The child comes to school possessing an abundance of kinaesthetic meanings for sensations. He already has *learned how to learn* with this medium. He has felt and touched objects. The object is hot or cold, soft or hard, round or straight.

Perhaps the primitivity of the kinaesthetic sense has not been sufficiently utilized in leading the child from the known to the unknown. For example, we do not associate the auditory sound of the word with the kinaesthetic meaning that the child already possesses for the word. It may well be that *all* children may profit from making associations between the various sense organs. They may profit from writing, hearing, and seeing the word.

The Sentence Method   The sentence method of teaching reading was emphasized especially in the early 1900's by Huey (42). Huey suggested that the sentence, not the word or letter, was the true unit in language. He inferred that therefore it also was the true unit in reading.

As we noted in Chapter 6, linguists today emphasize that reading is primarily a language process and that the major task facing the child is the mastery of the graphic system that reflects the spoken language system. Lefevre (49, pp. 247–248) suggests an analytical method of teaching reading emphasizing language patterns. He emphasizes that meaning comes only through the grasping of the language structures exemplified in a sentence. Meaning thus depends on the intonation, the word and sentence order, the grammatical inflections, and certain key function words. Only by reading structures can full meaning be attained. Or to put it in another way, unless the reader translates correctly the printed text into the intonation pattern of the writer, he may not be getting the meaning intended (49, p. 250).

Perhaps Huey was speaking of something quite different than method of word attack as indeed Lefevre does today. It may well be the sentence which is the basic unit of meaning, but the word, the letter, or the sound may be the basic unit of identification and recognition. We are more concerned at present with recognition than with comprehension, with identification rather than with reading. Meaningful reading seems to occur only when the reader comprehends the total sentence unit. However, few would suggest that the pupil should learn to identify sentences as units. The word seems to be the largest linguistic unit that readily lends itself to identification. Thus, the sentence method and the linguistic method may be the way we should read; they may have less significance for identification.

BEGINNING WITH THE WHOLE WORD

Much debate has centered about the question: "Should reading teaching begin with an analytic approach or the whole word or with a synthetic approach or a part of a word?" Most reading programs today begin by introducing the child to whole words.

Is there justification for beginning reading in this way? If so, what is the justification?

In the discussion that follows we are not attempting to refute the validity of the word method nor to suggest that it is the only valid method. We merely raise the question whether the validity of this method rests on the assumptions often advanced, and we shall try to state the reasons why beginning with the whole word seems best in most circumstances. Let us evaluate the arguments commonly advanced for beginning the teaching of reading with the whole word.

In 1885 Cattell and in 1898 Erdmann and Dodge demonstrated that in a given unit of time only three or four unrelated letters could be recognized, but that in the same unit of time it was possible to recognize two unrelated words containing as many as twelve letters (3, pp. 212–213).

These and other experiments like them and Gestalt psychology gave rise to the principle that the child characteristically reacts to the *whole* word rather than to its elements. As a consequence, the word became the unit of teaching in reading.

However, such an interpretation is not at all necessary. Studies have shown that even when every other letter has been deleted in a word or words, it frequently is possible to reconstruct the whole word. It is quite possible that the subjects in Cattell's experiment, for example, had learned to infer letters and hence the word, even though they did not actually recognize all the letters or even the total configuration of the word. In World War II, pilots were trained to interpret a fantastic amount of detail in one fixation and to describe it accurately, even though they did not see all the details. Brown (10, p. 70) notes that

> Letters in words follow sequential probabilities familiar to readers of English while letters at random are all equally probable at every juncture. It is quite possible, therefore, that Cattell's subjects were reading individual letters rather than "total word pictures" and were able to report more letters than they could possibly identify at very brief exposures because the additional letters could be inferred from those observed.[2]

Furthermore, in the experiments mentioned above the subjects already knew how to read. They were recognizing rather than identifying the words. Unfortunately, the appropriate method of recognizing a word may not be the appropriate method for teaching word identification. Even though the mature reader may react to the *total* word in recognition and meaningful interpretation, it does not follow that he does so in learning to identify the word (4). The unit of meaning and of recognition may not be the unit of identification. Or to put it in another way, words may be the basic meaning units but are not necessarily the basic units of visual identification or even of recognition.

[2] Reprinted with permission of The Macmillan Company from *Words and Things* by Roger Brown. Copyright 1958 by the Free Press.

The mature reader sees the word as a Gestalt or as a whole. The word's configuration or physiognomy stands out from the letters that compose the word, giving it individuality. The word's form becomes the figure and stands out from the ground and from the letters. The mature reader perceives the figure. He sees the characteristic features of the word.

The beginning reader has not attained such perceptual refinement. He may quite frequently see the letter as a distinct Gestalt or form, and indeed there is no difference between the perception of a letter and a word. The letter is as much a Gestalt as is the word. The simple fact is that mature readers are capable of perceiving more complex Gestalten than are beginning readers, but even they have to analyze some words into their parts.

The second major support for the whole-word method also came from Gestalt psychology. This theory teaches that the perceiver generally reacts not only to the whole but to the *meaningful* whole in perceiving reality. The person sees a house not as a bundle of parts, but as a distinct and organized unit. Reading teachers immediately inferred that in learning to read the child perceives the smallest linguistic unit that has meaning and that can stand alone as a part of an utterance. This unit is the word.

The correctness of this interpretation seems to depend upon the meaning of the word "meaningful." Although meaning is associated with the word, this is not what is meant by "meaningful" in Gestalt psychology. Meaning in this theory refers to the organization or structure rather than to the object or event to which the word refers. It is systematic meaning rather than referential meaning (10, p. 71).

Gestalt psychologists look upon perception and learning primarily as the structuring of experience. The learner must perceive the relationship between the parts and from this develops insight. Their experiments were concerned with the learning of meaningful and meaningless materials. Material is said to be meaningful if the person has had some experience with it, if he has organized it, if he has identified its structure, or if previous learning transfers to it. Meaningful materials, in this sense, are already learned materials.

Stroud (71, p. 437) points out that:

Meaning, insight, and logical relations are psychological phenomena and have no existence *sui generis* in material of learning. Material is not inherently meaningful; it is endowed with meaning by a reacting individual, and experience, or previous reaction, is a necessary condition. . . . To put the matter in another way, meaningful, insightful, and logical materials are partially learned already.[3]

[3] James B. Stroud, *Psychology in Education* (Longmans, Green and Company, 1956). Reprinted by permission, David McKay Company, Inc.

Unfortunately, in learning to read there is no such previous experience. The word form or its configuration is not any more meaningful than is a single letter. The learner does not "see" the meaningfulness of its structure. The word form becomes meaningful to the learner (here we are *not* dealing with referential meaning or with the task of associating meaning with the word) if he can see the interrelationship of its parts.

The word, *fitting,* is meaningful only if the pupil understands why it is pronounced *"fiting"* but written *fit-ting.* Each letter of the word receives its pronunciation or "meaningfulness" from the other parts of the word and the total word represents a different systematization or organization than the sum of its parts. Thus, the sound value of letters is established only through their appearance in the context of a word. Experience has shown that the spelling of the long *e* sound in words like wreath and reef often is confused because of the phonetic similarity of the final phonemes *f* and *th*; the long *e* sound in seek and beak is rarely misspelled because of the great phonetic dissimilarity between the initial *s* and *b* sounds (76).

The systematic meaningfulness of which Gestalt psychologists speak can only come through an understanding of the interrelationship of the parts. Only in this way can the pupil transfer his knowledge about a given word to others.

In the Gestalt use of the term, *meaningful,* the combination, *tac,* has just as much meaning to the child as has the word *cat.* True, after he has associated the word *cat* with a real or vicarious experience, the child will more readily learn it than he will learn *tac.* He is more interested in it, or to put it in another way, the word has greater ego reference for him or has meaning for him since he probably has seen and played with cats, but the form itself may still not be meaningful in the Gestalt use of the term.

Katona (44) gives an example of systematic meaning. He asked one group of subjects to learn the sequence, 5-8-12-15-19-22-26-29, from memory. A week later he asked them to reproduce the series. No one was able to do so. Another group learned the organization of the sequence of numbers, namely, that their differences were 3-4-3-4-3-4 respectively. Katona used the following technique to illustrate the organization:

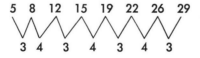

The latter group learned and retained the series because learning was "meaningful."

This connotation of meaning is quite different from the concept of referential meaning in reading. To say that a word is "meaningful" is not the same as saying that it has "meaning."

A third argument centers about the most desirable mode of learning. Much time and effort have been spent in establishing a difference between "whole methods" and "part methods" of learning (30, p. 242). This difference may not be entirely real. The "perceptual whole" is a relative term. It is not the same for all children in all circumstances. Furthermore, there is no evidence to indicate how much the so-called whole unit entails. The whole may be an entire novel, a chapter, a poem, a paragraph, a sentence, or a letter. Just as a word is both a "whole" and a "part," so also a letter is both a "whole" and a "part."

It is rather arbitrary to say that for every child the perceptual whole is the word. Surely, what constitutes the whole is dependent on the ability, experience, purposes, maturation, perceptual skill, and learning habits of the learner; hence, his general readiness for learning. It also depends on the nature of the materials being learned. Thus, at times it is wise to teach the principle or generalization. Other principles can only be developed inductively.

The psychology of individual differences would suggest that each child characteristically reacts to the "perceptual whole," but that for one child it may be the total word, for another, it may be a part of the word. In general, the whole child reacts, but he is not necessarily stimulated holistically.

Petty (60) for example, reports that some first graders prefer to draw form syncretically, whereas others tend to emphasize and select details. Muehl (56) also found that beginning readers discriminate among words of similar length on the basis of specific letter differences. Perception is holistic only if the form itself is quite simple and uncomplicated. If the "whole" is meaningless to the perceiver, the details then tend to dominate individual perception. What constitutes a "whole" is different from individual to individual, and is determined by the meaningfulness of that unit to the individual.

Interesting also are the results of eye-movement studies. These studies indicate that children rarely see one word per fixation. In the first grade not more than one-half of a word is usually seen. This means that the child must look at the parts of words, retain them in memory, and combine them mentally to form the total word.

To say that the whole-word method is the correct method of teaching word identification because children characteristically perceive wholes rather than parts is to ignore the basic relativity of the perceptual whole. This statement overlooks the fact that the smallest unit of meaningfulness in perception must necessarily be a whole.

It would seem that the three arguments commonly advanced for beginning with the whole word are of doubtful validity. Does this mean that the whole-word method is invalid? Although it is very difficult to prove that for any given child analytical methods harmonize more closely with the child's normal mode of learning than do synthetic methods, there are other valid reasons for beginning with the total word:

1. Any method of reading must keep meaning in the limelight. Reading is never complete without the apprehension of meaning. Reading is the process of securing meaning and it would seem that from the beginning the child should be dealing with meaningful language units (37). Thus the child from the beginning should be introduced to the smallest linguistic unit that can stand alone and that has meaning. This is the word. He should learn that he is responding to a symbol with which he can associate meaning—not necessarily systematic meaning but referential meaning. Words have meaning; the sounds of the individual letters in a word do not.

   Starting with the word *and* meaning makes learning to read an interesting and rewarding process from the beginning. These side effects perhaps have greater significance for successful learning and for the development of habitual reading than the method that is used.

2. The pupil has had numerous experiences with words, listening to them and speaking them.

3. There is a one-to-one relationship between the spoken word and the printed word symbol, even though the spelling irregularities are many

4. There are, finally, many words that cannot be learned letter by letter or sound by sound. These words often defy phonic analysis and must be learned as sight words.

EMPHASIZING PARTS OF WORDS FROM THE BEGINNING

Through the years the whole-word method has come to mean the sight method or the configuration method. This is not necessarily correct. The child must *see* the word if he wants to learn it, but the question still remains: What does he see? Does he see the total configuration or outline of the word, or does he react to the parts of the word? Of even greater importance, should he be taught to look for more than the word's general configuration?

For beginning reading the configuration method has been generally effective. However, the pupil also must become self-directive in learning. He must become an independent reader. He needs skill in analyzing those words that are not in his recognition vocabulary. In evaluating reading methods it seems legitimate to ask: Which method best develops the child's skill in attacking new words? Which method makes him self-directive in identifying new words?

Bruner (9) notes that in perception the person often goes beyond what the senses provide. We already have alluded to the ability of readers to recognize words when certain letters are deleted or to recognize numbers when numbers in a sequence are missing as in 1, 3, 9, and 3, 9, —. As soon as the person sees that the numbers are multiples of three, it becomes obvious that the missing number is twenty-seven. Studies also have shown that in the sentence, "George _____ was our first president," the word Washington is readily read into the sequence. Theories themselves are "good" only if they permit the learner to go beyond the objective data. The theory permits him to order past events and leads him to see new relationships in future data.

The above examples of redundancy are like those observed in grammar (58, p. 87). Thus, the singular subject calls for a verb ending in *s* (Jack sits); a time element calls for an appropriate tense (*Today,* I *am* king); a dependent clause calls for an independent clause (If you see him, call me); and the order of words itself is set (The boy sat on the log—the log sat on the boy). Changing the order usually alters the meaning.

The question of what the person learns in the above situation is not immediately answerable. Bruner (9, p. 44) believes that the *perceiver learns certain formal schemata that are used to order the probabilistic relationships between the data.*

In support of his assumption Bruner (9, p. 47) refers to a study by William Hull. Hull found that in learning to spell the good speller learned a general "coding system" which permitted him to reconstruct the sequence of letters. The good and poor spellers both learned, but *what* they learned was substantially different. Bruner notes that the poor speller learned words by rote; the good speller learned a system, based on the transitional probabilities that characterize letter sequences in English (9, p. 48).

Bruner (9, p. 49) adds that when the perceiver goes beyond what the senses give, he

> . . . does so by virtue of being able to place the present given in a more generic coding system and that one essentially "reads off" from the coding system additional information either on the basis of learned contingent probabilities or learned principles of relating material. Much of what has been called transfer of training can be fruitfully considered a case of applying learned coding systems to new events. Positive transfer represents a case where an appropriate

coding system is applied to a new array of events, negative transfer being a case either of misapplication of a coding system to new events or of the absence of a coding system that may be applied.[4]

The letters in the language are used in a way that permits us to reconstruct them from what we know about the surrounding letters. The letters follow one another in a predictable order. Some sequences never occur in English; others occur frequently. The letter *q* is only followed by *u*. The chances are rather good that the letter *p* completes the word *com act*. The probability of occurrence of the *p* is greater than that of any other letter. Listeners, even though they have not heard a letter or word, infer it from the context.

The three-year-old is using the context or the transitional probabilities that characterize the English language when he uses regular endings such as selled, runned, or mans for the irregular *sold, ran,* or *men,* and so does the first grader who reads come as *kōm*. Because he was dealing with an irregularity, he got into error. Thus, the letter sequence is not an exact indication of the pronunciation of a word. The pupil must learn that sometimes there are other alternatives, but the system of transitional probabilities or sequence is a valuable cue in perhaps 85 per cent of the cases.

What implications do the data that Bruner presents have for reading method? They *seem* to suggest that the child must develop a coding system that will permit him to simplify the task of having to learn to read thousands of words.

The child must develop independence in word attack. He must become self-directive in learning. He must develop an economical method, and he must develop a method that will provide him clues to other words.

The configuration method is a valuable technique, but it alone cannot guarantee mastery of the multiple words needed for independent reading. In fact, as we shall see later, the configuration method *per se* offers little opportunity for transfer of learning from one reading situation to another. The pupil, it seems, gains much from learning a system based on the probabilities that characterize the spoken-written or sound-print relationships of the English language. This seems possible in our present teaching of reading only through analysis of words, through learning a *system* of phonic and structural analysis.

Unquestionably, both the beginning reader and the mature reader (41, pp. 110–111) frequently identify a word through its general shape and configuration. They see the word as a unified symbol rather than as a collection of related letters.

[4] Jerome S. Bruner, "Going Beyond the Information Given," *Contemporary Approaches to Cognition* (Cambridge, Mass.: Harvard University Press, 1957). Reprinted by permission.

Experience has shown that the configuration method initially works with "most" children. The child learns the shape or configuration of the word, and his perception of the word is strengthened by the picture that accompanies the word, by using the word in a meaningful context, and by practicing it on flash cards, card games, tachistoscopes, and in spelling lessons.

Teachers of reading should take advantage of a word's general configuration. The length of the word, the number and variety of letters that it contains, and the ascending and descending letters are important clues to the identification of the word. For some children, the configuration method may be the only usable method. They cannot analyze the word into its parts, or have such poor auditory-discriminatory skills that they cannot deal with phonics.

Children differ in auditory, visual, and motor imagery. Some children simply cannot rely on a visual image; others rarely depend on auditory imagery. When the latter "read" a word, they may "see" the word; the former "hear" the word; and those with motor imagery "feel" the word. They recognize the word as one they "traced" previously.

Furthermore, the maturational pattern for each of those sensory modalities may fluctuate from one to another. A pupil may develop slowly in one, more rapidly in another. Others mature slowly in all despite good intellectual ability. Obviously, teaching methods must take these differences into account, and readiness programs should be directed to the development of the sensory modalities of each child.

There are other young children and poor readers who do not perceive clearly either the total configuration of the word or the details of the letters. The word tends to be a jumble of lines. Nothing stands out. In Gestalt terms, the figure and the ground are fused and the page looks like an undifferentiated mass. Such children have not acquired an understanding of the importance of particular details in letter shapes, and of their relationship to one another within the total word (65). Retarded readers, unable to analyze words, sometimes treat words as solid wholes defying analysis; or they may perceive the general structure of words only in a vague and inaccurate way without attending to the details. Vernon (75, p. 15) also notes that children may see letters as unanalyzable wholes whose structure cannot be differentiated.

The conclusion seems clear. There is no one method that works with *all* children. The configuration method is a useful method, especially in introducing the pupil to reading. However, the configuration method is not necessarily the only way, nor even the best way of developing independence and self-direction in reading.

Marchbanks and Levin (50), in a study of fifty kindergarten children and fifty first-grade children who had been taught by "the whole-word sentence method," found that the specific letters were much more important in determining recognition than was the overall shape of the word. The initial letter was the most salient cue, next came the final letter, and finally the middle letter. The least used cue was the word shape.

Children pay particular attention to the *parts* of words when they are required to discriminate between similar-appearing words. When the total word is not identifiable they attend to special elements and observe individual letters. Four- and five-year-old children and poor readers generally tend to identify words by certain key letters, letter arrangements, or other outstanding characteristics, and for this reason confuse them with other words having the same letter or characteristics.

Such children often are taught to use tricks to identify the word, but these tricks betray them. For example, the word *purple* is identified by the one ascending and the two descending letters. The configuration looks like this: ⎯⎯⎯ Unfortunately, the word *people* has the same visual configuration and the ascending and descending letters fall in the same place (73, p. 65).

Even in normal perception the perceiver may react to the particular characteristic rather than to the total configuration. Terman and Walcutt (73, pp. 59–60) note that the faces of Chinese persons look so much alike to Westerners that to discriminate them the perceiver must resort to the details that characterize the individual face.

Adults, who have become proficient in reading, need less and less visual stimulation to identify and interpret a word. The rapid reader is noted for his ability to use minimal visual and perceptual clues. A single letter may be an adequate cue, and the mature reader is quite conscious, even when reading rapidly, of a misspelling of a word such as *percieve*.

Unfortunately, we still find *some* teachers who put all their cards in the configuration basket. They teach reading as though the average child could and should learn each new word as a distinct form or configuration.

Betts (5, p. 8) notes that

Today there are too many first-grade classrooms in which the so-called "word method" of teaching *beginning* reading is used. When this so-called method is stripped of its "pedaguese," including the term *sight words*, it is merely a tell-the-child-the-word procedure. And telling isn't teaching! The word method, therefore, is a nothing-for-nothing proposition, emphasizing rote learning.[5]

[5] Emmett Albert Betts, "How Well Are We Teaching Reading?—Reply," *Controversial Issues in Reading*, Tenth Annual Reading Conference Proceedings, Lehigh University, 1 (April 1961) 8. Reprinted by permission.

The child cannot be taught the thousands of words that compose his language as individual units. In fact, some symbols such as ÷ must be thus learned. However, such an approach would make the English language ideographic, and it would turn the learning of reading into a conditioning process, thus unnecessarily complicating the process for the child.

The memory load that is created by having to learn hundreds of new and ever less discriminable words surely is excessive for some children, and may partially contribute to the negative reading attitudes that one sees so frequently among third and fourth graders.

As the differences between configurations become ever finer, with letters curving left and right (b-d) and upward and downward (n-u) (25, p. 129), the child may become confused, lose confidence, and turn against reading. He will have difficulty progressing because the problems of visual discrimination increase proportionately as the rate of the introduction of new words increases (40, p. 116).

Asking *all* children to recognize *all* words as configurations also

> . . . ignores the very basic fact that *printed words are symbols of sounds* and are made of letters which are symbols of sounds . . . a printed word has meaning *because it is a symbol of a sound,* a spoken word, that already has meaning to the child. It is not the configuration that means; it is the sound, *which the child already knows.* He does not have to memorize the configuration of a word for its meaning . . . he has to learn to recognize it instantly as a *sound.* The instant he hears it, he knows it . . . (56, pp. 50–51).

Terman and Walcutt (73, pp. 55–56) add that:

> For the child who does not know the alphabet either as printed letters or as symbols of sounds, the word on the page is a totally new squiggle that is presented to him as a *meaning* and therefore as a completely new learning act that is not related to anything else he knows. . . .[6]

Pooley (62, p. 41) suggests that:

> One of the principal learning procedures at the early stage is the association of printed letters, singly and in combination, with the typical sounds they represent and the synthesis of these sounds into patterns which the child can recognize as the words he already knows. Some words he will learn as wholes, without the need for analysis; but,

[6] From *Reading: Chaos and Cure* by Sibyl Terman and C. C. Walcutt. Copyright 1958, McGraw-Hill Book Company, Inc. Used with permission of McGraw-Hill Book Company.

increasingly as he meets new words, the power to deal with them analytically in terms of sound related to symbols is a valuable asset.[7]

The pupil must have an economical method, one that helps both to identify the word with which he is concerned and to use this present learning in the identification and recognition of other words. The method should provide the maximum possibilities for transfer. It should permit the child to benefit from consistent previous learning. It should prepare him to formulate inductively generalizations and rules that further aid word identification and recognition.

The child needs to develop a system for attacking words that allows him to use and apply what he has learned to other words. The configuration of a word is a pattern or Gestalt, but it has relatively little value in the identification of other words. The basic pattern or Gestalt in language seems to be the phoneme-phonogram interrelationship. The basic identification skill is the "seeing" of the sound in the printed word; the association of the phonogram with the phoneme. When the pupil learns a Gestalt for a word that is based on the perception of these interrelationships, he learns a code that is applicable to other words. It seems that this is best learned through a study of phonics and structural analysis.

McKee (52, p. 101) feels that the pupil should use only two aids in unlocking strange words: (1) the context and (2) the sounds that letters or groups of letters stand for in a word—hence phonics—and the pupil should always use them together, never either one alone.

Ausubel (4) notes that word recognition is more a matter of rational problem-solving than of random guessing. It is the process of lawfully decoding the unknown written word through the application of one's knowledge of grapheme-phoneme correspondences. It is not enough to know that the pupil needs to learn a coding system. The teacher needs to be able to organize his presentation of words in beginning reading in such a way that children can break the code rather than have to learn each word independently. Chapters 10 and 11 are aimed at this. Pupils need to learn how words are structured and how the arrangement of letters in a word controls the way the letters function.

The basic contribution of phonics instruction may be that it requires the child to visually study the word (51). Phonics instruction forces the child to look at the parts of a word and thus may lead to a somewhat different Gestalt than is seen if the word were perceived strictly as a unit. The artist sees a picture as a Gestalt, but his Gestalt is substantially more detailed and refined than that of the casual observer. Through

---

[7] Robert C. Pooley, "Reading and the Language Arts," *Development in and through Reading* (Chicago: The University of Chicago Press, 1961). Reprinted by permission.

phonics the pupil may learn to more adequately scrutinize the configuration and thus may develop the habit of being unsatisfied with a general, overall view of a word.

It is also apparent that even in the most rigid phonics program a certain number of words will be learned as sight words.

Knowing how to sound out words is also more than just a pronunciation skill. It is an effective way of increasing the child's *comprehension* vocabulary to the level of his speaking and listening vocabulary.

Durrell and Nicholson (24, pp. 264–265) point out that ultimate progress in reading is dependent on three factors: (*1*) The child must notice separate sounds in spoken words; (*2*) He must be able to see differences in printed letters and words; and (*3*) He must see the relationships between speech and the written word. He must be able to turn sound symbols into letter symbols and letter symbols into sound symbols. This, we would hope, would give the pupil the independence in reading that seems necessary for genuine achievement.

Over the last ten years the phonic method, both synthetic and analytic, has been much discussed. It is now generally accepted that phonics have a prominent place in a reading program. In fact, some feel that phonics instruction may well be more beneficial than any other skill in helping the pupil to develop a sight vocabulary and to become an independent reader. However, questions as to when and how we might introduce phonics most effectively are still being debated.

Phonics alone do not make a reading program. No amount of phonic training will lead the child to understand the meaning of a written word if the child has never associated an experience with its oral equivalent. Phonics are a method of identifying and recognizing words, and word recognition is only one aspect of the reading process. To be readers children must: develop a grasp of meaning, become accurate and independent in identifying words, and want to read (37, pp. 11–17).

Experience has shown that few readers become very proficient unless they manage to learn more than one way of attacking words. No one method is sufficient in and of itself. The very fact that pupils are different and that they do not learn by the same methods ought to keep the teacher from putting undue emphasis on any one method. What is food for one may well be poison for another.

In general, most methods of teaching reading have been found to be successful with some pupils in certain conditions. Thus, research (15, 31, 57) has shown that children who have been taught to read even by synthetic phonic methods frequently become independent readers. They have confidence in attacking new words, have relatively little difficulty with pronunciation, generally are good oral readers and spellers, are proficient in word meaning and word study skills (6), and often are good comprehenders.

A study (14) involving 1652 freshmen students at Stanford University, San Jose State College, and City College of San Francisco indicates that the less knowledge the student had of the relationships between the letter combinations which make up words and the sounds of those words, the poorer were his chances of being good in comprehension. The poorer the phonic ability, the poorer the student's reading seemed to be.

The most frequent criticism of the phonic method suggests that it leads to "word-calling" and verbalism. The slow learner may indeed become a better word-caller than a comprehender. The inadequacies, however, are inherent in the mind of the learner, not in the method.

In most classrooms phonic elements are not learned in isolation and meaning is not ignored. Such criticisms do not invalidate the argument that the child should make use of his language background and the sound of the spoken word to identify and to get to the meaning of the word. The sound of the word should be used to get to the meaning. If the child has been taught that what can be said also can be written, it seems most natural for him to want to work out the pronunciation of the printed word and then to associate with it the meaning that he previously associated with the spoken word. Reading in this sense is "the responding to visual forms with vocal or subvocal ones. The 'thoughtful' or 'meaningful' reactions that accompany or follow this process are responses to the vocalized or subvocalized forms and the underlying neurophysiology." (68)

Recently writers (70,72) have suggested that present reading programs spend too little time on the basic sounds and the basic sentence structure of the language. But these same people, while emphasizing the relationship between reading and linguistics and between the letters of the alphabet and the sounds of the language, intimate that this does not mean that the child should learn to associate sound with a *single* letter. This, they suggest, is the basic fault of synthetic phonic methods.

NEWER APPROACHES IN READING

We have recently seen the proliferation of methods, theories, approaches, and programs. Apart from configuration and phonic approaches, and basal, individualized, kinaesthetic, and special remedial approaches, which are covered in other parts of this book, there have been presented to educators models of various types that have sought to alter the stimulus situation in reading or that have sought to provide a more penetrating analysis of the reading process.

Unfortunately, some of the efforts to improve reading are perhaps characterized more by fervor than by perspective (53). "In some respects a salvation through innovation complex prevails. Ill-defined problems, partial solutions, and exaggerated claims are not unusual. . . . Change is equated with betterment. 'New' and 'different' by some queer semantics have become synonymous with 'better.' " [8]

We have divided these newer approaches into (1) those that emphasize method, that which the teacher does—hence the stimulus aspects—and (2) those that emphasize the pupil's capacities, potentials, and behavior, or the organism—especially the mediational aspects. Let us begin with stimulus approaches.

Stimulus Approaches

The relationship between the sounds of the English language and the way these are represented is not entirely consistent. Many approaches have been made to this problem. One approach is to change the word form. The printed symbols themselves are modified so as to make the relationship more consistent. Approaches which do this we have labelled stimulus approaches, because they emphasize the stimulus variables. The emphasis in these approaches is simply this. Change the nature of the stimulus in a given way, such as by changing the alphabet, and it will lead to easier and improved learning.

The Initial Teaching Alphabet (ITA)   Perhaps the most discussed stimulus model in the literature today is the Initial Teaching Alphabet Model (20,21,22). Pitman (61), its modern originator, spoke of the Augmented Roman Alphabet (ARA); the name has now been changed to Initial Teaching Alphabet (ITA). It is said to make reading easier because of the following:

1. Coding of the basic sound units of English is regularized. There is one symbol for each single sound.
2. The number of characters is reduced by using only lowercase letters.

Knutson (46) lists the following advantages of ITA: (1) The appearance of the letters is excellent motivation for failure-frustrated, allergic readers; (2) It offers greater opportunity for early and repetitive success; and (3) It is limited by a controlled vocabulary with its concomitant "level" stigma.

However, Fry (29), evaluating five of the 27 First Grade studies in which ITA was used, suggests that there is very little difference between the reading abilities of children in the United States taught in traditional orthography or ITA, but in each instance the pupils using ITA

[8] Miller, Melvin L., "Another Look at Reading and the Teaching of Reading." *Reading Horizons,* 7 (Summer, 1967) 157–163. Reprinted by permission.

scored higher on the oral word reading test. ITA, as indeed also some of the other approaches listed in this chapter, is not to be confused with the more legitimate methods of teaching reading. It is not a method and was never intended to be one (23); it merely presents different letter forms, forms which might be used in either a synthetic or analytic system.

The ITA model presents a total of 44 symbols. The basic thesis is that children should use a more reliable alphabet until they have acquired proficiency in it, at which point they should switch to the traditional alphabet and spelling.

Systems similar to the ITA system began as early as 1551. In that year John Hart suggested a new set of principles of spelling, and in 1569 in *Orthographie* he proposed to teach reading by using an alphabet that has as many letters as there are sounds or voices in speech. Alexander Ellis noted that by 1845 there were 26 "phonetic alphabets" for teaching reading, including those of Benjamin Franklin and Brigham Young.

In each of these early efforts there was an attempt to simplify materials or stimulus aspects by presenting a one-to-one correspondence between letters and sounds. Figure 8-1 illustrates the ITA alphabet.

Figure 8-1.   Initial Teaching Alphabet *

* Reproduced with permission of Initial Teaching Alphabet Publications, Inc., New York.

The Ten-vowel Modification Model   A model with similar emphasis as ITA is the "ten-vowel" modification of the alphabet by Leo G. Davis in *k-a-t spelz cat*[9] and Davis's transliteration of *McGuffey's First Reader.* Its basic change is the use of small capitals A-E-I-O-U to designate long vowels and lowercase a-e-i-o-u to designate short vowels. It is based on a 31-letter alphabet. Davis maintains that there are no reading problems; only spelling problems.

The Diacritical Marking System   Edward Fry (28) suggests the use of diacritical markings to indicate how each of the traditional letters should be pronounced. The diacritical markings are introduced to regularize the phoneme-grapheme relationship. Fry refers to this as the Diacritical Marking System or DMS. The diacritical markings are temporary, soon to be replaced by normal spelling and writing.

The value of the system is said to lie in: (*1*) the greater regularity of the phoneme-grapheme relationship (than, for example, in the ITA system); (*2*) the ease with which the child can transfer his learning to regular orthography, because the basic word form is preserved; and (*3*) the difficulty with spelling is not increased.

Words in Color   Gattegno (32,33,34), in *Words in Color,* proposes a synthetic phonic approach using color. Each of the 48 sounds is represented by a color, even though it is written in numerous ways. For example, the sound of short *i* may be written as *a* (senate), *ai* (mountain), *ay* (always), *e* (pretty), *ea* (guinea), *ee* (been), *ei* (forfeit), *eo* (pigeon), *ey* (money), *i* (sit), *ia* (carriage), *ie* (sieve), *o* (women), *u* (busy), *ui* (build), or *ẏ* (hymnal), but in Gattegno's system these letters would all be in red. Color thus is used to unify English even though it does not alter the spelling. Gattegno has found that 48 colors are sufficient to account for almost all the sounds in English.

The letter *a* colored white represents the *a* in *bat;* when colored blue-green, it is the *a* in *lane.* The *u* as in *but* is yellow, the *i* as in *pin* is red, the *e* as in *pet* is blue, and the *o* as in *pot* is orange. The consonant *p* is brown, the *t* is purple, *s* is dark lilac, and so on.

The color approach is based upon a definition of reading as the decoding of writing into speech. Meaning comes as the pupil discovers that the sounds of written words are like those of words he has both heard and spoken.

Linguistic Approaches   The linguistic approach logically fits in this section, but we have reserved the discussion of it for Chapter 10.

---

[9] This is available through Carlton Press, Inc., 84 Fifth Avenue, New York.

Chapter 10's main emphasis is linguistic phonics. The linguists maintain that the teaching of reading is not likely to be improved by emphasizing individual letter-to-sound correspondence through modification of the alphabet. Rather, they suggest that we emphasize the relationship or correspondence between letter patterns and sound patterns and that we help the pupil to use the correspondence rules already present in English (45).

Programmed Learning Model   Today numerous materials designed to teach reading are being presented in programmed form. Programmed materials are an innovation emphasizing self-instruction, increased pupil participation, and almost immediate feed-back of results. Programmed materials have the following obvious advantages (27):

1. They provide immediate knowledge of success or failure.
2. They permit each pupil to advance at his own success rate.
3. They require the pupil to progress through a logical sequence of steps of increasing difficulty, each step being so small that it can be met successfully and yet leading the pupil closer to full mastery.
4. They prohibit the by-passing of any step without mastery.
5. They bring the pupil into contact with the best minds—those who prepared the materials.
6. They require the pupil to be constantly active and alert and to construct his own response.
7. They provide for readiness by presenting material of appropriate difficulty.
8. They provide the teacher with a rather accurate measure of where the pupil is and thus may lead to more meaningful homework and study.
9. They involve the gradual removal of the stimulus. This has been described as fading.
10. They require the pupil to listen or read carefully and to give his full attention. Unlike in the classroom, the teaching material does not flow on without the pupil's attention. The machine sits idle if the learner is not concentrating on the task at hand.
11. The materials are actually pupil-made. The programming is continuously evaluated and corrected until ambiguities and gaps are removed.
12. They permit the teacher to help individual pupils because all the pupils are working in their own workbook.
13. The pupil actually has a longer reading period.

In the past few years, numerous programmed materials designed to teach reading skills have appeared. A mechanical programmed learning device is the Edison Responsive Environment or Edison Talking Typewriter (43).[10] The pupil sits in front of the E. R. E. (talking typewriter). He can reach only the typewriter keyboard. All other parts are behind a transparent shield. When he presses a key, the letter is printed in large size and a prerecorded voice names the letter. As soon as each of the letters is learned, more complicated programming is introduced. The pupil progresses from the alphabet to words, sentences, and stories. At more advanced levels he can type complete stories and read them aloud to be recorded and played back.

Initially, an electric typewriter was used. The fingernails of the child were painted in different colors to match colors on the keyboard. When the fingernail-keyboard colors matched, the machine worked; if they did not match, the typewriter did not work. In teaching reading, a picture of a cow with the letters c-o-w is flashed on a screen. The letters c-o-w are illuminated on the typewriter permitting the child to practice the letters and word. The illumination on the keyboard and the letters c-o-w on the screen gradually fade, and when the picture of the cow reappears, the child is expected to type c-o-w.

Here are some published programmed materials:

1. Brogan, Andrews and Hotchkiss, Emily, *Dialogue I: An Aural-Oral Course in Phonics* [Chester Electronic Laboratories, Inc., 1963]. The 31 tapes, accompanied by 62 booklets, provide a programmed phonics course for first grade or remedial groups.

2. Brown, James, *Programmed Vocabulary* [Appleton-Century-Crofts]. This is a packet of 320 printed originals containing a step-by-step lesson plan to improve word power and reading ability.

3. *Building Reading Power* [Charles E. Merrill Books, Inc.]. This programmed course for improving reading techniques is designed for students who read on or about the fifth-grade level. There are 15 different booklets, covering such topics as picture and verbal context, visual clues, definitions, synonyms, antonyms, context, prefixes, suffixes, main ideas, central thought of a paragraph, and details of a paragraph.

4. Deighton, Lee C., and Sanford, Adrian B., *et al.*, *The Macmillan Reading Spectrum*. This is a non-graded, multi-level program for building the vital reading skills. It consists of six word analysis booklets, six Vocabulary Development booklets, and

[10] Talking Typewriter (Edison Responsive Environment System). Responsive Environments Corporation, 21 East 40th Street, New York, New York.

six Reading Comprehension booklets. Placement tests are provided. The lessons in the skill booklets are self-directing and self-correcting. Included also are two sets of books, 60 in all, ranging from a second grade reading level to eighth grade.

5. Fry, Edward B., *Lessons for Self-Instruction in Basic Skills* [California Test Bureau, 1963]. This is designed for grades 3–9 and teaches reference skills, following directions, levels of interpretation and vocabulary development.

6. *Honor Products Programmed Materials* [Honor Products, Inc.]. These materials consist of a pushbutton testing machine and the following programs:

    a. *A Guide to Efficient Study* (ninth grade).
    b. *Building Words* (seventh grade).
    c. *Fun with Words-Homonyms* (second grade).
    d. *Persuasive Words—Effective Word Usage* (eighth grade).
    e. *Reading Comprehension* (ninth grade).
    f. *Synonyms and Antonyms* (ninth grade).
    g. *Vocabulary Building* (ninth grade).
    h. *Word Clues* (seventh grade).

7. *Imperial Primary Reading Program* [Imperial Productions, Inc., Kankakee, Illinois]. This is a self-teaching program for grades one to three on forty tapes.

8. *Michigan Successive Discrimination Language Program* [Ann Arbor Publishers, 711 North University, Ann Arbor, Michigan, 1964]. This programmed basal reading series covers auditory, visual, and space discrimination, letters, words, phrases, sentences, paragraphs, manuscript writing, phonemic analysis, spelling, oral composition, and comprehension.

9. *Peabody Rebus Reading Program* [American Guidance Service, Inc., Circle Pines, Minnesota]. This is a programmed approach to readiness and beginning reading instruction. It consists of two workbooks, using a vocabulary of picture words (Rebuses).

10. *Programmed Phonics* [Educators Publishing Service]. These two books, for grades four to six, are designed for remedial teaching of phonics. There are three general objectives: (1) to train the student to attribute the proper sound to each letter in a word or syllable; (2) to train the student to perceive aurally and visually, and to respond vocally to each letter in a syllable and each syllable in a word in a left-to-right sequential order; and (3) to train the student to read whole words accurately and quickly.

Assuming a fair understanding of initial and final consonant sounds, Books 1 and 2 teach a basic phonic repertory, including a review of difficult consonants and of all consonant blends. In addition, the student is trained to use principles of structural analysis and basic rules of pronunciation.

An aural-visual approach is used involving a workbook and either a tape or a script which may be read by the teacher. Each lesson presents several phonic elements through a series of auditory discrimination and dictations. The tape or script gives directions, prompts examples, and works through each frame and each page with the student. Having written a response, the student is informed immediately of the correctness or incorrectness of his answer. Correct answers are uncovered by moving a plastic mask down the page as the lesson progresses.

11. *Reading* [M. W. Sullivan, Behavioral Research Laboratories, Box 577, Palo Alto, California]. This is two-series program of eight books designed to develop basic alphabetic, phonic, and structural skills.

12. *Sullivan Programmed Reading* [Webster Division, McGraw-Hill Book Company]. This is a fully-developed phonic reading program consisting of a prereading series and series I, II, and III. In all 21 programmed workbooks are available.

13. Taylor, S., Frackenpohl, H., McDonald, A., and Jolene, N., *EDL Word Clues* [Educational Developmental Laboratories, 1962]. These are programmed workbooks, with seven to twelve reading level. Each Word Clues book consists of thirty lessons of ten words each.

Language-experience Approach[11] Another stimulus approach is the language-experience approach. It teaches beginners to read through associating print with meaningful personal experiences. The experience approach began some sixty years ago when Flora J. Cooke at the Chicago Institute and later at the Francis Parker School began putting on the blackboard children's oral expressions. It grew and developed as part of the Progressive Education Movement. The latter deemphasized the importance of systematic and sequential presentation of materials in favor of purpose, interest, and meaning. In 1934 Nila Smith termed this approach the "experience method," and recently it has been termed the language-experience approach.

The experience approach, advocated in *Learning to Read Through Experience* by R. Van Allen and Doris M. Lee (Appleton-Century-Crofts), and presented in the *Language-Experience Program* by Roach Van Allen and Caryce Allen (Encyclopaedia Britannica Press, Chicago),

[11] See Marjorie A. Crutchfield, "In Practice: The Language-Experience Approach to Reading," *Elementary English*, 43 (March, 1966) 285–288.

illustrates the language-experience approach in beginning reading. *Language Arts for Beginners, a Portfolio of Charts* (D. C. Heath) (64) provides the teacher with help in the use of experience charts. The personalized reading program as described in *Educator's Guide to Personalized Reading Instruction* (Prentice-Hall) is a classroom organizational pattern which permits the language-experience approach to operate.

Textfilm Reading Program   The textfilm reading program, originated by McCracken in the New Castle Experiment, features the use of correlated filmstrips to accompany each page of printed text.

The textfilm frame contains the same image as is in the textbook. Each lesson begins at the screen and ends in the textbook. This approach has demonstrated its usefulness in motivating children and in addition permits reading to begin at a far-point. It takes cognizance of the fact that at age six many children are farsighted and thus might more sensibly be taught to read at a distance.

Mediational Approaches

Let us now turn our attention to the mediational approaches. The mediational approaches emphasize the neurological, physiological, and chemical changes that accompany reading. They note that learning and indeed reading occur in a cranium. Some children do not learn to read because internal events have gone awry. Specialists in remedial reading are aware that faulty teaching methods per se are not always the cause of reading failure. The conditions limiting learning often appear to be not in the method but in the learner.

Some today lean toward a biological-neurological explanation of reading disability. Reading difficulties thus often are said to have been caused by damage to or dysfunction of certain localized areas of the brain or of other physiological mechanisms.

Delacato (18,19) has revived Orton's mixed dominance theory with some changes and has built a reading program on it. He believes that neurological development and organization of the human organism are the key to language and reading development and to language and reading difficulties. It is suggested that the basic difference between man and the animal world is that man has achieved cortical dominance, rather than cellular quantity. When the dominant hemisphere experiences certain trauma, loss of language skills results.

Delacato recommends that:

1. Children should be encouraged to engage in unified one-sided activity (e.g., Do not allow children to have double-holster gun

sets). Until preference for one side is evidenced, naturally both sides should be given equal opportunity to become dominant.

2. Children should not be allowed to suck the thumb of the dominant hand.

3. Parents should be sensitized to anoxia and head injuries as possible causes of language disturbance. Since crying and breath-holding may reduce cortical oxygen supply, they should be reduced to the minimum level.

4. All tonal activity, listening to music or singing, should be deleted in remedial teaching. Oral reading should be done in whispers, thus activating the dominant hemisphere and developing unilaterality.

5. Since poor readers lack cortical organization (they exhibit faulty posturalization in sleep) mothers should be taught to posturalize their children. From the age of nine weeks on children should be posturalized on their stomach when put to bed.

6. The reading activity should originate at the word sight level—learn words at sight through configuration. The language-experience approach is encouraged. Children are taught reading by wholes at the outset. To begin, they are given common experiences as a class group, such as going on a trip. Upon their return to the classroom the teacher and children discuss what they did and saw, and the teacher writes an "experience chart" which is dictated by the children. The experience chart is made in sentence and story form. After the sentences are recorded and read, they are broken down into meaningful phrases. Having learned to recognize sentences and phrases containing between 100 and 150 words via this method, the children are given books which, through proper teacher planning, will contain most of the words met via the experience charts.

7. Later a dualistic system of recognizing new words as wholes is used: recognizing them through small familiar words which make up the large words and through the sound components of words. No child should be taught the letter-sound method until he has established complete unilaterality, has complete mastery of left-to-right progression (this usually takes more time and effort for the left-handed children), and does not reverse letters or words.

8. Finally the teacher should evaluate how each child masters reading skills most efficiently, and should teach the child via the method which best meets his needs. No "one" method will be the most efficient for all children. At this point an eclectic approach to methods is ideal. If neurological organization has been achieved, method is secondary.

9. Peripheral activity . . . such as vision, dexterity, skills, phonetics,

various reading techniques, are meaningless in remediation if the total neurological organization is defective. The prerequisite to peripheral therapy is central neurological organization.

AN EVALUATION OF READING METHODS

Obviously, when one speaks of reading method, there are many divergent points of view, and it is just as obvious that one's point of view is the result of one's own, perhaps biased, interpretations. We believe in an eclectic point of view.[12]

Eclecticism generally is defined as "the selection and orderly combination of compatible features from diverse sources," the combination of valid elements from various theories into an harmonious whole. Few teachers have arrived at such a synthesis. Few teachers can honestly say that the approach which they are using is a systematic and orderly synthesis of data from various theories. And, yet, eclecticism of some kind seems necessary.

We thus propose an eclecticism for the *teacher* that encourages him to select from the great variety of approaches that one or combination of approaches which best meets the needs of the pupil. We propose that the selection of method or approach in teaching reading should be based on the individual differences of the learner. Perhaps instead of the word, eclecticism, we should borrow the phrase of Elizabeth Vasquez, a principal of Homestead School in Garden City, New York. She speaks of an "All-method Method" of teaching reading.

Today most teachers probably use a combination or eclectic approach. Some begin with the total word and then *more or less* simultaneously break it down into its phonemic elements (Analytic-Synthetic Method). Others begin with the phonemes and then combine these to form meaningful words (Synthetic-Analytic Method). In Chapter 10 we present a phonic approach which begins with the total word and which we have labelled "Linguistic Phonics."

The Rationale for Eclecticism

What is the rationale for a combination or eclectic approach in reading method? Why do most teachers today use both a synthetic and an an-

---

[12] For a more complete discussion of this position, see Emerald Dechant, "Why an Eclectic Approach in Reading Instruction?" *Vistas in Reading,* Proceedings of the Eleventh Annual Convention, International Reading Asssociation, Newark, 1967, pp. 28–32.

alytic approach, even though many disagree on the question of whether reading teaching should begin with an analytic or synthetic approach?

Research and experience have shown that for genuine independence in reading children need *both* analytic and synthetic approaches. Children need to observe the whole word and they need to look and listen for those characteristics that individualize a word.

Ames and Walker (1) studied fifth grade children and found that the better readers showed greater clarity, accuracy, and appreciation of detail and fewer gross global responses than did those who became poorer readers.

Goins (35,36) found that good readers were able to keep in mind the total configuration (word) or the total language pattern (sentence) while at the same time attending to parts of the word. The good reader is not preoccupied with details for their own sake. The poor reader is often preoccupied with details, frequently failing to assimilate the details into the whole. The good reader can shift from whole to part or from detail to whole. His perceptual approach shows flexibility and versatility (39, p. 284).

The analytic and the synthetic method are two partial and yet indispensable phases of the total learning process. The child must be able to synthesize the parts into a whole and to analyze the whole into its parts.

The implications are obvious. Synthesis and phonics are an integral part of the reading program. Phonics cannot be relegated to a separate phonics period, to be used only when some other method doesn't work.

The good reader probably is one who uses all the analytic-synthetic methods, intertwining them in such a way that he doesn't even know which one he is using at any given moment.

In general, *research and experience have shown that an analytical or whole-word approach has worked with most children.* They have, however, also shown with the same degree of validity and reliability that the analytic method has not worked with *all* children and that the synthetic method has worked with *some* children. No one method has been found to be equally satisfactory in all classrooms with all pupils.

The task facing teachers and psychologists today is that of identifying the pupil who learns best with either one or the other method. Who is the pupil that would best be introduced to reading through a synthetic approach? Who is the pupil that would best be introduced to reading through an analytic approach?

Both the synthetic and the analytic methods have something to offer in the teaching of reading. Effective reading results from a *flexibility* in behavior. This is a legitimate and, it seems, a valuable goal in teaching word attack skills.

As one scans the literature, listens to experts in the field, or observes practices in the classroom, one is amazed by the many methods of teaching reading. Each method is proposed as an answer to a reading problem; perhaps not *the* answer, but nevertheless an answer. There is not one advocate of a method who submits that his or her method does not work or who is unable to adduce evidence as to its effectiveness. And the fact is that children have become readers, indeed good readers, through analytic, synthetic, or combination approaches.

Thus, unless one is willing to call every researcher or practitioner who claims to have success with a given method a cheat, one has to accept that success may come by many paths. Since many different roads can and do eventually lead to reading proficiency, we are unwilling to accept that only one method, one approach, or one technique is successful with *all* children. There simply is not sufficient evidence in support of one approach that warrants universal allegiance to it as the supposedly best or only way of teaching reading.

A second argument for eclecticism is the fact that children are different and learn differently. Eclecticism is based on the assumption that until it is possible to standardize youth, it seems unwise to standardize reading method. If children were all alike, we might look for *the* method. Indeed, we would have found it long ago. If all children were identical twins, with identical experiences, we would not notice individual differences among them. And, without the individual differences, we would have no need for a variety of methods. If there were no differences, there would be no need to differentiate. But, the simple fact is that children are different from one another intellectually, physically, emotionally, socially, and perceptually, and they seem to be differentiated on the basis of the method that is beneficial to them. There is nothing wrong with the sight-word configuration. It becomes wrong when we use it exclusively with all children.

Teacher differences are a third reason for eclecticism.[13] The teacher's preferred mode of reaction may be as significant as the method of teaching that he is using. Two equally competent teachers may not be able to use the same method with equal effectiveness. Chall and Feldmann (13) found that teachers vary in their implementation of reading method and that teacher variables influence reading achievement. It may be as significant in the education of future teachers (and in your own personal success in teaching) that you and prospective teachers develop competency in method in line with your own natural style of responding and communicating. Some one of you, because of your personal makeup, may do a beautiful job with individualized reading; another, because of his personal characteristics, may be doomed to failure.

[13] See Emerald Dechant, "Teacher Differences and Reading Method," *Education*, 86 (September, 1965) 40–43.

The Consequences of Eclecticism

What does the acceptance of eclecticism imply? It implies, among other things: (*1*) that the teacher understand the differences in children; and (2) that the teacher become familiar with a host of reading methods.

We have already discussed the importance of the teacher's knowledge of the pupil that he is trying to teach. The effectiveness of the teacher's knowledge with a specific method depends to a great degree on his understanding of the pupil whom he wants to teach. This differential in knowledge of the learner quite frequently accounts for the fact that one teacher is successful with a particular method and another teacher fails. The really successful teacher is one who has developed an extraordinary sensitivity to the differences among children in the classroom and makes adjustments for them. A method of teaching is adequate only if the teacher knows enough about the child so that he can adapt the method to the specific child.

A second major consequence of accepting a position of eclecticism is a need to become more familiar with a great variety of methods of teaching reading. The teacher of reading today needs to be able to provide proper remediation all along the way. This means he needs to know what is best or probably best for a given child. It is not enough to know *a* method of teaching. It is necessary to know *the* method that is best for a *given* child. This means he must become familiar with a host of methods.

Teachers with the most novel of approaches to teaching reading often claim to be unusually successful with their method. It may be, and indeed often is so, that these teachers work harder or are more enthusiastic than the average teacher. But, it may also be true that their novel approach may be especially effective with some child because it meets his need in a special way. There are methods or specific approaches to teaching that make a world of difference for the individual child. One child benefits from one type of instruction, while another may not.

When the teacher is acceptant of the student, when he respects the individuality of the pupil, shows understanding and empathy, has deep faith in the improvability of the pupil, and identifies the pupil's area of confidence, we find that that teacher's pupils generally are successful (16). Because learning occurs in a relationship, the teacher's personality and his ability to enlist the child's active cooperation are often more important than the specific method used.

The simple fact is that other factors that make for disability in reading frequently pale into insignificance when the teacher is an interesting and an interested teacher. The teacher must be something of an expert in reading method, but he also must care for the pupil. Teaching method is not the final answer. The superiority of one method over another resides in such factors as teacher knowledge of and teacher enthusiasm for the method. Reading disability seems to require a predisposition in the pupil and an initial approach or method that ignores it.

Dawson (17), in evaluating the 28 first grade studies, writes: "The one element that was found absolutely essential for a successful program in reading is a competent teacher."

Bond and Dykstra (7,8), in a similar evaluation, concluded that it is the teacher that makes the difference and that no one method is significantly superior to any other method or such that it should be the one to be used exclusively.

Bond (7), in his summary evaluation, made these observations:

1. There is no one method that is so outstanding that it should be used to the exclusion of the others.
2. The effectiveness of any one approach appears to be increased when it is broadened by addition of other instructional components. . . .
3. Specific approaches to first-grade reading instruction appeared to increase children's achievement in certain instructional outcomes but are weak in other outcomes. . . .
4. . . . there was greater variation between the teachers within the methods than there was between the methods.[14]

The research[15] from the continuation of the first-grade studies into the second year suggests that:

1. Bond's evaluations of the first-year studies seem to be still valid.
2. The factor that made a difference was a good teacher . . . (7, p. 692). The wide variations in achievement means within each method, which far exceeded the differences between methods, seem to indicate that in this study the teacher was a far more important influence than the particular method used (7, p. 702).

SUMMARY

In this chapter we have discussed the two basic reading skills: word identification, and the association of meaning with a printed symbol. We have pointed out that a good reading program must give due con-

---

[14] Guy L. Bond, "First-grade Reading Studies: An Overview," *Elementary English*, 43 (May, 1966) 464–470. Reprinted with permission.

[15] See the *Reading Teacher*, 20 (May, 1967).

sideration to both identification and meaning. Neither one by itself is adequate.

We have emphasized the importance of both analysis and synthesis in reading and have suggested that neither the configuration nor the phonic method meets the needs of every pupil nor perhaps *all* the needs of even one pupil. However, since identification of words must be economical, must allow for the greatest amount of transfer, and since it is primarily the process of associating the visual symbol with its oral equivalent, there seems to be a need for the development of a coding system that permits the pupil to attack new words without having to learn a new configuration each time. The teaching of identification skills must make some provision for independence in word attack. *The ultimate goal is self-direction in the learning process.*

The pupil who depends totally on configuration skills finds progress increasingly more difficult because his identification problems increase as new words are introduced more and more rapidly (40, p. 16). Independence in reading does not seem possible without phonetic and structural analysis skills. Phonics training seems to equip the pupil with *one* general coding system that fosters development in independence. There are others.

We have every right to expect our children to learn to read more words in the first and second grade than they at present are capable of reading. Studies (65,66) show that the oral recognition vocabulary of first grade children may be as high as 26,363 words, although Ames (2) found that the median size of a pupil's understanding vocabulary in first grade is more like 13,000. Certainly, in six years of listening and speaking the child has learned many more words than we at present seem to be teaching him to read. It seems reasonable to expect children to learn to read, in grades one and two, a greater percentage of those words that are a part of their speaking and listening vocabulary.

Perhaps a few generalizations are apropos in closing this chapter.

1. Most children learn to read regardless of the method. Many different methods can and do eventually lead to reading proficiency. One type of program does not seem to be clearly superior to all others or best for all children.

2. There are methods or specific teaching approaches that make a world of difference for the individual child.

3. The method that works best for a given child depends on the individual child. Not all children profit to the same extent from a given method. What is good for slow learners may not work with gifted learners.

4. No one program seems to provide for all the child's reading requirements.

5. The "best" method for *most* children has both an analytical *and* a synthetic emphasis. There are few pure-configuration methods, and few programs ignore phonics completely.

6. Some teachers do not make use of the best that is available, but if the teacher is a good teacher, other factors often pale into insignificance. Differences in program effectiveness often can be attributed to teacher effectiveness.

7. A given method may well produce excellent results under one set of conditions, but may result in failure under a different set of circumstances.

What does good teaching include? In reading, good teaching seems to mean that the teacher devises techniques of instruction which help the pupil to construct a generic code or a coding system that has wider applicability in reading than would the rote identification of individual words. The code has wider application than in the situation in which it was learned. The child learns to "read off" from this generic code information that permits him to attack other words. Such learning maximizes the transfer of learning. The child, in a sense, is taught to be a better guesser by knowing the language system and the phonogram-phoneme interrelationships. The newer approaches in reading seem to be carrying out the implications of this statement. They are concerned with the utility of learning: Whether, if the pupil has learned one thing, he will be able to handle other situations without additional learning; Whether, if he has learned to identify some words, he also has learned a system that helps him to identify other words (9, p. 67).

Phonics is no longer a real issue in reading. All systematized approaches to reading teach phonics in one way or another. All approaches stress the importance of attaining meaning. All emphasize both an analytical and a synthetic approach.

However, there are differences as to the route to ultimate progress in reading. Should the earliest emphasis be on meaning or on word discrimination? [16] We have tried to show that this is a pseudo-question, that both are essential from the beginning. There must be a delicate balance between the two, lest the child be dragged too far afield in either. There must be a middle course between a complete discrimination approach in which pupils perhaps can recognize words but can't think with the materials and a meaning approach in which children might be able to enjoy reading but can't recognize the words.

In the configuration approach the printed word is directly associated with an idea; in the word-discrimination approach greater emphasis

[16] For a thorough discussion of this, see Theodore L. Harris, "Some Issues in Beginning Reading Instruction," *Journal of Educational Research*, 56 (September 1962) 5–19.

is placed on the association of the printed word with the spoken word for which the child has a meaning. The first of these has been an effective way for introducing reading. It seems that the second is essential to develop independence in reading.

The need for both approaches again seems indicated. Children need to see words as units, but they also need to pay attention to parts. We do not want to have children capable of reacting only to the whole, neither do we want them to become fixated on the parts.

The child, in this approach to reading, must be viewed as a learner capable of discrimination and generalization who can, with guidance, learn a generalized coding system which he can use in identifying numerous words not previously seen by him.

QUESTIONS FOR DISCUSSION

1. Discuss: "The quickest way to the meaning of a word is through its sound."
2. What has been the historical, psychololgical, and experiential basis for the analytic or word method?
3. Discuss the validity of the word method in the light of newer research and new interpretations of previous research.
4. By examples, illustrate the difference between systematic meaning and referential meaning.
5. Discuss Bruner's thesis that the good reader must develop some sort of coding system which permits the pupil to achieve independence in attacking words.
6. Discuss: Children react to the perceptual whole but this may be the total word or only a specific characteristic of that word such as an ascending letter.
7. Discuss the pros and cons of the question: Do children from infancy perceive the world in the fully articulated way that adults do?
8. Discuss the argument that children are not really being taught to read with meaning. The books contain words and concepts which are so simple that the child can't do anything but understand. How can one teach understanding if there is nothing left to understand?
9. Discuss: Using the context to guess an unknown word may be a harmful technique.
10. Discuss: Is the child characteristically reacting to the whole word or is he latching on to some particular element? Is there some justification for assuming that the pupil's response implies no more than the minimum of knowledge to reproduce it?
11. Discuss: Letters have meaning. The letter gives instructions to the voice

muscles and the order of the letters in words lets the reader know in what order the instructions are to be carried out.

12. Discuss:

    a. The quickest and most economical way to the meaning of the printed word generally is through its sound.

    b. The unit of meaning and of recognition may not be the unit of indentification.

    c. The basic pattern or Gestalt in language is the phoneme-phonogram interrelationship rather than the size or shape of the word.

    d. The perceptual whole is a relative term, dependent for its formation upon the ability, experience, purposes, maturation, perceptual skill, and learning habits of the learner.

    e. The good "identifier" of words learns a coding system based on the transitional probabilities that characterize letter sequences in English and that characterize the sound-print relationships of the language.

    f. When words are learned as configurations and as the number of words learned increases, the possibility for errors in recognition also increases.

    g. The basic identification skill is the "seeing" of the sound in the printed symbol.

    h. Word attack training gives better results with the average pupil than with the bright pupil. (The bright pupil generally acquires word attack skills through his everyday reading experience.)

    i. The more a child's achievement has been lowered by lack of attention and concentration, the more helpful is the kinaesthetic method.

    j. Pupils generally achieve significantly higher on a word recognition test when taught by a phonic method than when taught by a look-and-say method.

Introducing the
Elementary Reading Program

chapter 9

The elementary reading program is a many-sided program. In this chapter we are concerned with the major aspects of this program. What constitutes a good program? What must be taught in such a program? What are its aims and objectives? What, in general, is the best way to introduce the pupil to actual reading?

INTRODUCING THE PUPIL TO READING

The first grader has learned much about reading. He has looked at, heard, and used words.

When he begins first grade, he is asked to make a more formal and a more systematic attack on printed words. He must look at the form [of the word], speak the pronunciation, and understand the meaning. He needs to identify the word, and in the course of his elementary school years will learn to attack the word through phonetic analysis, through the word's shape or configuration, through the use of contextual clues, picture clues, through structural clues, through syllabication, or by using the dictionary. He must learn that a printed word has a form, that it has a pronunciation, and that it has a meaning. Reading is a *see, say,* and *comprehend* process.

Children early note that words have specific shapes or configurations, that some are short and others are long, and that some have ascending letters and others have descending letters. This information is most useful. Shape identifies a word for the child.

As noted in the previous chapter, major teaching tasks still remain. Children must be taught to identify the word by "seeing mentally" the pronunciation of the word, and if they have not already done so, they must learn that symbols have meaning or that they stand for something.

The beginning reading program is an extension of the child's readiness program. In the beginning program the child is formally introduced to reading materials, such as experience charts, preprimers, primers, and first readers.

The Experience Chart

Children have a natural inclination to want to talk about their experiences either as individuals or as groups. They may want to describe a mountain trip, the bottling of Coca Cola, the planting of a garden, or the harvesting of wheat. The teacher should use this language activity to introduce reading. He may write the description on the blackboard and eventually may transfer it to the tag-board. Later, especially in the upper grades, charts may be used to introduce old words in new contexts, to study rhyming, to develop creative thinking, to record classroom directions, to record steps in an experiment, or to summarize information.

Initially, however, the experience chart is a simple, meaningful, and highly motivating introduction to reading. The pupils report a common experience and the teacher prints it on the chalk board. The story or incident is changed by the teacher only when he needs to modify the vocabulary. The vocabulary normally is simple; the sentences are short; and three or four sentences complete the story.

The steps in making an experience chart are usually the following:

1. Provide for commonality of experience.
2. Have children discuss their experiences.
3. Record on the blackboard the key ideas.
4. Have children read the chart as a whole.
5. Isolate parts of the chart for specific emphasis.
6. Have children read again the chart as a whole.
7. Make a file of experience charts and label them "Our Big Book."
8. Have the children read the stories occasionally.

The child comes to school with a well-developed speaking language. This language reflects his home background and may deviate somewhat from the language he will be taught in school. Experience charts allow for a gradual transition to the formalized language in books. Moving from the known (child's spoken language) to the unknown (the written language) is good educational procedure and experience charts make this possible. They provide the pupil with his own model of sentence patterns and with experiences with which he is familiar.

Developing experience charts also teaches the child the natural relationships between the language arts (70, p. 263). He already has learned that what he can think he can say. Now he learns that what can be said can be written and what can be written can be read. The child learns that sounds can be put into written form and that the beginning sounds, middle sounds, and ending sounds can be graphically symbolized.

Basal Reading Materials

Although most teachers use experience charts of one form or another, few have thought of them as comprising the total reading fare. The need for sequential development in reading skills is difficult to satisfy by their use alone. Most children profit greatly from a steady progression through graded materials.

Such graded materials have come to be known as basal reading materials. They are designed to provide continuity in reading development and to provide training in *all* the basic reading skills. They aim at systematic instruction.

In the greatest number of schools the basal reader is still the most important material used in the reading program. Its importance seems especially significant in the primary years.

The basal reading program leads the pupil by logical and sequential steps to the mastery of the basic reading skills. It is perhaps true that basal readers in their attempt to provide systematic instruction, controlled vocabularies, and mastery of the basic reading skills have failed to some degree in providing purposeful reading. Be that as it may, they have been shown to be helpful in developing reading proficiency in most children. They represent what many people believe to be the "best" materials available for leading the child from the prereading stage to actual reading.

In the wake of the book, *Learning to Read: The Great Debate*[1] by Chall, will surely come new evaluations of the basal readers, but the simple fact is that the research supports the usefulness of the basal readers. Dawson (14), evaluating the 27 first-grade studies, notes: "No one method or type of teaching material was found to be adequate in itself; each one needed supplementation. . . . However, in most of the investigations where basal readers were used, results were favorable to the use

[1] McGraw-Hill Publishing Company, New York, 1968.

of such books. . . . Each method proved to be successful with certain pupils, less so with others. . . ." The results of the second-year extensions[2] of these studies seem to lead to the same overall evaluation.

Harris and Serwer (27) reported greater success with the basal reader method with the disadvantaged children than with the language-experience approach. McCanne (51) had similar results with children from Spanish-speaking homes.

It would seem that an adequate reading program must include teaching of the basic skills, must provide suitable materials to teach the skills, and should provide the proper reading content (30, p. 171). Because of the latter aspect, basal reading programs have always encouraged the use of supplementary materials.

Two philosophies and/or procedures of using reading materials have developed through the years. One of these, perhaps the most prevalent in the past, emphasized the sequential nature of materials. All children were required to master the sequence of skills; only the speed of introduction and the level of difficulty were modified. The second approach assigns greater responsibility to the learner in determining the continuity of learning (30, p. 172). This latter approach has been termed individualized reading. It makes the learner and his stage of development the major referents and relates instructional materials to them (30, p. 175).

Here is a list of the major basal reading series:

1. *The Alice and Jerry Basic Reading Program* [Harper and Row, Publishers].
2. *Bank Street Readers* [The Macmillan Company].
3. *Basic Reading Series* [J. B. Lippincott Company].
4. *Betts Basic Readers* [American Book Company].
5. *Building Reading Skills Series* [McCormick-Mathers].
6. *Catholic University of American Faith and Freedom Series* [Ginn and Company].
7. *Chandler Language-Experience Readers* [Chandler Publishing Company].
8. *City Schools Reading Program* [Follett Publishing Company].
9. *Developmental Reading Text-Workbooks* [Bobbs-Merrill].
10. *Developmental Reading Series* [Lyons and Carnahan].
11. *Easy Growth in Reading Series* [Holt, Rinehart, and Winston, Inc.].
12. *Economy Reading Workbooks* [Economy Company].
13. *Gateway to Reading Treasure Series* [Laidlaw Brothers].
14. *Get Ready to Read Series* [Bobbs-Merrill].

[2] For a description and detailed analysis of these programs in the second year see *The Second Grade Extension of First Grade Reading Studies*, The Reading Teacher, Volume 20, May 1967.

15. *Ginn Basic Readers* [Ginn and Company].
16. *Harper and Row Basic Reading Program* [Harper and Row, Publishers].
17. *Learning to Read Series* [Silver Burdett Company].
18. *The Linguistic Readers* [Harper and Row].
19. *The Macmillan Readers* [The Macmillan Company].
20. *Merrill Linguistic Readers* [Charles E. Merrill Books, Inc.].
21. *The New Basic Readers* [Scott, Foresman and Company].
22. *Open Court Basic Readers* [Open Court Publishing Company].
23. *Prose and Poetry Series* [L. W. Singer Company].
24. *The Quinlan Basic Readers* [Allyn and Bacon, Inc.].
25. *Reading Essentials Series* [Steck Vaughn Company].
26. *Reading for Interest Series,* Revised [D. C. Heath and Company].
27. *Reading for Meaning Series,* Revised Edition [Houghton Mifflin Company].
28. *Royal Road Readers* [Educators Publishing Service].
29. *Scott, Foresman Basic Reading Program* [Scott, Foresman and Company].
30. *Sheldon's Basic Reading Series* [Allyn and Bacon, Inc.].
31. *Sounds of Language Series* [Holt, Rinehart and Winston, Inc.].
32. *SRA Basic Reading Series* [Science Research Associates].
33. *Winston Basic Readers* [Holt, Rinehart, and Winston Inc.].

Preprimers, Primers, and First Readers

The first graded basal materials are usually the preprimers. These are extensions of the readiness materials and frequently contain stories with the same characters as were met in the readiness materials. The vocabulary is simple (perhaps too simple) and is systematically repeated. Primers and first readers are extensions of the preprimers.

The McKee series[3] contains three preprimers: *Tip, Tip and Mitten,* and *The Big Show.* These materials introduce the child to 60 words. *Tip* has five stories and 20 different words; *Tip and Mitten* has three stories and 25 new words; and *The Big Show* has three stories and 15 new words.

The same series has one primer, *Jack and Janet,* consisting of 11 stories and 91 new words. The first reader, *Up and Away,* has ten stories and introduces 164 new words.

Each of the readers is usually accompanied by a workbook that leads the child step-by-step through a carefully developed program of instruction. The workbook introduces the vocabulary and provides the experiential background needed for successful reading. It is especially

---

[3] *Reading for Meaning Series,* Houghton Mifflin Company, Boston.

useful in meeting individual needs, in stimulating interest in reading, in providing opportunities for practice, in varying instructional procedures, and in making optimum use of pupil and teacher time.

In some workbooks today there is an attempt to apply the same principles as do the best programmed learning materials. The pupil is introduced to word recognition and comprehension skills in small steps and advances to higher levels only after successful completion of the simpler task. The workbooks provide the repetition, self-competition, and day-to-day records that make it possible for the pupil to grow and for the teacher to diagnose and to remediate the pupil's inadequacies.

Teacher manuals are provided to guide the teacher in his day-to-day and even minute-to-minute teaching. Unfortunately, these may work against good reading instruction. The teacher may become so reliant upon workbooks and teacher manuals that he falls imperceptibly into the lock-step that he would be the first to abhor.

Reeve (61) analyzed the vocabulary of seven primary reading series (preprimers, primers, and first readers) published by Scott, Foresman and Company; Macmillan; Ginn and Company; Houghton Mifflin Company; Holt, Rinehart and Winston; Harper and Row; and Allyn and Bacon. She found that 633 different words were introduced, 109 words were common to all the series, and 41 were common to 6 series.

This study has a number of implications. The teacher who uses more than one reading series probably will want to concentrate on the 150 words which were common to most series. They are considered "basic" and will be especially useful in group activities such as experience charts, word games, or word drills. The study also revealed that one series introduced only four words not found in any of the other series; another series introduced as many as sixty-four words not found in the other series. The teacher needs to know this if he is to encourage a gradual progression from easy to more difficult materials.

Another analysis (30, pp. 177–178) of twelve basal reading programs revealed that the total vocabulary of preprimers and primers ranged from 121 to 189 words, that the total vocabulary for materials through sixth grade ranged from 3894 words to 4436, and that one new word was introduced at the rate of every 50 to 110 running words.

Olson (58), in an analysis of seven series, found that only 12 per cent of the total vocabulary appeared in five or more of the series. There were a total of 763 different words introduced through the first reader level. Olson lists the 92 words that were common to five or more series.

Recently, evaluations of basal reading series have emphasized the excessive vocabulary control that is exercised in writing them. The above studies give some credence to this charge. Is it necessary to repeat a word again and again?

In studies involving 412 children Gates (19) found that third-grade children of average ability, as a result of previous experiences in word recognition and comprehension, have only slightly more difficulty with the "new" words that are introduced in fourth-grade basal readers than with words met previously in basal readers. In fact, the top 25 per cent of youngsters in the last half of the second grade had such an easy time with both third- and fourth-grade words that vocabulary control seemed of little value. Pupils of below-average ability had only slightly more difficulty with the "new" fourth-grade words than with those words met prior to the second half of grade three. Pupils apparently met most so-called "new" words in their supplementary reading or had developed a method for attacking them, perhaps a form of coding system that we discussed in the previous chapter.

The assumption of basal readers seems to be that children must learn completely within a short time each and every word that they meet. There seems to be no other reason for the constant repetition of words. However, we know that learning rarely results in total mastery. The child in his language learning certainly progresses quite differently. He may hear or say a word only a few times and even then there may be a long interval of time before he hears it again.

The principle of vocabulary control used in basal materials may not be valid. Vocabulary control is more than simply limiting the number of words and their rate of introduction. Frequency of use is not a valid criterion either, and yet, these seem to be the primary criteria of control in the basal series.

Basal readers introduce the pupil to relatively few different words. However, he may meet numerous regular and irregular phoneme-phonogram relationships. One preprimer, for example, introduces the pupil to only twenty different words but in those twenty words the pupil meets the following: sixteen different consonants, the double consonant *ll* as in call, one beginning-consonant blend, the end-consonant blend *nd*, the combination *ck*, and the *z* sound of *s*; the short vowels *i, a, e,* and *o*; the long vowels *e, o,* and *i*; the vowel combinations *ay* and *ou*; the short *u* sound of *o*; the *ȯ* sound of *a* as in ball; the silent *e* preceded by a long *e* and *o* sound as in mere and bone; the long *i* sound in the combination *ind*; and the peculiar *e* sound in the word *the*.

Perhaps, a control of the phoneme-phonogram relationships, the internal structure of words, would be more desirable than control of the number of words, and would lead to more meaningful learning, to better transfer of learning from one situation to another, and to less interference with learning. The pupil needs to learn that parts of words are useful in attacking new words, and he cannot do so when he meets a novel phoneme-phonogram relationship in each new word. Introducing children in one short breath to the short sound of *o,* the long sound of *o,* the short *u* sound of *o,* and the combination *ome* pronounced əm (as in come) and ōm (as in home) will leave many pupils gasping for air.

Despite these inadequacies, and it seems that basal readers could be improved, the basal series have helped teacher after teacher to teach hundreds of pupils to read. From our frame of reference and in the light of the discussion in the previous chapter, they are perhaps most useful in the early stages of reading and when the child is taught through a configuration approach. In the light of Gates' study (19) on the upper levels they may frequently be more useful in developing the pupil's comprehension skills than in actually teaching independence and self-direction in identification of words. This is not bad. It simply means that they must be supplemented by other materials and, in fact, usually are.

The teacher must adjust the materials to the pupil. No materials will fit all pupils in even one classroom. Some children learn more slowly and have greater difficulty in comprehending than others. Little is gained from meaningless repetition for all pupils when it leaves the bright child with the feeling that the teacher can make a story last, and last, and last. Nothing more is gained from rushing the slow learner through a series because the schedule calls for it.

TEACHING READING

Before discussing additional ways of introducing reading content to the child, let us examine the actual process of learning to read.

In some form or another reading in its earliest stages, such as of experience charts or preprimers, involves picture reading, association of sound with the total word, and use of context to get the meaning intended. We are in addition recommending that the child should from the beginning learn to name the letters, learn to write the letters, and learn to associate sound with the beginning consonant letter and the median vowel. The last three steps are necessary if the pupil is to attain independence in reading. Let us look at each of these steps.

Picture Reading

In the preprimer, the child is introduced to picture reading. A picture may accompany each thought unit, which at this level is a line of print. The picture gives clues to the meaning of the words and is the child's first attempt to use the context, even though picture context, to infer the word. The teacher points out that the picture is trying to tell the reader the same thing that the words convey.

As the child looks at the picture of Tip and Tom (Figure 9-1), the teacher may point out the specific details in the picture. Pointing to the title of the story, he shows the pupil that this is a story about Tip and Tom and that the title tells him this. Then, making certain that the pupil is looking at the words he says: "This says: Tip and Tom."

Figure 9-1.   Tip and Tom

Perhaps too many pictures accompany most preprimer and primer materials. Reading often becomes an exercise in picture reading, rather than in identification and understanding of the word. The pictures may even be distracting to a few beginners (85). King and Muehl (37), however, found that when the words were similar, faster learning resulted when the word was accompanied by a picture or when the child said the word rather than simply hearing it. They thus concluded that pictures should probably not be dispensed with in teaching sight-words or in beginning reading material as some writers of beginning reading material have done.

Weintraub (86) suggests that pictures may be simply pretty, may depict what is in the text, or may build a concept that is too difficult to develop through the use of words alone. They may also have motivational value. The research indicates that colored illustrations are preferred by young children over black and white, but that realism takes priority over color (86).

Association of Sound with the Whole Word

The teacher next prints the word *Tom* on the chalk board. If the reading exercise is an experience chart, the words will already be on the blackboard and the pupils will "read" the whole chart. The teacher will point out key words, asking each pupil to look at the word and say "Tom." The teacher asks: "What does it say?" Later he may teach the child that what a word *says* is a clue to what it *means*. The child must learn that the sound of the word, if the meaning of the spoken word is known to him, is usually a clue to its meaning. The child should realize that printed words are talk written down and that he has spoken similar words and sentences time and time again.

Since the method of sounding recommended here and which we discuss in detail in Chapter 10 is the analytical method of sounding (31) or perhaps the linguistic phonic method (3, p. 28), we begin with the whole word. It is hoped that the child will learn the phonemes of the language and apply them in learning to identify new words by repeatedly hearing and "seeing" them in meaningful words. Key charts are made for every vowel and consonant sound, and the pupil should refer to these when in doubt. For example, *bat* may be the key word for the initial *b* sound in words. The key words, since they frequently are accompanied by pictures, should be the only possible name for the picture.

As noted in the previous chapter, the distinction in actual practice between whole-word sounding and the configuration-recognition method of identifying words is not as great as it appears. Sounding whole words may be an optimum method for teaching the configuration of words. Many children, who have been taught to "look at the word," probably pay as much or more attention to the *sound* of the word than to its shape. Heilman (29, p. 106)[4] notes that: "Those who have mastered the process of reading are likely to lose sight of the many factors which must mesh at a given moment if success in reading is to be achieved. It is much easier to describe how to teach reading than to state specifically how children *learn* this process."

Use of the Verbal Context

The pupil also needs to learn that he can use the verbal or semantic and grammatical or structural *context* to arrive at the pronunciation and the meaning of the word (55). Research (43,21) indicates that pupils read words more quickly when the words are preceded by a context word, and they read them more quickly when the cue is grammatical (the dove) than when it is semantic (bird dove). Goodman (21) found that reading a word in a list is much more difficult than reading the word in a story.

The child should always ask: Does the word make sense in the sentence? What word would make sense in the sentence? The child thus fits the word into its environment and from it may get his first pronunciation clue.

[4] Arthur W. Heilman, *Principles and Practices of Teaching Reading* (Columbus: Charles E. Merrill Books, Inc., 1961). Reprinted by permission.

Leary (42) points out the value of teaching a word in context:

> Train a child to anticipate probable meaning, to infer an unknown word from its total context, to skip a word and read on to derive its probable meaning, to check the context clue with the form of the word, to search the context for a description or explanation that will identify the word, and he will have acquired the most important single aid to word recognition. For, regardless of what word he perceives, if it doesn't "make sense" in its setting, his perception has been in error.[5]

Linguists emphasize that the grammatical or structural context is just as important as the verbal or meaning context "in making language comprehensible and in framing and delimiting and defining sentence elements . . . (22)."

Unfortunately, the verbal and/or grammatical context, especially in preprimers, primers, and first readers, frequently is not of much help (53, p. 98). *Tom has a ball* gives little help in identifying the word *ball*. And *Nan bought the dog* gives little basis for inferring the word *bought*. It might be *sees, has,* or *liked*. Nevertheless, as the child advances in reading he must learn that when a word has more than one meaning only the context or the sentence structure may give the clue to the specific meaning intended.

In the beginning reading exercises, the teacher should be careful:

1. That context clues are not overemphasized.
2. That the reading exercise does not contain too many strange words.
3. That the child does not become frustrated in his attempts to unlock the word.

Learning the Names of the Letters

The child gradually needs to learn the names of the letters of the alphabet. Most children come to school knowing some of them, but few know all of them. The teacher must systematically introduce the letters and teach their names. He may select the word "Tom" from an experience story. He asks the children to look at the word, "Tom," containing the separate letters *T, o, m*. The teacher explains the differences among the letters, uses letter cards to fixate the association between the letter form

---

[5] Bernice E. Leary, "Developing Word Perception Skills in Middle and Upper Grades," *Current Problems in Reading Instruction* (Pittsburgh: University of Pittsburgh Press, 1950). Reprinted by permission.

and its name, and introduces the child to the capital and the lower case letter.

The teacher may use various techniques for teaching the letters.[6] The teacher may have cards containing a single capital or lower case letter; cards containing the same capital and lower case letter; and cards containing more than one letter. The latter requires the pupil to discriminate one letter from another letter. If the pupil has difficulty in discriminating one letter from another, as, for example, between *p* and *b*, the teacher may point out the peculiar characteristics of each letter. The stroke of *b* is above the line; that of *p* goes below the line. If the child cannot associate correctly the capital letter with the appropriate lower case letter, he must be drilled in this phase.

The Manuscript Formation of the Letter

After the child has learned the name of the individual letter, he is ready to learn how to write the letter. Again, many children, especially those who have attended kindergarten, will have developed some proficiency in writing the letters. Others may not have written any letters or at least have no familiarity with the correct formation.

At present, manuscript, script, or printscript is the first mode of writing taught the child. It was introduced into this country in 1921 by Marjorie Wise. It consists of sanserif letters, that is, letters without ornamentation.

The chief reason for using manuscript writing is that the child is more ready for it. Manuscript writing is easier to acquire, is more simple, is more legible, and seems to have more transfer value than cursive writing. In manuscript writing the letters are not joined, and the form of the letters is like that met in reading. This permits the pupil to compare what he writes with what he reads. Children don't experience as much difficulty with the straight vertical lines, circles, and part circles used in manuscript writing as with the more complex forms used in cursive writing.

Association of Sound with the Beginning Consonant and Medial Vowel Letter

Finally, the pupil must learn to associate a sound with the letter that he can name and perhaps write. It is important that he hear the sound in the natural context of the word. *T* is not a *tuh* sound. It has a distinct sound as a part of the word *Tom*. This phase is described at length in

---

[6] See also Chapter 7, the section on "Developing a Knowledge of the Alphabet."

Chapters 10 and 11 and is perhaps most necessary in acquiring independence in reading.

GROUP VS. INDIVIDUALIZED INSTRUCTION

Reading method always functions in the context of a specific type of classroom organization, but "a plan of organization is not a method of teaching. It is a facilitator of method, perhaps, but no more." (35) Either the classroom is organized on a group basis with some attempt at individualization, or individualized instruction is emphasized and groups are formed as needed.

Historically classrooms have been organized into groups and the emphasis has been upon the development of a group organization that would permit the greatest amount of individual growth.

Unfortunately, the search for a happy balance between grouping and individualization is still in progress.

In the 1880's educators were already complaining about the lock-step in reading education. The complaint was that all pupils were forced to advance along a common front at the same rate of speed. Each child had the same book, was asked to learn the same material, and was judged by the same academic standards.

Ability Grouping

With the increased emphasis on individual differences in the 1920's and with the publication of the Twenty-fourth Yearbook of the National Society for the Study of Education, entitled *Adapting the School to Individual Differences,* came a new classroom organization. It was termed ability grouping and for some time was thought to be the answer to the problem. In this approach pupils of the same ability used the same basic reader and it was assumed that their individual needs were being met.

Unfortunately, pupils commonly were divided into three groups, the average, above average, and below average. The child rarely was able to move from one level to another.

Individualized Reading

In an attempt to overcome some of the inadequacies of ability grouping there arose in the early 1960's an interest in individualized reading.

This approach suggested that the child *seeks* for what he is physiologically and psychologically ready, and that he shows his readiness through the spontaneous *selection* of the materials that he wants to read.

Self-selection is considered to be a necessary aspect of individualized reading. Teachers have always encouraged the child to explore reading materials apart from those that he used in the classroom. Perhaps, in individualized reading, the pupil is encouraged to take a more active part in the selection of the materials.

The advantages claimed for individualized reading are many. Perhaps, the most significant is the attitudinal change in the learner (10). Pupils seem to be more interested in reading. They read more at home. They show more interest in improvement and develop more favorable attitudes toward school in general. They often show improvement in work habits, self-motivation, and self-confidence. They seem to engage in more independent thinking and show better self-management.

In individualized reading, the purposes for reading are primarily individual and only secondarily group. The group serves as a sounding board for the individual to test the accuracy of the ideas acquired and to permit him the luxury of sharing the knowledge and insight that he has acquired.

The teacher thus works with the individual, detecting his needs and providing for these needs as the pupil's work reveals them. He keeps an accurate record of the pupil's accomplishments and inadequacies and helps him to pace his activities in accordance with his interests, aptitudes, and previous achievements. The teacher is not the prime director of the learning process and indeed never has been. Teaching may be a group process, but learning has always been an individual process.

Individualized reading does not seem suitable for pupils who cannot work independently or who cannot select or pace themselves wisely, and it is not economical when instruction can be provided more simply and in less time in a group situation than in a one-to-one teacher-pupil conference. And skills are not learned simply by reading. The poor reader does not become a good reader by selecting and reading materials that he enjoys. Practice of itself is not enough.

The Need for Eclecticism in Classroom Organization

In *Psychology in Teaching Reading* (67, pp. 383–389) the principles that should guide classroom groupings were outlined. It was pointed out that total homogeneous groups are never possible, and that when formed, groupings should be related to the specific learning task. Groups are occasioned when pupils show a commonality of achievement, interest, or need. Children may be grouped to help each other in a learning activity. Such groups may be labelled team groups. Children may be grouped when they show the need for the same skill development.

Groups should be changed (28) when pupils give evidence of growth or when their reading needs can be better met in another group. More specifically, a child might be moved from one group to another because of excessive absence, because he does not understand words, because he has not learned certain basic skills, because the book is too difficult, or because he is falling too far behind others in the group. He may move because he has shown rapid improvement in an area or because he might profit from the exposure to a faster moving group. At times, the teacher may simply want to know what a trial in a new group might do.

Obviously, class organization is only one phase of the total reading program. To group heterogeneously, homogeneously, or individually is not the total answer.

The good basal program has always had some aspects of the individualized program, and the individualized program does not eliminate all group aspects. If indeed we do believe in the individuality of the learner, then it is difficult to ignore either approach, for one child may learn better in group situations, another in independent study. And even the same child may learn better when shifting from one approach to another as the occasion and his own needs demand.

Total individualization of instruction thus may not be individualizing the reading program. For some children it may be an inappropriate organization. Individualization really means that the teacher accommodates the situation to the child and not the child to the situation. He does not force him entirely either into a group structure, nor into an individualized, one-to-one, pupil-teacher structure. We now realize that some types of learning may best be obtained through individualized instruction; others, through group instruction. Groups of five may be best for discussion purposes; groups of two or three may be better for practice exercises (56); and the teacher may best be able to test the pupil's comprehension of what he read individually.

Thus, the teacher's role ultimately is determined by the situation in which he finds himself. Sometimes he must become quite directive and sometimes he functions best in a permissive, laissez-faire role. He moves between the two extremes, neither advocating a "just-let-them-read" point of view, nor limiting all the child's reading to the basal reader. He avoids both the "turn-them-loose, permissive" approach and the "stick-strictly-to-the-textbook" approach (2).

The instructional procedures must be altered to accommodate individuals within the group. "Taking the child where he is" does not simply mean selecting materials on his grade level. Emphasis must be placed on his specific needs.

Individualized reading and grouping are not incompatible. A teacher-child conference is a group. Sometimes, the teacher will have three, five, or as many as eight youngsters about him. All in the group may need help in the same reading skills, many want to discuss the same story, or may want to read aloud to each other. Children may be grouped on an interest basis, need basis, or for social reasons. It is even possible to subgroup within ability groupings and to individualize instruction in each of them. Some children learn better with a friend. A study by Bradley (9) indicates that children worked better in pairs than under the direction of a teacher or when working alone.

When pupils work on experience charts, they may work in groups. When beginning sounds are taught, initial instruction may begin on a class basis. Education cannot become so individual that socialization is ignored. The child is by nature individual; with learning he becomes a social animal. The pupil whose reading experiences are limited to one-to-one sessions with his teacher or who reads always alone is missing an important part of education, perhaps even of reading education.

There are even occasions when the entire class can and should work together. There *never* is and never has been justification for "total class teaching of reading (80, p. 97)."

Mobile groups based on constantly changing objectives and the needs of the children imply a constant awareness of the individuality of the learner. It is possible that the best and the poorest reader will be in the same group. Both may need help in a specific reading skill. Flexible groups thus are ever-changing and make the attainment of immediate objectives that are consistent with immediate needs possible (40).

Recent studies have not resolved the issues of organization. Vite (81), in analyzing seven controlled studies, found that four favored individualized reading and three favored grouping. Sister M. Marita (47), evaluating three types of grouping, including individualized grouping, found no clear superiority of one over the other and concluded that the whole-class pattern in a child-centered context might be as useful as any others. McDonald and others (52) found that first-grade children taught individually did not have greater reading achievement than others who were taught in groups. Hillson and others (32) reported that children in a nongraded plan scored significantly higher on word and paragraph meaning than children grouped on the basis of ability. Lambert (41), in a study involving over 600 pupils in grades one and six, reported significant gains in reading and study skills for pupils who were grouped regularly, but not so for those grouped on a pupil team basis; in the second year, the team groups showed greater gains. Williams (88) reported no significant differences in achievement between comparative groups of pupils who attended graded and nongraded primary schools. Newport (57), evaluating the Joplin interclass ability grouping plan—where fourth through sixth-grade pupils are grouped homogeneously without regard to grade level, reported on nine studies of the plan and concluded that the results of most studies have not favored the plan, but interclass grouping seemed as effective as ability grouping within the self-contained classroom. In general, parental, teacher, and pupil acceptance of the plan was good, but pupils in the low group expressed dissatisfaction and would rather be transferred to higher groups (36). Goldberg et al. (20) reported that the findings concerning ability groupings are inconclusive. Justman (34) found that reducing the range of ability in fourth grade was not associated with increased achievement in reading.

Despite these findings, the easiest study to find is one expounding the strengths of either the basal or individualized approach. Each has its defenders and its antagonists. Unfortunately, many studies either do not control teacher competence, pupil abilities, and teacher-pupil motivations, or they compare a poor "basal" program with a good individualized approach or a poor individualized approach with a good basal program.

The Developmental Reading Program has little quarrel with attempts to individualize the reading program. It does insist that principles of child development should guide the methods and procedures used. With this in mind, let us make a few observations:

1. There are times when it is desirable to teach a class as a whole.
2. Grouping may reduce or narrow, but it will not completely eliminate the range of differences in a class.
3. Combinations of group and individual instruction seem at present to be indicated.
4. No organizational plan of itself insures reading success.
5. If the individualized reading approach is used, the teacher should keep a card on each book, questions to test the pupil's comprehension, numbers of pages that have material suitable for oral reading, and a list of the vocabulary.
6. The reading program should make provision for the progressive development of skills. Certainly, the basal program is a great asset here. Children may make their selections from a teacher-preselected list of books. Each such shelf of books might contain one basic reader that the child must read prior to going on to other books.
7. The effectiveness of the program depends on the number and quality of reading materials. There is a need for many basal and supplementary readers, magazines, and tradebooks on all levels of instruction. As important is the teacher's familiarity with the content and reading difficulty of the books.

No reading program is complete that does not provide the opportunity for the child to move beyond the basal materials. Children need to read enjoyable literary material. They need to experience poetry and prose; they need to read animal stories, fiction, folk tales, and fairy tales. The basal program requires development in comprehension, word analysis, and vocabulary. The literature program provides skill in following the sequence of events in a story, in predicting outcomes, in distinguishing between the real and the fanciful, and in reading between the lines. The well-balanced program lets children explore their literary heritage. It extends their horizons, stimulates their imagination, fuels their intellect, and whets their interest.

Today's reading program cannot afford to ignore the values of either the group approach, whether in a basal or other program, or the individualized approach. The good teacher will vary his approach from child to child and from day to day and from hour to hour. It is not necessary to assume that using basal readers excludes individualization, nor that individualization must omit sequential skill development. Both grouping and individualization have something to contribute to the reading program.

THE PRIMARY PROGRAM

The primary reading program extends usually through the first three grades of school. Because of the composition of the grades, a beginning reader may be learning what some other reader will learn only toward the very end of the primary years.

Primary reading is concerned most with initiating the pupil to the basic reading skills. During this period the pupil normally learns to read. He expands his sight vocabulary and becomes increasingly proficient in attacking new words. He becomes versed in structural and phonetic analysis.

His ability to deal with concepts and the meanings of words is similarly expanded. He learns new meanings for words and is introduced to figurative meanings. The pupil makes a beginning in mastering study skills and oral reading skills. He develops his reading habits, interests, and tastes. He reads for enjoyment as well as for learning purposes. He reads for information, interpretation, and appreciation.

Knowing what skills to teach is not enough for the teacher. He must decide what skills a specific child needs and can learn; he must know what method to use in teaching the skill; and he must be able to construct and use special projects that illustrate, organize, and develop the skills.

Since learning to read is such an individual process, it seems illogical to suggest that certain learnings are peculiar to first grade, second grade, or third grade. *Skill development does not come in capsule form.* One cannot dish out to third graders the third-grade capsule and to fourth graders the fourth-grade capsule. It would seem more logical to identify the sequence, if indeed there is any, in which the skills are to be introduced and then to identify the level at which the pupil is performing. Only in this way can the teacher provide for each one's needs.

Thus we will postpone an outline of the reading skills for the elementary years until we discuss the intermediate reading program. There is justification for this. All teachers in the elementary grades should be familiar with the *total* reading program. Each teacher should appreciate its continuity. He should know at what level the pupil is working, what he has learned, and what he probably needs to learn. Introduction of reading skills is useless unless the child's subsequent reading experiences serve to maintain those skills (89).

It is not possible to determine precisely when a child learns to read, when he reads to learn, or when he develops an appreciation and taste for reading. Although the goals of teaching reading are constantly changing, every significant reading skill has its beginning in the earliest school years. The kindergarten youngster learns to appreciate, to evaluate, to organize, to think and read critically, to draw inferences, to apply ideas, and to follow directions. Thus there is some value in listing the general reading skills.

In general, these may be divided into the following seven broad areas:

1. Perceptual Skills
2. Literal Comprehension Skills
3. Word Recognition Skills
4. Interpretative and Appreciative Skills
5. Reading-Study Skills
6. Rate of Comprehension Skills
7. Oral-Reading Skills

THE INTERMEDIATE READING PROGRAM

Although in the intermediate grades most emphasis is put on "reading for learning," many pupils have not yet acquired the reading skills needed to do this. Thus, for some pupils this period is actually a continuation in the basic skills program. They need to learn the more advanced basic reading skills. The child who is deficient in the basic reading skills does not improve his reading by reading more. Such reading only reinforces his faulty habits. He needs guidance in reading skill development.

For others, the intermediate grades are a period of refinement. They learn how to use the context to glean from it the one specific meaning intended. They learn to read critically. Their vocabularies expand rapidly so they can digest newspapers, magazines, and the many textbooks that they now encounter. They develop lasting reading interests and tastes, and appreciation for prose, poetry, and drama.

Because there is a great emphasis on textbooks which require high-level reading ability and proficiency in reading-study skills, the pupil needs to handle many more reading tasks. The sentence structure becomes more difficult; new and more difficult meanings for words are required; and idiomatic and figurative expressions must be handled. The amount of reading greatly increases, requiring the pupil to read at a more rapid pace. The reading demands of the intermediate grades call for flexibility in approach. The pupil must learn to gauge his rate and even his accuracy of comprehension to many different purposes for reading.

The elementary school pupil reads for various purposes. He may read for an over-all view, for main ideas, or to note details. On more advanced levels he may read to solve problems, to understand the organization, or to appreciate literary form.

In the learning of basic skills there obviously are differences among children in *rate* of learning. The differences in learning *capacity* are just as significant. Some children may never master all the skills. This again reinforces the need for individualization of each pupil's reading program. The teacher must start the child at the point of success that he has attained and must permit him to advance as far as he can as rapidly as he can.

Let us list the skills that the child should learn during his primary and/or intermediate years:

1. Perception Skills
   a. Visual perception of form
   b. Visual perception of capital and lower-case letters and words
   c. Auditory perception of sounds
   d. Recognition of rhyming words
   e. Ability to move eyes from left to right and make accurate return sweeps
   f. Increased eye span
2. Comprehension Skills
   a. Matching words with pictures
   b. Associating meaning with word symbols
   c. Inferring meanings from context clues
   d. Inferring meanings from word clues—roots, suffixes, prefixes, compounds
   e. Matching words with definitions
   f. Recognizing antonyms and synonyms
   g. Associating printed word symbols with other symbols such as:
      (1) musical notes, clef, sharp, flat, rest

      (2) mathematical signs—plus, minus, half-dollar, cent, circle, triangle

      (3) maps, charts, graphs

      (4) diacritical marks in the dictionary

  h. Developing meaning for ever larger units of language: sentences, paragraphs, etc.

  i. Finding main ideas in paragraphs

  j. Recognizing and organizing facts and details

  k. Ability to recognize literary form

  l. Ability to detect the writer's purpose

3. Word Attack Skills

  a. Using word configuration clues

  b. Using contextual clues

  c. Learning structural analysis clues

      (1) inflectional endings

      (2) words ending in *ing*

      (3) doubling the consonant before adding *ing*

      (4) compound words

      (5) prefixes and suffixes

      (6) the apostrophe *s*

      (7) the past tense with *ed*

      (8) the plural with *es*

      (9) the contractions

      (10) syllabication

  d. Learning phonic skills

4. Reading Study Skills

  a. Dictionary skills

      (1) definition—Select correct meaning that fits the context

      (2) alphabetizing

      (3) syllabication

      (4) accent and guide words

      (5) use of the thumb index

      (6) pronunciation key

      (7) diacritical marks

  b. Location and reference skills—use of encyclopedias, almanacs, magazines, card catalogues, etc.

      (1) locating specific information in a textbook

      (2) locating material in the index

      (3) ability to interpret cross references and to use the table of contents, glossary, and footnotes

  c. Use of maps, charts, tables, and footnotes

  d. Use of library resources: card catalogue, indexes

  e. Organization skills

      (1) selecting main ideas

(2) ability to follow directions

(3) arranging events and items in sequence

(4) putting together ideas from various sources

(5) summarizing

(6) outlining

(7) note taking

(8) ability to retain and apply what has been read

(9) ability to use study-methods, such as the SQRRR method—
surveying, questioning, reading, recitation, review

(10) ability to read in specific content-areas

5. Interpretative and Appreciative Skills
   a. Evaluate what is read
   b. Predict outcomes
   c. Perceive relationships or comparisons
   d. Suspend judgment
   e. Draw inferences and conclusions
   f. Deal with figurative and picturesque language
   g. Detect bias
   h. Detect author's mood and purpose
   i. Filter facts
   j. Differentiate between fact and opinion
   k. Weigh facts as to their importance
   l. Analyze opinions

6. Rate of Comprehension Skills
   a. Left-to-right eye movements
   b. Reduction of regressions
   c. Phrase reading
   d. Reduction of vocalization
   e. Ability to choose an appropriate reading technique—flexibility
   f. Scan for specific information
   g. Skimming skills

7. Oral Reading Skills
   a. Keep eye ahead of voice
   b. Enunciate clearly
   c. Pronounce correctly
   d. Read in thought units
   e. Vary pitch and volume of voice
   f. Adapt voice to size of room and audience

RATE SKILLS

We single out rate skills for detailed discussion here because all the
other reading skills to be developed in the elementary school have been
discussed or will be discussed in subsequent chapters. Perception skills

are discussed in Chapters 2 and 7, meaning skills in Chapter 12, word attack skills in Chapters 10 and 11, study skills, interpretative skills, and purposive reading in Chapter 13, and oral reading skills in Chapter 2.

In a previous article (15)[7] the author pointed out that rate of reading frequently has been described as rate of comprehension. Perhaps it is better described as speed in grasping the meanings intended by the writer. To read is to comprehend, but one may comprehend at a slow rate or at a relatively more rapid rate.

Thus, rapidity in reading has value in its own right and should be investigated as a separate skill. There are fast readers, average readers, and slow readers and it seems more desirable to be a rapid reader than a slow reader.

The superior reader supposedly pushes his eyes across the page as rapidly as his comprehension permits. This may or may not be good. No one can work at top efficiency all the time and there is no great necessity in even wanting to. There really is little advantage in rapidly proceeding through a newspaper if, after the reader has finished, he doesn't know what to do with his time. The proofreader gets better results if he is completely accurate the first time than if, because of too much speed, he has to reread the materials.

Thus slow reading is not necessarily poor reading. It affords the reader an opportunity to evaluate, to linger, to enjoy the beauty of the description (much as the traveler who stops to see points of scenic interest), and to read between the lines. At times, slowness is beauty. To read slowly, to think critically, and to feel deeply may be true enrichment.

That many readers read much more slowly than they could is an obvious fact. That others read as rapidly as their comprehension abilities allow may also be true. And for these, rate improvement training is of little value.

Fast readers and slow readers may or may not comprehend well, but sometimes the fast reader comprehends better than the slow reader. This happens when the fast reader is reading approximately as rapidly as his comprehension abilities allow and when the slow reader is reading more slowly than his comprehension permits, thus allowing time for the mind to wander from the task.

Rate of reading, of course, is not the ultimate goal in reading. The ultimate aim is comprehension according to one's abilities and needs. This means that the good reader is a flexible reader.[8] Just as cars have

---

[7] Emerald Dechant, "Rate of Comprehension—Needed Research," in *Changing Concepts of Reading Instruction*, ed. by J. Allen Figurel, International Reading Association Conference Proceedings, 6 Scholastic Magazines, New York (1961). Used by permission. This article has been frequently quoted or paraphrased in this section.

[8] The *Reading Versatility Test* by Arthur S. McDonald, Marquette University, measures flexibility of reading. It is designed for pupils in the fifth through the ninth grade.

in them the power to go slowly or to go rapidly as the occasion demands, so also the good reader can slow down or speed up as the nature of the material and his own needs change. He can shift gears in reading.

Rate of reading should always be dependent on the purposes, intelligence, and experience and knowledge of the reader and upon the difficulty level of the material. The rate is always dependent on the reader's motivation and his psychological and physical state, his mastery of the basic reading skills, and the format of the materials. More specifically, factors that affect speed and comprehension are (65): size of type, type style, blackness and sharpness of print, quality and tone of the paper, size of the page, organization of the material, amount of white space, kind and placement of illustrations, headings and subheadings, clarity of the writing, the field of knowledge from which the writing is drawn, the complexity of the ideas, the author's style, the kind of writing (poetry, narrative, or descriptive), the reader's personality, the way the reader feels (sleepy, alert, calm, nervous), the reader's mental ability, reading skill, and his likes and dislikes, the environment in which reading occurs, the reader's background of experience, his purpose, and his interest in the field or area in which he is reading, and his familiarity with the peculiarities of style and phraseology of the author.

Efficiency in reading means simply this; with some purposes and some materials one should read slowly; with others, one should read more rapidly. This means that the reader should read as rapidly as possible, always meeting the comprehension specifications that he has set for himself or that the task has set for him (65).

It makes little sense to prod along at a snail's pace if one can read rapidly and still understand the materials. If the reader cannot understand what he is reading, then a slower rate is called for. The good driver slows down his car in snow, on ice, around curves, in city traffic, and whenever he is not sure of the conditions of the road. He thus transmits more power to the wheels while at the same time going slowly enough so that he can view the entire situation carefully. The good reader slows down whenever he needs to do so to understand what he is reading. When he doesn't understand, he is in as much trouble as is the driver whose car is stuck in mud. It may be necessary to slow down to a crawl so that he can use more of his thinking power.

The reader gets into trouble in reading and must read more slowly when the writer's style is too difficult; when the ideas are too abstract; when he is trying to learn and to remember what he is reading; when he is following directions such as the carrying out of an experiment; when he is reading poetry; when he is reading critically—trying to evaluate what he reads; and when he reads such specialized materials as science.

It is interesting to note that when the good reader reduces his speed, he does so for a purpose. It does not create a gap between his reading rate and thinking rate. He reduces his speed because the materials require him to think more slowly. The good reader seeks to increase his understanding without sacrificing speed unnecessarily, or he may want to increase his speed without sacrificing his understanding. In short, he is a flexible reader. The flexible reader gears his reading rate to his thinking rate.

Rate improvement cannot be built on inadequate word identification and word recognition skills. It cannot be built on an experimental background that keeps the reader from understanding what he is reading. It cannot be built upon immaturity in intellectual development.

On the other hand, there is little doubt that rate of comprehension can be improved. Students on the high school and college level and adults who have undertaken some form of rate improvement training do increase their speed and generally will read faster than those who have not had such training.

Advocates of rate improvement programs claim that such programs also may lead to increased accuracy in perception, more accurate and more rapid visual discrimination, wider span of apprehension, better attention and concentration, shorter reaction time, fewer regressions, a decrease in the number and duration of fixations, reduction of vocalization, better comprehension, and general improvement in perceptual skills.

Let us take a look at the vast array of gadgetry available today which is intended to help the pupil to develop these skills. These gadgets might be grouped into tachistoscopes, accelerating devices, and other reading-related instruments.

Tachistoscopes

Tachistoscopes expose numbers, letters, words, or other images for short periods of time, usually ranging from $1/100$ to $1\frac{1}{2}$ seconds. Most training on these machines is at the higher speeds.

The tachistoscope, whether individual or group, primarily develops the person's perceptual intake skills. By forcing the pupil to cope with intake speeds of $1/10$ of a second or less the tachistoscope requires the pupil to see more rapidly, more accurately, and more orderly; to pay better attention to what was seen; and to organize what he has seen. He also has to develop better directional attack.

Since the tachistoscopic span is greater than the span in normal reading, researchers have always asked: What are the effects of tachistoscopic training, and is there any value in increasing the tachistoscopic span?

A tachistoscopic exposure is followed by a period of "nonreading" in which the person can assimilate and integrate what he saw; in reading, there is continuous perceptual activity, the images overlap each other, and there is relatively little time to assimilate and interpret (16). Obviously, increasing the tachistoscopic span further seems to be of little value in reading. The training should be directed rather toward developing the intake aspect of perception and toward improving the seeing skills as a basis for better reading rather than toward developing reading skills per se (16).

"Seeing" can be improved and tachistoscopic training is one of the better ways of doing this. It has been used in the armed services, in remedial reading, in orthoptics, in teaching spelling and arithmetic, in art and business education, and even in physical education. In each instance the emphasis has been on the development of general accuracy in seeing and remembering. This is of value in all learning situations in which the pupil must come to understanding through the use of vision (73, p. 6).

There are many by-products of tachistoscopic training. The pupil learns self-discipline, better habits of work, better eye-hand coordination, and improves his focusing ability.

Tachistoscopic training has greatest value in the elementary years when the pupil is learning to "see." Since much of the material is designed to develop accuracy of seeing and the retention of the particular placement of certain elements (for example, the pupil needs to see and remember 24571 in a definite order), it may have value in a word-attack program.

Here is a list of tachistoscopes available today:

1. *AVR Eye-Span Trainer* (AVR E-S-T 10) [Audio-Visual Research]. This plastic mechanism offers a simple hand-operated shutter device for training in rapid recognition of numbers, words, money amounts, phrases, etc. Slides are available for elementary, junior high, senior high, college, and adult level.

2. *AVR Flash-Tachment* [Audio-Visual Research]. This is a simple attachment that converts any filmstrip projector into a tachistoscope. Speeds range from 1/25 to 1/100 of a second.

3. *EDL Flash-X* [Educational Developmental Laboratories]. In this device the pupil flicks the tab opening the shutter device for 1/25 of a second. The pupil records what he saw and then checks his answer. Discs are provided covering such areas as readiness, primary recognition, numbers, sight vocabulary, arithmetic, and spelling.

4. *EDL Tach-X Tachistoscope* [Educational Development Laboratories]. Images (numbers, pictures, letters or words) can be projected on a screen for as long as 1½ seconds or as briefly as 1/100 of a second. The Tach-X is designed to develop visual

discrimination and memory. Filmstrips range from the readiness to adult level. Exercises such as the following are very effective. "Watch the screen. Ready?" The Tach-X flashes y ¡ ¡ ¡ ¡. "Which letter was different?" The letters are shown again so the pupil can check for accuracy. Constant illumination is maintained and the words flash in and out of focus.

5. *Electro-Tach* [Lafayette Instrument Company]. This is a near-point tachistoscopic training instrument for use at all age levels. The exposures are electronically controlled and range from 1/100 to 1 second. Training cards available cover digits, jumbled letters, words, phrases, sentences, and familiar objects.

6. *Flashmaster* [Keystone View Company]. This device used with overhead projector forms a tachistoscope. The flashmeter is multibladed and has the following times: 1/2; 1/5; 1/10; 1/25; 1/50; 1/100 of a second.

7. *Phrase Flasher* [Reading Laboratory, Inc.]. This tachistoscope device is accompanied by a 940 card set of simple digits, words, and paragraphs.

8. *Rapid Reading Kit* [Better Reading Program, Inc.]. This is a self-help program designed to develop speed in comprehension. it includes: the Visualizer, practice slides, *Reading Skill Book*, *Progress Records*, and *Improvement Guide*, and two *Reading Raters*. Phrases are up to 5 words long and exposure is up to 1/100 second.

9. *Speed-I-O-Scope* [Society for Visual Education]. This flash mechanism with shutterlike device mounts on a standard still projector. Speeds range from 1/100 second to 1 second.

10. *Tachistoscope* [Lafayette Instrument Company]. This all-purpose group tachistoscope permits exposures of 1, 1/2, 1/10, 1/25, 1/50, and 1/100 seconds. It is usable with any make of projector. The tachistoscopic attachment is adaptable to all makes of projectors.

11. *Tachisto-Flasher* [Science Research Associates]. This shutter mechanism, when set in front of the lens of a film strip projector, converts it into a tachistoscope.

12. *Tachisto-Viewer* [Learning Through Seeing, Inc.]. This tachisto-scope filmstrip viewer has speeds of 1/5 to 1/40 second. Filmstrips are provided to develop word recognition skills, spelling skills, and speed of visual perception.

Accelerating Devices

The accelerating devices provide rate training for the competent readers. The *Controlled Reader*, for example, presents materials in a left-to-right direction at a pre-determined rate. A moving slot travels across the screen in a left-to-right direction, covering and uncovering the materials as it moves along (74, p. 4).

Such devices lead to a reduction in fixations and regressions, better attention and concentration, more rapid thinking, and improved organization of what is read.

Once the pupil has attained a speed of 450 to 500 words, the words may be more satisfactorily uncovered a line at a time.

Accelerating devices are most useful in the upper elementary years and in junior high school.

Much group training with accelerators is at far-point. This is undesirable for children with myopic vision and for those who have difficulties with fusion because they are required to improve rate while handicapped visually (69). At far-point the person also can "read" more words than in normal reading. It is possible that this explains the relatively little transfer that occurs from machine programs to normal book reading.

Here is a list of some accelerators on the market today:

1. *AVR Reading Rateometer* [Audio-Visual Research]. Three models of this machine are available. The standard model (model A) has a range of from 70 to 2500 words per minute. Model B offers a range from 20 to 500 words per minute. Model C offers a range of 140 to 5000 words per minute. Each model is equipped with a pacing T-bar that moves down the page at a constant rate.

2. *Cenco Pacer* [Cenco Center]. A reading pacer with 14 sequential lesson rolls and a student workbook form the materials for this program usable with the slow learner.

3. *Controlled Reader* [Educational Developmental Laboratories]. A moving slot (picture) travels from left to right across the screen or a full line may be uncovered at a time. It permits speeds of from 60 to 1000 words per minute. Filmstrips are available from the kindergarten to the adult level, and question books and story books accompany each level.

4. *Craig Reader* [Craig Research, Inc.]. The Craig Reader adjusts to permit reading speeds of 100 to 2000 words per minute. The machine uses slide units rather than film. The slides contain twelve film frames in each slide. Twelve programs from elementary to university level are available.

5. *EDL Controlled Reader Jr.* This machine is similar to the Controlled Reader but is more economical for individual use.

6. *Keystone Reading Pacer* [Keystone View Company]. This device has a pointer which moves at speeds from 50 to 1000 words per

minute. The pacer shuts itself off when the bottom of the page is reached and begins as it is moved to the top of the next page.

7. *NRI Speed-Reading Machine* [National Reading Institute]. The automated speed reading program includes the above machine, equipped with a self-timing device that enables an automatic increase in speed. This machine comes with programmed reading rolls that are fed through the machine.

8. *PDL Perceptoscope* [Perceptual Development Laboratories]. This projector serves as accelerator, projector, tachistoscope, or timer. Speeds may be varied on ten films from 120 to 4300 words per minute.

9. *Readamatic Pacer* [Americana Interstate Corporation]. This pacer, quite similar in design to the Reading Rateometer, can very speeds from 100 to 1000 words per minute.

10. *Shadowscope Reading Pacer* [Psychotechnics, Inc.]. The Shadowscope is designed for junior high level and up. The reading speeds may be varied from 125 to 2000 words per minute.

11. *SRA Reading Accelerator* [Science Research Associates]. Model III offers rate adjustments of from less than 30 to more than 3000 words per minute. Model IV is a plastic portable.

12. *Tachomatic* [Psychotechnics, Inc.]. The Tachomatic film projector is designed for reading training at all levels, including that of adults. It utilizes a special film and highspeed mechanism to project series of words in a narrow band across a screen. The rate may be varied from very slow to motion picture speeds and the fixations may be one, two, or three per line.

Reading-related Machines

The reading teacher might also have use for one of the following machines in his reading program.

1. *Aud-X* [Educational Developmental Laboratories]. As students listen to interesting stories, they watch the screen to learn new words. Each time the narrator pronounces one of the several words being taught in a lesson, it appears on the screen in exact synchronization with its pronunciation. In follow-up word study lessons, students discover the graphic and sound qualities of words through the unique sight-sound synchronization afforded by the Aud-X. Though the students may be part of a small group during Aud-X sessions, each one listens, looks, and responds in an individual manner. Through its auto-instructional capability, the

      Aud-X makes an important contribution to truly individualized learning.

2. *Delacato Stereo-Reading Service* [Keystone View Company]. This service with stereo reader is designed for remedial use with pupils who suffer from laterality confusions. It develops binocular reading. The Zweig-Bruno Stereo-Tracing Exercises, to be used with the Stereo-Reader, are effective in the correction of letter reversals, letter substitutions, in-word reversals, and poor hand-eye coordination.

3. *Language Master Machine* [Hoover Brothers]. This machine comes with cards designed to teach vocabulary, sounds of English, phonics, etc.

4. *Leavell Language Development Service* [Keystone View Company]. This service with instrument develops eye control and hand-eye coordination. It is useful with mirror writers and children who reverse.

Skimming and Scanning

The only machine available today that is designed to develop the skimming skill is the *EDL Skimmer*. This machine is equipped with a bead of light that travels down the center fold of the book at the rate of one-half minute per page or about 800 to 1000 words per minute. This informs the reader how rapidly he should proceed and keeps him perceptually alert. The device is useful also in developing scanning skills.

Skimming is selective reading. In skimming the reader chooses what he wants to read. He selects those sentences, clauses, and phrases which best serve his purposes. He gets a general impression of the selection and decides on the basis of his examination whether to read the selection more intensively. He takes a quick glance at the table of contents, the index, the chapter titles, the paragraph headings, the topic sentences, and the summary. These provide valuable clues to the main idea.

In scanning, the reader runs his eyes down the page with the purpose of finding an answer to a specific question.

We scan a crowd to find a certain person; we scan a bowl of candy for the right piece; and we scan over a box of tools for a plier. In reading, we scan to find an answer to a particular question, to locate a specific date or number, or to locate a reference, a name, a city, or a quotation.

Skimming and scanning are not accelerated reading. In them the reader switches from looking to reading to looking and so on. In fact, there may be less reading than looking and when the person reads he reads in the usual way (23).

Research tends to indicate that reading rates above 800 words per minute are in the nature of skimming and scanning. The reader characteristically omits part of the content and reads with considerably less comprehension (72, p. 6).

Skimming usually takes the form of preview, overview, or review (71, pp. 34–37). Skimming for preview purposes has already been described. In skimming for overview purposes the reader gets a general impression of the content. He reads more of the material than when doing preview skimming. He looks for the writer's organization, thinks along with the writer, and notes the transitions. Skimming for review is a useful technique in preparing for tests or to increase retention generally.

When the pupil should be taught to skim is difficult to say. Taylor and Frackenpohl (72, pp. 9–12) have identified the *type* of pupil who is ready for selective reading. The pupil must be a flexible reader. He needs visual coordination. He must have developed a proper directional attack, and must be able to organize a series of data. He must be able to identify words rapidly, must retain them, and must relate them to each other. He must develop attention and concentration, while maintaining his composure. He must be relaxed and willing to settle for less than complete comprehension.

Do skimming and scanning have any place in the elementary school? It is doubtful that any significant usage of them is made in the primary years. However, in the intermediate years the good reader can apply scanning in his use of the index, the dictionary, or a glossary. He can use skimming to survey a chapter. In fact, the first step in effective study or intensive reading involves previewing, surveying, or skimming.[9]

To skim, the pupil must develop a new perceptual skill. In selective reading "looking" is as important as is reading. The person must look back and forth and down the page in a "floating" manner as it were (72, p. 11). He learns to take in words, ideas, and organization at a subliminal level.

Teaching the pupil to skim may advance through many stages. Perhaps the first is the changing of the pupil's attitude (71, p. 36). The pupil must realize that partial comprehension meets certain needs. He should be taught that the title of an article by itself gives a general overview. Each pupil has read stories with a title and has probably been told what the title tells him. Generally, the title identifies the content or subject matter.

The table of contents describes the book. It is like a grocery advertisement in a newspaper. The advertisement gives a glimpse of the stock inside the store. It tries to interest the perceiver enough to get him to visit the store and to examine the contents more closely.

Scanning requires similar but also different skills. Much of a scan-

---

[9] For a description of how to teach skimming, see: Irwin Weiss, "Skimming Practice," *English Journal,* 56 (January, 1967) 135–137.

ner's skill lies in knowing what he is looking for and in predicting how the specific point that he is trying to find is stated. For example, distances usually are stated in terms of miles, feet, minutes, or hours.

Let us give an example of how scanning might be taught. The exercise suggested here is for the reader of this book rather than for the elementary pupil.

Use the scanning technique as *you* try to find the answer to the following question: "How many children suffer from the condition known as retinoblastoma?"

Retinoblastoma is a cancer found in the eyes of infants and young children. It is somewhat like a tumor. The Retinoblastoma Clinic in the Institute of Ophthalmology of the Columbia-Presbyterian Medical Center in New York specializes in its treatment. Approximately one of every 23,000 children is affected by it. Children are born with it and hence the condition is congenital.

The first symptoms consist of a yellowish-white reflection in the pupil of the eye. When the tumors are small, radiation treatment is frequently successful. At more advanced stages, the eye has to be removed. If this is not done, the cancer spreads and death ultimately occurs.

Evaluation of Machine Programs

No one would suggest that reading instruments make a total program. On the other hand, few would deny that they have a legitimate role in a balanced reading program. In evaluating their effectiveness one must always be cautious in generalizing from one instrument to all others. Each has its own strength and weakness and must be separately evaluated.

However, there are certain principles that guide all evaluations. It is not enough to simply look for rate gains. The reader's relative efficiency is more than rate; it is also a function of the fixations and regressions $(RE) = \dfrac{Rate}{Fixations + Regressions}$. An increase in rate is meaningful only when it is accompanied by a reduction in fixations and regressions.

Mechanical devices are motivating. They may even increase comprehension achievement; however, they cannot increase comprehension potential. They merely help the mind to operate on a level approximating its potential.

Persons working with mechanical devices repeatedly have noticed among pupils an increase in interest in reading and in a desire to improve their reading skills. For some of these a successful experience in a machine program may develop a new attitude toward reading generally which may lead to improved performance in a number of areas including rate of comprehension.

It thus frequently is impossible to attribute rate improvements to machines alone. Increased motivation and increased teacher effectiveness may be as significant. No one would suggest that because no gains are made that the machine is necessarily useless. Neither can one infer that because gains were made in a machine program that these were the sole result of the machine. The effectiveness of any mechanical device depends on the user.

How good then are these gadgets? Tinker (79) makes the following observations:

1. Reading speed can be improved, but it is not at all certain that the gains are lasting.
2. Improved rate is not automatically transferred to other types of material.
3. There is evidence to indicate that pacers and accelerating devices are more effective developers of reading rate than are tachistoscopes. Tinker adds, "The tachistoscope is without value for increasing speed of reading."
4. The improvement through mechanical devices is no greater than that resulting from motivated reading alone. However, Maxwell and Mueller (50), in a study involving 40 college students, found that those students who were given specific techniques for improving their speed showed significantly greater gains than either the control group or the group which was simply "motivated" to increase rate.
5. Pacing devices often are emphasized more than the processes of perception, apprehension, and assimilation, with a resultant decrease in flexibility.
6. There is perhaps too much of an emphasis upon "oculomotor mechanics."

There are still other concerns that constantly perplex the practitioner. For example: What is optimal reading speed on specific materials and how can it be determined? Which rate skills should receive most reinforcement? What are the side effects of speed programs? In some programs the pupil is taught rhythmic phraseology. Yet, the good reader is a flexible reader. Normal reading is continuous textual and non-rhythmic reading.

Finally, what is the pupil learning in rate improvement programs using tachistoscopic and/or other mechanical devices? Fletcher (18) found that when three equivalent forms are used in testing the pupil's performance, at the end of the first, second, and last tachistoscopic training session, most of the gains are found to occur between the first and second session. The technique of rapid performance on a tachistoscope seems to be acquired rather quickly.

What implications do all the data about reading rate have for the elementary reading program?

There seems to be little justification for emphasis on speed of reading in the primary school years. The intermediate pupil on the other hand must be taught to adjust his reading speed to the materials and his purposes for reading. He must be taught, either through book or machine programs, facility and speed in perceiving words and relating them to their meaning. He must be taught to read in thought units. He must be helped to overcome faulty habits such as moving his lips, pointing to words, or moving the head while reading.

The pupil must be encouraged to move his eyes as rapidly across the line of print as is possible. Too frequently, the pupil can read faster but he has developed the habit of moving slowly. To overcome this habit the pupil should time himself on passages of a particular length. In the beginning the passages should be simple and interesting. If the print is in narrow columns, as in newspapers, the pupil should be encouraged to make only one fixation per line, forcing himself to move the eyes down the page.

The pupil is constantly tempted to regress so that he can read more accurately. Normally this may be good procedure, but it does not lead to increased speed. The pupil must fight against this. He can be helped to overcome excessive caution by cutting a slot out of a piece of paper and moving the paper down the page. This forces him to move ahead and keeps him from looking back or too far ahead. Another device consists simply of a sheet of paper which he may move down the page, covering a line at a time.

The pupil must learn that there is no best rate of reading. The good reader uses a flexible approach in reading. He uses a greater variety of approaches when reading, even though he may have learned this skill on his own (66). His reading varies in speed from very slow, to moderate, to very fast; from detailed analysis of what he reads to skimming and scanning. Even his comprehension tends to be flexible. Some materials need to be understood thoroughly; others, only generally. Certain parts of a textbook must be read intensively; others may be skimmed. The flexible reader may read very rapidly or even skip those parts that are trivial, already known, or that have no bearing upon his goals and purposes.

The flexible reader knows what he wants from the material. He has asked himself: Need I to understand only the main idea, the supporting facts, or a combination of these? Am I reading for pleasure or for information? What is my purpose?

The flexible reader also has developed a flexible attitude toward reading. He realizes that different reading situations call for different ways of reading. He reads differently when reading newspapers, magazines, advertisements, encyclopedias, textbooks, novels, how-to-do-it books, and editorials.

It is not enough to know what a flexible reader does. Elementary and high school students need to be taught the ability to behave flexibly when reading, and Harris et al. (26) found in a two-week program with fourth-grade children that this can be done. Exercises like the following teach what flexibility in reading is all about.

Exercise I

This lesson is on flexibility in reading. How should you read the following? Which would you read most rapidly? Most slowly? Try to arrange the exercises in an order of increasing speed.

1. *Changing a mixed number to an improper fraction*
   To change a mixed number (3½) to an improper fraction (value is one or more than one) multiply the whole number by the denominator of the fraction and add the numerator of the fraction to this product. The sum of the product and the numerator is then written over the denominator.

2. *Johannson-Patterson Fight*
   With barely a minute gone the challenger Ingemar Johannson unleashed a right that sent Patterson helplessly toward the floor. Patterson recovered quickly but in another twenty seconds he again was sprawled on the canvas. Again Patterson rose. Suddenly, Patterson's left landed on the jaw of the challenger. Down went Johannson with a thud. History had been made in the first round of the fight. Three knockdowns and still no knockout.

It is obvious that the speed of reading these short paragraphs will change depending on one's purposes and one's familiarity with the material. One would read them more slowly if it was necessary to know every little detail; one would read them more rapidly, if one needed only general information. Thus, knowing why one is reading them is of first importance.

Similar exercises on the pupil's level can be developed to teach the various rate skills. The following are examples of such exercises:

1. Have the pupil read simple materials as rapidly as he can.
2. Have pupils time their reading of an article whose number of words they know.
3. Have the pupil skim a page in a textbook to find the answer to a question, to locate a new word, or to identify a quotation.
4. Have the pupil skim an encyclopedia article for a specific fact.
5. Have pupils determine purposes for reading and then discuss appropriateness of various rates for various reading purposes.

The aim of these exercises is not the development of an absolute reading rate. The pupil should develop an attitude favorable to reading at the rate that his comprehension and the nature of the materials allow. He should become unfavorably disposed to needlessly slow reading.

READABILITY

The level of comprehension that the pupil will attain is dependent upon the readability of the materials that he uses. If the major aim of reading is the comprehension of meaning, the teacher must be interested in the measurement of the comprehensibility of materials. He wants some means for quantifying his statements about the difficulty of material. It is not enough to say that reading material is difficult or easy. He must have reference points or a scale with which to judge printed materials.

Readability is not an easily defined concept. It involves an interaction between reader and book. Because communication between writer and reader seldom is perfect, readability rarely can be absolute. It usually is a matter of degree. The teacher thus must make some practical decisions as to the degree of understanding that is necessary before a book may be considered readable by a child at a certain grade level. In short, he must determine how much the reader must get from the printed material before it becomes readable for him.

The concept of readability generally refers to the success that the average individual has with a book. Dale and Chall (13) point out that readability refers to those elements within printed material that affect the success that a group of readers have with it.

Unfortunately, the teacher cannot be completely satisfied with this concept. A book that is readable for one child may not be readable for another child even if he has the same general level of reading ability. The teacher cannot make prescriptions for the average individual. He must make decisions for a specific child.

One approach to the study of the readability of books is to ask teachers or librarians to rate books according to difficulty. This has been tried and has been found to be inadequate. Teachers and librarians are not proficient in designating the grade-level for which a given book is written. It is doubtful that they have a greater degree of accuracy in picking the right book for the individual youngster.

Another approach was made by Vogel and Washburne (82,83). They surveyed 37,000 children and developed the Winnetka Graded Book List. This list contained 700 books that children from the second to the eleventh grade claimed to have read and enjoyed. The grade placement of each book was found by determining the average reading ability of the children who read and enjoyed the book.

Teachers frequently use a similar technique. In helping children choose books, they select books somewhat below the pupil's estimated level of reading ability. They obtain a rough estimate of the appropriateness of a book by having the child read orally. They choose two or three selections of 100 words each from the book for the pupil to read, noting the errors as the child reads orally. If he misses more than five words out of a hundred or has less than 85 to 95 per cent comprehension, the child is directed to another book.

A third approach is to develop and apply a readability formula to the book. Since 1923, more than thirty such formulas have been developed. Generally, the authors of these have attempted to identify the factors that make materials difficult to read. The factors most agreed upon are vocabulary, or some aspect of word difficulty, usually frequency (39), some aspect of sentence difficulty, usually length, and the number of prepositional phrases. Hunt (33), however, found that clause length may be a better index of language maturity than sentence length or number of subordinate clauses. He notes that when writers build up long clauses, the reader must break them down.

Vocabulary seems to be the most significant determinant of reading comprehension. Materials are more easily understood when there are few different words than when there are many. They are more difficult when they contain words that call for concepts that are strange and rare. Easy materials generally contain short, simple sentences or clauses with few prepositional phrases.

The goal in developing readability formulas is to get the highest degree of prediction while having to deal with the smallest number of factors. Thus, although the abstractness of the words, the organization and format of the materials, the interest and purposes of the reader, and the experience background of the reader influence the readability of materials, these elements have not been incorporated into readability formulas.

The formulas that have been used most widely are those of Flesch (17), Dale-Chall (12), Lorge (44), Yoakam (90), and Spache (68). The Flesch formula appears to be most useful with adult materials; the Dale-Chall and Yoakam formulas, with middle and upper-grade materials; and the Spache and Vogel-Washburne (83) formulas, with primary level materials.

Figure 9-2 is a graph, developed by Fry, that has the advantage of simplicity in estimating level of difficulty.

Readability formulas are not a panacea for meeting comprehension problems. They frequently yield different results and fail to measure

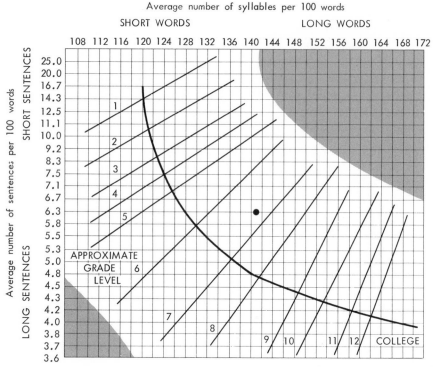

Average number of syllables per 100 words

SHORT WORDS   LONG WORDS

Figure 9-2. Graph for Estimating Readability

Directions: Randomly select three 100-word passages from a book or an article. Plot average number of syllables and average number of words per sentence on the graph to determine the grade level of the material. Choose more passages per book if great variability is observed and conclude that the book has uneven readability. Few books will fall in the gray area, but when they do, grade level scores are invalid.

Example:	*syllables*	*sentences*
first 100 words	124	6.6
second 100 words	141	5.5
third 100 words	158	6.8
average	141	6.3

Readability: 7th grade (see dot plotted on graph)

many elements considered important for readability. However, they are useful in giving a relative estimate of the difficulty of books, in determining the sequence to be followed in recommending books to a child, and in detecting the difficult words and sentences in the book (11).

Each teacher should become familiar with the formula that is designed for reading materials on the level that he is teaching. He will be better prepared to put the right book in the right hands at the right time. The pupil profits greatly. If he understands what he reads, he will be more interested, will read more rapidly, will retain it better, and will be less frustrated.

Developed by Taylor (75), the cloze procedure is the most recent trend in measuring readability (38,87). This procedure deletes words in a prose selection and measures the success the reader has in supplying the words which have been deleted. It is assumed that the individual's score is an index of his ability to comprehend reading matter. Bormuth (4,5,6,7) feels that the cloze tests are reliable and valid predictors of the comprehension difficulties of a passage and furthermore that they have an advantage in that they permit computerization.

Hafner (24) used the cloze procedure to identify the student who tends to use information not near the blank. He noted that the poor reader "apparently does not take advantage of the structure of the material." It is suggested that the student who does not use the information to complete the blank may be deficient in ability to reason (24).

Using cloze procedures with fourth graders, Ruddell (63) found that the more nearly the patterns of language structure in written material approximate the child's oral language structure, the better the pupil tends to comprehend the material.

Louthan (45) found that when articles and possessive or other pronouns were deleted from a passage that subjects received better comprehension scores. The explanation is offered that deleting such noun determiners forces the reader to be unusually aware of the noun. Perhaps the attention of poor readers should be focused on the meaning-bearing words—nouns, verbs, and specific modifiers (25). MacGintie (48), however, notes that missing words can frequently be identified without an understanding of the passage. It is possible that cloze tests are measures of language redundancy rather than of comprehension (84). Teachers can improve the readability of materials by adding illustrative and explanatory materials in lectures, discussion, and written materials (25).

Other studies have shown a high correlation (.73, .69, .72) between word deletion tests and test of intelligence. Hafner (24) reported that poorer readers in college as measured by cloze procedures were less rapid workers on the cloze task, were less able to use contextual clues to meaning, were less intelligent and less knowledgeable, and were less able to reason well than the better readers.

The style of the author is another determiner of performance on cloze tests (8). It might be profitable for the literature teacher to vary approaches to different authors and various works of literature.

EFFICIENCY IN READING

Although comprehension is of primary importance, efficiency in reading is worthy of attention. The mature reader not only is a comprehending reader; he comprehends at a satisfactory rate.

Here we are concerned particularly with legibility. Since legibility greatly influences the speed with which the reader can digest materials, legibility becomes an important factor in reading. It is related to such factors as illumination, line width, color of paper and print, type size, contrast, and leading. These factors are not so directly related to the comprehensibility of what is being read as they are to the efficiency with which the reading is done.

Type Sizes[10]

One of the factors that affect legibility is type size. Generally readers prefer 11 point type, with 10 and 12 point type next, and finally 9 and 8 point type (60, p. 148). However, 9, 10, 11, and 12 point type are equally legible in a line of appropriate length and with two-point leading (60, p. 80). Children read best with 14 to 18 point type.

Studies (54,78) indicate that speed of reading is not a valid criterion for determining the effect of type sizes on reading ease below the fourth-grade level. Speed is not an important characteristic of reading at this stage. The pupil is concerned more with the recognition and interpretation of what he reads. Marks (49) found that type size and face did alter reading competency; color, double spacing, and underlining did not. The best evidence indicates that the type size should be between 14 and 18 point in grade one, between 12 and 14 points in grades two and three, and between 10 and 12 points in the upper grades (78).

Too large or too small type results in more fixations, more regressions, and a smaller perception span (77). Figure 9-3 illustrates the various type sizes.

Kinds of Type

Studies generally have indicated that roman print is more legible than italic type; lower case type is more readable than capitals; book print is more readable than typewriter type; and lightface type is more legible

---

[10] In printing, the standard measurements are the pica and the point. The pica is about one-sixth of an inch and the point is about one-seventy-second of an inch. Thus, 72 points or 6 picas equal one inch.

8 point

16. This band of men and women set sail for the new world where they could live in peace. There was great rejoicing when

9 point

16. This band of men and women set sail for the new world where they could live in peace. There was great

10 point

16. This band of men and women set sail for the new world where they could live in peace. There was

11 point

16. This band of men and women set sail for the new world where they could live in peace. There

12 point

16. This band of men and women set sail for the new world where they could live in

14 point

16. This band of men and women set sail for the new world where they could

Figure 9-3.   Variations in Type Size*

than boldface. Readers also prefer lower case over italics but differences in reading speed are not significant. Figure 9-4 illustrates various styles of face type.

Leading

Increased leading[11] aids reading ease and promotes speed of reading. Generally a two-point leading is used with adult materials. Most preprimers use approximately a 12 point leading. Tinker (78) recommends a 4 to 6 point leading in grade one, a 3 to 4 point leading in grade two, and a 2 to 3 point leading in grades 3 and 4.

* From Fig. 7, p. 33, *How to Make Type Readable* by Donald G. Paterson and Miles A. Tinker. Copyright 1940 by Harper & Brothers; renewed 1968 by Margaret Paterson. By permission of Harper & Row, Publishers.

[11] Amount of leading is the distance between two lines of print.

Times Roman

3. This morning my mother asked me to find out what time it was. I therefore ran just as rapidly

Garamond

3. This morning my mother asked me to find out what time it was. I therefore ran just as rapidly as I

Fairfield

3. This morning my mother asked me to find out what time it was. I therefore ran just as rapidly as

Bodoni Bold

3. This morning my mother asked me to find out what time it was. I therefore ran

Caledonia

3. This morning my mother asked me to find out what time it was. I therefore ran just as rap-

Spartan Medium

3. This morning my mother asked me to find out what time it was. I therefore ran just as rapidly as I

Typewriter

3. This morning my mother asked me to find out what time it was. I

Figure 9-4. Variations in Type Style *

The width of the line can vary greatly without serious effect upon the speed of reading. Although the variation may be from 16 to 30 picas in the primary grades, generally it lies somewhere between 18 and 24 (78). With adults the variation is even greater, quite commonly from 14 to 31 picas (from $2\frac{1}{3}$ inches to $5\frac{1}{6}$ inches) if the line has 2 point leading and is set in solid 10 point type (60, p. 148). In Table 9-1 we have summarized Tinker's (78) recommendations for primary reading materials.

Adult readers generally prefer lines from about 17 to 28 picas in

* From Fig. 4, p. 14. *How To Make Type Readable* by Donald G. Paterson and Miles A. Tinker. Copyright 1940 by Harper & Brothers; renewed 1968 by Margaret Paterson. By permission of Harper & Row, Publishers.

TABLE 9-1   Recommended Type Sizes, Leading, and Line Widths
for the Primary Grades and Above

	Grade I	Grade II and Grade III	Grade IV and Above
Size of Type	14–18 point	12–14 points	10–12 points
Leading	4–6 point	3–4 points	2 points
Line Width	19–20 picas	19–22 picas	19–24 picas

length. When the lines are too short or too long, the reader tends to make more fixations and to read fewer words per fixation. Long lines make it more difficult to make the proper return sweep. Short lines lead to choppy reading because the eye does not use peripheral vision effectively (78).

Illumination

Luckiesh and Moss (46, p. 345) recommend 20 to 50 footcandles[12] for ordinary and prolonged reading and 50 to 100 footcandles for difficult and prolonged reading. Tinker (76) suggests that with 10 point type an intensity of from 10 to 15 footcandles is sufficient for ordinary reading conditions. Russell (64, p. 100) believes that ordinary reading requires from fifteen to twenty footcandles for efficient work and higher intensities for detailed and prolonged work.

Color and Contrast

The efficiency of illumination depends on the number of footcandles, but also on the reflection factor of the surface. Contrasts of color between paper and print and contrast of illumination in the room are important factors for ease of seeing. We refer to these as brightness factors.

The black letters on the page receive as much light as the paper itself, but reflect only about one-fortieth as much light (60, p. 306). Generally black print on a light background is a good combination for ease of readability.

Reading efficiency also is decreased by strong contrasts in illumination within the room. The amount of illumination provided in the classroom by the light from the sun varies both with the weather outside and with the location in the room. This situation creates unequal illumination

---

[12] A hundred-watt bulb gives an illumination of 100 footcandles one foot away; 25 footcandles, two feet away; and about 11 footcandles, three feet away.

in the classroom and may need to be remedied with artificial light. The surface of the paper generally should be rough enough so that glare is minimized (78).

SUMMARY

This chapter has concentrated on some aspects of the elementary reading program. It has discussed such varied aspects as (1) formal introduction of reading teaching; (2) materials for the beginning program; (3) the steps in teaching reading; (4) group versus individualized instruction; (5) the primary and intermediate reading program; and (6) the significance of reading rate, readability, and legibility.

Perhaps we have put too much emphasis on the skills to be learned. However, other values of reading, such as interest in reading and good literature, and personal growth and development in and through reading, will accrue to the child if he has developed the necessary skills to be a good reader. One of the basic principles in motivational theory is that persons are "driven" or motivated to use their skills and abilities. The person who can see will want to use his visual skills, and the good reader generally wants to read.

QUESTIONS FOR DISCUSSION

1. Examine two "experience charts" and discuss the values and limitations of each for the teaching of reading.
2. What are the chief purposes of basal reading materials, and in your estimation, how well have these purposes been met by these materials?
3. Compare the vocabulary control in basal reading series with that in some of the more prominent phonetic systems. What are the criteria of control and which seems more undesirable to you?
4. What are the steps in the actual teaching of reading?
5. What is the advantage of the analytical method of sounding?
6. Explain and discuss the implications of the statement: The teacher is not the prime director of the learning process.
7. Explain: Total individualization of instruction may not be individualizing the reading program.
8. Evaluate flexible or mobile subgrouping.
9. Discuss: Slow reading is not necessarily poor reading.
10. Discuss: Mechanical devices cannot increase comprehension potential.

Introducing the Pupil to Linguistic Phonics

chapter 10

In Chapter 8 we examined the various methods of teaching reading. We intimated that an eclectic or combination approach is probably best and that the teaching of reading might best begin with the total word, but that for genuine independence in reading the parts of words should be emphasized from the beginning. The pupil must become self-directive in the process of identifying new words. The linguistic phonics program can offer much in this regard, and for this reason we treat it in the following two chapters.

Phonetic instruction (and consequently phonetic analysis) is not reading; it is only *one* of the skills required for successful reading. It is not even the only method of word attack. Other ways of identifying and recognizing a word are: through the use of picture clues, the use of the configuration of the word, the use of context clues, and structural analysis. Weber (46) found that children use all types of cues (phonic, grammatical, and meaning) to recognize words, but he also noted that toward the end of first grade children become more reliant upon phonic cues. The high-achieving children used phonic cues to a greater degree than did the nonachievers.

Word attack skills are needed to attain one of the basic goals of teaching reading. It is hoped that the reader eventually will commit the word so well to memory that he can respond to it spontaneously without having "to figure it out." Each word should then become a sight word that is instantly recognized.

Chapters 10 and 11 are essentially a summary of another book by the author, entitled *Linguistics, Phonics, and the Teaching of Reading* (Springfield, Ill.: Charles C Thomas, Publisher, 1969).

TERMINOLOGY

Before getting into the specifics of linguistic phonics instruction, let us clarify a few terms.

1. *Phonics* is the study of the speech equivalents of printed symbols and the use of this knowledge in identifying and pronouncing printed words (25, p. 324). It is learning which involves the association of the appearance of a letter or letter combinations with a given sound (25, p. 330). It is the study of sound-letter relationships in reading and spelling. It represents the various teaching practices that aim to develop the pupil's ability to sound out a word by matching individual letters by which a word is spelled with the specific sounds which these letters say. *Phonic analysis* is the actual process of sounding out letters or letter combinations to arrive at the pronunciation of the word.

2. *Phonetics* is the study of the sounds used in speech, including their pronunciations, the symbolization of the sounds, and the action of the larynx, tongue, and lips in sound production. Phonetics does not concern itself with the ways words are spelled by the traditional alphabet. It seeks to develop phonetic alphabets which represent graphically the actual pronunciations of linguistic forms. Dictionaries contain phonetic transliterations.

3. *Phonemics* is the study of the speech sounds that are used in a language. It is thus a study of phonemes. Phonemic analysis deals only with those sounds that are significant in the language (the phonemes) and ignores the nonsignificant differences (the allophones). The *p* sound in *pet, spot, suppose,* and *top* is slightly different in each instance, but the difference is considered to be nonsignificant. The phonemes are the smallest sound units in a language. Phonemes combine to form morphemes which are the smallest units of language that can bear meaning. The written phoneme is a grapheme, and the writing of graphemes in proper order to form morphemes is orthography or spelling.

4. *The Alphabet* is a set of graphic shapes that represent the phonemes of the language.

5. *Word Analysis* is an inclusive term which subsumes all methods of attacking words. Phonics is one form of word analysis.

6. *Phonic or Phonetic Method*—There are various methods of teaching reading. The phonic method is often considered to be a synthetic method because it begins with the word element or the sound of the letter and gradually advances to the total word. This designation is actually in error. There are some "phonic methods" that are termed "whole word phonics" which begin with the total word.

7. *A linguist* is a scientist who studies a language in terms of its basic structure, including sound patterns, stress, intonation, and syntactic structure

8. *Linguistic Phonics*—We have titled this chapter, "Introducing the Pupil to Linguistic Phonics," because we recommend that the letter be sounded only in the context of the total word. This approach sometimes is referred to as the phonemic-word approach because the structure of the language is studied through symbol-sound relationships in whole words (38). It is our view that comparing and contrasting basic spelling patterns with the appropriate or correlative sound patterns lead to independence in attacking new words. Thus, the individual letter is never sounded; it is only named. The sounds represented by *b, c, d* exist only in the context of a word or syllable. The *o* combination with *y,* as in boy, has a distinct sound; its sound depends on the pattern in which it occurs. Blending, which is a common problem in phonics, ought not to be a problem in a linguistic approach.

Whenever the word phonics is used alone in this chapter, it is meant to signify whole-word phonics as opposed to synthetic phonics.

THE PHONETIC CONSISTENCY OF OUR LANGUAGE

The teaching of reading has paid relatively little attention to the phonic consistency of the English language. And yet, Hanna and Moore (23) found English to be 86.9 per cent phonetic. We do not mean that English is less phonetic than other languages. It is not correct to say that one language is more phonetic than another. All languages, in that they involve the use of phonemes or speech sounds, are phonetic. One language may have a more consistent spelling system and thus is more alphabetic than another. Thus, Hanna and Moore (23) report that single consonants are represented by regular spellings about 90 per cent of the time.

It is not difficult to find examples of the problems that one would encounter if one assumed that the English language provided a completely consistent spelling system for the sounds of the language. As we saw in Chapter 8, systems like ITA and Words in Color are attempts to provide this consistency and to deal with the inconsistencies.

Ever so often in the literature somebody pokes fun at anyone who talks of phonic consistency. George Bernard Shaw asserted, years ago, that the word *fish* might just as well be spelled *ghoti*. There is no doubt that the *f* sound is sometimes spelled *gh* (enough); the short *i* sound, as *o* (women); and the *sh* sound, as *ti* (nation). But, as Lefevre (34, p. 182) notes, "in spelling practice, not a one of the three phonemes is regularly represented in these positions by these graphemes. The *gh* is never used initially; *ti* representing [sh] does not occur finally but medially—the initial part of a suffix such as *-tion* or *tiate;* and *o* as [short i] occurs precisely once in English, in the word *women*." [1]

The correspondence between written and spoken English is weak if one attempts to relate individual letters and sounds, but if the graphemic unit is a letter pattern, words, or word groups, a high degree of correspondence is found (31).

Levin and Watson (35,36) found that training on regular sound-to-spelling correspondences was less than optimal for transfer. Levin suggests that it seems reasonable early in one's schooling to simultaneously learn more than one associated sound to letters and letter groups. The indication is that this will lead to greater flexibility in trying out sounds when the child meets new instances. The study showed that dual associations were more difficult to acquire, but that once acquired they facilitated the child's learning to read new words. It is our contention therefore:

1. That pupils learn to associate letter and sound patterns. The relationship emphasized by the linguistic approach is not letter-to-sound, but rather letter patterns to sound patterns.

    The first task is to break the alphabetic code and to grade words according to their phonetic difficulty, not their semantic difficulty (3). The pupil should be taught to associate specific letters in words with specific sounds without conscious analysis of a word into its individual sounds by presenting the whole word in lists and contexts (3). There should be no analysis of individual sounds as occurs in phonics. Reading should not be confused with the infant's acquisition of speech sounds.

2. That the pupil be taught from the beginning that nearly every generalization has exceptions and that if the word does not make sense in the sentence that he try another approach. We need to teach him *flexibility*.

[1] Carl A. Lefevre, *Linguistics and the Teaching of Reading* (New York: McGraw-Hill Book Company, 1964). Reprinted by permission.

3. That the exceptions be taught immediately from the beginning as *sight* words and that they be clearly labelled as exceptions. The pupil might benefit from this introduction of variation; however, this does not mean that he should be exposed to the total range of variation.

The reading program should be flexible enough to include words which are irregular if these words are needed to make the language more meaningful. It should provide contextual settings for words that permit them to be learned in a more natural linguistic environment (9).

One of the chief objections to phonic and/or linguistic programs has been the limitation that it has put on initial reading materials. Such controlled materials are often viewed as uninteresting and quite meaningless. Edwards (17, p. 356), however, notes:

"Sophisticated adult readers who react negatively to the content of materials based on the principle of controlled vocabulary input are projecting their own desires for richness of meaning because they have already mastered the decoding process. The beginning reader, on the other hand, is intrigued by the magic of the decoding process, and success in the mastery of this process might well provide adequate motivation at the initial stages of learning to read." Any student of foreign languages will attest to the thrill of being able to read: "I am big." [2]

Nevertheless, the child's reading vocabulary probably does not need to be controlled to the extent that it now is. The child's early language training in the home is not structured for him. He hears thousands of words and learns to understand and to speak them. His training is sequential only as he makes it so. No one formally teaches him the word.

The results with individualized reading also tend to indicate that the child learns much more than is formally taught him. He in fact masters that for which he is psychologically, physiologically, and mentally ready.

However, there seems to be value in some control. *We suggest control in his phonic vocabulary* (not in the number of words necessarily but in the rate of introduction of phoneme-phonogram pattern relationships) *so that he will more quickly master the principles that undergird language structure. This*

[2] Thomas J. Edwards, "Teaching Reading: A Critique," pp. 349–362 in John Money (ed.), *The Disabled Reader* (Baltimore: Johns Hopkins Press, 1966). Reprinted by permission.

control seems sensible only when formally teaching skills of phonic analysis. Introducing the pupil to the phonetic consistencies will make him more conscious of the sounds in words, and having learned the principles that guide their relative consistency, he will be able to attack hundreds of words that he has not previously seen in print.

When a word is met in the child's reading that is alphabetic, it should be taught as such. Thus, if the pupil reads *cat* and he has experienced the *k* sound of *c*, the short *a* sound, and *t*, it should be pointed out to him that the spelling is quite regular. There is no great virtue in teaching this word as a sight word. If in reading he comes across such a word as *come,* it should be taught immediately as a sight word. If the word is actually regular (came) but he has not yet been formally introduced to such words or to the principles governing the sounding of such a word, the word might simply be pronounced and teaching of the appropriate word analysis skills might be deferred until later. There is no reason to insist that the child should learn it as a sight word, or as a configuration, if by application of the principle of pacing, the pupil will soon know it and understand it as a phonetically consistent word.

4.   That the best way of breaking the language code may not yet have been developed, but it seems easier to break the code when the child is introduced to words in which the letters behave consistently.

5.   That rather than establish a new system in which there is a separate symbol for each sound, such as *I T A* or even such a distinctive cueing device as Words in Color, it is better to teach the present system, emphasizing the consistency of sound-symbol patterns most often encountered (44).

6.   That the pupil develop the habit of "reading through" words by proceeding from left to right (27, p. 335). The order of the letters in a word symbolizes the time-order in which the sounds are made, but it seems far safer to teach the pupil to sound the whole word.

LINGUISTIC SYSTEMS OF TEACHING READING [3]

Since we have termed our approach linguistic phonics, it may be advantageous to summarize various linguistic systems of teaching reading.

[3] See Deanna Bartkowiak, "Linguistics and Reading: Four Views," *Elementary English*, 44 (April, 1967) 386–391.

There is really no linguistic method; all methods of teaching reading are linguistic methods in that they teach the comprehension of linguistic material (29).

Linguists emphasize that reading is primarily a language process and that the major task facing the child is the mastery of the graphic system that reflects the spoken language system. The linguist maintains that he has more to offer than a retreat back to synthetic phonics.

Bloomfield & Barnhart (7, 8) presented in 1961 a linguistic approach in *Let's Read: A Linguistic Approach*. The central thesis of the Bloomfield-Barnhart method is that there is an inseparable relationship between the words as printed and the sounds for which the letters are conventional signs, and that converting letters to meaning requires from the beginning a concentration upon letter and sound to bring about as rapidly as possible an automatic association between them (40). Barnhart (8, p. 9) points out that Bloomfield's system is a linguistic system of teaching reading which separates the problem of the study of word-form from the study of word-meaning. He notes that children come to school knowing how to speak the English language, but they do not know how to read the form of words.

Bloomfield makes the following points:

1. In spite of its many imperfections, the system of writing used in the English language is basically alphabetic, and reading is merely the act of responding vocally to the printed letter as it functions with other letters. The alphabetic nature of our writing is most obvious when we put together a combination of letters to make a word. The linguistic emphasis thus is not so much on the representation of a single phoneme, but rather of a pattern of phonemes. The emphasis is on the relationship between patterns of phonemes and patterns of graphemes, especially between spoken words and written words. The linguist admits that the correspondence between written and spoken English often is weak if one relates individual letters and sounds, but notes that the correspondence between letter patterns and word groups is high (20,21,22). The letter is not sounded alone; it is sounded only in the context of other letters or the word.

2. In order to read alphabetic writing the reader must have developed an ingrained habit of producing the phonemes of the language when he sees the written marks which conventionally represent these phonemes (8).

3. English writing is alphabetic, but only imperfectly so. The child should not be introduced to the exceptions until he has mastered the regularities of the language. The child's early reading experiences should be dealing with letters and sounds as they function in

monosyllabic regular words. Hildreth (27, p. 348) notes that it is easier to learn the relationships among sound elements within words by studying monosyllabic words. When all words are three-letter words the pupil cannot use the length of the word to identify it, and quite frequently he cannot use the configuration: *bat, hat.* Both words obviously have the same configuration. The words should contain only short vowels. Long vowel sounds, diphthongs, consonant blends, speech consonants, and words containing silent letters should be introduced only after the pupil has mastered some of the phonetic consistencies of the language. The goal of this approach to reading instruction is to familiarize children with the phonetic consistencies of the language as a basis for generalizations to new words. In beginning reading materials, every letter should represent only one single phoneme. The pupil must learn the equation: *printed letter = speech sound to be spoken.*

The first material should contain no words with silent letters (*knit*), none with double letters (be*ll*), and none with combinations of letters having a special value (*ea* as in bean). Letters such as *x* or *q* should also be delayed until later.

4. Bloomfield decries the fact that synthetic phonic methods isolate speech sounds. Synthetic phonics proceeds as though the child were being taught to speak. Phonemes do not occur by themselves and should not be taught in isolation.

5. The child should first be taught the names of the letters. Presenting the letters in color increases interest and emphasizes shape. Writing of the letters should be delayed until after reading has begun.

Lefevre (33,34, pp. 247–278), having a different emphasis than Bloomfield, adapted linguistic ideas to meaningful reading. He suggests an analytical method of teaching reading emphasizing language patterns. He emphasized that meaning comes only through the grasping of the language structure exemplified in a sentence. Meaning thus depends on the intonation, the word and sentence order, the grammatical inflections, and certain key function words. Intonation, or the pauses and stresses in oral language, are represented by (*1*) capital letters, periods, semicolons, and question marks, (*2*) by the order of the words, (*3*) by grammatical inflections signaling tense, number, and possession, and (*4*) by such function words as *the, when, nevertheless,* or *because.* Only by reading structures can full meaning be attained. Or, to put it another way, unless the reader translates correctly the printed text into the intonation pattern of the writer, he may not be getting the meaning intended.

Bloomfield felt that initial teaching of reading for meaning is incorrect and that meaning will come quite naturally as the alphabetic code or principle is discovered. Lefevre is critical of Bloomfield's approach, criticizing him for confining himself largely to phonemic analysis and for neglecting intonation and syntax.

Lefevre makes the following observations:

1. "To comprehend printed matter, the reader must perceive entire language structures as wholes—as unitary meaning-bearing patterns." (34, p. XI) Reading requires "recognition and interpretation of the graphic counterparts of entire spoken utterances as unitary meaning-bearing patterns; this is reading comprehension." (32)[4]
2. Lefevre decries the emphasis on letters and words as the significant units of language (34, p. XVII). He notes that in English the most significant structures are intonation patterns, grammatical and syntactical word groups, clauses, and sentences. Words are relatively minor elements in meaning-bearing patterns. The pupil needs to be taught to read by language patterns that carry meaning. Word-order provides one of the most reliable clues to the total meaning-bearing pattern. Intonation is another. The child should be taught first to read and write the language patterns he brings to school.
3. Writing and print are mnemonic devices whose chief function is to effect recall of entire language patterns, especially sentence-level utterances (34, p. 4).
4. Misapprehension of the relationships between spoken and printed language or sentence patterns is a decisive element in reading failures (34, pp. 4–5). The basic fault in poor reading is poor sentence sense, often demonstrated orally in word calling. The crippled reader's worst fault is literal word calling or word-by-word reading with virtually no sentence sense (34, p. 23). The poor reader registers only random elements (words)—many can't even do this and that is why we need phonics—but miss language structures altogether.
5. Children taught to read with chief emphasis on larger patterns than words develop their own generalizations of spelling-sound relationships (phonics). If they do not, special instructions may need to be devised to help them (34, p. 6). Although attention to word analysis and spelling may be necessary, isolated words must be brought back into the larger patterns and structures that function linguistically and carry meaning; this is true reading (34, p. 174).
6. "The essence of reading and writing readiness is the child's understanding that the language he hears and speaks can be represented

---

[4] All quotes are from Carl A. Lefevre, *Linguistics and the Teaching of Reading* (New York: McGraw-Hill Book Company, 1964). Reprinted by permission.

graphically in writing and print; and that the writing and print he sees can say something to him." (34, p. 39)

Soffièti's system (42), that of Daniels and Diack (13,14,15) proposed in the *Royal Road Readers,* and Fries' system (19) are basically linguistic systems. Daniels and Diack call their system "the phonic word method." They teach letter meanings functionally in words and do not isolate speech sounds. Soffièti emphasizes, contrary to Bloomfield, the importance of meaning, structure, and form clues, but he nevertheless stresses the importance of beginning with words in which each letter has only one phonetic value.

Fries,[5] in *Linguistics and Reading,* offers the following suggestions for the teaching of reading:

1. The process of learning to read "is *the process of transfer* from the auditory signs for language signals [sounds], which the child has already learned, to the new visual signs [letters] for the same signals (19, p. 120)." "Both reading and talking have the same set of language signals for language *reception.* In talking, contrastive bundles of sound features represent these signals; in reading, contrastive patterns of spelling represent these same signals (19, p. 188)."
2. Writing represents the *time* sequence of auditory patterns [sounds follow one another in time] by means of a sequence of *direction in space* (19, p. 121). In English writing the space-direction is a horizontal sequence of graphic shapes from left to right.
3. "The first set of recognition responses to be developed by the pupil are those for the letters of our alphabet. The letters that appear in our spelling patterns must be identified as contrasting shapes (19, p. 190)." The ability to identify and distinguish the graphic shapes does not necessarily mean attaching the conventional names to these distinctive shapes, even though the names are very useful in checking the identification response (19, p. 124).
4. There must be no attempt to connect the letters themselves with sounds. Nor should the groups of letters (such as IT, IF, FIT, HIT, AT, HAT) be treated at this preliminary stage as words to be pronounced and connected with meanings (19, p. 194).

    The approach advocated by Fries rests upon the same foundation as does phonics, namely, the relation between sound patterns of the words and the letter symbols of the alphabet, but it differs

---

[5] All quotes are from Charles C. Fries, *Linguistics and Reading* [Reference 19], Copyright 1963 by Charles Carpenter Fries. Reprinted by permission of Holt, Rinehart and Winston, Inc.

in that the relation is not such as to lead to the matching of specific letters with each of the physical sounds of the language (19, p. 146). Reading is not the matching of words, letter by letter, with words, sound by sound. Furthermore, the pronunciation of a word is not a fusion or blending of the sounds represented by the individual letters. "The relation of the sound patterns of the 'words' to the letter symbols of our alphabet is not a *one-for-one correspondence between the isolated individual letters of the spelling and specific separate phonetic features of the sound pattern.* The 'phonics' approach of (a) isolating and in many instances trying to pronounce the individual 'sounds' of a word, and (b) seeking to learn the 'sounds each letter makes' has had some merit, for it served to turn attention to the fact that our language sounds and alphabet spellings are indeed related. Because of that fact, 'phonics,' in spite of all the critical discussion and all the evidence brought against its assumptions and practices, has persisted (19, p. 146)."

"Instead of the approach through trying to match individual letters and separate sound units, we must develop the automatic habits of responding to the contrastive features of *spelling-patterns as identifying the word-patterns they represent.* For example, even in the three letter word . . . *man,* it is not the single letter A that indicates the vowel sound [ae]. It is the spelling-pattern *m a n* in contrast with the spelling-pattern *m a n e* or that of *m e a n* that signals the different vowel phonemes that make these three different words. Each of these three is one of the major regular spelling-patterns of English . . . (19, p. 200)."

5. This spelling-pattern approach, learning to respond to the contrastive features that separate and identify whole word-patterns, is a word-method. "The essential difference between this spelling pattern approach and the usual 'word-method' lies in the kind of identifying characteristics used to recognize the words. The systematic materials used here to build up the habits of automatic recognition responses to the contrasts of the major spelling-patterns leave no uncertainty in the identifying characteristics that mark off one written word from another. These are the identifying characteristics of the language itself as incorporated in the patterns of our alphabetic spelling (19, p. 201)."

6. a. "The words used, that is, the sound-patterns of the words themselves and the particular meanings selected, must include only those within the *actual linguistic experience* of the pupil. The beginning reading stage must use only the language material already in the full control of the pupil; it is not the time to strive to increase the range of that control (19, p. 202)."

b. "The grammatical signals must also include only those within the pupil's linguistic experience. By the age of four or five, however, most native speakers of English will have full control of practically all the basic grammatical signals of their language . . . (19, p. 202)."

c. "Not all the words familiar to the pupil in the transfer stage of reading can be used for the materials of practice. It is essential *throughout this stage* that the words selected for the practice materials be only those for which the *spelling-patterns fit those that have been introduced and practiced or those that are being introduced* (19, p. 202)."

d. ". . . The simple contrasts used should always be of items within a whole pattern, never of items less than a word . . . (19, p. 202)."

e. "At the beginning and for considerable time thereafter the teacher pronounces in *normal talking fashion* each new word and each pair of contrastive words as it is introduced and makes sure that the pupil, from that pronunciation, identifies the words as ones he knows (19, p. 203)."

f. "Only complete words are pronounced. The pronunciation for the 'word' is thus attached to the total spelling-pattern that represents that word. The spelling-pattern *cat* represents the word /kaet/ as pronounced. . . . The understanding of the difference that any particular letter makes in the spelling-pattern is built up out of the experience of pronouncing a variety of word pairs with minimum differences in their spelling patterns.

CAT—AT
CAT—RAT
CAT—PAT

We avoid completely such a question as 'What does the letter C say?' (19, pp. 203–204)."

7. "And yet if the reader is to learn to read well, that is, if the graphic devices are to function as fully for him as reader as all the sound-patterns of speech do for him as hearer, there must be some way by which he can learn to supply with some degree of fullness and accuracy the meanings contributed to speech by the patterns of intonation and stress. As a matter of fact, all of us who read with some maturity and the few who read with extraordinary insight and understanding, do, as they read, carry along and build up such a cumulative comprehension of so much of the total meanings of a discourse that their automatic recog-

nition-responses *fill in the appropriate intonation and stress patterns* (19, pp. 206–207)."

"Teachers should never allow to pass any oral reading of any sentence that does not display in the features of pitch sequence and stress an understanding or some understanding of the total meaning. The very least that teachers should accept at the beginning, is the 'saying' of a sentence, after it has been 'mechanically read,' as the child would 'talk' it to a companion. Later, intonation patterns can be marked on material that is to be read aloud. Children can very soon quite consciously judge the significance or the fitness of an intonation sequence, for they are *not*, at the age of five or six, learning to *use* intonation sequences. They have already learned them as they have learned to understand speech directed to them. Now, in their learning to read, they are simply becoming conscious of their existence as they are brought to realize that 'reading' must substitute for the 'understanding of talk' (19, p. 207)."

"In other words, the second stage of the development of reading ability is complete not only when the responses to the spelling-patterns have become so automatic that the contrastive features of these bundles of the graphic shapes themselves sink below the threshold of attention leaving only consciousness of the body of meaning as it develops, but especially when the cumulative understanding of this body of meaning enables the reader to supply, to produce for materials read 'at sight,' those portions of the language signals, the appropriate patterns of intonation and stress that are not represented or only partially represented in the graphic materials given for the eye. We have, therefore, called this stage of reading development the 'productive' stage. The case for oral reading today rests primarily on the need to develop 'productive reading' (19, p. 208)."

It seems that before the pupil can do what Lefevre wants him to do, the pupil must be able to do what Bloomfield and Fries are most interested in. They are emphasizing the importance of being able to identify the word; they thus have a lot to offer in word identification. Lefevre is more concerned with the total reading act and thus has much to offer in word comprehension. But since context is often invaluable in identifying a word, Lefevre's ideas have meaning also when the pupil cannot identify the word, for unless the word makes sense in the sentence, both in meaning sense and structurally, word identification was faulty.

THE ORDER OF PRIORITY IN SOUNDS

There is some order of priority in sounds. The Institute of Logopedics at the University of Wichita uses the term, "Order of Primitivity," to refer to the order of the development of the sounds in the language. This order is *m, p, b, t, d, n, h, w, f, v, k, g, th, sh, zh, ch, j, s, z, r,* and *l.* The mechanics of the articulatory process developed physiologically from the integration of the basic chewing, sucking, swallowing, and similar vegetative reflexes. Experience shows that when a child suffers a speech loss, the loss is in reverse order. The last sounds to be developed are the first sounds to be lost.

Many errors in reading arise from the fact that children cannot or do not discriminate certain sounds orally and consequently neither make the sound properly nor form the proper association between the spoken element and the written element. The teacher must determine *what phonetic elements should be taught, in what order* they should be taught, and *how* they might be taught best.

There are stages in the development of general reading skills, of word attack skills, and of specific phonic skills. The teacher must know what the goals of achievement are at each level for each of these. He must realize that children progress at different rates through the various levels and that they differ from one another in the levels they ultimately attain. This makes the identification of a natural sequence in teaching phonic skills even more important.

This sequence is not used for the setting of definite standards of attainment for all children, but rather for the guidance of teachers in their attempt to provide for individual differences. Each child must be let through the sequence at a rate at which he can succeed. Thus, there really are no first-grade skills. There is only a sequence of skills through which children normally should proceed. *This sequence the teacher must identify.*

Word recognition skills are important. Proper training in them increases independence in attacking words, improves comprehension, and leads to more accurate pronunciations. Perhaps as significant is the fact that they are not acquired in a year or two. Training needs to be continuous, it needs to be applied in many situations, and it needs to be sequential.

Davis (16,39) reports that some six-year-old children have not mastered *l, r, s, th, sh, zh, z,* and *wh.* Van Riper and Butler (45, p. 64) report that most of the articulatory errors made by primary children involve *f, l, r, s, sh, k, th,* and *ch,* and that elementary children have most difficulty with *r, s, l, th.* Hildreth (27) points out that the *k, q, v, x, y,* and *z* should be introduced last.

There are other reasons for not using certain letters in initial phonic (and possibly reading) exercises. The letter *x,* for example, represents six distinct sounds. It has the sound of *ks* in box, of *gz* in exist, of *ksh* in anxious, of *gzh* in luxurious, of *z* in xylophone, and of *gksh* in anxious (angshus). The letter *q* occurs only with *u* and then has the sound of *kw.* The letter *k* is readily confused with the much more used hard *c.*

Because of these data the following letters might best be excluded from early *phonic* experiences: *k, q, v, x, y, z.* There is no great advantage in introducing them. Relatively few words use these sounds. A word like *you* may be taught as a sight word. This does not mean that these sounds are not introduced in the first grade. Some youngsters may be able to handle them almost immediately.

The letters themselves present problems for the pupil. Popp (41) found that the most frequently confused pairs of letters in rank order by nonreading kindergarteners were: p-q, d-b, d-q, d-p, b-p, h-u, i-l, k-y, t-u, c-e, d-h, h-n, h-y, j-k, and n-u. Coleman (12) found that p-q and d-b were more often confused by preschoolers than they were correctly identified.

THE SEQUENCE OF PHONIC SKILLS

Before getting involved in the minute details of phonetic analysis, and let us from the start say that few children or even adults fully master these details, let us suggest one sequence in which phonic skills might be taught. In the two chapters that follow, the program for teaching phonic skills looks something like this:

Chapter 10

1. Teaching the initial consonant sounds and beginning consonant substitution

    a. *M, T, B, H, P, N*   d. *K, Q*
    b. *D, W, G, C, J*   e. *V, X, Y, Z*
    c. *F, L, R, S*   f. Soft sounds of *C* and *G*

2. Teaching the short vowel sounds
3. Teaching the ending consonants
4. Teaching structural analysis skills

Chapter 11

5. The two- and three-letter consonant blends
6. Speech consonants *ch, sh, th, wh, gh, ph*

7.   The long vowels

   a. *a, e, i, o, u, y*
   b. long vowel plus silent *e*
   c. *ai, ay, ea, ee, oa, oe, ow*
   d. *er, ir, or, ur,* and *wa*
   e. the diphthongs—*ei, ie, oi, oy, oo, ou, au, aw, ow, ew, ue*

8.   Syllabication and Accentuation
9.   Silent letters
10. Special problems of two- and three-syllable words.

The program suggested above is necessarily flexible. We have presented what we feel is one way of setting up a logical sequence. Other writers may prefer a different sequence (2). It is quite probable that children rarely learn the materials in any prescribed order.

THE BEGINNING CONSONANT

Initial reading exercises, as was pointed out in the previous chapter, are designed to develop a basic recognition vocabulary. In working toward this goal the pupil is asked:

1.   to do picture reading;
2.   to associate sounds with the whole word;
3.   to use the context both for identifying the word and for understanding its meaning;
4.   to learn the names of the individual letters;
5.   to write the letters; and
6.   to associate sounds with the beginning consonant and with the median vowel.

The pupil must learn to hear sounds in words, to see phonograms or to notice the letter or letters that represent the sounds of whole words, and to blend phonograms.

The major aim in this initial stage is to teach: (*1*) the consonants in the beginning position; (*2*) the short vowels within monosyllabic words; and (*3*) a phonetic and a sight or recognition vocabulary. The child needs to learn what is meant when the teacher says: "This word begins with an *m, t, b, h, p,* or *n* sound." He must also learn to deal with consonant substitution. He needs to learn what changing of the initial consonant does to the sound and the meaning of the word.

For years, educators have debated the question whether consonants or vowels should be introduced first. Perhaps the question is invalid. If pupils are to begin with complete words, consonants and vowels must necessarily be introduced concomitantly. The reasons for systematic and formal studying of consonants first usually include the following:

1. There is a greater correspondence between the consonant sounds and the letters used to represent them than between the vowel sounds and the letters used to represent them. Fifteen consonants (*b, d, f, h, j, k, l, m, n, p, r, t, v, w,* and *y*) have only one sound each.

2. Consonant letters are more significant in the perceptual image of a word; (thus, "j–hnn– – h–t th– b–s–b–ll" is more readily identified than "–o– –ie –i– – –e –a–e–a– –"), McKee (37, p. 74) notes that if the pupil knows letter-sound associations for the consonants and if he understands that each printed word in his reading matter is one which makes sense in the context, the pupil can do a lot of independent reading without having been taught letter-sound associations for vowels. McKee adds that the pupil cannot possibly read much if he knows letter-sound associations for vowels, but does not know them for consonants.

3. Consonant letters to a great degree determine the sound of the vowel, whereas vowels rarely affect the sound of the consonant. Thus, in one-syllable words the vowel is usually short when it is in the beginning or the middle position and followed by a consonant

4. Most of the words met in beginning reading begin with consonants.

5. It makes sense to have the child work through the word from left to right and this means beginning with the first letter, which commonly is a consonant.

Teaching the Beginning Consonant

During the first phase of the child's experience with linguistic phonics the pupil should learn how to sound the common consonants. Many children will have mastered all the skills required at this level in the readiness program. They can name most letters and have associated the appropriate sound with the letters. For others, teaching tasks remain. Teaching beginning consonants basically involves the development of auditory, visual, and kinesthetic discrimination of the sound. Teaching the initial *b* sound, for example consists of the following steps:

1. The teacher may pronounce some words that begin with the *b* sound such as bat, bib, bug, boy, etc. The *b* sound may be slightly elongated or stressed, but it should not be distorted. The child may also be taught the mouth geography of the

sound. And, it is useful to identify each sound with a little jingle.

Boys, boys	Cat, cat	Dog, dog
Lets have some fun.	Your purr is sweet,	Chew your bone,
Come out and play	But you have stickers	That will keep you
When your work is done.	In your feet.	Close at home.[5]

2. The teacher asks the pupils what they noticed about the initial sound. Were the initial sounds alike or different?

3. The teacher pronounces words, some of which begin with a *b* sound and some of which do not. The pupils raise their hand when the word begins with the *b* sound.

4. The pupils give other words beginning with a *b* sound. The teacher may accept any word which begins with a *b*. Such combinations as *br* are acceptable at this stage. The teacher may ask if there is anyone in the class whose name begins with a *b* sound.

5. The teacher prints the letter *b* on the blackboard and writes out words such as bed, bat, bib, bug, or any other word beginning with a *b* that the youngsters mentioned. He may put pictures on the chalkboard to make the lesson more meaningful, and the pupils may be asked to pronounce the name of the pictured objects. It is useful to have *key* pictures for each of the sounds to be taught. The teacher may associate the *b* with a picture of a bed and call it "the bed sound." The pupils may be asked to come to the blackboard and draw a line around any pictures whose names begin with the *b* sound.

6. The teacher writes a name under each picture whose name begins with *b*.

7. The pupils are told to look carefully at the letter beginning each of the words under the picture, and the teacher gives the letter a name. The teacher again sounds the words making sure that the pupils listen carefully to the sound at the beginning of each word.

8. The pupils next are taught to associate the *b* sound with both the capital and lower case letter *b*. They may be shown that a word like *Ben,* which begins with a capital letter is sounded in the beginning just like the word bed. It is helpful to show the pupils that if a personal name begins with *b*, the capital *B* must be used.

---

[5] Courtesy of Avis Griffith, Lillian Peak, and Dorothy M. Randle.

9. The pupils then read the words in unison.
10. The pupils next print the letter *b*, both capital and lower case.

Workbook and other teacher-prepared materials may then be used to teach the consonant sounds and the technique of consonant substitution. For exercises that are illustrative, please consult Emerald Dechant, *Linguistics, Phonics, and the Teaching of Reading* (Springfield, Ill.: Charles C Thomas, Publisher, 1969).

The Letters B, C, D, G, H, J, M, N, P, T, W

We have already suggested that it might help to introduce sounds in a given order. Although the teaching of any consonant follows the procedures outlined above, some sounds might be deferred for later teaching because they are more difficult to sound. Table 10-1 lists monosyllabic words containing short vowels that are helpful in teaching the consonants *b, c* (sounded k), *d, g, h, j, m, n, p, t,* and *w* in the beginning position.

The pupil should gradually develop a sense of the structure of words. When the words are organized into linguistic spelling patterns (38), as in Table 10-2, the pupil should see words not as sight words but as words having a similar structure.

The Letters F, L, R, and S

Having mastered the eleven consonants suggested above, the pupil might next be introduced to words containing the *f, l, r,* and *s* sounds. Teachers will find that children generally have much more difficulty articulating these sounds than those that have been considered previously. In some instances it is absolutely necessary to teach the placement in the mouth (the mouth geography) for each sound. The child must be taught the lip and tongue position required in making the sound. Adding these four sounds, *f, l, r,* and *s,* to the pupil's repertoire permits the teacher to introduce many additional phonetically-consistent words. You will notice, however, from Table 10-3 that many of these monosyllabic words are not consistent.

There needs to be specific teaching of each of the following:

1. The words in Table 10-3 introduce additional *a* sounds: the *a* (ȯ) sound in all, call, fall, gall, ball, and wall, and the *a* (ä) sound in bar, car, far, jar, mar, par, and tar. The pupil should note that *a* followed by *r* in monosyllabic words is the *ä* sound. These words may be learned as the "car" words. When *a* is followed by *l* it has the *ȯ* sound, and the words may be identified as the "all" words. These variant sounds of *a* should not

TABLE 10-1   Monosyllabic Words Formed by *B, C, D, G, H, J, M, N, P, T,* and *W*

bad	cab	dad	gab	had	jab	Mac
bag	cam	Dad	gad	ham	jag	mad
ban	can	dam	gag	hem	jam	man
bat	cap	Dan	gap	hen	Jan	map
bed	cat	den	get	hid	Jed	mat
beg	cob	did	God	him	jet	men
bet	cod	dig	got	hit	jib	met
bib	cog	dim	gum	hog	jig	Mig
bid	con	din	gun	hop	Jim	mob
big	cop	dip	gut	hot	job	mop
bin	cot	Doc		hub	jog	mud
bit	cub	dog		hug	jot	mug
Bob	cud	don		hum	jug	mum
bog	cup	Don		hut	jut	
bud	cut	dot				
Bud		dub				
bug		dug				
bun						
but						

nab	pad	pig	tab	tin	was (wäz)
nag	Pam	pin	tag	tip	web
Nan	pan	Pip	tam	Tip	wed
nap	pat	pit	tan	tit-tat	wet
Ned	Pat	pop	tap	Tom	wig
net	peg	pot	tat	ton (tən)	win
nib	Peg	pun	Ted	top	wit
nip	pen	pup	ten	tot	won (wən)
nod	pep	put (pút)	tic	tub	
not	pet		Tim	tug	
nub				tut	
nun					
nut					

be taught until the pupil has mastered the short sounds of the vowels.

2.   The pupil also must learn that quite commonly monosyllabic words ending in an *f, l,* and *s* sound double the final consonant letter.[6] He must learn that in these words only one written letter is pronounced and that in spelling he must use two letters to reproduce the sound.[7]

---

[6] Exceptions to this rule are: as, bus, clef, gas, has, his, if, is, nil, of, pal, plus, pus, this, thus, us, was, yes; also beef, dwarf, golf, half, loaf, meal, mail, roof, self, soil, thief, wheel, and wolf.

[7] Some other words fit this pattern: ebb, egg, add, fizz, buzz, fuzz.

TABLE 10-2   Word Structure

	a	e	i	o	u
b	bat	bet	bit		but
c	cat			cot	cut
d				dot	
e					
f	fat		fit		
g		get		got	gut
h	hat		hit	hot	hut
i					
j		jet		jot	jut
k			kit		
l		let	lit	lot	
m	mat	met	mitt		
n	Nat	net		not	nut
o					
p	pat	pet	pit	pot	
q					
r	rat			rot	rut
s	sat	set	sit		
t	tat			tot	
u					
v	vat	vet			
w		wet	wit		
x					
y		yet			
z					

3. Words ending in double *ll* preceded by *u* sometimes are pronounced as *ù* and sometimes as short *u* sound: thus *bull, full, pull,* but also *cull, dull, gull, hull, lull, mull,* and *null.* For this reason *full* and *pull* may be introduced as sight words at this level of phonic development.

4. Even though the *ər* sound as in *cur* and the *ȯ* sound as in *for* and *boss* are listed in the vocabulary in Table 10-2, these sounds should not be introduced at this time. Thus, the words *her* and *for* should be introduced as sight words. The words *log, of, war, son,* and *was* must also be learned as sight words.

5. The letter *s* frequently is pronounced as a *z*. We have listed some of these words: as, has, his, is, and was. This pronouncing of *s* as *z* generally occurs
    a. at the end of some monosyllabic words (as, has, his, is, was)
    b. when the *s* occurs between two vowels; and
    c. after *j, s, x, z, sh, zh,* and *ch,* the *s* is an *es;* after *f, k, p, t,*

TABLE 10-3   Monosyllabic Words Formed by *B, C, D, F, G, H, J, L, M, N, P, R, S, T, W* and the Short Vowels

as (az)	fop	lag	or (ór)	rod	sip
	for (fór)	lap		rot	sir (sər)
bus	fun	led	pal	rub	sit
	fir (fər)	leg	pus	rug	sob
cur (kər)	fur (fər)	let		rum	sod
		lid	rag	run	son (sən)
fad	gas	lip	ram	rut	sop
fag	Gus	lit	ran		sub
fan		log (lóg)	rap	sad	sun
fat	has (haz)	lop	rat	sag	sum
fed	her (hər)	lot	red	Sal	sup
fen	his (hiz)	lug	rib	Sam	
fib			rid	sap	us
fig	if	nor (nôr)	rig	sat	
fin	is (iz)		rim	set	was (wäz)
fit		of (ov)	rip	Sid	
fog	lad	off (óf)	rob	sin	

Ending in ff	*Ending in ar*	*Ending in rr*	*Ending in ss*		
buff	bar (bär)	err (ər)	bass	hiss	muss
cuff	car	burr (bər)	mass	miss	
duff	far	purr (pər)	pass		
huff	jar			joss	
muff	mar		Bess	boss (bós)	
puff	par		less	moss (mós)	
riff-raff	tar		mess	toss (tós)	
ruff	war (wór)				

Ending in ll

all (ól)	bell	Bill	cull
ball	dell	dill	dull
call	fell	fill	gull
fall	hell	hill	hull
gall	jell	ill	lull
hall	mell	Jill	mull
pall	Nell	mill	null
tall	sell	pill	bull (búl)
wall	tell	rill	full (fúl)
	well	sill	pull (púl)
		till	
		will	

and unvoiced *th,* the *s* is simply an *s;* after all other consonants the *s* is a *z.*

The Letters *K* and *Q*

In the letters *k* and *q,* the consonant blends *nk* and *sk,* and the speech consonant *ck,* the pupil meets new phonic problems. The pupil needs to learn that certain sounds can be written in two ways. The much more common hard *c* and the *k* have the same sound. If the child remembers that the *k* sounds like all the *c* sounds he has met thus far, he should have little difficulty pronouncing the words correctly.

The letter *k* doesn't occur too frequently at the beginning of the word. In this position it is more commonly the letter *c.* However, the *k* is much more frequent than the *c* at the end of the word. This knowledge should be especially helpful in spelling.

The letter *q* occurs only in the combination *qu* and usually has the sound of *kw.* It also may be simply a *k* as in liquor. Occasionally, the *kw* sound is separated as in liquid (lik'wid). *Que* at the end of a word is simply a *k* sound: unique, clique, critique.[8]

Table 10-4 lists some common monosyllabic words illustrating the *k, ck, nk, sk,* and the *qu* sounds.

An analysis of these words shows that most of them are phonetically consistent. The following observations, however, are in order:

1. The speech consonant, *ck,* at the end of the word, preceded by a short vowel, is simply *k* as, for example, in back, click, cluck, crick, crock, deck, Dick, duck, hack, hock, lack, lock, luck, nick, peck, pick, pluck, prick, rock, sack, sick, slack, slick, snack, sock, speck, stick. Bailey (1) found this rule had 100 per cent validity.
2. *Ank* is *angk* as in bank, blank, drank, flank, frank, plank, prank, sank, spank, swank, and tank.
3. *Ink* is *ingk* as in kink, blink, brink, clink, drink, ink, pink, mink, rink, stink.
4. *Unk* is *əngk* as in bunk, dunk, flunk, junk, plunk, punk, skunk, spunk, stunk
5. *Onk* is *ängk* as in honk or *əngk* as in monk.
6. *Kn* is simply an *n* as in knack, knell, knit, knock, knob, knoll, and knot. *Gn* is simply *n* as in gnash, gnat, and gnaw.
7. *Iss* is *is* as in kiss; *iff* is *if* as in skiff; *ill* is *il* as in skill; *aff* is *af* as in quaff; *ell* is *el* as in quell.

[8] It may be desirable to introduce the pupil to the *gu* combination at this time. Examples are: guard, guess, guest, guide, guilt, guardhouse, guilty, guitar, intrigue, safeguard. The *gu* in penguin is pronounced *gw.*

TABLE 10-4   Monosyllabic Words Formed with *K* and *Q* and the
Previously Learned Consonants and Vowels

ark	crock	hock	knell	park	rock	speck
ask		honk	knit	peck		spunk
	dark	hulk	knob	pick	sack	stack
back	deck	husk	knock	plank	sank	stalk*
balk*	Dick		knoll*	pluck	sick	stark
bank	disk	ilk	knot	plunk	silk	stick
bark	drank	ink		prank	skid	stink
bask	drink		lack	prick	skiff	stock
beck	duck	junk	lark	punk	skill	stuck
black	dunk		lock		skim	stunk
blank	dusk	keg	luck	quack	skin	sulk
blink		kept		quaff	skip	swank
brink		kick	mark	quart*	skit	
brisk	elk	kid	mask	quell	skulk	tack
buck	flank	kill	milk	quest	skull	talk*
bulk	flask	kiln*	mink	quick	skunk	tank
	flunk	kilt	monk	quill	slack	task
calk*	folk*	kin	muck	quilt	slick	tick
cask	frank	king	musk	quit	slink	trek
click	Frank	kink			smock	trick
clink	frisk	kiss	nick	rack	snack	
cluck		kit	Nick	rink	sock	walk*
crick	hack	knack		risk	spank	wick
						wink

* Balk (bȯk); calk (kȯk); folk (fōk); kiln (kil, kiln); knoll (nōl); stalk (stȯk); talk (tȯk); walk (wȯk); quart (kwȯrt).

8.   *A* when followed by *r* as in ark, bark, dark, lark, mark, park, stark, and quart is the ä sound.

The Letters V, X, Y, Z

The four letters *v, x, y, z* commonly are the most difficult for the child to learn. The letter *x* spells six different sounds. Generally, it is either the the *ks* or the *gz* sounds.

The consonant *y* is a palatal semivowel corresponding to the German *j* sound. It occurs only before vowels.

The letter *z* has two pronunciations: *z* and *zh*. The *v* has only one sound.

The pupil must become familiar with the sounds represented by these letters by familiarizing himself with words that contain them. The following lists of words illustrate the various sounds.

V sound: brave, breve, cave, clove, cove, crave, curve, dive, dove, drive, drove, Eve, eve, five, gave, give, grave, have, heave, hive, hives, jive, knave, live, love, move, pave, peeve, prove, rave, rove, save, salve, selves, sleeve, solve, starve, stove, vail, vain, vale, value, van, vane, vase, vast, vat, veal, veer, veil, vein, vend, vent, verb, vest, vet, vex, vie, view, vile, vim, vine, vise, vogue, voice, void, volt, vote, vouch, waive, wave, wives, wove.

Ks sound of x: ax, box, coax, fix, fox, flax, flex, flux, hex, hoax, jinx, lax, Max, mix, next, ox, pix, pox, pyx, Rex, sex, six, tax, text, vex, wax.

Y sound: yacht, yak, yams, yank, yap, yard, yarn, yawn, yea, year, yearn, yeast, yegg, yell, yelp, yen, yes, yet, yield, yip, yoke, yolk, yond, you, young, your, youth, yowl, yule.

Z sound: adz, blaze, breeze, bronze, buzz, craze, daze, doze, faze, fez, fizz, freeze, frieze, froze, fuzz, gauze, gaze, glaze, graze, haze, jazz, phiz, prize, quiz, raze, razz, size, sneeze, snooze, squeeze, waltz, wheeze, zeal, zest, zinc, zing, zip, zone, zoo, zoom.

The Soft Sounds of C and G

The pupil already has learned the hard sound of *c* and *g*. He also must become familiar with their soft sounds. *C* and *g* generally have a soft sound before *e*, *i*, or *y*;[9] *c* becomes an *s* as in cede and *g* becomes a *j* as in age. Emans (18) found that this generalization had a 90 per cent utility. In the exceptions, the *c* is pronounced *sh*. The most common exceptions to the *g* rule are: get, girl, give, tiger, and finger.

The soft sound at the end of a word usually is spelled *ce* (dance), *ge* (age), or *dge* (badge).[10] *Dge* occurs after short vowels; after a consonant the sound is spelled by *ge* (change). In words borrowed from the French (rouge, garage, mirage) *g* is a *zh* sound. The letter *c* also may have a *sh* sound as in vicious or ocean or a *s* sound as in sacrifice. This occurs in words of more than one syllable.

Here are some common one-syllable words containing the soft *c* sound:

bounce	dunce	lace	place	space
brace	face	lance	pounce	splice
cede	farce	mice	prance	spruce
cell	fence	mince	price	stance
cent	fierce	nice	prince	thence
chance	fleece	niece	quince	thrice
choice	flounce	once	race	trace
cinch	force	ounce	scarce	trance
cite	glance	pace	since	trice
cyst	grace	peace	slice	twice
dance	hence	pence	sluice	vice
deuce	ice	piece	source	whence
dice	juice	pierce		wince

[9] When c is soft before a, it is written as ç.
[10] In polysyllabic words it may be written as a *dg* (badger) at the end of a syllable.

Here are words illustrating the soft *g* sound:

age	dodge	germ	liege	sledge
badge	doge	gibe	lodge	sludge
barge	dredge	gist	merge	smudge
beige	edge	gorge	nudge	splurge
bilge	flange	gouge	page	sponge
blunge	fledge	grange	pledge	stage
bridge	forge	grudge	plunge	stooge
budge	fringe	gurge	purge	strange
bulge	fudge	hedge	rage	surge
cage	gage	hinge	range	tinge
change	gauge	hodge-podge	ridge	trudge
charge	gem	huge	rouge	urge
cringe	gene	judge	sage	verge
dirge	gent	large	siege	wage
			singe	wedge

The pupil might benefit in the learning of these words if they are grouped as follows:

bounce	fence	barge	change	gurge
flounce	hence	charge	grange	purge
ounce	pence	large	range	splurge
pounce	thence		strange	surge
	whence	budge		urge
chance		fudge	dredge	
dance	mince	grudge	edge	
glance	prince	judge	fledge	
lance	since	nudge	hedge	
prance	wince	sludge	pledge	
stance		smudge	sledge	
trance		trudge	wedge	

TEACHING THE SHORT VOWEL

Children early learn to articulate both the short and the long vowel sounds. The short vowels are usually introduced before the long vowels because they occur most frequently in monosyllabic words, are phonetically more consistent, and occur more frequently in words that the pupil meets in initial reading. The most natural sequence in learning the vowels seems to be: learning the meaning of vowel, learning the short vowel sounds, learning the long vowel sounds, learning to discriminate between the short and long vowel, learning the effect of adding an *e* to a syllable containing a short vowel in the medial position, and learning the sound of two vowels written together.

Teaching the short vowel usually proceeds through the following steps:

1. The teacher pronounces some words that contain the short *a* sound such as *bat, fat, cat, rat, cap, sat, Ann, at, am, and, apple,* etc. The *a* sound may be slightly elongated. This teaches the pupil to listen for the short vowel sound.

2. The teacher asks the pupils what they noticed about the middle sound in the words that he gave: cap, bat, cat, etc. Were the middle sounds alike or different?

3. The teacher then may pronounce words, some of which contain the short vowel sound and some of which do not. The pupils raise their hands when the word contains the short *a* sound.

4. The pupils pronounce the words and are asked to give other words containing the short *a* sound. The teacher may ask if there is anyone in the class whose name contains a short *a* sound.

5. The pupil is taught that the sound he has been hearing in the words given by the teacher is the short *a* sound.

6. The teacher prints the letter *a* on the blackboard and writes out words such as at, am, bat, mat, pat, hat, etc. He underlines the short *a* sound and notes that in each instance a consonant follows the vowel. The pupil is told that there are five vowels, *a, e, i, o, u,* and that each of these has a long and a short sound. "Today we are learning the short *a* sound." The teacher may give a key picture for each of the vowel sounds. For *a,* it might be apple; for *e,* an egg or elephant; for *i,* Indian or ink; for *o,* ox or ostrich; and for *u* umbrella. The teacher may associate the short *a* with an apple and may call it the "apple sound." The teacher may post different pictures on the blackboard and may ask the pupils to draw a line under any pictures whose names contain a short *a* sound.

7. The teacher then writes a name under each picture whose name contains a short *a* sound. He underlines the short *a* and notes that it is called the short *a* sound. He again sounds the words, moving his finger across the word from left to right, and makes sure that the pupils listen carefully to the sound in the middle of the word. He gives the short *a* sound a slight emphasis.

8. The pupils say the words in unison or individually.

9. The pupils next are taught to associate the short *a* sound with both the capital and lower case letter. They may be shown

that a word like apple may be written with a lower case *a* or a capital *A*.

10. The pupils next print the letter *a,* both the capital and lower case.

Workbook and other teacher-prepared materials may then be used to teach the sounds. For illustrative exercises consult Emerald Dechant, *Linguistics, Phonics, and the Teaching of Reading* (Springfield, Ill.: Charles C Thomas, Publisher, 1969).

The *o* frequently is pronounced as a short *u.* The following mono- and polysyllabic words are illustrative:

come	blossom	gallop	mongrel	salmon
does	boredom	galop	monkey	scaffold
done	bottom	godson	month	season
dove	button	govern	monthly	seldom
glove	cannon	grandson	mormon	sermon
love	carrot	hammock	mother	smother
none	canyon	handsome	mutton	shovel
one	color	havoc	oneself	stomach
shove	comfort	honey	oneway	scallop
some	coming	idol	oven	someone
son	common	income	parrot	sometime
ton	compass	kingdom	patron	sometimes
won	confront	lemon	phantom	someway
abbot	cotton	lesson	pilot	summon
above	cover	lonesome	pivot	symbol
among	crayon	loveless	piston	symptom
apron	donkey	lovely	poison	synod
atom	dragon	loving	prison	tendon
bacon	dozen	mammon	purpose	tiresome
ballot	falcon	mammoth	random	wagon
baron	felon	matron	ransom	welcome
beacon	flagon	melon	reason	wisdom
become	freedom	method	reckon	zealot
bigot	frontal	Monday	ribbon	
bishop	gallon	money	riot	

It is interesting to note that in most instances the *o* is followed by *m, n, p, t,* or *v.*

An exercise such as the following teaches the short *u* sound of *o.* Have the pupil circle the correct pronunciation.

1. A ton $\left[\begin{matrix} \text{tun} \\ \text{ton} \end{matrix} \right]$ of gold

2. A lot $\left[\begin{matrix} \text{lot} \\ \text{lut} \end{matrix} \right]$ of fish.

3. A son $\left[\begin{array}{c} \text{son} \\ \text{sun} \end{array}\right]$ of Jim.

4. He has done $\left[\begin{array}{c} \text{dun} \\ \text{don} \end{array}\right]$ his job.

An analysis of two-syllable words reveals that the letter preceding the final letter in a word often is silent when followed by *n* or *l*. Thus:

bison	garden	lesson	metal	prison
bitten	glisten	lighten	model	redden
button	glutton	listen	mitten	rotten
chosen	gotten	madden	mutton	sadden
christen	hasten	maiden	pardon	sharpen
cotton	hidden	mason	parson	sudden
dozen	kitten	mantel	petal	tassel
frozen	lessen	medal	pistol	tighten
				widen

TEACHING THE END CONSONANT

It would appear logical that after the pupil has learned to deal with the consonants in the beginning position and the short vowel in the medial position, he might learn to deal with the consonant in the end position.

The techniques which were useful in teaching the beginning consonant can be used in teaching end-consonant substitution. These are:

1. The teacher pronounces some words which end with the *t* sound such as hat, but, net, nut. The end sound may be slightly elongated or stressed, but it should not be distorted.
2. The teacher asks the pupils what they noticed about the end sound. Were the sounds alike or different?
3. The pupils are asked to give other words ending with a *t* sound.
4. The teacher pronounces words, some of which end with the *t* sound and some of which do not. The pupils raise their hands when the word ends with a *t* sound. The teacher may put pictures (such as those illustrated in Figure 10-1) on the board and ask the pupils to name the picture. He then may ask them to identify the pictures or words that have the same ending sound.
5. The teacher prints the letter *t* on the blackboard and writes out the words, *hat, but, net,* and *nut,* or any other word ending with a *t* that the youngsters mentioned.

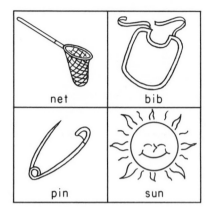

Figure 10-1

6. The pupils are told to look carefully at the letter ending each of the words. The teacher again sounds the words, making sure that the pupils listen carefully to the sound at the end of each word.

7. The pupils read the words in unison.

8. The teacher shows the pupil that substituting one final consonant for another completely changes the word. The word pet, for example, may become pen or pep; tan may become tap or tab. The pupil must learn that changing of the final consonant both alters the word and falsifies the meaning. In the sentence, "Bob wants a pet," changing the *t* on pet to an *n* alters the meaning of the utterance. At this stage the pupil is learning consonant substitution.

Workbooks and other teacher-prepared materials may then be used to teach the end sounds. Teaching of phonograms, rhyming, and of end consonants is very similar. For illustrative exercises, see Emerald Dechant, *Linguistics, Phonics, and the Teaching of Reading* (Springfield, Ill.: Charles C Thomas, Publisher, 1969).

One of the basic sound-sense patterns in the language is the phonogram. Some even suggest that the phonogram is *the* natural unit of the English language. The phonogram is a closed syllable which begins with a vowel (eg, eb, ac, in, ill, ate, ing, oat, etc.) and which produces a single speech sound. The phonogram is generally phonetically stable and regular in sounding, its form is consistent, and it has a basic utility in reading.

Joos (30, p. 90)[11] notes: "It is a characteristic of English vowels that

[11] Loyal W. Joos, "Linguistics for the Dyslexic," pp. 83–92, in *The Disabled Reader,* ed. by John Money (Baltimore: Johns Hopkins Press, 1966). Reprinted by permission.

their sounding is regulated (in most cases) by the letter pattern which follows the vowel. Since the phonogram has the vowel plus its following letter pattern, the reader soon learns to see the entire pattern as a unit. Experience has shown that this is exactly what happens; pupils taught to analyze words into phonograms quickly learn to read sound-symbol patterns and are safely past letter-by-letter perception (11).

Jones writes:

> . . . the stability of the phonogram eliminates much of the tedious teaching of rules. For example, if *ite, ate, ike, oat, ain, air,* etc. are taught as graphemes demanding an immediate oral response, the deductive teaching of vowel rules can be postponed until a later date when such teaching will not "slow up" the beginner's progress. Of course, I would advocate teaching only one phoneme per grapheme at first (green, seen, queen, not been).

A student of reading quickly recognizes the similarity between the phonogram method [12] and the "word family" approach. The phonogram method, however, is different in that:

1. Spacing is the key to the utilization of a grapheme-phoneme correspondence that is natural in the flow of the language. Usually two and never more than four words containing the same phonogram should be introduced in any one passage.
2. Pupils learning phonogram analysis are moved as quickly as possible from monosyllabic words to words containing more than one syllable. Thus pupils learn that *an* is a stable unit whether it occurs in initial, medial, or lateral positions: initial– *an*imal; medial-adv*an*cing; and lateral–r*an*.

By the time the pupil has mastered the beginning and end consonants and short vowels, he should be able to deal with the following phonograms:[13]

ab	eb	ib	ob	ub
ac	ed	ic	od	ud
ad	eg	id	og	uff
aff	ell	if	om	ug
ag	em	iff	on	ull (dull)
am	en	ig	op	um
				(continued)

[12] The phonogram method was developed by Virginia W. Jones, George T. Gabriel, and Loyal W. Joos, and is presented in *The Phonogram Method: A New Approach to First Grade Reading.* Materials are available through Virginia Jones, State University College, Oswego, New York.

[13] Schmitt, Hall and McCreary Company, Minneapolis, offers two sets of cards in booklet form which illustrate various phonograms and phonogram families.

an	ep	ill	ot	un
as	et	in		us
at	ex	ip		ut
		is		
		iss		
		it		
		ix		

In addition, he probably will have learned such common endings as *all, ar, off, oll, oss,* and *alk.* Some other phonograms that the pupil might profitably learn in the elementary years are:

and	ee	ike	oke	unk
ake	eet	ing	ook	uy
ay	eep	ine	own	ure
ack	ent	ight	oy	ush
ank	ead	ich	ouse	
arne	ease	ilk	ome	
arn	eat	ith	ool	
alk	ern	ird	ow	
arm	eak	ink	oom	
aid	een	ick	oot	
age	eel	ile	ore	
atch	eek	int	orse	
	eech	igh	out	
		itch	our	
			ove	
			old	
			ood	
			ough	
			oil	
			onk	
			ought	
			orn	
			oast	
			ound	

TEACHING STRUCTURAL ANALYSIS SKILLS

The pupil rather early needs to develop some skill in structural analysis. In fact, structural analysis may logically precede phonetic analysis. Structural analysis is possible with three kinds of words. A word may have an inflectional ending such as *s, es, ed,* or, *ing;* it may be a derived word, being constructed from a root, a suffix and/or a prefix; or it may be a compound word.

In the initial stage the child commonly is introduced to two kinds of words which may be analyzed structurally. The child learns that the *s* can change the word in two ways: (*1*) It changes the verb into third person singular; and (*2*) It makes a noun plural in form. The teaching of the *s* plural is easier when it is accompanied by another word in the sentence that suggests the plural. The sentence, *Tom has ten pet pups,* is an example of this.

As the pupil's skill in structural analysis develops, he may identify two simple words in one larger word. He may see *tea* and *pot* in teapot; *some* and *thing* in something; or *bat* and *boy* in batboy.

Frequently, he may be able to identify by sight only one of the two words and will identify the other through picture reading, contextual clues, or phonetic clues. The ability to see little words—and they should be words—in bigger words is helpful in pronouncing the word.

And he gradually learns to break the word into its syllables and to handle words composed of roots, prefixes, and suffixes.

Syllabication must receive attention at all levels of reading instruction. For most pupils, learning in this area is greatest during the intermediate grades. However, even in the first grade the pupil must be trained to hear and see the distinct vowel sounds that occur in a word. Gradually, some children will learn that the number of vowel sounds indicates the number of syllables in a word.

In the primary grades structural analysis is the following:

1. Teaching of the common word ending *s*.
2. Teaching the compounds such as gunman, hotdog.
3. Teaching two-syllable words—beginning with words ending in *ing*.
4. Teaching the past tense with *ed*.
5. Teaching the plural with *es*.
6. Teaching simple prefixes and suffixes.
7. Teaching the apostrophe *s*.
8. Teaching simply syllabication.

Hanson (24) found that variant endings (*s, ing, ed, er*) can be taught in first grade and should be used in preprimers, primers, and first readers. He reports on studies by Dolch and Osborne which point out that the three most common syllables are *ing, ed,* and *er*. A child who early learns *ing* will be able to transfer this knowledge to hundreds of words.

Betts (5) has outlined the steps in applying phonics skills to the syllables of words:

1. **The pupil must first learn to hear the number of syllables in spoken words.**

2. He must learn to identify syllables in printed words. Early in the grades the pupil needs to learn that some words ending in ed have only one syllable (cooked); others have two syllables (landed).

3. He must learn to accent the proper syllable. Accentuation should be taught only after the pupil has mastered steps one and two and after having learned something about prefixes and suffixes. These latter rarely are accented (intend, fishing).

4. He must learn to apply phonic skills to the separate vowels in words;
   a. He applies the short-vowel rule to the stressed syllable (rabbit).
   b. He identifies such vowel-phonograms as ar, er, ir, or, ur.

5. He must check if the word makes sense in the sentence.

Let us look more closely at each of the above eight teaching tasks.

Teaching S

The s may be used to form the third person singular of a verb or to convert a noun into its plural form. Beginning with the vocabulary that the pupil already knows, the pupil is shown what the addition of s does to the word. Here are examples of both uses:

s with a verb			s with a noun			
bats	hits	nabs	bibs	caps	guns	nets
bets	hops	pets	buns	cats	hats	nuts
bids	hugs	tags	bags	cobs	hens	pans
cuts	jabs	taps	beds	cubs	huts	pens
digs	jigs	tips	buds	cups	hogs	pins
dims	mops	tugs	bugs	dens	jobs	pots
gets		wins	cabs	dogs	pigs	pups
			cans			

Table 10-5 illustrates the various pronunciations of s at the end of words. For exercises to teach third-person singular s, plural s, and the pronunciation of s, see Emerald Dechant, *Linguistics, Phonics, and the Teaching of Reading* (Springfield, Ill.: Charles C Thomas, Publisher, 1969).

Teaching the Compounds

The pupil may be introduced to two syllable words through simple compounds. The pupil needs to learn that one syllable words have only one

TABLE 10-5   The Sound of S

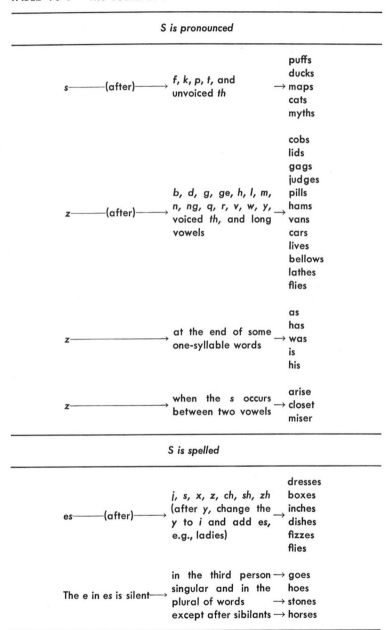

S is pronounced			
s———(after)———→	f, k, p, t, and unvoiced *th*	→	puffs ducks maps cats myths
z———(after)———→	b, d, g, ge, h, l, m, n, ng, q, r, v, w, y, voiced *th*, and long vowels	→	cobs lids gags judges pills hams vans cars lives bellows lathes flies
z————————→	at the end of some one-syllable words	→	as has was is his
z————————→	when the s occurs between two vowels	→	arise closet miser
S is spelled			
es———(after)———→	j, s, x, z, ch, sh, zh (after y, change the y to i and add es, e.g., ladies)	→	dresses boxes inches dishes fizzes flies
The e in es is silent———→	in the third person singular and in the plural of words except after sibilants	→ → →	goes hoes stones horses

vowel sound and that compounds each have two vowels that are sounded and therefore are called two-syllable words. He probably needs to learn this inductively. Burmeister (11) found that when the vowel is a vowel combination (*ai, oa,* etc.), the generalization "Every vowel combination means a syllable" was correct 85 per cent of the time.

A syllable is that part of a word which contains a vowel and which receives some stress. The syllable is very helpful in attacking new words. After all, monosyllabic words are merely syllables to which we have given a meaning. Hildreth (27, p. 151) notes that "The syllable, not the phoneme, is the basic unit of speech articulation. . . ." There are two kinds of syllabication: one for writing and one for pronunciation. The former is inconsistent and generally one must consult the dictionary to be certain.

There are numerous simple compounds that are teachable at the primary level. For example:

bedbug	cobweb	hamlet	onset	titbit
bellhop	cutup	hellcat	pell-mell	tiptop
bigtop	dishpan	hubbub	pigpen	tomcat
bigwig	forbid	humbug	popgun	tomtom
bulldog	forget	into	sunlit	upon
carhop	godson	mudsill	sunset	upset
cannot	gunman	offset	sunup	wigwag

On more advanced levels the pupil should learn more difficult words, beginning with those compounds that keep the basic meaning of each word making up the compound. For example, a classroom is a room where class is held. Other words useful in teaching this skill are: byways, breakdown, campfire, cornstalk, cowboy, earthquake, eyelash, hillside, hilltop, limestone, railroad, rosebush, watchman, weekend, steamboat, workbook, snowshoes, sawdust, sandhill, and newsboy.

Frequently, the meaning of the compound is completely new, e.g., broadcast, township, or wholesale. Some compounds are written as two words, e.g., ice cream, living room, dining room, sea power, post office, oil painting, air brake, parcel post, money order, or school spirit.

Whenever a compound word is used as a modifier and occurs before the word that it modifies, it is hyphenated. We speak of living-room furniture and a high-school dance. The hyphen also is used with self (self-denial, self-confidence, self-control) and with compound numbers from 21 to 99 (twenty-six men).

A list of additional compounds follows.

airplane	eyebrow	nighttime	sundown
backbone	eyelash	northwest	sunset
bagpipe	farmland	outgrow	sunshade
barnyard	fireman	outline	sunshine
baseball	fishhook	outskirts	sunstroke
bedside	foreman	pancake	sunup
bedtime	footprint	plaything	tadpole
beehive	footstep	playtime	toothbrush
beeline	footstool	quicksand	touchdown
blacktop	grandstand	railroad	township
bobcat	grapevine	rainbow	trailways
bobsled	graveyard	ransack	treetop
bobwhite	gumdrop	roommate	upkeep
boldface	halfway	rosebush	uplift
bloodshed	hedgerow	sandhill	upset
boxcar	himself	sawdust	vineyard
broadcast	hillside	seacoast	warehouse
broomstick	hilltop	schoolroom	watchman
breakdown	horseback	seesaw	waylay
byways	inland	shipshape	weekend
campfire	inside	sideline	wholesale
cardboard	instep	sidetrack	wigwag
childhood	itself	signpost	wishbone
classmate	kidnap	smokestack	withdraw
classroom	limestone	snowshoes	within
corkscrew	lookout	soapsuds	without
cornstalk	makeshift	stagecoach	withstand
cowboy	mankind	starfish	windshield
daylight	maybe	statehood	woodpile
dragnet	milkman	steamboat	woodland
drumstick	milkshake	subway	workbook
earthquake	milkweed	sunburn	yardstick
elsewhere	newsboy	sunburst	yearbook
		Sunday	yuletide

For exercises in teaching compounds, see: Emerald Dechant, *Linguistics, Phonics, and the Teaching of Reading* (Springfield, Ill.: Charles C Thomas, Publisher, 1969).

Teaching —*ing*

After dealing with simple compounds, the pupil is ready to learn the ending *ing*. The teacher demonstrates how *ing* can be added to verbs to form two-syllable words: hitting, batting, getting, hopping, running, tagging, tugging, nagging, and winning. The pupil should note that the consonant is doubled before adding the *ing* and that the second consonant is silent. Emans (18) reports that this rule has a 91 per cent utility. Bailey (1) found it had 98 per cent utility. The exceptions are usually the result of a prefix or suffix being added (illegal) or *ly* being added to a root word ending in *l* as in dreadfully.

After the pupil can deal successfully with long vowels in various combinations and after he has mastered the regular uses of *ing* as discussed above, he needs to expand his uses for *ing*. Whenever *ing* is added to monosyllabic words ending in a vowel, diphthong, or double vowel (being, playing, fleeing, hoeing), to monosyllabic words ending in a single consonant preceded by a double vowel (aiding), to monosyllabic words ending in a double consonant (arming), or to words ending in ow (blowing), no doubling of the letter preceding *ing* occurs. Monosyllabic words ending in a silent *e* drop the final *e* before adding *ing* (bake-baking). The first vowel receives its long sound in reading.

The principles suggested apply not only to *ing* but to any suffix beginning with a vowel. The most common such suffixes are: able, ably, ability, age, ance, ant, ard, ary, ation, ed, en, ence, ent, er, ern, ery, es, est, ion, ish, ity, ive, or, ous, and y. Words ending in *ce* or *ge* retain the *e* before a suffix beginning with *a* or *o*.

The lists of words provided below illustrate these principles in all of their applications.

1. When *ing* is added to monosyllabic words ending in a vowel, diphthong, or double vowel and to words ending in ow, no doubling of the letter preceding the *ing* occurs.

being	flaying	freeing	growing
doing	playing	seeing	knowing
going	praying	hoeing	mowing
crying	saying	shoeing	rowing
flying	slaying	blowing	showing
frying	spraying	bowling	slowing
prying	staying	crowing	snowing
spying	straying	flowing	throwing
trying	fleeing	glowing	towing

2. When *ing* is added to monosyllabic words ending in a single consonant preceded by a double vowel, no doubling of the letter preceding the *ing* occurs.

aiding	creeping	coasting	cleaning
claiming	feeding	floating	cheating
failing	feeling	loading	dreaming
nailing	keeping	roasting	leaking
painting	boasting	beating	bleeding

3. When *ing* is added to monosyllabic words ending in a double consonant, no doubling of the consonant before *ing* occurs.

asking	drinking	hunting	singing
barking	dusting	kissing	fighting
bringing	falling	milking	holding
dressing	farming	missing	kicking
drilling	helping	rocking	pulling

4. When *ing* is added to monosyllabic words ending in a silent
    e, the e is dropped before adding *ing*.

baking	giving	praising
biting	hiding	smiling
coming	living	smoking
diving	making	taking
driving	moving	

The Past Tense with *ed*

The pupil also must be introduced to the past tense formed by *ed*. In
reading *ed* the child meets certain problems. The *e* is silent (begged,
canned) except after *d* and *t* (batted, nodded). The *d* is pronounced as
a *t* after the voiceless consonants such as *c, ch, f* (puffed), *h, k* (peeked),
p (dipped), *s, sh* (wished), *t,* or *th.* The past participle of *dream, learn,*
and *spell* may be pronounced with a *t* or a *d* sound.

The following lists of words exemplify the rule:

1. The *e* in *ed* is silent except after *d* and *t*:

batted	dusted	lasted	skidded
cheated	folded	nodded	started
dated	hated	planted	twisted
dotted	hunted	punted	waited
drifted	landed	scolded	wanted

2. The *d* is pronounced as a *t* after soft *c, ch, f, h, k, p, s, sh, t,* and
    th.

clapped	asked	huffed	dressed
helped	baked	puffed	kissed
hoped	barked	stuffed	missed
ripped	kicked	lunched	passed
roped	talked	preached	wished

Prefixes and Suffixes

We are reserving the teaching of prefixes and suffixes for the most part
until Chapter 12. However, the teaching of simple prefixes and suffixes

begins early in the elementary school years. The most common prefixes are (10,43):

ab (from)	*dis* (apart)	*ob, op, ov* (against)
ad, a, ap, at (to)	*en* (in)	*pre* (before)
be (by)	*ex, e* (out of)	*pro* (in front of)
com, con, col (with)	*in, en, im, em* (into)	*re* (back, again)
de (from)	*in* (not)	*sub* (under)
		un (not)

The Possessive Case and Contractions

The possessive case needs to be introduced to the pupil in the primary grades. The pupil also needs to become familiar with the use of the apostrophe in contractions. The teacher must illustrate the use of the possessive and the apostrophe and must develop exercises that elicit from the pupil the correct application of the possessive rule.

The apostrophe is used also with contractions, thus: don't (do not); let's (let us); hasn't (has not); didn't (did not); can't (can not); I'm (I am); I'll (I will); I've (I have); haven't (have not); hadn't (had not); isn't (is not); wasn't (was not); he's (he is); he'll (he will); she's (she is); she'll (she will); you're (you are); you'll (you will); we're (we are); we'll (we will); they're (they are); and they'll (they will).

In this instance the apostrophe indicates that one or more letters have been omitted.

An exercise similar to the following, requiring the pupil to match appropriate pairs, may be used to teach simple contractions on the first- and second-grade level.

does not	wasn't
can not	hasn't
will not	doesn't
was not	won't
has not	can't

SUMMARY

The initial phonic exercises should have one chief function: that of developing a reading vocabulary. This may be done in many ways. It is possible to form a direct association between meaning and the printed symbol. In this case the word is identified through its shape and configuration or through picture reading. Another approach continues auditory and visual discrimination training and involves phonetic and structural analysis. The child associates the *whole word* with a sound, but from the beginning identifies letters or groups of letters that recur repeatedly in words and that constantly have the same sound. These parts of words give clues to the sounds of other words, thus helping the child both to pronounce and indirectly to associate meaning with the printed symbol. This method starts with the initial consonant and teaches the child to read through the word. This means proceeding from left to right, much as in reading a sentence.

There is little research to indicate which words children should learn first. Present assumptions in this regard are based on frequency count. But is this a valid criterion? Bloomer (6) notes that word length may be a more important consideration than frequency of use. The longer the word, the more difficult it is. We believe that vocabulary control in the linguistic phonics program should be based on the regularity of the grapheme-phoneme pattern; on phonetic difficulty, not semantic difficulty. We are concerned most with teaching those words that most aid in the acquisition of a vocabulary.

The materials in this chapter are in no way intended to constitute a reading program or to limit the child's reading. It is not necessary for each pupil to learn on the spot each new word that he encounters. The development of a recognition vocabulary should be based on (*1*) the acquisition of words that can only be learned by sight or configuration; (*2*) the acquaintance with numerous words that only gradually become a part of the pupil's reading vocabulary (no great emphasis should be put on these in early reading); and (*3*) *the acquisition of a method that permits the pupil to work out the pronunciation of new words.* This chapter has been concerned primarily with the teaching of this last aspect. The pupil must be systematically trained in the development of such a method.

QUESTIONS FOR DISCUSSION

1. Distinguish between phonics and phonetics and discuss the implications of these for the teaching of reading.
2. What phonic skills should each learner possess?
3. What are the relative merits of the various methods of sounding words?
4. Adduce arguments to support Soffiètti's position on the nature of the pupil's first reading materials?
5. Examine a basal reading series, identifying points of similarity and difference between the phonics program presented there and the program recommended in this book.
6. Adduce arguments both for and against the introduction of linguistic phonics instruction from the beginning.

7. What is the meaning of phonic readiness?
8. Outline briefly the sequence for the teaching of phonic skills proposed by three reputable authorities.
9. Discuss the importance of structural analysis in the teaching of reading.
10. Discuss the arguments for teaching phonics through phonemically-regular words, synthetically, and/or through sight words.
11. Adduce evidence from five different studies that reading teachers need more background in phonics.

Advancing the Child's
Phonic Skills

chapter 11

If each child had to learn formally every principle or generalization proposed in Chapters 10 and 11 before he learned to read, few might be termed readers, and those of us who are readers would gladly exclaim, "Thank God, I have learned to read." Yet the good reader has a functional knowledge of the linguistic phonic skills.

It would seem that the artful teacher needs a much vaster, more systematic, and more generalized knowledge than the good reader. He needs to know *why* a word is pronounced as it is.

The various sections of these chapters can be used as *references* when the teacher needs to teach specific skills in the classroom. This does not tie the teacher to the sequence suggested in this book. In each instance we have presented common monosyllabic words that best illustrate the sound that is being considered.

Thus, we have preferred to be complete rather than to limit the analysis to skills usually acquired during the elementary school years. Since this book is written for teachers, a complete program will be presented which may be adapted to individual classroom needs.

In the previous chapter emphasis was on the use of single consonants and short vowels in attacking new words. The pupil on this level learned to substitute a single consonant or a short vowel. If he knew the word *cat,* he should have learned to decipher *bat;* and, if he knew the word *bet,* he should have learned to decipher *but.* Furthermore, if he knew the word *cat,* he should now be able to attack the word *cats;* and, if he knew *sit,* he now should be able to handle *sits.*

This chapter introduces the pupil to the remaining skills of word attack. It teaches consonant blends, the speech consonants, the long vowels, such vowel combinations as *ai, ay, ea, ee, oa,* or *oe,* the special combinations, *ar, ir, or, er,* and *ur,* the diphthongs, syllabication and accentuation, silent letters, and the special phonetic and structural problems associated with two- and three-syllable words.

In this chapter, then, we are concerned primarily with the learning of:

1. The consonant blends in the initial and final position.
2. The speech consonants *ch, sh, th, wh, gh, ph.*
3. The long vowels:
   a. *a, e, i, o, u, y*
   b. Long vowels plus silent *e*
   c. *ai, ay, ea, ee, oa, oe, ow*
   d. The diphthongs: *au, aw, oi, oy, oo*
   e. *er, ir, or, ur,* and *wa.*
4. Syllabication and accentuation
   a. The *ly* ending
   b. The *le* ending.
5. Silent letters
6. Special problems of two- and three-syllable words
7. Common sight words.

Let us begin with consonant blends.

TEACHING THE BEGINNING CONSONANT BLENDS

The consonant blends must be distinguished from the speech consonants, *ch, sh, th, wh, ck, gh, ph, qu,* and *ng.* These latter are digraphs and thus are two consonants that have a single speech sound. The consonant blends, on the other hand, consist of two or more letters each having its own distinct sound. The following consonant blends occur: *bl, br, chr, cl, cr, dr, dw, fl, fr, gl, gr, nk, pl, pr, sc, scr, shr, sk, sl, sm, sn, sp, sq, spl, spr, sch, st, str, thr, tr,* and *tw.*

Since the early phonic experiences emphasized primarily the short vowel sounds, the pupil should have little difficulty pronouncing the following phonograms.

a—ab, ac, ad, aff, ag, all, am, an, ap, ar, ass, at
e—eb, ec, ed, eff, eg, ell, em, en, ep, ess, et
i—ib, ic, id, iff, ig, ill, im, in, ip, iss, it

o—ob, oc, od, og, om, on, op, ot
u—ub, uc, ud, uff, ug, ull, um, un, up, uss, ut

Most of these syllables he has pronounced as parts of words. He also has learned to make initial consonant substitution. He has learned that by changing the initial consonant he can change *cab* to *dab, gab,* or *nab.*

Now he must extend this process. Instead of substituting one consonant for another, he substitutes two consonants for one. Thus *cab* becomes *crab, grab, scab, slab,* or *stab.*

Teaching the initial consonant blend begins with the same procedure as the teaching of the beginning consonant. This was outlined in Chapter 10, and you may want to refer to page 303.

The pupil also needs to learn to deal with the three-letter blends: *chr, sch, scr, shr, spl, spr, str,* and *thr.* Here are common monosyllabic words beginning with these combinations:

Chr—Christ, chrome
Sch—scheme, school
Scr—screech, screen, scroll, script, scrunch
Shr—shrank, shred, shrewd, shriek, shrill, shrimp, shrine, shrink, shroud, shrub, shrug
Spl—splash, spleen, splice, splint, split, splotch, splurge
Spr—sprain, sprang, sprawl, spray, spread, spree, spring, sprint, sprite, sprout, spruce, sprung, spray
Str—strafe, strain, strait, strand, strap, straw, stray, streak, stream, street, strength, stress, stretch, stride, strife, strike, string, stripe, strive, strode, stroll, strong, strove, stray, struck, strung
Thr—thrash, thread, threat, three, thresh, threw, thrice, thrift, thrill, throat, throb, throng, through, throw, thrush, thrust

The consonant trigraphs, such as *chm* (drachm) and *ght* (thought), representing a single speech sound, should be taught after the pupil has mastered three-letter blends.

TEACHING THE ENDING CONSONANT BLENDS

After the pupil has learned to handle some of the beginning consonant blends, he is ready to learn the end consonant blends.

Table 11-1 provides a list of numerous monosyllabic words that are phonetically consistent and that end in double consonants, some of which are consonant blends.

TABLE 11-1   Monosyllabic Words Containing Double Consonants at the End

Words that Have Been Formed From the Letters,
M, T, B, H, P, N, C, D, G, J, W, F, L, R, S, and the Short Vowels

act	calf*	fact	helm	pact	salt	stung
alb	cant	fang	help	palm*	sand	stunt
alms*	card	farm	hemp	pang	sang	sung
alp	carp	fast	hest	pant	scald	swang
and	cart	felt	hilt	pants	scalp	swept
ant	cast	fend	hint	parr	scant	swift
apt	clamp	film	hiss	part	scarf	swing
arc	clasp	Finn	hump	pass	scull	
arm	cleft	fist	hunt	past	sect	
arms	climb*	flint		pelt	self	tact
art	clump	flung	imp	pest	send	talc
Art	clung	fond	inn	ping	sent	tamp
asp	craft	font	ism*	plant	sift	tang
	cramp	front*		plump	silt	tend
	crest		jest	pomp	sing	tent
	crimp	gang	jilt	pond	slang	test
bald*	crisp	garb	jump	primp	slant	tilt
balm*	crumb*	gasp	just	print	slept	ting
band	crust	gilt		pulp	sling	tint
bang	cult	gland	lamb*	pump	slump	tomb*
bard		glint	lamp	punt	slung	tramp
barn		golf	land	putt	small	trend
belt	damp	graft	lard		smart	trump
bend	darn	grand	last		smell	trust
bent	dart	grant	lens	raft	smelt	twang
best	deft	grasp	limb*	ramp	snarl	twist
blast	dent	grist		rang	sniff	
blend	dint	grunt	malt	rant	spasm	want*
blest	disc	gulp	marc	rapt	specs	weld
blimp	draft	gump	mast	rasp	spend	wend
blond	drift	gust	meld	rend	spent	went
blunt	duct		mend	rest	stamp	wept
bomb*	dumb*		mint	rift	stand	west
bond	dump	half*	mist	ring	start	wind
brand	dung	hand	mitt	romp	stilt	wing
bring	dust	harm	must	rump	sting	wings
brunt	dwarf	harp		rung	stint	wisp
bump	dwell	hasp		runt	stomp	wolf*
bunt		hast	nest	rust	stump	womb*
bust	end	held	numb*			

* These words should be learned as sight words: alms (ȧmz); bomb (bäm); calf (kaf); climb (klīm); crumb (krəm); dumb (dəm); front (frənt); half (haf); ism (iz′m); lamb (lam); limb (lim); numb (nəm); palm (päm); tomb (tüm); want (wänt or wȯnt); wolf (wu̇lf); womb (wüm).

THE SPEECH CONSONANTS: *ch, sh, th, wh, gh, ph*

The pupil already has had experience with digraphs or with two letters having one sound, especially with *ck* and *qu*. Now we extend this principle to the speech consonants, *ch, sh, th, wh, gh,* and *ph.* Digraphs are not a blend of two letters; the sound is distinctive.

The Digraph *Ch*

The digraph *ch* may have four distinct sounds: *ch, j, sh,* and *k.*[1] The unvoiced *ch* is a combination of *t* and *sh.* Sometimes it is pronounced as a voiced *j,* as in spinach. It is equivalent to *sh* in words of French derivation such as cache, chagrin, chef, Chicago, creche, gauche, machine, machinery, and mustache. It has a *k* sound in some words derived from the Greek and Hebrew as chasm, chorus, Christ, chrism, Christmas, chrome, Enoch, and scheme, and also in ache, backache, chemist, chloride, choral, technic, technique, headache, orchid, school, and Czech. In drachm, schism, yacht, and fuchsia the *ch* is silent. Here are some common words exemplifying the regular *ch* sound:

arch	change	chin	couch	leach	preach	squelch
batch	chant	chip	crotch	leech	punch	stanch
beach	chap	chirp	crutch	lunch	quench	starch
beech	charge	choice	ditch	lurch	ranch	staunch
belch	charm	choke	drench	march	reach	stench
bench	chart	choose	dutch	match	retch	stitch
birch	chase	chop	each	mooch	rich	stretch
bleach	chaste	chore	etch	much	roach	switch
blotch	chat	chose	fetch	mulch	scorch	teach
botch	cheap	chow	filch	munch	scotch	thatch
branch	cheat	chuck	flinch	notch	scratch	torch
breach	check	chug	flitch	ouch	screech	touch
breech	cheek	chum	French	parch	scrunch	trench
broach	cheer	chunk	grouch	patch	search	twitch
brooch	cheese	church	gulch	paunch	sketch	vetch
bunch	chess	churl	hatch	peach	slouch	vouch
catch	chest	churn	haunch	perch	smirch	watch
chaff	chew	chute	hitch	pinch	smooch	welch
chain	chick	cinch	hunch	pitch	smutch	winch
chair	chide	clench	inch	poach	snatch	witch
chalk	chief	clinch	itch	pooch	snitch	wrench
champ	child	clutch	latch	porch	speech	wretch
chance	chill	coach	launch	pouch	splotch	

[1] This is another way of saying that the *ch, j, sh,* and *k* sounds can be spelled as *ch.* For a complete listing of multiple spellings of consonants see Appendix I at the end of the book.

The digraph *sh* presents no special reading difficulties. Some common words exemplifying the sound are:

ash	mesh	share	shell	shop
bash	mush	shark	sherd	shorn
brash	plush	sharp	shield	short
brush	rash	shave	shift	should
bush	rush	shawl	shin	shout
cash	sash	shay	shine	shove
clash	shade	she	ship	show
dash	shaft	sheaf	shirk	shun
dish	shag	shear	shirt	slash
fish	shake	sheath	shoal	slush
flush	shale	sheathe	shoat	smash
fresh	shall	sheave	shock	smutsh
frosh	shalt	shed	shod	splash
gnash	sham	sheen	shoe	squash
harsh	shame	sheep	shone	trash
hush	shank	sheer	shoo	wish
josh	shan't	sheet	shook	
lash	shape	shelf	shoot	

The *th,* on the other hand, may be the voiceless *th* or the voiced *th.* The final *th* usually is voiceless except in smooth, with, and in *the* endings as, for example, in bathe. Some verbs (mouth, bequeath, and smooth) have dropped the final *e* but still follow the rule. Some nouns with a voiceless singular (mouth) have a voiced plural. Generally when the final *ths* is preceded by a short vowel sound (deaths) or by a consonant (months), it is unvoiced. The words, cloths, truths, youths, and wreathes, may have either. Initial *th* in such words as the, them, there, this, and thither, is voiced. *Th* in Thomas, Esther, and Thompson is simply a *t.*

The following words illustrate the *th* sound in monosyllabic words:

Voiceless th

bath	depth	health	Smith	thief
berth	doth	hearth	sooth	thigh
birth	earth	heath	south	thin
booth	faith	mirth	strength	thing
breadth	fifth	mouth	teeth	think
breath	filth	myth	thank	third
broth	forth	ninth	thatch	thirst
cloth	fourth	north	thaw	thong
couth	froth	oath	theft	thorn
dearth	growth	sixth	theme	thought
death	hath	sloth	thick	thrash

(continued)

thread	thrift	throw	tooth	worth
threat	thrill	thrush	truth	wraith
three	throat	thrust	twelfth	wrath
thresh	throb	thud	warmth	wreath
threw	throng	thump	wealth	youth
thrice	through	thwart	width	

Voiced th

baths	smooth	their	these	though
bathe	soothe	them	they	thus
breathe	that	then	this	thy
clothe	the	thence	those	with
scathe	thee	there	thou	wreathe
scythe				writhe

The Digraphs *Wh*, *Gh*, *Ph*

The combination *wh* may be pronounced as *hw* or simply as *h*. The combination, *gh*, may be pronounced as a simple *g*; it may be an *f*; or it may be silent. We have seen that in the combination *igh* the *gh* is silent. *Ph* commonly is an *f* sound. It also may be sounded as *v* (Stephen), as a *p* (diphthong, diphtheria, naphtha), or it may be silent (phtalin).

Here are words that illustrate the observations just made:

Wh sound—whack, whale, wharf, what, wheat, wheel, wheeze, whelm, whelp, when, whence, where, whet, whew (hwu, hu), which, whiff, whig, while, whilst, whim, whine, whip, whirl, whish, who (hü), whoa, whole (hōl), whom (hüm), whoop (hüp), whose (hüz), why

Silent *Gh*—aught, bough, bought, brought, caught, dough, drought, eight, freight, height, light, naught, neigh, night, nought, ought, plough, sleigh, sought, straight, though, thought, through, weight, wrought

Gh as *f*—cough, draught, laugh, rough, slough, tough, trough

Gh as *g*—ghost, ghoul

Ph as *f*—phase, phew, phlegm, phone, phrase

THE LONG VOWELS

Up to this time, with exception of the *ä* sound in the *ar* words, we have mentioned the short *a* sound as in hat, the short *e* sound as in met, the short *i* sound as in bit, the short *o* sound as in hot, and the short *u* sound as in hut. The pupil also needs to learn the long *a* sound as in fate and stare; the long *e* sound as in mete; the long *i* sound as in bite; the long *o* sound as in so, and the special *o* sounds as in off and in orb; and the long *u* sound as in use and lute. In *use* the *u* is pronounced as yü and in *lute* it is pronounced as *ü*. The former sound occurs regularly after *b, c, f, g, h, k, m, p,* and *v* and at the beginning of a word. After the other consonants usage varies. The ü sound is common after *j, r,* and *l* when these consonants are preceded by another consonant as in brute. The pupil also must learn the sound of *u* in such words as *fur*.

Since the short vowel occurs much more frequently than the long vowel, the pupil customarily should sound the vowel as a short sound. If the word thus formed does not sound like a word that he already knows or if it doesn't make sense in the context, then another attempt must be made.

There are three principles that may help more advanced pupils in arriving at the correct word. These principles are the principle of variability, the principle of position, and the principle of silentness.

Before delving into these, a few observations seem in order.

1. The pupil learns vowel generalizations or rules best by *frequent* experiences with words that exemplify the rule.
2. These experiences should be *consistent*. Thus, any of the exceptions mentioned in this, or for that matter in any other section, should be learned as sight words.
3. Only those rules which have wide applicability are worth teaching.

The Principle of Variability

The principle of variability simply means that the pronunciation of the written vowel may change from one word to another. The *e* sound may be short as in bed, or long as in he. The pupil gradually must learn and apply the following variations:

a	e	i	o	u	y
a (hat)	e (bed)	i (bit)	ä (lot)	ə (hut)	y (crypt)
ā (fade)	ē (mete)	ī (bite)	ō (so)	yü (use)	ȳ (cry)
ä (car)			ȯ (off)	ü (lute)	
e (ə) (care)			ȯ (orb)	u̇ (pull)	

The Principle of Position

The second principle to be learned is the principle of position. The sound of the vowel changes depending upon its position in the word.

After the pupil has mastered the sound of vowels in the beginning or medial position in monosyllabic words, he should be ready to deal with the short sound of the vowel in one-syllable words in which a single vowel beginning the word is followed by a single consonant: for example, am, an, as, at, Ed, if, in, is, it, of, on, up, and us.[2] The first vowel rule then may be stated thus: *A single vowel at the beginning or in the middle of a one syllable word usually is short.* Emans (6) found that this rule had 80 per cent utility. The pupil needs to be taught that *r* generally modifies the vowel sound (car, her, sir, for, fur).

The pupil also must learn the long vowel sounds. He first should learn that long vowels generally have the same sound as that indicated by their names. The vowel receives a long sound when a single vowel comes at the end of a one-syllable word: for example, a, be, he,she, me, we, I, go, ho, no, so, by, cry, fly, fry, my, ply, pry, sky, sly, spry, spy, sty, try, why, wry.[3] A second rule may be stated thus: *A single vowel at the end of a one-syllable word usually is long.* This rule is readily applied and is easily learned.

Sometimes the vowel occurs in the middle of a word but does not follow the principle of position. The vowel is a long vowel.

> long *i*—blight,[4] bright, fight, flight, fright, high, knight, light, might, nigh, night, plight, right, sigh, sight, slight, thigh, tight; bind, blind, find, grind, hind, kind, mind, rind, wind; child, mild, wild; pint; climb.[5]
>
> long *o*—bold, cold, fold, gold, hold, mold, old, scold, sold, told; boll, droll, knoll, poll, roll, toll, scroll, stroll; bolt, colt, jolt; gross; ghost, host, most, post; both; comb; don't, won't.

Frequently the *o* has the ò sound of *o* and it occurs in the following words: log; broth, cloth, froth, moth; boss, cross, dross, floss, gloss, joss, loss, moss, toss; cost, frost, lost; gong, long, prong, song, strong, throng, tongs; honk; off, scoff; loft, oft, soft; cough, trough.

The Principle of Silentness

The third principle to be learned is that of silentness. Some vowels in words are not pronounced. When the letter *e* comes at the end of a

---

[2] Or is an exception. Note that the rule is valid only if a single consonant follows, although the *e* in egg is short. The *o* in off is long.

[3] Exceptions are: *ha, do, to,* and *who*. These really are not exceptions to the rule, since the vowels are long, but the words are not phonetic.

[4] The *gh* is silent—common two-syllable words with long *i* and silent *gh* are: brightness, highness, lightness, higher, highest, highway, lightning, midnight, flashlight, delight, tonight, overnight, mighty, moonight, and sunlight.

[5] The letter *b* is silent.

monosyllabic word, it frequently is silent. In addition, the normally short sound in the middle of the word becomes a long vowel. A third rule may be stated thus: *In one-syllable words in which there are two vowels, the second one being a silent e preceded by a single consonant, the initial vowel is long.* Emans (6) reports that this rule has about 70 per cent utility if words ending in *le* (ankle) and *ive* (live) are accepted as exceptions to it.

Since the pupil has heard and spoken many monosyllabic words that exemplify this rule, it is desirable to consider such words next. Table 11-2 lists words that follow this principle.

A new sound occurs in the following words: bare, blare, care, dare, fare, flare, glare, hare, mare, pare, rare, scare, snare, spare, stare, and ware. This *a* e(ə) is a more open sound than the long *a* sound and occurs commonly in accented syllables and/or in conjunction with the *r* sound. There is no great need to distinguish it for the pupil from the long *a* sound.

The pupil must learn further extensions of the principle of silentness. *In certain vowel combinations, for example, ai, ay, ea, ee, oa, oe, ow, the second letter may be silent and the first is long.* Table 11-3 shows various monosyllabic words that follow this rule:

In an analysis of vowel-vowel combinations which have one sound, Burmeister (4) found that the *ai* combination has the long ā sound 74 per cent of the time;[6] in 16 per cent of the cases, it is followed by *r* and is pronounced e(ə) as in air, chair, fair, flair, hair, lair, pair, and stair. The other pronunciations should be learned as sight words: aisle, plaid, said, mountain, villain, again.

The *ay* combination has a long *a* sound almost 95 per cent of the time (4); common exceptions are aye, says, yesterday.

The *ee* combination is pronounced as long *e* about 85 per cent of the time (4); the words, beer, cheer, deer, jeer, peer, queer, sheer, sneer, steer, and veer, have the *i*(ə) sound. This is a lowered long *e* sound and occurs only in conjunction with *r*. It occurs about 12 per cent of the time (4). A common exception is *been.*

The *oa* combination is sounded like a long *o* 94 per cent of the time. The *oa*, pronounced as in broad, occurs the remaining six per cent of the time.

The *oe* combination occurs much less frequently than *oa* and its pronunciation is much less consistent. It is pronounced as long *o*, 60 per cent of the time; as long *e*, 23 per cent of the time; and as *oo*,

[6] Emans (6) found that this observation had 83 per cent utility. There are obviously going to be variations in these findings because of differences in types of materials from which words are taken, in method of word selection, in phonemic systems, and in definition of what is a short and long vowel (3).

TABLE 11-2   Monosyllabic Words With a Silent *E* at the End and a Long Vowel Sound in the Middle of the Word

ape	crude	flake	June	muse	quite	slime	tile
are*	cruse	flame		mute	quote	slope	time
ate	cube	flare	Kate			smile	tire
	cute	fluke	kite	name	rake	smite	tome
babe		fuse		nape	rape	smoke	tone
bade	dame		lake	nine	rare	smote	tote
bake	Dane	gale	lame	node	rate	snake	trade
bale	dare	game	lane	none*	ride	snare	tribe
bane	date	gape	late	nose	rife	snipe	tripe
base	dime	gate	life	note	rile	snore	tube
bate	dine	give*	line	nude	rime	sole	tune
bide	dire	glade	lobe		ripe	some*	twine
bike	dome	glare	lode	ode	rise	spade	
bile	done*	gone*	lone	one*	rite	spare	vale
bite	dope	grate	lube		robe	spate	vane
blade	dose	grime	lure		rode	spike	vile
blame	dote	gripe	lute	pale	role	spine	vine
bone	dove*	grope		pane	rope	spire	vise
bore	drape		made	Pete	rude	spite	vote
bride	drive	hare	make	pike	rule	spume	
brine	drove	hate	mane	pile		stake	wade
brute	dude	have*	mare	pine	safe	stale	wake
	duke	here	mate	pipe	sake	stare	wane
cake	dupe	hide	mere	plane	sale	stile	ware
came		hike	mete	plate	sate	stipe	waste
cane	eke	hire	Mike	plebe	scale	stoke	were*
cape		hole	mike	plume	scape	stole	wide
care		home	mile	poke	scare	sure	wife
chore	fade	hone	mine	pole	scope	swine	wile
clove	fake	hope	mire	pope	sere	swipe	wine
code	fame	hose	mite	pose	shake		wipe
coke	fare		mode	prime	side	take	wire
come*	fate	jade	mole	probe	sire	tale	wise
cone	fife	Jane	mope	prone	site	tame	
cope	file	jibe	mote	prose	skate	tape	yoke
crate	fine	joke	move*	prune	slate	tide	Yule
crime	fire	Jude	mule	pure	slide	tike	

* These are exceptions and should be learned by sight. In summary, these are: are (är), come (kəm) done (dən), dove (dəv), give (giv), gone (gȯn), have (hav), move (müv), none (nən), one (wən), some (səm) and were (wər). O frequently is a short *u* as in some, come, dove, love, done, none, one.

in such words as shoe, snowshoe, canoe, and horseshoe, 18 per cent of the time (4). A common exception is does.

The *ow* combination is listed here because in some instances it follows the general principle of silentness. In *ow,* the *w* is not pro-

TABLE 11-3

Ai as ā	maize	clay	eel	reel	coal	goes
aid	paid	day	feed	see	coast	hoe
aide	pail	flay	feel	seed	coat	Joe
ail	paint	gay	feet	seem	croak	shoe*
aim	pair	hay	flee	seen	float	toe
ain't	plaid*	may	fleet	seep	foal	
air	plaint	nay	free	sleek	foam	Ow as ō
aisle*	praise	play	geese	sleep	gloam	blow
bail	quail	pray	Greek	sleet	gloat	bow
bait	quaint	ray	green	sneer	goad	bowl
braid	raid	say	greet	speed	goal	crow
brail	rain	says*	heed	steed	goat	flow
brain	raise	slay	heel	steel	groan	flown
claim	said*	stay	jeep	steep	load	glow
drain	sail	tray	jeer	steer	loaf	grow
fail	saint	way	keel	sweep	loam	grown
faille	slain		keen	sweet	loan	know
fain	snail	Ee as ē	keep	teem	moan	low
faint	staid	bee	knee	teens	moat	mow
fair	stain	beech	kneel	tree	oak	owe
flail	stair	beef	leek	tweed	oat	own
flair	tail	been*	lees	tweet	road	row
gain	taint	beer	meet	wee	roam	show
gait	trail	beet	need	weed	roan	slow
hail	train	bleed	peek	week	roast	snow
hair	trait	breed	peel	weep	soak	stow
jail	waif	creed	peep		soap	throw
laid	wail	creek	peer	Oa as ō	toad	tow
lain	waist	creel	preen	boar	toast	
lair	wait	creep	queen	board		
maid		creese	queer	boast	Oe as ō	
mail	Ay as ā	deed	reed	boat	doe	
maim	aye*	deem	reef	broad*	does*	
main	bay	deep	reek	cloak	foe	

* Aisle (īl); plaid (plad); said (sed); aye (ī); says (sez); been (bin); broad (bròd); does (dəz); shoe (shü); the ee followed by r is always i(ə).

nounced, and the *o* is given its long sound 50 per cent of the time. Forty-eight per cent of the time it is pronounced as *ow* in town.

The principle of silentness also applies to certain words having an *ea* combination. This group of words is by far the least consistent. The pupil will have to learn many of the words as sight words. In attacking words with the *ea* combination the pupil's best guess is the long *e* sound. It occurs about 50 per cent of the time (4). The next most common

TABLE 11-4

			Ea*		
Ea		Ear			
e	ā	i(ə)	e(ə)	ə	ä
bread	great	clear	bear	earl	heart
breadth	break	dear	pear	dearth	hearth
breast	steak	beard	swear	earn	
breath		ear	wear	earth	
dead		fear		hearse	
deaf		gear		pearl	
dealt		hear		search	
death		near			
dread		rear			
dreamt		sear			
head		shear			
health		smear			
lead		spear			
meant		tear			
read					
realm					
spread					
stealth					
sweat					
thread					
threat					
tread					
wealth					

* Some two-syllable words with *ea* pronounced as short e are: abreast, headache, ahead, already, baldhead, behead, blockhead, breakfast, bullhead, deadbeat, deaden, deadeye, deadly, deafen, deafmute, dreadful, feather, headlight, headlong, headstrong, healthful, healthy, heaven, heavy, hothead, instead, jealous, leather, meadow, measure, pleasant, peasant, pleasure, ready, redhead, retread, steady, sweater, threaten, weapon, weather, wealthy. In heartbreak and heartburn it is *ä*. In impearl, learned, rehearse, searching, unearth, and research it is *ə*.

usage is that of the short *e* as in bread. The pupil must learn that break and steak are pronounced as brāk and stāk. The ending *ear* may be pronounced four ways: as i(ə) in beard, clear, dear, ear, fear, gear, hear, near, rear, sear, shear, smear, and spear; as e(ə) in bear, pear, swear, wear; as ə in dearth, earl, earn, earth, hearse, and pearl; and as *ä* in heart and hearth. In diagrammatic form the various pronunciations for *ea,* omitting the long *e* sound, may be categorized as in Table 11-4.

The following *ea* combinations are pronounced as long *e:*

beach	cleave	gleam	leak	plea	seat	teach
bead	creak	glean	lean	plead	sheaf	team
beak	cream	grease	leap	please	sheath	tease
beam	crease	greave	lease	pleat	sheathe	treat
bean	deal	heal	leave	preach	sheave	veal
beast	dean	heap	meal	reach	sleave	weak
beat	dream	heat	mean	read	sneak	weal
bleach	each	heath	neat	ream	speak	weave
bleak	ease	heave	pea	reap	squeal	wheat
bleat	east	jean	peace	reave	stead	wreak
breach	eat	knead	peach	screak	steal	wreath
breathe	feast	lea	peak	scream	steam	wreathe
cheap	feat	lead	peaked	sea	streak	
clean	flea	leaf	peal	seal	stream	
cheat	freak	league	peat	seam	tea	

THE DIPHTHONGS

Diphthongs are vowel combinations that have a single sound. The sound is distinct from that represented by either of the single letters. The most common such combinations are: *au, aw, oi, oy, oo.*

Au and Aw

The combination *au* is pronounced *ò* (ought) 94 per cent of the time (4); the principal exceptions are draught, gauge, aunt, chauffeur, and laugh. *Aw* is pronounced as *ò* (law) 100 per cent of the time (4), when it occurs at the end of the word or syllable or is followed by *k, l,* or *n.*

Au as ò—aught, caught, caulk, cause, craunch, daub, daunt, fault, faun, flaunt, fraud, Gaul, gaunt, gauze, haul, haunch, haunt, jaunt, laud, launch, mauve, naught, naughty, Paul, paunch, pause, raught, sauce, Saul, staunch, taught, taunt, vault, vaunt, applaud, applause, assault, auburn, audit, auger, augment, augur, August, austere, auto, because, caucus, causal, dauntless, default, defraud, laundress, naughty, saucepan, saucer, saucy, slaughter.

Aw as ò—awe, awl, awn, bawl, brawl, brawn, claw, craw, crawl, dawn, draw, drawl, drawn, fawn, flaw, gawk, hawk, jaw, law, lawn, paw, pawn, raw, saw, scrawl, shawl, slaw, spawn, sprawl, squaw, squawk, straw, thaw, trawl, awesome, brawny, awful, awning, bylaw, drawer, drawing, gnawing, hacksaw, in-law, jigsaw, lawful, lawless, lawsuit, lawyer, pawnshop, rawhide, tawny.

Oi and Oy

The sound of *oi,* as in boil, occurs 98 per cent of the time (4). It occurs in the following words: boil, broil, choice, coil, coin, droit, foil, foist, hoist, join, joint, joist, moist, noise, oil, point, poise, soil, spoil, toil, voice, void, appoint, avoid, boiler, cloister, foible, jointly, jointweed, noisy, recoil, rejoice, rejoin, toilet, toiler, topsoil, uncoil, and unsoiled. A common exception is choir.

The sound of *oy* as in boy also occurs 98 per cent of the time. Common words are: coy, joy, Roy, soy, toy, Troy, alloy, bellboy, boycott, boyhood, boyish, convoy, cowboy, decoy, deploy, destroy, enjoy, envoy, joyful, loyal, oyster, royal, and tomboy. An exception is coyote.

The Combination Oo

Oo is pronounced as *ü* (bloom) 59 per cent of the time (4); as *u̇* (cook) 36 per cent of the time (4); as *ō* (door); and as short *u* (blood).[7] The latter two occur infrequently and should be taught as exceptions. The combination, *ook,* occurs frequently enough in words that one may speak of the *ook* words. Some examples are: book, brook, cook, crook, hook, nook, rook, shook, and took. Only spook is an exception.

The following words are illustrative of the *oo* combinations:

Oo as *ü*—bloom, boo, boom, boon, boost, boat, booth, booze, brood, broom, choose, coo, cool, coon, coop, coot, croon, doom, drool, droop, food, fool, gloom, goof, goon, goose, groom, groove, hoof, hoop, moo, mooch, mood, moon, moose, moot, noose, pooch, pool, proof, roof, room, roost, root, school, scoop, scoot, shoo, shoot, sloop, smooch, smooth, snoop, snoot, snooze, soon, sooth, soothe, spook, spool, spoon, stooge, stoop, swoon, swoop, too, tool, toot, tooth, troop, whoop, zoo, zoom, baboon, balloon, ballroom, bamboo, bassoon, bedroom, behoove, blooming, booby, booster, bootleg, bridegroom, caboose, cartoon, classroom, cocoon, cooler, coolie, disproof, doodle, fooling, foodstuff, foolish, gloomy, homeroom, igloo, moonlight, moonshine, mushroom, noodle, noonday, noontime, papoose, platoon, raccoon, reproof, roofing, roomette, roommate, rooster, rootbeer, saloon, storeroom, toothache, toothbrush, toothpick.

Oo as *u̇*—barefoot, bookend, bookmark, bookworm, childhood, cookbook, footstool, football, footbridge, foothill, footnote, girlhood, goodness, lookout, manhood, redwood, rookie, sooty, woodpile, woodshed, woodsman, woodwork, lookout, book, brook, cook, crook, foot, good, hood, hook, look, nook, shook, soot, stood, took, wood, wool.

[7] Emans (6) found that the *ü* sound occurred 74 per cent of the time in his study; the *u̇* sound, 26 per cent.

Oo as ō—brooch, door, floor, doorstep, doorway, doorsill.

Oo as
short u—blood, flood, bloodshed, bloodshot, bloodstain, bloody floodlight.

OTHER VOWEL COMBINATIONS

There are a number of other vowel combinations which occur frequently enough to be included in this survey. They are: *ei, ey, ew, ie, ou, ow, ue,* and *ui.*

The Combination *Ei (Ey)*

A common pronunciation for *ei* is that of a long *a.* It occurs 40 per cent of the time (4). The following words are illustrative: beige, deign, feign, feint, heir, heiress, reign, rein, reindeer, seine, skein, their, veil, vein, eight, freight, neigh, sleigh, weigh, and weight.

In about 26 per cent of the cases (4), *ei* is simply pronounced as a long *e,* the second vowel being silent. Thus we have ceiling, deceive, conceive, receive, perceive, leisure, seize, either, neither.

The *ei* may be pronounced as long *i:* height; short *e:* heifer; and short *i:* forfeit and sovereign.

The *ey* is pronounced as short *i* 58 per cent of the time (4): barley, honey, kidney, parley. It is pronounced as long *a* 20 per cent of the time (4): hey, obey, prey, they, whey. It occurs as long *i:* eye, eyeball, eyebrow, eyelash; and as long *e:* key, keyboard, keyhole, passkey.

The Combination *Ie*

Ie generally is a long *e* (36 per cent of the time); a short *i* (19 per cent); or a long *i* (17 per cent) (4). The long *i* sound is common when *ie* is at the end of a word and in the ending *ied.* The following words are illustrative of the various sounds for *ie:*

Long e—bier, brief, chief, fief, field, fiend, fierce, frieze, grief, grieve, lief, liege, mien, niece, piece, pier, pierce, priest, shield, shriek, siege, thief, tier, wield, yield, achieve, backfield, belief, believe, cashier, frontier, grievance, grievous, hygiene, priestly, rabies, relief, retrieve, timepiece, wieldy.

Long i —die, fie, fried, lie, pie, tried, vie, allied, applied, belie, implied, tie-up, untie, untried.

Short e—friend, befriend, friendless, friendly, friendship.

Short i—sieve.

The Combination Ou

Ou has numerous pronunciations: as *ou* in blouse; as long *o* in course; as *ü* in coop; as *u̇* in could; as *o̥* in bought; as short *u* in touch; and as *ȯ* in cough. Certainly, the most common sounds are *ou*, 35 per cent of the time (4); as the schwa sound of *ou* in rigorous, 41 per cent; as *ü* (soup), 7 per cent; and as *ō*, 6 per cent. The child should learn the "ought" words and the "could" words. He must learn the pronunciation of such common words as tough, cough, tour, and your.

The following words may be used to teach the various sounds:

Ou as *ou*—blouse, bough, bounce, bound, bout, cloud, clout, couch, count, crouch, douse, drought, flounce, flour, foul, found, fount, gouge, gout, grouch, ground, hound, hour, house, loud, mound, mount, mouse, mouth, noun, ouch, ounce, our, oust, out, pouch, plough, pounce, pound, pout, proud, round, rout, scour, scout, shout, shroud, abound, about, account, aground, aloud, around, arouse, astound, background, blockhouse, blowout, bouncing, bounty, cloudburst, cloudy, compound, counsel, county, devour, devout, discount, doghouse, enounce, flounder, greenhouse, greyhound, guardhouse, housecoat, household, housemaid, housewife, house-work, icehouse, mountain, mounted, mounting, mouthful, ourself, ouster, outboard, outbreak, outburst, outcome, outcry, outdoors, outer, outfit, outing, outlaw, outlay, outlet, outlive, outmost, out-post, output, outrage, outright, outsell, outshine, outside, outskirt, outsmart, outward, outwards, outweigh, outwork, playhouse, pronoun, pronounce, propound, recount, renounce, rounding, round-ness, roundup, rousing, southwest, stoutness, trousers.

Ou as *ō*—course, court, dough, four, fourth, furlough, mould, mourn, pour, soul, source, though, although, doughnut, thorough, courtroom, courtship, courtyard, discourse, doughnut, fourteen, fourthly, mourning, poultry, recourse, resource.

Ou as *ü*—coup, couth, croup, ghoul, group, rouge, route, soup, through, wound, you, youth, cougar, coupon, detour.

Ou as short *u*—cousin, country, couple, double, enough, tough, rough, roughage, roughen, roughly, roughness, touch, trouble, young, famous, touch-back, touchy, toughen, grievous, jealous, monstrous, pious.

Ou as *o̥*—bought, brought, cough, nought, fought, ought, sought, thought, wrought.

Ou as *u̇*—could, should, tour, would, your.

Ou as *ə*—adjourn, journal, journey, flourish.

The Combination Ow

The pupil already has learned the long *o* sound of *ow*. He also must learn the *ou* sound of *ow*. This sound at the end of the word usually is written as *ow* and occurs in the following words:

> bow, brow, brown, browse, chow, clown, cow, cowl, crowd, crown, down, dowse, drown, drowse, frown, gown, growl, how, howl, jowl, owl, plow, prow, prowl, scowl, sow, town, wow, allow, avow, breakdown, chowchow, cowbell, cowbird, cowboy, cowhide, dowry, endow, flower, Howard, howdy, nightgown, powder, power, powwow, prowess, renowned, towel, tower, township, uptown.

The Combinations Ew, Ue, Ui

The pupil has learned two sounds for the long *u:* the yü sound and the ü sound after *j, r, bl, fl, pl, cl, gl,* and *sl.* The yü sound is regularly used after *b, c, f, g, h, k, m, p,* and *v.* He must apply the same principles to the *ew, ue, w,* and *ew* combinations:

> ew as yü—ewe, few, hew, lewd, mew, new, pew, phew, skew, spew, stew, thew, view, whew, sinew, askew, nephew, newly, newness, renew, review.
>
> ew as ü—blew, brew, crew, drew, flew, grew, Jew, screw, shrewd, slew, threw, Hebrew, jewel, Jewess.
>
> ue as yü—cue, due, hue, imbue, statue, tissue.
>
> ue as ü—blue, clue, flue, glue, rue, slue, true, accrue, bluegill, bluegrass, blueprint, construe, gruesome, rueful, untrue, sue, statue, tissue.
>
> ui as yü—suit, nuisance.
>
> ui as ü—bruise, cruise, juice, sluice, suit, grapefruit, fruitcake, juicy, recruit.
>
> eu as yü—deuce, feud, Europe, feudal, Teuton, neural, neuter, neutral, neutron.

The *yü* sound of *ew* occurs 61 per cent of the time; the *ü* sound, 34 per cent (4). Ew also occurs as long *o:* sew.

The *yü* sound of *ue* occurs 63 per cent of the time; the *ü* sound, 37 per cent of the time (4).

The *yü* sound of *ui* occurs 24 per cent of the time; the *ü* sound, 29 per cent; and the short *i* sound, 47 per cent (4). Emans (6) found in his study that *ui* had a short *i* sound 79 per cent of the time: build, built, guilt, guilty, building. An exception is suite.

The *yü* sound of *eu* occurs 72 per cent of the time (4).

The vowel combinations in order of frequency of occurrence according to Burmeister (4) are: *ou, ea, ai, oo, ee, ow, au, ie, oa, ay, oi, ei, aw, ey, ew, oy, ue, eu, ui,* and *oe.*

Burmeister (4) points out that phonemes for vowel-pairs tend to fall into the following categories:

1. The first vowel may do the talking, as in *ai, ay, ea, ee, oa,* or *ow* and say its name. *Ea* may be long e or short e; *ow* may be long o or *ou.*
2. The two vowels may blend: *au, aw, oi, oy, oo; oo* may sound as in lagoon or wood.
3. The two vowels may create a new sound: *ei, ow, ey, ew.*

Sabaroff (10) identifies five basic vowel patterns:

1. The single (or short) vowel pattern as in bat or at.
2. The open vowel pattern as in he, she or me.
3. The vowel with final e pattern as in rope or use.
4. The double vowel pattern as in rain.
5. The modified vowel pattern as in bird, as in word, or as in a*ll.*

He points out that instruction should begin with words in pattern 1.

The pupil needs to learn the basic generalizations that govern sounding. The child should see how the rule fits the words that he has learned. He should be asked to provide other words that follow the same rule.

Perhaps the sound of the individual vowels is best learned through practice with actual words. However, the rules and principles have their value. In fact, generalizations are not necessarily learned best inductively. If this were so, many theories would forever elude us. Sometimes, it seems to be more effective to state the generalization explicitly.

TEACHING THE LONG VOWELS

In teaching the vowels the child initially looks at a picture, pronounces its name, and identifies the short sound. The teacher may ask: "What vowel sound occurs in the word *cat?* In the word *bell?*"

Next the pupil should be taught to discriminate between the short and the long vowel. What sound occurs in the word *mule?* In the word *go?* Are these short sounds or long sounds? Why? The teacher asks the child to look at words like came, flame, and dame. How many vowels are pronounced? Which vowel is silent? What happens to the first vowel when the *e* is silent and is preceded by a single consonant?

For exercises useful in teaching the various vowel sounds, see Emerald Dechant, *Linguistics, Phonics, and the Teaching of Reading* (Springfield, Ill.: Charles C Thomas, Publisher, 1969).

THE EFFECT OF R ON A PRECEDING VOWEL

The pupil also must be able to cope with *ar, er, or, ir,* and *ur.* The consonant sometimes influences the sound of the vowel. The letter *r,* when following a single vowel, changes the sound of the vowel. The vowel is neither long nor short. Bailey (2) found that this generalization was true 86 per cent of the time. The pupil already has some experience with this phenomenon. The *a* in monosyllables when followed by *r* or when followed by *r* plus another consonant is the *ä* sound as in bar, car, art, arm, far, and mar.

Unfortunately, not all *a*'s followed by *r* are pronounced as *ä*. When the *r* is followed by a silent *e* as in care or fare or when it is the final letter in an accented syllable and is followed by a vowel, as in parent or Mary, the *a* frequently is pronounced e(ə). However, the *a* may be a short vowel in this last instance: for example, paradise and paradox. When the *a* is the final letter in an unaccented syllable and is followed by an *r* in the next syllable it is ə: thus, maroon and cataract.

In the suffix *ar,* as in ward, and in some final syllables, *ar* is pronounced (ə)*r*: thus, liar, granular, westward, pillar, dollar, orchard, Tartar, circular, lizard, sugar, grammar, collar, wizard, lizard, and mustard. In the suffix *ary,* *ar* is pronounced as *er*: thus, stationary, legendary, and sanitary.

Er in monosyllabic words (her), generally in accented syllables (revert), and in unaccented syllables in which the *er* is followed by a consonant (adverb) is sounded as ə*r*. When it names a person (baker) or has a comparative meaning (hotter), it is usually pronounced as (ə)*r*. It may also be *er* as in meridian, *i*(ə) as in here, or *e*(ə) as in there, where, ferry, herring, very, or perish.

Ir is sounded as ə*r* in monosyllables (firm) and in accented syllables (firkin). It may be sounded as ə(*r*) (tapir), ī*r* (dire), or i*r* (virile, irrelevant, irritate).

Or is sounded as ə*r* when *or* follows *w* as in word.[8] In other monosyllabic words it is sounded as ō or as ȯ. The *or* may be pronounced as ə(*r*) (inventor) or may become ä*r* or ŏ*r* as in coral or torrid. It usually is

---

[8] The exception is worn.

pronounced ə(r) when it names a person (doctor) or a quality or condition (horror).

Ur is sounded as ər in monosyllabic words and in the accented syllable of polysyllabic words. *Ur* also may be ə(r) (liturgy), ür (cure), and u̇ (sure, jury, hurrah, rural).

When *ar, er, ir, or,* or *ur* are followed by a second *r*, the vowel is usually short: thus, barrel, barren, sparrow, arrest, barrack, derrick, error, terrier, errand, mirror, borrow, horror, sorry, corrupt, torrent, torrid.

The vowel also is short when the *r* is followed by a vowel: thus, charity, tariff, lariat, parachute, paratroop, parasol, parapet, parallel, parasite, parable, ceremony, America, very, inherit, peril, verify, merit, cleric, spirit, miracle, direct, quorum.

Sometimes the *r* is separated from the vowel preceding it and has no effect on its pronunciation: thus, arise, around, arena, spiral, Irish, erect, erupt, hero, irate, siren, uranium, pirate, virus, furious, spirant, wiry, glory, tyrant, mores, oral, story, Tory.

The following lists of words illustrate the various combinations of the vowel with the *r* in monosyllabic words:

er as ər—berg, berth, clerk, err, erst, fern, germ, her, herd, jerk, kern, merge, nerve, per, perch, perk, pert, serf, serge, serve, sherd, stern, swerve, term, tern, verge, verse, versed, wert.

ir as ər—birch, bird, birth, chirp, dirge, dirt, fir, firm, firn,[9] first, flirt, firth, gird, girl, girt, girth, irk, Kirk, mirk, mirth, quirk, shirk, shirt, skirt, squirm, squirt, stir, third, twirl, whirl.

or as ȯ—born, cord, cork, corn, for, gorge, horn, horse, Lord, morn, Morse, norm, Norse, north, or, orb, scorch, scorn, short, snort, sort, sport, stork, storm, torch, tort, worn.

or as ər—word, work, world, worm, worse, worst, wort, worth.

ur as ər—blur, blurb, blurt, burg, burn, burnt, burp, burr, burse, burst, church, churn, curb, curd, curl, curse, curt, curve, durst, fur, furl, gurge, hurl, hurt, lurch, lurk, nurse, purge, purse, scurf, slur, spur, spurge, spurn, spurt, surf, surge, turf, Turk, turn, urge, urn.

THE EFFECT OF **W** ON **A**

The *w* changes the sound of *a* much as the *r* changes the sound of *e, i,* or *u*. The *a* may become a short *o* or an ȯ. The following words are illustrative:

[9] Firn has a short *i*.

wa as wă
    (short o)—swab, swamp, swan, swap, swat, wad, wand, want, was, wash,
        wasp, watch, watt, what, swallow, tightwad, waffle, wallet,
        wallop, wanting, washing, washrag, washcloth, washer, wash-
        room, watchdog, watchful, watchman, wattage, whitewash.

wa as ô—dwarf, swarm, war, ward, warm, warp, wart, walleye, walnut,
        warble, warden, wardrobe, warlike, warmly, warming, warrant.

However, there are exceptions to the above: way, sway.

SYLLABICATION

Up to this point we have not emphasized the principles that govern accentuation and syllabication. Glass (8) questions the value of syllabication. He notes that usually the syllabication is done after the sounds in
words become known. No one in his study seemed to use syllabication
rules to discover the sounds in words; rather, the sounds were used to
determine syllable division. Glass adds: "Word analysis is not needed once
the sound of the word is known" and asks: "Why syllabicate?" Schell (11)
raises the same question. Glass concludes that he can discover no reason
why syllabication activities should be included in a word analysis program.

At any rate, the good reader knows how to divide words accurately
and rapidly. This does not mean that he divides every word that he
comes to in his reading or that he knows the rule for dividing it. The
former would slow down his reading and might even interfere with good
comprehension. The latter is not necessary for good reading.

The first principle to be learned is that every syllable contains
a sounded vowel. At times, a vowel itself constitutes a syllable: a-corn, I,
vi-o-let, lin-e-ar, lin-e-al, cer-e-al, o-pen, i-de-a. A syllable thus is defined
as a unit of pronunciation consisting of a vowel sound alone or with one
or more consonant sounds and pronounced with one impulse.

The pupil also must learn that a syllable may contain more than
one vowel. The number of syllables a word has is dependent upon the
number of vowels heard, not on the number of vowels seen.

There are two kinds of syllables: closed syllables and open syllables.
A closed syllable is one that ends with a consonant: thus, *cat*, ba*sis*, and
magne*tic*. The vowel in a closed syllable is usually a short vowel. There
are some common exceptions. These were discussed previously in this
chapter under the heading, "Principle of Position."

An open syllable is one that ends in a vowel: thus, *cry*, *by*. At one
time the *y* at the end of a word was often pronounced as a short *i*; today,
it is a long *e*. Below is a list of words with the *y* pronounced as long *e*
The vowel in an open syllable is usually a long vowel.

ably	cocky	grimy	kingly	pigmy	sloppy
army	collie	grisly	kinky	pity	smelly
baby	copy	grumpy	kitty	plenty	snappy
badly	crabby	gusty	lackey	poppy	soggy
baldy	cranky	handy	lady	pussy	sorry
barley	dimly	happy	lanky	putty	spotty
belfry	drafty	hardy	lassie	rally	study
belly	empty	hasty	lately	Randy	stiffly
berry	entry	hefty	lily	ruddy	sultry
body	flaky	Henry	madly	rummy	sunny
brandy	foggy	hobby	manly	rusty	taffy
buddy	folly	holy	marry	sadly	tally
buggy	fifty	homely	muddy	Sally	tinny
bumpy	filly	humbly	nasty	scabby	tippy
bunny	funny	hungry	nifty	scanty	tipsy
busy	froggy	jelly	nippy	Scotty	Tommy
cabby	gladly	jiffy	pantry	sentry	twenty
candy	glory	jolly	pappy	silly	ugly
carry	grassy	jumpy	parley	simply	wiggly
clammy	gravy	Kenny	party	singly	windy
classy	greasy	kidney	penny	sissy	
clumsy	greedy	kindly			

Rule I

When two consonants follow a vowel, as in after, kitten, pencil, summer, and butter, the word is divided between the two consonants, and the first syllable ends with the first consonant. In instances of this kind the second consonant is silent when the consonants are the same. Since the first vowel is followed by a consonant, it tends to be a short vowel.

The pupil must be shown that not all double consonants can be divided. Consonant blends and speech consonants fall into this category.

Rule II

When only one consonant or a digraph follows a vowel, as in paper, bacon, prefer, begun, and reshape, the word usually is divided after the first vowel and the consonant or consonant digraph begins the second syllable. The first vowel, in that it ends a syllable, is usually a long vowel, thus: si/lent, no/mad, ba/sin, da/tum, mi/nus, to/tal, ha/zel, si/nus, fa/tal, ca/det, ce/ment, etc.

Exceptions and Observations

One: Not all words follow the rule. For example, planet, solid, robin, travel, study, record,[10] river, primer,[10] present,[10] cabin, tropic, power, timid, habit, pity, body, quiver, copy, lily, bigot, calico, atom,

---

[10] These may be divided according to both rules, dependent upon their meaning in the sentence.

honor, venom, olive, legend, lemon, valid, limit, dragon, wagon, digit, solid, cherish, volume, lizard, snivel, cherub, and profit join the consonant to the first vowel. This makes the first vowel short and the accent is on the first syllable.

Two: The suffix *ed* is a syllable only when it follows the sound *d* or *t*.

Three: Whenever two or more consonants appear between two vowels, the pupil must learn to look for consonant blends or speech consonants. These are never divided: thus, gam-bler, mi-grate.

Four: Whenever *le* ends a word and is preceded by a consonant, the last syllable consists of the consonant and the *le*. We divide thus: ta-ble, mid-dle, peo-ple. When *le* is preceded by *ck*, *le* is a separate syllable: freck/le, buck/le. The *e* in *ble, the, ple,* and *dle* is silent. Some authors, however, suggest that *le* says *el* with *e* being shorter than usual and called schwa.

Observe that in *tle* the *t* sometimes is silent and at times may be pronounced. Thus in battle, bottle, brittle, mantle, cattle, little, rattle, and tattle the *t* is pronounced; in castle, hustle, jostle, and rustle (words in which *tle* follows the letter *s*), it is silent.

able	cradle	kettle	raffle	scuttle
ankle	dazzle	kindle	ramble	stable
apple	dimple	little	rattle	steeple
babble	double	mantle	riddle	struggle
battle	fable	maple	rifle	table
beetle	fondle	marble	ripple	tackle
Bible	fumble	mangle[11]	rubble	tangle[11]
bicycle	gable	meddle	ruffle	tattle
bobble	gamble	middle	rustle	temple
bottle	gargle	mingle[11]	saddle	tickle
brittle	gentle	muddle	sample	tingle[11]
bubble	giggle	muffle	scuffle	title
buckle	grumble	mumble	simple	trample
bugle	haggle	muscle	single[11]	trifle
bundle	handle	nimble	sizzle	triple
bungle[11]	humble	nibble	smuggle	treble
cable	hustle	nipple	sniffle	tremble
cackle	jiggle	paddle	snuggle	tumble
candle	jingle[11]	pebble	spangle[11]	turtle
castle	little	pickle	sparkle	twinkle
cattle	jostle	pimple	swindle	uncle
circle	juggle	puddle	stubble	waggle
coddle	jumble	purple	supple	wiggle
crackle	jungle[11]	puzzle	scuffle	wriggle
		rabble		

[11] When *gle* is preceded by *n*, it is pronounced as gg'l.

Five: Sometimes it is necessary to divide between two vowels: create. Common words in which this occurs are the following:

ai—archaic, laity, mosaic
ea—cereal, create, delineate, fealty, ideal, laureate, lineate, linear, permeate
ei—being, deity, reinforce, reinstate, spontaneity
eu—museum, nucleus
ie—client, diet, dietary, expedient, orient, piety, propriety, quiet, science
oa—coadjutor, coagulate, oasis
oe—coefficient, coerce, coexist, poem
oi—egoist, going
oo—cooperate, coordinate, zoology
ue—cruel, duel, duet, fluent, fuel, gruel, influence, minuet
ui—altruism, ambiguity, annuity, fluid, fruition

Six: In a compound word the division comes between the two words
making up the compound: post-man.

Seven: Prefixes and suffixes are usually set apart from the rest of
the word: in-sist, hott-est.

ACCENTUATION

A word of two or more syllables generally is pronounced with more stress
on one syllable. This is termed accent. In dictionaries the accent mark
(′) is placed just after the syllable that receives major stress. In words of
three or more syllables there may be a secondary accent such as in lo′co
mo′tive.

The teaching of accentuation is usually put off until the pupil is
well advanced in phonic analysis and word analysis generally. After the
pupil has learned the meaning of accent and the way the dictionary
identifies the accent or stress point, he may gradually be introduced to
the following rules:

1. Generally, words of two syllables in which two consonants
    follow the first vowel accent the first syllable: thus, *after, kit-
    ten, puppet,* and *butter.* This rule has 81 per cent utility (2).
2. When a two-syllable word contains two vowels in the second
    syllable but only one is pronounced, the second syllable gen-
    erally is accented: *abide, abode, above, about, aboard, delay,*
    and *proceed.* Usually, the last syllable is long.

3.   Compound words usually carry the primary accent on (or within) the first word: bellhop, bulldog, carhop, dishpan, godson, humbug, pigpen. There are many exceptions to this rule: forbid.
4.   Syllables beginning with a consonant followed by *le* (circle, rabble) are not accented.
5.   In three-syllable words in which the suffix is preceded by a single consonant, as in *adviser, exciting, translated,* and *refusal* or in *piloted, traveled,* and *shivered,* the accent may be on the first or second syllable. It is on the first syllable except when the root word (advise, excite, translate, and refuse) ends in *e* and the last syllable is accented.
6.   In general, the accent is placed on alternate syllables (dis'-ap-point'-ment). Frequently, the accented syllable is followed by two unaccented syllables (san'-i-ty). At times the accent is on alternate syllables and the last two syllables are unaccented (op'-por-tun'-i-ty).[12]
7.   Root words when preceded by prefixes or followed by suffixes usually are accented (amuse, amusement).
8.   Words ending in *ion, ity, ic, ical, ian, ial,* or *ious* have the accent immediately before these suffixes (consternation, athletic, immersion, industrial, harmonious, humidity, psychological, historian). This rule is valid 95 per cent of the time (6).
9.   Words of three or more syllables ending in a silent *e* usually accent the third last syllable (graduate, accommodate, anticipate).
10.   Homographs or words with identical spellings receive their accent from the context in which they are used (con'tract-contract').

In introducing the pupil to accent and syllabication, the teacher needs to use words that the pupil knows. Repeated exercise with actual words will help the pupil to obtain a functional knowledge of the generalizations stated above.

Initially the teacher may pronounce a word orally and may let the pupils indicate by one or two fingers whether the word has one or two syllables or whether the accent falls on the first or second syllable. Gradually, the pupil should learn to write a word, divide it, indicate its accent, and at the upper grade levels may give the rules which govern its syllabication and accentuation.

---

[12] Josephine Rudd, *Word Attack Manual* (Cambridge, Massachusetts: Educators Publishing Service, 1961), p. 119.

SILENT LETTERS

Sometime in his reading education the pupil should learn that certain consonants are not pronounced. When this situation prevails, the word frequently needs to be taught as a sight word. There are, however, some observations that apply consistently. For example, when a consonant is doubled, the first often is silent: *hitting*. The following are other examples in which a consonant is silent:

Silent b after m:	bomb, bomber, bombproof, bombshell, climb, crumb, dumb, lamb, limb, numb, plumber, plumbing, succumb, thumb, tomb, womb
Silent b before all consonants except l & r:	bdellium, debt, debtor, doubt, doubtful, subtle
Silent c:	czar, indict, victuals
Silent ch:	drachm, fuchsia schism, yacht
Silent c after s:	ascend, ascent, descend, descent, scene, scenic, scent, scepter, muscle, science, scissor, transcend
Silent d:	adjunct, adjust, handkerchief, handsome, Wednesday
Silent d before g:	badger, dodger, edge, fudge, etc.
Silent g before n:	align, arraign, benign, campaign, design, ensign, feign, foreign, gnarl, gnash, gnat, gnaw, gnome, malign, reign, resign, sign, signer, signpost
Silent gh:	eight, freight, neigh, neighbor, sleigh, straight, straighten, weigh, weight[13]
Silent h:	aghast, ah, diarrhea, Durham, exhaust, exhibit, forehead, ghost, heir, hemorrhage, honest, honestly, honor, hour, hourly, myrrh, oh, rhesus, rhetoric, rhinestone, rhinoceros, rhubarb, rhumb, rhyme, rhythm, rhythmic, shepherd, Thomas, Thomism, Thompson, vehement, vehicle
Silent k before n:	knack, knap, knapsack, knave, knead, knee, kneel, knelt, knew, knife, knight, knit, knob, knock, knoll, knot, know, knowledge, knuckle[14]
Silent l:	almond, alms, balk, balmy, behalf, calf, calk, calm, chalk, embalm, folk, folklore, half, jaywalk, kinsfolk, kiln, palm, polka, psalm, salmon, solder, talk, walk, would, yolk

[13] Bailey (2) found that *gh* is silent 100 per cent of the time when it precedes *t*.
[14] This observation has 100 per cent utility (2).

Silent n after m:	autumn, column, condemn, damn, damned, hymn, hymnal, solemn, solemnly
Silent p:	corps, cupboard, pneumatic, pneumonia, psalm, psalmist, psalter, pseudo, psychiatry, psyche, psychic, raspberry, receipt
Silent s:	aisle, fuchsia, Arkansas, bas-relief, Carlisle, chamois, corps, debris, Illinois, island, isle, Louisville, rendezvous, St. Louis, viscount
Silent t:	bustle, castle, chasten, chestnut, Christmas, fasten, hasten, hautboy, hustle, listen, Matthew, mortgage, mustn't, often, soften, thistle, whistle
Silent th:	asthma
Silent w:[15]	awry, answer, boatswain, bowler, enwrap, own, owner, rewrite, sword, swordfish, swordsman, toward, two, who, whole, wholeness, wholesale, wholesome, wholly, whom, whose, wrack, wraith, wrangle, wrangler, wrapper, wrath, wreak, wreath, wreck, wreckage, wren, wrench, wrest, wrestle, wrestling, wretch, wring, wrinkle, wrist, wristband, writ, write, writer, writing, writhe, wrong, wrongly, wrote, wroth, wrought, wrung, wry, and in the ending ow as in snow

MULTISYLLABIC WORDS

Multisyllabic words introduce numerous problems not usually met in one-syllable words. For example, in one-syllable words one expects a long middle vowel when the word ends in a silent *e:* thus dame, dine, plume. This rule does not apply in some multisyllabic words. For example:

ace = əs:	solace, furnace, Horace, menace, palace, preface, surface
age = ij:	adage, baggage, bandage, bondage, breakage, cabbage, carnage, carriage, cleavage, coinage, cottage, courage, damage, dosage, drainage, forage, garbage, homage, hostage, image, language, leakage, luggage, manage, marriage, message, mileage, mortgage, orphanage, package, passage, pillage, postage, pottage, roughage, rummage, salvage, sausage, savage, scrimmage, sewage, seepage, soilage, soakage, spoilage, village, vintage, voltage, voyage, wastage, wattage, wreckage, yardage

[15] The *w* is always silent before r (2).

ege = *ēg:*   renege

ege = *ej:*   college

ege = *ij:*   privilege

ige = *ēzh:*   prestige

ase = *əs:*   purchase

ate = *ət:*   chocolate, climate, deliberate, delicate, delegate, desolate, duplicate, frigate, palate, prelate, private, senate, separate, temperate

ice = *əs:*   chalice, complice, crevice, justice, malice, notice, novice, office,
practice, service

ice = *ēs:*   caprice, police

ile = *il:*   agile, docile, fertile, fragile, futile, hostile, missile, mobile, reptile,
servile, sterile, tractile, virile[16]

ile = *ēl:*   automobile, castile

ine = *in:*   doctrine, engine, ermine, famine, genuine, urine, but also long *i*
as in divine, turpentine

ine = *ēn:*   carbine, machine, marine, morphine, ravine, routine, sardine, vac-
cine, vaseline

ise = *əs:*   premise, promise, treatise

ise = *ēs:*   valise

ite = *ət:*   respite

ive = *iv:*   active, captive, festive, massive, motive, passive, tractive

ive = *ēv:*   naive

uce = *əs:*   lettuce

The following are examples of other problems in reading multi-syllabic words:

ain = *ən:*   bargain, Britain, captain, certain, chaplain, chieftain,
curtain, fountain, mountain, villain

ay = *ē:*   always, Monday, yesterday

ia = *i:*   marriage, parliament

ience = *shens:*   patience

ce, ci, si, ti, as sh: ocean; electrician, musician, physician, politician; cordial,

[16] The chief exception is gentile; also note exile, crocodile, reconcile, juvenile, in-
fantile; mercantile and versatile have both pronunciations.

social, racial, special, facial, glacial, official, special; ancient, sufficient, efficient; precious, spacious, delicious, conscious, ferocious, cautious, gracious, spacious, vicious; mission, cession, decision, fusion, lesion, occasion, passion, pension, tension, torsion, version; action, attention, auction, caption, caution, definition, diction, edition, faction, fraction, friction, function, junction, ignition, lotion, mention, motion, nation, notion, option, portion, potion, sanction, section, station, traction, unction; partial, martial, nuptial, confidential, residential, potential; tertian; patient, patience, quotient, transient; ambitious; militia

$s = sh$: mansion, nauseous, issue, tissue

$s = zh$: vision, visual, usury, fusion

sure = chǝr; shǝr; zhǝr: censure, measure, pleasure, pressure, treasure, tonsure

$i = y$: familiar, peculiar, genius, behavior, junior, senior, guardian, Indian, brilliant, Italian, valiant, billion, champion, companion, million, onion, opinion, union, Spaniard, spaniel, congenial, convenience, convenient, obedient, Muriel, Daniel, William, Julia, California, Virginia, Pennsylvania, Celia, India, Columbia, Philadelphia, period, radio, curious, furious, glorious, serious

$i = $ long e: broccolli, ski, spaghetti, police, machine, antique, physique, technique, unique, clique, pique, intrigue, fatigue, simile, facsimile, recipe

$du + r = $ jǝr: procedure, verdure[17]

$tu + r = $ chǝr: capture, creature, culture, departure, feature, fracture, furniture, future, fixture, gesture, lecture, mixture, nature, pasture, picture, puncture, stature, suture, tincture, texture, torture, venture, vulture; nature is an exception.

$tu + $ any other letter = chǝ: actual, mutual, virtue, virtuous

zure = zhǝr: seizure, azure

COMMON SIGHT WORDS

The following list of words contains some common words that should be taught as sight words.

[17] Common exceptions are *endure* and *mature*.

above	cousin	heart	pretty	tough
again	cover	hearth	pull	tour
against	do	his	push	toward
aisle	dog	hour	put	trouble
already	does	into	rough	two
always	done	is	said	very
another	don't	isle	says	walk
answer	double	knew	sew	wand
anxious	dove	laugh	shoe	want
any	dozen	leopard	some	war
are	eight	live	someone	was
as	enough	lived	something	wash
aunt	eye	log	sometime	wasp
been	father	love	son	were
blood	flood	many	steak	what
both	four	mother	sugar	where
break	friend	move	sure	who
build	from	Mr.	swap	whom
bull	front	Mrs.	swat	whose
bury	full	none	talk	wind
busy	get	of	the	wolf
business	girl	off	there	women
buy	give	often	thought	won
canoe	glove	once	to	won't
choir	goes	one	today	would
come	gone	only	together	write
coming	half	own	ton	you
cough	has	other	too	young
could	have	people	touch	your
country				

SUMMARY

In this chapter we examined additional aspects of linguistic and phonic proficiency. It is impossible to suggest at what time children should have mastered these skills or indeed whether they ever need to master all of them. Teaching must be adjusted to individual needs.

Throughout the preceding two chapters we have emphasized what ought to be taught. There seem to be many benefits in teaching whole-word phonics. We find it profitable to introduce the child to the phonetic element through the whole word. This does not mean that another approach will not work. It does mean that since reading is a meaningful process the child should keep meaning foremost in his mind. This is best done through a whole-word approach.

From the beginning the child is taught to perceive the sounds in words. He also is taught to notice that some words have the same elements and that they sound alike. Finally, he either infers himself or is taught that he can get to the pronunciation and indirectly to the meaning of a word by noticing the elements in new words and sounding them as he sounded them in other words that he has learned. The pupil must learn that numerous words have some similarity in sound and that he can use this knowledge in attacking other words.

He needs to learn the phoneme-grapheme system by induction rather than by deduction. Rules should grow out of the situations that the pupil deals with. Finally, isolated words should always be brought back into the larger patterns and structures that function linguistically and which carry meaning.

QUESTIONS FOR DISCUSSION

1. Discuss two parallel programs for teaching consonant blends and speech consonants.
2. Discuss the principles of variability, position, and silentness and give means for teaching them at the first-, second-, and third-grade level. When would you, if ever, switch from a functional to formal teaching of the principles?
3. Illustrate the difference between the voiceless *th* and the voiced *th* by describing the mouth geography of each.
4. Develop a sequential program for teaching the *ar, er, ir, or,* and *ur* combinations in monosyllabic words.
5. Is there a recommended way for teaching the pupil to substitute a consonant blend for a single consonant at the beginning of a word? Discuss the various techniques.

ADVANCING THE PUPIL'S
READING SKILLS

part V

Part V consists of two chapters: Chapter 12, which deals with "Developing a Meaningful Vocabulary," and Chapter 13, which is devoted to "Advancing the Pupil's Comprehension Skills." A reading program must provide for the development of meaning for both the individual word and the larger units of meaning. This is the purpose of Chapters 12 and 13.

Developing a
Meaningful Vocabulary

chapter 12

A reading program must make some provision for the development of meaning by the pupil. A prime requisite for reading is the association of meaning with a given symbol. Unless the pupil can associate meaning with a symbol, he has not learned to read. Understanding must escape him and reading without understanding is verbalism.

The pupil also must interpret meaning in its broader contextual sense. The word has meaning as part of a sentence, the sentence as part of a paragraph, and the paragraph as a part of the story. This phase we will discuss in Chapter 13. In this chapter we will concern ourselves with the association of meaning with the individual symbol. Association of meaning with a symbol cannot occur unless the person has had some experience, whether real or vicarious, with that something for which the symbol stands. The word, apple, for example, has no meaning to the child who has never had either a first-hand or vicarious experience with an apple. The child must first have an experience with an apple if he is to be able to *read* the word apple.

Most children have little difficulty with the concepts and the vocabulary needed for beginning reading. The average child experiences his first real difficulties with meaning in the third grade. Content-area reading introduces rapidly a new vocabulary that the pupil must master. However, children with a bilingual background and those who come from low socioeconomic homes or are of dull intelligence generally experience serious meaning difficulties much earlier.

PROBLEMS IN DEVELOPING MEANING

Developing word meaning is one of the teacher's most important tasks. Even though the pupil possesses the meanings needed for the comprehension of the reading materials available to him, the teacher constantly must expand the child's meanings and check upon the adequacies of his present meanings.

Dawson and Bamman (7, p. 113) tell the story of a five-year-old boy who complained to his father that Molly had called him stupid. Upon questioning the boy, the father found that young Richard wasn't concerned about being insulted, but rather about the wrong use of the word *stupid*. Richard complained: "Well, dad, you know. Stupid is a woman driving a car!"

Another father recently had a similar experience with his child. He had just bought her a box of Cracker Jacks. He asked her: "Is the popcorn good?" Her reply was: "This is Cracker Jack." He again asked her: "Isn't that popcorn?" Again she informed him that it was Cracker Jack, not popcorn.

Most of us have had similar experiences. Children frequently have not had sufficient experience to appreciate all the connotations of a word. Generally, even if they have a broader understanding of the word, they are content to settle for the first meaning that comes to mind. Poor readers especially tend to accept the first meaning that pops into their minds (18, p. 62).

Children also many times have not learned that words can have more than one meaning. For example, the word *run* can mean "to move swiftly"; "to go back and forth" as in the sentence, "The boat runs between Georgia and New York"; to run as in an election; to win a race (the horse ran first); to turn a wheel; to run in debt; to run (trace) the story back to its source; to run (smuggle) contraband; and to run a store. These are only a few examples. In addition, we speak of a run of fish, a run of bad fortune, a run on the bank, the running brook, the ordinary run of people, or a cattle run.

Multiple meanings and pronunciations are not the only ambiguities of language that hinder communication and that make the apprehension of meaning difficult. Two words may have the same meaning; two words, although pronounced alike, may have different spellings and meanings; and words may have generic or specific meanings. Numerous idiomatic expressions also add to the reader's predicament. We speak (8, p. 254) of "facing the music," "leaving no stone unturned," or "breaking the ice with someone."

Growth in meaning and vocabulary has many levels. The child must develop precision in meaning; he must become acquainted with multiple meanings; he must learn specific and generic meanings; he must interpret idiomatic expressions; and for successful speech and writing he must be able to call to mind the word needed and then apply it correctly.

Some children have not learned to look for meaning. Usually, pupils will read the word, associate with it the sound of the spoken word, and take to it the meaning that they previously associated with the spoken word. However, this process does not always take place. Some pupils must be formally taught to make the inference.

Certainly, the grasping of meaning is important for learning. Educational psychologists have found that students prefer to deal with materials that have meaning. They apply meaningful data more easily, and they remember meaningful data for longer periods of time.

CONCEPTUALIZATION

In Chapter 1 we indicated that success in reading frequently depends on the pupil's ability to think of the word in an abstract way. This process we call conceptualization and the end result is a concept.

One would think that volumes would have been written on concept development and the teaching of concepts, but such is not the case. Carroll (4) notes that meaning has been considered the province of a branch of linguistics called *semantics,* but concept is almost anybody's oyster.

Concepts develop from experience, and their richness and scope are in direct proportion to the richness and scope of the individual's experience. This is perhaps another way of saying that concepts are the result of practicing something. The most important reason for the difference between the adult's concepts and those of the child is the differential in experience and knowledge. And, frequently, the significant reason for differences in learning is the differential in experience.

Concepts are idiosyncratic because they reside in a particular person with a particular history of experiences that have led him to classify experiences in particular ways (4). Perception and cognition always "go beyond the information given." They include a reading of the past experience. That which the person adds is the sum total of the retained and organized effects of past experience. The individual perceives his world in terms of "what he is" as much as "what it is" (20, pp. 140–141).

Even animals show a need for experience early in life. A dog that is raised in an environment in which he is freed from all physical hazards will show peculiarly inept behavior when put into a more normal environment. He will bump his head on a low pipe twenty or more times without any apparent learning. He will react ineptly to fire and pain. It takes learning and experience to profit from experience. And some children in the classroom sometimes have not had the experience necessary to acquire school learning. Educators thus far have not been able to discriminate between the child who does not learn because of inadequate biology and maturation and the one who does not and indeed cannot learn because of inadequate prior experience.

Every teacher has real concern with the comprehension abilities of his students. Can they integrate experience into larger meaningful wholes? A more basic question might be: Do they have the experiences and are they able to differentiate and to systematize the details necessary for comprehension?

The evidence shows that not all persons characteristically use conceptual thought. Experience with the *Vigotsky Test of Concept Formation* indicates also that concept formation is distinct from intelligence. Those who do best on this test are not necessarily the most intelligent. The evidence shows that children grow in their conceptualization.

A concept requires both abstraction (this isolates the property—abstract concept) and generalization (this applies it to several objects—general concept). A word is the verbal expression of a concept.

Teachers sometimes assume that a young child possesses a concept because he can and does use a "class" name. He will speak of a "flower," a "dog," or a "cat." We might assume that he has a class concept when in reality he is thinking of a specific flower, dog, or cat in his experience.

At other times, especially at the upper grade levels, the pupil may even be able to give a definition for a class name. Too frequently, this simply means that the student has learned to verbalize by rote.

The development of meanings or concepts follows a characteristic pattern. First, the child must learn to discriminate one object from another. Gradually, with repeated experience with similar objects, he acquires new layers of meaning and his perceptions become increasingly wider, richer, more diversified, and more complex.[1] He learns to identify the essential and the nonessential characteristics of the various realities in his environment. He proceeds from simple experience to concept via abstraction and finally arrives at categorization. He is able to categorize when he can group objects or experiences into classes.

Let us examine more closely the steps in the development of meaning.

[1] Perception thus is unidirectional (always growing richer and irreversible).

Concepts are possible only when the pupil has had experience with the actual phenomena that are to be conceptualized (17, p. 136).[2] Thus the initial step in the development of meaning is the differentiation of realities within one's environment or *experience with the concrete reality.* There is no perceptual activity without sensory experience. The attainment of a higher level of abstraction requires a corresponding broadening of experience with objective reality. In general, the broader the concept, the more abstract it is and the greater the experience needed for its formation.

The evidence indicates that there are stages in the development of meaning. The initial perceptual level is characterized by reaction on a concrete level. At this level each object is distinct, having no commonalities with any other objects. The end result is a percept. It is an impression of an object obtained solely through the senses.

> First there is sensation. . . . But, beyond the initial stages of infancy we never experience pure sensation. The present sensation is always linked with past similar sensations. The mind's awareness of this (present plus past sensations) is designated as perception. Thus, this house is like others I have seen; it has a roof, windows, doors, and so forth. Imagination and memory keep the still concrete images in our mind. This is the image or the phantasm, and at this stage it retains individual colors, shapes, and the like. Now, the active intellect, by reason of its inherent power, abstracts the essence from the image. It does this by removing all of the individual, concrete characteristics. The essence is presented to the passive (or cognitive) intellect which, in turn, gives us the concept. The idea is not this, or that house, but it is an immaterial representation of what is common to all houses (25).[3]

Perception is an intermediate step between sensation and conception. It is something more than sensation because the organism is reacting; it is not yet abstraction or conception because it always occurs in the presence of an object or thing (26, p. 101). Perception is an ordering of sensory experience on a relatively concrete and specific level; concepts are a higher and more abstract level of cognitive functioning (20, p. 142).

---

[2] *Universalia non sunt res subsistes, sed habent esse solum in singularibus* (St. Thomas, *Contra Gentiles,* I, 64). Concepts are not existing realities. They exist only in the particular.

[3] John Travers, "A Return to Sanity in Learning Theory," *Catholic Educational Review,* 61 (January, 1963) 16–25. Reprinted by permission.

The concrete becomes abstract only when the learner moves from the "here and now" to the "not here, not now." Travers (26, p. 101) notes:

> So, perception is a process by which the individual transforms the separate stimuli of the environment into an *awareness* of objects. His personal, *past* experiences merge with *this* sensation and organize them into a pattern which produces awareness. If you meet for the first time a boy, or a girl, with bright red hair, you do not react to hair, then eyes, nose, mouth, and so forth. But, because of your extensive experience with people, you respond to a *person* whose outstanding characteristic might be flaming hair.[4]

In Chapter 15 we note that attention is selective. Even though some stimuli pass the absolute threshold—the point at which we sense something—they may never reach the level of awareness, because man chooses what he wants to react to. This is what we mean by perceptual readiness.

One of the best ways of leading children to the development of concepts is to give them an opportunity to experience both examples and nonexamples of the concept under consideration. Awareness is built only through the discrimination and differentiation of stimuli. An example of a concept contains all the basic features; a nonexample contains only some or none of the essential features. If one were to teach the concept, cat, one would necessarily show the child cats of various kinds, sizes, and colors. One might also show him dogs, gradually chickens, or other animals. The child would learn to identify the individual objects, but he would also learn to discriminate one from the other. Activity programs are an outgrowth of the need for actual concrete experience.

At this level of conceptual development the emphasis is on simplicity and clarity of examples. The cats are all the domestic kind. Only later will the child be introduced to the various shadings and meanings that might be associated with the concept cat.

In developing a more general concept such as loyalty, it is necessary to present numerous examples of loyal and disloyal behavior. The child might be told about a loyal dog, but also about a disloyal servant.

Perceptual Schematism

A higher level of reaction is termed "perceptual schematism" by Scheerer (22). The term refers essentially to the internal representation in perception. On this level the incoming sensory data are grouped into their

---

[4] John F. Travers, *Learning: Analysis and Application*, p. 101 (New York: David McKay Co., Inc., 1965). By permission.

most natural Gestalt or organization. The furry little animal with a white stripe down its back is perceived as a "skunk." The configuration takes on meaning. This meaning allows the perceiver to react with the experience of sameness upon subsequent contact with another object. Skunks can vary within a certain range (their inessential characteristics may change within a prescribed limit) and the perceiver will still react thus: "Ah, another skunk." If the variants are too great in the light of the perceiver's experience, no recognition will occur. The concept includes a certain unchanging core of experience—the invariant characteristic—and encompasses all possible variations.

The meaning that follows sensation is the result of learning. Travers (26, p. 102) notes that it is doubtful that the human, once he grows beyond infancy, ever experiences pure sensation. Even the most outlandish object would evoke the reaction, "It looks like . . . ." The perceiver tends to combine this sensation with past experiences and this is exactly what is meant by perception.

Contextual Perception

The percept may have a third meaning. An object can take on meaning by being characteristically associated with other objects or experiential events. Thus, "A bat is used to hit a ball." It may also mean a placental mammal with wings. Daddy means "the person who fills my bottle at two o'clock in the morning." It has been shown that a brain-injured patient cannot name an egg until the experimenter breaks the shell. Only then will the patient peel the egg and name it. He cannot identify objects without reference to the action he directs toward them (13).

A person can be said to understand something if he knows how to use it. A person can use an idea if he has found that it works in a given situation. Here we are in the area of multiple meanings, and the context or the way in which the object is used determines the specific meaning. It is the context in which the word occurs that gives it part of its meaning. Scheerer (22) refers to this as an object's or word's "meaning sphere." The multiplicity of meaning on this level is experienced but is not acquired through abstraction proper.

Perception of Differences

Concept formation requires accurate discrimination of essential and nonessential characteristics. If we take a child to see an airplane, he will note hundreds of specific bits of data. Some of these he must ignore and some of them he must hang on to if he is to form an adequate concept of airplane. The size of the airplane, its color, and the number of seats are features that are not essential characteristics. On the other hand, there are certain characteristics that the concept of airplane includes. He will have to note that an airplane is an aircraft with fixed wings and that it is driven by a screw propeller or a rearward jet.

The child's meaning for an object may omit certain characteristics or it may include too many. Young children tend to overgeneralize. To a small child, all men are daddy and all women are mother. Errors of overgeneralization are errors in discrimination of similar objects, persons, or events. Only through experience will the child learn that one man is daddy, another his uncle, and another his grandfather. And, only with experience will the child learn that some airplanes are colored red and others blue and that color is not an essential characteristic. We have already spoken of perceptual veridicality. The sensations that are caused by the stimuli impinging on the organism determine the accuracy of one's concepts. If there is a distortion in the sensation, it is almost certain that the concept will be similarly distorted.

Abstract Concept

The next stage in perceptual development is the concept itself. The concept is actually the end result of abstraction. Abstraction isolates the essential properties and the end result might be termed an abstract concept. Scheerer (21, p. 126) provides us with a definition of an abstract concept. He writes:

> Concepts are psychologically operative when the invariant relationship between the properties of an object, an action, or an idea is grasped, and when the communality of characteristics that is invariant can be abstracted from a variety of changing aspects.[5]

The concept in a sense annuls presence in order to arrive at representation (5, p. 307). This is possible only through abstraction. A concept permits its possessor to make sorting and labelling responses that others who do not possess the concept cannot do.

Concepts are formed in three ways. They may be reactions to specific events; they may arise through the relation of one concept to another; and they may represent the creative activity of an individual. The concept expressed through the word, phlogiston, is an example of creative concept formation (1, pp. 232–233).

The development of a concept requires a distillation of the essential and invarying similarities from a series of related objects or events. To

---

[5] Martin Scheerer, "Cognitive Theory," *Handbook of Social Psychology,* Volume I, ed. by Gardner Lindzey (Reading, Mass.: Addison-Wesley Publishing Company, 1954). Reprinted by permission.

form an adequate concept of "dog" there will have taken place the activation of some (and probably several) of the receptor processes in response not only to one dog but to several kinds of dogs. Indeed, communication would be seriously jeopardized if a boy's concept of dog were based on his responses to St. Bernard dogs alone and another boy had had experience with Chihuahuas only. It is necessary, also, that there be a recognition that numerous creatures which bear fur, walk on four feet, and have pads on their feet are *not* dogs. The child gradually learns to restrict his usage of the word *dog* to those instances which are regarded as positive by the speech community. In so doing, the learner often makes false responses, either false positives as by calling a nondog a dog or false negatives as by believing that a dog is a noninstance of the concept.

In the development of a concept of the word "house," the child's first understanding of the term (or experience with it) may have been through a picture of a house in an alphabet book. From this, of course, he cannot have developed an adequate concept of the term "house." Ideally, his experience should include firsthand as well as vicarious encounters with various types of houses. His understanding of the written or spoken symbol "house" must be broadened through experience so that it includes cottages, mansions, native huts, houses made of various materials and of different colors, and a knowledge that the term implies a structure for people to live in. It also includes the realization that there are somewhat similar structures (hospitals, office buildings) which are not termed houses. His concept of "house" develops from his various experiences with the object and the term. And the impact of his culture will, of course, have an influence on his concept.

We see, then, that the development of a concept involves *abstracting* or seeing the similarities within a framework which involves dissimilarities. Piaget, as we do above, draws a distinction between perceptual and conceptual processes. He does not lump together, as the Gestaltists did, all cognitive processes. A concept keeps its character irrespective of the context or pattern into which it is put. The concepts "number" or "mile" are stable from one time to the next. Not so with perceptions. They vary from person to person and are determined by the pattern of which they are a common component.

Categorization

Finally, the child must learn to categorize. He must group his experiences into classes. Abstraction isolates the basic characteristic, and categorization applies it to more objects. The word or verbal symbol in turn is the verbal expression of a concept. Scheerer (21, p. 126) notes that:

The name for an individual object in daily life does not refer to the specific uniqueness of the object; the name signifies the object as a representative of a category—an exemplification of all the possible variations allowed for by its invariant characteristics.[6]

Travers (26, p. 96) notes that a word symbolizes a classification (tree) or a generalization (loyalty). Whether it "cloaks" or "molds" the category is unimportant. What is significant is that the word represents abstraction and that a person's use of language is an excellent clue to the level of abstraction.

Bruner (1, p. 1) suggests that to categorize is to render discriminable different things equivalent; it is to group the objects and events and people around us into classes; and it is to respond to them in terms of their class membership rather than their uniqueness.

At this stage of the development of meaning, the child may be able to use the word *cat* to refer to an even broader class of objects. At this level we are not thinking of the various kinds of domestic animals. Rather, the child's concept of cat is broadened to include lions, tigers, leopards, jaguars, cougars, lynxes, wildcats, and cheetahs, all of which belong to the cat family.

Figure 12-1 summarizes the process of the development of meaning. It illustrates how the perceiver moves from sensation to perception and more specifically from concrete percept to abstract perception, concept, and categorization.

GENERALIZATION

The process of generalization needs comment. Pavlov observed generalization in his early experiments and termed it irradiation. He found that changing the tone of the bell within a certain frequency range still led to the conditioned response. Even though conditioning is to a tone of 750 hertz (cycles per second), the dog will respond also to one of 690 and to one of 810. Here we have an instance of stimulus generalization.

Stimulus generalization and the concept of "equivalent stimuli" are the same. Equivalent stimuli are stimuli that occasion a similar response. If stimulus generalization did not occur, the child would not respond correctly to the word "cat" if it were written in capitals. On the other

[6] Martin Scheerer, "Cognitive Theory," *Handbook of Social Psychology,* Volume I, ed. by Gardner Lindzey (Reading, Mass.: Addison-Wesley Publishing Company, 1954). Reprinted by permission.

Figure 12-1

Sensation

External | Internal

Perception

Concrete ————————————————————————— Abstract

Step I	Step II	Step III	Step IV

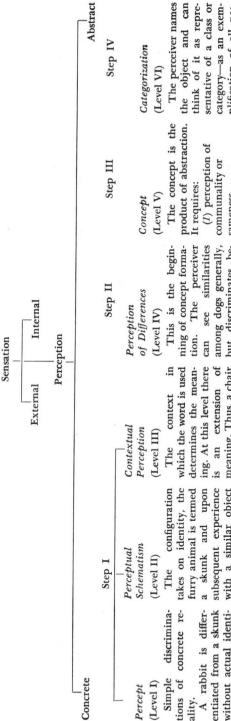

Step I

Percept
(Level I)

Simple discriminations of concrete reality.

A rabbit is differentiated from a skunk without actual identification of the object as a rabbit.

Perceptual Schematism
(Level II)

The configuration takes on identity, the furry animal is termed a skunk and upon subsequent experience with a similar object the perceiver will say, "Ah, another skunk." This stage is often confused with abstraction. A child may see similarities but doesn't think abstractly because he doesn't see the essential and invariant characteristics.

Step II

Contextual Perception
(Level III)

The context in which the word is used determines the meaning. At this level there is an extension of meaning. Thus, a chair can be used to wash the ceiling or to send a man to his death. Objects will take on new meanings dependent upon the context in which they are used.

Perception of Differences
(Level IV)

This is the beginning of concept formation. The perceiver can see similarities among dogs generally, but discriminates between collies, mongrels, rat terriers, etc. He discriminates one dog from another dog; this is more than simple discrimination of difference that occurs in Level I. Perceiver who cannot operate on this level will under- or overgeneralize.

Step III

Concept
(Level V)

The concept is the product of abstraction. It requires:

(*1*) perception of communality or sameness.

(*2*) perception of invariant characteristics.

(*3*) abstraction of invariant characteristics from a variety of changing aspects.

Step IV

Categorization
(Level VI)

The perceiver names the object and can think of it as representative of a class or category—as an exemplification of all possible variations permitted by its invariant characteristics.

hand, if the child did not discriminate the word "cat" from all other words, he would not be able to learn to read. A child who has learned to respond to the stimulus *the* with the response "the" may make the same response to words like *then, there,* and *their.* Stimulus generalization may occur because the words are quite similar.

Stimulus generalization is a genuine problem in the classroom. All teachers have experienced the situation in which the student will answer a question different from the one that was asked. The teacher might ask: Would the question that I asked have elicited the same response if I had asked it in a slightly different manner?

The error responses that occur because of faulty generalization can be eliminated through extinction. Pavlov demonstrated that when the US is omitted in the normal conditioning sequence, the CR decreases and eventually disappears. If S_1, S_2, and S_3 call forth R but the experimenter wants only S_1, to do so, he will have to associate the US with S_1, but not with S_2 or S_3. S_1, then, becomes a "discriminated stimulus," and the entire process is termed discrimination. Bugelski (2, p. 44) notes that the process of education might be termed the formation of ever finer discriminations.

Bugelski (2, p. 48) adds that generalization is a two-edged sword. On the negative side, teachers realize that learners will respond to similarities in stimuli, and, if these are undesired, they must make educational adjustments for this. Teachers confuse students by bringing up exceptions to rules, but rules with exceptions are not really rules.

On the positive side, generalization can be expected to lead to desirable behavior to similar stimulus situations. In the areas of spelling and reading, pupils can be helped if the teacher groups words that contain the same sounds. The exceptions should be given discrimination training.

In response generalization, the learner comes to associate various responses with a single stimulus. Some children respond to "saw" once with the oral "saw" and sometimes the oral "was." It becomes imperative that teachers spell out in clear detail what is required of the student. He should not be permitted to get by with rough approximations of the proper response. If he is permitted this, he will learn the approximations rather than the correct response. Bugelski (2, p. 48) notes that if a teacher pronounces a word for a pupil or permits the student to mispronounce the word without the pupil himself actually having to say the word correctly, the pupil may merely learn that the teacher sometimes corrects him.

Of interest here, in the light of the previous discussions, is the fact that *categorization is an instance of response generalization.* When the learner perceives that one verbal symbol applies to a variety of objects (the word "cat" refers to lions, tigers, wildcats, etc.) or when one object is a representative of a category (the word "cat" is an example of a class of objects), then he has made a response generalization. When he learns that a word has multiple meanings, he is making a response generalization.

A concept, as we noted above, is a generalization. The concept chair refers not only to one object of furniture but also to a whole group of objects. On the basis of his categorizations, the learner or perceiver makes additional generalizations. He observes numerous events, categorizes them, relates them to one another, and comes up with a higher order generalization. This is nothing more than the identification of relationship and perhaps a statement of proposition that relates two concepts. A generalization is nothing more than the incorporation of two or more experiences into a more comprehensive and new meaning (10, p. 58).

TECHNIQUES FOR TEACHING MEANING

Before discussing the techniques for teaching meaning, let us examine a few principles that should guide the teacher in the development of meaning. The following seem especially pertinent:

1. Each new level of meaning requires a corresponding broadening of experience with objective reality.
2. The quality of meaning is greatly influenced by the quantity and quality of previously acquired meanings and concepts. Thus the teacher must build upon the child's previous background of experience.

The teacher's major task in the development of meaning is to select the materials and experiences that will aid the child to become more discriminative and learn to generalize. Unfortunately, there is no clear-cut evidence that suggests what materials to use in the teaching of specific concepts. This leaves much to guess work and taxes the teacher's ingenuity.

The major question then is this: How can the teacher help the child to develop meaning? Generally, the approaches to the teaching of meaning are twofold: (*1*) the direct-experience approach such as through the visitation of a farm or the acting out of an activity, or (*2*) the vicarious experience approach such as through pictures, storytelling, or the use of radio. The vicarious experience approach in the classroom comes to mean: (*a*) direct vocabulary instructions; (*b*) incidental instruction of vocabulary; and (*c*) wide or extensive reading.

Chapter 7 discussed numerous activities of a direct and vicarious experience nature that are helpful in teaching meaning to kindergarten and first-grade youngsters.

However, since some third and fourth graders have not learned certain primary-level skills and since primary youngsters at times have advanced far beyond their grade level, the teacher must constantly adapt skill reading to the individual pupil's level of achievement. The so-called first-grade comprehension skill needs to be constantly maintained. Thus, the techniques discussed in Chapter 7 warrant repetition. They are:

1. Experience with the concrete object
2. Labelling
3. Learning to read pictures
4. Conversation and story telling
5. Description, riddle, rhyme, and puzzle games
6. Audiovisual aids
7. Dramatization, marionette and puppet shows, pageants, and operettas
8. Constructing and using picture dictionaries
9. Use of oral and written directions
10. Fitting objects and words into categories

Each of these techniques can be applied on upper-grade levels. For example, "Learning to Read Pictures" may be "Interpreting Charts, Graphs, and Maps" on the fourth- and fifth-grade level. "Labelling" may consist of labelling instruments in a science laboratory.

Durrell (8a) has published materials for the itermediate level designed to develop categorization skills. Entitled *Word Analysis Practice,* the materials require the pupil to read words and to classify each one under one of three suggested categories. The intermediate series consists of three sets of thirty cards each. Set one contains 720 words and is usable at low fourth-grade level; sets two and three contain 1200 words each and may be used with pupils on the fourth- to the sixth-grade level.

Studies (23,27) tend to indicate that vocabulary study is beneficial, but that pupils with average or above average ability profit more than those of below average ability. Pupils also tend to learn words better if they have an immediate need to use them. Finally, a combination of methods in teaching seems to be better than the use of any one alone. Some common methods might be meaningful dictionary work, word study in context, use of context clues, attention to multiple meanings and figurative language, study of the history and etymology of words, application of new words in oral and written language, and wide reading (15).

Let us now look at some of these more advanced meaning skills. Perhaps the first of these is the need for increased competency in the use of the context to arrive at the appropriate meaning.

Study and Analysis of the Context

The child's first reading experiences encourage him to use the verbal context in which the word occurs to decipher the meaning of the sentence. Reading teachers have always suggested that the child should look at the word, and that he should not guess; now the teacher encourages the child to see whether the word makes sense in the sentence (16). The teacher today suggests that the pupil *anticipate* and *predict* meaning. He should think along with the author. If youngsters learn to anticipate probable meaning, they also have learned a most useful means of word identification.

Skill in using the context needs constant refinement, and indeed it becomes increasingly more valuable as the pupil advances through school. Some pupils rely too much on the context. They pay little attention to the details. Their reading makes sense but sometimes it is not the meaning intended by the writer. Their counterparts are those readers who are so preoccupied with details that they read a word into the sentence that makes little or no sense.

McCullough (16) suggests that the pupil use pictures, his own experience, the verbal context, indications of comparison and contrast, the accompanying synonym, the summarizing word (the word is a summary of the ideas just presented or about to be presented), or the definition as clues to what the word means.

The pupil gradually needs to expand both the number and the quality of the meanings that he attaches to a single word. Many words, even in the "simplest" of books, have more than one meaning. Frequently only by understanding the verbal context can the pupil select the meaning intended by the writer.

Here are some simple means for teaching the importance of the context in meaningful reading.

The pupil may learn to anticipate meaning through exercises that require the addition of a single word to complete the meaning of the sentence. For example, the sentence, "The boy fell ...... the stairs," allows for little deviation in meaning. Other exercises might be: "Father bought the apples at the ...... (store, story)." "A dog is an ...... (animal, vegetable)." "There are ...... (three, tree) boxes on the table." "He is sick. Call a ...." "Pass the salt and ...." "Pamela picked up a ...... (house, hammer, harvest)." "Each boy wore a new ...... (dress, uniform, apron)."

Sometimes the exercise presents a sentence that is complete but that contains a wrong word. The pupil is asked to eliminate the wrong word and to substitute a correct one in its place. Examples of such exercises may be: "Father brought the apples at the store"; "There are tree boxes on the table"; or "Pamela picked up a flour."

An exercise like the following teaches both the usefulness of the context in apprehending the correct meaning and the fine shades of meaning that a word may have.

> Read the following sentences. The word *run* is used in each of the sentences, but it has a different meaning in each. Write the meaning of the word run in the blanks provided.
>
> 1. The boat runs between Georgia and New York. *sails between*
> 2. The two-year-old filly ran first in the Belmont Stakes. *won the race*
> 3. I ran the story back to its source. *traced*
> 4. We saw a run of fish. *school of fish*
> 5. The man had a run of bad fortune. *series of bad luck*
> 6. The brook runs by the cottage. *lies near*
> 7. He belongs to the ordinary run of people. *common kind*
> 8. He runs contrabrand between the Middle East and Europe. *smuggles*

The sentence context frequently gives the meaning of a word by either defining it or by giving a synonym for the word. For example:

> Read the following sentences. Select the proper meaning for the underlined word from those suggested to you.
>
> 1. Johnny <u>drew</u> a picture of Mary on the blackboard.
>   a. to pull or cause to follow
>   b. to attract
>   c. to represent by drawing, to delineate
>   d. to withdraw
> 2. The horse <u>drew</u> a wagon behind him loaded with garden vegetables.
>   a. to pull or cause to follow
>   b. to attract
>   c. to represent by drawing, to delineate
>   d. to withdraw
> 3. There are many <u>utensils</u> or instruments that one uses daily in a kitchen, a bakery, or on a farm.
>   a. a vessel used in a kitchen
>   b. a tool or instrument
> 4. The pupils are studying the structure of the <u>bat</u>. It is the only placental mammal that is capable of flying.
>   a. a stick or club used to hit a ball
>   b. a placental mammal
>   c. a gliderlike bomb

5. The seats upon which we were to sit were _littered_ with paper and other trash. In fact, they were absolutely filthy.
   a. to put into disorder
   b. a stretcher for carrying sick people

At the upper grade levels the pupil should learn to identify the writer's style. Shaw (24, p. 239) points out that a writer's rhetorical and grammatical contrivances characterize his writing. "Like the ice cream cone, which is both container and confection, a writer's contrivances not only support ideas, but also are digestible themselves." [7] The writer has so many peculiar characteristics that upon reading some of his work again the reader finds that he has a better conception of what the writer is trying to say. The mood of the writer colors the meaning of what is written and frequently can be identified only by reading between the lines.

The reader operates in the context of a special writer, but to get the most out of what he reads he also should become familiar with the rhetorical devices used in a poem, play, short story, essay, novel, or bibliography (24). The title, topical headings, topic sentences, graphs, and summarizing sentences are additional clues to meaning. For example, the title at the head of an article helps the reader anticipate what is to come.

Finally, the structure of the phrase, sentence, and paragraph serves as a clue to the fuller meaning of what is written.

> Rhetorical terms of coherence are also guides to reading comprehension of a paragraph. Conjunctions are common links. The correlative conjunctions (both—and, not only—but also, either—or) mark pairing of ideas. Subordinating conjunctions signal special connections, as cause-effect relationships (because, since, so that), conditions (if, unless, although), contrast (whereas, while), and time relationships (as, before, when, after). Besides pure conjunctions, certain adverbs have conjunctive impact (however, therefore, nevertheless, hence, similarly, conversely, accordingly), as have directive expressions (for example, on the other hand, in conclusion, in other words) (24, p. 243).[7]

These words and phrases have meaning only as parts of sentences or paragraphs. The sentence itself has meaning in the larger context of the paragraph.

In such a sentence as "Ed was talkative while Bill remained taciturn," (16) the sentence structure provides the parallelism and the contrast necessary for understanding the word _taciturn_.

[7] Philip Shaw, "Rhetorical Guides to Reading Comprehension," _The Reading Teacher_, 11 (April 1958) 239–243. Reprinted by permission.

Synonyms and Antonyms

The pupil reaps much benefit from exercises with the synonyms of words. Initially this exercise is oral. The teacher asks: "What word has the same meaning as *big*?" This exercise is more meaningful when the pupil uses the word in a sentence and then substitutes his suggested synonym in its place.

Matching of words with definitions is another exercise of this nature. The following exercise is an example:

	Choices
This is a piece of clothing	handkerchief
This comes out of the chimney	blanket
This is a place in which to pray	medicine
This we use to cover ourselves	smoke
This we use when we blow our noses	dress
This we use when we are sick	church

Antonyms are words opposite in meaning to certain other words. The pupil perhaps best learns meanings for words such as *fat, father, come, hot, high, up, wide, today, night, big, hate, old, back, warm, boy, long, white, yes, yesterday, happy, shut, stay, dark, after, asleep, cry, ugly, under,* and *empty* by contrasting them with their opposites. The teacher may ask the pupil to select the antonym for a given word from a list of three or four words. Thus: Warm—hot, cold, cool, chilly.

Sentences such as the following teach opposites:

1. Today the sky is bright, but yesterday it was . . . .
2. Do you like sweet or . . . . pickles?
3. Do you want to be . . . . or last in the parade?

Qualifying Words

The meaning of a sentence sometimes is dependent upon key qualifying words. Such words are: *all, always, almost, many, more, most, less, few, only,* and *none.* Additional words are *nearly, likely, probably, in all probability, true, false, some, usually, frequently, never, sometimes, little, much, great,* and *small.* The ability to interpret these words is especially helpful in taking objective tests.

The following exercises teach pupils the effect that these words have on the meaning of a sentence:

1. Provide sentences containing a qualifying word (The table was set with *many* kinds of fruit) and ask pupils to study the exact meaning of the sentence. In the sentence, "Johnny fell into deep water," how deep is deep?
2. Have pupils write pairs of sentences in which the qualifying words mean about the same thing. Let them differentiate the meaning in the two sentences. For example:
   a. (1) Johnny had a small toy.
      (2) The toy was so tiny that Johnny had difficulty playing with it.
   b. (1) Most boys like to fish.
      (2) Almost all boys like to fish.

Overworked Words and Phrases

Overworked words and phrases are words that have lost much of their meaning. Some common words are: divine, grand, great, keen, awful, nice, lovely, perfect, swell, terrible, thing, lot, fit, and wonderful (3, p. 60).

Similes and metaphors such as "shaking like a leaf," "white as snow," "I could eat a horse," or "raining cats and dogs" probably are overworked.

The following exercise will help pupils to become more discriminative in their choice of words.

Substitute a more descriptive word for the italicized word in each sentence or rewrite the sentence keeping the meaning intended.

1. The party was *divine*.
2. We had a *grand* time.
3. Isn't he *keen*?
4. She looked simply *awful*.

Analogous to overworked words, but not the same, is the use of words by youth today. Here are such words including the meaning that they are intended to convey:

big daddy ....an older person
bread ....money
tube ....television
cool ....wonderful
who rattled your cage? ......who asked for your opinion?

Homonyms

Homonyms are words that are sounded alike but that have different spellings and meanings. They frequently lead to recognition and meaning difficulties. To illustrate their difference in the early grades the teacher must use them in meaningful context. Thus, the difference between *blue* and *blew* is brought out in the following sentences:

1. The wind blew down the house.
2. Mary wore a blue dress.

Following is a list of some common homonyms:

ate—eight	hair—hare	rain—rein	vane—vein—vain
	haul—hall	rap—wrap	
base—bass	heel—heal	read—reed	wade—weighed
be—bee	here—hear	read—red	waist—waste
bear—bare	hour—our	road—rode	wait—weight
beat—beet			wave—waive
berth—birth	made—maid	sail—sale	way—weigh
blue—blew	mail—male	sea—see	week—weak
bow—bough	meet—meat	seen—scene	whole—hole
break—brake		sew—so	wood—would
buy—by	new—knew	sight—site—cite	write—right
	night—knight	some—sum	wrote—rote
course—coarse	no—know	steak—stake	
	not—knot	steal—steel	
dear—deer		sun—son	
do—dew	one—won		
	owe—oh	tail—tale	
fair—fare		their—there	
fir—fur	pain—pane	through—threw	
flee—flea	pair—pare	to—too—two	
flower—flour	peace—piece		
forth—fourth	plane—plain		
four—for	principal—principle		

Roots, Prefixes, and Suffixes

Being able to break a word into its root, prefix, and suffix is a valuable skill in developing meaning for a word. This, however, is not enough. The pupil also must know the meaning of the root, prefix, and suffix.

In teaching the pupil the structural skill here indicated the teacher must follow definite steps. He must show the pupil that most two- and three-syllable words are composed of a root, prefix, and/or suffix. He next develops meaning for the words root, prefix, and suffix.

The root is the main part of a word. It is the reservoir of meaning. The prefix is that something which is put before the main part of a word or that which is put at the beginning of a word. The word, prefix, is composed of a root and a prefix. It comes from the Latin root, *figere,* meaning to put or fix and the Latin prefix, *prae,* meaning before or at the beginning of.

The teacher should demonstrate to the pupil that prefixes change the meaning of a word, much as an adjective changes the meaning of a noun. In the sentence, "The test was very difficult," the word difficult is an adjective, and it changes the meaning of the word test. The test could have been described as easy. Prefixes work in a similar way. Circumnavigate is composed of the prefix *circum* and the root *navigare.* *Navigare* is a Latin word meaning to sail. The prefix *circum* means around, and the entire word, circumnavigate, means to sail around. The prefix *circum* thus changes the meaning of the root by indicating that in this instance *navigare* isn't just sailing, but is actually a particular type of sailing.

The suffix is another part of many two- or three-syllable words. It comes at the end of the word. It comes from the Latin words, *sub* and *figere,* meaning to add on. The suffix frequently indicates what part of speech the word is. Thus, *ly* in badly is a suffix and usually indicates that the word is an adverb. The *ion* in condition is a suffix and usually indicates that the word is a noun.

Four combinations of root, prefix, and suffix are immediately indicated:

1. Root by itself as in *stand*
2. Prefix + root as in *prefix*
3. Root + suffix as in *badly*
4. Prefix + root + suffix as in *insisting*

Finally the pupil may be taught that when two roots are combined to form a word, the word is termed a compound word.

Studies have shown that a few Latin and Greek roots are very helpful in deciphering the meanings of thousands of words. Approximately twenty prefixes account for something like 85 per cent of the prefixes used in words. There also are some key suffixes.

Here is a list of nineteen common Latin roots:

Infinitive	Meaning	Examples
agere, ago, egi, actum	to act, do, arouse, to set in motion, drive, transact, sue	agent, act, action, actuality, actual, active, actor
capere, capio, cessi, cessum	to give ground, to yield, to seize	seceded, cede, secession

Infinitive	Meaning	Examples
ducere, duco, duxi, ductum	lead	duct, conduct, ductile, abduct, seduce
facere, facio, feci, factum	to do, make	fact, factory, benefit, factor, fashion, factual
ferre, fero, tuli, (tolerabilis tollere, tolerare), latum	bear, carry	ferry, oblation, tolerate, ferret, tolerant, toleration, transfer
legere, lego, legi, lectum	choose, collect, gather, read	elect, reelect, select, lector, lecturer, legendary
mittere, mitto, misi, missum	send	emit, mission, remit, submit, admit, missive
movere, moveo, movi, motum	move, arouse, excite	move, mobility, movable, movement, mover, movie
plicare (complicare), complico, complicavi, complicatum	to fold, confuse	complicate, duplicate, plicate, complication
ponere, pono, posui, positum	put, place	pose, opposite, post, position
portare, porto, portavi, portatum	carry	comport, port, export, import, report
regere, rego, rexi, rectum	to rule, guide, direct	direct, regular, rector, rectory, rex
scribere, scribo, scripsi, scriptum	to write	script, transcript, manuscript, inscription
specere, specio, spexi, spectum	to see	specious, specter, spectre, inspect
stare, sto, steti, statum	to stand, remain, endure	statue, insist, stationary, station
tenere, teneo, tenui, tentum	hold, have	tenuto, tenet, tenor, tenaculum
tendere, tendo, tentendi, tentum (tensum)	stretch out, extend, march toward	tend, tendency, tension, tender
venire, venio, veni, ventum	to come	event, convene, convention
videre, video, vidi, visum	to see	view, vision, visible, visit

Greek roots also are helpful in arriving at the meanings of words. Here are twenty Greek roots, of which the first two are by far the most common.

graphein—grapho, gegrapha	to write, inscribe	graph, phonograph, monograph, graphic
legein, lego	to tell, to say	(see *logos*)
aer	air, atmosphere	aerodonetics, aerate
autos	self	automatic, automobile

bios	life	autobiography, biography
geos	earth, land	geologist, geometry
heteros	other	heterodox, heterogeneity
homoios	like, same	homogeneity, homogenous
logos	word, thought, study of	geology, biology
micros	small	microscope, microcosm
monos	alone, only, once, one	monochord, monochrome
philos	friend	Philadelphia, philanthropy
phone	sound, tone, voice	telephone, phonic
physis	nature	physics, physical
polys	many	polygamy, polygamist
pseudos	lie, false	pseudonym, pseudoclassic
psyche	breath, life, spirit	psychometry, psychopath
sophos	wise, clever	philosopher, philosophy
telos	end	telephone, telegraph, television
tele	far	

The pupil will learn to use roots in figuring out the meaning of words through an exercise similar to the following.

> Here is a list of nine roots: *act* (to act), *capt* (to seize), *duct* (to lead), *mov* (to move), *port* (to carry), *script* (to write), *vis* (to see), *graph* (to write), and *auto* (by itself). Look now at the series of words below and identify the root that is used in each of the three words. Write the meaning of each of the words, using the dictionary when necessary.
>
> 1. active, actor, action ————— (*act*)
>   a. quality of being active, busy, energetic.
>   b. one who acts, a doer.
>   c. an act, the process of acting.
> 2. captor, captive, captured ————
> 3. abduct, ductile, deduct ————
> 4. movable, movement, mover ————
> 5. export, import, report ————
> 6. transcript, inscription, manuscript ————
> 7. visual, vision, visible ————
> 8. monograph, biography, graphic ————
> 9. automobile, automatic, autobiography ————

Twenty prefixes that are used rather frequently follow.

ab, a	away from, from	*ad, a, ap, at*	to, toward
be	by	*com, co, cor,*	with
de	from	*con, col*	
epi	upon	*dis, di*	apart
in, en, im, em	in, into	*ex, e*	out of
inter	between	*in, ir, il*	not
non	not	*mis*	wrong
pre	before	*ob, op, of*	against
re	back	*pro*	in front of
trans	across	*sub*	under
		un	not

Of less importance are:

ante	before	*circum*	around
contra	against	*intra, intre*	inside, within
per	through	*post*	after
amphi (ambi)	around, on	*super*	above
	both sides	*anti*	against
dia	through	*peri*	around
syn	together		

One of the best ways of helping the student to increase his vocabulary is to run the root word through the prefix-assembly line.

intra		ad
inter		ab
in (not)		mis
in		non
ex		ob
epi		per
dis	*Root*	peri
dia	*Word*	post
de	*"Port"*	pre
contra		pro
com		re
circum		sub
be		super
anti		syn
ante		trans
amphi		un

Running the root word *port* through this sequence suggests the following words: comport, deport, export, import, report, transport, and support.

Another exercise requires the pupil to work out the meaning of a word when the prefix and its meaning are given. Thus:

	Prefix	Meaning of Prefix	Meaning of Word
transport	trans	across	. . . .
deduct	de	from, away from	. . . .
import	in	into	. . . .
subscript	sub	under	. . . .
invisible	in	not	. . . .
inactive	in	not	. . . .
unable	un	not	. . . .
adduce	ad	to, toward	. . . .
compose	com	with	. . . .
export	ex	out of	. . . .

A third exercise requires the pupil to identify the word when the meaning and the prefix are given. Thus:

1. to send out of the country (ex) ———— export
2. to send into the country (in) ————
3. to turn a pupil away from school (ex) ————

There also are many suffixes that are helpful in working out the meanings of words. The following are common:

able, ible	capable of, worthy	durable, credible
age	act or state of	bondage, dotage
acy	quality of	lunacy, piracy
al, eal, ial	on account of, related to	judicial, terminal
ance, ence, ancy, ency	act or fact of doing, quality, state of	violence, temperance
ant	quality of one who	reliant, truant
ar, er, or	agent	scholar, author
dom	state, condition, fact of being	wisdom, kingdom
en	made of, to make	woolen, strengthen
eur	one who	amateur
ful	full of	graceful, blissful
fy	to make	falsify
ible, ile	capable of being	legible, docile
ier	one who	carrier
ic, ac	like, made of	maniac, metallic
ism	fact of being	barbarism
ity, ty	state of	unity, ability
ize	to put to, to make	memorize, modernize
less	without	motionless
let, et	small	cornet, hamlet
ly	like, characteristic	ably
ment	state or quality or act of doing	accomplishment
ness	state of	blindness

ous, ious, eous	abounding in, full of	joyous, courteous
tion, sion, xion	action, state of being, result	condition, tension
ty	quality or state of	liberty
ward	toward	southward

An exercise like the following develops the pupil's knowledge of the suffixes.

Using the list of suffixes and the meanings provided, select the word that says the same thing as the <u>underlined words</u> in each of the following sentences.

1. The dog was <u>watching</u> the child carefully lest he wander onto the street.
    a. watchful
    b. watcher
2. The sky was <u>without a cloud.</u>
    a. cloudless
    b. cloudy
3. The man <u>did not move a muscle.</u> He waited for the judge's verdict.
    a. movable
    b. motionless
4. Are you the man who <u>will help me</u> with this job?
    a. helpful
    b. helper
5. The United States is constantly forced to <u>bring</u> its armed forces up to modern standards.
    a. modern
    b. modernize

Programmed learning is an effective aid in teaching structural skills. The following is an example:

Most two- and three-syllable words are composed of a root, prefix and/or suffix: thus inscription is composed of in (prefix), script (root), and ion (suffix). The root *script* (meaning writing) gives the essential meaning of the word; the prefix *in* modifies or changes the basic root meaning and indicates that the writing is upon something; and the suffix *ion* indicates the part of speech of the word. Here, the word is a noun.

Read the items on the right side of the page and try to answer the question. All answers are either completions or a choice of one of three possibilities. Then slide the piece of cardboard on the left down the page, one question at a time. The correct answer will be shown.

1. One-syllable words contain only a (a) prefix (b) root (c) suffix

1. root

2. The _____ is that part which is written before the root.

2. prefix

3. The prefix changes the _____ of the root word.

3. meaning

4. The prefix *in* may mean *not*. The meaning of the word inactive then is _____.

4. not active

5. The prefix *in* may also mean *in* or *into*. In the sentence "The army will induct ten men," the meaning of the word *induct is* (a) not to lead (b) to take into (c) not to take.

5. take into

6. The prefix, *in*, meaning *not*, may be written as *in, im, ir,* or *il*. The meaning of *il*legible is then _____.

6. not legible

7. The meaning of *ir*religious is _____.

7. not religious

8. The meaning of *im*material is _____.

8. not material

9. The various forms that *in* takes to say *not* are _____, _____, _____, and _____.

9. im, in, il, ir

10. The prefix, *in*, meaning *in* or *into*, may be written as *en, im,* or *em*. The meaning of *en*chained in the sentence "The man was enchained" is the man was put _____.

10. in chains

11. The meaning of enclose is to close or hem _____.

11. in

12. The meaning of immigrate is to _____.

12. migrate into

Compound Words

The pupil also must learn that sometimes root and root are combined to form compound words. Some of these keep the basic meaning of each root; others have a completely new meaning. We discussed the problems and techniques of teaching compounds in Chapter 10.

Figurative and Idiomatic Expressions

We already have indicated that numerous idiomatic expressions also add to the reader's predicament. We speak (8, p. 254) of "facing the music," "leaving no stone unturned," or "breaking the ice with someone." We suggest that someone's "hands were tied" or that he is "cutting the ground from under someone." We speak of a "Jack-of-all-trades," a "devil-may-care" attitude, and of someone being "penny-wise-and-pound-foolish." We speak of George Washington as the "father of our country"; we are as cozy as a "bug in a rug"; the wind "whistles"; and the rain "patters"; someone jumps as if "he had been shot" or runs out of the door "like a shot." A bill is thrown into the legislative hopper; a candidate sweeps the field; the United States is a melting pot; and someone almost dies laughing (3). Embler (9) lists numerous similar metaphors: to be down-and-out; to be looked down upon; to be at the bottom of the heap; high living; ladder to success; social climber; too keyed up; to settle down; down to earth; going to the root of the matter; big wheel; great guy; soft drink; hot-headed; cold-hearted; be in hot water; frozen with fear; square meal; dead pan; kiss of death; to be out of line; open minded; and heavy heart.

Groesbeck (12, p. 75), in an analysis of four third-grade readers, *Looking Ahead* and *Climbing Higher* by Houghton Mifflin Company and *Finding New Neighbors* and *Friends Far and Near* by Ginn & Company, found that these contained 424 figurative expressions. Two fourth-grade readers (*High Roads* by Houghton Mifflin Company and *Roads to Everywhere* by Ginn & Company) contained 845 figurative expressions. The fifth-grade readers contained an even greater number.

Obviously, the elementary pupil has a real need to master figurative reading skills. Unfortunately, most children interpret expressions literally. They seem to be unconscious of both the figurative use of language and of their own inaccuracies in interpretation (12).

Figurative language differs from the literal or standard construction; figures of speech are the various types of departures from the literal form. Table 12-1 lists the major figures of speech.

Here are some sentences taken chiefly from Groesbeck (8)[8] which illustrate the various figures of speech:

1. George Washington was the *Father of our country*. (metaphor)
2. I laughed until I thought *I would die*. (hyperbole)

[8] Reprinted by permission of the author.

TABLE 12-1   Figures of Speech

Figures of Resemblance	Figures of Contrast and Satire	Others
Allegory	Antithesis	
Onomatopoeia	Epigram	Hyperbole
Personification	Irony	Euphemism
Metaphor	Apostrophe	Synecdoche
Simile		
Metonomy		

An *allegory* is the prolonged metaphor: eg. *Pilgrim's Progress.*
Onomatopoeia is the use of words whose sounds suggest the meaning.
A *metaphor* is simply an analogy or an expression of comparison: unlike the simile, the metaphor does not use *as* or *like* (You're a clumsy ox.).
Personification is the endowment of an inanimate object or abstract idea with personal attributes.
A *simile* compares two objects or actions and usually joins them with *as* or *like*: for example: My car goes like the wind.
Antithesis is the contrasting of ideas.
An *epigram* is a short, terse, satirical, or witty statement.
Metonomy is the use of one word for the other, the first word being suggestive of the other: for example: The woman keeps a good table.
An *hyperbole* is an exaggeration; *euphemism* is the substitution of an inoffensive expression for one that is unpleasant; *apostrophe* is the addressing of the living as dead or the absent as present; and *synecdoche* is the use of the part for the whole.

3. He jumped *as if he had been shot from a cannon.* (hyperbole)
4. I was just *tickled to death.* (hyperbole)
5. She was *as happy as a lark.* (simile)
6. She turned *white as snow* at the news. (simile)
7. He raced *like lightning* down the street. (simile)
8. Her face turned as *red as a beet.* (simile)
9. The summer months sure *fly by.* (personification)
10. He was so angry he was *boiling.* (hyperbole)
11. Her eyes *sparkled like stars.* (simile)
12. The squirrel *froze* in its tracks. (metaphor)
13. The floods *clapped their hands.* (personification)
14. Long *fingers* of early sunlight came through the trees. (metaphor)
15. I came within sight of the *forks of the road.* (metaphor)
16. "Zzzinggg! Yowww!" howled the saw. (onomatopoeia and personification)
17. Neighbors from *near and far* gathered there. (antithesis)
18. That's a *fine way to act* when company is here! (irony)
19. The moon *looked* through a clear bit of sky. (personification)
20. *Arise dead sons* of the land and sweep the enemy from our shores. (apostrophe)
21. The *pen* is mightier than the sword. (metonomy)

22. She *gave her hand* in marriage. (synecdoche)
23. He didn't *raise a finger.* (synecdoche)

The pupil may be taught figurative reading skills with exercises similar to the test questions in the *Figurative Language Matching Test* (12). The following items are taken from this test.[9] The pupil is required to pick from the three choices the one that best explains the underlined words in the context of the sentence.

Item   1, Grade 3.   They had so much fun playing that the <u>minutes</u> flew by.
a. Minutes can fly like birds.
b. Time went very fast.
c. The minutes were riding on an airplane.

Item 23, Grade 3.   He <u>raced like lightning</u> down the track.
a. He was frightened by the lightning.
b. He ran fast down the track.
c. He tried to run faster than the lightning.

Item   4, Grade 4.   Sara <u>stood glued</u> to the ground.
a. She did not move.
b. She stepped in some glue.
c. Her feet were fastened tightly to the ground.

Item   8, Grade 5.   Minneapolis and St. Paul are <u>twin cities.</u>
a. They look very much alike.
b. Many twins live in these cities.
c. They grew up side by side.

Item 23, Grade 5.   We <u>hung on by the skin of our teeth.</u>
a. We hung on to the skin of our teeth.
b. Our teeth were hanging by the skin.
c. We just barely hung on.

Other exercises require the pupil:

1. To read poetry or prose and to underline the figure of speech.
2. To indicate what type of figure of speech it is.
3. To complete statements like the following: "I'm hungry enough to eat a . . . ."

[9] Reprinted by permission of the author.

Exercises requiring the pupil to complete similes are especially helpful (19, p. 153). For example:

black as	clear as . . . .
wise as	sober as . . . .
white as	hungry as . . . .
busy as	sly as . . . .
quick as	happy as . . . .

Perhaps, the meaning of figurative language can be best illustrated by pictures. Look at the samples on p. 393. In each instance the pupil is asked to check the picture that best gives the meaning of the sentence.

Developing Skill in Using Punctuation Marks as Clues to Meaning

Punctuation frequently is looked upon merely as a discipline in writing rather than as a help in reading (6). Yet, the writer punctuates not for himself but for his reader. Punctuation is not only a set of rules to be learned but rather a means to facilitate the grasp of meaning.

Punctuation (11) replaces the intonation pattern in speech—the pauses, pitch, and stress. Intonation in speech is used to convey surprise, anger, or satire; it also indicates whether the utterance makes a statement, gives a command, or asks a question. In written language the comma and semicolon indicate a pause. The comma is used also to set off a non-restrictive clause, to note a series, and to set off an appositive. The period is used to end a statement; the question mark, to end a question; and the exclamation mark, to end a command. The question mark indicates that in speech there would be a sharp rise in voice and then a drop back to the normal level. The colon indicates that something additional is about to be written.

Here are a few exercises that teach the skill of reading punctuation:

1. a. *Mary has a kitten.*
   b. *Mary has a kitten?*
   This teaches the difference between a sentence that tells and one that asks. The only different elements in the two sentences are the question mark and the period.

2. a. *The school, kitchen, cafeteria, and auditorium are offbounds during regular school hours.*
   b. *The school kitchen, cafeteria, and auditorium are offbounds during regular school hours.*

1. Boats were dancing up and down on the waves.

A   B   A ____
               B ____

2. Another Indian bit the dust.

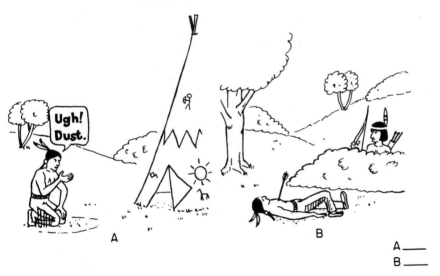

A   B   A ____
               B ____

3. The ship plows the sea.*

A   B   A ____
               B ____

* The sentences and illustrations are from Groesbeck (12) and are used with her permission.

The comma after the word, school, in sentence *a* falsifies the intended meaning.

3. *a. Will you send me a catalog?*
   b. Will you send me a catalog.

Sentence *a* asks a question; sentence *b* is a polite request disguised as a question and thus is followed by a period.

Study of the Dictionary, Text Glossaries, and Word Lists

Glossaries become important as soon as children engage in any type of content-area reading. The teacher discusses the new words that will be met in today's lesson. He identifies the word through its visual form, its pronunciation, accent, and meaning. The discussion is completed when the word is met in its contextual setting. In this way teacher and pupil develop their own glossary.

Although the pupil has learned to use the context and other clues to decipher the meaning of words, he sometimes must go to the dictionary. In the intermediate years the dictionary becomes a very useful tool. To be able to use it correctly, the pupil needs:

1. to develop alphabetization skills. He should be able to arrange words in alphabetical order according to the first, the first two, and the first three letters.
2. to understand guide words.
3. to understand dictionary symbols: the breve, the macron, the circumflex, the tilde, etc.
4. to use the dictionary to work out the pronunciation of words, to help him in his spelling, and to identify the accent of words, the derivation of words, and the part of speech that the word is.
5. to use the dictionary to learn the various meanings of words.

Simple exercises designed to teach alphabetization are (3, 69–71):

a. Put the following letters into alphabetical order:
   1. b, k, q, r, w, c, a.
   2. c, r, l, m, y, z, f.

b. Write in the spaces provided the letter that immediately precedes and follows the one given:
   1. _____ k _____   3. _____ g _____
   2. _____ r _____   4. _____ f _____

c. Check as true or false each of the following statements:
   1. M comes before *l*:   True_____ False_____
   2. R comes after *q*:   True_____ False_____

d. Alphabetize the following:

speech	cook
analogy	flower
root	material
nature	derby

This exercise requires simple alphabetization according to the first letter. The next exercise requires the pupil to go to the second letter.

e. Alphabetize the following:

cook	chunk	out
careful	city	

The pupil also needs to learn to analyze the definitions given in a dictionary. A good definition puts something into a class of things and then differentiates that something from all other members of that class. Thus the word rocket is defined as a firework (this is the class concept) that consists of a case filled with combustible material and that is fastened to a guiding stick (these are the aspects that differentiate it from other fireworks).

An exercise requiring the pupil to look up the word in the dictionary and to note both its class aspects and its *differentia* is helpful in teaching the dictionary as a device for broadening meaning. Thus:

Term	Class	Differentia
raccoon		
buffalo		
porcupine		
bronco		
coyote		

Another exercise requires the pupil to associate the meaning of an underlined word in a sentence with possible meanings of that word. Thus:

LaCrosse is the county seat of Rush County.

a. way of sitting
b. the thing on which one sits
c. a center of government
d. the buttocks

Study of Word Origins and Change

Numerous other vocabulary exercises help to enlarge the vocabulary and broaden meanings. The most common are: a study of word origins; study of the new terms recently added to the language; exploration of the encyclopedia; and the study of word lists.

A recent article by Warren (28) has outlined a program for leading the pupil beyond the simple fact that words mean something. It is a program designed to familiarize the pupil with the nature, origin, and growth of words.

Warren recommends that we *begin with the origin of surnames*. For example, names like Baker, Butler, Binder, Bishop, Cook, Brewer, Dechant, Dreher, Engel, Geist, Guard, Hunter, King, Miner, Miller, Pfeifer, Rider, Sander, Schuchman, Schumacher, Shearer, Skinner, Smith, Spicer, Taylor, Teller, Walker, and Weaver identify occupations.

Other surnames represent objects: for example, Ball, Bell; some surnames identify certain characteristics of an object or person: thus, Belle, Breit, Fair, Good; some identify colors: Black, Braun, Brown, Gray, Green, Roth, Schwartz (Schwartzkopf), and White; and finally, some are animal names: thus, Beaver, Bee, Bird, Crow, or Ochs.

The teacher also may find it useful to familiarize the student with the history and origins of the names of streets, parks, rivers, countries, and states. Each of them has a history.

The *second step* in studying word origins may be an analysis of the foreign origin of many words. The Dutch, the French, the Germans, and the Italians have given us many words. Let us list just a few: Italian (soprano, piccolo, piano, contralto); French (carburetor, chauffeur, coupe, beau, chateau, trousseau, chamois, machine, boudoir, bouquet, barrage, croquet, sachet, ballet); and German (kindergarten, waltz, sauerkraut, wiener). Words of Latin and Greek origin are so numerous that a list is not necessary.

A *third phase* of the study of origins is an analysis of how words disappear, change, or appear. Language is man's tool and he has always used it for his convenience. He has discarded certain words, added others, and frequently has associated new meanings with old words.

The last 25 years have witnessed a lot of language activity. Numerous new words have been coined (14,17,28). Here are just a few:

ack-ack	amtrac	audiophile	babushka
bamboo curtain	bazooka	beachhead	bebop
bellyland	big wheel	blitz	boogie-woogie
brainwashing	calypso	cloverleaf	crew cut
de-icer	deltiology	discophile	emcee
freeway	genocide	ghetto	goldbrick
grassroots	hardtop	Hi Fi	intercom
junkie	liquidate	megaton	me-too-ism
Molotov cocktail	to needle	oscar	pedal pushers
ponytail	poodle cut	prefab	rabbit ears
rev	rhubarb	satellite	schmoe
snow (television)	spelunker	split-level house	supermarket

Warren (28) notes that the pupil needs to look upon good English as up-to-date English. The dictionary thus is not the ultimate authority. It lists acceptable and unacceptable words (illit., arch., and obs.) People decide what is correct.

Study of Technical Vocabularies

Finally, the pupil should become familiar with the technical vocabularies of the content areas. Only by knowing them can the pupil read with meaning in those areas.

A SUMMARY OF TECHNIQUES FOR IMPROVING VOCABULARY

The intermediate-grade pupil needs to have before him a constant reminder and summary of the techniques useful in building a vocabulary. A summary chart containing some of the following principles or techniques may be hung in the classroom.

How to Improve Your Vocabulary

1. Broaden your experiences. Be alert for new ideas and always learn to describe them in clean terminology. Read and discuss. Listen and write!
2. Develop a regular and systematic method of studying words.
3. Keep a vocabulary notebook, or 3 x 5 cards, in which you write the words you want to master. Include the pronunciation and meanings of the word.
4. Learn first the common meaning of the word. Gradually expand your knowledge to include special meanings.
5. Study the word in its context.
6. Associate the word with a mental picture.
7. Break the word into its basic elements—the root, prefix, and suffix. In the case of a compound word break it into its simple words.
8. Associate the root word with its synonyms (words with similar meanings) and antonyms (words with opposite meanings).
9. Study carefully those words that are pronounced alike, but that have different spellings. Such words are called homonyms. Examples of these words are: f-a-r-e–f-a-i-r.
10. Use the new words in writing and in speech.
11. Develop an interest in the origin of words.

12. Introduce yourself to the new words in the language: for example: boycott, carpool, de-icer, or three-D.

13. Learn the fine shades of meanings of words. Instead of the word little, you may at times wish to use small, minute, microscopic, puny, tiny, petty, dwarfed, stunted, diminutive, Liliputian, short, or miniature.

14. Finally, study the technical vocabulary of your subject matter.

SUMMARY

To be a reader the child must be able to identify words and to associate some meaning with them. Unfortunately, he cannot do this unless he has had the opportunity to develop meaning. Generally, meaning is acquired through some form of direct or vicarious experience. Perhaps our emphasis on learning from experience is too great. We might emphasize more learning from instruction and this has been the intent of this chapter.

Ideas and experiences can be expressed in many ways. Each writer has his own modes of expression. Because of this the teacher must develop in children the ability to gather meaning from the context and to decipher the author's rhetorical and grammatical contrivances.

QUESTIONS FOR DISCUSSION

1. What are some of the hindrances to the easy development of meanings for words?
2. What are the advantages of meaningful learning?
3. What is conceptualization?
4. Describe the characteristic pattern in the development of meanings or concepts.
5. Distinguish the three meanings for percept.
6. What are some appropriate techniques for teaching meaning at the kindergarten level?
7. What are some additional appropriate techniques for teaching meaning at the primary and intermediate levels?
8. Discuss and illustrate the various ways that the context may be used to infer the meaning of a word.
9. Discuss the value of film-readers.
10. Discuss ways of developing meaning for figurative expressions.
11. What dictionary skills should the pupil develop in the intermediate years?

12. What is meant by the "class" and "differentia" aspects of a definition? Illustrate your answer.
13. Discuss:
    a. Facility in conceptualization is a function of previous experience in concept formation. The progression in concept formation is from the simple to the complex; from diffuse to differentiated; from egocentric to objective; from specific to general; and from inconsistent to consistent.
    b. Concepts are possible only when the pupil has had experience with the actual phenomena that are to be conceptualized.
    c. Concepts are formed when the individual perceives the communality of characteristics among a variety of changing aspects. He perceives likenesses and differences.

Advancing the Pupil's Comprehension Skills

chapter 13

The goal of all reading is the comprehension of meaning. The *initial* step in this process (which we discussed in the previous chapter) is the association of an experience with a given symbol. This is absolutely necessary, but it is the most elemental form of comprehension. Complete meaning is not conveyed by a single word. The good reader learns to interpret words in their contextual setting. He comprehends words as parts of sentences, sentences as parts of paragraphs, and paragraphs as parts of stories.

Meaningful reading includes not only a literal interpretation of an author's words, but also an interpretation of his mood, tone, feeling, and attitude. The reader must comprehend the implied meanings and prejudices of the writer. He must recognize summary statements, make inferences and applications, and see the broader implications of a passage. He must familiarize himself with the time and place in which the words were written. He must use the periods, commas, quotation marks, and questions as aids to interpretation.

Too often we involve the pupil in the retrieval of the trivial factual data of a story (17). Comprehension questions asked over a story often are directed at literal comprehension rather than at getting broad understandings. The pupil quickly learns to parrot back an endless recollection of trivia. The purpose of this chapter then is to help teachers to instruct the pupil to look for intricate relationships, implications, subtle meanings, conjectures, evaluations, and inferences.

400

COMPREHENSION SKILLS

Comprehension involves a complex of abilities. The good comprehender possesses the ability to:

1. associate experiences and meaning with the graphic symbol.
2. react to the sensory images (visual, auditory, kinesthetic, taste, smell) suggested by words.
3. interpret verbal connotations and denotations.
4. understand words in context and to select the meaning that fits the context.
5. give meaning to units of increasing size: the phrase, clause, sentence, paragraph, and whole selection.
6. detect and understand the main ideas.
7. recognize significant details.
8. interpret the organization.
9. answer questions about a printed passage.
10. follow directions.
11. perceive relationships: part-whole; cause-effect; general-specific; place, sequence, size, and time.
12. interpret figurative expressions.
13. make inferences and draw conclusions, supply implied details, and evaluate what is read.
14. identify and evaluate character traits, reactions, and motives.
15. anticipate outcomes.
16. recognize and understand the writer's purpose.
17. recognize literary and semantic devices and identify the tone, mood, and intent or purpose of the writer.
18. determine whether the text affirms, denies, or fails to express an opinion about a supposed fact or condition.
19. identify the antecedents of such words as *who, some,* or *they.*
20. retain ideas.
21. apply ideas and integrate them with one's past experience.

This chapter, being intended to help the pupil to move from elemental comprehension to the higher-level skills mentioned above, describes the development of comprehension skills, location skills, and ability to read charts, maps, and graphs.

DEVELOPING COMPREHENSION SKILLS

Of major importance for interpretative reading is a purpose for reading. The purposeful reader is an interested reader. If the pupil is to understand what he is reading, he must know why he is reading. He must know whether to read for information, to solve a problem, to follow directions, to be entertained, to obtain details, to draw a conclusion, to verify a statement, to summarize, or to criticize. As already mentioned, learning to comprehend involves a complex of skills. In the previous chapter the first of these skills was discussed. Let us add a few words here about the significance of word meaning.

Word Meaning

Studies generally indicate that vocabulary is highly related to comprehension. Vineyard and Massey (49) found that even when intelligence is held constant there still is a sufficiently high relationship between comprehension and vocabulary proficiency to justify attempts to improve comprehension through vocabulary training. To comprehend, the pupil must have a knowledge of word meanings and be able to select the correct meaning from the context (7).

Fortunately, it appears that children have a far greater knowledge of the meaning of words than we usually credit to them. First graders generally have a speaking vocabulary of over 2500 words (39) and possibly a recognition vocabulary of over 20,000 words (33,38). Certainly, no teacher ever taught a child even most of the words that he knows.

Certain principles should guide the teacher in the development of word meanings (11).

1. *Most words have more than one meaning.* Generally, the more frequently a word is used, the more meanings it tends to have.
2. *The specific meaning elicited by a word is a function of the context in which the word occurs.* This is not only the verbal context but also the cultural and structural context.
3. *The number of meanings actually elicited by a word depends on the number and quality of experiences that the reader has associated with the word.*
4. *The pupil has numerous means at his disposal for developing word meanings.* These were discussed in Chapters 7 and 12. He may use the context. The word may be explained to him by giving a synonym, by classifying the word, and by pointing out differences and similarities. Or, the meaning of the word may be illustrated through activities, picture clues, structural analysis, and the dictionary.

Perhaps, we have not paid enough attention to the sense appeal of words. Words make the reader hear, see, taste, smell, and touch. The following words are examples:

Touch (feeling)	Sight	Sound	Taste	Smell
cold	green	mellow	sweet	fresh
warm	rippled	bang	sour	pungent
hot	spotted	crash	bitter	stuffy
rough	glistening	thud	salty	fragrant
bumpy	ruffle	bellow		choking

The underlined words in the following sentences are examples of words that appeal to the senses and that encourage meaningful reading.

1. "Icicles hanging from cabin roofs dripped continuously, and the snow beneath was peppered with holes where the drops of water fell in the softening snow." [1]
2. "The sap was watery thin and sweet and icy cold." [1]
3. "Even though spring was on the way, the fire felt good in the snapping, stinging cold of an early morning in the woods." [1]

Phrase Meaning

Phrase reading is not synonymous with word reading. A phrase is more than the sum of the individual words that it contains. The meaning of phrases like "to spin a yarn," "to throw away one's money," or "to pitch a tent" cannot be ciphered from individual words. In the previous chapter we gave numerous examples of similar idiomatic and figurative phraseology.

In developing the pupil's phrase-reading skill an exercise like the following is useful:

Phrase	Synonym
1. big wheel	
2. great guy	
3. soft drink	
4. hot-headed	
5. cold-hearted	

Sentence Meaning

In Chapter 8 we noted the importance of the sentence as the basic unit of meaning. Meaningful reading implies an understanding and an interpretation of language patterns. The full meaning of a sentence de-

[1] Mabel O'Donnell, *Singing Wheels, The Alice and Jerry Basic Readers.* "Spring's in the Air," p. 342. Copyright © 1957, 1954, 1947, 1940 by Harper & Row, Publishers; reprinted by permission of the publisher.

pends on the punctuation, the word order, the grammatical inflections signaling tense, number, and possession, and on such key words as *because* or *nevertheless*. Until the reader translates correctly the printed text into the intonation pattern of the writer, he may not be getting the meaning intended.

Reading materials usually do not come in single word or phrase units. The meaning of a sentence is not obtained by piling up, as it were, the meanings of individual words. The pupil must learn to master the skills of relating the various words that form a meaningful sequence in a sentence. Unfortunately the dynamics of converting single word meanings into the total thought of a sentence or paragraph has not been sufficiently investigated.

The elementary pupil must learn that all sentences have a "who" or "what" and often answer the questions: "Where?," "When?," "Why?," and "How?." The reader may realistically be described as a news reporter. The good reporter answers the above questions in his story and the good reader identifies the answers in print.

The following sample exercises taken from the *Read and Listen Workbook* (2, p. 33)[2] teach the pupil to look for answers to who, what, when, where, and how in his reading:

> **Read the sentences below. Then answer the questions that follow in the blanks provided.**
>
> **1. Late last night a burglar entered the home of Adam Mullins at 22 Clay Street apparently to steal several valuable paintings.**
>   Who or what?
>   What happened?
>   Where?
>   When?
>   Why?
> **2. A large oak tree was blown down by the wind across Sardis Street during the storm last week.**
>   Who or what?
>   What happened?
>   Where?
>   When?
>   How?

Sentences are parts of paragraphs receiving both their full meaning from the context in which they occur and giving meaning to the sen-

[2] Copyright 1961 by Educational Developmental Laboratories; reprinted by permission.

tences that surround them. Thus, some sentences are introductory or lead-in sentences; some are transitional sentences; and some are concluding sentences. An exercise similar to the following will teach the pupil to identify the type of sentence being used and to read for implied meaning:

Select from the three choices (I, T, C) the one that best describes each of the following sentences.

I—Introductory Sentence
T—Transitional Sentence
C—Concluding Sentence

1. There are three chief reasons for studying government.
2. Finally, democracy is based upon the acceptance of these responsibilities.
3. In addition to knowledge and skills there must be the willingness to work with one's talents.

Paragraph Meaning

Paragraphs are basically a series of sentences that give one basic idea. All the sentences are written in such a way that they relate to one another.

The following exercises present ways of teaching paragraph interpretation:

1. *Have pupils select from a series of sentences the one that doesn't stay on the topic.*

    It was the last of the seventh. The Mexican juniors were about to bring home the Little League baseball championship. It was ten degrees below zero in Canada. The crowd was on its feet eagerly waiting for the final pitch of the game.

2. *Have pupils select the topic sentence or the sentences which best summarize the main idea of a paragraph.*

    The western Indian tribes feared Kit, but they respected him. They knew his word was good. They knew that once he had given his word he would keep it. Although he spent his life fighting them, the Indians knew they would find him fair in his dealings with them.[3]

3. *Have pupils identify the technique that the writer is using to get his point across. Is he piling up details? Does he open with a*

generalization and then go on to list supporting details? Does he use repetition or contrast to get his point across? Does he use a chronological sequence?

1. *Piling Up Details?*

   Kit Carson was a great scout and Indian fighter. He was also an explorer, a hunter, and a trapper. His real name was Christopher Carson, but he became famous as Kit Carson.[3]

2. *Chronological Sequence:*

   'I am twenty years old,' said Kit. 'For three years I have been traveling the plains. I went with a wagon train from Missouri to Santa Fe. I lived there for a while. Then I went with a train to El Paso and back.'[3]

Reading the Context

Although contextual reading skills have been discussed in previous chapters, a few comments seem in place.

The development of the contextual reading skill begins in the kindergarten. The teacher reads a short anecdote and lets the pupil predict the ending. Proficiency here requires careful reading, the ability to hold in mind what one has read, and to make certain inferences.

Context offers the reader many types of clues to word, sentence, and paragraph meaning. It may provide a definition of a word, may relate it to previous experiences, may associate it with a whole word whose meaning is known, may provide a synonym, and it may indicate the mood and the tone that the writer attaches to the word.

Reading for the Main Idea

The aim of this chapter is to help the child to bring maximum meaning to the printed page. The chapter on speech development pointed out the need of helping the pupil to state the main idea. In teaching listening emphasis is on the importance of listening for the main idea. The reader also must learn *to read for the main idea.*

The ability to identify the main idea is necessary for interpretation and understanding of what is written. It is based on an accurate comprehension of the word, the phrase, and the sentence. All the other interpretative reading skills are secondary. Children who do not get the main idea cannot identify the theme of a paragraph, do not understand the implied meanings, and usually cannot organize or summarize what they have read.

[3] Frank L. Beals, *Kit Carson*, American Adventure Series, p. 10. Copyright 1960, 1941 by Harper & Row, Publishers; reprinted by permission of the publishers.

Dawson and Bamman (9, pp. 178–179)[4] give the following list of suggestions in order of difficulty for helping the child to find the main idea:

1. Read a short selection and select the best title, from several listed for the selection.
2. Read a short selection and give it a title, in the child's own words.
3. Read the title of a chapter and attempt to predict what the author is going to say.
4. Read the introduction of a chapter and note carefully just what the author has outlined.
5. Read the summary of a chapter and tell, in a simple sentence, what the chapter covered.
6. Read a paragraph and reduce it to a simple sentence, by paraphrasing the author.
7. Rapidly skim the titles and the subheads of a selection and attempt to list details which will give a general impression of the entire selection.
8. Read the first and last sentences of an entire selection.
9. Turn each subhead or subtitle into a question. The answer to that question will be the main idea of the paragraph or paragraphs.
10. Give the children a newspaper and present them with a clearly stated problem. Ask them to skim rapidly for a solution to that problem. In the beginning, it is best to confine the exercise to a single selection from the newspaper.

The following exercises illustrate how some of these suggestions may be put into practice:

1. *Select the Best Title*
   It was a summer's day late in the 1870's. High in the southern sky the hot noonday sun blazed down upon ripening grainfields and far-reaching stretches of unbroken prairie. Not a breeze rippled the prairie grasses! Not a birdcall broke the hot, dead stillness in which ears attuned to listening might have heard the corn grow.[5]
   Which of the following titles best fits the paragraph?
   a. The Stillness of a Hot Summer Afternoon
   b. A Hot Afternoon

[4] Mildred A. Dawson and Henry A. Bamman, *Fundamentals of Basic Reading Instruction.* Copyright 1959, Longmans, Green & Co., Inc. Reprinted by permission, David McKay Co., Inc.
[5] Mabel O'Donnell, *Engine Whistles, The Alice and Jerry Basic Readers,* "Puffing Billy," p. 5. Copyright 1957, 1954, 1947, 1942 by Harper & Row, Publishers; reprinted by permission of the publishers.

2. *Find the Answer to a Question*
Neither sunlight, an east window, nor the boom of Fourth of July could bring the stir and brightness of a summer's morning into that bedroom! Nothing could give a cheery look to the dull brown wallpaper, the heavy marble-topped dresser and table, and the long curtains which began at the window tops and reached out over the carpet-covered floor beneath.
    a. Was the room bright and cheery?
    b. What sentences support your answer? [6]

Robinson (31) suggests that the pupil first learn to identify the main idea of a sentence. He may be taught this skill by being required to underline key words. He then moves to identifying the key sentence in a paragraph. This is the topic sentence. However, some paragraphs do not have a single sentence that summarizes the main idea. Thus, the third step consists of teaching the pupil to make an inference from a series of sentences as to what the basic idea is. Eventually the pupil needs to learn that a main idea may be spread over two or three paragraphs.

Reading for Details

After the child has had some success in reading for and stating the main idea, he is ready to read for details. Reading for details becomes important after the third grade, especially in science, geography, arithmetic, home economics, and history.

Learning to follow directions through reading essentially is reading for details. In directions every little step is significant. The pupil must give full attention and must look for a definite sequence of data (9, p. 182). This process is particularly important in doing arithmetic and in carrying out experiments.

Initially the child may learn to arrange pictures in proper sequence to tell a story. Learning how to develop a simple paragraph is a further step in this process. The pupil may be taught how to read to answer a specific question. He is tested on a paragraph to see whether he remembers significant details.

The following activities promote reading for detail:

1. Have children look at a picture and then let them describe what they saw.

[6] Mabel O'Donnell, *Engine Whistles, The Alice and Jerry Basic Readers,* "Fourth of July," p. 41. Copyright 1957, 1954, 1947, 1942 by Harper & Row, Publishers; reprinted by permission of the publishers.

2. Ask children to note the details in a paragraph after you have stated the main idea.

3. Have children read a paragraph into which have been inserted some irrelevant sentences and let them identify these sentences.

4. After the pupils have read a paragraph, let them choose from a prepared group of sentences those that agree or disagree with the paragraph.

5. Present three paragraphs and let the pupils determine which of the last two supports and logically follows the first paragraph.

6. Analyze a written paragraph into its main and supporting ideas by making a formal outline of it.

7. Let children read and then carry out simple directions on how to do something or how to play a game. Children may develop direction charts. Common activities are: how to care for a plant, pet, or garden; how to cook a simple dish; how to make a dictionary; how to use the reading table.

8. Ask questions about the paragraph; multiple choice, completion, and true-false questions are especially appropriate in eliciting answers concerning the details of a paragraph.

9. Develop a chart, diagram, or map of the sequence of events.

The following exercises illustrate some of these techniques:

1. *Answer Specific Questions about a Paragraph*
   The only parts of the animals that had a market value were the hides and fat, or tallow. If the ranchers could have sold the meat, too, then they would have made a lot of money. But there were no railroads to ship the cattle to markets in the north and east.[7]
   a. Which parts of animals had a market value?
   b. Why did meat not have a market value?

2. *Put a Check Mark after Each of the Following Sentences that Might Be Included under the Topic, "Life on the Farm."*
   a. Johnny liked the sound of milk shooting into his pail.
   b. The sound of railroad cars passing by his window lulled him to sleep.
   c. Frank woke each morning with the rooster's first call.

Reading for the Organization

The good reader also comprehends the organization of what is being read. He thinks with the reading material, outlining it as he goes along.

[7] Shannon Garst and Warren Garst, *Cowboys and Cattle Trails,* American Adventure Series, p. 5. Copyright 1962, 1948 by Harper & Row, Publishers; reprinted by permission of the publishers.

He sees the relationship between the main and subordinate ideas and arranges these in some logical order. He utilizes materials from many sources and is able to draw conclusions.

Reading in the content areas especially depends upon proficiency in this skill. Textbooks have a characteristic paragraph organization. The topic sentence sets the theme of the paragraph. There follows a sequence of details. The paragraph is concluded by a summarizing sentence.

Numerous activities help the pupil to learn how to organize what he is reading. The following are suggested:

1. Ask the pupil to retell a story that he has read.
2. Have the pupil group a series of pictures in a logical or chronological sequence.
3. Let the pupil group a series of details about a main idea.
4. Let the pupil develop an outline for a story, with headings and subheadings.
5. Have the pupil arrange records, directions, or ideas in a sequential order.
6. Have the pupil assemble various bits of information and group them into an informative story.

The pupil should be taught to watch for time sequences in paragraphs (indicated by such words as *next, while, when, later*), to look for organization according to position or degree, to look for categorization (hoofed mammals, winged mammals, toothless mammals, and sea mammals), and to look for comparisons, contrasts, and cause-and-effect organizations.

Let us illustrate a few of these:

Organization According to Time-Sequence

John's pretty, young mother had died when he was a baby. He wished he could remember her. His father had been a preacher. He had died in 1861 when John was four years old. The boy could dimly remember him as a tall, kindly man.[8]

Organization According to Contrast

Among the many varieties of wheat are winter wheat and spring wheat. Winter wheat is planted in the autumn; spring wheat is planted in the spring. Winter wheat is harvested about three weeks earlier than spring wheat. Spring wheat is planted in the colder areas such

[8] Shannon Garst and Warren Garst, *Cowboys and Cattle Trails,* American Adventure Series, p. 4. Copyright 1962, 1948 by Harper & Row, Publishers; reprinted by permission of the publishers.

as the Dakotas and Canada. Winter wheat is most common in less severe winter areas such as Kansas, Nebraska, and Oklahoma.

Organization on a Cause-Effect Basis

What causes a cyclone, a tornado, and a hurricane? A cyclone is caused by a low-pressure area in which the winds move counterclockwise in a spiralling upward fashion. A tornado also is a low-pressure area but smaller and more violent than a cyclone. A hurricane is a huge mass of air whirling about a calm center.

The organizing of what is read also is an important part of effective learning or integrative reading. There are various approaches to this task. Summarizing, outlining, note making, and combinations of these have been recommended.[9] The specific approach used is not so important as that the student perceive the interrelationship between the various elements.

Summarizing   Summaries help to preserve the essential facts and the main ideas in capsule form. They are especially necessary when the pupil is not using his own book.

Summaries are particularly useful when reading literature, essays, or social science materials; they are not so useful in chemistry, physics, or biology. A summary or synopsis is all that may be necessary in reading the former. As for the latter, a summary usually is more lengthy than the original.

Exercises similar to the following teach the summarizing skill.

1. *Have pupils select the main idea of a paragraph from four possible choices:*

   Transportation developed step by step. In the beginning man used logs to move down the stream. The lake or stream was the first roadway. Then man taught the animal to pull heavy loads on sledges. The land became the natural roadway. Finally, man discovered the wheel. This led to the invention of the stagecoach.

   A good summary for the paragraph might be:

   a. Man used logs to move down the streams.
   b. The problems of transportation were overcome by the invention of the wheel.
   c. Transportation passed through the stages of log travel, sledge travel, and stagecoach travel.
   d. The land became the natural roadway.

[9] For a summary of the research on outlining, underlining, note taking, and summarizing see Sartain (36), *Educational Leadership*, 16 (December 1958), 155–160.

2. *Have pupils note how various writers introduce the topic or summarizing idea.*

In the following paragraph the writer asks a question and his *answer* to the question summarizes the paragraph:

What is success? Was Napoleon successful? What about Stalin, Hitler, or Michelangelo? Is that man successful who accomplishes the task that he set for himself? In other words, does success consist in getting what one wants? I doubt it. I believe success consists in being the best that one can be. Success must be measured by its effects upon man and society. The emphasis must be on being the best, not necessarily on getting the greatest rewards. The good plumber is a success; the lousy philosopher is a failure. And, the good plumber is an asset to both himself and society.

A good summary for the paragraph might be:

  a. That man is successful who accomplishes the task that he sets for himself.
  b. Success consists in being the best that one can be and it must be measured by its effects on man and society.
  c. Rewards are a significant aspect of success.

3. *Have pupils read poetry and select the best summary from a series of four choices.*

Poetry usually presents one main idea or moral and that main idea summarizes what the poem has to say. In poetry all the words are so interrelated that they dovetail into one main idea. Thus:

> Not enjoyment, and not sorrow,
> Is our destined end or way:
> But to act, that each to-morrow
> Find us farther than to-day.
> —*Psalm of Life*, Longfellow

A summary of this poem might be:

  a. Man must take what comes.
  b. Man can do something about his destiny.
  c. All of us are doomed to sorrow.

4. *Have pupils outline graphically a paragraph on a scientific topic.*

Scientific materials are difficult to summarize. Graphs, charts, maps, formulas, and definitions rarely can be summarized.

Trees

There are two kinds of trees. Some have leaves that drop off during one particular season of each year. Others keep their leaves for much longer periods of time. The latter are called evergreens.

Evergreens are of various types. Those with very narrow leaves are the pine, the cedar, the spruce, and the hemlock. Broadleaved evergreens are the palm and the live oak.

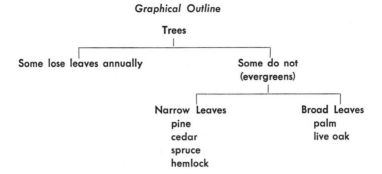

Graphical Outline

Other techniques useful in developing the summarizing skill are:

1. Have pupils summarize a message so that it would be suitable for sending by telegram (reduce a fifty-word message to a twenty-word message).

2. Have pupils write summaries of stories that they have read.

3. Have pupils select from three summaries that which best summarizes a series of paragraphs.

4. Have pupils identify the moral of a statement or paragraph. For example:

    > A goat had wandered from the herd, and the young goatherd tried to get him back. After calling in vain, he threw a stone that broke one of the goat's horns.
    > The alarmed lad wept and begged the goat not to tell his master. But the goat replied, "My broken horn will tell the story, even if I do not utter a word." [10]

    The moral might be: "Facts speak louder than words."

5. Have pupils organize and summarize materials from a variety of sources.

6. Have pupils write headlines for the school paper.

Outlining   Outlining is just another way of organizing information. It is closely related to summarizing. When the reader owns the book, he sometimes outlines by underlining and by using letters and numbers to designate main and subordinate points.

The pupil should be taught to look for the organization early in the primary grades. In his earliest picture reading he learns to follow a sequence of events. In his first stories he learns to identify the main

---

[10] *Basic Reading Skills for Junior High School Use* (Chicago: Scott, Foresman & Company, 1957), p. 161. Reprinted by permission. Other similar exercises will be found on pages 160–61 of this source.

idea. Gradually, he will learn to put the story with its main idea and its supporting details into a simple outline. The outline should identify the major idea and show the relation of supporting details in a logical, sequential order.

Outlining is not easy. Many speakers and writers do not have a clear-cut outline. Others, because not all pupils immediately grasp what is said, repeat or elaborate at great length. This may tend to make their presentation seem unorganized. As the pupil attempts to outline such a presentation, he needs to ignore the unimportant details. He must select the essentials from the nonessentials.

Once the pupil understands the organization, he is ready to put this organization into an outline form. He starts by listing the major points. Points of lesser importance that support the main ideas are indented. Indentation gives clues to the organization.

Sometimes the pupil may want both to indent and to letter and number the headings. Roman numerals represent major headings; headings of next-highest significance or second-order headings are indented and prefaced by capital letters; headings or points that support second-order headings, hence third-order headings, are preceded by Arabic numerals; finally, fourth-order points are preceded by lowercase letters.

The pupil may use a topic approach or a sentence (or question) approach in outlining. Thus, the first major point may simply be "A definition of photosynthesis." Or, it may be put into a complete sentence such as, "What is the definition of photosynthesis?" Either technique is satisfactory.

The outline, like any other summarization, has certain limitations. It does not contain the original material. It cannot contain everything that was said or written. But, in the beginning at least, it may be better for the pupil to write too much rather than not enough. An outline that is too skimpy is not very useful. It must contain enough material so that the pupil will see the relationships between the facts, ideas, or statements made. The perceiving of relationships is true organization.

Teaching the pupil to outline may be done in many ways:

1. Have pupils organize a series of objects into specific categories.
2. Have pupils select the two or three main ideas in a series of paragraphs.
3. Have them group details about each of several main ideas.
4. Teach outline form.
5. Have pupils check their outlines against teacher-prepared outlines over the same material.
6. Have pupils fill in the details in an outline for which they have been given the major ideas.

I.
    A.
    B.
II.
    A.
    B.

This exercise may be simplified by giving the pupils the four statements that should be used to complete the paragraph, but requiring them to put them in the proper order.

Underlining   Another form of organizing information is underlining. Many pupils use underlining of key words and phrases in a book to organize what they have read. Unfortunately, the technique used is frequently not good. The pupil reads and underlines words and phrases in a hit-and-miss fashion. He finds out too late that his underlining was not planned. In short, it does not show the organization of what was read. When the pupil returns to the underlining later, he finds that he no longer can decipher the reasons for underlining. Underlining thus may become a poor substitute for the thinking and organizing that accompanies good reading.

Proper underlining requires the pupil:

1. To survey the chapter.
2. To read the chapter.
3. To mentally familiarize himself with the organization of the chapter.
4. To underline main ideas and supporting details after having read each paragraph.
5. To underline only those words and phrases that actually indicate the organization of the paragraph.

Commonly, the pupil should underline the topic sentence. This sentence gives him the main idea of the paragraph. Frequently, he may want to underline only a key word or phrase in the topic sentence. The good reader, using a skimming technique, learns to know the major content of a book simply by detecting the topic sentences and then associating them with one another.

Proper underlining also means that the pupil must underline the key subtopics or supporting ideas. This includes key words or key phrases.

A useful technique is to number the subpoints or facts that support the main idea. The pupil's memory for these facts will be improved and in review they will stand out more forcibly if he numbers them.

When underlining, the pupil should have a code of symbols that he can use consistently. Thus, the topic sentence may have two lines under it; the supporting details have only one line under the key words.

Pupils frequently use a vertical bar in the margin to indicate an area of importance. An S in the margin may indicate that at that point the writer has summarized what he has said. A question mark in the margin indicates that here is a section that the learner doesn't understand. A circle frequently is used to indicate new and technical words used in the paragraph.

Some writers disparage underlining. However, one might ask: Why spend time taking notes on something that one can have in its entirety? Underlining prevents the learner from taking too few notes. It also permits him, during review, to again read the entire paragraph if, in the meantime, he has lost the trend of thought.

Note Making   Effective note making is a high-level study or integrative reading skill. It requires attention, concentration, skillful reading and listening, and the putting into practice of one's organizing abilities.

The making of good notes whether in reading or in listening requires the pupil to learn to write notes and to pay attention at the same time. The making of notes is certainly more than a secretarial job. Digestion and learning should be taking place. However, all notes do not need to be in the pupil's own words. Usually there is nothing wrong with the teacher's words, if the pupil understands them. Comprehension is the prime consideration. The pupil should learn to listen and read for meaning rather than for mere words.

The pupil needs to be taught to focus on the main idea and on those points that support the main idea. The pupil's notes should be a clue to the organization of the original material.

There are three basic forms of note making:

1. *The Paragraph*—This is probably most easily developed, but frequently is not the best organized. Each paragraph represents a new idea.
2. *The Sentence*—This is better than the paragraph form in that it attempts to organize the material by stating a series of sentences. It thus also may be easier to use in review.
3. *The Outline*—This provides the best opportunity for organization.

Obviously, the best notes seem to be written in outline form. Charts, diagrams, and illustrations should be included in the outline. The writer or speaker frequently summarizes in a simple drawing hours of lecture or written material. Charts frequently show the organization of an entire discussion.

The pupil should learn to read for the topic sentence. This gives the main idea. He also must read for the supporting details, for the speaker's organization, and for transitional words that give clues to the entire paragraph or chapter.

Such cue words or phrases as *"The main point is," "There are three major ideas represented here," "I will discuss three major issues,"* or *"The uses of lye are"* indicate that the writer is about to present major ideas.

Words like *besides, furthermore, moreover, likewise,* and *in addition* indicate that a supporting idea is about to be introduced. Words like *first, in the first place,* or *second* indicate that a number of subpoints will be introduced. Words like *consequently, therefore, hence, thus, thereupon,* or *accordingly* indicate that the point now being made flows from previous statements. Words like *finally* or *in conclusion* indicate that a summary is about to be made.

Words like *but, however, whereas, nevertheless, notwithstanding, on the contrary,* or *yet* indicate that a contradictory statement or point of view is about to be introduced.

It is not uncommon to find a conscientious pupil failing to get significant results from note making. Perhaps the notes themselves are adequate, but the pupil has not taken the pains to organize them. He has written them on any piece of paper available. Unfortunately, when the time comes for review, he no longer can locate the odd bits of paper or, if he can find them, he no longer knows what comes first and what comes next.

Some pupils may be too wordy. Simplicity is the key to good note making. Thoroughness, however, should not be ignored. The pupil must learn to take enough notes so that, if after the lecture he spends a few moments on them, he can organize them into a representation of the lecture or of his reading. This is impossible when he takes notes only over those elements that he does not understand.[11]

Finally, notes must be reworked. They should not be rewritten, but as soon as possible they should be revised. The more recently the pupil has written them, the better will be his memory for the content that they contain and the more easily will he be able to organize them. Notes do not change physically, but unless the pupil rereads them and reworks them immediately, he will lose much information. It is the pupil who loses that "something" required to make notes meaningful.

In summary, let us suggest a few guidelines for effective note making. The pupil should learn to:

[11] Eisner and Rohde (13) found that making notes after the lecture was just as effective as making them during the lecture. Perhaps, if pupils were trained to delay note making, retention would generally improve. Notes are only an aid to learning, not learning.

1. Use a standard 8½" × 11" notebook.
2. Use a loose-leaf notebook, not clipboards, small pads, or ordinary writing tablets.
3. Divide his paper into two sections: the right side of the page to be used for actual note taking, the left margin for personal comments. Below the notes and personal comments may be written the summary.
4. Number each page, entitle notes, and begin each new topic on a new page.
5. Keep notes from different classes in separate notebooks or separate them with dividers or tabs.
6. Take notes in ink.
7. Use only one side of the page.
8. Make notes brief and to the point.
9. Use quotation marks whenever the writer's or the speaker's words are quoted.
10. Copy definitions, formulas, and statistics exactly. They usually cannot be shortened.
11. Move on if a point is missed. Allow room to add it later.
12. Combine notes on the same topic.
13. Make notes of those items that are emphasized, frequently repeated, on which there will be an examination, and that are written on the blackboard.
14. Make a table of contents for the notebook.
15. Organize notes, indenting supporting points and subtopics.

Reading for Evaluation (Critical Reading)

Smith (41) states that critical reading "involves the literal comprehension, and interpretation skills, but it goes further than either of these in that the reader evaluates, and passes personal judgment on the quality, value, accuracy and truthfulness of what is read." [12]

Eller and Wolf (14) define critical reading ability as "the cluster of skills involved in evaluation of the validity, accuracy or intellectual . . . worthwhileness of a unit of printed matter." Olson (26) says critical reading involves "the reader's ability to recognize the author's intent or point of view, distinguishing fact from opinion and making judgments and inferences."

The pupil must constantly read to evaluate. The good comprehender is a critical reader. He checks the truth, logic, reliability, and accuracy of what is written. He looks for contradictory material. He relates

---

[12] Nila B. Smith, "Reading for Depth," *Reading and Inquiry*, International Reading Association Proceedings, 1965, 10, p. 118. Reprinted by permission.

the material to his experience. He distinguishes fact from fiction, is concerned with the timeliness of the material, and tries to understand the author's motives.

The critical reader is as much interested in why something is said as in what is said. He is sensitive to how words are used and is slightly suspicious of the author's biases. He pays particular attention to words with several meanings. He checks copyright data, the author's reputation, and the publisher's past performances. He looks for errors of reasoning, of analogy, of over generalization, of over simplification, and of distortion. He looks for one-sided presentations, prejudices, biases, faulty inferences, and propaganda. He avoids jumping to quick conclusions.

The development of critical reading should begin in the preschool years. It cannot be delayed until the later grades (20). Children can make critical evaluations of printed materials at very early ages, provided the content lies within their background of experience. If critical evaluations of material are to take place, the pupil will have to be skilled in word recognition and comprehension. He must enjoy a high level of reading performance (18).

The teacher can and must lessen the difficulties of critical reading, among which are the following (26): use of a single textbook, the halo effect that is attached to the printed word, the desire on the part of school people to avoid controversial subjects, the emphasis on conformity, and the natural involvement of our own prejudices and emotions.

Huelsmann (19) mentions three ways of teaching critical reading: the direct approach, the incidental approach, and the functional approach. Kottmeyer (23) experimented with a direct approach. Newspapers, magazines, editorials, and cartoons were read critically. Pupils were given definitions of propaganda techniques and sought to discover their presence in the materials read. The functional approach is one in which class materials are taught with the definite purpose of promoting critical skills. The least effective is an incidental approach. It refers to the training in critical reading that may come as a mere by-product of social studies learning.

Russell (35) recommends group discussion as a way of getting at assumptions or preconceptions. Artley (2) suggests that the essential process is one of raising questions or of setting up situations based on reading that require an evaluative response and then by a process of guidance, helping the child to think his way through to an answer. A simple technique is to stop the pupil before he comes to the writer's conclusion and to let him state all the possible solutions.

Harvison (18, p. 246) points out that teachers will have to depend upon their own creativity and initiative in teaching critical reading, particularly in the primary grades. Activities are as many and as varied as the teacher's imagination permits. On the primary level the pupil can be taught to react critically to pictures and stories; in the intermediate grades the pupil may be encouraged to read many texts to find answers, with the emphasis being on problem solving, inductive thinking, and frequent verbal expression among pupils.

The critical reader reads all materials in a questioning way. He constantly asks: Why? He is constantly concerned lest the writer's prejudices, biases, or assumptions may be coloring his presentation and consequently lead to an acceptance of a wrong point of view.

The critical reader reads beyond the materials. He is not satisfied with the simple statements. He uses his previous experiences and previous learning to understand fully what he is reading.

The critical reader thinks with the writer. He formulates the question clearly, checks the authenticity of the materials, evaluates the author's credentials, looks for errors in reasoning, and develops a sensitivity to the rightness or wrongness of what is presented.

The critical reader suspends judgment until the writer has finished his argument. As he proceeds with the material he asks himself: Is the author consistent? Is he logical? Are his motives noble? Are his facts true? Are his conclusions correct?

Critical reading is slow, sentence by sentence, and thought by thought reading. It requires the reader to analyze carefully the writer's words, his purpose, and his implications.

Let us look at these:

Words   Many words can be used by writers to arouse unfavorable feelings toward a person or an idea. For example, the words fascist, communist, or socialist usually arouse antagonism and distrust. In some circles to be labelled a Negro, Jew, or Catholic may leave similar impressions. The words, conservative, capitalist, warmonger, isolationist, progressive educator, selfish, conformist, world-minded, idealist, overzealous, and liberal, similarly mean many things to many people.

Purpose   What is the writer's purpose? Does he wish to inform or to entertain, to teach or to move emotionally? Is his motive open or hidden? The reader should constantly ask: Who would benefit if I agreed with the speaker or writer? What kind of evidence does he bring forth?

Implications   It is obvious that the reader must prepare himself so that he can detect generalities, fallacious reasoning, and unwarranted clichés. As citizens, as buyers of somebody's products, or as pupils in a classroom individuals are constantly subject to writings that attempt to make them think in a given way. They are asked to give allegiance to one thing and to turn against something else.

Some common techniques used by speakers and writers to sway public opinion are:

1. False or glittering generalization
2. Bias or prejudice
3. Unwarranted inference or cliché
4. Confusion of fact and opinion
5. Distortion of truth
6. Begging the question
7. False analogy
8. Error in inductive or deductive reasoning
9. Ignoring alternatives
10. Oversimplification
11. Changing the meaning of terms
12. Misleading headline
13. Failure to cite sources for one's information
14. Using prominent names to bolster one's point of view (testimonial)
15. Assuming all relationships are causal
16. Use of bandwagon appeals
17. Use of questionable sampling
18. Appeal to emotion rather than to intellect
19. Relating only one side
20. *Argumentum ad hominem*—Getting the reader to accept a conclusion by ridiculing the opposition, by snubbing it, or by ridiculing the person who holds the argument rather than by attacking the argument. Name-calling is a common such technique.
21. Use of straw men, straw issues, outright lies, digs, and snide remarks.
22. Transfer techniques (I'm Jimmy Jackson, I drink Mayberry.)

The pupil early in life needs to learn to interpret what he reads. The teacher may develop the critical reading skill with exercises similar to the following:

1. Teach pupils to discriminate between factual news reporting and editorial writing.
2. Have pupils identify the types of writing that are more likely to state the facts, that indulge in the bantering about of personal opinion, or that specialize in propaganda.
3. Have pupils select from three or four stated purposes the one that best represents the writer's purpose.

4. Have pupils select from a list of words those that tend to arouse the emotions of the reader.

5. Have pupils match given propaganda techniques with statements such as the following:

Propaganda Techniques

a. Citation of an authority or a testimonial
b. Bandwagon or everybody is doing it technique
c. Glittering generality
d. Transfer technique (similar to testimonial, but the person doesn't say anything directly associated with what is being advocated or recommended)
e. Name calling

Statements

_____ 1. Mr. Bott says there is no need to fear snakes.
_____ 2. Everybody is going to Lakewood Park on Sunday afternoon.
_____ 3. Grand Park is the finest park in central Missouri.
_____ 4. Don't be a wallflower.
_____ 5. A and B tastes best. Everybody drinks A and B.
_____ 6. We have the finest and the world's largest industrial facilities.
_____ 7. When you wear a hat you are more of a man and people hire men.
_____ 8. There's nothing like wood to add to the decor of your home.
_____ 9. The best music comes from a Cunningham radio.
_____10. People who know drink their beer out of a glass.
_____11. Theresa Pond, movie star, uses Market soap.
_____12. You will look better in a Manor shirt.
_____13. Fifty million people carry Blue-White Insurance.[13]

Reading for Learning

Complete reading is said to involve four steps: recognition, understanding, reaction, and integration. Ultimately, it is hoped that the reading a child does will influence and direct some future activity. In a very real sense, then, whenever the child integrates what he is reading, he is

[13] This exercise is effective only if the pupils have been taught the various propaganda techniques.

studying. This may be the ultimate in comprehension. Gray (15) points out that integration is "the heart of the learning act in reading."

Here we are concerned primarily with a method of integrative reading. Such a method is that proposed by Robinson (32, 33, pp. 13–14). It involves five steps: survey, question, read, recite, and review (SQ3R).

How good is the SQ3R method? Donald (12) found that the use of the SQ3R method on the junior high level resulted in a significant difference in factual type of knowledge of content material. The method seemed to develop better powers of organization, association, and critical thinking. Berg and Rentel (3), after a review of the research data, concluded that students need guidance to develop study skills, and that students who enroll in study skills courses do in fact raise their grade point averages.

Various modifications of the SQ3R method are available today. Pauk (27) developed a reading technique for prose, poetry, and drama called the EVOKER System—explore, vocabulary, oral reading, key ideas, evaluations, and recapitulation. Johnson (21) developed the Three-level Outlining Method. It requires the pupil to outline and to locate information.

Survey   Surveying is the first step in the SQ3R method and is the process of becoming familiar with the broad outlines, the chapter title, the main headings, the topic sentences, and the summary.

The good student gets an over-all picture of what he is reading or studying. The reason is obvious. The driver consults a road map before venturing on a trip. The race driver drives the course many times before the actual race. The diner surveys a menu. In rapid fashion he notices the dinners, sandwiches, appetizers, and drinks, and the prices do not escape him. The baseball player checks the infield for chuck holes, and the general surveys the terrain before initiating his attack. Each of these persons wants to know what lies ahead so he may proceed with the proper technique. The pupil must know what type of article he is reading before he can choose his techniques well.

In surveying a book, the *title* tells in general what the book is about; the *preface* gives a more detailed statement. In it the writer tells why he wrote the book and what he seeks to accomplish.

The *table of contents* gives a more detailed outline of the book. It gives clues to the writer's organization.

The chapter *titles, headings,* and *summaries* should come next. The headings are especially important. They are the cues to the chapter organization. In general, the chapter title tells the main idea. The major headings give the broad outlines of the chapter and show how the writer supports the main idea. Under each major heading may be one or more side headings.

The *topic sentence* in each paragraph is especially important. It summarizes the paragraph. It contains the main idea of the paragraph and usually is the first sentence in a paragraph. However, sometimes it occurs at the end of the paragraph, in the middle of the paragraph, or simply may not be stated.

Surveying thus allows the reader to "warm-up" to the reading task ahead. It gives an over-all view of the material.

Elementary teachers have always prepared the pupil for the reading task. They have made certain that the child had the necessary experience for understanding and that he had a purpose for reading. This is what surveying accomplishes for the more mature pupil.

Skimming frequently is used in previewing. Skimming gives a quick glimpse at the organization. It is a sort of threshing process in which the wheat is separated from the chaff. The reader is after certain information or perhaps wishes to decide whether or not to read the selection more intensively.

Question   The second step in integrative reading is the question. Sometimes the writer poses questions at the beginning or at the end of the chapter. The teacher may suggest questions as a part of the assignment. The pupil should become able to make his own questions. In doing this, he may turn the main headings or italicized words into questions. The teacher has many questions at his disposal. His questions may call for memorization, evaluation, recall, recognition, comparison, summarization, discussion, analysis, decision making, outlining, illustration, refutation, and inductive or deductive thinking (16, p. 253).

A pupil should readily see the value of this process. Formulating questions encourages the reader to seek answers as he reads. Many writers suggest that pupils write down these questions as a basis for review. Additional questions may be added during the actual reading.

Here are a few suggestions about asking questions:

1.   The pupil should ask questions *before* he reads rather than *after* reading. He must turn the chapter title, the headings, unfamiliar terms, etc., into questions.
2.   He should ask questions during reading.
3.   He should try to answer his questions before actually beginning reading.

Read   The third phase of an effective study procedure is *purposeful reading*. Let us examine some of the objectives of purposeful reading. The reader should:

1. Have a definite reason for his reading
2. Define clearly the problem that he wishes to solve
3. Focus his attention on the main points
4. Try to group the supporting details with the main idea
5. Keep in mind the nature of the assignment
6. Pay special attention to illustrations of all kinds, graphs, maps, charts
7. Be a flexible reader, adjusting his rate to the purpose of the reading and the nature of the material
8. Try to remember that he is seeking to answer questions

Study-type reading frequently is intensive reading. It is careful, rather slow reading with emphasis upon remembering details (42, p. 29). Intensive reading requires that upon reaching the end of the chapter the reader recognize the main idea. He should know where the author was heading and how he got there. He tends to form an outline of what he has read. He sees the major and supporting points.

Recite   The fourth phase of Robinson's SQ3R study method is literally a self-examination. Here the pupil attempts to answer the questions that he has posed without referring to his notes or other aids. Only when he fails should he consult his notes or refer to the book. One study method has been labelled a "self-recitation method" because of the great importance of recitation in learning. Recitation directs our attention to specific questions, thereby aiding concentration. Concentration is a by-product of having a goal that challenges the person's whole mind (28).

Self-recitation makes a number of contributions to effective learning. The pupil immediately is aware of how well he read, how accurately he accomplished his purposes, and whether he can express his newfound knowledge in his own words. If he can verbalize his knowledge to his own satisfaction, generally he can also explain or recite to another. Recitation is the heart of effective study; it is the seeking of answers to self-imposed questions and of putting new learnings into one's own words.

Review   The fifth and final phase of Robinson's method is review. Study is not complete until it includes a plan for retention. If learning is to be of any use in later situations, the child must remember what he has learned. Actually, remembering itself is defined in various ways. We say that one remembers data if he recalls them, can relearn them more quickly, recognizes them, can use them in test situations, or uses them to learn something else more easily. Perhaps the most important criterion of retention is the transfer that is made from the school situation to the life situation, to future acquisition of knowledge, and to future behavior.

Review becomes a relatively simple process if the reading has been done correctly. If the pupil developed an outline, wrote out questions for himself, developed the textbook into an outline, or made a summary, he may use any one of these as the basis for a good review.

Review, whether through notes or through rereading, should be an exercise in critical reading and thinking. Basically there are two methods of review: symbolical review and review by reimpression. Reimpression is the type of review that occurs when the person rereads. Symbolical review is done through recall, self-recitation, class discussions, tests, summaries, and lecture notes. This type of review encourages thinking, assimilation, integration, and organization. It is review with a purpose and with an eye on application.

Developing Study Skill   Educational Developmental Laboratories supplies a study skills library designed to help the pupil to develop the essential study skills and to improve his reading in the content areas. The program is planned as a sequential twelve-year program. It emphasizes reading in science and social studies and provides training in reference skills. At present materials are available for grades four through nine. A similar program is offered by Science Research Associates. Both are described in Appendix VI.

Mahoney (24) outlines various study skills, estimates the grade level on which they are to be taught, and suggests tools and methods used in teaching them. She covers teaching of the alphabet, dictionary, parts of a book, encyclopedia, library skills, study methods, and research skills.

Location Skills   The good pupil is one who has learned "to find the facts." He knows how to locate information. This means a familiarity with library aids, with library resources, the Dewey Classification system and card catalog, the various indices, encyclopedias, and almanacs, but it also means the ability to find the desired material within a book, a chapter, a paragraph, or a sentence. It means that he knows how to use a table of contents, an appendix, and the footnotes.

At the primary level location skills begin with the learning of the alphabetical sequence. The pupil needs to know which letters precede and follow a given letter. He needs to learn that indices and dictionaries are based on an alphabetical order. He must become familiar with the guide words (usually in the upper left-hand and upper right-hand corner) used in dictionaries to indicate the first and last entry words on a given page.

Although reference materials and their use are discussed later, at the primary level the pupil should have experience with the following materials:

1. Picture dictionaries
2. Picture and regular encyclopedias such as *Compton's Pictured Encyclopedia,* The *World Book Encyclopedia,* or *Junior Britannica.*
3. Glossaries.

Exercises useful in developing dictionary, encyclopedia, and alphabetizing skills at this level are:

1. Ask the pupil to supply a missing letter in a series of alphabetized letters.
2. Have the pupil arrange letters or words in an alphabetical order.
3. Ask the pupil to supply the preceding and following letter. Thus:

    ——— k ———   ——— o ———
    ——— b ———   ——— p ———
    ——— x ———   ——— d ———
    ——— s ———   ——— f ———

4. Let the pupil arrange a series of last names in alphabetical order.
5. Have the pupil locate the pages on which an encyclopedia treats given content matter. "On what page would you find something about George Washington?" "Find a description of an elephant." "In what volume(s) and on what page or pages is atomic energy discussed?"
6. Teach the pupil how to use the volume designation on the back of encyclopedias to locate quickly the subject matter for which he is looking.
7. Teach the meaning and use of guide words and cross references in encyclopedias.

At the intermediate level especially the pupil must be able to locate materials needed in the preparation of his assignments. There is a high degree of relationship between a pupil's ability to locate and use reference materials and the grades that he gets in school.

READING MAPS, CHARTS, AND GRAPHS

Sometimes, the writer cannot put into words accurately what he wants to say. Writers thus frequently use pictures, illustrations, maps, charts, graphs, and diagrams to explain more fully than is possible through words. Unfortunately, the pupil gets from these materials what is intended only if he can read the new symbols that the writer incorporates into these illustrations. He needs to learn to read the terms, colors, and other symbols that occur on the illustrations.

Research (50) indicates that children can be taught to read maps, charts, and graphs, perhaps as early as first grade. The more capable first-grade children can learn to handle simple graphs. Children can interpret pictorial graphs most easily; next in order of difficulty come circle or pie graphs, two-dimensional graphs, and line graphs. Vertical bar graphs seem to be easier to read than horizontal bar graphs. Finally, the type of graph used depends on the materials and the context in which it is used.

Reading Maps

Map reading requires numerous skills. The pupil needs to identify natural features such as rivers and lakes; land shapes such as continents and islands; and man-made features such as railroads and highways. He needs to know the meanings of gulf, bay, earth, distance, scale, latitude, longitude, sphere, hemisphere, pole, and equator. He needs to be able to read map symbols.

He needs to read physical and political maps of the United States, of North America, and the World. He needs to read maps depicting crops, rainfall, population, vegetation, wind belts, and ocean routes. He must learn to read maps of cities. And he should be able to read topographic and polar maps.

At the earliest level the pupil will learn simple concepts of direction (north, south, east, west), of distance, and of scale. He next advances to a recognition of large land and water forms on the globe and he may learn to identify water, land, forests, and mountains by their color designation. Gradually, his learning becomes more specific. He will learn to locate continents, seas, oceans, and countries on a map.

In the upper elementary grades the pupil usually learns to use map symbols, scales, and legends. He learns to find and use the equator, longitude, and latitude, and he can understand the causes of night and day and of the seasons. He translates latitude into miles and longitude into time. He becomes familiar with the poles, the arctic and antarctic circles, the Tropic of Capricorn and the Tropic of Cancer. He understands meridians and parallels. He develops further skill in location, in direction (upstream, downstream, etc.), in identifying natural features (continents, countries, islands, peninsulas, oceans, rivers, lakes, gulfs, mountains, plains, deserts, etc.), and in identifying cultural features (cities, capitals, railroads, industries, crops).

He learns that in the tropics it is warm all year; that between the tropics and the arctic-antarctic circles the temperature varies from season to season; that near the poles it is cold all year.

Rushdoony (34) found that third graders can be taught the map-reading skills usually taught in grades four and five, and he recommends that readiness for such teaching be developed in grades one and two.

Teaching the pupil to read maps includes the following steps:

1. Studying the title of the map
2. Studying each symbol (the legend)
3. Noting direction on the map
4. Analyzing and applying the map scale
5. Relating the area under study to a more general or larger area (Kansas in relation to the United States)

Thompson (47) describes how to teach pupils in grades 4–8 to draw maps from memory. Pupils begin by tracing the outline of a map of California, for example, with the index finger.

The following exercises are helpful in teaching map skills:

1. Relate map study to pictures and aerial photographs.
2. Teach direction in the classroom; teach the meaning of up and down; demonstrate that at noon shadows are to the north.
3. Demonstrate how a small map or globe represents a large territory.
4. Make a map of the child's home town or of his immediate environment (school building, school grounds).
5. Let pupils answer true or false statements such as the following:
   a. My home is north of the post office.
   b. East of our school is the public library.
6. Have children locate their city on a map.
7. Have children trace the route of boats moving upstream.
8. Teach that shading from green through yellow, brown, and red indicates an increase in altitude.
9. Require pupils to find answers for questions such as the following:
   a. How many continents are there?
   b. How do you know that the earth is round?
   c. What route did Balboa take?
   d. What changes have occurred in the map of Europe as a result of World War II?
   e. What time is it in Tokyo and London when it is 6 p.m. in New York?

10. Require the pupil to locate on the map an example of each of the following:

archipelago	coast line	highland	ocean
basin	continent	inlet	peninsula
bay	delta	island	plateau
boundary	desert	isthmus	port
branch	dike	jungle	reef
canyon	divide	lake	river
cape	estuary	marsh	sea
channel	fiord	mesa	strait
city	gulf	mountain	swamp
cliff	harbor	oasis	tributary
			valley

A chart such as Figure 13-1 is useful in teaching the meaning of these terms.

Figure 13-1   Geographical Terms*

*This "Geographical Terms Chart" is published by the George F. Cram Company, Inc., Indianapolis, and is reproduced by permission.

11. Require the pupil to match picture symbols with word symbols (Figure 13-2).

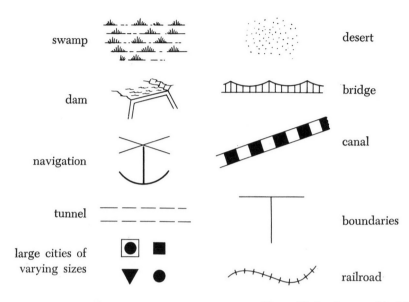

Figure 13-2   Geographical Symbols

12. Teach the representation of elevation and slope through contour lines.

13. Study the meanings of terms such as:

apogee	isobar	altitude
contour line	isotherm	longitude
divide	meridian	parallel
equinox	perigee	meridian
international date line	satellite	Mercator's projections

14. Require pupil to answer questions based on maps. For example:

   a. In Africa, the rainfall around the equator (see *Figure 13-3*) is generally heavier than either north or south of the equator.
     a. true
     b. false

   b. North of the equator there is very little vegetation (see *Figure 13-4*).

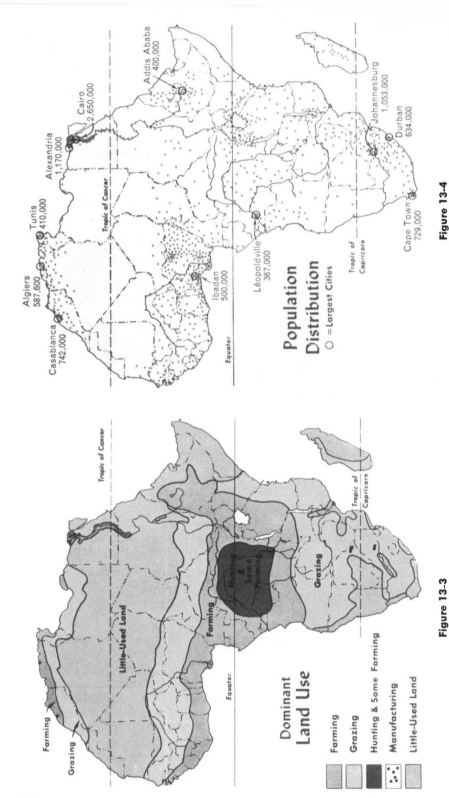

Figure 13-4

Population Distribution

○ = Largest Cities

Addis Ababa 400,000
Cairo 2,650,000
Alexandria 1,170,000
Tunis 410,000
Algiers 587,600
Casablanca 742,000
Ibadan 500,000
Léopoldville 367,000
Johannesburg 1,053,000
Durban 634,000
Cape Town 729,000

Tropic of Cancer
Tropic of Capricorn
Equator

Figure 13-3

Dominant Land Use

Farming
Grazing
Hunting & Some Farming
Manufacturing
Little-Used Land

Little-Used Land
Farming
Grazing
Manufacturing & Some Farming
Farming
Grazing

Tropic of Cancer
Tropic of Capricorn
Equator

The maps here and on page 433 are from *Exploring the Old World,* ©1957 by O. Stuart Hamer, Orlando W. Stephenson, Ralph S. Yohe, Ben F. Ahlschwede, Dwight W. Follett, and Herbert H. Gross. Used by permission.

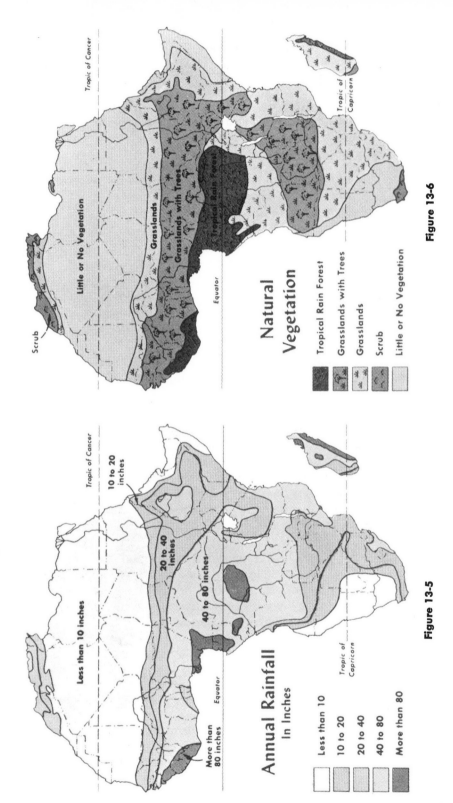

Natural Vegetation

Tropical Rain Forest
Grasslands with Trees
Grasslands
Scrub
Little or No Vegetation

Figure 13-6

Annual Rainfall
In Inches

Less than 10
10 to 20
20 to 40
40 to 80
More than 80

Figure 13-5

433

a. true
b. false

c. Farming is most common near the equator (see *Figure 13-5*).
   a. true
   b. false

d. The population near the Tropic of Cancer is more dense than near the equator (see *Figure 13-6*).
   a. true
   b. false

Reading Graphs

Another important skill is the ability to read graphs. There are four kinds of graphs. The *pictorial* graph (see Figure 13-7) in which the units are expressed in picture form is the easiest to read. It uses pictures to show relationships between realities. The *bar* graph (see Figure 13-8) compares the size of quantities. It expresses amounts. For example, one may want to compare the heights of various buildings or dams in the United States; the number of ticket sales made by the boys and girls in a class; or the number of deaths that are attributable to various causes such as drowning, car accidents, and airplane accidents. In each instance, the bar graph shows how much more or less one type is than another. A bar graph may be either vertical or horizontal.

The *line* graph (see Figure 13-9) shows changes between quantities. It indicates what has happened over a period of time. It indicates whether there has been an increase or a decrease, for example, in the amount of rain each month of the year, in the price of foods, in daily temperature, etc.

The *circle* (see Figure 13-10) graph shows the relation of parts to a whole. It may be used, for example, to indicate the percentage of A's, B's, C's, and D's in a certain class; how much of the family budget goes to food, clothing, shelter, savings, car, miscellaneous; or the percentage of the school budget that is allotted for salaries, maintenance, and the general operation of the school plant.

To read graphs of one kind or another the pupil should learn to observe the following steps:

1. Read the title of the graph—this tells what the graph is about.
2. Discover what is being compared—persons, places, or things.
3. Be able to interpret the legend and the meaning of the vertical and horizontal axis.

4. Identify the scale of measure that has been used. What does each figure represent?
5. Discover what conclusions can be drawn from the graph.

On pages 83 and 84 of the *Listen and Read Workbook* (1) we have presented various graphs. With each graph is an accompanying set of questions that checks upon the pupil's ability to *read* it.

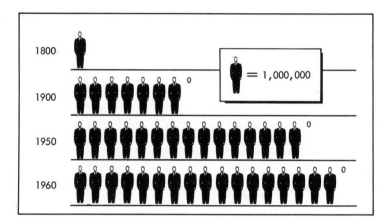

Figure 13-7.   Pictorial Graph (*Pictograph*)*

1. The population of the United States in 1900 was more than seven times that in 1800.
    ———true
    ———false

2. Between 1950 and 1960 the population grew approximately twenty million.
    ———true
    ———false

* Figures 13-7 through 13-10 are reprinted by permission from the *Listen and Read Workbook*, copyright 1961 by Educational Developmental Laboratories.

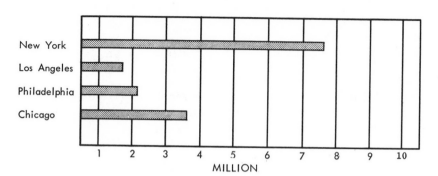

Figure 13-8.   Bar Graph

1. The population of New York City is about
   a.   8,000,000.
   b.   7,000,000.
   c.   800,000.
   d. 8,000,000,000.

2. The City of Los Angeles has more people than the City of Philadelphia.
   ———true
   ———false

3. The City of New York is more than twice as large as the City of Chicago.
   ———true
   ———false

The teacher may require the pupil to develop:

1. A bar graph showing the ticket sales of the following groups: 6th graders, 200; seventh graders, 350; eighth graders, 300; fourth graders, 220.
2. A bar graph showing the percentage of voters who turned out in various countries in recent elections: Austria, 95 per cent; Greece, 85 per cent; Korea, 80 per cent; United States, 60 per cent.
3. A bar graph showing the death rates per 100,000 occurring in 1950 as a result of various illnesses: pneumonia, 31; tuberculosis, 22; cancer, 139; heart, 355; appendicitis, 2; all accidents, 60.
4. A bar graph showing the battle deaths in World War II for the following countries: Austria, 380,000; China, 1,325,000; Germany,

3,250,000; Japan, 1,270,000; Poland, 664,000; Rumania, 350,000; Russia, 6,115,000; England, 357,000; United States, 291,000.

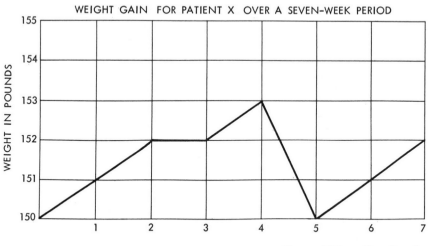

Figure 13-9.   Line Graph

1. Patient X weighed the least during the second week.
   _____true
   _____false

2. Patient X weighed the most in the fourth week.
   _____true
   _____false

3. Patient X weighed eleven pounds more at the end of the seven-week period.
   _____true
   _____false

Have the pupils draw line graphs for the following:

1. A graph showing John's percentile scores on four weekly tests: week 1, 92; week 2, 85; week 3, 65; week 4, 98.
2. A line graph showing the increase and decrease in battle deaths in various wars in which the United States was involved: Revolutionary War, 4,435; War of 1812, 2,260; Mexican War, 1,733; Civil War, 140,414; Spanish-American War, 385; World War I, 53,402; World War II, 291,557; Korean War, 33,629.

STATUS OF KANSAS HIGH SCHOOL GRADUATES, 1960*

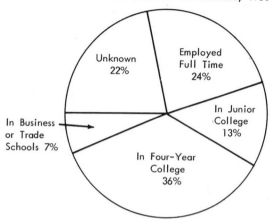

Figure 13-10.   Circle Graph

1. How many of the high school graduates attend junior college?
2. What percentage of graduates attend business or trade schools?

Pupils may be required to draw circle graphs for the following:

1. A hotel spends 28¢ of each dollar for services and supplies; 19¢ for food; 37¢ for payroll; and 16¢ for maintenance and repair.
2. In 1957 the world population was 2,795 million. Of these, 225 million were in Africa; 189 million in North America; 192 million in Latin America; 1,556 million in Asia; 618 million in Europe and Asiatic Russia; and 15 million in Oceania.

Requiring the pupil to construct his own graphs is an effective teaching technique. The teacher should prepare for pupils a guide both for the development of graphs and for the interpretation of them.

Reading Tables

A table is a simple listing of facts and information. In reading a table the pupil should first look at the title. He then should look at the headings of the various columns with their major headings and subheadings, if there are any. Finally, he must read the details. These usually are written in the left-hand column. Table 13-1, from the *Listen and Read Workbook* (1, p. 85), teaches all of these skills.

TABLE 13-1   Average Retail Prices of Foods in Cents, 1950, 1952, 1954

Food and Unit	1950	1952	1954
Coffee, 1 lb.	79	86	110
Sugar, 5 lbs.	48	51	52
Butter, 1 lb.	72	85	72
Bacon, 1 lb.	63	64	81

If the pupil has learned to read tables, he should be able to answer questions like the following[14]:

1. The title of the table indicates that the prices given are in cents.
   _____true
   _____false

2. The title of the paragraph indicates that wholesale prices are given.
   _____true
   _____false

3. The average price of butter in 1950 was 85 cents.
   _____true
   _____false

4. Only butter showed no increase in 1954 over 1952.
   _____true
   _____false

5. The lowest price per pound of any item listed is sugar.
   _____true
   _____false

Reading Charts

Possibly the most common chart is the "flow chart." It shows the flow of organization. The pupil needs to be able to read it in social studies. Figure 13-11 shows one such chart.

[14] *Listen and Read Workbook* (1, p. 85). Copyright 1961 by Educational Developmental Laboratories; reprinted by permission.

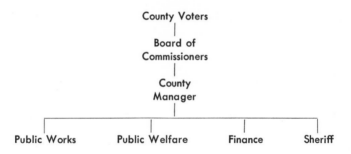

Figure 13-11.   County Manager Plan

Reading Diagrams

Finally, the pupil must learn to read diagrams. An illustration of such a diagram is given in the *Listen and Read Workbook* (1, p. 86).

COMPREHENSION IN A SPECIFIC CONTENT AREA

In the course of this and the previous chapters we have discussed numerous reading skills. We have emphasized the importance of grasping the main idea, of surveying materials, of choosing appropriate reading rates, of interpreting graphs, maps, charts, tables, and diagrams, of reading for a purpose, of organizing what one reads, of drawing inferences, and of retaining and applying what has been learned.

In the content areas, these and all other reading skills are needed for successful comprehension. In addition, in the content areas each of these reading skills must be applied to the specific content area in a particular way.

It is no longer possible to hold that all reading skills will transfer from one field to another. Reading is not a generalized ability that the pupil learns once and for all time. Rather, reading is a composite of many skills, each varying with the situation.

The vocabulary is a distinct problem in each of the content areas. Thus, Stauffer (43), comparing the vocabulary appearing in primary arithmetic, science, and health texts with the vocabulary of basal readers for grades one through three, found that 1331 words in arithmetic, 900 words in health, and 809 words in science did not appear in the basal readers.

Let us take a short look at some of the major content areas, and let us attempt to identify some of the factors that cause reading difficulties. The reader who wishes more extensive coverage of reading in the content areas might consult such books as *Effective Reading in Social Studies* and *Effective Reading in Science,* both by David L. Shepherd.

Literature [15]

Reading literature requires special appreciation of the mood and style of the author. It requires interpretative reading and emotional involvement by the reader. The reader needs to read with his mind and with his emotions. He must find in literature splotches of the ever-flowing stream of human behavior and emotions. He must analyze the characters, appreciate the style, and digest the sequence of development (48). It requires literal understanding, symbolic interpretation, and an appreciation of the relevance of literature to life (29).

Fiction is a biography of conflict in human motives (25, pp. 211–213). It traces the conflict from its inception to its conclusion. Since motives are "within" the person, the writer must "psychoanalyze" the individual, report what the person is saying to himself, use soliloquies or asides in which the person tells the audience what his motives are, or portray the person's motives through his appearance, speech, or action. The successful reader of literature must understand these literary contrivances of the author and read between the lines for a comprehension of the basic meaning.

Each literary form has its own mode of expression. In poetry the writer communicates through words and concepts and also through tone, mood, repetition, rhythm, and rhyme. In essays the mood may take on a formal, pedantic, humorous, satiric, philosophical, inspirational, persuasive, or political form. The short story presents its own literary contrivances. It is characterized by uniformity of tone and plot and by dramatic intensity.

To appreciate novels, short stories, poems, and plays the pupil must learn to analyze the elements of plot, characterization, style, and theme.

Plot. The pupil must learn to ask himself a series of questions. Did I like the ending? How would I have changed it? Did the writer use surprise, suspense, or mystery to keep me interested? What was the conflict or major motive of the story? What are the time and place settings? Is it fanciful or realistic literature?

An exercise similar to the following teaches the pupil to appreciate plot:

Read the following sentences and select the word that best characterizes the plot:

[15] See Helene W. Hartley, "Teaching the Reading of Literature in the Elementary School," *Challenge and Experiment in Reading,* International Reading Association Conference Proceedings, 7 (1962), 43–45.

1. We stood on the bridge not knowing whether to go forward, backward, or just remain where we were. In front of us and behind, the flood waters were rushing across the highway. Broken tree limbs, barrels, and household goods were floating by.

   This series of sentences indicates that the plot is based upon:
   a. surprise
   b. suspense
   c. adventure
   d. intrigue

2. How wonderful it would be if the world were really at peace. There wouldn't be this constant distrust among all of us. Men and women could intermingle freely with each other. They would be free from the fear of atomic destruction.

   This series of sentences indicates that the plot is:
   a. fanciful
   b. realistic

The pupil also must learn to appreciate *characterization*. The pupil should ask: What character did I like best? Which one would I like to be? Were the characters true to life?

The pupil learns characterization skills by analyzing statements and answering certain questions about them. For example:

1. The man just sat. His eyes stared into empty space. No smile or grin ever adorned his face. When he spoke, it was about the wickedness of man and the burning fires of hell.

   This series of sentences describes a person who is probably:
   a. discontented with life
   b. satisfied with life
   c. successful in life
   d. proud of living

2. The wrinkled old man with curved back was ambling toward the park. Behind him in droves came the pat-pat of little feet. Little ones and not so little ones were laughing and jumping trying to get his attention.

   This series of sentences describes an old man who:
   a. is discontented with life
   b. enjoys the little things of life
   c. has few friends
   d. is considered an old fogy

Or, the teacher may require the pupil to underline one of three words that best characterizes the person described in key sentences. For example:

1. Jim grabbed Johnny by the shoulder and threw him against the wall. "That's for ratting on me."

    Jim is generous, *unethical*, brave.

2. Mary's eyes shot darts of fire at anyone who in the slightest way disagreed with her.

    Mary is rude, generous, *opinionated*.

The third element is *style*. What was the writer's style? What figures of speech did he use? What was the general mood or tone of the writing?

Exercises such as the following may teach the pupil to read for style.

1. We were awakened by the sound of a man trying to break open the door. Quietly my father peered out of the window but there was only darkness. The noise continued. My father got his revolver from the closet, loaded it, and we advanced toward the door with trepidation.

    This series of sentences describes a set of circumstances character-ized by:
       a. annoyance
       b. dismay
       c. fright
       d. anger

2. Lori wiggled and crawled and splashed in the pool. It was her first outing for the summer and what an occasion it was.

    This series of sentences describes a little girl who is:
       a. comfortable
       b. contented
       c. joyful
       d. successful

3. All afternoon Marie thought of what would happen when her father would come home. She had just broken her father's favorite pipe. Then the moment came. Dad was just pulling up his ash tray and said, "Honey, where is my pipe?"

She is:
   a. ashamed
   b. embarrassed
   c. guilty
   d. shy

The fourth element is the *theme*. What was the moral of the story? Which character best exemplified the morals and ideals of the writer? How do the morals and ideals portrayed fit with the reader's morals?

Social Studies[16]

Reading in the social studies is a special skill and one that the pupil is called upon to use innumerable times. The pupil must learn a new verbal vocabulary. He must be able to deal with detailed information in historical sequence, with cause and effect relationships, and with critical reading. He also must learn to handle new symbols: maps, charts, diagrams, and graphs (40).

In teaching the pupil to read social studies content one must begin with social studies materials. The teacher must know what specific skills to teach and how they should be taught.

Let us dwell on the *how:*

1.   Call attention to the new words, duplicate them for the pupil, use them in the appropriate context, and require pupils to use them.
2.   Use films, charts, etc., to illustrate new concepts.
3.   Require pupils to read for specific purposes: to answer a question, to identify the cause, to outline, etc.
4.   Provide numerous activities that stimulate critical thinking and analysis.
5.   Test and constantly evaluate the pupil's proficiency in reading social studies materials (46, p. 147).
6.   Make assignments specific enough so the pupil will know how to read (46, p. 149). For example, the teacher may require the pupil to identify the author's point of view.

Mathematics

Reading in mathematics requires the pupil to comprehend a new set of symbols. He must react to numerical symbols that synthesize verbal sym-

---

[16] For additional discussion see: Paul A. Witty, "The Role of Reading in the Social Studies," *Elementary English,* 39 (October 1962) 562–69; also: Helen Huus, "Antidote for Apathy—Acquiring Reading Skills for Social Studies," *Challenge and Experiment in Reading,* International Reading Association Conference Proceedings, 7 (1962), 81–88.

bols. He must be able to read and to compute. He must read deductively. He must translate formulas into meaningful relationships, and, generally, he must read slowly.

In mathematics, comprehension is not limited to the understanding of a story. It is not even limited to the understanding of one experiment. One concept is built on another in mathematics and can have meaning only on the basis of the understood meaning of the former. In no other area is it more true than in mathematics that new learning depends upon previous learning. Smith (40) identified the following writing patterns in mathematical textbooks: classification, explanation of a technical process, instructions for an experiment, detailed statement of facts, descriptive problem solving, abbreviations and equations, mathematical problems, and various combinations of each of the above. These patterns point up the diverse reading tasks a pupil must be prepared to handle.

The pupil should early be introduced into the steps of reading mathematics. Bond and Wagner (5, p. 317) point out that the child must know what the problem calls for, what facts are needed for the solution, what steps are appropriate in leading to a solution, and what is the probable answer.

In learning to read in mathematics the pupil should:

1. Read for main ideas.
2. Read for organization, listing perhaps in one column the points given and in the second the points needed.
3. Translate the verbal symbols into mathematical symbols and formulas.
4. Read for relationships and translate these into an equation.
5. Analyze carefully all mathematical symbols and formulas.
6. Analyze carefully all graphs, figures, illustrations, etc.
7. Follow a definite procedure:
   a. learn the meaning of all words.
   b. find what the problem asks for.
   c. decide what facts are needed to find a solution to the problem.
   d. decide what mathematical process is required (addition, subtraction, etc.).
   e. identify the order for solving the problem.
8. Make a drawing of the problem. A problem such as the following can be easily represented by a drawing:

   > Harry has fifteen pictures. If he can paste three pictures on each page of his scrapbook, how many pages will be filled?

9. Study the contrast between the way words are used in mathematics and in other areas.

10. Learn the proper symbols and abbreviations: ft. = foot; $7^3 =$ 343.

Does direct instruction in reading help in mathematics? Call and Wiggin (6) devised an experiment to answer just this question. They concluded that teaching specialized mathematical reading-study skills had a definite effect on the ability to solve mathematical word problems. The experimental group did better even when reading abilities and mathematical aptitude were controlled. Their procedures are described in sufficient detail to permit replication.

Science[17]

Reading in science requires the ability to follow a sequence of events. It requires an orderly, systematic approach, including the ability to classify, categorize, and memorize (48). The technical vocabulary must be mastered, the formulas must be learned, and theory must be understood.

Directions become a very important factor. The success of an experiment depends on the pupil's ability to follow directions. Reading in science as in mathematics usually is careful, analytical, and slow. It puts a premium on inductive reasoning and on detail. Every formula, chart, or graph is important. It demands a problem-solving approach similar to the steps of the scientific method. The pupil must learn to follow the scientist as he states the problem, enumerates the facts, formulates his hunch or hypothesis, investigates the facts to test the hypothesis, works toward his conclusion, and makes his verification. He must observe the facts, keep them in mind, relate them to each other, and determine whether or not they support a theory.

Science materials present the following additional difficulties:

1. Many of the terms are of a mathematical nature.
2. Many common words are used in a special sense (*force, body*).
3. Statements are concise (laws, definitions, formulas).

The teacher can help the pupil by:

1. Simplifying the vocabulary for most pupils—a meteorologist is simply a weatherman. The pupil needs to be taught how to comprehend technical symbols, graphs, maps, charts, diagrams, formulas, scales, and equations.
2. Having pupils read for the main idea—"The purpose of this experiment is . . ."

[17] See Don H. Parker, "Developing Reading in a Science Program," *Challenge and Experiment in Reading,* International Reading Association Conference Proceedings, 7 (1962), 88–90.

3. Having pupils organize the material, jotting down the steps in an experiment.
4. Using films to illustrate and develop concepts.
5. Helping pupils adjust reading speed to the difficulty of the material, the purposes for the reading, and the pupil's own familiarity with it.
6. Helping pupils to evaluate the competency of the writer or experimenter.
7. Teaching pupils to use the problem-solving technique: formulation of the hypotheses; collation of the evidence; evaluation and organization of the evidence; forming of a conclusion; and testing the conclusion.
8. Teaching pupils to recognize the sequence of steps.
9. Conducting hunts for information requiring the use of bibliographies, encyclopedias, card catalogue, etc.
10. Directing the pupils in developing summaries and outlines.
11. Having pupils express formulas in their own words.

SUMMARY

Essentially, this chapter has concerned itself with advancing the child's comprehension skills. From a literal interpretation we must lead him to cause-and-effect reasoning, drawing inferences, arriving at conclusions, and making generalizations. From mere obtaining of the facts we lead him to the interpretation of the deeper meanings.

Although each of the specific skills discussed here reaches its culmination only in the upper grades and frequently not even then, the teacher of reading, as indeed all teachers, must encourage the development of each early in the primary grades. Even critical reading should begin in the primary grades. It is not "what to teach" but "how to teach" the skills that causes difficulty.

One of the prime tasks of the elementary school is that of teaching the pupil how to learn. The chapter has emphasized the use of reading for learning purposes.

Unfortunately, the ability to comprehend printed material is not entirely subject to development. Teaching cannot accomplish everything. The ability to remember word meanings and the ability to reason with verbal concepts are probably a part of the child's native endowment. It is doubtful that even an optimum environment can do much to remedy inadequate brain development. Skill development is subject to the potentialities that already exist.

QUESTIONS FOR DISCUSSION

1. What comprehension skills seem not amenable to training? Which seem most amenable to training?
2. What principles in addition to those mentioned in this chapter should guide the teacher in the development of word meanings?
3. What types of organization do paragraphs normally fall into? Either write or locate materials that illustrate various organizations and that might be used at a third, fifth, or seventh grade level.
4. What is critical reading? How might newspapers be used to develop critical reading skills?
5. Discuss Robinson's SQ3R method and its appropriateness in the primary grades.
6. Discuss the special problems of map reading.
7. Discuss four kinds of graphs and the problems they present in interpretation.
8. What are the special reading problems in literature, mathematics, science, and social studies and how might they be dealt with in the daily class session?
9. Discuss:
   a. The specific meaning elicited by a word is a function of the context in which it occurs.
   b. Drill and training in comprehension increase comprehension achievement rather than comprehension potential.
   c. Comprehension depends upon a vocabulary factor, intelligence factor, perceptual factor, interpretation-of-language factor (getting meaning from context), and speech factor.
   d. Organizing of what is read as by summarizing or outlining is positively related to comprehension.
   e. The closer the reading skills stressed in a reading program are to the skills used in a specific content area, the more transfer occurs and the more the child tends to learn when reading in that area.

DIAGNOSTIC TEACHING
OF READING

part VI

In previous chapters we were most concerned with how a pupil becomes a reader; in part VI we look at the problem of reading disability, outlining the procedure for diagnosing reading disability and for remediating difficulties that do exist. Part VI helps the teacher to identify the symptoms of disability and suggests ways of dealing with the symptoms. It outlines for the classroom teacher a program for the retarded reader.

Retarded readers may well be with us always; at any rate, there is at present no reading method or approach that guarantees total freedom from retardation. The teacher thus needs to become versed in dealing with the child who is drifting or has drifted into trouble. This is the significance of Chapter 14.

Chapter 14 is a summary of another book by the author, entitled *Diagnosis and Remediation of Reading Disability* (West Nyack, N.Y.: Parker Publishing Company, 1968). You may also want to consult Emerald Dechant, *Detection and Correction of Reading Difficulties; Readings and Commentary* (New York: Appleton-Century-Crofts, 1970).

Diagnosis and Remediation

Before we get into the more technical aspects of diagnosis and remediation, let us make a few general observations about the prevention of reading disabilities.

Many educators today are concerned that we may be overemphasizing remediation and ignoring prevention. Their fears are not entirely groundless. In too many instances the best teachers are removed from regular classroom teaching and put into the role of special or remedial reading teacher. This may lead to poorer instruction in the classroom and increased numbers of children with reading problems. It may well be that we are thus producing retarded readers at a rate much faster than we will ever be able to remediate.

Although we have done a better job of remediation than of prevention, it is far better to prevent than to remediate; it is far better that we deal with the problem in the classroom rather than wait until the pupil acquires a reading disability.

Prevention is not an easy task. No one has found the appropriate preventions, or we would not have the number of reading disabilities that we do have. Perhaps we have not looked for ways of preventing reading disability but merely have been satisfied with cures.

Reading failures can be prevented only if every lesson is a diagnostic and, in a sense, a remedial lesson. Perhaps even then many failures cannot be prevented, but the teacher must operate on the assumption that failures can be prevented, and it is only through accurate and continuous diagnosis of the child's needs and difficulties, of his assets and strengths, that the teacher can modify instruction to meet these needs. Continuous diagnosis is a must in the reading classroom; prevention is its end-product. Diagnosis identifies minor difficulties before they become disabilities and thus occasions adjustments in instruction that might remove these difficulties.

It is not uncommon for the teacher to observe within the classroom children who fit the following descriptions. Jane has completed the readiness program but still cannot identify rhyming words. Dick has missed a significant amount of reading instruction because he was ill. June has an abnormal amount of difficulty with similar-appearing words such as *them* and *then*. Pat, in reading orally, gets the meaning but cannot say some of the words. Jim has difficulty remembering such high frequency words as *in* or *the*.

Others are developing habits of word-by-word reading, of vocalizing, of backtracking, of daydreaming while reading, of rereading, of plodding along at a snail's pace, of word blocking, of following words with their finger, or of moving the head from side to side rather than moving their eyes across the page.

Serious problems? No, but these innocuous difficulties tend to snowball. Most remedial cases are probably instances of "an accumulation of unmet reading needs." Reading deficiency begins with simple inadequacies. Despite the good work of the classroom teacher, some pupils lose increasingly more ground with each year of school attendance. Retardation is cumulative.

To detect and diagnose the incipient reading problems, then, is a prime responsibility of the teacher. Prevention of reading difficulties should begin before the child begins formal reading instruction and continue throughout his entire school year. Prevention is best brought about by diagnosis of and constant alertness to any incipient or existing difficulty.

The child with a reading disability must have the benefits of recognition (25). His problem needs to be identified early, or he will grow up with the disability intact. Beyond a certain point he no longer may be interested in or be able to benefit from educational recognition (25).

It does not make sense to delay remedial instruction until, say, the third grade. We cannot permit children to become imprisoned in faulty learning habits. At the first instance the teacher notices that the child is not progressing satisfactorily, diagnostic study and appropriate remedial education are indicated. As Eisenberg (22) notes:

> We would not hear of delaying therapy for rheumatic fever because not every patient incurs a valvulitis; we would not consider deferring laparotomy for a suspected appendicitis because diagnosis is imprecise and not every appendix perforates.

Schiffman (61), in a survey of 10,000 children, found that pupils with reading problems who were identified and received remedial education in the second grade had ten times as great a chance for successful outcome of the remedial treatment as those identified only at the ninth-grade level.

DEFINITION OF DIAGNOSIS

Diagnosis is defined in *Webster's New Collegiate Dictionary* as the art or act of recognizing disease from its symptoms. Brueckner (10, p. 2) notes that educational diagnosis refers to the techniques by which one discovers and evaluates the strengths and weaknesses of an individual. The diagnostician gathers data and then on the basis of the analysis and interpretation of these data suggests developmental or remedial measures.

Tiegs (66, p. 5) adds that educational diagnosis

. . . is the basis of intelligent teaching. Its function is to facilitate the optimum development of every pupil. The following activities should become routine: determining for each pupil (1) which of his factors of intelligence are strong and which are weak, (2) whether he learns better through language or non-language materials and situations, (3) what his unattained objectives are, and (4) the nature of his desires, his fears, and his frustrations.[1]

Diagnosis is an identification of weakness or strength from an observation of symptoms. It is an inference from performance. It must include assessment of both level of performance (reading retardation) and manner of performance (inability to integrate visual stimuli). It is concerned with determining the nature of the problem, identifying the constellation of factors that produced it, and finding a point of attack.

PRINCIPLES OF DIAGNOSIS

As one scans the literature on diagnosis, a few general principles emerge:

1. Diagnosis begins with each pupil's unique instructional needs:
   a. What can he do?

---

[1] From *Educational Bulletin No. 18*, "Educational Diagnosis," 1959 Revision, by Ernest W. Tiegs. By permission of California Test Bureau, a Division of McGraw-Hill Book Company, Del Monte Research Part, Monterey, California.

   b. What are his difficulties?

   c. What are the causes of his difficulties?

   d. What can be done to remedy his difficulties?

2. Diagnosis is a continuous process.

3. Diagnosis should be directed toward formulating methods of remediation. Educational diagnosis is productive only if it is translated into specific educational strategies.

4. Diagnosis and remediation are no longer the special privileges of the slow or retarded learner—they are extended to the gifted and the average as well.

5. Diagnosis may be concerned merely with the symptomatology, but genuine diagnosis looks toward the causes of the symptoms. The diagnostic viewpoint is that behavior is caused. The teacher thus needs to understand the causes of inadequate performance rather than to blame the pupil for it. The child should not be labelled dumb or lazy, even though each may be a cause once in a while.

6. The causes of pupil inadequacy are usually multiple rather than single or unitary.

7. The teacher needs more than simply skill in diagnosing the causes of the child's difficulty. He needs ability to modify instruction to meet the need identified by diagnosis.

8. Decisions based on diagnosis should flow from a pattern of test scores and a variety of other data.

9. The analysis of reading difficulties is primarily an *educational-analysis* task; it is best done by an experienced teacher who knows the essential elements of reading instruction (21, 354–355).

Steps in Diagnosis

Diagnosis leads to an ever more detailed study of the problem. It begins in reading with simple observation and possibly a survey test and ends up with a hypothesis for remediation. It involves the identification and description of the problem, the discovery of the causes, and projection of remediation required. More specifically, the steps of the diagnostic procedure may be the following:[2]

   1. The Over-all Screening Process—Compare expected functioning level as determined by IQ and other test and personal data with actual functioning level as determined by the reading

---

[2] Bateman, Barbara. "Learning Disabilities—Yesterday, Today, and Tomorrow." *Exceptional Children*, 31 (December, 1965) 167–176.

survey test or by other less formal procedures. This is the level
of *survey diagnosis* and consists chiefly of classroom screening.

2. Diagnostic Testing—Describe the condition more specifically,
checking on such specifics as knowledge of vocabulary, inability
to associate sound with the beginning consonant, inability to
phrase correctly, or reversal problems. Informal observations
of the pupil's reading and diagnostic testing will help to identify the difficulties. This is the level of *specific diagnosis* and is
identified with individual diagnosis.

3. Detailed Investigation of Causality—Make an analysis of the
disability, looking for the correlates of disability. If the test
results in Step 2 show a weakness in phonic skills, the pupil's
auditory discrimination might be checked. This is the level of
intensive diagnosis and is associated with identifying the underlying causes of the reading disability.

4. Remediation—Finally, draw up a program of remediation. Diagnosis is complete only when remediation occurs. The diag-
nostic-remedial process is a single process.

STEP 1: THE SCREENING PROCESS

Let us assume that we have a typical elementary school that has about
500 children and in which the administration and staff want to begin a
special reading program for those children who are more or less retarded
in reading. The immediate aim will be to reduce the number of pupils
for this special education to something below 500.

Screening separates those persons who are most likely to need special attention from those who are not likely to need it. It is commonly
applied to large groups of pupils by classroom teachers. This first step
tends to be comprehensive in *breadth*; the later steps in diagnosis are
more comprehensive in *depth*. Screening procedures should be simple,
fairly quick, inexpensive, valid, reliable, and productive.

For many children we do not need a detailed diagnosis. A more
general diagnosis is sufficient. It is enough in most instances that we
acquire sufficient knowledge about the 500 children or the 30 children
in a given classroom so that instruction might be adjusted to the group.
This over-all screening process should identify the over-all reading proficiency of the group or class, help to adjust instruction to individual
differences within the group, and locate those pupils who are in need
of further analysis of their disability.

There needs to be adequate provision for remediation of most
reading disability cases in the regular classroom. One factor that oper-

ates against remediation in the regular classroom is the high pupil-teacher ratio. It is difficult to provide individual remediation when there are 30 children, all clamoring for the teacher's time and attention.

The Nature of Retardation

Perhaps the first prerequisite for anyone associated with the reading program, and indeed the educational program, is to have a clear conception of the meaning of retardation. There is a difference between slow learners, reluctant readers, experientially-deprived readers, and retarded readers. Table 14-1 delineates some of these differences.

TABLE 14-1   Characteristics of Various Poor Readers

Slow Learner	Reluctant Reader	Disadvantaged Reader	Retarded Reader
ability level below 90 IQ ↓ generally reads on ability level ↓ generally reads below grade level ↓ instruction needs to be adapted to his limited ability—the pace of instruction and teacher expectations must be realistic	can read but will not ↓ the root of the reading difficulties is the mental attitude of the pupil ↓ solution to the reading problem begins with a change of attitude	potential often far exceeds performance ↓ generally can learn and wants to learn ↓ lacks adequate oral language because of inadequate experience ↓ does not look upon reading as life-related ↓ often feels alienated from the larger social structure ↓ often is deficient in auditory attention ↓ needs to learn how to learn	is usually of average or above average intelligence, although a retarded reader could also be a slow learner ↓ does not read on ability level ↓ may or may not be reading below grade level ↓ may show blocks to learning, especially emotional or neurological, which keep him from learning to read.

Retardation generally is defined in relation to level of general development, with perhaps the greater emphasis being on mental development. Retardation is associated with slower progress than is expected. A retarded reader is one whose reading capacity is considerably greater than his reading achievement. Bryant (11) notes that disability is always dependent upon the material and methods used in instruction. A child may not be able to learn by one method, but he may not be "disabled" if a different method is used.

A reader is also more or less retarded. The retarded reader of 50 years ago was more likely to be a pupil who could not read. Today, he often is a pupil who is not reading as well as he might. Durrell (20, p. 270) notes that a retardation of six months at the first grade level is more serious than is a retardation of six months at the sixth grade level. Harris (31, p. 299) does not consider a first-grade child retarded unless his reading age is at least six months below his mental age. The difference between performance and potential ought to be at least nine months for children in grades four and five and about a year in grades six and above.

Reading Potential

The first diagnostic step involves an analysis of (1) reading potential or reading expectancy level and (2) reading achievement. This presents the teacher with a knowledge of what the child's present level of achievement is and to what level he might progress.

Various ways of assessing reading potential have been tried. The tests most frequently used to assess reading potential are intelligence or scholastic aptitude tests. These tests often provide IQ or mental age scores.

Since the idea is to obtain intelligence or scholastic aptitude test scores on all 500 children in our sample school, or perhaps on a class of 30, it is recommended that the first test be a group paper and pencil test. Tests useful for this purpose are:

1. California Test of Mental Maturity
2. Kuhlmann-Anderson IQ Test
3. Kuhlmann-Finch IQ Test
4. Otis-Lennon Mental Ability Test
5. SRA Primary Mental Abilities Test

Each of these and other scholastic aptitude tests are described in Appendix II. Most primary tests use pictures and thus can generally be used with retarded readers. Tests for fourth grade and above usually require reading. Some of these, however, provide nonverbal scores, and these scores can give clues for diagnosis. When the verbal score is substantially lower than the nonverbal score, the teacher might suspect that the pupil's performance on the verbal sections is limited by the lack of reading ability. The test is thus an unfair test for him. It often places the poor reader in the dull-normal category, thus underestimating his real ability.

Probably, every child whose IQ score falls below 90 or below the twenty-fifth percentile on a test requiring reading should be given another intelligence or scholastic aptitude test. Another IQ test should also be given when the pupil's reading level score as determined by a reading achievement test is significantly below his grade level. This means that perhaps 25 per cent or 125 pupils of the original group of 500 need retesting. It may mean that from six to eight pupils in a given classroom need to be retested. Their abilities need to be measured by a test that does not require reading to get the correct answer. Here is a list of tests that are specifically designed to deal with this problem. Some of them may be administered to a group of children and others must be given individually. Some of the latter require special training for their administration.

Group
1.   IPAT Culture Fair Intelligence Tests

Individual
1.   Columbia Mental Maturity Scale
2.   Full Range Picture Vocabulary Test
3.   Peabody Picture Vocabulary Test
4.   Quick Test
5.   Slosson Intelligence Test for Children and Adults
6.   Stanford-Binet Intelligence Scales
7.   Wechsler Intelligence Scale for Children

Each of these tests is also described in Appendix II.

The IQ score should not be used as an absolute measure. A mechanical formula cannot decide for us when a pupil *is* a retarded reader, and it cannot tell us when the child is no longer a disabled reader (44). Nevertheless, the IQ, though perhaps too simple an estimate of the pupil's present academic potential, is the best that we have. It is indicative of the minimum that we might expect from the pupil; it is certainly not indicative of the maximum of which he is capable.

As was noted in Chapter 7, reading potential or readiness for reading instruction on the kindergarten–first-grade level also may be assessed through readiness tests.

There is a third way of estimating the pupil's potential. The pupil's listening ability is a good indicator of the level on which the pupil could be reading. Reading might be defined as listening through print. The following tests provide a measure of the pupil's listening comprehension.

1. *Stroud-Hieronymus Primary Reading Profiles* [Houghton Mifflin Company]. This test is designed for first and second grade levels and measures aptitude for reading, auditory association, word recognition, word attack, and interpretation and comprehension. Test 1, *Aptitude for Reading,* is a listening test, requiring no reading of any kind. Its purpose is to indicate the pupil's aptitude to understand spoken language, informative language, and directions, as well as his ability to associate the meaning of the pictures with what he hears.

2. *Botel Reading Inventory* [Follett Publishing Company]. This inventory for grades 1–12 has a section entitled "Word Opposites Listening Test." There are ten multiple choice items at each level. Each item consists of four or five words, and the pupil must find a word in each line that is the opposite of the first word.

3. *Sequential Tests of Educational Progress: Listening* [Cooperative Test Division, Educational Testing Services]. This listening test is part of a larger battery of tests usable on grade levels four to fourteen.

4. *Brown-Carlson Listening Comprehension Test* [Harcourt, Brace and World]. This test for grades nine-adult measures five important listening skills—immediate recall, following directions, recognizing transitions, recognizing word meanings, and lecture comprehension.

5. *Durrell Listening-Reading Series* [Harcourt, Brace and World]. This test provides a comparison of children's listening and reading ability in order to identify those pupils who are in need of special help. The series consists of a Reading Test and parallel Listening Test. The series is available for grades 7–9.

Reading Achievement

Having discovered the approximate potential of the 500 youngsters, or the 30 in the individual classroom, it is next necessary to get an estimate of their reading achievement. A reading survey test should be administered to each of the pupils.

The survey test is concerned with general achievement and typically is the first reading achievement test that the teacher will use. Usually it emphasizes vocabulary knowledge, comprehension of sentences or paragraphs, and perhaps speed of comprehension. It gives a general picture by identifying broad areas in which the pupil excels or is weak. It may tell, for example, that a certain child is reading at a level typical of children one or more grades above or below his present grade level. It indicates the general level of pupil progress and provides data for determining a pupil's proper grade placement and the reading materials that he should be expected to use with understanding.

Some common survey tests are the following:

1.   California Reading Test
2.   Durrell-Sullivan Reading Capacity and Achievement Test
3.   Gates-MacGinitie Reading Tests
4.   Iowa Silent Reading Test
5.   Metropolitan Reading Test

Each of these and other survey tests are described in Appendix III.

After having obtained the intelligence test score and the survey reading test scores, it is possible to identify the number of students whose reading scores are significantly below their intelligence or scholastic aptitude test score.

For a discussion of how to analyze test data, see Emerald Dechant, *Diagnosis and Remediation of Reading Disability* (West Nyack, N.Y.: Parker Publishing Company, 1968), pp. 19–24.

STEP 2: DIAGNOSTIC TESTING

Diagnostic testing continues the diagnostic process begun in Step 1 and is the beginning of detailed diagnosis. It is directed toward defining the actual nature of the individual's reading difficulties and toward identifying the conditions causing them. It is a detailed investigation of the symptoms of reading disability, leading to a clinical diagnosis. Here the teacher is not satisfied to know that the pupil is reading on a second-grade level when in fact he might be able to read on a fourth-grade level. The teacher wants to know the specific reasons for the over-all low performance: Is it the inability to attack words? Is it the limited vocabulary? Is it the failure to use context? Is it the lack of ability in auditory blending? Is it an orientational difficulty? Or is it a combination of factors?

Smith and Carrigan (63, p. 91) note that diagnosis must be based on a careful investigation of the symptoms, on psychological test behavior, and often on intensive clinical case studies. "Such dead-end diagnosis as 'he isn't trying'; 'he needs more discipline'; 'he's neurotic'; 'too much pressure from his parents'; 'the trouble is, the schools don't teach phonics any more'—such conscience balms must be replaced with a clinical diagnosis." [3]

Step 2 thus is a specific, an individual, and a clinical diagnosis. It is a detailed analysis of the reading problems of pupils identified in step 1 as retarded readers. Let's assume that about 20 per cent of the pupils

[3] D. E. P. Smith and Patricia M. Carrigan, *The Nature of Reading Disability* (New York: Harcourt, Brace and Company, Inc., 1959). Reprinted by permission.

studied in step 1 are actually retarded in reading. It is now necessary to determine what their specific difficulties are and where, whether in the regular classroom or in the remedial room, their difficulties might best be taken care of.

In many schools, the classroom teacher is still the person primarily responsible for the diagnosis and remediation of reading problems. In others, the teacher is assisted by a remedial teacher or a reading specialist. This special reading teacher might then direct the diagnostic process or actually do the diagnosing himself.

Step 2 should include, if possible, the personal data sheet, a learning and behavior checklist, and a formal or informal inventory, an oral reading test, or a diagnostic test. Let us begin with the personal data sheet.

Personal Data Sheet

The first report on each pupil who was revealed in step 1 to be reading significantly below his ability should summarize personal data on the pupil. This report might be used as the referral form from the classroom teacher to the special teacher if this becomes necessary. It might also be sent to the pupil's new teacher when the pupil moves from one grade to another. In this way, the new teacher would have some knowledge of the pupil's needs and could then adjust his instruction to the pupil.

The personal data sheet includes such data as pupil's name, age, grade level, address, his previous grades, his attendance record, statements about his health, standardized test results, a compilation of the anecdotal reports by other teachers, and most of all the reason for the referral. The reason may be that the pupil is not reading up to ability level. The statement might simply read: "The test results indicate that he is reading about one grade level below his ability"; "He has a mental age of ten, but is reading like the average eight year old"; or, "His reading level is substantially below his listening comprehension level."

Whether the pupil is referred or kept in the regular classroom, it is imperative that the teacher know at least in a general sense what the problem is. The remaining instruments discussed in this chapter delve more deeply into the pupil's more specific problems and symptoms.

A form similar to Figure 14-1 might be used to compile the basic information of a pupil.

Learning and Behavior Checklist

There is also a need for another report, detailing the pupil's behavior and learning problems in the classroom. It is designed to summarize information about the child's usual scholastic performance and interac-

Figure 14-1. **Personal Data Sheet**

Pupil's Name _____ Birthdate _____
                                                                              Mo.   Day   Year

Parent's Name _____ Age _____ Grade _____

Address_____ Phone _____

Academic Progress
  Report last year's grade(s)

Attendance Record
  Number of days absent for each grade: K _____ 1 _____ 2 _____ 3 _____ 4 _____
                                                          5 _____ 6 _____ 7 _____ 8 _____

Health
  (List physical infirmities, accidents, and severe illnesses as listed in school record).

Standardized Tests
  (Include all test results available—intelligence tests, achievement tests, etc.)

| *Date Given* | *Name of Test* | *Score by* | |
| | | *Grade Level* | *Percentile* |

Reason for Referral

Anecdotal Reports or Comments of Former Teachers (Report on back of this page)

                                        Signed _____

                                        Position _____

Date of report _____ 19____

---

tion in classroom affairs. A checklist, such as the one in Chapter 2 in *Diagnosis and Remediation of Reading Disability* (16, pp. 29–32), might be completed by the teacher on each pupil who is significantly retarded in reading.

Formal or Informal Inventory

A teacher's prime task (or the special teacher's as the case might be) with the retarded may be to identify the pupil's frustration, instructional, and independent reading level. To do this, he may administer additional individual intelligence tests, such as the *Wechsler Intelligence Scale for Children* (WISC) or the *Revised Stanford-Binet Scale* and additional achievement tests, but he certainly makes use of informal and formal reading inventories.

The *WISC* consists of subtests that have proven useful in diagnosis. Neville (48) found that poor readers score low on the Arithmetic, Coding, and Information subtests, and score relatively higher on the Picture Arrangement and Picture Completion. Reid and Schoer (56) also reported readers scored significantly lower on the Arithmetic subtest of the *WISC* but showed relative high performance on the Picture Completion subtest. The retarded readers likewise scored lower on the Digit Span and Similarities subtests. Ekwall (24) found that 43 retarded readers in grades four, five, and six scored significantly low on Information, Arithmetic, and Digit Span and significantly high on Picture Completion, Block Design, Picture Arrangement, Object Assembly, and Coding. Sawyer (60) reports that the Wechsler subscales did discriminate between severely disabled and mildly disabled readers.

Informal Inventories   The classroom teacher has probably already used informal procedures in gauging the reader's achievement as well as his frustration, instructional, or independent level. He frequently determines the level of the child's performance through an informal analysis of the pupil's oral reading.

Betts (6) considers a child to be reading on a frustration level if he reads with less than 75 per cent comprehension and less than 90 per cent of accuracy. He reads on an instructional level if he reads with 75 per cent comprehension and 95 per cent accuracy in word recognition. He reads on an independent level if he reads with 90 per cent comprehension and with 99 per cent accuracy in word recognition. Elder (23) reports that children can use materials for instructional purposes in which they know 88–89 per cent of the words.

Generally, the teacher will select a passage for the pupil to read orally. The teacher ought to have picked out the passages, made a readability check on each, and have some questions prepared to measure pupil competency before he uses a given book to make an informal check on a pupil's reading. The reading by the pupil tells something of the pupil's background of experience, of his vocabulary knowledge, of his reading habits (slowness in reading, lip movements, or finger pointing), of his comprehension, and of his specific difficulties.

As the child reads, the teacher looks for pupil interest in materials, pupil concentration or apathy, the speed with which he completes his work; the willingness to read orally, and the ability to follow directions. The first sign indicative of poor reading is often the pupil's attitude toward reading. A pupil who does not read well generally is not willing to read aloud. He would rather hear others.

The teacher notes whether the child's oral reading indicates deficiencies in sight reading, in vocabulary, in structural or phonetic analysis, in comprehension, in eye-voice span, in phrasing, or in inflection. He checks whether in his silent reading the pupil follows instructions, reads for meaning, and uses the context to determine the meaning of the story. He is interested in whether the learner hears and sees likenesses and differences in letters and words. He evaluates the pupil's expressive and receptive abilities in the oral language area.

Smith, in *Graded Selections for Informal Reading Diagnosis: Grades One through Three,* 1959 and in *Graded Selections for Informal Reading Diagnosis: Grades Four through Six,* 1963, both published by New York University Press, lists passages for use in informal diagnosis. The reading passages are presented with questions and answers and with vocabulary checks useful in detecting word recognition difficulties.

Inventories help the teacher to determine changes in instructional, frustration, and independent reading level and to detect improvements or continuing inadequacies in dealing with individual reading skills. They provide a good measure of the child's true growth. Other devices such as the following may be used to aid informal diagnosis.

1. Keep samples of classroom work.
2. Make an anecdotal record of the child's reading behavior.
3. Have the pupil write a reading autobiography.
4. Place a transparency over the book from which the child reads to check errors that can be analyzed later.
5. Make a tape recording of the pupil's reading.

Formal Inventories   Many classroom teachers use formal or standardized inventories to gauge a child's reading level. These are usually compilations of graded reading selections with questions prepared in advance to test the reader's comprehension.

Frequently, the formal inventory is administered by the special or remedial reading teacher to pupils identified as retarded readers. He is especially interested in a more detailed diagnosis of the pupil's reading deficiencies. He is not satisfied with an over-all estimate of the pupil's reading ability, but wants to know specific strengths and weaknesses.

Two good standardized inventories are the *Botel Reading Inventory* and the *Classroom Reading Inventory*.[4] The *Botel Reading Inventory,* designed for grades 1–12 and published by Follett Publishing Company, obtains an estimate of the pupil's instructional, independent, and frustration reading level. It is useful only when the reading level is below fourth grade. The inventory consists of two tests: *Phonics Mastery Test* and the *Reading Placement Test.*

Standardized tests often overestimate the child's reading ability (15), and thus greater reliance needs to be placed upon the results of formal and informal reading inventories. Betts (6, pp. 450–451) felt tests place children at their frustration level; Harris (31, p. 180) thinks that they identify the instructional level rather than the independent level. Sipay (62) found that standardized tests overestimate the pupil's instructional level of fourth graders by about one grade level and underestimate the frustration by about one grade level, leading him to conclude that it is impossible to generalize as to whether standardized tests indicate the frustration or instructional level.

The Botel inventory suggests that a pupil is reading on an instructional level when the pupil can recognize and pronounce 70–90 per cent of the words in the Word Recognition Test and when he can comprehend 70–80 per cent of the words in the Word Opposites Test. The pupil is reading on a frustration level when he fails to recognize more than five per cent of the running words in the Botel inventory (this is equivalent to 70 per cent on other lists) and shows less than 70 per cent comprehension. Pupils reading on this level tend to dislike reading, are anxious, read orally with poor rhythm and timing, and point to words.

Another inventory, *The Classroom Reading Inventory,* has recently been developed by Nicholas Silvaroli and is published by Wm. C. Brown Company, 135 South Locust Street, Dubuque, Iowa. It is designed specifically for teachers who have not had prior experience with individual diagnostic reading measures. The chief purpose of the inventory is to identify the frustration, instructional, and independent reading level of the pupil. It is useful in grades two through eight.

The Classroom Reading Inventory is composed of two main parts: Part I, Graded Word Lists, and Part II, Graded Oral Paragraphs. Part III, A Graded Spelling Survey, may also be administered. Parts I and II must be administered individually; Part III may be administered to

---

[4] The *Standard Reading Inventory* by Robert A. McCracken is available through Pioneer Printing Company, Bellingham, Washington. It is usable on preprimer through seventh-grade level.

groups. The inventory may be administered quite easily in about 15 minutes.

Dolch Basic Sight Word List   Other inventories or checks that isolate specific areas might be constructed. For example, the classroom or special teacher will learn much about a child's reading by having him respond to a test over the Dolch Basic Sight Word List.

If the pupil knows up to 75 of these words, he may be reading at a preprimer level; up to 120, on the primer level; up to 170, on the first reader level; up to 210, on the second reader level; up to 220, on the third reader level. A child is given credit for knowing the word if he can pronounce it or if he corrects the word immediately after pronouncing it.

Inventories have an advantage in that they provide some clues as to why a pupil pronounced the word in a peculiar way, why he reversed letters, or why he skipped a word. In diagnosing, we are especially interested in the causes of errors. Our interest does not cease with a yes or no answer; we want to know why and how the child got his answer. It is, for example, quite common at the first grade level for a child to recognize a word by means of irrelevant clues (e.g., identification of words with an erasure mark or a torn edge in the book or on the word card).

In using inventories we generally are trying to determine what books a child can read independently and how difficult an assigned reading can be and still be used as instructional material. Although, unfortunately, grade-level designations furnished by the publishers of many books are far from accurate, the experienced teacher can select a suitable set of books and other materials for use in informal determinations of children's reading abilities. The informal reading inventory analysis is more clinical in nature than test interpretation, but studies (41,43) show that teachers are quite accurate in predicting children's readiness for reading. However, Emans (26) did not find that the experienced teachers in his study were particularly apt in determining the reading deficiencies of children without the benefit of diagnostic testing.

The classroom teacher should forward to the remedial teacher or to the reading clinic the results of any informal or formal inventories that he administered to the retarded reader while he was in the regular classroom.

Oral Reading Tests

Oral Reading Tests are helpful both in measuring pupil reading achievement (especially in oral reading) and in making diagnostic evaluations. They possess many of the same advantages as the reading inventories in that they permit the teacher to detect the errors made by the pupil and to identify the reasons why the error was made.

Here is a list of some common oral reading tests:

1. Gilmore Oral Reading Test
2. Leavell Analytical Oral Reading Test
3. Slosson Oral Reading Test
4. New Gray Oral Reading Test

Each of these tests is described in Appendix V.

Oral reading tests are very useful in the diagnosis of reading difficulties. There is strong evidence to suggest that the oral reading errors of a pupil tend to be carried over to silent reading. The oral reading test thus reveals pupil strengths and weaknesses and suggests the kinds and types of reading experiences which should be provided. Analysis of pupil errors should help to identify areas where most of the mistakes occur and toward which remedial teaching ought to be directed.

Diagnostic Reading Tests

The diagnostic reading test, like some of the instruments already described, seeks to discover specific strengths and weaknesses. It is especially useful in planning remedial procedures. It is no doubt possible to make a successful diagnosis without using any objective test measures, just as it is possible for a physician to diagnose a disease correctly without x-ray analysis. However, for the most part diagnostic tests prove helpful.

The survey test, the type given in step 1, tells us, for example, that a boy or girl who is in fifth grade is reading at a level typical for third graders. The diagnostic test, on the other hand, identifies the pupil's specific deficiencies, his inability to work out unfamiliar words, his inability to blend sounds, or his tendency to reverse. It helps to locate those areas of deficiencies that need to be investigated further. It also may indicate which instructional adjustments are needed. It provides the basis for planning remedial teaching of such specifics as word analysis or phonic skills.

The following diagnostic tests have demonstrated their usefulness in diagnosis:

1. Bond-Clymer-Hoyt Silent Reading Diagnostic Test
2. Doren Diagnostic Reading Test
3. Durrell Analysis of Reading Difficulty
4. Gates-McKillop Reading Diagnostic Test
5. Roswell-Chall Diagnostic Reading Test
6. Spache Diagnostic Reading Scales

Each of these diagnostic tests along with others is described in Appendix IV.

The *Durrell Analysis of Reading Difficulty*, as an example, is designed for grades one through six. Testing time is usually from 30 to 45 minutes. It consists of the following subtests:

1. Oral Reading Test
2. Silent Reading Test
3. Listening Comprehension Test
4. Word Recognition and Word Analysis Test
5. Naming Letters
6. Identifying Letters Named
7. Matching Letters
8. Writing Letters
9. Visual Memory for Words
10. Hearing Sounds in Words
11. Learning to Hear Sounds in Words
12. Learning Rate
13. Phonic Spelling of Words
14. Spelling Test
15. Handwriting Test

The teacher may want to give tests such as the following to evaluate even more closely a pupil's problem:

1. Auditory Discrimination Test, Language Research Associates, Chicago, Illinois.
2. California Phonics Survey Test, California Test Bureau.
3. Illinois Test of Psycholinguistic Abilities, Institute for Research on Exceptional Children, University of Illinois.
4. Leavell Hand-Eye Coordination Test, Keystone View Company.
5. Marianne Frostig Developmental Test of Visual Perception, Consulting Psychologists Press, Palo Alto, California.
6. McKee Inventory of Phonetic Skills, Houghton Mifflin Company.
7. Mills Learning Methods Test, Mills Center, Fort Lauderdale, Florida.
8. Perceptual Forms Test, Winter Haven Lions Publication Committee, P.O. Box 1045, Winter Haven, Florida.
9. Phonics Knowledge Survey, Columbia University.
10. Phonics Mastery Test, Follett Publishing Company.
11. Robbins Speech Sound Discrimination and Verbal Imagery Type Tests, Expression Company, Magnolia, Massachusetts

12. Roswell-Chall Auditory Blending Test, Essay Press, P.O. Box 5, Planetarium Station, New York, N.Y.
13. Screening Test for Identifying Children with Specific Language Disability, Educators Publishing Service, Cambridge, Massachusetts.

The Symptomatology of Reading Disability

What is the significance of step 2? It is an intensive study of the symptoms of reading disability. At this level we are still concerned primarily with identifying the areas of difficulty. We are dealing with symptomatology.

Many reading disabilities become disabilities because teachers are not familiar with some of the symptoms of disability. The result is that some reading needs are not met, leading to disability cases. It is obvious that a clear identification of the symptoms of reading disability is needed.

Symptoms are observable characteristics which help the teacher to make some educated guesses about the pupil's reading problems. Symptoms rarely appear singly. There usually is a pattern of symptoms, a syndrome that characterizes the individual reading disability case. The teacher needs to know the pattern, must attempt to understand it, and must have the educational know-how to deal with the syndrome. The diagnostic responsibility of the classroom teacher or the reading specialist is to identify the pattern of symptoms, relate it to the appropriate skill area or areas, and plan a program to correct the deficiency. The interpretation of the syndrome pattern is much more significant than are the data themselves.

The Developmental Reading Program

Let us again look at pupils found to be retarded. Our concern is to decide the type of help the pupil needs and where he can best receive help. Perhaps at this time we should take a look at various phases of the total reading program. Authorities in the field speak of the developmental reading program, the corrective reading program, and the remedial reading program.

The developmental program emphasizes reading instruction that is designed to develop systematically the skills and abilities considered essential at each level of reading advancement. It thus encompasses also the corrective and remedial program. Perhaps we should then speak of developmental, corrective, and remedial instruction. Developmental instruction is the type of instruction that is given to the majority of children in the regular classroom.

Corrective instruction consists of remedial activities usually carried on by the regular classroom teacher within the framework of regular classroom instruction. Corrective instruction is provided when the entire class or a small group of pupils is deficient in a particular skill. Corrective reading deals with the problems of the partial disability case, that type of pupil who can identify words and comprehend what he reads, but only after great difficulty. The pupil may not have been ready for initial reading experiences, instruction may have consistently been above or below his level of ability, or classroom stimulation may have been inadequate.

Remedial instruction consists of remedial activities taking place outside of the framework of regular class instruction and is usually conducted by a special teacher of reading. Remedial instruction should thus be restricted to a small clinical group with severe symptoms of reading retardation—those having difficulty mastering even the simplest mechanics of reading. Such pupils are often identified as word blind, alexiac, or dylexiac learners. They have difficulty in remembering whole word patterns, do not learn easily by the sight method, and show orientational difficulties. The total reading program might schematically be portrayed as in Figure 14-2.

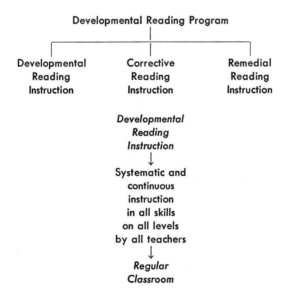

Figure 14-2

If the pupil has a reading problem and if he is not a slow learner, a reluctant reader, or a disadvantaged reader, he needs corrective or remedial instruction and should be able to be classified as either a case of general retardation, specific retardation, or remedial disability case. Table 14-2 describes in greater detail the characteristics of the corrective reader with general or specific retardation.

TABLE 14-2   Characteristics of the Corrective Reader

Case of General Retardation	Case of Specific Retardation
The reading level is substantially lower than the mental age, but no other specific problem exists. He is a case of partial disability. ↓	There is a definite weakness in a given area. This is usually a skill weakness. ↓
He is a pupil who learns only after undue and laborious effort; he is like the underweight child whose eating habits are not conducive to gaining weight but who, if he follows the proper diet, will gain. He learns after inhibiting factors have been removed. ↓	This is a case of reading retardation not complicated by neurological difficulties. ↓
The pupil may not have been ready for initial reading experiences and thus fell further and further behind as his schooling continued. ↓	Learning capacity is adequate, but deficiencies in regard to certain specifics in word analysis or comprehension indicate that he has not profited from regular class work as well as he might. He has missed or has not profited from basic instruction in a given area. ↓
Instruction and reading materials generally have been above the pupil's level of ability and above his level of achievement in word-recognition and comprehension skills. ↓	Although each pupil presents a distinct pattern of acquisition and remediation, there will usually be others in the class with similar problems. ↓
He perhaps was absent from school at critical periods. ↓	His over-all reading performance may be high over-all in relation to his ability, but diagnostic testing will reveal a low subscore on a test. ↓
He perhaps was not stimulated to learn because instruction was below his ability level. ↓	There is usually a need for training in the area of weakness rather than a need for total remediation in the basic skills. ↓
The reading profile of the generally retarded pupil is relatively uniform. ↓	The pupil should be kept in the regular classroom in which reading is taught to subgroups of three to five.
He needs more experience in reading, including systematic instruction at his level of ability. Usually a visual-auditory technique or method is adequate. He does not need a VAKT method of teaching such as the Fernald or Gillingham method. There is a need for major adjustment in materials and instruction and for a reading program that motivates the pupil to learn. ↓	
On the secondary level, the pupil may be referred to the remedial teacher. ↓	
The pupil should be kept in the regular classroom.	

The remedial reader is not so easily described. Even though experts agree that the remedial reader is actually a constellation of characteristics and subtypes, there is a great deal of confusion about terminology and even about the identifying characteristics of various levels of retardation.

We divide remedial readers into four types. This is another way of saying there are four types of severe reading disability or of wordblindness. Figure 14-3 illustrates these types.

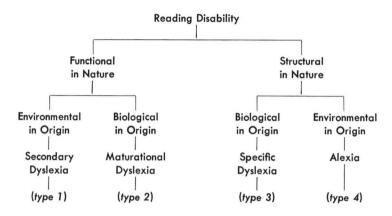

Figure 14-3 Characteristics of the Remedial Reader

Secondary Dyslexia   Secondary dyslexia or type 1 is often termed a secondary reading disability. It is by far the most common form of disability seen in remedial readers. This syndrome is characterized as follows:

1. The pupil's problems are more severe than those of the corrective reader, and include inability to use contextual clues, poor comprehension, wild guessing at words, inability to deal with individual letter sounds, reversal tendency, and difficulty in structural analysis.
2. There usually is no single identifiable cause of the disability. Multiple causality is indicated, with the reading disability closely related to intellectual, emotional, environmental, psychological or educational factors. It is probable that some factor is the precipitating cause; other factors are contributing causes.
3. The major cause is not attributable to dysfunction or delayed development of the brain. The capacity to read is intact. The causative factors are exogenous, that is, the disability is not innate or the result of a deficit in structure or functioning of the brain. There is usually no familial history of reading disability. This child reads poorly, but he has a normal reading potential. His reading differs from the normal in quantity but not in quality.
4. A therapeutic diagnosis is adequate. Bond and Tinker (8, p. 153) note:

In studying a disabled reader, whether in the classroom or clinic, the diagnosis should be concerned with the collection of information necessary for planning a corrective program. There are two types of diagnosis—etiological and therapeutic. Etiological diagnosis is concerned with finding out what caused a child to get into difficulty. Such a search is often impossible and frequently useless for formulating a remedial program. It is of little use, for example, to search the records and find a child is in difficulty in reading in the fourth grade because he was absent from school with the measles when he was in the first grade. Nothing can be done now to give him the help that should have been available when he returned to school after a month's absence during the first grade. A body of such information, collected and summarized for research purposes, would be most useful for the prevention of reading difficulties, but it is not now useful for the immediate job of correcting a reading disability that began several years earlier.

Therapeutic diagnosis is concerned with the conditions that are now present in the child in order to give direction to a program of re-education. The diagnostician concerned with therapeutic diagnosis searches for the reading strengths and limitations of a child and for any characteristics within this child's present environment or makeup that need to be corrected before this remedial instruction can be successful, or for conditions that need to be adjusted to before he can be expected to make maximum progress. The diagnostician would be more concerned about a current hearing loss, for example, than he would be about finding out that the child was in difficulty because he had had a temporary hearing loss several years ago.[4]

5. The pupil should be taught in small groups in a remedial setting. Remedial teaching is usually successful with this type of learner.

Chapters 3–4 discuss the causes of secondary reading disability in detail.

Maturational Dyslexia   Type 2 or maturational dyslexia indicates the presence of some brain pathology, but it is not aphasic in nature. There is no structural defect, deficiency, or loss. It is more like aplasia in that the neural tissues have failed to develop. There is an absence of function rather than a loss of function. The condition flows from cerebral immaturity or a maturational lag or slowness in certain specialized aspects of neurological development. There is delayed or irregular neurological development. The potential is there, but it has not yet been

[4] Guy L. Bond and Miles A. Tinker, *Reading Difficulties: Their Diagnosis and Correction*, Appleton-Century-Crofts, 1967. Reprinted by permission.

realized. He is a late bloomer. He is not yet matured but is capable of maturing.

The characteristics that identify this reader are very much like those of type 3. Delacato's description of reading disability, with its emphasis on neurological maturity, neurological organization, and hemispheric dominance, fits here.

Specific Dyslexia   Specific dyslexia or type 3 goes by various names: primary reading disability, specific reading disability, congenital reading disability, constitutional reading disability, developmental dyslexia, and congenital wordblindness. It is difficult to describe because "there is no single clinical feature which can be accepted as pathognomonic (16*a*)." There is no invariable common core of symptoms. It is a massive unreadiness for reading (45). It is a failure to learn to read even though the child has had appropriate instruction, comes from a culturally-adequate home, is properly motivated, has adequate sensory equipment, has normal intelligence, and shows no gross neurological defect or brain pathology (22, p. 14). Retardation nevertheless is based on some organic incapacity (51*a*). The neurological signs are minimal. There is need for an etiological diagnosis.

The pupil is deficient in even the most fundamental basic reading skills. It is almost as though the pupil had never been in school. Remedial instruction often seems to have little effect, and where it is effective, it may well be that the pupil is a type 2 case rather than a genuine case of specific dyslexia.

It is not always possible to distinguish between specific dyslexia and dyslexia of a neurological nature. In fact, there is no foolproof way of diagnosing specific dyslexia; no one has uncovered a telltale symptom or group of symptoms that are exclusive to the syndrome of specific dyslexia and which are not found in other cases of reading retardation, but whatever the etiology of reading retardation may be, the principles of remediation seem the same or at least are very similar.

The following characteristics identify the dyslexic:

1. The dyslexic reader is usually a boy, although girls also can be dyslexic. Delacato suggests that boys have bigger heads and so the incidence of difficult birth is greater among boys. This does not mean that the disability is inherited. It simply means that predisposing conditions are present in certain families. It may be that reading disability is related to the bodily structure of the woman which in some instances causes difficulty of birth.

2. His IQ is usually in the normal range, but Verbal IQ tends to be significantly below the Performance IQ.

3. There is more persistent and frequent left-right confusion.
   a. There is a reversal of concepts: floor for ceiling, go for stop, east for west. The dyslexic frequently makes kinetic reversals. He reads entire words backwards, e.g., saw–was. He may perform as well if the book is held upside down.
   b. Penmanship is characterized by poorly formed and irregular characters, untidiness, malalignment, omissions, linkages which are too short or too long, and fusion of letters. Drawing and copying are poor.
   c. He comes from families in which there is left-handedness or language disorders or both.
   d. He shows evidence of delayed or incomplete establishment of one-sided motor preferences. He tends to be left-handed, ambidextrous, or shows mixed dominance. These orientational problems may not be present in the older dyslexic. On earlier age levels, lack of form perception and of directional sense and dyslexia may go hand in hand. A faulty sense of direction ought not be confused with crossed dominance. Benton, in *Right-Left Discrimination and Finger Localization* (New York: Hoeber, 1959), describes how to identify the person with right-left disorientation.
4. He often has speech difficulties and poor auditory discrimination. Stuttering, lisping, stammering and cluttering often are quite noticeable.
5. He is more likely to have been premature or to have survived some complication of pregnancy.
6. He is generally an underachiever.
7. He is hyperactive, distractive, distractable, impulsive, shows poor motor coordination, has a short attention span, and perseverates excessively.
8. He has difficulty in spatial relationships and in figure-ground perception.
9. Dyslexic children may divide into three patterns (7a):
   a. Auditory dyslexics: They may show deficits in symbol-sound integration, cannot develop phonic skills, or cannot auditorize. Their ability to visualize may be quite normal. They are visual learners and may best be taught initially through a whole-word configuration or sight method. They remember the shapes of the letters, but cannot associate the proper phoneme with the proper shape. They need to be taught to do this.
   b. Visual dyslexics: They cannot develop gestalts for letters or words, showing little ability to visualize. They are weak in visual imagery, have poor visual memory, and poor visual

discrimination skill. Initial remedial teaching might begin with tactile-kinesthetic techniques (The Fernald Method) if they have not yet acquired visual recognition for letters. Remedial phonics, such as the Orton-Gillingham approach, might be used if letter recognition has occurred.

c. Auditory-visual dyslexics: This group represents a combination of groups one and two. The child cannot read by sight or by ear.

10. There is an associative learning disability, making it impossible for him to associate experiences and meaning with symbols or to associate symbol with symbol. This pupil will ask again and again for help with the same word. He has great difficulty with visual recognition and recall of familiar words. He may also experience difficulty learning other symbols such as number or music symbols. Both visual and auditory symbols fail to achieve identity. He cannot associate sounds with visual symbols. The pupil cannot deal with letters and words as symbols and thus cannot integrate the meaningfulness of written material. He does not experience the "flash," global identification of a word as a whole and cannot synthesize the word out of its component letter units. He cannot see or identify the word as an entity, but also ignores many details in words. The letter standing alone has no language identity. *S* may be described as a traffic sign. He may be totally deficient in word attack or in comprehension. His reading is arrhythmical and replete with word recognition errors.

a. The pupil cannot pronounce unfamiliar words. He has a tendency to guess wildly at words. He pays attention to specific letters and guesses wildly at the rest; horse becomes house. His rendition of a word is often phonetically unrelated to the desired response (dog becomes chay). He cannot put the sounds together so as to constitute a word. He can spell b-a-n-a-n-a, but cannot pronounce it.

b. He confuses similar appearing words, e.g., bed-fed.

c. He frequently loses his place in reading and does not move easily from the end of one line to the beginning of another line.

d. He vocalizes excessively while reading silently.

e. He demonstrates more vowel, consonant, reversal, omission, addition, substitution, perserveration, and repetition errors.

f. He has marked difficulty in blending sounds to produce a word.

g. Comprehension tends to be poor, but he is also an exceedingly slow reader.

11.   The reading behavior of the dyslexic is extremely variable. On a given day he may reverse; the following day no reversal problems appear.

The reading teacher must realize that we do not have all the answers to reading disability. There simply is not a remedy for every disability. Children may fail even under the most favorable educational circumstances.

Alexia   Alexia or type 4 is the loss of the ability to read as a result of damage, injury, or lesion to the association and connection areas in and around the angular gyrus of the dominant cerebral hemisphere (51a). For most of us this is the left hemisphere. Here there is clear brain pathology which prevents the pupil from becoming a reader. The pupil may see black marks on paper, but does not recognize that they represent words. The past history of such an individual often reveals normal speech development initially. There may be no family history of reading difficulty. Instructional techniques alone cannot come directly to grips with the reading problem; this is a reader who is neurologically unable to read. The symptoms of reading disability are much like those that are seen in type 3.

The Teacher's Task

As the teacher works with the symptomatology in a given case, he should ask himself four questions (70):

1.   Did the pupil make the same error on both easy and difficult material or were his errors chiefly the result of having to read material which for him was on a frustration level? Diagnostic conclusions and remediation should not be based on errors made on material that is clearly too difficult for the pupil.
2.   Were his slowness in reading and his constant need to regress while reading the result of poor reading skill or simply of his desire to read carefully? Diagnostic conclusions should not be based on comprehension errors made over material the pupil did not have time to read. Sometimes, the pupil's reading grade level is inaccurate because he answered questions incorrectly on a test that he did not have time to finish.
3.   Was the pupil's performance reliable, or was it poorer than usual because he was nervous, upset, or distracted during the testing situations?
4.   Was the pupil's poor reading performance basically in the area of comprehension skills, word-identification skills, rate skills, oral reading, or a combination of these?

STEP 3: A DETAILED INVESTIGATION OF CAUSALITY

Step 3 of diagnostic procedure is a thorough analysis of the reading disability leading to an identification of the causal factors involved. It is the level of intensive diagnosis, a detailed study of the correlates of disability.

Chapters 3 and 4 looked at some of the major causes of reading disability. We discussed such areas as inadequate experiential background, inadequate language background, inadequate maturation, inadequacies in intellectual-social-emotional development, lack of motivation, instructional inadequacies, visual and auditory inadequacy, and deficiencies in other physical-physiological areas.

An important question is surely: "So what? You know the causes of reading disability, but what can you do about it?"

The teacher can do something about the causes of reading disability by:

1. Providing preparatory experiences necessary for learning.
2. Using and developing reading materials that present experiences familiar to the children being taught and that capitalize on the pupil's preferred modes of learning.
3. Helping children to develop their listening skills.
4. Helping children to articulate the sounds of the language.
5. Providing language training along with reading instruction.
6. Providing appropriate environmental stimulations so that maturational development may progress at an appropriate rate. Let instruction march slightly, but only slightly, ahead of the child's maturation process.
7. Using intelligence test scores and other data to gear the instructional program to the ability level of the pupil.
8. Striving to expand the intelligence level of all children.
9. Checking the child for:
    a. signs of illness or over-all poor health.
    b. visual problems.
    c. hearing problems.
10. Looking for symptoms of neurological disturbances and referring the child to a specialist if this is indicated.
11. Teaching reading in such a way as to enhance the social-emotional development of the learner and so as to whet his appetite for reading.
12. Constantly evaluating his teaching.

But even more important than the above is the need to develop competency in hooking symptoms to their proper cause. The special or remedial reading teacher is by definition an expert in tying together symptom and cause. The classroom teacher can become quite expert in doing the same thing.

It requires considerable skill and care to transfer the diagnostic data into an accurate prescription that can serve as the basis for remediation. In making the transfer we must recognize certain dangers. Sometimes the learner's symptoms may lead us to take faulty steps toward his remediation. What may appear to be the cause of his difficulty may be quite unrelated to it or may even be a result or symptom of his problems. But skill and experience in the translation of diagnostic data and an earnest desire to help each student attain the highest goals that his capabilities permit should serve as a firm foundation for remediation.

The two symptoms in Table 14-3 are common symptoms of reading disability. But what is their cause? We have suggested four possible ones for symptom 1 (there are others) and three for symptom 2 and have suggested remediation in each instance. This is the type of skill needed by the classroom teacher.

TABLE 14-3   Two Common Symptoms of Reading Disability

Symptom	Possible Cause	Possible Remedy
1. Inability to remember a letter visually or makes frequent substitutions of words.	a. Poor vision.	a. Check and remediate visual defect. Have pupil engage in exercises teaching discrimination of letters.
	b. Inability to tie letters together and remember them (c-a-t). Poor visual memory span.	b. Provide tracing exercises to develop a "feel" for the word; stress training in visual discrimination of words.
	c. Reverses letters and so can't discriminate and remember them (b-d).	c. Check if he also reverses nonsense syllables. Have pupil engage in exercises designed to change the pattern.
	d. Inattention, not wanting to learn.	d. Use language-experience approach.
2. Inability to discriminate word sounds. For example, the teacher might say, "Now listen for the sound pig . . . big, dig, pig, pick." The child cannot deal with this problem.	a. Poor hearing—poor auditory acuity.	a. Check hearing and consult doctor.
	b. Speech defects: "Father becomes fodder," "Shishter for sister," "Kool for school."	b. Provide training in articulation.
	c. Poor auditory discrimination.	c. Seat child near teacher; check for high tone deafness and watch for sounds f, v, s, z, sh, zh, th, t, d, p, b, k, and g; provide exercises in auditory discrimination.

As one completes this third step, the chances are that the following has been done:

1. A case history has been compiled.
2. The pupil's capacity has been analyzed including, if possible, the results of hearing tests, visual screening tests, eye-movement data, hand and eye preference tests.
3. The level of oral and silent reading achievement has been determined.
4. The reading problem has been identified.
5. The factors that interfere with reading have been isolated.
6. The data have been collated and interpreted.

The written report of the diagnosis should include recommendations as to *how* the child should be taught and should suggest materials that may be used in teaching. It should outline specific weaknesses in word analysis and in comprehension. There might be statements about the child's spontaneity or lack of it in correcting his own errors; statements about the ease or lack of it with which the pupil develops insight into phonic generalizations; statements about the pupil's awareness or lack of awareness of phonetic differences in words; or statements about the reasons why the pupil substitutes words of similar meaning.

The teacher needs to become expert in reading the causes of reading disability. Smith and Carrigan (63) note:

> **Clinicians are like a small group standing beside a river full of drowning people. The victims are being swept seaward by the current of time. The clinicians can pull out a few, but the rest are lost. Few of the group are willing to go upstream to find out how the victims get into the river in the first place.**[5]

The teacher needs to know how the disabled reader gets into the river in the first place. To do this, he needs to be able to read the causes of reading disability. It is not enough to know the symptoms. The symptom has to be hooked up with the proper cause. Only in this way is remediation of reading disability possible.

STEP 4: REMEDIATION

Step 4 of diagnostic procedure is actually the development of a plan for remediation. Identification of symptoms and causes is simply not enough.

---

[5] D. E. P. Smith and Patricia Carrigan, *The Nature of Reading Disability*, p. 6. (New York: Harcourt, Brace and Company, Inc., 1959). Reprinted with permission.

Diagnosis is meant to lead to remediation; it must serve as a blueprint from which remediation is structured. From a study of the diagnostic data, the teacher evolves a plan by and through which it is hoped the learner will improve in reading. The principles which we will discuss later in this section should help the teacher to formulate such a plan. They are basic procedures and principles that should guide all remedial instruction, irrespective of the type of reading disability.

This section thus deals with four questions: What decisions or what knowledge does the teacher of reading need before he can plan an effective remedial program? What principles should guide remedial instruction? What are the skills that must be developed in all remedial programs? And how can a corrective or remedial program be organized? Let us consider the first of these.

Decisions Required of the Teacher

Somehow, either on his own or with specially skilled help if it is available, the teacher must identify the child's problems and then plan and carry through the best possible corrective measures. This requires certain decisions based on particular information.

1. The teacher must decide whether the pupil actually is a retarded reader rather than a child of low ability. If he is a retarded reader, he must identify the nature of his retardation.
2. He must decide what type of teaching is needed.
3. He must determine whether the needed remedial work can best be done in the classroom or in separate facilities and, if in the classroom, whether individually or in a subgroup.
4. He must make an estimate of the proper length of the instructional period. The length will depend upon the skill being taught and on the physical well-being and social-emotional maturity of the child.
5. He must determine the most efficient methods and materials that can be used. He needs to determine what the difficulty level of the materials should be and whether the materials are interesting to the pupil. Bond and Tinker (8, p. 454) emphasize ". . . there should be no compromise with difficulty even to get material of high interest."
6. He must be alert to and decide how to make adjustments for the child's special interests, for any emotional or physical defects, or conditions in the child's home and community environment that may block his reading growth.
7. He must be alert to and decide how to deal with the environmental factors, institutional factors, that might be keeping the pupil from progressing in reading.

8. He must decide how to interpret to the pupil the progress he might make.

9. He must plan independent work activities for the pupil.

Principles of Remediation

Remedial teachers have developed certain principles that should guide all remedial or corrective instruction. A general observation might be that the principles underlying remedial or corrective reading instruction are basically the same that govern developmental reading instruction. Of these principles, the following seem most significant.

1. Develop a plan of remediation, put it on paper, and refer to it frequently as remediation progresses. Incidental teaching is simply inadequate with the retarded reader. Write flexibility into the plan. There needs to be flexibility in materials, methods, and attitudes.

2. Discover the child's area and level of confidence. Start where the pupil knows something. Nothing succeeds quite like success. One of the most therapeutic experiences for reading disability cases is success. Thus remedial instruction should begin at the level at which the pupil can be successful, probably about one grade level below the pupil's ability. It must begin where the pupil is, not where the curriculum guide suggests that sixth-grade learners on the average are. It should begin with short assignments, inspire confidence, and restore status to the child in the eyes of his peers, his parents, and teachers.

   In dealing with corrective or remedial cases it is necessary to remember that:

   a. The pupil is generally anxious and fearful of discussing his problem with an adult.

   b. His anxiety and guilt are especially high when he has experienced disapproval of his parents. Reich (55) notes that over every remedial reading case hovers an anxious parent: a parent who is overprotective, disappointed, and often feels guilty himself.

   c. The pupil's "don't care" attitude toward reading frequently is a "do care very much" attitude. (8, p. 183) It is a safety valve that permits the pupil to save face. Both teacher and parent should permit the pupil to have this apparent attitude without developing a feeling of guilt on the part of the pupil.

3. The corrective or remedial methods are hardly distinct from developmental methods. One cannot "reteach" a pupil who

never learned. One cannot remedy what was always lacking. Children receiving remedial education are distinct from normal readers in that they did not learn as a result of the educational procedures that were effective with most children. All the principles that apply to effective developmental instruction also apply to what is termed remedial teaching. The good teacher, whatever his title may be, starts at the child's present reading level, builds self-confidence in reading, and uses a variety of reading methods. Perhaps the remedial teacher is somewhat more permissive, delves more precisely into the causes of the reading problem, uses a greater variety of materials and motivational devices, and individualizes the program to a greater degree. The methods and principles of remedial teaching and developmental teaching are distinguishable, if at all, by the emphasis on individualization. Remedial reading is not a magic hocus-pocus of special methods, but a more intense and personal application of the techniques used with all others. Consequently, it is the nature of the child rather than the nature of the teaching that distinguishes the two procedures. Remedial measures are not curealls. They do not correct and eliminate all reading difficulties.

4. Develop those skills and abilities which are most necessary for immediate successful reading.

5. Remediation should be based on and accompanied by continuous diagnosis. This identifies areas that need unteaching and helps to identify the pupil who is ready for regular classroom instruction.

6. No one symptom, error, or mistake of itself implies an ailment or a general deficiency. Even the best reader will err at times.

7. Perfect results on a test do not mean complete mastery. An average score of second-grade level, on any test, does not mean that all the pupil's reading skills are on a second-grade level. It is not uncommon to find children getting the correct answer through the use of an incorrect method. By incorrect method is meant any method that will hinder future progress (such as guessing).

8. The child's symptoms, if not correctly interpreted, may lead the teacher to provide the improper remediation. The so-called cause, upon careful analysis, frequently is found to be an effect of poor reading. The teacher thus expects from the expert psychological insight into why a given method is recommended. Too often, the expert comes up with a diagnosis

such as "He is a dyslexic reader," without any recommendations as to the type of program to follow. The expert's diagnosis must be translated into "what to do" in the classroom. It is the going from the diagnostic hypothesis to the remedial method that is the difficult task.

9. The pattern of symptoms is usually more significant than the individual symptom.

10. Cures do not necessarily mean that the correct method of cure has been found. The intangibles of teacher-pupil motivations and teacher effectiveness generally play an important role. The good teacher may have good results regardless of method used. The poor teacher may experience only failure.

11. No remedial method has universal application. Methods of instruction should be selected which are in harmony with the best mode of learning for a given child.

12. The teacher's personality and his ability to enlist each child's active cooperation are often more important than the specific method used. Learning occurs in a relationship. Rapport is a subtle thing. The pupil needs to develop a desire to learn.

In dealing with remedial cases, psychotherapeutic principles should be incorporated into the process. The teacher should:

a. Develop a constructive relationship with the pupil (rapport). Drop the role of an authoritative teacher. Become an interested teacher.

b. Be a genuine person.

c. Give total and unequivocal acceptance of the pupil despite his frequent failures in school.

d. Have complete faith in the pupil's improvableness and ability to read. It is a fact that if the significant adults in a pupil's life believe that he can succeed, his chances for success are appreciably improved.

e. Develop a feeling of empathy, not sympathy. Objectivity must be maintained. If sympathy develops, the pupil feels that he has to please his teacher and that he cannot make mistakes. This often leads to tension (39,59).

f. Have a structured, well-defined program. The remedial program is more structured than the psychotherapeutic session.

g. Arouse interest by judicious choice of materials.

If the corrective or remedial teacher provides a relationship in which he is (a) genuine, internally consistent; (b) acceptant, prizing the learner as a person of worth; (c) empathically understanding of the learner's private world of feelings and attitudes, then certain changes are likely to occur in the learner. Some of these changes are: the learner becomes (*a*) more realistic in his self-perceptions; (*b*) more confident and self-directing; (*c*) more positively valued by himself; (*d*) less likely to repress elements of his experience; (*e*) more mature, and adaptive in his behavior; (*f*) less upset by stress and quicker to recover from it; (*g*) more like the healthy, integrated, well-functioning person in his personality structure; and (*h*) a better learner (58).

13. No two reading disability cases probably stem from the same source, have exactly the same pattern, or need the same instruction.

14. Select materials that the pupil can handle and in which he is interested. To do this, the teacher needs to know the pupil's instructional level. It is very important to remember that reading skills don't operate in a vacuum. The teacher needs proper materials, perhaps packets and kits, however, "packets and kits are fine for practice, tackling the dummy, but practice isn't to be confused with playing the game, of football or reading." It is often not what materials that are used with retarded readers that is most significant, but rather what the teacher does with the materials.

15. Instill in the pupil a feeling of responsibility for his own progress. Progress charts should be developed. The units of improvement need to be small enough so that progress can be recorded at frequent intervals.

16. Some remedial approaches, if used flexibly, appear applicable to reading disability cases almost irrespective of cause.

17. Remedial sessions must be adapted to the pupil. Half-hour sessions are probably suitable for third and fourth graders; eighth graders might be able to handle hour-long sessions.

18. When we speak of remedial reading or reading disability, we often imply that there is a basic deficiency in the learner that impedes progress. It may be helpful to remind ourselves that the basic deficiency may be poor teaching.

Improvement in reading is not necessarily brought about by spending more money, by bringing in consultants, by buying more gadgets and mechanical devices, or by resorting to newer approaches. Outstanding instructional programs in reading will be achieved "only through outstanding instruction." (33) This means, as Heilman notes, that "we must develop practices which are totally in accord with what we know about pupil-learning and what we know about reading and its relation to all school learning." [6]

Individualization of instruction is the chief identifying mark of good teaching and is totally dependent upon pupil diagnosis. The wise teacher identifies individual differences and teaches each pupil accordingly. The aim of remediation is to direct a pupil into that set of learning experiences most appropriate for him. The teacher thus must be extraordinarily sensitive to the needs of the learner.

But what if the diagnosis is incorrect? This would obviously result in wrong remediation; the greater the error in diagnosis, the greater might be the harm. We all realize that even the best diagnosis often is not totally reliable. The diagnostic information is fallible, but this does not make it worthless. It does mean that the degree of differentiation in remediation that should be attempted is directly proportional to the accuracy of the diagnosis. It would seem wise, then, to begin remediation by using those principles, methods, and procedures that are developmentally sound. Only gradually and with great care should the remediation depart from these.

The diagnostic-remediation process may be viewed as a matter of obtaining and transmitting information. Diagnosis brings forth information about the pupil. We have suggested in this chapter a positive and direct way of doing this by observation, questionnaire, inventory, and test. Another approach is to begin the remediation process with the problem as the pupil presents it and to help the pupil rather immediately in solving it. This latter approach consists of observing the pupil, working with him, and studying, analyzing, and remediating during actual instruction and practice in reading. This approach calls for the use of few tests.

One teacher might want to narrow the point where remediation might be applied. He is confident that he can and actually has identified the significant areas of difficulty. A second teacher believes that it is not possible to predict what areas will be significant in the case before him. He prefers to risk some loss of time in order to avoid the risk of overlooking a significant area. The first teacher would thus at once plunge into a reading diagnosis. The second teacher would fear that such a direct attack might actually cause the pupil to fail to mention the real reason of why he hates reading.

Each teacher is gambling. It would appear that if the teacher strongly believes, because of his experience and knowledge, that the

[6] Heilman, Arthur W. "Moving Faster Toward Outstanding Instructional Programs." *Vistas in Reading*, Proceedings of the Eleventh Annual Convention, International Reading Association, Newark, 1967, pp. 273–76. Reprinted by permission.

significant area is to be found in a limited area, he should study that area with maximum precision (17). It would appear that experienced teachers would be safer in doing this than inexperienced teachers.

Systematic Instruction in the Basic Reading Skills

Today it is fashionable to assert that most reading failures are the result of faulty approaches in beginning reading. Chall (15) notes that with regard to where the problem lies, whether in the initial reading approach or in the deficiencies of the child, there probably is an interaction effect between the two. "Severe reading disability seems to require both—a predisposition in the child and an initial approach that ignores it."

As already suggested, we do not like the term "remedial reading program." Remediation along with diagnosis is an integral phase of the developmental program. Diagnosis and remediation must accompany all effective teaching. The developmental program is responsible for systematic reading instruction at all school levels. It includes developmental, corrective (34a), and remedial instruction. We have used the term "corrective instruction of reading" to refer to situations in which remedial activities are carried on in the regular classroom. When the remediation occurs outside of the regular classroom, we have termed it remedial teaching. It seems clear that in an ideal situation or some sort of educational utopia, where there would be no retardation, the concept of and need for remedial teaching might disappear.

Corrective instruction usually occurs in the regular classroom. If a special teacher is available, the pupil might be assigned to him several times a week for 45 to 60 minutes.

Corrective instruction stresses sequential development in word attack and comprehension skills but uses special techniques and materials and concentrates on a particular reading deficiency. The corrective program is in addition to regular reading instruction.

Remedial teaching, because of its expensiveness, is necessarily limited. It is a slow process, on a one-to-one basis or at most on the basis of one teacher to three to eight pupils. Because of the expenses involved, "even when a special remedial teacher is available, it is likely that instruction will need to be individualized rather than strictly individual (50, p. 73)."

The school thus needs to limit the number of pupils that will find themselves in a remedial classroom. As we have already noted, some poor readers, and in this group belong slow learners reading up to their ability, reluctant readers, and the disadvantaged readers, for the most part should be kept in the regular classroom. Some retarded readers need corrective reading but can still stay in the regular classroom. Only the severely retarded readers need to be taken out for full-time special instruction.

Remedial teaching or corrective teaching is not justified if it is not different from regular reading instruction. The instruction needs to be on a broader basis. *The corrective or remedial teacher needs to be completely familiar with the skills to be taught at all levels. He must be able to telescope, as it were, the total reading program into a relatively brief period of instruction. He must appreciate and understand the continuity of the total reading program.*

The two basic reading skills are still identification of the word or sentence and association of meaning with it. Many professional books devote major sections to the development of these skills. In Chapter 8 of our book, *Diagnosis and Remediation of Reading Disability* (West Nyack, N.Y.: Parker Publishing Company), we list numerous additional skill-improvement materials useful in the development of these skills. Here are some of these. Each of these along with many other materials is described more fully in the above book.

Word Attack Materials

1. *Basic Reading Series* [J. B. Lippincott Company], Grades 1–8.
2. *Building Reading Skills* [McCormick Mathers Publishing Company], Grades 1–6.
3. *Cordts Phonetic Books* [Benefic Press], three levels.
4. *Dialog I* [Chester Electronics Laboratories].
5. *Early to Read Series* [Initial Teaching Alphabet Publications], Grade 1.
6. *Eye and Ear Fun* [Webster Publishing Company], Grades 1–6.
7. *A First Course in Phonic Reading* and *A Second Course in Phonic Reading* [Educators Publishing Service], Grades 1–6.
8. *A First Course In Remedial Reading* [Educators Publishing Service], Grades 2–3.
9. *First Phonics* [Educators Publishing Service], Grade 1.
10. *Happy Times with Sounds Series* [Allyn and Bacon, Inc.], four books.
11. *Hayes Mastery Phonics Workbooks* [Beckley-Cardy Company], six books.
12. *I Learn to Read* [Kenworthy Educational Service], Grades 1–4.
13. *Instructor Basic Phonics Series* [F. A. Owen Publishing Company], Grades 1–5.
14. *Iroquois Phonics Series* [Charles E. Merrill, Inc.], three workbooks.
15. *It's Time for Phonics* [Webster Publishing Company], Grades K–3.

16. *Landon Phonics Program* [Chandler Publishing Company], Grades K–3.
17. *Linguistic Readers* [Harper and Row].
18. *Listen and Learn With Phonics Records* [Beckley-Cardy Company], Beginning Phonics.
19. *New Auditory Visual Response Phonics* [Polyphone Company], tape program.
20. *Phonetic Keys to Reading* [Economy Company], Grades 1–3.
21. *A Phonetic Reader Series* [Educators Publishing Service], Grades 1–6.
22. *Phonics is Fun* [Modern Curriculum Press], Grades 1–3.
23. *Phonovisual Method* [Phonovisual Products, Inc.], Primary Grades.
24. *Reading Along with Me Series* [Columbia University], Grades K–3.
25. *Reading Essential Series and Teaching Aids* [Steck Company].
26. *Reading With Phonics* [J. B. Lippincott Company], Grades 1–3.
27. *Sounds We Use* [Wilcox and Follett], Grades 1–3.
28. *Speech-to-Print Phonics* [Harcourt, Brace and World], Readiness.
29. *Time for Phonics* [Webster Publishing Company], Grades 1–3.
30. *Words in Color* [Learning Materials, Inc.], Beginning Reading.

Comprehension Materials

1. Reading Laboratories:
   a. *EDL. Listen and Read Program* [Educational Developmental Laboratories].
   b. *SRA Reading Laboratory* [Science Research Associates].
   c. *Literature Sampler* [Learning Materials, Inc.].
   d. *Tactics in Reading* [Scott, Foresman & Company].
   e. *Webster Classroom Reading Clinic* [Webster Division, McGraw-Hill Book Company].
   f. *Reading Spectrum* [Macmillan Company].
   g. *Sullivan Reading Program* [Webster Division, McGraw-Hill Book Company], 21 levels.
2. *Be a Better Reader Series* [Prentice-Hall, Inc.], Grades 4–12.
3. *Building Reading Skills* [McCormick-Mathers Publishing Company], Grades 1–6.
4. *Cowboy Sam Workbooks* [Beckley-Cardy Company], Primer–Grade 3.
5. *Developmental Reading Text Workbooks* [Bobbs-Merrill Co., Inc.], Grades 1–6.
6. *The Everyreader Series* [Webster Publishing Company], Remedial–fourth grade.
7. *Gates-Peardon Practice Exercises in Reading* [Bureau of Publications], Grades 1–7.

8. *McCall-Crabbs Standard Test Lessons in Reading* [Bureau of Publications], Grades 2–12.
9. *New Goals in Reading* [Steck-Vaughn Company], Grades 4–6.
10. *New Practice Readers* [Webster Publishing Company], Grades 2–8.
11. *New Reading Skilltext Series* [J. B. Lippincott Company], Grades 1–6.
12. *Reading Attainment System* [Grolier Educational Corporation], Grades 3–4.
13. *Reading Essentials Series* [Steck-Vaughn Company], Grades 1–8.
14. *Reading for Meaning Series* [J. B. Lippincott Company], Grades 4–12.
15. *Reading-Thinking Skills* [Continental Press, Inc.], Preprimer–6.
16. *Specific Skill Series* [Barnell Loft, Ltd.], Grades 1–6.

Organizing for Corrective and Remedial Reading

Historically, classrooms have been organized into groups and the emphasis has been upon the development of a group organization that would permit the greatest amount of individual growth.

Unfortunately, the search for a happy balance between grouping and individualization is still in progress. It is our feeling that heterogeneous grouping with mobile flexible subgrouping, rather than homogeneous grouping, has the most to offer in the regular classroom. Flexible subgrouping seems especially helpful in dealing with the problems of the pupil who needs corrective reading instruction. It permits the organization of clusters or subgroups of pupils with common reading needs.

Corrective Reading in the Classroom   As we have stated previously, corrective reading instruction should be reserved for the regular classroom. A few cautions are in order. Corrective instruction cannot be so organized as to embarrass the child and should certainly not be substituted for such pleasurable activities as recess or physical education. Neither should it give the appearance of simply being squeezed into the school day.

Because of the nature of the pupil needing corrective or remedial reading, drill sessions should necessarily be short. This means that on the lower elementary levels pupils may move from one group to another at fifteen or even ten minute intervals, if there are three groups.

The classroom teacher needs to spend some time with the entire class at the beginning of the class to introduce a new unit or topic or to give special assignments and directions. He may want to teach the entire class if he finds that all or most of the pupils are deficient in a particular skill, such as the rules of punctuation. He probably needs to spend some time with the entire group at the end of the class to summarize and to make homework assignments. Between the beginning few moments and the end of the class the teacher frequently will find it necessary to group the youngsters according to their similarity of needs. Table 14-4 shows an organization of the reading period that makes group instruction possible and permits greater individualization through the process of subgrouping.

TABLE 14-4   The Reading Hour

9:00–9:10	Common activities
9:10–9:55	Subgrouping within the classroom
9:55–10:00	Common subgrouping activities

Group I	Group II	Group III
9:10–9:25	9:10–9:25	9:10–9:25
Directed reading	Free reading	Reading group with teacher
(Practice on what has been taught)	(Application of what has been taught)	(Actual teaching)
1. Workbooks 2. Mimeographed seatwork 3. Questions on the board to answer 4. Use of programmed materials 5. Use of listening stations	1. Games 2. Free reading of library books—recreational reading	1. Basal reading instruction 2. Specific skill instruction
9:25–9:40	9:25–9:40	9:25–9:40
Free reading	Reading with teacher	Directed reading
9:40–9:55	9:40–9:55	9:40–9:55
Reading with teacher	Directed reading	Free reading

The organization suggested in the table permits the teacher to have simultaneously three groups, each at a different level of reading performance, each using its own set of materials, and each advancing at its own success level. Dividing the class into three groups according to reading levels or needs permits the teacher to use basal readers more closely approximating the individual pupil's achievement level. At another time, one group may be working on word recognition, another on comprehension, and a third on rate improvement, even though the youngsters composing a given group might be reading on different levels. Thus a child reading on third-grade level might be working with one reading on a fourth-grade level. Both of them may need help with diphthongs, consonants, or speech consonants.

If the situation prevails where all children on the same reading level are grouped together for reading instruction as in the Joplin plan, there still may be need of flexible subgrouping on a learning-activity basis in the classroom. There still might be three groups: those receiving actual instruction, those practicing what has been taught, and those applying what has been taught. Children also may be subgrouped on an interest basis. In the ungraded primary, the pupils move from level to level on the basis of their achievement.

Even with a reduction of the teacher-pupil ratio and with subgrouping, there is no easy solution to children's reading problems. The teacher may need outside help. One pattern of organization for corrective instruction may include the use of additional teachers or aides. The use of team teaching or of reserve or supplemental teachers to work with small groups has been found beneficial. Some schools assign a master teacher to work directly with the teacher during the regular reading period. The remedial reading teacher may help the classroom teacher by giving classroom demonstrations in the use of specific methods or materials. It may be possible to use parents or aides to help children listen to tapes, do workbook exercises, listen to children's oral reading, or make comprehension checks. The teacher may initiate team learning, in which pupils subgroup as a team and work together in the learning of new concepts, in applying skills, or in reviewing. Tutoring, a situation in which one pupil works with one or more pupils who need help, has been used by many teachers.

Staggered scheduling is another organizational device useful in planning developmental and corrective reading instruction. In the developmental setting staggered scheduling is sometimes labelled divided-day, split-day, extended-day, or staggered-day organization. It provides a reading period in the morning with one-half of the class, which arrives early, and another period in the afternoon with the other half of the class, that stays late. Warner's study (68) indicates that this form of organization is advantageous to both teacher and pupil and results in superior reading achievement.

In the corrective setting, those youngsters who are to be kept in the regular classroom but who need special help in reading may be asked to report to school an hour early or leave an hour late. Lunch periods could be staggered for similar effect.

Remedial Reading   Pupils who are seriously retarded may have to be taken out of the regular classroom and put into a special room where a remedial reading teacher or a special teacher will work with them. Sometimes there is no classroom space available, and the school may have to use mobile equipment. In another school the remedial teacher may function out of the reading materials center.

Regardless of where the remedial room is, it should probably have two glass-partitioned offices: one for the remedial teacher and one for testing purposes. The glass partition permits the teacher to observe the testing from his own office. The room should also contain an audiovisual center, small group practice rooms, individual practice cubicles, desks, chairs, bookshelves, and office furniture. The reading room should make provision for a testing room and for individual practice cubicles.

Organizing for *remedial* instruction requires that pupils be dismissed from the regular classroom at scheduled times during the regular school day so that they can go to the remedial classroom for special instruction. The pupil reports to the remedial class for perhaps one lesson per day and then returns to his own classroom. It is important that we get the pupil back to the regular classroom as soon as possible. We recommend, therefore, that every nine weeks the following question should be asked and answered about every pupil: "Is he ready to be excused from the remedial class?"

Remedial instruction may be given during a regular study period or during a subject-matter class which requires reading for efficient performance. Sometimes the pupil is given remedial instruction before school begins or after school ends. In some schools remedial instruction is provided during the homeroom or the activity period. In other schools remedial instruction becomes a part of the English class.

The remedial room should be equipped with audiovisual materials of various types, filmstrip projector, tachistoscopes, accelerating devices, record players, children's records, tape recorder, listening stations, flashcards, and art supplies. It should contain books of all types, supplementary readers, programmed reading materials, multilevel reading laboratories, testing and diagnostic materials, magazines, games, and all kinds of word recognition and comprehension development materials.

MEETING INDIVIDUAL NEEDS

Up to this point we have looked at the four steps of the diagnostic process. The remainder of the chapter will deal with the problems of special types of learners, remedial methods, and the evaluation of remedial instruction. Let us begin with the needs of the slow learners, disadvantaged readers, and gifted readers. We have already described the dyslexic reader and the reluctant reader.

Each of these groups needs a slightly different reading program and remediation needs to be adapted to individual needs. For example, we need to present different stimuli, and we need to present them in a different way for the learner who is deficient because of inadequate capacity than we do for the one who is deficient because of a verbally impoverished environment. Let us then first look at the slow learner.

The Slow Learner

The slow learner may or may not be retarded in terms of his ability level, but he is almost always retarded as to grade level. He generally has an IQ of between 70 and 90. This pupil begins to read at age seven or later, will read slowly and haltingly, and is achieving below grade level in areas other than reading, such as spelling or arithmetic. He does not need a remedial program. In fact, pushing him may only hurt him. He may interpret it as dissatisfaction with his wholehearted efforts.

Certainly major adjustments must be made for the slow learner in the context of the developmental reading program and in the rate at which he is expected to progress through it. He requires a longer readiness program than does the average child. To begin formal reading instruction before the slow learner has attained a mental age of six or more is often to waste the time of both teacher and pupil and will result in pupil discouragement. The extended readiness program of the slow learner should emphasize social interaction, storytelling, arts and crafts, dramatizing, music, and recreational activities. Reading charts built from the direct experiences of the children are especially useful. These charts will be read and reread with pride and satisfaction by mentally retarded pupils at chronological ages considerably beyond those at which they can be used with children whose IQ scores are above 90. In the early stages of learning, listening will need to be stressed more than reading.

The teacher needs to give detailed and simplified directions for all work, providing concrete illustrations and short range projects resulting in frequent rewards. There must be frequent rereading of materials, more use of oral reading, and an emphasis on physical activity and specific, concrete projects in connection with the learning experiences.

In the slow learner's reading program, it is necessary to spend considerable time on phonetic and structural analysis and, frequently, to encourage lip movements, vocalization, and pointing at the word. The emphasis should be on word knowledge and the mastery of simple comprehension skills. The slow learner cannot use context clues as well as children of average intelligence. He makes more vowel errors and omits more sounds.

The slow learner appears to have little need for rapid reading skills. He will not read many different materials. He has a difficult time reading for practical purposes. The reading of the slow learner, especially when he is about ready to leave school, should be functional in nature. He needs to learn the working vocabulary required to function effectively as an American citizen.

From his experience with slow learners, Kirk (38, pp 174–175)[7] suggests that the teacher should keep the following in mind:

1. It should not be expected that the slow learner should learn to read at the life age of six when he enters the first grade. . . .
2. His rate of learning to read is slower than that of other children. . . .
3. Throughout his school career the slow learner has not been able to succeed in reading like other children. . . .
4. Health and poorer environmental handicaps have been found more frequently in the slow learner, thus contributing to his reading retardation.
5. Other school subjects, like history, geography, and even arithmetic computation, are difficult for him since they require efficient reading habits.
6. Due to difficulties in reading, lack of interest in recreational reading, and avoidance of an unpleasant task, reading does not become a part of the life of a slow learner.

The teacher can help this pupil in the regular classroom:

1. By providing a friendly, accepting, and encouraging relationship. Teacher attitudes substantially affect the performance of the slow learner. The teacher must believe in the improvableness of the learner.
2. By creating a learning environment where simple reading is important. Teach him to read road signs, city directories, a letter from a friend, want ads, newspapers, an application blank, a menu.
3. By pacing the learning according to the pupil's ability.
   a. Introduce only a few materials at any given time.
   b. Review daily.
   c. Introduce materials in varied contexts.
   d. Simplify materials, explanations, and techniques.

[7] Samuel A. Kirk, "Characteristics of Slow Learners and Needed Adjustments in Reading," *Classroom Techniques in Improving Reading*, Supplementary Educational Monographs, No. 69 (Chicago: University of Chicago Press, 1949), pp. 172–76. Reprinted by permission.

The basic vocabulary needs to be carefully controlled. Instead of using many different primers or readers, build many reading situations which require the pupil to use his limited vocabulary over and over again. The use of workbooks is especially recommended.

4. By coordinating all the language arts. Reading orally to the pupil is very beneficial. Let the pupil do oral reading. Sometimes he needs to hear himself say the word to understand what he is reading.

5. By not underestimating the slow learner's ability to learn. Don't simply let him do busy work, draw aimlessly, trace and copy words and sentences.

6. By having the pupil see his progress every day. Nothing succeeds like observed and tangible success.
   a. Have him keep a card file of words that he has learned to spell or read.
   b. Have him construct a picture dictionary, perhaps of shop tools. The teacher needs to provide opportunities for the pupil to "shine" in some area.

7. By providing drill on new words:
   a. Let the pupil write, pronounce, and read the word.
   b. Use all the sense avenues.

8. By providing ample opportunity for review and repetition. The slow learner profits greatly from repetition. He may get the gist of a story only in spurts. Each rereading adds more to his understanding.

9. By giving special attention to eye movements and line-to-line sequence.

10. By individualizing instruction. The teacher needs to give as much individual help as possible.

11. By not putting him into a remedial program simply because he is reading below grade level.

12. By using concrete illustrations to develop concepts and generalizations.

13. By providing short-range goals. Projects should not be too long.

14. By emphasizing the visual and auditory characteristics of words. Word analysis is very helpful. The teacher needs to emphasize sound symbols.

15. By breaking complex learning tasks into small steps. The use of programmed materials and teaching machines is especially recommended for slow learners. They divide the task into small steps and use frequent repetition and other supportive cues to make the correct response dominant.

16. By employing a variety of teaching techniques.

17. By familiarizing himself with methods of teaching specifically designed for the slow learner. Among these are the following:
    a. Kirk: *Teaching Reading to Slow-Learning Children* [Houghton-Mifflin].
    b. Bruechner and Bond: *Diagnosis and Treatment of Learning Difficulties* [Appleton-Century-Crofts].
    c. Featherstone: *Teaching the Slow Learner* [Columbia University].
    d. Monroe and Backus: *Remedial Reading* [Houghton Mifflin].
    e. Kephart, N. C.: *The Slow Learner in the Classroom* [Charles W. Merrill Books, Inc.].

The Disadvantaged Reader

With four of our fourteen largest cities having one deprived child for every two of their population and with it being estimated that by 1970 the other ten cities will share an identical ratio (47) and since many of these children are poor readers and are thus educationally handicapped, there is need to look closely at the reading needs of these children. The problem is even more acute if, as some social scientists claim, one of three youngsters in the country as a whole is educationally deprived.

The disadvantaged child or the experientially-deprived child belongs to no single race or color. Peoples of varied colors and national origins are poor and experientially-deprived and fail to achieve the goals established by the main stream of society (7).

What characterizes the disadvantaged child? (7,57)

1. He lacks a proper self-image. He feels alienated from the larger social structure.
2. He expects little from life and has little academic drive. He has a weak sense of the future and seems to lack ambition.
3. He tends to be afflicted with more health and physical difficulties.
4. He is deficient in language development, has a limited vocabulary, and even though he uses short sentences, these are sprinkled with grammatical errors. Sentence structure is faulty.
5. He has mastered the public language (this uses simple declaratory sentences) but cannot deal with the formal language. His language contains few clauses or structural complexities. He does not use the school language.
6. He has more perceptual difficulties. He recognizes fewer objects than most children. He is deficient in auditory attention and interpretation skills and experiences great difficulty in blending sounds. He learns less from what he hears than does the middle class child. Cohen (16) believes most disad-

vantaged children tend to be visual rather than auditory or phonic readers, but emphasizes that a linguistic-phonic program should be built into the beginning reading program.

7. He tends to perform poorly on tests and his achievement in school is low. He is slow at cognitive tasks. He is unaware of the ground rules for success in school. He is not willing to sit still while having to read, "Look, Jane! Look!," to get in a line in a hurry, or to do meaningless homework (16).

8. His reading achievement tends to be substantially below his ability level.

9. He learns more readily through a physical and concrete approach.

10. If he is a boy, he values masculinity and views intellectual activities as unmasculine.

11. His attention span is short, and he is not motivated by long-range goals.

12. His experiential background is meagre. He does not have the experience to make words meaningful.

The need for concerted effort to improve the language and reading skills of the disadvantaged child is apparent. The following techniques might prove helpful (42,69,49,54):

1. Make every effort to obtain a true estimate of the pupil's potential. The *Wechsler Intelligence Scale for Children,* the *Stanford-Binet Intelligence Scale,* the *I. P. A. T. Culture Fair Intelligence Test,* or a similar test should be used to obtain an IQ or mental age score. Do not use tests which only hammer home the point that the pupil is stupid.

2. Teach disadvantaged children to "learn how to learn." They do not know what it means to be taught.

3. Build on oral language as a prerequisite to dealing with printed language. This child will not know a word like steeple, although a dozen steeples may be visible from the classroom window. Develop experiential and oral meanings for words. The Peabody Language Development Kit (American Guidance Service, Inc., Minneapolis) and the Ginn Language Kit A provide a systematic program of language experiences on the first grade level.

4. Develop speaking-reading-writing relationships through the use of experience stories, audiovisual devices, and concrete illustrations. Many visual stimuli should be presented together with the verbal stimuli. Make tapes of the pupil's oral reading.

5. Teach reading as a life-related process. When saying: "We

wash our hands," have the children do it and write the sentences on the blackboard for them to read. Experientially-deprived children perhaps more so than any other group learn by doing. In the middle and upper grades the pupil needs to develop an awareness that reading is important. Too often, the fact that he cannot read causes him little concern.

6. Make frequent use of experiences charts. Permit children to verbalize and to communicate orally. Reading assignments should be brief and concrete.

7. Display books strategically and attractively for personal and group examination. Show a filmstrip about a book; read from a book. Make available materials that present his own ethnic group in a good light. Instead of trying to get him to adopt a new culture, help him to improve within the framework of his own culture.

8. Only gradually introduce books as readers, moving back and forth from charts to books as the situation demands.

9. Give special attention to readiness for reading and for learning. Be reasonably certain that pupils have a chance of understanding the materials.

10. Do not limit the approach in reading to any one method or one approach.

11. Teach phonics and structural analysis as means of figuring out the pronunciation of words. Few disadvantaged children know either the alphabet of letters or the alphabet of sounds. Emphasize visual and auditory discrimination, but especially auditory discrimination.

     Disadvantaged children profit from a great deal of auditory and visual perception activities. The *Michigan Successive Discrimination Listening Program* and the *Frostig Program for the Development of Visual Perception* stress such activities. A new program with similar emphasis is *Readiness for Learning: A Program for Visual and Auditory Perceptual-Motor Training* by J. B. Lippincott. It is designed for kindergarten–first grade level.

12. Provide an atmosphere of trust where the pupil can learn self-assurance and self-direction, raise his aspirational level, and develop pride in himself. For example, choral reading may be used to great advantage. This permits the pupil to respond and yet it does not single him out if he makes an error. Programmed materials give him all the time he wants or needs without pressuring him for an answer. They permit him to check on his own answer without subjecting him to embarrassment because the teacher or another pupil saw his error or

deficiency. The teacher must proceed on the assumption that the pupil can improve.

13. Make use of materials that are specifically designed for culturally-deprived children. The Detroit city schools have been using multicultural readers. Some recommend the use of the Montessori approach. *The Progressive Choice Reading Program,* described later in this chapter, is designed specifically for the disadvantaged child. Another program on junior high–senior high school level for disadvantaged children is *Reading in High Gear* by Science Research Associates. The *Miami Linguistic Readers,* D. C. Heath and Company, form a two-year beginning reading program for bilingual and culturally disadvantaged pupils. Books available are: *Biff and Tiff, Kid Kit and the Catfish, Nat the Rat, Tug Duck and Buzz Bug, The Sack Hut, On the Rock in the Pond, The Picnic Ship, Hot Corn Muffins, The Camping Trip,* and *The Magic Bean.* A new brochure, *A Reading List for Disadvantaged Youth,* is available through the American Library Association. Another source of books is Allan C. Ornstein, "101 Books for Teaching the Disadvantaged," *Journal of Reading,* 10 (May, 1967), 546–551. *Dandy Dog's Early Learning Program,* American Book Company, is a combination book-record program useful with slow learners and nonEnglish speaking children. The teacher of experientially-deprived children will also want to become familiar with:

a. Bloom, B. S., Allison Davis, and Robert Hess. *Compensatory Education for Cultural Deprivation.* [Holt, Rinehart and Winston, Inc., 1965].

b. Frost, Joe L., and Glenn R. Hawkes. *The Disadvantaged Child: Issues and Innovations.* [Houghton Mifflin Company, 1966].

c. Gowan, John C. and George D. Demos, ed. *The Disadvantaged and Potential Dropout.* [Charles C Thomas, 1966].

d. Bereiter, Carl and Siegfried Englemann. *Teaching Disadvantaged Children in the Preschool.* [Prentice-Hall, Inc., 1966].

e. Ansara, Alice. *A Guide to the Teaching of Reading* (for teachers of the disadvantaged). [Educators Publishing Service].

f. Taba, Hilda and Deborah Elkins. *Teaching Strategies for the Culturally Disadvantaged.* [Rand McNally & Co., Skokie, Illinois, 1966].

g. Strom, Robert D. *Teaching in the Slum School.* [Charles E. Merrill Books, Inc., Columbus, 1965].

h. Webster, S. W., ed. *The Disadvantaged Learner: Knowing, Understanding, Educating.* [Chandler Publishing Company, 1966].

14. Greatly expand the amount of time that is devoted to reading instruction. On the upper-grade levels put special emphasis on study skills.

15. Structure the reading program in such a way that the pupil thinks of reading as the process of bringing meaning to the page (36). Don't ask the child, "What does this word mean?" His answer will probably be wrong. Rather, ask him: "What does this word make you think of?" Such a question preserves his self-concept and allows the teacher to develop new or additional meanings.

16. Take an attitude of "positive expectancy" (65) toward the pupil, focusing on his assets rather than his weaknesses. As Niemeyer, President of Bank Street College, notes: "A major reason for low achievement among children in poor neighborhoods is the low expectation as to their learning capacity held by teachers."

The following suggestions might prove helpful in organizing the reading program for the disadvantaged pupil:

1. Use team teaching, permitting the grouping of children into very small groups when needed. Disadvantaged children might be assigned to small classrooms or subgrouped for specific teaching.

2. Have half of the children report an hour early and leave an hour early; the other half comes an hour later, providing the teacher with a smaller group at both ends of the day. Reading and related language arts may be taught in these periods of reduced class size. Lunch periods might also be staggered with similar effect.

3. Reduce the teacher-pupil ratio.

4. Use "reserve teachers" or "supplemental teachers" to work with groups of eight to twelve for one hour each day to help the lowest reading groups.

5. Assign "master teachers" on the basis of one master teacher to six to ten less experienced teachers to help them and to work with small groups.

6. Use "remedial reading teachers" to give demonstrations for classroom teachers, and to secure needed materials for teaching reading.

7. Use parents in the classroom as aides to help children listen to tapes and to use the library and to help the teacher with record keeping.

8. Use counselors, psychiatric social workers, psychologists,

nurses, secretaries, speech specialists, etc., as consultants in dealing with the more severe cases.

The disadvantaged learner is essentially inexperienced in language. He knows too few words and too few meanings. The teacher must accept his manner of expression but must guide the learner toward using complete sentences. This learner's language, while quite adequate away from school, is not adequate for success in school. Engaging the learner in conversation, fostering language development through role playing and dramatic representation, and reading aloud to him each day are all good procedures to use in developing language competency.

The Gifted Learner

Too often in a discussion of reading, the needs of the gifted learner are overlooked. Whereas most gifted children are probably reading substantially above grade level, there are many whose reading achievement is substantially below their ability level. In fact, many of them are seriously retarded. Helping these children to achieve appropriate educational growth requires that the teacher know how to identify the gifted, to know their characteristics as learners, and to know how to make educational adjustments to meet their needs.

Identification of the Gifted Learner   To identify the gifted learner, we must reach some agreement as to what we mean by gifted. In the case of the slow learner, our criterion was low IQ. However, the IQ as the criterion of giftedness is not completely satisfactory for at least two reasons: (1) although low IQ generally guarantees low accomplishment, high IQ does not guarantee high accomplishment, and (2) although the gifted learner generally learns anything quite easily, frequently gifted children are highly successful in one area and less successful in others. Thus Witty (71) would consider a child gifted if his performance is consistently remarkable in any valuable line of human activity.

Generally, however, standardized intelligence test results have been used as criteria both to identify the gifted and to define giftedness even though tests are never completely reliable or valid and some types of gifted children do not express their full capabilities on intelligence tests. Even when we use high IQ as our criterion, we still must decide the specific range of IQ levels that is to mark giftedness. A person generally is considered gifted if he has an IQ of 130 or above, although some programs use a higher cutoff point (4).

In defining giftedness the recent trend has been to combine intelligence with other criteria. Guilford (30), for example, suggests that we must look well beyond the boundaries of the IQ if we are to fathom the domain of creativity.

Perhaps one should speak of the intellectually bright as the "gifted learners" and of those who show special excellence in a specific area such as in the arts, mechanics, creative writing, or in social and political leadership as the "specially gifted." Certainly, some distinction is needed. The child with special abilities or aptitudes may or may not be superior in general academic areas such as reading.

Although there has been much discussion of creativity within the last ten years, the concept has not been clearly defined. The tests of creativity do not agree on what they measure (67), and information concerning the reliability and validity of the tests is sparse (14). Nevertheless, Yamamota (72) feels that if giftedness is identified with high scores on intelligence, almost 70 per cent of the most highly creative individuals in our society would be overlooked.

Characteristics of the Gifted Learner   As a group, children with superior IQ's are less neurotic, less selfish, more self-sufficient, more mature socially, more self-confident, taller, heavier, and healthier than average children. Their major strength, however, is their academic prowess. They tend to learn through association rather than through rote memory. They perceive relationships and like to deal with abstractions. They are curious, creative, and imaginative. They tend to work individually, but they enjoy preparing and giving oral and written reports, organizing and cataloguing materials and information, and sharing their experiences with their classmates. They tend to write both prose and poetry creatively and effectively. Frequently what they choose to read and learn is on an adult level and they are attracted to school subjects that require abstraction. Also, their social consciousness and responses indicate a higher degree of maturity than do those of average children.

Summaries (4,5,40, p. 308) of the characteristics of the gifted include the following points:

1. The gifted child frequently learns to walk earlier than the average child.
2. His speech development begins earlier and develops more rapidly.
3. He is probably more active than average children, and more curious about new situations.
4. Chances are about 50–50 that if he is gifted he will learn to read before entering school and early develop an interest in mastering words.

5. He will probably like school, more because of his desire for knowledge than for the challenge presented to him.
6. He is more likely to participate in a larger number of extra-curricular activities.
7. When he is allowed to elect subjects, he will prefer the harder ones.
8. He is taller, healthier, and physically more attractive than the average of the population. He frequently is the first born child and the parents tend to be well educated. There is a greater evidence of giftedness among boys than among girls.
9. He learns early to live with himself and with others, possessing greater personal and social adjustment.
10. His adjustment to school and learning is superior.
11. He performs at a superior level in academic situations.
12. He has better attitudes toward and more interest in intellectual activities.
13. He learns through abstraction, association, and coding rather than through rote memory.
14. He exhibits a high degree of sensitivity to discovering and solving problems and to feelings of his fellow man.
15. He is more independent, more dynamic, more practical, and more utilitarian.
16. He prefers projects involving complexity, novelty, and decision-making to tasks that are cut and dried.
17. He prefers to compare and to criticize rather than gain simple mastery of facts and skills.

The Need for Guidance of the Gifted   The tremendous potential of the gifted child for academic achievement and social leadership carries with it a high challenge and responsibility for educational guidance. This calls for creative teaching. The following points summarize some of the problems the teacher will meet in teaching the gifted learner.

1. Gifted learners are likely to become irritated by the repetition which slow learners need to reinforce their learning.
2. Even if the pupil has not learned to read, readiness programs tend to be unchallenging because the gifted learner learns in a fraction of the time that others require.
3. The pupil is usually desirous of reading for learning purposes.
4. Materials are often too simple.
5. The pupil early needs to be exposed to critical reading, rate improvement, use of the dictionary, and content area reading. He needs guidance in appreciation, in detecting mood and tone, and in recognizing literary devices. He needs to question

and evaluate the authority of the source material. He must learn to identify the author's purpose, to understand inferences, to anticipate outcomes, and to analyze the author's style.

6. In teaching the gifted learner the teacher should emphasize such things as abstracting principles and significant interrelationships, synthesizing facts and drawing conclusions, tracing themes and analyzing their importance to the selection as a whole, and criticizing on the basis of all the various forces involved.

7. The intellectual qualities of the gifted often render superfluous traditional patterns of classroom instruction. The pupil needs problem-centered teaching and pupil-teacher planning.

8. The teacher must know when to guide, when to direct, and when to get out of the way.

9. The teacher must help the pupil to develop intrinsic rather than extrinsic motivations.

10. The gifted are not impressed by tight scheduling, close supervision, rigid administration, authoritative teaching, and traditional forms of evaluation (28).

11. The pupil needs to be provided broad exposure to and immersion in content (51). He needs to be taught to see interdisciplinary relationships and to reorganize knowledge. He needs active encounters with academic knowledge.

12. There is need for basic changes in the curriculum rather than simply "patchwork adjustments."

Educational Adjustments for the Gifted Learner   Various procedures have been suggested for adjusting instruction to the needs of the gifted child. However, as Hildreth (34) notes, the number of schools offering special programs for the gifted still does not nearly match special programs for slow learners. Generally, the adjustments have taken one of the following forms (35):

1. Honors courses.
2. Seminars, especially on the high school level. These often are for noncredit.
3. Special course work.
4. Noncurricular grouping: This brings pupils together in drama, crafts, language, music, etc.
5. Regular classroom grouping.
6. Credit by examination.
7. Telescoped curriculum: This provides a two-year program in one year.

8. Early admissions: especially on high school and college level.
9. Extra courses for credit.
10. Sectioning: Pupils of all levels of ability are together in the morning, but in the afternoon the more able participate in a special program.
11. Acceleration: Student attitudes toward acceleration are positive and favorable (37).
12. Enrichment in the regular classroom: The best form of adjustment still may be a diversification of instruction by a competent teacher.

REMEDIAL METHODS

This chapter would not be complete without a résumé of remedial methods. We have already indicated that there is no one best method for teaching reading and there is no one best remedial or corrective method. There may be a best method for a given learner. There may be a best method for a special segment of the learner population. There may even be a best method for a given teacher because he is most comfortable with it. The teacher of reading thus has to look at many methods. Because he doesn't know whose brand of reading method is the best buy, he has to consider a variety of possibilities, each of which might have some merit and validity in a specific teaching situation.

It is not possible to survey all remedial methods, but the following are some key ones.[8]

Monroe Method

Numerous writers have advocated phonetic methods both for remedial work and as a general portion of the developmental program. Monroe (46, pp. 111–136) in 1932 evolved a synthetic phonetic approach using considerable repetition and drill. The basic emphasis was the development of auditory discrimination. Pictures are mounted on cards and the child is taught to identify initial consonants and consonants followed by a vowel. After a few of these phonetic elements are known, blending is begun. Gradually, the child is initiated into the reading of specially written stories. Tracing is used in this method as the need arises, but the child uses a pencil rather than the forefinger for tracing. Monroe found her method to be highly successful with serious reading dis-

[8] For a more detailed discussion, see Dechant, Emerald, *Diagnosis and Remediation of Reading Disability* (New York: Parker Publishing Company, 1968).

ability cases and with children who have great difficulty in making visual associations.

Fernald Method (27)

The steps in the Fernald method vary from word tracing to word analysis and are determined somewhat by the ability and progress of the child. At the lower ranges of achievement, the child selects a word that he wishes to learn. The teacher writes the word on paper in large script or print. The child may even dictate a sentence such as "I like my mother." The teacher records this on paper. There is little or no control of the vocabulary. The child then traces each word with the forefinger, saying each part of the word as he does the tracing. The process continues until the child can write the word without the benefit of the copy. The child's fingers must make contact with the paper as he traces. Words thus learned are later typewritten and then included in stories for the child to read. As new words are learned, they are collected by the pupil in an alphabetical file. As the child advances, tracing may cease entirely, but pronouncing the word while writing it is always an essential feature.

The kinesthetic method develops through four stages:

1. Tracing, calling and writing the word.
   a. The teacher writes the word for the pupil in large print, perhaps on the chalkboard.
   b. The pupil traces the word, pronouncing the word in syllables as he traces.
   c. The pupil tries to write the word, repeating steps one and two if he is unable to do so.
2. Writing without tracing. Gradually the pupil attempts to write new words without having to trace them.
3. Recognizing the word. The pupil gradually comes to recognize the word on sight. He learns the printed word by saying it to himself before writing.
4. Word analysis. The pupil is taught to break the word into smaller parts. He now recognizes words by their similarity to words that he already knows.

The kinesthetic method is time-consuming, but it has many advantages. It teaches left-to-right orientation, and the sound of the word is associated with the visual stimulus. The child seems to acquire phonic skills without having formal training, and he develops skills in syllabication. The method is designed especially for clinical use and requires almost constant direction from the teacher.

The Hegge, Kirk, and Kirk Grapho-Vocal Method (32) requires the pupil to sound out and write each word. The pupil pronounces the word entirely phonetically (synthetic phonics) and later writes the word from dictation. The steps thus are:

1. Sound the words letter by letter.
2. Blend the sounds together.
3. Pronounce the words.
4. Write the words.

Fernald's method is a VAKT (visual, auditory, kinesthetic, and tactile) method. There are similar methods labelled only VAK. In these, the pupil does not do any tracing of the word.

The Unified Phonics Methods

The Unified Phonics Method by Spalding and Spalding[9] is a phonics method which teaches reading through a spelling-writing approach and through a study of some 70 phonograms in the English language. These are single letters or letter combinations which represent 45 basic sounds. The authors recommend their program as a beginning reading program and suggest that through the use of this program remedial reading will not be needed later. The steps in teaching are the following (pp. 40–42):

1. Teach the phonograms by having pupils say in unison the one or more sounds of each of the phonograms.
2. The pupil writes each phonogram. The letters are not named.
3. Any phonogram of two or more letters is called by its sound. Thus *eigh* is *a*.
4. Have children write words from the Ayres list.
5. Teach the basic laws of spelling.
6. Reading is begun only when the pupils have learned enough words to comprehend instantly the meaning of a sentence.

The Color Phonics System

The Color Phonics System[10] presents the letters in color in such a way that once the principle of coding has been mastered the pupil can immediately identify the sound. The method is designed to be used with the dyslexic reader. It is not to be used with the color blind or

---

[9] Romalda Bishop Spalding and Walter T. Spalding, *The Writing Road to Reading* (New York: Whiteside, Inc., William Morrow & Co., Inc., 1962).
[10] Color Phonics System (Cambridge, Mass.: Educators Publishing Service, 301 Vassar Street).

with the brain injured suffering from color agnosia. The system is based, among others, on the following assumptions:

1. The most successful techniques for teaching dyslexics are founded on a phonetic basis.
2. Each letter should be taught separately or in given combinations which can be arranged and rearranged again and again in various orders. Bannatyne (3) believes that the fundamental neuropsychological deficit of the dyslexic child is the inability to sequence correctly, especially auditorily. The pupil must vocalize constantly, sounding out the successive phonemes which make up a word.
3. The dyslexic child has difficulty mastering the irregular orthography of the English language, but replacing the irregular phonetic structure of the language with a regular one requires the child to transfer to the traditional orthography at a later date. As the dyslexic child finds it extremely difficult to memorize a set of sound-symbol associations, an additional set of symbols for the same sounds is scarcely likely to solve his problems (3, p. 196). Color coding permits the child to identify the sound in a direct way.
4. The pupil must overlearn sound-symbol associations through a variety of stimuli and sensory pathways.

Bannatyne (3) believes that the Color Phonics System can be used in conjunction with the Fernald Method, the Gillingham Method, or Daniel's and Diack's systems as developed through the Royal Road Readers. For teaching with this system the following points are emphasized by Bannatyne:

1. If the child suffers from severe dyslexia, the teacher usually begins with the phonetically regular words and short sentences, and initially short vowels. Consonants are introduced later.
2. The vowels are printed in red. The pupil learns that there must never be a word or syllable without a red letter (the letter *y* has a red band because it can be used as a vowel).
3. At all times, words are broken up into syllables whenever the individual letters are used. One technique which helps the child with breaking a word into syllables, memorizing colors, and spelling generally is the use of rhymes and rhyming.
4. A problem frequently encountered is that of blending phonemes. Frequently, the inability to blend is a direct result of faulty teaching, inasmuch as the pupil has learned to voice unvoiced consonants by adding unwanted vowels. The word *lit* cannot be

blended if the *l* is pronounced *luh*. More often than not, this inability to synthesize sounds into meaningful speech is an aspect of the primary inability of the dyslexic to sequence auditory material in the absence of auditory sounds. Clear vocalization and auditory sequencing of words are the most important requisite for successful remediation.

5. There are only two methods for facilitating blending. The first is to tell the child to form his mouth in preparation for saying the initial consonant of a syllable but then to say the following vowel instead. This technique is useful when the initial consonants are unvoiced ones anyway. The second technique consists of demonstrating a single syllable in two parts, namely, the initial consonant and the remainder of the syllable as a whole. Thus cat is taught not as c a t, *but as* c at. At the same time, the word, *cat,* as a *gestalt,* is presented in both its written and spoken forms, and these are simultaneously analyzed into their component letters and phonemes.

6. The child is introduced to the twenty or so spelling rules one by one. He is given plenty of practice in applying the rules. In the long run, it is easier for a dyslexic, with his weak verbal memory, to remember a few set principles than thousands of those arbitrary letter-sound sequences called (printed) words.

7. Gradually, the black vowels replace the colored ones.

The Progressive Choice Reading Method

The Progressive Choice Reading Method [11] is an outgrowth of studies by Myron Woolman. Two programs based on Woolman's ideas are available today. The first of these, entitled *Lift Off to Reading*[12] is useful with educable and trainable mental retardates, culturally disadvantaged, the emotionally disturbed, bilinguals, and dyslexics. *Reading in High Gear*[13] is designed for older, underachieving, culturally disadvantaged readers at the adolescent level. Woolman emphasizes elements in words. He begins with a "target word" by discussing its meaning. The learner then must differentiate the linear and curvilinear components which compose the letters of the target word. These components are then combined into individual letters and discrimination of the letters is stressed. The pupil next writes the letter by tracing the letter, finally writing the letter without tracing. The third step consists of

[11] M. Woolman, *The Progressive Choice Reading Program* (Washington, D. C.: Institute of Educational Research, Inc., 1962).
[12] M. Woolman, *Lift Off to Reading* (Chicago: Science Research Associates, 1966).
[13] M. Woolman, *Reading in High Gear* (Chicago: Science Research Associates, 1965).

learning the sound that is most commonly associated with the letter. Woolman teaches the *g*, for example, as *guh*, noting that this is a necessary crutch in the beginning and that the pupil quickly gets rid of it when he has mastered a "feeling" for the consonant. The pupil must utter the sound when he sees the printed form of the letter and he must write the letter when he hears it pronounced for him. Fourthly, the reader must learn to combine various vowels and consonants into single sounds. Finally, the pupil must read and write the "target words."

Gillingham Method

The Gillingham method [14] is a multisensory approach emphasizing the linguistic and graphic regularities of English words. It is termed an alphaphonetic method and begins by teaching the child a few short vowels and consonants that have only one sound. It does not use letters that, if reversed, become new letters. Thus initially it steers clear of letters like *b* and *d*. It is a combination method, using the auditory, visual, and kinesthetic sense avenues. It is a synthetic phonics system rather than an analytical phonics approach. The teaching processes that result in the association of the visual, auditory, and kinesthetic processes are called linkages. The method consists of eight such linkages.

Linkage 1. The name of the letter is associated with the printed symbol; then the sound of the letter is associated with the symbol.

Linkage 2. The teacher makes the letter and explains its form. The pupil traces it, copies it, and writes it from memory. The teacher directs the pupil to move in the right direction and to begin in the right place when making the letters.

Linkage 3. The phonogram is shown to the pupil and he names it. The child learns to associate the letter with its "look" and its "feel." He learns to form the symbol without looking at the paper as he writes.

Linkage 4. The teacher says the phoneme, and the child writes it.

Linkage 5. The child is shown the letter and asked to sound it. The teacher moves the child's hand to form the letter, and the child sounds it.

Linkage 6. The teacher gives the name of the phonogram, and the pupil gives the sound.

[14] Anna Gillingham and Bessie W. Stillman, *Remedial Training for Children With Specific Disability in Reading, Spelling, and Penmanship* (Cambridge: Educators Publishing Service, 1966). Available also are: *Phonetic Drill Cards, Phonetic Word Cards, Syllable Concept, Little Stories,* and *Introduction of Diphthongs.*

Linkage 7. The teacher makes the sound, and the pupil gives the name of the letter.

Linkage 8. The teacher makes the sound, and the pupil writes the phonogram. Sometimes the pupil writes without looking at the paper and also names the letter.

Using the multisensory approach, the Gillingham method introduces the linguistic and graphically regular words first. Only gradually the pupil is introduced to exceptions.

EVALUATING REMEDIAL INSTRUCTION

The reading teacher, whether in or out of the regular classroom, must constantly evaluate his instruction. He needs to determine the effectiveness of various procedures in terms of the gains in reading achievement. Over the course of years many quite different procedures have been suggested for evaluating remedial teaching, but too few data are available concerning their relative effectiveness. And for that matter, some writers actually challenge the effectiveness of special methods of remediation. Young (73), for example, suggests that the personality of the teacher and his ability to enlist each child's active cooperation are more important than the specific method used. On the other hand, numerous studies on remedial and diagnostic methods indicate that reading difficulties can be either entirely or at least largely eliminated.

Balow (2) found that remedial instruction was effective in dealing with the problems of the disabled reader, but he also notes that severe reading disability is not corrected by short term intensive treatment, but that it should be considered a relatively chronic illness needing long term treatment rather than the short course typically organized in current programs. Buerger (13) also reports that children who received remedial instruction demonstrated significant reading gains, but they did not make greater long term educational progress than other children who did not receive remedial instruction.

Rankin and Tracy (52,53) list three methods of measuring and evaluating individual differences in reading improvement.

1. *Crude gain.* In this situation comparable tests are given before (the pretest) and after (the posttest) a remedial program. The score at the start of the program is subtracted from the score at the end of the program, and the difference is considered as improvement. Children will naturally show improvement if a difficult

test is given in the beginning and if an easier test is administered after the completion of the program.

2. *Percentage gain.* In this approach the gain between the pre- and posttest is expressed as a percentage of the initial score. The formula then is:

$$\text{per cent of gain} = \frac{\text{pretest} - \text{posttest.}}{\text{posttest}}$$

3. *Residual gain.* This is the difference between the actual posttest score and the score that was predictable from the pretest score. For a discussion of this third procedure the reader may want to consult the articles by Rankin and Tracy in the *Journal of Reading*, March, 1965, and March, 1967.

Many faulty conclusions apparently have been drawn from reading research because residual gain was not considered. As Sommerfield (64) points out, there is a natural tendency for those people who score at the extremes of a distribution on the first test to score closer to the mean of the distribution on the second test. The scores tend to regress toward the mean.

Although the research worker can use control groups or make statistical corrections to eliminate regression effects, this frequently is not done.

Dolch (19, p. 80) has cautioned that research can come up with the wrong answer unless it is carefully planned and watched. He recommends vigilance in these areas:

1. Compare equal teachers working equally hard.
2. Compare pupils of equal ability and equal home influences.
3. Compare equal school time and emphasis.
4. Watch carefully size of class.
5. Beware of misleading averages.
6. Watch for unmeasured results.

In discussing these points, Dolch emphasizes that the teacher using the method frequently is far more important than the method used. Numerous variables enter into any experiment. Sommerfield (64, p. 56) indicates that the reported results of experimental reading programs may be influenced by the subjects involved, the techniques and materials used, the conditions under which the study was done, the tests that were employed, the statistical devices used, and perhaps the bias or misinterpretations of the investigator.

Studies often do not make allowance for the differences in both skill and motivation among teachers. Control groups are taught by the "regular" teachers; experimental groups are taught by teachers who have a special interest in the project and can give more time to their students. Studies do not control for the Hawthorne effect,[15] which is the learning that results simply because the program is new and presents for students and teachers alike an opportunity for recognition. Brownell (9) notes that the critical determinant of achievement is teaching competency rather than the system of instruction. He also notes that results frequently are evaluated by means of test scores, but this is not necessarily what is educationally significant. The measurable is not necessarily the significant, and the significant is not necessarily measurable. There are no published tests available that measure how well students read to gain information in specific courses. In this area general reading tests are of limited value. In many instances achievement at the moment is evaluated; the transfer value of what has been learned is rarely evaluated. There may also be differences in motivation between the pupils in a control group using the regular methods and the experimental group using a new method.

Weiner notes that to evaluate changes in reading behavior we must consider all relevant functions: perceptual, integrative, and motivational. We need to evaluate processes rather than simply end-products, measurable and nonmeasurable changes, and changes in self-concept and attitudes as a result of remedial programs. We need to find ways of analyzing the process that produced the outcome and of determining cause-and-effect relationships. When assessing process, we encounter such difficult-to-evaluate variables as student-teacher interaction, attitudes, interests, and enthusiasm. Weiner notes that evidence of improvement is greater accuracy in responses to printed material, greater dependability, greater retention of and confidence in one's responses, and greater speed.

In advancing a clinical concept of assessment Weiner stresses the qualitative aspects of assessment and suggests that "gains should be measured from the point of actual departure and not from an arbitrary zero point on a grade-level scale . . . the pupils in need of such services start not from scratch, as the saying goes, but from behind scratch." [16]

---

[15] Willard J. Congreve, "Implementing and Evaluating the Use of Innovations," *Innovation and Change in Reading Instruction*, 67th Yearbook of the National Society for the Study of Education (Chicago: University of Chicago Press, 1968), pp. 291–319.

[16] Bluma B. Weiner, "Dimensions of Assessment," *Exceptional Children*, 28 (September, 1961), pp. 483–86.

SUMMARY

This chapter outlines the diagnostic remedial process. It draws a distinction between developmental, corrective, and remedial instruction. It deals with the specific problems of teaching the slow learner, the gifted learner, and the disadvantaged reader. It takes a look at various remedial methods, and it offers ideas on evaluating remedial methods.

QUESTIONS FOR DISCUSSION

1. Discuss prevention of reading disability as an important principle in the teaching of reading.
2. What does a comprehensive individual diagnosis consist of?
3. What are the criteria for estimating a child's independent reading level?
4. Compare the advantages and disadvantages of the informal and formal reading inventory.
5. Which diagnostic test would you recommend for grade levels four through six?
6. Identify basic symptoms of reading disability and suggest possible causes for each. How would you go about identifying the specific cause?
7. Suggest four possible classroom organizations that make allowance for corrective instruction.
8. Differentiate between the needs of the slow learner and the disadvantaged child.
9. List the factors to be considered when evaluating the effectiveness of remedial instruction.

THEORY AND PRACTICE
IN TEACHING

part VII

Previous sections of this book have concerned themselves with the most significant aspects of the *teaching of reading*. The continual concern has been how the teacher might improve his instruction and thus the pupil's learning. We were particularly interested in how the teacher can help the pupil to learn to read. In many instances, the relationship between practice and theory was not spelled out. Thus, the book to this point has emphasized methodology, relegating theory to a secondary role.

In this last section more emphasis will be put on the theory behind teaching. Theory, especially learning theory, must provide the unifying concept of this book. Theory gives direction and helps to evaluate practice. Learning is what the teacher is trying to promote. Only by knowing what learning is and how it must be encouraged and promoted can he hope to provide effective teaching. *Even if the teacher knew his subject twice as well as he now does, the pupil would not necessarily learn more. The average teacher needs more knowledge in the area of learning.*

There is today a mutually rewarding relationship between educator and psychologist. The educator examines closely the findings of psychology and so hopes to improve the curriculum, materials used in teaching, and methods of instruction. The psychologist uses the school as a laboratory to test his ideas. It is the common interest in the learning process that links education and psychology. Even the best teacher knows that there is much room for improvement; there are better ways of doing things. He is daily perplexed with instructional-learning problems. He knows better than anyone else that he needs to improve his understanding of the teaching-learning process.

Understanding the Reading-Learning Process

If the teacher fully understood how the pupil learns to read, the teaching of reading would be rather simple. Unfortunately, this is not the case. The teacher thus is faced with the task of constantly checking his teaching practices against theory and experimentation. He needs to know *why* certain methods work and why some do not.

Too frequently education has been concerned with "what works" rather than with "why it works." Perhaps this is as it should be. As teachers we are primarily interested in creating effective learning situations. We wish to help children to learn. Why they learn better under one approach than under another does not seem quite so important as the fact that they do learn better. Thus, the teacher asks: What is taking place? What will happen if I try this method? He frequently fails to ask: What may account for this event? Why is method *A* more effective than method *B?*

Professional teaching is more than a technique; it is a science as well as an art. Teachers are artists rather than mere technicians. Techniques are inert and lifeless; the learner is active. The teacher cannot impulsively apply a "cookbook" recipe to learning problems. He may be content to give first place to the art of effective teaching, but for highest excellence in teaching he generally must know also its scientific basis. He must know the *why* in order to perform the *how*. He must understand the *learner* as well as or better than *what is learned*. He needs to have an interest in the broader aspects of learning even though this may not lead to immediate practical results.

TEACHING [1]

Teaching is a "system of actions directed to pupils (49, p. 233)." How well a child learns frequently is dependent upon the educational provisions that the teacher makes for the child. The teacher constantly expands the pupil's meanings by broadening his experience or by helping him to recombine and to perceive new relationships between his existent knowledge and ideas.

Snow (50) points out that teaching often means simply instruction. It is something that is provided from without the learner and results in a flow of information to the student. Education is something more than that. It is not simply the pouring in of a glob of information.[2] Education more correctly refers to the internal process of learning. Where the former description emphasizes the stimulus aspects, the latter emphasizes those things that the pupil does and assigns a greater role to the pupil in the learning process. Education includes both instruction and learning. Learning is the correlative of instruction. Indeed, if the pupil has not learned, he may not have been taught. A criterion of effective teaching is effective learning on the part of the pupil.

The major task facing educators generally and reading teachers particularly is the individualization of instruction. The teacher teaches groups of children, but even the most carefully selected or homogeneous group is still composed of individuals. Thus learning is always an individual process. The learner is an individual and the criteria for effective teaching vary from individual to individual.

The meaning of the previous chapters is this: the teacher cannot devote most of his time and effort to finding out how the *average individual* performs. We are told that poor readers come from homes of lower socioeconomic standing, tend to dislike school, have more auditory and visual defects, and cannot analyze or synthesize.

Many good readers have similar problems and characteristics, but they do not become poor readers. What is the explanation? The whole complex of causes, correlates, and reasons why children fail in reading presents a new pattern of organization for each individual. Each child has his own organization and his own rate and level of growth and development. Just because the child is intellectually able, this is no assurance that all other aspects of his growth and development are in perfect synchronization.

---

[1] For a perceptive discussion of the ingredients of effective teaching, see Calvin E. Harbin, *Teaching Power* (New York: Philosophical Library, Inc., 1967).

[2] Arthur W. Combs at the Fifteenth Annual Meeting of the Kansas Personnel and Guidance Association, Wichita, Kansas, March 30, 1963.

The teacher cannot offer group prescriptions. He must provide a reading program and reading materials that fit the needs of each child and that permit each pupil to advance according to his own abilities and needs. He must provide for the development of each child's unique constellation of characteristics.

To be effective, teachers must know the pupil's individualness. Without this knowledge they cannot provide meaningful learning experiences. Without this knowledge all the rules and generalizations are empty for these are modified and changed in and by every individual. Without this knowledge, the teacher cannot adapt his responses, his rules, and generalizations to the individual.

This does not mean, however, that the teacher can ignore the group and its characteristics. In fact, it may even be dangerous to prescribe too narrowly, or to individualize teaching too much, especially when diagnosis and knowledge of the individual is limited. At times, it may even be wiser to teach a group as a group and to treat individuals as alike rather than to instruct singly. To teach a student incorrectly because of faulty differentiation is worse than to teach all students similarly. Frequently, the best indication as to what the individual is like is the average of the group, and the best provision for individual differences may be instruction that fits the average.

This does not mean that differentiation of instruction is universally harmful. It does mean that the teacher must take greater pains in diagnosis. It means that he must recognize the inaccuracy of much of his diagnosis. It means that generally instruction and remediation for the individual should differ only slightly from instruction for the group. It means that irreversible decisions should be avoided.[3]

Thus, the sound reading program today emphasizes the need for broadening the child's interests; it provides for readiness, gradually preparing the pupil for new words, new meanings, and new reading demands; it gives sequential development of the basic reading skills; it utilizes group dynamics and group instruction; and it provides a series of graded, integrated, and organized materials. Skills are best taught when the pupil is ready for learning them, when the teacher has a plan for presentation, when the teacher has a share in pacing the pupil, and when there is a systematic attempt to maintain the skill.

THE DETERMINANTS OF READING SUCCESS

As mentioned previously, teaching is a series of actions directed toward pupils, and the teacher is the prime stimulator of pupils. He must

[3] For a detailed discussion see Lee J. Cronbach, "The Counselor's Problems from the Perspective of Communication Theory," in *New Perspectives in Counseling*, Vivian H. Hewer, ed., University of Minnesota Press, 1955, 3–19.

present the material so clearly that the pupil's attention is focused completely on the task at hand. Attention is not given to a lecture that is "sound and fury signifying nothing" or to a teacher who doesn't have knowledge worthy of the pupil's attention.

However, stimulation is not enough. As we noted in Chapters 3 and 4, there are certain conditions that may prevent adequate learning. In Table 15-1 we have outlined the various factors inherent in the learning task itself, in the method used, in the individual, and in the institution, that are worthy of the teacher's consideration. Effective learning (and hence effective teaching) commonly does not occur unless the teacher understands the nature of these factors and makes adjustments for them.

Downey speaks of the last three phases listed in the table below as the substantive dimension (task), the procedural dimension (method), and the environmental dimension (institution). He points out (10, p. 188) that a change in any single aspect will result in a modification of all other aspects.

Let us comment briefly on each of the four major determinants of reading achievement.

Individual Variables

Reading achievement is variable because children are different. They have different biological and environmental backgrounds, and if the teacher is to know how and when to teach what, he must know and understand those factors that make children different. The quantity and quality of reading achievement depend upon the pupil's conscious and unconscious receptiveness to what is taught in the classroom or to what is experienced informally (64, pp. 39–40). Only the pupil controls the entrance of sense impressions. He may let them in and permit them to become percepts and concepts or he can reject them.

In general, the psychology of individual differences indicates that:

1. Children achieve at different rates.
2. The differences in achievement increase as children advance through school, being as much as four grades at the first grade level and as much as nine and ten grades at the sixth grade level.
3. Native endowment or biology plays a large role in the development of any child. The child's biological characteristics are prime factors in making him an individual.
4. Intra-individual differences may be as great or greater than the differences between individuals.
5. The achievements of individuals often are marked by spurts and plateaus.

TABLE 15-1   The Determinants of Reading Success

Individual Variables	Task Variables	Method Variables	Institutional Variables
(The Learner or the Pupil's Receptivity to Learning—The Nature of the Learner)	(That Which Is to Be Learned or the Concepts, Skills, and Habits)	(The Way It Is Learned or the Experiences by Which the Pupil Learns)	(The Setting in Which It Is Learned —The Institution)
Psychology of Reading	*Reading Content*	*Reading Method*	*Educational Setting*
1. Experiential Background— Previous Learning	1. Perception Skills	1. Synthetic Method a. alphabet b. phonic c. syllable	1. Attitudinal Variables a. resistance to or acceptance of change b. expectations of school staff
2. Maturational Development	2. Comprehension Skills	2. Analytic Method a. word b. phrase c. sentence	2. Classroom Variables a. type of organization b. size of instructional unit
3. Language and Speech Development	3. Word-attack Skills	3. Kinesthetic Method	3. Teacher Variables
4. Intellectual Development	4. Reading-study Skills	4. Eclectic Method	4. Procedural Variables a. grading practices b. policy of retention and promotion c. type of control
5. Physical Health and Energy	5. Interpretative Skills	5. Basal Approach	5. Facilities a. Laboratory Facilities b. Library Facilities c. Materials d. Availability of Referral Sources
6. Visual Adequacy	6. Rate of Comprehension Skills	6. Individualized Approach	
7. Auditory Adequacy	7. Oral Reading Skills	7. ITA	

(continued)

TABLE 15-1 (*continued*)

Individual Variables	Task Variables	Method Variables	Institutional Variables
(The Learner or the Pupil's Receptivity to Learning—The Nature of the Learner)	(That Which Is to Be Learned or the Concepts, Skills, and Habits)	(The Way It Is Learned or the Experiences by Which the Pupil Learns)	(The Setting in Which It Is Learned —The Institution)
Psychology of Reading	Reading Content	Reading Method	Educational Setting
8. Adequate Brain Development		8. Words in Color	
9. Interest, Curiosity, and Motivation		9. Linguistic Method	
10. Social and Emotional Readiness		10. Programmed Learning Model	
11. Sex		11. Language Experience Approach	
12. Self-discipline for Learning		12. Textfilm Approach	

6. Environmental factors may serve as equalizers among individuals. They may tend to make unequals more equal and more similar. Teaching may encourage mediocrity.
7. Membership in a group may lead to the wrong attribution of a certain characteristic to an individual. "All of your brothers are bright, why are you not achieving like them?"
8. The rate of teaching (pacing) must be suited to the child's pace of learning. Thus, it is an error to presume that the pupil develops meanings and concepts from a single brief explanation.

Through the course of this book we have said nothing about discipline and yet self-discipline is as much an individual variable as are the child's intellectual skills and may have as much influence on the learning of reading as do many of the factors discussed in Chapters 3 and 4. Discipline sets the stage for learning. Without self-control and positive motivation, few pupils will direct consistent effort toward the acquisition of reading skills, habits, and interest.

Discipline does not mean complete permissiveness. It does not mean only reward and approval. Discipline does not function in a class-room where everybody talks at once, where the teacher is ignored, and where teachers are abused if they exercise their authority.

Discipline may mean the imposition of external standards, and it may mean punishment and reproof. A pupil who has a psychological reason for misbehaving is not thereby absolved from moral accountability (1, p. 29). Ausubel (1, p. 29) adds that the teacher's dignity is just as important as is the pupil's. It is just as wrong for the pupil to abuse the teacher as for the teacher to abuse the pupil.

Some would suggest that children should not be inhibited. On the contrary, without inhibition there is no discipline and experience has shown that self-discipline in the adult rests on the firm foundation of external inhibitions in childhood.

Children always *believe* that what they are doing is the best for them. This does not mean that their judgment is always correct. They are not always sensitive to their needs. The present interests and opinions of pupils are hardly reliable guideposts for designing a curriculum or for formulating standards of classroom behavior (1, p. 30).

Discipline is not merely a *means* to learning; it is an important *goal* of learning. Discipline is necessary for learning, but the pupil also must learn discipline.

Children must learn that the teacher inevitably must in one form or another become a restrictive force to their free use of self-directed freedom (63). The freedom or autonomy that pupils seek sometimes is self-destructive and contrary to the goals of a democratic society in which individuals are cooperative and interrelated persons. Pupils must learn that belonging to a society means to sacrifice some degree of in-dividual liberty.

Task Variables

The major portion of this book has been devoted to the identification and development of the reading skills. The pupil must be taught per-ception skills, comprehension skills, word-attack skills, study skills, inter-pretative skills, rate skills, and oral reading skills. He must be taught to recognize the symbol and to take meaning to it.

In previous chapters we have offered some guidelines as to when and how these skills should be developed. Some of these guidelines may warrant repetition:

1. The child seeks for what he is physiologically and psycholog-ically ready.
2. Because of the composition of grades, a beginning reader may be learning what some other reader will learn only toward the very end of the primary years.

3. Knowing what skills to teach is not enough for the teacher. He must decide what skills a specific child needs and can learn; he must know what method to use in teaching the skill; and he must be able to construct and use special projects that illustrate, organize, and develop the skills.
4. Skill development does not come in capsule form. One cannot dish out to third graders the third-grade capsule and to fourth graders the fourth-grade capsule.
5. Every teacher should be familiar with the total skill-development program so that he can perceive its continuity.
6. Introduction of skills is useless unless the pupil's subsequent reading experiences serve to maintain those skills.
7. Every reading skill has its beginning in the earliest school years.
8. There are differences among children in rate of learning. The differences in learning capacity are just as significant. Some children may never master all the skills.
9. A skill that is more difficult for the average third grader may be relatively easier for a specific third grader.

Method Variables

Chapter 8 discussed and evaluated the various methods of teaching reading. In this chapter we will discuss the additional factors of motivation, incentives, and practice. Let us first say a few words about attention and perception.

Attention is selective in that the learner selects from his experience the elements to which he wishes to attend. He lets only certain elements into consciousness. He is constantly bombarded by stimuli, both from within and from without. Hundreds of stimuli are constantly competing with each other for the dominant position.

That the learner considers some stimuli more deserving of his attention than others or that some stimuli are higher in the hierarchy of attention value is of great benefit. The clap of thunder and the streak of lightning may save him from a good drenching.

Attention also is integrative in that the perceiver sometimes can attend to more stimuli if the stimuli are part of a pattern. In reading, our perceptions frequently move from whole to detail and from details to whole. We peripherally attend to the whole when focusing on the part and to the parts when focusing on the whole. Like a camera, we may take in breadth while subsuming detail, or we may focus sharply upon detail while subsuming the whole (51, p. 183).

Attention also is an energizer in that it elicits the expenditure of human energy and inhibits its expenditure for other tasks. Concentration in one area results in less energy being available in other areas. It has been shown (51, p. 186) through electrodes implanted in the auditory pathway in the brain stem of cats that when the cat "attends" to two mice in a bottle, auditory stimuli are not transmitted. In our analysis of vision we found that for children with visual defects whose total energy is devoted to the maintenance of single and clear vision, concentration upon learning tasks becomes impossible or extremely difficult.

Institutional Variables

The teaching of reading functions in a sociological matrix (2) in which the interaction of numerous persons and groups (children, parents, teachers, schoolboards, departments of education, colleges, press, etc.) determines what will be taught, how it will be taught, by whom it will be taught, and when it will be taught. This matrix determines what research will be done, how it will be interpreted, and how it will be applied. It determines who will be promoted and retained; how the school will be organized; what provisions will be made for the slow and the rapid learner; how large classes will be; what grading systems will be used; and whether classes will be grouped homogeneously or heterogeneously.

STIMULUS-RESPONSE THEORIES OF LEARNING: AN OVERVIEW

The teacher's prime task is to get children to learn, so he obviously needs to know how learning takes place. He needs to know how to provide the conditions for effective learning.

Through the years various schools of learning have arisen. In fact, if one wanted to do justice to even one of them, an entire book would have to be devoted to the task.

The usefulness of learning theories for the teacher has always been questioned, and no fully satisfactory answer has been found. The psychologist finds it difficult to apply learning theory to school situations. The gap between theory and research and practice has never been satisfactorily bridged. The basic reason for this is that learning theory must be founded on carefully controlled experimentation, but unfortunately, experimentation with children is often a complex and forbidding task. Rigidity and control, which are the major strengths of laboratory research, are the very factors that often make accurate research in the classroom forbidding, if not impossible. Certain applications, however, can and should be made.

Learning theories can be divided into Stimulus-Response Theories and Field Theories. Each of these major divisions has its supporters, and each may be subdivided into numerous segments. Figure 15–1 illustrates this.

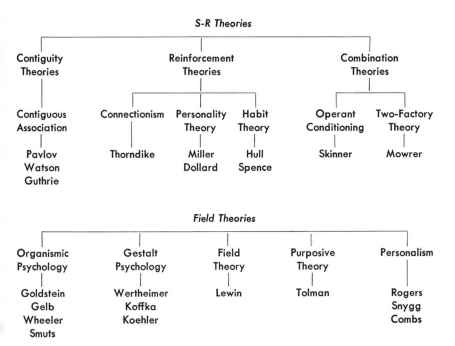

Figure 15-1.   Theories of Learning

S-R theorists suggest that in any activity there are three basic elements: the situation or stimulus, the response that a given person makes to the situation or stimulus, and the connection or association between the stimulus and the response. This connection is referred to as an S-R bond. The S-R theorist focuses on the response or the observable action and suggests that what the organism learns is the response. For example, the pupil learns to type words; he learns to read a word; or he learns to kick a football. The pupil is learning an action or a response.

The S-R theorist thus considers learning to be the process of forming new bonds and organizing them into a system of bonds which may be called knowledge. He defines learning as: "The acquisition of new behavior patterns or the strengthening or weakening of old behavior patterns as a result of practice (48, p. 210)." Kingsley and Garry (24, p. 12) state that "Learning is the process by which behavior . . . is originated or changed through practice or training. . . ." Such a definition of learning suggests that we learn by doing something or by experiencing.

S-R theorists generally assert their predilection for conditioning, which to them is the clearest and most simple instance of a response to a stimulus. This is the simplest form of learning in S-R theory.

FIELD THEORIES: AN OVERVIEW

The field theorists, on the other hand, emphasize cognitive processes, purposive behavior, the organizational nature of the learning process, contemporary experience, and wholes rather than parts.

Emphasis on Cognitive Processes

Whereas S-R theorists emphasize the observable response or the peripheral events, field theorists emphasize the perceptual process or understanding, conscious experience, and meaning. Gestaltists took issue with the proposition that all learning consisted of simple connections of responses to stimuli, without recourse to ideas or thought processes. The Gestalt psychologist is more interested in what the child *understands* than in what he *does*; he is more interested in man's ability to conceptualize, reason, and form judgments.

The field theorist suggests that the meaning that an experience has for the person experiencing may be as significant as the experience itself. He studies the effect that a change in the structure of meanings or perceptions may have on behavior. He is a firm believer that psychology is enriched when it finds the lawful relationships between inner meanings and external behavior.

The field theorist thus stresses that learning is both a perceptual as well as an associative process. He suggests that learning is guided by intervening mental processes which may be labelled cognition, thought, or perception.

Emphasis on Purposive Behavior

Field theorists also emphasize that man is purposive and not subject entirely to instincts, as Freudianism would lead us to believe, nor is he an entirely passive being who is the prey of stimuli, as some S-R thinking might suggest. There are stable, central processes which integrate behavior and give purpose to it. Man lives a life which is not entirely explained by previous conditionings or the unconscious. He is interested in inner meanings (43), in purposes, goals, values, choice, perceptions of self, and in man as a self-determining and self-actualizing system.

Emphasis on Learning as an Organizational Process

In field theories, learning is defined as a change in perception and is the result of a new organization of experience. Learning is an organizational response to a stimulus, an active process resulting in a new organization. The field theorist maintains that man is constantly acting upon the environment, structuring it, and bettering his perception of it, not simply reacting to it.

Learning thus proceeds by reorganization rather than by accretion. When the pupil suddenly realizes that multiplication is simply another form of addition, the flash of understanding that comes at this single trial is not simply the result of adding up S-R connections. The learner now perceives previously acquired learning in a better way. The differentiations result from a change in perceptual structure either through a new organization of past experiences or by the addition of novel experiences.

What is learned? The field theorist maintains that the learner discovers and understands relationships between the various elements of the present stimulus situation or between those of the present and the past.

The meaning that the learner assigns to the stimulus is an indication of how he has organized experience. It is a sign of his peculiar organization. The meaning that he takes to a word, such as beauty, comes from within him more than from the stimulus situation, and while determined by his previous experiences, to be sure, it is not entirely so. It is also determined by the learner's constitutional makeup, the quality and organization of his experiences, by his affective state, and by his culture. The learner reacts as an organized whole.

The stages in perception are, then: (*1*) a pattern of stimulation, (*2*) an organization, and (*3*) a response to the product of organization.

Emphasis on the Contemporary Experience

The field-theoretical approach to learning emphasizes the primacy of the contemporary pattern, organization, field, or Gestalt rather than the past history or experiences of the organism. The S-R theorist endorses a historical viewpoint and suggests that responses and response patterns are the accumulation of numerous trials. When a new problem is met, in his view, the learner calls upon his previous habits and responds to the new situation in terms of previous responses to similar aspects or elements, or he varies his responses, using a trial-and-error approach, until he achieves a correct response.

The field theorist believes that the learner comes up with an organization fit to meet the demands of the present situation. He admits that in solving problems past experience is useful, but suggests that the present structuring of the problem may prevent or enhance the possibilities of a solution.

Perhaps no individual is ever completely free to behave on the basis of the present situation. Previous experiences have developed a set or pattern of behavior that is difficult to change. The retarded reader, even if he now sincerely wants to be a good reader, must live with his previous inapplication. But, each new situation has within it the potentiality for change. The pupil can usually make positive advances toward new goals and achievements. He has the potentiality for growth.

Emphasis on Wholes Rather than Parts

Field theorists all maintain that one can deal better with organisms by observing the total organism. In this sense all are organismic psychologists, who emphasize the functional belongingness of parts to the whole and suggest that organismic events are best understood if they are examined in the pattern into which they belong. Let us now look at the various theorists in more detail.

THORNDIKE'S CONNECTIONISM

Learning theory for years was associated with the name of Edward L. Thorndike (54,55,56,57,58; 1874–1949). He initiated systematic laboratory investigations of animal learning and produced the first formalized associationistic learning theory. Most of Thorndike's experiments were done with cats. Usually a hungry cat was placed in a box or cage which had a loop or string hanging from the top or that contained a latch that, if the cat operated it, would open the door and the way to escape. The cat was rewarded with food or fish if it learned to manipulate the latch or to pull the string that opened the door. Thorndike noted that initially in such a situation the cat will walk around, claw, bite, and dash back and forth. It will usually take a long time before the cat either pulls the string or operates the latch, freeing it from the cage.

With repeated exposure to the box, the cat becomes more proficient in performing the response that immediately precedes the opening of the door and the attainment of food and gets out of the box much more quickly. Thorndike suggested that the cat gradually stamped in the correct responses and stamped out the incorrect ones. He pointed out that the cat, when confronted with the problem of getting out of the cage, selects the proper response from a series of possible responses and connects it with the appropriate stimulus. He termed such learning trial-and-error learning.

Thorndike believed that more complex learning should be broken into more simple learning and that human learning could be essentially explained by animal or trial-and-error learning.

The Law of Readiness

Thorndike developed various "laws" to explain the learning of the cat and the learning of the pupil in the classroom. One of these was the Law of Readiness. Thorndike gave readiness a physiological interpretation, suggesting that when a tendency to act is aroused through preparatory adjustments, sets, or attitudes, carrying out the act is satisfying and not acting is annoying. Readiness thus is a preparation for action.

Thorndike's concept of readiness is roughly analogous to attention or motivation for learning. All of us have watched a cat readying itself to pounce upon its prey. We also have seen many children who come to school with a set to read. They are psychologically ready. They have the proper attitudes and sets to attend to the reading task. Sometimes, however, the learner does not have a "felt need to learn," and not much learning occurs. Teachers then must prepare the pupil for learning. They must arouse curiosity and in other ways appeal to the needs of the child.

Readiness also has acquired a maturational interpretation. In this connection it means that the organism should be mature enough to make the responses required for learning. Readiness then is defined (as was done in Chapter 7) as the developmental stage at which constitutional factors have prepared the pupil for instruction. Learning readiness for a given task also may be described as the teachable moment for that task.

The Law of Exercise

A second law formulated by Thorndike is the Law of Exercise (57). It is sometimes termed the law of use and disuse and asserts that practice is necessary for learning and that when practice is discontinued, learning deteriorates. To learn, the organism must do something. And whenever a response is made to a given stimulus, the response becomes associated with that stimulus, and the more frequently that response is made to the stimulus the stronger the association becomes.

Thorndike found that the more frequently the cat was put into the cage and managed to escape, the more quickly it was able to solve the problem when again put into the cage. Pupils generally become better in word recognition the more frequently they see the word.

We cannot measure learning. To answer the question, "Has the pupil learned?," we must know how well the pupil was doing prior to practice and how well he is doing now. If he could read 200 words per minute and after a period of practice increased this to 300 words per minute, we say that he has learned. We note the changes in his performance and from these surmise that learning has occurred. Learning is an inference from performance.

All theories of learning have to find some place for practice. The child looks at the word for the seventy-fifth time for the same reason that he did the first time. In fact, sometimes the learner breaks a habit by actually practicing the habit (9,11,62, pp. 199–200). Our suggestions on how to overcome reversals include this technique.

Learning is basically a perceptual or psychological process. Learning to read is basically a perceptual process. But, reading also is a *skill* that is learned, and skills are learned best through practice.

This means that the teacher must find ways and means of developing the skills to be learned. He must guide pupils through the processes and provide them with the materials that are necessary for the attainment of the objective.

There are two types of practice: varied practice and repetitive practice. Varied practice or range of experience permits the learner to reorganize his experiences at increasingly higher levels of abstractness and clarity. Through this type of practice meanings are extended and refined. Repetitive practice implies a constant repetition of the same experience. It is most effective when a skill has been "learned" correctly and practice is initiated to make the skill habitual. Repetitive practice of what has been done incorrectly merely makes the performer more proficient in doing the wrong thing.

Fortunately, in most learning situations the two types are combined. Practice is varied so as to bring the performance ever closer to the model and it is repetitive so as to increase proficiency in correct performance and to promote retention.

The characteristics of practice may be summarized as follows:

1. Practice or repetition *per se* does not cause learning. The child's practice must be both motivated and rewarded. In school situations practice should be slightly varied from session to session. The pupil should not be required to do the same thing over and over again. Practice should mean increasingly higher levels of performance.

2. Members of a group tend to keep the same relative position during practice.

3. Members of a group tend to become more different rather than more alike as a result of practice. Practice increases individual differences.

4. In general, distributed practice is better than massed practice. This is particularly so when motivation and consequently the attention span are high.

5. Generally, the greater a child's rate of learning, the less practice is necessary for learning to read.

Motivation and Learning

Thorndike recognized that practice is not the sole determinant of learning; it does not itself cause learning. He found that a blindfolded person did not improve in his ability to draw a line three inches long regardless of the number of practices. Practice is important only because of the conditions that operate during practice. Thorndike recognized that improvement in performance requires certain motivations. The learner improved his performance only if he was interested in his work, if he was interested in improving himself, if the material to be learned had special significance for him, if he was attentive to the situation, and if he had a problem-solving attitude.

A casual observation of behavior and learning tends to indicate that they are motivated. Already in 1921 Woodworth had recognized motivation as a psychological principle. He noted:

> We have to find room in our stimulus-response psychology for action persistently steered in a certain direction by some cause acting from within the individual. We must find room for internal states that last for a time and direct action (65, p. 71).[4]

Motivation is the *why* of human behavior. It initiates, sustains, and directs behavior toward a goal (30, p. 48). It arouses the learner, moves him, wakes him up as it were, and tenses him just enough for action.

In discussing motivation, the problem of terminology is immediately apparent. What is a need? What is a goal? What is a motive? What is an incentive?

Needs are a want or a lack, whether it be a mineral, vitamin, or dietary component or even an environmental condition (34, p. 2). They may exist apart from motive or drive. If a rat lacks Vitamin D, it will develop rickets. The rat needs Vitamin D, but may have no drive to

---

[4] R. S. Woodworth, *Psychology* (New York: Holt, Rinehart and Winston, Inc., 1921). Reprinted by permission.

seek the vitamins. Needs might also be described as more or less stable tendencies to be motivated in specific ways (33, p. 84). They are the underlying states out of which specific motivations arise (33, p. 125).

In most situations goals and needs are closely related. Needs frequently are developed through goal-seeking behavior that is constantly rewarded or reinforced. A child who gets the esteem of his parents by getting good grades in school soon develops a "need" for good grades. Behavior thus may be said to be either directed toward environmental goals or toward the satisfaction of one's needs.

Motives or drives are within the person. They initiate activity in the direction of a goal—an object or condition that satisfies the need that gave rise to the drive or motive in the first place. Motives are internal conditions, energies, or forces that impel the learner toward a goal.

The motive is inferred from the behavior and is an outgrowth of a need. A child who has a need for recognition may be motivated to do well in school. A boy who has a need for aggression may be motivated to show his hostile feelings by giving someone a black eye. Need seems to be a broader concept than motive. Motives imply a specific mode of satisfying a need. The person who has a need for affection may on a given occasion be motivated to behave in one way; on another occasion, in another. Each time he is trying to satisfy the same need.

Incentives are also an important determinant of behavior. Behavior that leads to a need-satisfying goal or to a goal that is reinforced externally is more likely to reoccur when the need arises again.

Incentives sometimes refer simply to the object that satisfies the motive. In this sense it is an environmental and an external element that stimulates a drive in the direction of a goal. Food thus may be termed an incentive if the person seeking it is hungry. In this instance goal and incentive are the same. Incentive can also mean a secondary goal that encourages and elicits behavior in the direction of the primary goal or toward the satisfaction of a basic need. Thus a child may be given candy for getting good grades.

A discussion of motivation seeks to answer two questions (21, p. 490): (*1*) Why does a person act? (*2*) Why does a person act the way he does?

Traditionally, psychologists have believed that the motivated person is constantly concerned with reducing tension within the nervous system. Thus, in answer to the question, "Why does a person act?" psychologists have said: "The person either is *driven* by primary, internal stimuli which arise when there is a homeostatic or organic imbalance or he is *driven* by external stimuli of a painful nature." These two forms of stimuli make the organism active. They bring the organism into the state of excitation that has been labelled drive. Drives or motives thus are conditions within the organism that initiate activity in the direction of a goal—

tension or pain reduction. *Need* is a state of tension created by organic deficiencies or by painful external stimuli. Figure 15-2 summarizes the drive-reduction theory.

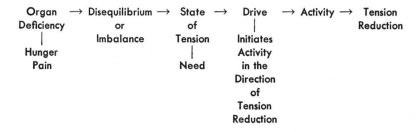

Figure 15-2.   Drive-Reduction Theory

Much of this theorizing has been "supported" by the work of Claude Bernard, Walter B. Cannon, and Curt Richter. Cannon (7) applied the term homeostasis to the internal physiological balance among the bodily tissues. Thus, the temperature of the body, the acidity base and the sugar concentration of the blood, and the water and salt balance can deviate only slightly without injury to the organism.

Whenever the organism cannot maintain the balance among the tissues, the organism is "motivated" to action. Thus, when the posterior lobes of the pituitary gland of a rat are removed, the animal will drink a great deal of water. A rat that has the thyroid or pituitary gland removed will build larger nests to compensate for a drop in bodily temperature. A rat without the adrenal glands will drink large amounts of salt solution (41). A rat without a pancreas, and consequently diabetic, avoids sugar and eats a large amount of fat. A rat without a parathyroid chooses solutions with a large amount of calcium (41). Lack of calcium secretion by the parathyroid results in too much alkalinity and may lead to tetany. Extreme acid conditions as in diabetes and nephritis lead to coma.

The drive-reduction theory presumes that the organism is essentially inactive when not motivated by internal or external stimuli. However, experience shows that persons are active when neither homeostatic drive or painful external stimuli are present. This is explained thus: Certain innocuous stimuli acquire the capacity to "motivate" by being associated with either painful or homeostatic needs.

Conditioned or learned drives do in fact motivate behavior. Thus rats shocked in a white box will attempt to escape when returned to the white box even though no shocking occurs.

An experiment like the following demonstrates this. A rat is placed in a box with two compartments. Compartment A has white walls and a grid floor; compartment B has black walls and a wooden floor. The rat is permitted to explore the compartments. Then it is put in the white compartment and given a strong shock. The rat will escape into the black compartment. Gradually, the rat avoids the white compartment even when no shock occurs. Learning theorists interpret the events as meaning that the rat has learned to fear the white compartment. The fear drive, a composite of the pain of the shock and the strong internal stimuli such as tensing of the muscles and increased heart rate that accompanies the shock, becomes a motivator of learning in its own right. If the opening to the black compartment is sealed, the rat will learn to turn a wheel opening the door in the white compartment, even though no shocking occurs.

This experiment demonstrates that fear can be learned, that fear thus learned functions as a drive by increasing the activity of the organism, and that secondary drives can motivate new learning.

If a child whenever he is self-directive, independent, or self-assertive is punished, he will soon learn to fear any self-assertive situations and will behave only in a submissive way. Being submissive brings him the release from fear that entering the black compartment brings the rat. Frequently, such a child will acquire a neurotic fear of action. Only by bringing him back, perhaps through counseling, to the original fear-producing situation and by his seeing the great difference between the original situation and the present will he be able to overcome his fear. We often find that such an individual not only fears self-assertive situations, but also is afraid to admit that he would like to be self-assertive.

As a result of experiments such as our example with the rat, many psychologists have assumed that all motives are ultimately reducible to organic needs.

Why does a person act the way that he does? The traditional answer has been "habit." Those ways of reducing drive or tension that were effective in the past are resorted to in the present. Freud's emphasis on the significance of the first five years of life upon later development was based on this. It is pointed out that the major issues of development and human relationship (dependence, deprivation, discipline, autonomy, sex, and aggression) are met early in life and that the first patterns of response set up precedents which leave the child less free to react differently later (62, p. 113).

Hunt (21, pp. 489–492), after outlining the traditional approach to motivation, calls for certain reinterpretations. He questions the assumptions that *all* behavior is motivated by homeostatic need, painful stimulation, or conditioned stimuli for these. He notes that children play most when they are homeostatically satisfied. Well-fed monkeys solve problems. Man characteristically is unable to resign himself to rest and equilibrium. The tension—the need to act and to learn—seems to be in the brain rather than in the stomach. The electroencephalograms (EEG's) indicate that the brain cells are constantly active. Hunt (21, p. 493) concludes that organisms characteristically show intrinsic activity and that to live means to act. Furthermore, the needs for self-esteem, esteem of others, curiosity, security, and aggression seem to motivate behavior in their own right and function like the physiological drives of hunger, pain, thirst, and sex. To be human means to yearn for the esteem of others, for self-realization, and for personal adequacy.

Studies indicate that the concept of drive must include drives other than those that reduce biological needs. We have evidence that exploration, curiosity, and manipulation function as separate and independent drives. These activity drives are related to the use and exercise of capacities of various kinds. We might speak of a drive for muscular activity, for sensory activity, for intellectual activity, or for social response. The normal organism is curious and wants to find out, explore, and discover. It wants to interact with its environment. To be an organism is to be active. The organism is self-determining and self-stimulating. The energies for manipulative and exploratory behavior are found in the living cells of the nervous system.

A part of the organism's "internal environment" may well be its need structure and its energy level (4, p. 178). The small child leaves a diary of his daily activities as he leaves a trail, touching and handling objects. Even the infant's daily activities are characterized by visual exploration, visual curiosity, and tactual and manipulative behavior. The child acts as though it had a need to see and to touch. A healthy pupil seeks activity and does not satisfy his needs by listening to and watching the teacher. The school program must be adapted to this activity need of the pupil.

Goldstein (15, p. 197) suggests that normal behavior corresponds to a continual change of tension, and tension of a certain level impels the organism to actualize itself through activity. For Goldstein, there is only one drive, namely, that of self-actualization. The organism has certain potentialities that need to be actualized or realized.

It also seems that activity or the expenditure of energy is pleasurable *per se*. Rats learn when the only opportunity for reinforcement is the pressing of a lever (36).

Nissen (35, p. 300) suggests that there is a biogenic drive to explore, to perceive, and to want to know. "Capacity is its own motivation." If one can see, one wants to see. If one can know, one wants to know. Manipulative behavior is a type of functioning for which the body is designed.

The import of all this is that the motivating condition frequently seems to be psychological. Pupils strive for self-enhancement, self-realization, and self-actualization. They seek for personal adequacy. Motives, it seems, need not always be pleasurable or reduce physiological tension.

Teachers thus need to pay attention to the physical conditions of pupils in the classroom. Travers (60, p. 98) notes that an unchanging environment in the classroom approaches the boundary of sensory deprivation. Stimuli must be varied to produce maximum results. If the teacher uses the same techniques, day after day, the material tends to become meaningless. Instructors should continually change their methods and appeal to as many senses as possible. Even though a pupil may learn better visually, stimulating the other senses may provide greater motivation, lead to more vigorous response, and eventually lead to better learning.

Our conception of the nervous system as a feedback loop system supplies us with another mechanism for motivation. Hunt (21, p. 86) notes that the motivational feedback system is much like a room thermostat. The temperature at which the thermostat is set is a standard against which the temperature of the room is continually being tested. If the temperature of the room falls below this standard, there is an incongruity which starts the furnace, which continues to operate until the room temperature has reached the standard, whereupon it is shut off.

Hunt notes that several classes of similarly operating standards can be identified for human beings:

1. The comfort standard, in which incongruity is equivalent to pain.
2. The homeostatic standard, in which incongruity is hunger or thirst.
3. The sex standard.
4. A fourth class or standard appears to consist of the ongoing inputs. Just as one never hears the clock until it has stopped, so any change in these ongoing inputs brings attention and excitement.
5. Expectations in which an incongruity might be, for example, poor grades.
6. Ideals.

Incongruity (13,14) with any of these standards instigates action. Hunt (21, pp. 499–500) notes that an individual constantly strives for consistency; when a stimulus is perceived as not belonging with existing cognitions, tension is aroused, and the organism will attempt to restore the system to balance. When his expectations are not fulfilled, dissonance occurs.

Whenever the pupil realizes that there is a disparity between what he is or can do and what he wants to be or could do, a cognitive dissonance results. The pupil is then *motivated* to become more adequate and to reduce the dissonance. Thus, learning may be motivated not so much by what the teacher does or by after-the-learning events such as rewards and punishments, as by what the learner wants, is interested in, or by what he feels will enhance his self-esteem and personal worth. The motivating condition begins within and is more psychological than physiological.

Motivation then is the end-product of having a goal and being prevented from the attainment of that goal by some barrier, whether physiological or psychological. Not being able to attain one's goal creates tension and results in cognitive dissonance.

When the incongruity or dissonance is slight, it is accommodated or may be tackled as a problem to be solved; when the dissonance is too great, when it is so great that the person cannot accommodate it, the person may become fearful, defensive, or avoid it. A pupil who fears failure in learning to read may not apply himself at all, thereby preserving his self-concept. He reasons thus: "I could learn to read if I really wanted to."

Motives for the laymen mean *wants, desires, purposes,* and *goals.* The hungry person doesn't feel *driven* to food; rather he feels that he *wants* it. Sinnott (46, p. 96) points out that:

> The conception of goal rather than drive as the basis of motivation is much more in harmony with a philosophy that puts the encouragement of high ideals and aspirations as the best means of elevating mankind rather than with one which depends on environment and conditioning and finally on physiological mechanisms to do so.[5]

Man wants, desires, and is goal-seeking. His behavior is influenced not so much by his past experiences as by his expectations.

The learner learns more readily and retention is more permanent when he *wants* to learn, when he actively participates in the learning task, when he perceives the meaningfulness of the task, or when he is moving toward a goal. The goal-directed movements of the learner must be interpreted as his attempts to secure for himself what he interprets as success. Success may be simply the desire to do a good job or to meet a challenge.

Objects also have motivating powers. Ice cream, for example, has qualities other than hunger satisfaction which attract the little child. Learning tasks have varying degrees of attraction and challenge. Reading materials are more or less interesting and children are most motivated by comprehensible and interesting subject matter. The key to human learning may be motivation aroused by external stimuli.

[5] Edmund W. Sinnott, *Matter, Mind, and Man* (New York: Harper & Row, Publishers, 1957). Reprinted by permission.

It is of course necessary that the teacher remember that children from different status levels in society will be characterized by different motivational systems, will have different goal expectancies, and will be motivated by different kinds of rewards. Since the average American school typically has children from practically all levels of society, the teacher is faced with the complex problem of motivating children who have different need systems.

The Law of Effect

Thorndike also developed the Law of Effect (57, p. 176). As we already mentioned, Thorndike suggested that the learner uses a trial-and-error approach until he hits upon the correct response, which tends to be repeated because of the operation of the Law of Effect. When after a series of exploratory movements the cat pulls the string or operates the latch, it is able to escape and is rewarded with food for having solved the problem. This successful event intensifies the association between the stimulus and the response.

Learning frequently requires the accompaniment of a rewarding situation. As indicated in Chapter 2, each perceptual experience has its emotional matrix. All experiences tend to involve feeling. They may be accompanied by "satisfying" feelings or by "feelings of annoyance." The learner will turn to experiences that satisfy and turn away from those that annoy. In either case, the individual is said to have been "rewarded" or the behavior to have been reinforced.

Rewarding situations are usually referred to as incentives. These are goal objects toward which a behavior sequence is directed.

There are many reinforcers of human behavior: rewards, punishments, praise, blame, group recognition, knowledge of progress, friendly conferences, or encouragement. Just as not all children are similarly motivated, so also what is rewarding to one child may not be rewarding to another.

Here are a few general principles:

1. Behavior that is reinforced tends to recur and learning that is reinforced comes more easily and is more permanent. Some theorists have said, "you cannot learn without doing"; others add: "you won't do anything without being rewarded."

2. Learning that is accompanied by reward is preferable to learning that is under the control of punishment. Punishment may only confirm the child's feeling that school is not for him and that it is a place to be avoided.

3. Reward is more effective when it closely follows the desired behavior or learning.

4. Learning that brings intrinsic rewards (the sense of satisfaction in achieving personal goals) is preferable to learning that is rewarded extrinsically.

5. Information about what is good performance, knowledge of one's success and failure, and the opportunity to explore one's curiosity and to broaden one's experience may be effective reinforcement situations.

6. Rewards should not be so dominant in the learning situation that the child strives primarily for their attainment rather than for the attainment of educational goals.

7. Reinforcement at regular intervals is most effective in eliciting new behavior; reinforcement at varying intervals more readily maintains the behavior. Thus, "pop quizzes" more readily maintain the habit of study than do regularly scheduled examinations.

The pupil needs to "see" the inherent worth of the learning task. The task must be worthwhile to him. It must be interesting and enticing. He needs to feel that the teacher has his good in mind. He learns to respect a teacher who modifies his teaching to fit his learning needs. He respects a teacher who doesn't demand that the pupil develop full competency. The good teacher does not believe that concepts are learned once and for always. The pupil needs repeated experience with the same task. The teacher must remember that though competence is necessary for academic success, it is not any more necessary than is confidence.

All pupils are motivated. Sometimes the major problem is to pry it loose. The good teacher uses kindness, recognition, praise, a friendly conference, or a pat on the shoulder. He tries to make the learning of reading a satisfying experience. He capitalizes on the pupil's curiosity and on his desire for improvement. He uses the pupil's identification with him to lead the pupil to greater accomplishment. He encourages excellence. He upsets the pupil's equilibrium and enlarges his expectations. But above all, he makes education something that the pupil wants. *Good entertainment is educational and good education is entertaining.*

When education becomes entertaining, the teacher does not have to threaten the pupil with punishment, with failure, or with a slip to be taken home to his parents. A pupil so threatened will work just hard enough and long enough to get the teacher off his back. Having accomplished this he falls back to his normal way of behaving.

Finally, we may have become so engrossed with the idea of incentives that we may forget that some children tend to learn better through imitation than through reinforcement. Some teachers are effective precisely because they have become persons to be imitated.

The Law of Belongingness

Thorndike likewise developed the Law of Belongingness. According to this principle, an association is more easily learned if the response belongs to the situation. Hilgard (19, pp. 28–29) gives an illustration. He notes that in the sentences "John is a butcher. Henry is a carpenter," the association between the words, "John and butcher," is a stronger one than the association between "butcher and Henry," even though the latter two words are more contiguous. The reason is that the subject and the predicate have a more natural belongingness one with the other than has the end of one sentence with the beginning of another.

The Law of Belongingness has application to teaching. For example, it stresses the importance of context. The child will learn and remember words better if he can immediately use them in meaningful reading or writing.

Summary

Thorndike identified the following steps in trial-and-error learning:

1. A need, a problem, a discomfort, or a goal to be attained. Much teaching in the classroom is wasted simply because the learner does not feel a need. The rat will not run a maze if it is not hungry. A pupil will not learn if he has no need for what is to be learned.
2. A great variety of activity with numerous responses being made to the situation.
3. A gradual elimination of unsuccessful responses. During the early trials, learning is crude and exploratory, the responses are undifferentiated, and the successes are accidental, without any awareness of what leads to what or of the relationship of the mechanism to the opening of the door.
4. A gradual consolidation of the learning and the acquisition of the most direct solution to the problem. It should be noted that the one response is stamped in and the others are stamped out, not by the perception of the relationship, but rather through the operation of the Law of Effect.
5. A gradual discovery of the functional relationship between the stimulus and the response, between the mechanism and the opening of the door on the box. Many would suggest that insightful learning occurs at this point.

In Thorndike's experiments the stimulus was held constant, and the responses were permitted to vary. The organism was taught to select the proper response from a complex of responses and to associate it with a given stimulus. Learning was perceived as a process of response selection.

The teacher's task, according to Thorndike, is to identify the responses that must be connected to a given stimulus or stimulus situation, to organize the learning situation in the best way possible for eliciting the correct response, and finally to reward the correct response. The teacher should know what responses the pupil is capable of making, should be able to identify tasks that are within the potential of the pupil to make, and should graduate these tasks from simple to complex. The problem solver, with repeated trials in the same situation, gradually eliminates wrong responses until only the correct ones remain. Repetition and reward gradually stamp in the correct response and eliminate the incorrect responses.

Bugelski (6, p. 54) notes that Thorndike made certain assumptions; the first of which is that learning is blind, dumb, and mechanical. The animal appears to react at random, and eventually one random reaction is followed by the attainment of a satisfier. Bugelski points out, however, that the animal in Thorndike's puzzle box cannot "understand" the relationship between the stimuli, the responses, and the effects. It cannot even see the pulleys and the connection of the string with the door.

GUTHRIE'S CONTIGUOUS ASSOCIATION

By the time Guthrie made his presence felt, Watson had already developed behaviorism and Pavlov had discovered conditioning. To understand Guthrie's contribution, it is useful to take a look at the contributions of Watson and Pavlov.

The Behaviorism of Watson

John B. Watson (1878–1958) laid the ground work for S-R theories. His behavioristic emphasis led him away from a study of what people "think" and "feel" to what people do. He insisted on an objective study of behavior. In 1913 in "Psychology as the Behaviorist Views It" (60a) Watson defined behavior as movements of muscles. Speech was movements of the muscles of the throat, thought was "subvocal speech," and behavior was learned through conditioning and could be subdivided into a series of conditioned reflexes.

Watson's view of conditioning was based on Pavlov, and complex and new behaviors represented for him a combination of simple reflexes.

Watson felt that when a rat learns to run to the goal box at the end of a maze, it simply learns the series of mechanical leg and body movements involved in turning left or right. He suggested that all differences in ability and personality were learned through conditioning. This concept easily fit in with "traditional American pragmatic bias in favor of action rather than thought or feeling"; in the United States it still is "what a man does that counts, not what he says or thinks or feels." (32, p. 297)

Pavlov's Classical Conditioning

Let us review Pavlov's classical conditioning experiment, which is an example of stimulus selection learning. Pavlov (40) found that a dog salivated immediately when food was placed in its mouth. This he termed the unconditioned reflex (UR). In a simple experiment, a tuning fork was sounded (conditioned stimulus or CS) and about 7 or 8 seconds later the dog was presented with a plate of powdered food (unconditioned stimulus or US). Initially the tone did not arouse a salivary response, but after 30 associations between tone and food, the sound alone caused the dog to salivate 60 drops (conditioned response or CR). The dog had become conditioned to the tone.

The meat powder served as a reinforcement because it produced a much greater flow of saliva than did the tuning fork. It had about the same function as Thorndike's reward. The meat (US) reinforced the association between the tuning fork and the salivary response much as the food in Thorndike's experiments reinforced the association between the string and the clawing or pulling.

The Law of Contiguity

Guthrie had only one law: "A combination of stimuli which has accompanied a movement will on its recurrence tend to be followed by that movement." (16, p. 23) This law has been termed the Law of Contiguity and has been paraphrased in many ways. Kingsley and Garry (24, p. 98) suggest that it might mean: "We repeat what we learn and we learn what we do." It might also mean that if you do something in a given situation, when that situation occurs again, you will do the same thing. Contiguity simply means that if stimuli act at the same time that a response occurs, the response will tend to reoccur on subsequent occasions whenever the stimuli are present. The pupil, who responds to *was* with *saw,* will on the next presentation of the stimulus *was* tend to respond again with *saw.*

Guthrie rejected the Law of Relative Frequency, which suggested that the strength of the stimulus-response connection increased with practice. For Guthrie, it was either all or nothing on the occasion of the first pairing between the stimulus and the response. He believed in one trial-learning. He felt that the stimulus pattern gains its full associative strength on the occasion of its first pairing with a response. Guthrie (16, pp. 79–80, 88) notes, for example, that sometimes a habit is established with one repetition, that a person can recall a name after hearing it only once, that fear is born out of one experience, that one doesn't have to practice getting up at eight when he has gotten up at 7:30 for years, and that a man may stop smoking all at once after smoking for years. Frequently, learning that is occasioned by one experience seems to be accompanied by strong emotional response.

Guthrie, however, did not completely reject the value of practice. He gave reasons why practice and repetition lead to improvement. Guthrie notes (16, pp. 85–86) that practice is necessary to break a habit because numerous stimuli usually can elicit the response and that each of these must be inhibited. Thus the smoking habit may be elicited by the sight of tobacco, the aroma of another's pipe, finishing of a meal, or sitting on a bank fishing. Each of these in the past became signals for smoking.

He suggested that whereas Thorndike was concerned with end results (scores on tests or correct response made), he himself was concerned only with movements. Each activity (swinging of a bat) consists of a complex of individual movements, and improvement and learning are not attained by frequent swinging of a bat, but rather by increasing the number of correct movements in swinging the bat (balance of the body, position of the feet, position of the hands, keeping one's eye on the ball) and by reducing the number of incorrect movements in the total complex of movements comprising the total activity. Each time a person swings a bat, if new learning is to occur, there will be movement more correct than before. Improvement occurs because the learner gradually replaces the erroneous movements that he still is making with correct ones (e.g., he may improve his stance). Thus, additional practice gives more opportunity to master the myriad of movements comprising a complex stimulus-response situation. And the end result is improvement in the total performance.

Skills thus represent a population or complex of habits but each habit, of the hundreds comprising a single skill, is learned completely at full strength in a single performance. The learner does not learn the skill with the first pairing of a stimulus and a response because the skill is a complex of many stimulus-response pairings. But the strength of the stimulus-response bond is at its maximum at its first pairing. Guthrie thus drew a distinction between the acts and movements and noted that, although acts, such as swinging a bat, are usually measured, it is the movements that are actually conditioned as response.

Guthrie suggested that "What is learned" are movements. Other theorists suggested that we learn habits or relationships. Which is correct?

In an experimental study Logan (31) asked the following question. Does the organism learn a fast or a slow response? When reinforcement is delayed, a rat will run the maze more slowly than if it is rewarded immediately. Is the rat learning the molar response of running or the micro-molar response of running at a particular speed?

Could it be that when the teacher tells the child, "Take your time in doing these addition problems but be right," that the child is being taught to "behave more slowly when adding"?

Logan found that students tend to repeat information at the same rate as it was learned and that performance deteriorates when the required speed of performance is increased.

SKINNER'S OPERANT CONDITIONING

Skinner's major contribution perhaps is his distinction between respondent and operant behavior.[6] Previous theories had suggested that all responses were to some specific stimulus, and when no external stimulation was observed, internal stimuli were postulated. Skinner felt this was begging the question and suggested that some behaviors simply do not have an identifiable stimulus. Responses which have a known stimulus are termed *respondents* (knee jerk after a blow on the patellar tendon, an eyeblink that follows a loud noise, fear that accompanies the sight of a vicious animal, or an answer to a teacher's specific question); those responses whose stimulus is not known are termed *operants*. Operant conditioning[7] is frequently termed instrumental conditioning because the organism must make a response, and the response makes possible or is instrumental in the achievement of the goal or reward. In the Skinner box, depressing of the lever by the rat or pecking of a key by the pigeon

[6] Some major works of Skinner are: *The Behavior of Organisms: An Experimental Analysis*, 1938; *Science and Human Behavior*, 1953; "Are Theories of Learning Necessary?" *Psychological Review*, 57 (July, 1950), pp. 193–216; *Verbal Behavior*, 1957.

[7] See Frank M. Hewett, "Teaching Reading to an Autistic Boy Through Operant Conditioning," *The Reading Teacher*, 17 (May, 1964) pp. 613–18; Roger Addison and Lloyd Homme, "The Reinforcing Event (EV) Menu," *National Society for Programmed Instruction Journal*, 4 (January, 1966); also Werner K. Honig, *ed.*, *Operant Behavior: Areas of Research and Application* (New York, Appleton-Century-Crofts, 1966).

leads to food; pulling the plunger of a vending machine does so in the case of humans. Reinforcement is dependent upon making the correct response.

Skinner has devoted much effort to developing operant behavior or to shaping behavior. He has trained pigeons to play a type of Ping-Pong, with the pigeon pecking a ball back and forth across a table. When the ball gets by one pigeon, the behavior of the other pigeon is reinforced. In another experiment Skinner taught a pigeon to bowl.

Shaping of behavior thus does not wait until the learner makes the desired response exactly correct. Operant learning may be quite gradual. At first, it may be necessary to reinforce gross approximations to the final response. These successive approximations gradually result in making the correct response.

According to Skinner, the first task of the teacher is to get the pupil to express himself in some observable way so that it will be possible to reinforce his behavior in some way. Skinner suggests that any activity that is to be learned must be divided into numerous small steps and that reinforcement must accompany the learning of each discrete step. His thinking has lead to programmed materials.

Skinner (47) emphasized the importance for teachers of analyzing the reinforcing contingencies in the classroom. What reinforcers are available? He notes that a teacher may be tempted to dismiss a class when discipline has broken down. This simply reinforces what the teacher is trying to prevent. A teacher might more profitably dismiss the class a few minutes early when all are working well. A few repetitions of this may lead to fewer discipline problems. Skinner felt that every reinforcement counts. He suggests that we should reinforce even if the child doesn't know what he is doing.

Skinner outlines the steps to be taken in teaching or in shaping behavior:

1. Analyze the skill to be learned; know what it requires the learner to do and make certain that it is within the learner's capacity.
2. Prepare the learner for learning. Create a psychological readiness for learning.
3. Use immediate rewards. Reward each successful movement in the sequence.
4. Provide an opportunity for learning.

The experimenter may want to train the learner to respond to a stimulus only when another stimulus is also present. He may reinforce the bar-pressing response only when a light is on and may not reinforce bar pressing when the light is off. The light is termed the discriminative stimulus or the cue stimulus. Darkness is termed a delta stimulus.

This principle is very useful in the classroom. A child, learning to read, sees many word symbols on a page. To only one word, perhaps, he must learn to respond with something like "this word says cat." The teacher is constantly reinforcing the *cat* response to one given word. The word then becomes a discriminative stimulus for one specific sound.

HULL'S HABIT THEORY

Clark L. Hull (1884–1952)[8] was concerned with the stimulus (the input), the response (the output), and the organism. His was an S-O-R theory rather than an S-R theory. This simply means that the stimulus (S) affects the organism (O), and the resultant response (R) is the product of both the stimulus and the organism. In his equations Hull sought to account for the activity of the organism.

Hull was not simply concerned with the stimulus and the response, but wanted to know the factors *within* the individual that affect the response. Hull sought to quantify all the variables in learning. This attempt of Hull has special meaning for the teacher, for the practitioner in the classroom will make fewer mistakes if he considers all possible variables.

Reaction Potential

Hull's theory focuses on performance, and so reaction potential (sEr) assumes a major role. sEr is the total tendency to make a given response to a given stimulus. It is an active readiness to make the response, to perform. It is dependent upon previous habit strength, drive, incentive motivation or reinforcement, and intensity of the stimulus.

For Hull, learning involves the strengthening or establishment of connections or habits. As learning occurs, an internal factor, which was termed habit strength (sHr), is strengthened. The tendency to respond (sEr) thus depends upon habit strength or on previous learning. It might be said that a pupil's tendency to read is dependent at least partially on previous habits of reading. The pupil who has read a lot in the past will tend to read more than the pupil who has read only infrequently.

Habit strength is the strength of the bond between a stimulus and a response, a bond which is built up through reinforced practice. Habit strength, designated sHr, with *s* referring to stimulus, *r* to response, and *H* for habit, increases with practice. As the number of reinforced trials

[8] Among Hull's major works are: *Aptitude Testing*, 1928; *Mathematico-Deductive Theory and Rote Learning*, 1940; *Essentials of Behavior*, 1951; *A Behavior System*, 1952.

or responses increases, so also will habit strength. The first association between s and r leads to the development of a strong connection or habit.

The tendency to respond is dependent also on drive (D) and incentive motivation (K). When a rat has eaten its fill, it will tend to fall asleep in a maze. This illustrates that performance depends on learning but also on drive and incentive motivation. Their interaction thus is multiplicative rather than additive. Reduce any one of them to zero and there is no performance. To determine what behavior will occur in a given situation, it is necessary to multiply the drive level of the organism by the level of learning attained. In other words, sEr is the product of $D \times K \times$ sHr.

Reaction potential (sEr) is also a function of stimulus intensity (V). The person tends to react to the stimulus of greatest intensity. When there is excessive stimulation, minor stimuli are usually not detected. The noise of a locomotive moving by the classroom forces the teacher to raise his voice, but the pupil frequently will still concentrate on the loudest noise or stimulus.

Let us apply these ideas to reading. Reading is a response. The ability to respond through reading is dependent on the many variables that affect performance. The tendency to read (sEr) is a function of previous habits of reading, of motivation, of the reinforcement value of reading, and of the proximity with which reinforcement follows reading.

We find that the more reading the child did before instruction starts (sHr), the greater the desire to read, and the better reading satisfies personal motives, the more interesting reading becomes and thus the closer it comes to being a motive in its own right. The greater the reinforcement value of reading or the closer reinforcement follows actual reading, the greater is the tendency to read.

Some children do not read even though they profess a great desire to do so. Perhaps reading constantly conflicts with television, and television may be the stronger stimulus, thus preventing reading. Perhaps reading has never been made meaningful because it has not been followed by satisfying aftereffects. The habit of reading thus may never have been learned.

Effective Reaction Potential

Hull also spoke of an organism's effective reaction potential (sĒr). The effective reaction potential is equivalent to sEr − Īr or the inhibitory factors, which Hull termed reactive inhibition (Ir) and conditioned inhibition (sIr). When the inhibitory factors are stronger than sEr, no reaction will occur. The total inhibitory tendency (Īr) is equal to Ir plus sIr.

The factors that inhibit performance are numerous, the most obvious of which is fatigue (Ir). As an organism continues to perform, as a student continues to read, for example, the tendency to read is gradually lessened. Reactive inhibition or Ir is generated each time a response is made. The greater the number of responses, and hence the greater the effort needed to make a response, the greater is the reactive inhibition. When the organism ceases to make responses, naturally Ir is reduced.

Otto (37,38,39) found that poor achievers accumulate reactive inhibition more rapidly than good achievers and that poor readers accumulate it more rapidly than good readers.

sIr is the conditioned nonactivity that is brought on by Ir. If the organism rests too long, it gradually develops the habit of not responding, becomes lazy, and avoids work. This is especially so when the organism is in the presence of stimuli normally associated with "not working." A comfortable easy chair or a beautiful green lawn may become a conditioned stimulus for resting.

If the inhibitory factors are too great, even a well-established habit may not show up in performance. The same occurs in the absence of drive or incentives.

The effective tendency to read (sĒr) is equal to the total tendency to read minus the inhibitory factors (Īr) that tend to block performance. Among the more obvious inhibitory factors in reading are health, fatigue, amount of energy needed for reading, and the number of unreinforced reading experiences. The greater the amount of energy the reader must expend in reading, the less he tends to read. The more difficult the materials, the quicker the student becomes fatigued, and the less reading will be done. The more frequently reading is unrewarded, the less the pupil tends to read. A pupil who reads but does not understand tends to lose interest in reading. And we find that the pupil who does not read gradually develops the habit of "not reading."

Momentary Reaction Potential

Hull likewise spoke of momentary reaction potential (sĖr). This is equivalent to sĒr − sOr or the organism's oscillation potential; it serves as another way of describing variability in behavior. The organism generally may have a tendency to perform well, but at a given moment cannot do so.

A person's tendency to respond through reading is subject to a certain amount of variability. On certain days a child may not care to read or to play piano regardless of the fact that the class schedule calls for reading or that it is time for practice on the piano. Thus perfect prediction of behavior is not possible.

The diagram in Figure 15-3 summarizes Hull's theory.

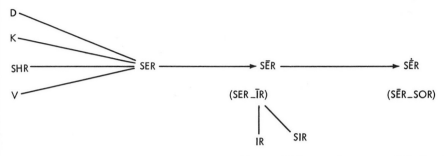

Figure 15-3.   A Summary of Hull's Theory

FIELD THEORY

A second major group of learning theories are the field theories. As shown in Figure 15-2, numerous psychologies representing variant shades of approach might be included in this group. We will concern ourselves primarily with three branches, namely Gestalt Psychology, Field Theory *per se* as seen in the writings of Kurt Lewin, and the Purposivism of Tolman. Field Theory began with Gestalt Psychology, and Gestalt Psychology was primarily concerned with perception.

The Perceptual Process

The phenomenon of apparent movement, generally called the phi-phenomenon, gave impetus to the field interpretations of the nature of perception. Motion pictures are an excellent example of apparent movement. The projected images from the individual frames of the film have no movement; the movement is only apparent. The light in the neon advertising signs is perceived as moving from one place to another, but actually as the light in one place is turned off, another light goes on.

Certainly in these instances what is apprehended by the viewer involves sensory data not presently available to the senses. There is an implication here that the incoming sensory data are in some way retained, processed, and reorganized by the viewer. Some intermediary step takes place between the sensory input and the response.

Going Beyond the Sensory Data

Chapters 2 and 8 emphasized two facts: (*1*) that we can come to know the external world and (*2*) that we go beyond what the senses provide.

Perception has characteristics which cannot be derived from sensation alone.

Here, we wish to explore this last concept more fully. In looking at a chair the senses are not really in contact with the chair at all. What hits the rods and the cones of the retina is a series of light rays that are reflected from the chair. In looking at a circle the person organizes the incoming impulses into a circle even though the pattern (the Gestalt) on the retina is not circular. This presents the perceiver with a peculiar difficulty. Although the light rays are the *cause* of his perceptions, he perceives not the light rays, but the geographical object (26, p. 79). His behavior is determined by the object and not by the light rays.

Because of the above situation the field theorist draws a distinction between the light rays—the proximal stimuli, and the object—the distal stimulus. Generally, psychologists refer to the proximal stimulus as simply the stimulus. Figure 15-4 illustrates the various steps in perception.

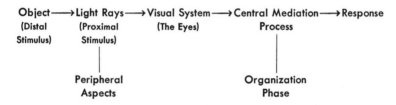

Figure 15-4.   The Perceptual Process

The problem has always been: how do the proximal stimuli come to signify the distal stimulus? This, the field theorist identifies as the problem of cognition.

The field theorist is not particularly concerned with the "know-ability" of external reality. He accepts the validity of the senses. He assumes that he can know the external world, even though he realizes that many errors may creep into his perceptions.

As a matter of fact, because the perceiver masters the outer world through his perceptions, he rarely ever knows the true nature of things. His perceptions commonly attain only partial truth because he responds to outer reality in his own way.

> Were we in perception chiefly passive, could the things of the outer world impress themselves immediately upon our minds and thus stamp their nature upon it, they would necessarily always leave behind the same ideas, so that a variety of apprehension would be impossible and inexplicable (27, p. 4).

The Central Intermediary

To explain *what* (not necessarily *how*) occurs when the person perceives, for example, a chair, cognitive theorists have suggested that the organism's response is determined not only by the proximal stimuli (the light rays) or even the geographical object or experience but also, and perhaps chiefly, by a central process within the organism. This central process influences the person's reactions to the stimulus and provides him with a representation of the distal stimulus or environmental-geographical object or experience (44). Field theorists refer to this representational process as cognition.

That in reality there is a central intermediary is indicated by experimental data. Hebb (17, pp. 48, 52–57) gives a few examples.

Pavlov's dog salivated to the sound of the bell only when he was hungry. When he was satisfied he was not "set" to respond. The same stimulus pattern 8, 2 may lead to the response 10, 4, 6, 16 depending upon the particular "set" to respond. The response will change as the learner is told to add, divide, subtract, or multiply. A monkey that likes both lettuce and bananas will reject lettuce if he is expecting bananas as the reward for successful completion of a task.

These data indicate that "set" depends on a neural trace of one kind or another that gradually develops activity of its own without the benefit of an immediate sensory stimulation. Set is analogous to closing a switch in the switchboard of the central nervous system, thus getting the organism "set" to respond in a predetermined way to the incoming data (17, p. 64). Some sets depend on the blood chemistry (hunger or lack of it in the dog); others depend on neural processes (the lettuce and the banana).

It is most common to hear the pupil say: "I can't concentrate. My attention is constantly wandering." In a sense he is not set to respond to the learning task. Langman (28, p. 31) notes that poor readers cannot attend to the *significant* visual stimuli in word recognition situations. Furthermore, they become distracted by less pertinent stimuli.

In Chapter 8 we noted that poor readers do not perceive the importance of particular details in letter shapes and of their relationships to one another.

We also noted that the poor reader has a special set in responding to words. He tends to think of them in their specific rather than their generic sense.

Set results in the imposition of an organization or meaning upon all incoming sensory data. And each learner is "set" to respond in one way or another; he is set or physiologically and psychologically ready to respond to some details rather than to others.

In reading, set makes the difference between the nonreader's observation of a multiplicity of irregular marks arranged in horizontal lines on a page, and the reader's recognition of combinations of letters composing familiar and meaning-associated patterns (28, p. 32)[9]

The Role of Experience and Organization

One of our first observations is that the cognitive representation (for example, of the meaning of the word democracy) has many characteristics which are not in the immediate stimulus-situation at all, but are to be found in the past experiences of the organism (environmental) and/or in its organizational (biological) response characteristics. If the organism cannot organize the stimuli or cannot form habit linkages, there is little hope that perception will reach a level adequate for thinking.

The organizational response characteristics of the organism are especially interesting. Studies show that "higher" animals perceive relationships which "lower" animals cannot. The spider monkey, for example, cannot grasp the principle of similarity, but the chimpanzee does so very readily.

Lashley (29) notes that all animals learn[10] but not all can learn the same thing. What is learned differentiates their organizational ability and this essentially seems to be biologically determined. It frequently is not the experience that guarantees the solution of the problem, but rather the organizational pattern or the biological inheritance into which the experience is fitted.

Perceptions and the Reading Process

Up to this point, we have identified two basic facts: (1) A central process intervenes between the stimulus and the response; (2) This process modifies the stimulus or afferent materials. Cognition organizes the incoming data into a meaningful pattern. William James (23, p. 103) noted that *"whilst part of what we perceive comes through our senses from the object before us, another part* (and it may be the greater part) *always comes . . . out of our head."*

[9] Muriel Potter Langman, "The Reading Process: A Descriptive, Interdisciplinary Approach," *Genetic Psychology Monographs*, 62 (August 1960) 1–40, The Journal Press, Reprinted by permission.

[10] To define intelligence as the capacity to learn does not discriminate between human and animal intelligence.

Our definition of reading, given in Chapter 2, emphasizes the perceptual nature of reading. Reading was described as the process of giving significance to graphic symbols by relating them to one's own fund of experience. Thus, the meaning is not something inherent in a word; meaning at least partly comes from within the reader.

The definition didn't stop there. It indicated that the meaning of a word is a function of experience. The meaning of a perception generally is based on the perceiver's previous experiences. Thus, Lange (27, p. 21) notes that "we see and hear not only with the eye and ear, but quite as much with the help of our present knowledge, with the apperceiving content of the mind."

Numerous studies have demonstrated that our past experiences influence our reaction to printed or graphic symbols. Chall (8), for example, administered a short true-false test of information about tuberculosis to one hundred sixth and eighth graders and had them read a selection on tuberculosis. Those who made high scores on the information test also tended to score high on the reading selection. Chall notes that reading enlarges our experience, but that the greater one's experience, the more profitable one's reading tends to be (8).

Perceptions rarely are completely representative of external reality. Perception rarely is totally veridical. It is at most an approximate representation. Thus it is rare for two persons to have exactly the same meaning or experiential content associated with a word.

The concept is really a creation of an individual mind and cannot be shared directly. Teachers sometimes behave as though they could share concepts; all they can do is to transmit the words that symbolize the concept. Words sometimes do not convey accurately what is intended and what is intended may not represent accurately the event or experience.

Brunswik (5, p. 10) refers to the degree of distal-proximal similarity as "ecological validity." [11] Generally, the perceiver (as also the reader) calls upon his previous experiences and assumes that the perception that was most successful in the past is the most likely to be correct now. However, numerous experiments have shown that since the perceiver interprets sense data on the basis of his past experience, his interpretation at times is in error.

Generally, the greater the number of experiences and the richer their quality, the greater are the chances for veridicality, but even the most veridical perception may be an inadequate representation of the concrete object or experience. Perception normally remains a representation.

---

[11] Ecology here means the environmental realities that surround the organism (5, p. 6).

THE FIELD CONCEPT

To explain the facts of perceptual organization, psychologists have introduced the field concept. The field, sometimes labelled the perceptual or phenomenal field, refers to the "more or less fluid organization of meanings existing for every individual at any instant (9, p. 20)." Combs and Snygg add that the perceptual field is *"the entire universe, including himself, as it is experienced by the individual at the instant of action* (p. 20)." [12]

Since no two individuals have had the same experiences, they cannot have the same perceptual field. Thus the fields of others often seem to us full of error and inadequacy in meaning. We refer to another as prejudiced and bigoted and he in turn may think the same of us. Two children playing in a sand box may live in entirely different worlds.

The field concept has special applicability in the classroom. "The classroom is a special kind of social field since the relationships involved in group dynamics, attention, discipline, and the like, permeate the atmosphere of the entire class and affect the learning process. The teacher's reaction to the discipline problem of one student is reflected in the 'feeling' of the class. It is impossible to deal with just one youngster— the influence of the total classroom atmosphere is brought to bear on all students." (60, p. 188)[13]

The significant fact is that the perceptual field is a major determinant of the individual's reactions to external reality or to a word. Wife and husband see completely different realities in looking at a sink full of dishes. Two readers see the word democracy and take completely different meanings to the term. Each one's behavior is determined by his own perceptual field. Each behaves according to how things *seem* to him. He may not actually be responding to the external reality. He more characteristically responds to the *meanings* that each bit of reality has for him.

In summary then, a central process, termed cognition, intervenes between the stimulus and the response and organizes the incoming data into some sort of pattern. This pattern is significantly different from the mass of detail that composes the stimulus situation, because each new stimulus or experience is fitted into a pattern of previous experience. The response or the meaning that is taken to a word consequently is not learning; it is not organization; it is a sign that perceptual organization or learning has occurred.

The child's response to a word may or may not be adequate. He

[12] Arthur W. Combs and Donald Snygg, *Individual Behavior,* revised edition (New York: Harper & Row, Publishers, 1959). Reprinted by permission.
[13] John F. Travers, *Learning: Analysis and Application* (New York: David McKay Co., Inc., 1965), p. 188. Reprinted by permission.

will react on the basis of his past experience, and if this has been inadequate, his response of necessity must be inadequate. His meaning for the word will be inadequate.

Thus the "meaning" of one's perceptions is almost entirely at the mercy of one's past experience and/or his organizational characteristics. Without the proper experience the reader cannot respond with the proper meaning to the writer's words. If he cannot assimilate experience and use it in understanding reality, he cannot react meaningfully. If he cannot recognize the word, he cannot bring meaning to it. Thus, the prime emphasis in reading must be on meaning, but if the pupil cannot identify the word or has not had the appropriate experience, meaningful reading is out of his reach.

Characteristics of the Perceptual Field

The perceptual field has numerous characteristics. Let us examine these.

1. The perceptual field of any person usually is much greater than the physical environment. The person's response to stimuli includes past memory traces or residues of neural activity that enter into and change the present field of forces. It consists of the total content of his perceptions. Reactions to words, for example, are dependent on the reader's phenomenal field at the time of action. They are a function of the person's innate endowment, of the quality, number, organization, and reconstruction of prior experiences, of his affective state, and of his culture. They are genuinely organismic reactions. The "whole" child reads. He reads something of himself *into* the written or printed word.

2. The perceptual field usually is much smaller than it might be. The perceptual field of any individual includes only a small fraction of the objects and meanings that might be present. Some bring a greater number and a much higher quality of meanings to a stimulus situation or to a word or words than do others, but few exhaust the total aggregate of meanings.

   Generally, as the number of meanings and experiences connoted by a word increases, the more difficult it is to understand the full meaning of such a word. The reliability of the initial perception of a word decreases as the number of meanings that may be associated with the word increases. A six-year-old child's perception of a word tends to be more reliable if the printed word suggests only one meaning than if it suggests ten different meanings. In teaching reading more emphasis should perhaps be put on the fact that words have multiple meanings. The pupil needs to learn to look for new and unfamiliar meanings.

3. The perceptual field has a characteristic figure-ground organization. This means that there are varying degrees of awareness of stimuli. Some stimuli are primary; others are secondary. What the perceiver is aware of is termed the figure and the rest is the ground.

    The figure in perception is variable. The person's attention may wander, and with each figure-ground change comes a change of meaning. The same proximal stimuli can become signs for various distal objects.

    The proximal stimuli from the picture of art are the same for all individuals, but what is "seen" in or signified by the picture is totally distinct for the artist and for the average layman. The pupil in the classroom may "see" something quite different in the reading task than does the teacher. The pupil's meaning for words changes as he attends with varying degrees of awareness to previous experiences. His reaction to the reading task is determined by his attention on pleasant reading-associated experiences or on unpleasant ones.

    Certainly, the proximal stimuli do not determine fully the nature of the perception. What is perceived frequently is not what actually is seen or experienced, but rather what the perceiver believes he saw or experienced or what the perceived things signify.[14] Individuals perceive objects and events in a way that best fits their perceptual field at the moment.

4. Various proximal stimuli can become a sign or a symbol for the same referent. This process, frequently labelled stimulus generalization or irradiation, is explained in field theory by improper differentiation. If the stimulus is incompletely differentiated, it will be confused with similar stimuli. In reading numerous errors arise because of this simple fact. The child who reverses, who sees *was* and reads *saw*, makes such an error. He has confused the sign. The explanation of reversals as an inability to locate symbols in space fits this thesis. Reversals frequently may be simply stimuli that are not completely differentiated from all others.

---

[14] The witness in court presents such a problem (9, p. 85). It is sometimes difficult to determine whether the witness actually saw a given individual at the scene of the crime or whether he believes that "he must have been there." In Chapter 8 we noted that it is quite possible for the perceiver to say that he "perceived whole words" when in reality he may have inferred the existence of other letters and hence the word.

Observations and Inferences

The data thus far discussed lead to certain observations and inferences.

1. The teacher must constantly test the validity of the learner's perceptions and his meanings for words. The pupil's experience may have been too meagre. His standards for judging the validity of his perceptions are based on experience. When his perceptions are in error, he must learn to correct his representation. This is best accomplished through the acquisition of new experiences.

2. Meaning may be presumed to lie on a continuum extending from a minimum of meaning at the left to a maximum of meaning at the right. The concept "tree" lies somewhat to the left of the concept "beauty." Yet, the tree specialist perhaps associates a vaster wealth of meaning with the word "tree" than most people have associated with the word "beauty." Obviously, meaning varies from person to person, from time to time, from perception to perception, and hence from experience to experience.

   Since we usually respond to words with our whole biology and experience, our perception of words is very personalistic. Even the most abstract term may lose its abstractness because we cannot react without being ourselves. Thus in a very real sense, our reactions are always intentional, individualistic, specific, or concrete and never quite communicable. We respond to the world in our own way. Children respond to the world in their own way. They respond as children. Their meanings are frequently peculiar to them. Many classroom activities, exhortations, and motivations do not serve their purpose because an adult communicates and interprets adult meanings. The pupil does not "see" the reason for the technique, project, or exercise.

3. The whole (the total field) is greater than the sum of its parts. A picture is more than spots of paint; a cartoon or joke is more than the sum of its sentences; a musical composition is more than a series of notes; a word is more than a series of letters; and the meaning of a perception is more than the number of sensations.

   Sometimes behavior is directed by only a part of the field. This happens when the young man tries to pick up a cigarette from the floor mat and ends up with his car parked in a pasture. It happens when the moviegoer becomes so engrossed with the images and the problems of the people on a screen that he loses all sense of life around him and shares their sorrows. He may cry unashamedly, something which he would not do if the people around him were more clearly in figure (9, p. 26).

In reading it happens when the pupil latches on to only a very limited or literal meaning. It happens when he reacts only concretely to a communication that calls for a generic response. It happens when the pupil identifies a word by some such part characteristic as an ascending or descending letter and confuses the word with another that has a similar characteristic (people-purple).

DIFFERENTIATION

The emergence of a new figure from the ground, or the process by which certain aspects of the perceptual field become figure, is called differentiation. The child gradually differentiates "Daddy" (figure) from all other men (ground). The learner, faced with the problem of multiple meaning of words, differentiates one specific meaning from a number of meanings.

The field theorist has to explain how the specific figure is selected from all the possible alternative organizations. Why does the learner take one specific meaning to the word, for example, democracy? We have here, according to Gestalt psychologists, an instance, not of stimulus nor indeed of response selection, but rather a case of perceptual selection. The organism is stimulated, and of all the possible perceptual organizations that might be made of the incoming sensory data one eventually emerges. This organization then becomes a determinant of the response. Figure 15-5 illustrates the process.

Selection is not a good term to describe perceptual organization. The Gestaltists spoke of how the organization *emerged*. The laws of organization likewise are not principles of connection, but rather state which structures will arise or emerge.

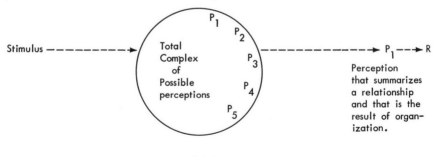

Perceptual Selection

Figure 15-5.   Perceptual Selection

The reader may assume that individual differentiations and hence the perceptual field are completely private. At times this may be true, but usually it is not. Individuals of the same culture, whose contacts with the external reality are similar and indeed where the objects are essentially similar, have many things in common. Human beings living in the same environment generally make similar differentiations.

Only because of this are we capable of communicating with one another. We already noted that the major determinants of meaning are: culture, experience, ability to reconstruct experience, previous experience in concept formation, one's native endowment, one's affective state, and the context in which the word occurs. The more alike the above elements are in both communicator and perceiver, the better the communication tends to be.

Persons with similar experience both make similar differentiations and have similar perceptual fields. Unfortunately, the learner's differentiations often are quite limited. Chapters 3 and 4 contain much evidence concerning the inhibitory factors in learning to read. Reading retardation results because the child cannot make the proper differentiations required for mastery of the reading task.

Differentiations take time and the teacher must constantly make adjustments for this. The application of white paint at the choice points in an otherwise completely black maze leads to quicker and more accurate learning by the rat. In reading, the method of teaching can be simplified or made unnecessarily difficult. The teacher can arrange the learning situation in such a way that the differentiations come easily or are immediately obvious. Teaching machines essentially strive to make each step to be learned so simple and small that it can be taken with great confidence and success.

Learning is a change in performance whether physiological or psychological as a result of a differentiation within the perceptual field. It is an active process resulting in a new organization. It is an emergence of new figures, entities, and characteristics from an undifferentiated ground. Hull's concept of the habit hierarchy is an analogous one. Learning thus may be an increasing or raising of the strength of a specific response in a hierarchy of responses. The differentiations result from a change in the figure-group structure either through a new organization of past experiences or by the addition of novel experiences.

To the question, "What is learned?," the S-R theorist answered, "habit"; the field psychologist, on the other hand, says it is a differentiation. The theories are perhaps closer than they seem.

For the S-R theorist, the end result of practice is *habit*. Thus, the pupil with repeated practice learns to respond automatically to the words on the page. He doesn't have to figure out the pronunciation of each word. For the field theorist, habit is more than a fixed sequence of acts that are neurologically determined; it more frequently is the result of learned insights. Habits, although they seem automatic and occur without awareness, are low-level perceptual differentiations. The person performs them with minimum or no awareness. They are more ground than figure. Dunlap (11) overcame the habit of typing *hte* for *the* only after he actually brought back into figure the *hte* by typing it. The differentiation now was clear and he could break the habit. Emphasizing *the* would not have removed from the ground (conscious or unconscious) the previously-learned *hte*.

According to Gestalt psychologists, a restructuring of the perceptual field frequently results in sudden solutions to problems. Behaviorists, so the Gestaltists maintained, placed animals in situations entirely foreign to them. It was not the animal that was behaving stupidly; rather, the situation itself was stupid. The levers and mechanical devices were usually above the animal's level of comprehension. Naturally, confronted with such situations the animal could not engage in genuine problem-solving activity, and the S-R theorist could falsely conclude that learning is a simple trial-and-error process.

Koehler, in experiments with chimps in 1913–1917 at Tenerife, in the Canary Islands, set about to devise experiments which permitted the organism to show insightful learning. Young chimpanzees were placed in a room to the ceiling of which was fastened a banana. The banana served as a lure. Some distance from the banana and on the floor was a wooden box. Initially all chimpanzees jumped repeatedly toward the banana, but could not reach it. One of the chimps, Sultan by name, soon ceased his jumping and paced back and forth across the room. He stopped for a moment in front of the box. He moved the box under the banana, climbed on top of the box, and jumped from the box toward the banana, which he now was able to get. Sultan apparently grasped a relationship between box and "getting the banana." He had "learned" and then made the appropriate response.

The type of behavior exhibited by the chimp was termed insightful learning. Insight, however, is not an explanation of learning. It is not correct to define learning as a change in performance as a result of insight. Insight does not cause learning any more than practice causes learning. Insight occurs when the differentiation of a relationship is made as a result of the restructuring of the field. Insight is an end-product of having perceived a relationship. It is a combination and reorganization of preexistent perceptions. In such instances we find that the child readily repeats the correct solution and applies what he has learned to new situations.

It does not seem necessary that all correct solutions be insightful. The pupil can "learn" the correct response through a trial-and-error approach or through simple conditioning. In classical conditioning the subject is totally unaware of what he is "learning." Thus, in Pavlov's conditioning experiment the dog was unaware of the fact that he was learning to salivate to the sound of the bell.

In other learning situations the learner may at times not know which of two or three alternatives is the correct response. On a pure chance basis he selects the correct response. This may be termed trial-and-error learning. On subsequent occasions he may continue making the "correct" response because "it worked the last time." This we would not term trial-and-error learning. Whenever previous experience is used to solve a problem, even though the learner is totally unaware of how he combined preexistent perceptions with the present situation to arrive at the proper solution, the learner is no longer acting on a chance basis. He probably is engaging in some form of perceptual learning, elemental though it be.

In most "insightful situations" the learner has a relatively high degree of awareness of "what leads to what" or of what leads to the correct solution. This perception of relationships may be encouraged in the classroom through either inductive or deductive teaching methods. Thus the pupil may be shown the principle or relationship directly (deductive method—the principle is stated for him) or he may learn the relationship by reasoning from specific fact to the generalization (inductive method).

We have suggested in Chapter 8 that the pupil quite frequently develops a *system* of attacking words. It is better if the pupil is taught such a system and if teaching procedure prepares for it. This will lead more readily to insightful response by the pupil in attacking new words.

Hilgard (19, pp. 234–237) notes that insight or the perception of relationships is more readily attained by the more intelligent and more experienced person. These persons can make sharper differentiations in the field. Hilgard also points out that some experimental arrangements are more favorable to insightful behavior than others. He (20, pp. 61–62)[15] notes:

> I have elsewhere pointed out that most of these attacks on insight really missed the main point, which was not one trial or sudden learning but, rather, how the manner in which a problem is presented permits the appropriate use of past experience. The issue is not over either the influence of past experience or sudden learning; it is over learning with understanding, in which the components of a problem are so laid out that their natural relations become evident and a sensible solution is possible. The criticism of association theory is not

[15] Ernest R. Hilgard, "The Place of Gestalt Psychology and Field Theories in Contemporary Learning Theory," *Theories of Learning and Instruction,* Sixty-third Yearbook of the National Society of the Study of Education (Chicago: University of Chicago Press, 1964), pp. 54–77. Reprinted by permission.

based on the importance assigned to past experiences but rather, on the notion that past experience guarantees the solution of a problem, no matter how the problem is presented. The insight point of view is that, with sufficient past experience, some problems are more difficult than others owing to their display or structural features; some learners can, to be sure, solve the more difficult problems because of experience with the particular kind of display, others because they are better able to generalize and not be misled by the display.

The experimenter in the laboratory and the teacher in the classroom can arrange the situation in such a way that the subject or the child cannot behave insightfully. Thus it has been demonstrated that with proper materials and with proper levels of difficulty the five-year-old can learn to read; with less well-prepared materials even the seven-year-old may not learn. Children, no less than animals, can be put in situations in which they can show only trial-and-error learning.

Past experiences, and the transfer that is made from the past situation to the present, surely play a major role in the development of insight. These experiences and transfer are a necessary condition, for it is only by seeing relationships among events that the pupil can generalize. Thus, materials are meaningful or insightful because they are partially learned materials (53, p. 437). Insight occurs only when transfer is made from one situation to another.

Stroud (53, p. 437) points out that:

Meaning, insight, and logical relations are psychological phenomena and have no existence *sui generis* in material of learning. Material is not inherently meaningful; it is endowed with meaning by a reacting individual, and experience, or previous reaction, is a necessary condi-

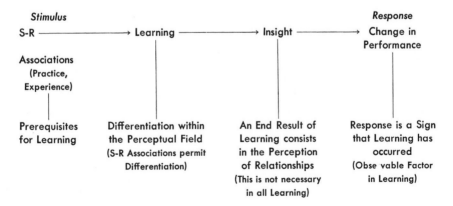

Figure 15-6.   Learning

tion. . . . To put the matter in another way, meaningful, insightful, and logical materials are partially learned already.[16]

In Figure 15-6 we have attempted to summarize the basic elements in the process of moving from stimulus to response.

KURT LEWIN AND EDWARD TOLMAN

Gestalt psychology developed out of the work and writings of Max Wertheimer (1880–1943), Kurt Koffka (1886–1941), and Wolfgang Koehler (1887–1967).[17]

Lewin's[18] chief point of emphasis, in the Gestaltist tradition, was perhaps his insistence that analysis of behavior should begin with the total situation. He felt that theory should be multidimensional in scope, embracing a network of interacting variables rather than simply a pair of variables.

Lewin emphasized the need for a psychological analysis of behavior. For example, typing is not simply the accretion of S-R connections or even movements, as Guthrie suggested. Lewin pointed out that what the beginner is doing and what the proficient typist is doing are distinct. In Chapter 8 we pointed out that the child who is just beginning to learn to read and the skilled reader are identifying the word and reading in completely different ways.

Tolman's[19] theory put major emphasis on the development of expectancies. Expectancy is represented by $S_1R_1S_2$ much as an association is represented by S-R; S_1 refers to the elicitor of an expectancy; R_1, to the response following this perception; and S_2, to the expectandum or significate, that something which is expected or the goal of the expectancy. The following example illustrates how an expectancy is formed. "When this *button* (S_1) is pressed (R_1), I *expect* to hear the ringing *doorbell* (S_2)" (19, p. 446). An expectancy refers to this process, prior to any oc-

[16] James B. Stroud, *Psychology in Education*, Copyright 1956, David McKay Co., Inc. Reprinted by permission David McKay Co., Inc.

[17] Some key works of the Gestalt psychologists are: *Productive Thinking*, 1945, by Wertheimer; *The Growth of the Mind*, 1924, and *Principles of Gestalt Psychology*, 1955, by Koffka; and *The Intelligenzprufuengen an Menschenaffen* (*The Mentality of Apes*), 1917; and *Gestalt Psychology*, 1929, by Koehler.

[18] Important writings of Kurt Lewin are the following: *Dynamic Theory of Personality*, 1935; *Principles of Topological Psychology*, 1936; *Resolving Social Conflicts*, 1948; *Field Theory in Social Science*, 1951; "Field Theory and Learning," in *The Psychology of Learning*, pp. 215–242. Forty-first Yearbook of the National Society for the Study of Education, Part II, 1942.

[19] Tolman's works include: *Purposive Behavior in Animals and Man*, 1932; *Drives Toward War*, 1942; *Principles of Purposive Behavior in Psychology: A Study of a Science*, Vol. II, 92–157, ed. by S. Koch, 1959.

currence of action. When the bell rings, my expectancy is confirmed and the attractiveness of the button is increased. The next time I wish to ring the doorbell, I push the button. Thus the incentive power of the doorbell will depend on my need to ring the doorbell as well as on the attractiveness of the button.

Tolman says that the learner follows signs to a goal, is getting a "feel" of the situation, and is learning meanings rather than movements. He learns sign-significate relationships or means-end relationships, that is, means to the goal. Learning involves the formation of a relationship between stimuli. In terms of Tolman's thinking, if S_1 occurs, we expect S_2. This is another way of saying, given S_1, I judge or assert or suppose that S_2 will follow. This is cognition. An illusion results when S_1 is not followed by S_2. An error of omission occurs when S_1 is judged to be S_2 alone when in reality it is also S_3, S_4, etc.

Tolman's expectancy theory posits that in the presence of certain signs the learner expects to find a certain goal or goal object if he follows the customary behavior route.

Thorndike had said in answer to the question, "What is learned?," that we learn S-R bonds and that reward explains how we learn. Tolman insisted that we learn the whole sequence—the connection and the reward. The rat in essence learns the "good path with food at the end" better than the "bad path without food." It learns the relationship between what it does and the reward. The animal learns "a path as one where it expects to find food," and another path as "one where it does not expect to find food." The animal learns an expectancy.

S-R AND FIELD THEORIES COMPARED

We are in a position now to delineate the differences between S-R and Field Theories of Learning. Learning theorists in common have sought to discover and specify the experimental variables that control and determine behavioral changes that occur with practice, experience, or perception, and furthermore they have tried to formulate the functional interrelationships or laws that hold between these variables.

All theorists agree that the observable response is a function of the physical and social world and the condition of the organism. Furthermore, as we observe responses, we note changes in response and infer that these are accompanied by certain internal changes. These internal changes or hypothetical learning factors in turn affect present performance. Theorists agree that these internal events have their character partly determined by the impinging stimulus and partly by various organic states and past experience, but they disagree as to their conception of these hypothetical learning factors.

Psychologists today maintain that behavior is lawfully related to antecedent events, that phenomena are lawful, that the relationships can be quantitatively described (22) and that "science is concerned with the formulation of general, invariant functional relations between antecedent events and consequents." (45, p. 696)

Behavior is lawful. Some call it deterministic. Sells (45, p. 696)[20] notes that:

> All contemporary theorists implicitly or explicitly accept the principle of the multiple determination of behavior, which implies neither stimuli nor responses occur in isolation, but rather in patterned, sequential, and ordered complex relationships.

The field theorist believes that the way an organism behaves is not entirely subject to preceding experimental conditions, past experience, the physiological state, or even the present environment. He maintains that even if one could predict with 100 per cent accuracy the behavior of a given organism, it is not necessary to infer that the organism's behavior is determined. The human organism, especially, is perceived as being a person who embodies the dimension of subjective freedom. He can transcend the material universe. He is able, in the words of Rogers, "to live dimensions of his life which are not fully or adequately contained in a description of his conditionings or his unconscious."

The cognitive psychologist thinks that learning is part of a larger problem of perceptual organization; the S-R theorist, that it is a matter of stimulus-response connections, bonds, associations, or habits. The cognitive theorist feels that learning involves the association or organization of perceptual processes. Conditioning is interpreted as being a reorganization of perceptual systems built about the conditioned and the unconditioned stimulus. The S-R theorist insists that the association is between stimulus and response mechanisms, between receptor or sensory and effector or motor processes. Perhaps, as Spence (52) says, both types of association occur in learning.

For the field theorist the inner world of the individual is a significant datum and it sometimes has a more significant influence upon behavior than the external environmental stimulus. Rogers (43, p. 125) found that the degree of self-understanding by the individual was the best predictor of the behavior of 75 delinquents. This phenomenal variable was much more closely related to future behavior ($r = .84$) than was the observable external environment (family environment, $r = .36$).

In general, all theorists agree on the following points: learning

[20] S. B. Sells, "An Interactionist Looks at the Environment," *American Psychologist*, 18 (November, 1963), pp. 696–702. Reprinted by permission.

situations involve stimuli and responses; motives initiate and direct behavior; responses are organized for the attainment of goals or ends; and goals, when attained and leading to the satisfaction of motives, also lead to the establishment of responses or expectancies. Hull spoke of drive, stimulus, response, and reinforcement; Lewin spoke of tension, path, vector, and valence; and Tolman, of demand, sign, expectancy, and goal object.

Hebb (18) notes that Gestalt psychology is not an alternative to S-R learning theory; it has had rather a complementary and a corrective influence. It called for more adequate statement of the problem and for more adequate consideration of cognitive and innate factors.

Let us now take a more specific look at the differences between S-R and field theories. We have perhaps exaggerated some differences, but hope that thus the various views might be better delineated.

Stimulus-Response Theories	*Field* or *Cognitive Theories*

Basic Philosophy

Reductionistic	*Emergentistic*
S-R theorists generally accept two principles. The first, termed phylogenetic reductionism, implies that higher evolutionary stages of development do not differ fundamentally from lower stages. The higher levels are treated as more complex only in the sense of containing more elements. The assumption is that that which has fewer elements is more simple than that which has more. No qualitative changes or differences in learning are admitted. S-R theorists have assumed that the laws of learning are the same for different phylogenetic levels. When attempts have been made to explain human learning, they have extrapolated human learning from rat learning. Cognition is explained in this way. Assuming that the speech-writing relationship is only a phoneme-grapheme relationship is an error in some areas of linguistics today and is clearly reductionistic.	The emphasis is on the living organism, which has characteristics that are not explainable by the elements of which it is composed. Life, and especially human life, is a unique phenomenon that has emerged from a complex organization of simpler elements, and this combination of elements has resulted in something qualitatively different and that is not predictable from a knowledge of those elements.
The second principle, termed ontogenetic reductionism, assumes that that which is genetically early is more fundamental than that which occurs later. The past is more important than the present. Adult behavior is explained on the basis of earlier acquired reactions.	This view maintains that the learning of each species is significantly different. Indeed, the learning of each learner may be distinct. A teacher may give four children the same directions for making paper hands on a clock (the stimulus is identical), but four different types of clocks will emerge.
	The laws of organization are not principles of connection. They state which structures will arise or emerge. This view emphasizes the forming and molding process in the classroom and the child's modifiability and flexibility.

Viewpoint
or Approach

Peripheralistic

S-R theorists are concerned in the main with observable physiological events. They tend to be peripheralistic, maintaining that psychological processes may be conceived as relatively simple or mechanical links between peripheral events or receptor stimulations at one end and effector activities at the other end. In general, the assumption is that when afferent neural materials come into the brain they tend to keep their independent existence. All the stimulus aspects which act on the organism get habit-linkages with the response. This assumption has been labelled the constancy hypothesis, and is probably not held in its strictest sense by any theorist.

A teacher who accepts this view is likely to emphasize the attainment of the correct response rather than the thought process used in getting the correct answer. A reading teacher may find himself at the end of a day feeding phonogram-phoneme relationships to children and caring only if the right response comes back.

Centralistic

Cognitive theorists are more concerned with central intermediaries—with perception, understanding, personal involvement—and with psychological tension systems. They give major importance in their explanation of behavior to events in the brain. Stimulus-response connections are explained physiologically by the Gestalt group. They assume that a one-to-one relationship exists between experience and brain fields. This doctrine of isomorphism holds that brain fields and experience are topologically identical. The brain is like a map, representing experience.

The teacher pays a great deal of attention to the pupil's thought process and will give credit if the pupil has used the correct thought process, even though the answer might be wrong. The teacher does not like to reward guessing or "accidental" solutions.

Units of Behavior

Molecular

Early behaviorism put major emphasis on physiological aspects, on muscular movements, and on glandular activities. Neobehaviorists speak of stimulus situations and molar activities, such as pressing a bar or running down an alley. They stress total response to patterns of stimuli. Nevertheless, emphasis still is on minute details and component parts. Analysis of behavior begins with parts and parts have meaning in isolation.

The phonic methods of teaching reading which begin with the individual letters and sounds are molecular approaches.

Molar

The emphasis is placed on the whole, and parts in a whole have meaning because of their relationship to wholes. Parts in a whole get their characteristics from the context in which they occur. Water is no longer water when broken into elements. Goldstein notes that reflexes, as they are defined by S-R theorists, can occur only when they are artificially isolated as by severing the spinal cord. The field theorist maintains that one cannot so isolate the reflex and still hope to be studying the same type of behavior as when the reflex acts via the whole organism.

Phonic systems which begin with the whole word are molar systems.

Means Used to Describe Learning

Connectionism

Learning is the forming and strengthening or weakening of specific bonds or connections between S-R. Learning is an additive process.

In learning to spell, the pupil needs to learn the sequence of the letters. Gradually wrong responses drop out, and the correct response, being more recent and more frequent, is substituted. Learning to read or the forming of word-meaning connections is an additive process. Each time the "word plus meaning situation" occurs, the connection is strengthened.

Cognition

Learning is the organizational response to a stimulus. It is a change in perceptual organization. Learning is a growth process involving the whole organism. Learning proceeds by reorganization rather than by accretion.

Learning to read requires the development of a coding system which organizes bits of knowledge into a meaningful whole, often resulting in a rule or generalization.

Types of Learning Emphasized

Trial and Error

The emphasis is on chance success and learning by selection and connection.

A sixth-grade boy who could not produce an R one day accidentally produced the sound when mispronouncing a word without an R. The teacher immediately strengthened this response and eventually the R became a part of the pupil's sound alphabet. The kindergarten child will select pieces of puzzle at random and will try to make them fit without attention to shape, size, or color.

Problem-solving

Learning by perception, insight, and intelligent behavior are primary. Emphasis is upon the importance of structuring. The assumption is that the learner generally seeks insightful solutions to problems and engages in trial and error only if the problem is too difficult.

A boy who was having special difficulty with S one day remarked in glee, "I've got it, you just have to close your teeth every time you come to an S or your tongue will come out."

The teacher bears the responsibility of structuring the learning situation in such a way that the child is not a random or chance learner, but so he can perceive relationships. Habits are easier to learn when interrelationships are perceived.

What Is Learned?

Response

The S-R theorist suggests that the learner learns habits or responses. The response is learned. Mowrer disagrees. He suggests that the rat doesn't learn to press the bar when

Cognitive Structure

The organism discovers and understands relationships. It learns that the bar can become a food-obtaining object. It learns a cognition that when it makes the response in it is hungry. The organism learns a motive rather than a habit. The rat already knows how to press the bar. The rat learns to *want* to press the bar when it is hungry.

The response is a muscular or glandular process that depends upon stimulation.

Education is the learning of as many useful responses as is possible. Education builds a reservoir of responses to be used as the occasion demands.

the future a reward will follow. It learns an expectancy or cognitive anticipation that if a given act is performed, there will occur a special consequence. The organism learns meaning rather than movements.

The response is a sign that learning has occurred.

Education includes the learning of facts, but facts are best learned when the learner perceives them as serving a purpose that is significant to him. While working with addition of fractions, children often solve a problem such as $\frac{3}{4} + \frac{2}{8} = ?$, but many of them are stumped when they face problems such as $? - \frac{3}{8} = \frac{2}{8}$. Before they have any continuous success with this type of problem, they have to work with rewriting the formula, addend + addend = sum. Once they discover the relationship of the various parts of the formula and are able to analyze their problems, their difficulties are alleviated. At first many will rewrite their problems as addition problems, but gradually many just habitually add the given elements to find the sum without rewriting.

Capacity

Emphasis on Learning

Learning capacity depends upon the number of bonds and their availability. The assumption is that the mere adding of bonds will result in a new and qualitatively different type of functioning.

As an S-R theorist, the teacher would attribute the child's difficulties in reading to lack of bond formation. Helping the slow learner is essentially a matter of exposing him to more S-R connections.

Emphasis on Biology and Physiology

There are differences in the ability to differentiate and restructure the field and these are predominantly biological.

The interaction between the organism and the environment, the cognitive representation, is brought about by the inborn and experiential resources of the learner. All organisms learn, but some learn more than others, and the differences in learning are explained to a great degree by the organism's response characteristics, which are biologically determined rather than by environmental differences or opportunities.

Practice

Practice must be rewarded to be effective. Practice is important because it permits rewards to act upon connections. The emphasis

Practice or repetitious exposure may lead to new insights and perceptions of relationships.

is on getting the learner to make the proper responses or to go through the necessary movements.

The field theorist rejects repetitive drill as inadequate, a drill which seemingly is indicated by the "path-wearing, bond-forming principle of conditioning, leading to supposedly lowered synaptic resistance along preferred neural pathways." (3)

Field theorists point out that insight may be achieved without repetition. Humans do not have to jump from a 50-story building to know that they should not jump. It is common occurrence that the better pupil will do well on a spelling test even though the words may not have been formally studied previously. However, he will show more crossing out, erasing, and respelling. He works out the words by applying principles of phonics and word construction.

Motivation and Reinforcement

Motives are synonymous with organic drives. Rewards strengthen specific bonds and neighboring bonds.

The emphasis is on external reinforcement. A father is S-R oriented when he promises his boy a bicycle for getting good grades.

Attention is explained through purposive behavior of the organism. Motives are products of disequilibrium within the life space. Goals modify performance and learning. They confirm expectations, thus providing closure. Closure produces the satisfying tension-reducing state that comes with the termination of an activity. The emphasis, especially by Lewin, is on internal rather than external motivation and reinforcement.

Transfer

The emphasis is on the theory of identical elements. An example in the classroom of transfer by the theory of identical elements is in spelling. The child soon learns that when a single consonant is preceded by a single vowel in an accented syllable which is at the end of a word, the consonant is usually doubled before adding a suffix beginning with a vowel. Whenever he encounters this situation, he doubles the final consonant because of transferring his knowledge from one identical situation to another.

Field theorists speak of transposition rather than of transfer. Similarity consists of common patterns, configurations, or relationships rather than of identical piecemeal elements. Transposition means that the organism in novel situations reacts to relationships rather than to similarities of content. A rat rewarded if he goes to B, an exit smaller than A, will select C in preference to B when confronted with B and C, if C is still smaller than B. He reacts to the relationship "smaller." He is transferring a relationship from the first situation to the second.

Nature of Reality

Reality equals material existence. Reality exists in a physical environment. A chair exists and it is reality.

Reality and existence are distinct. Reality for the field theorist is "meaning." An object may exist, but have no meaning for a given individual. A child has no meaning for playing jacks if he has never watched or played the game. The words, bumper crops, have no meaning to a child who associates bumper with automobile bumpers. Actions are based on one's interpretation of existences.

SUMMARY AND CONCLUSION

The reading-learning process involves usually two persons: the teacher and the pupil. The teacher commonly is an indispensable ingredient of the learning process, but hardly any more so than the pupil. Education is essentially the internal process of learning and this occurs within a pupil. Learning is individual and until the teacher understands the nature of this individualness, he may not be able to teach the pupil in an optimum way.

In order that the teacher may individualize or personalize education for the pupil, he must understand the variables or factors that affect learning. This chapter discussed the determinants of reading success and broadly categorized them as: individual variables, task variables, method variables, and institutional variables.

The individual variables, those factors within the learner that make learning an individual process, were discussed at length in Chapters 3, 4, and 5. The task variables, those factors inherent in the learning task that make the learning of reading more or less difficult, were discussed in Chapters 3, 7, 9, 10, 11, 12, 13, and 14. The method variables were discussed generally throughout the entire book, but specifically in Chapters 8, 10, and 11. And the institutional variables were discussed in a general way throughout the book.

When the teacher and child meet, a major part of the teacher's armament must be knowledge of principles of learning.

The following statements summarize learning principles discussed in this chapter that are particularly applicable in dealing with learning problems in the classroom.

1. All learning involves a stimulus (S), response (R), and a connection between the stimulus and the response. The pupil is stimulated by a book (S) and reads words, sentences, and paragraphs (R).

2. Learning proceeds best when the learner understands what he is doing.
   a. Teachers need to be aware that sometimes the pupil comes up with the correct response by accident or by guessing, *without understanding why his answer is correct.*
   b. The teacher needs to determine whether to reward the correct response, the correct process, or only the correct response when it is accompanied by the correct process.
3. Learning is an associative process, but also a perceptual process.
4. The pupil learns by doing, learning occurs under conditions of practice, and overlearning is of crucial importance to poor readers. Children generally become better in word recognition the more frequently they see the word. However, practice or repetition *per se* does not cause learning. The pupil's practice must be both motivated and rewarded and it should be slightly varied from session to session.
5. The learner learns best when he is psychologically and physiologically ready to respond to the stimulus. The learner needs a proper attitude, should be ready to attend to the stimulus, and should have a felt need to learn. He needs also to have adequate maturity for learning. The learner will not respond unless he is motivated and he cannot learn unless he responds. The reader's performance will improve only if he is interested in his work, if he is interested in improving himself, if the material to be learned has special significance for himself, and if he is attentive to the situation. Reduce motivations to zero, and there is no performance and, hence, no learning.
6. The learner cannot learn without doing, but he won't do anything without being rewarded. The best rewards in the reading setting are often pleasant pupil-teacher relationships, permissiveness on the part of the teacher, and feelings of success. The teacher must divide the learning situation into numerous small steps and must reward the learning of each discrete step.
7. Learning is often a matter of present organization and reorganization, not simply past accretion. Perhaps no individual is ever completely free to behave on the basis of the present situation. Previous experiences have developed a set or pattern of behavior that is difficult to change. The retarded reader, even if he now sincerely wants to be a good reader, must live with his previous inapplications. But, each new situation has within it the potentiality for change. The pupil can usually

make positive advances toward new goals and achievements. He has the potentiality for growth.

8. Letters might best be taught to most children as parts of a whole word, but the perceptual whole for the retarded reader often is the single letter. The size of the unit of instruction depends on the nature of the pupil, and many retarded readers benefit greatly from a synthetic-phonetic approach.

9. The teacher needs to ask himself whether he is trying to get the pupil to substitute one stimulus for another or whether he wants to elicit the correct response. In teaching the child to read, we obviously have a case of stimulus substitution. In essence we are asking the child to bring to the written word the same meanings that he previously attached to the spoken word.

10. Reading also involves response selection. A child who can read *the* and *there* may not be too sure of *their*. He makes provisional tries at the word and when he comes up with the correct pronunciational response the teacher reinforces this response, thus gradually stamping it in. Thus, from a series of possible responses the child gradually learns to select the correct response.

11. Each activity (reading of a sentence, for example) consists of a complex of individual movements, and improvement and learning are not necessarily attained by *much* reading but rather by increasing the number of correct movements in reading (moving from left to right, proper identification of the word, association of the proper meaning with the word, development of proper eye movements) and by reducing the number of incorrect movements (excessive regressions, improper word attack, etc.) in the total complex of movements comprising the total capacity. Improvement occurs because the learner gradually replaces the erroneous movements that he still is making with correct ones. Thus additional practice gives more opportunity to master the myriad of movements comprising a complex total performance.

This view of the learning of a skill certainly emphasizes the need for the teaching of specific habits. Telling a retarded reader "to read" is not specific enough. We need to teach specific habits in specific situations. This requires careful job analysis, leading to an identification of all specific movements. The curriculum, methods and materials must be so specific that they will serve as proper stimuli to call forth appropriate responses. It is not enough to identify large, all-embracing abilities such as "gaining a sight vocabulary." It is necessary to break the broad area into basic subskills, such as the ability to discriminate between sounds, to see elements within a word, and to blend the elements into the total word.

12. When a stimulus is followed by a response, there is a tendency for the same response to occur when the stimulus recurs (Law of Contiguity). The pupil who responds to *was* with *saw* on the next presentation of the stimulus, *was*, tends to respond again with *saw*. In the classroom, much teaching follows this contiguity principle. The teacher shows the child a card containing the word "cat" and says "cat," and the assumption is that the child will, upon subsequent occasions, say the word "cat" when the same printed stimulus is presented alone.

It is important, especially when learning is a one-shot or a one-trial affair, that the teacher not permit the learner to leave a learning situation without performing the response correctly. A pupil should read the word correctly before going on to another word. Bugelski (6, p. 104) notes: "Here, teachers can also see the folly of allowing children to do homework without having the answers supplied. Such homework is not training or practice. It is a *test*." [21]

The reader should not "get by" with approximations of the correct answer (6, p. 103). The pupil should not be permitted simply to get a "general idea." Teachers frequently give partial credit for partially correct answers. Partially correct answers such as reading *their* for *them* are in fact totally wrong. Bugelski (6, p. 103) notes that "Too many students are rated as 'knowing what to do' without being able to do."

It may well be that when the teacher says to the reader, "read with care," the pupil is not learning the molar response of reading but rather the micromolar response "when you read, read slowly."

13. If the learner tends to repeat the response that was made most recently in the presence of the stimulus (Law of Relative Recency), the teacher should exercise great care, especially with the retarded reader, in not permitting extraneous materials to come between the stimulus and response. The teacher must see to it that when the response is made, it is made to the proper stimulus and not to any of many other possible stimuli that may have intervened. Too frequently in teaching, by the time the proper response occurs, the original stimulus

---

[21] From *The Psychology of Learning Applied to Teaching*, by B. R. Bugelski, Copyright 1964 by The Bobbs-Merrill Company, Inc.; reprinted by permission of the publisher.

situation has disappeared. The teacher must take great care that the necessary stimuli are so distinct for the pupil that he cannot help but see the connection between a given stimulus and the objective of teaching.

14. The teacher will make fewer mistakes in teaching if he analyzes all the variables in behavior. This idea is expressed well in both Hull's S-R theory and in Lewin's field theory. There are multiple causes of behavior. Some children do not read even though they profess a great desire to do so. Perhaps reading constantly conflicts with television and television may be the stronger stimulus, thus preventing reading.

Another factor that inhibits performance in reading is fatigue. As an organism continues to perform, as the retarded reader continues to read, for example, the tendency to read is gradually lessened. The pupil's tendency to perform may be lessened also by such factors as defective vision.

15. Hull's habit hierarchy concept has implications in education. Whenever a stimulus is presented to an organism, the organism generally is capable of responding in one or more ways. All the responses possible in the situation may be thought of as comprising a hierarchy of responses, each of which has a certain probability of occurring. Education thus might be a "changing of relative positions in a hierarchy." (6, pp. 74–75)

Learning requires the elimination of faulty habits or competitive responses or of those members in the hierarchy that have higher probability. If these constantly intrude, learning cannot occur. As all teachers have seen, sometimes it is more difficult to undo a wrong habit or to unlearn what has been learned faultily than to teach from scratch the correct procedure to a student. A "correct" baseball stance is easier to assume by the beginning player than by one in whom an incorrect procedure has become ingrained.

As Bugelski (6, p. 80) notes, the habit-family hierarchy concept also indicates the great value in teaching a variety of methods for reaching a goal. The student needs to learn to switch approaches to solve problems when necessary.

We have already suggested that learning is also a psychological and perceptual process. The incoming data (stimuli) are retained, processed, and reorganized by the viewer. This intermediary step, which is initiated by a stimulus and culminates in a response, is termed perception. This process modifies the stimulus data.

The facts of perception as they apply to the teaching of reading are essentially these:

1. Perception goes beyond sensation. Recognition of a word is not reading. The pupil must react with meaning and this frequently requires the organization of previous experiences. This is perception.

2. Perception of a word or the meaning taken to a word or series of words is usually representational, neither representing wholly or completely the meaning intended. The child uses his previous experience to interpret the words of others. At times his perceptions are in error. The teacher must check on the adequacy of the pupil's experiences and meanings.

   The meanings taken to a word usually are many more than one, but also far fewer than they could be. The greater the number of meanings that are associable with a word, the more difficult it is to understand such a word and the less reliable the individual learner's meaning for such a word tends to be. This is why pupils have difficulty with multiple meanings of words.

3. The meaning comes from the learner rather than from the word and is determined primarily by the learner's previous experiences but also by his own constitutional make-up, by the number, quality, and organization of his experiences, by his ability to reconstruct his own experiences, by his affective state, and by his culture. The learner reacts as an organized whole.

4. The central process that controls the learner's particular re-action to printed materials or that modifies the stimulus materials is termed cognition and depends on adequate neural functioning.

5. Perceptions and hence meanings for words are really creations of the individual's mind and usually cannot be shared directly. Thus teachers rarely share concepts; they merely transmit words that symbolize concepts which in turn represent experiences. The teacher can only permit pupils to examine the insights which he offers with the hope that they will see their meaningfulness.

6. The sum total of the learner's biology and experiences and his perception of them are termed the learner's perceptional field. This field of psychological and physical, physiological, and social forces as they impinge upon the learner's perceptions at the moment of action, determine his reactions to reality, to reading itself, and to words. Simply put, each

learner behaves according to how things *seem* to him. He reads something of himself *into* the written or printed word. Rogers (42, pp. 483–484) notes that each person lives in a continually changing world of experience and he reacts to the field as it is perceived. For him, it is reality.

7. The reaction to a word, the meaning in other words, is an indication that the learner has organized his experiences in a specific way. The response is a sign that perceptual organization or learning has occurred.

8. The perceptual organization characteristically is one of figure-ground. That of which the learner is aware is termed the figure.

9. The figure-ground relationship is variable or, to put it in another way, the focus of attention may change. With each figure-ground change comes a change in meaning. Today learning to read may be challenging; tomorrow it may be discouraging and undesirable.

10. The process whereby a figure arises from a ground is called differentiation. The pupil must be taught to use his experience and the context to differentiate the correct meaning from a series of meanings.

11. Communication is the process of understanding another's perceptual field or perceptual figure-ground organization. This is an essential ingredient in being able to teach effectively.

12. The child's differentiations are prevented or inhibited by such factors as visual or auditory inadequacies, brain injuries, lack of intelligence, lack of experience, etc. Learning retardation frequently results because the pupil cannot make the proper differentiations required for mastery of the learning task.

Differentiations take time, and the teacher must constantly make adjustments for this. Thus the application of white paint at the choice points in an otherwise completely black maze leads to quicker and more accurate learning by the rat. In classroom learning, the method of teaching can be simplified or made unnecessarily difficult. The teacher can arrange the learning situation in such a way that the differentiations come easily or are more difficult. Teaching machines essentially strive to make each step to be learned so simple and small that it can be taken with great confidence and success. With the retarded reader in particular, the learning task needs to be presented in structured, carefully-planned steps.

The manner in which a problem is presented determines

at least in some way whether past experiences can be used appropriately or not. Some classroom arrangements are more conducive than others to the elicitation of insightful solutions. The evidence indicates that with retarded readers, who often are weak in the visual association–memory area, materials should be presented through the auditory and kinesthetic channels.

13. Learning is a differentiation within the perceptual field and usually results in a behavioral or performance change.

14. Learning in the classroom functions best when it involves a movement toward a goal. Learning occurs most easily when it represents the goal-directed attempt of the learner to satisfy his needs (42, p. 491). The teacher should emphasize the processes in learning or the steps toward a goal rather than merely the end product or the correct answer.

15. Learning is chiefly under the influence of the learner's perceptual field at the moment of action. Children learn best by surveying the situation and grasping relationships by perceiving meaningful relationships among the elements of the goal toward which they are striving.

16. Learning to read requires an association between a stimulus (the word) and a response (the meaning) and is most easily brought about when the printed symbol is associated with a spoken word for which the pupil has previously learned a meaning under conditions of spaced and varied practice.

17. Repetitive practice usually is necessary to make habitual or to stamp in the association between the printed and spoken word and to develop accurate identification and recognition of the printed symbol.

18. Practice must be motivated. The pupil learns best when he *wants* to learn a word and its meaning. Emotion, especially that which causes unpleasantness or anxiety, facilitates learning or goal-directed behavior. An individual thus stimulated seeks for the goal. He feels unhappy when he doesn't know. This is cognitive dissonance and it is a more effective motivator than such after-the-learning events as rewards or punishments.

19. Cognitive dissonance may become too great—the pupil may become fearful or feel that removal of cognitive dissonance by learning to read would interfere too much with previously formed cognitive structures or self-concepts and thus may become fearful and avoid the goal. Sometimes he will feel that attainment of the goal (learning to read) is not worth the

difficulties he will encounter in surmounting the barriers that prevent him from attaining the goal.

Learning proceeds best when the task is challenging but still within the potentiality of the pupil. The pupil must have sufficient interest in the task to use the responses of which he is capable. The pupil needs experience in setting realistic goals, goals neither so low as to elicit little effort nor so high as to discourage him from trying altogether or that in his opinion foredoom him to failure.

20. Sometimes learning is not motivated by cognitive dissonance and thus must be reinforced by rewards, praise, recognition, knowledge of progress, encouragement, blame, or punishment. Rewards and punishments are effective because they change the values of various parts of the psychological field for the pupil.

21. Transfer of learning to new tasks is best promoted by the perception of the interrelationships within the situation and by actual experience in applying the principles to new situations. The pupil should see, for example, the interrelationships between letters in words and apply this knowledge to new words.

22. Learning proceeds best when the pupil knows or senses that the teacher understands him and when the conditions of learning enhance the personal and social development of the learner.

23. The best way to understand the pupil's behavior is from the "internal frame of reference of the individual himself." (42, p. 494)

24. It is not enough to understand the child's perceptions. At any moment, there are forces, both physical and social, that influence the child's behavior and of which the child may be unaware. The child is not necessarily the best judge of what is good for him, of why he behaves the way he does, or of how he may best learn.

25. Educational experiences are either:
    a. ignored or denied perceptual awareness.
    b. accepted or admitted to perceptual awareness and incorporated into one's self-concept.
    c. perceived in a distorted way.
    Some children simply don't want to learn to read; some want to because it satisfies some need; and there are those who, conscious of some threat in reading, do not make any effort to read while at the same time professing a great desire to

want to learn to read. The pupil seems to respond to threat without knowing what causes the threat (42, p. 506).

The teacher must interpret the classroom behavior of the pupil from the pupil's point of view. The child does not react to classroom situations as the teacher sees them, but rather as he sees them. The pupil learns only what he wants to learn and he responds to the environment as he has created it for himself.

If the teacher looks upon behavior or performance as being determined and influenced at the moment of behaving by the learner's perceptions, he at once sees the lawfulness and purpose of much of the pupil's behavior in the classroom. Behavior in the classroom is not without its reasons. It invariably looks to the pupil as being the most effective and most reasonable thing for him to do. It is only through a change of his perceptions that the learner later may see its "unreasonableness."

Reading experiences in school thus must satisfy the needs of the pupil. They must lead to personal enhancement. Only in this way will the pupil become and remain an active participant in the learning process. If his needs are not satisfied, he will revert to laziness, inattention, and perhaps even hostility. He will turn to other objectives and goals. Reading must satisfy his needs or he will turn away from it.

The simple fact is that learning occurs only if the pupil wants it to occur. Adult attempts to "force" learning rarely are effective. The best laid plans for retention or promotion, passing or failure, go awry if the pupil prefers other self-enhancing experiences more than he hates the censorious grade.

Teaching is rarely only a matter of presenting subject matter. Each bit of subject matter has a *meaning* for the pupil and on it depends whether the pupil will learn or reject, whether he will simply acquire or make learning a part of living. It is not uncommon to find pupils who learn to read, but who rarely read.

In a school, where the teacher is concerned with the meanings that realities have for the perceiver, methods of teaching are not hard and fast. No method completely fits the nature of the pupil or the teacher's personality or provides for the goals of education at all times. Methods of teaching are always individual. Even if a method should work, that is, if the pupil is willing to accept it without reluctance, this may well fall short of good teaching. Its usefulness, as indeed that of all educational procedures, is not independent of the meaning that it has for the pupil. Above all, method should become a stimulus that will activate the pupil's own dormant resources, that will actuate the pupil's potentialities, and that will develop within the pupil independent and self-directive behavior.

We close this chapter and this book with a quote from Tolman:

> What, by way of summary, can we now say as to the contributions of us rodent psychologists to human behavior? What is it that we rat runners still have to contribute to the understanding of the deeds and the misdeeds, the absurdities and the tragedies of our friend, and our enemy—*homo sapiens?* The answer is that, whereas man's successes, persistences, and socially unacceptable divagations—that is, his intelligences, his motivations, and his instabilities—are all ultimately shaped and materialized by specific cultures, it is still true that most of the formal underlying laws of intelligence, motivation, and instability can still be studied in rats as well as, and more easily than, in men.
>
> And as a final peroration, let it be noted that rats live in cages; they do not go on binges the night before one has planned an experiment; they do not kill each other off in wars; they do not invent engines of destruction, and, if they did, they would not be so inept about controlling such engines; they do not go in for either class conflicts or race conflicts; they avoid politics, economics, and papers on psychology. They are marvelous, pure and delightful. And, as soon as I possibly can, I am going to climb back again out on that good old phylogenetic limb and sit there, this time right side up and unashamed, wiggling my whiskers at all the silly, yet at the same time far too complicated, specimens of *homo sapiens,* whom I shall see strutting and fighting and messing things up, down there on the ground below me (59).[22]

QUESTIONS FOR DISCUSSION

1. When would total individualization of the reading program be inappropriate?
2. What is teaching?
3. What is the importance of the organizational aspects in learning?
4. Classify the determinants of reading success.
5. What basic facts are taught by the psychology of individual differences?
6. Explain: Environmental factors may serve as equalizers among individuals.
7. Discuss the nature of discipline and distinguish it from license.
8. Harmonize the fact that the pupil may have psychological reasons for misbehaving with demands for moral accountability.
9. Discuss the importance of discipline as a goal of learning.
10. What is the role of attention in perception?
11. What is the nature of perception?

[22] E. C. Tolman, "A Stimulus-Expectancy Need-Cathexis Psychology," *Science,* Vol. 101 (16 February, 1945), 160–66. Reprinted by permission.

12. What is the meaning of set and discuss its implications in reading?
13. What is the significance of Hebb's physiological and Smith's chemical emphasis?
14. Explain reversal errors as a symptom of ACh & ChE dysfunctioning.
15. Is it possible to share directly one's concepts with another person?
16. What is the meaning of "field" in field theories of learning?
17. Illustrate how the "perceptual field" influences the meaning content that the pupil takes to a word, sentence, or paragraph.
18. Explain the figure-ground organization of the perceptual field.
19. Explain: What is perceived frequently is not what actually is seen but what the perceiver believes he saw.
20. Define differentiation, learning, insight, communication, and transfer.
21. What are the basic tenets of field theorists?
22. Discuss:
    a. All learning requires at least one performance, one association between a stimulus and a response.
    b. The strength of the contiguous stimulus-response connection gradually weakens and eventually becomes extinguished when no reinforcement accompanies its occurrence. Learning to read is a function of *meaningful* reinforcement. (Reinforcement must have meaning for the child. The words of praise of one person may motivate while those of another do not.)
    c. The good reader is differentiated from the poor reader in that he has made more distinct associative connections and he needs fewer cues to arouse responses. (He requires less and less stimulation to make more and more responses. This applies both to the perception as well as the recognition of words. Each word suggests a wider range of meaning, and he needs fewer cues to recognize a word.)

Appendices

APPENDIX I *Multiple Spellings*

Multiple Spellings of Certain Consonants

Ch: The *ch* sound may be spelled as *ch* (church) or as *tu* (nature, actual, future).

D: The *d* sound in verbs frequently is spelled *ed*. Thus for example, we have begged, bragged, canned, and crammed. Usually the sound is spelled simply by *d* as in bed, fed, and red.

F: The *f* sound may be spelled as *f, ph,* or *gh*. In the words, fad, fan, fat, fed, and for, the *f* is spelled as *f*. In cough, draught, laugh, rough, tough, trough and enough the *f* is spelled as *gh*. In phase, phew, phlegm, phone, and phrase the *f* is spelled as *ph*. The *ph* spelling is common in scientific and medical terms of Greek origin, such as morphine, lymphatic, diaphragm, and diphtheria.

J: The *j* sound is spelled as *g* (magic), *ge* (page), *dg* (judgment), *dge* (judge), *ch* (Greenwich), and *di* (soldier). The most common spellings are *j, g, ge,* and *dge*. The *j* sound is spelled as *j* in jam, jet, Jim, job; it is spelled as *g* in gem, gene, germ, gist; it is spelled as *ge* in age, barge, gauge, hinge; and it is spelled as *dge* in badge, bridge, budge, and dodge. The common spellings for *j* at the end of words are *ge* and *dge*.

K: The *k* sound is spelled as *c* (call), *cc* (account), *ch* (choir), *ck* (back), *cu* (biscuit), *k* (rank), *qu* (liquor), and *que* (clique). The *c* spelling of *k* is most common, such as cat, can, come, and came. Before *e* and *i* the initial *k* sound usually is spelled with a *k*. Thus we have the following words: keg, kept, kick, kid, kill, kin, and king. *K* is also used in khaki and kangaroo.

A final *k* sound preceded by a consonant is usually spelled as *k:* thus, ark, ask, balk, bark, and bask. When the final *k* sound is preceded by a short vowel sound as in back, beck, black, buck, and click, it is spelled as *ck*. A final *k* sound preceded by a long vowel has two options—eke or eak, oak or oke. In a medial position when the *k* sound begins a new syllable it is usually spelled *c*. There are many exceptions: yokel, market, basket, trinket, blanket, tinkle, twinkle, wrinkle, lamkin, and manikin.

The student should become familiar with the various combinations of *act, ect, ict, oct, uct,* and *inct,* as in the words fact, compact, elect, reject, depict, evict, concoct, conduct, instruct, and instinct.

In words ending in *et* and *le* as ticket, jacket, pocket, rocket, bucket, tackle, sickle, and trickle, the first syllable usually ends in *ck*. The *k* sound is spelled as *ch* in many Greek words: chasm, choir, Christ, chrism, chrome, and scheme. It appears also, for example, in ache, archive, chaos, chorus, school, character, chronology, echo, epoch, lichen, orchid, drachma, and troche.

Finally, the *k* sound may be spelled as *que:* thus, clique, unique, antique, and mosque.

Ks: The *ks* sound is spelled as *ks, cks, cs, ks,* and *x*. Nouns ending in *k* form their plural by adding an *s;* the third person singular of verbs also ends in *s*. Usually, the *ks* sound at the end of words is an *x;* thus: fix, mix, six. The *ks* sound may be spelled as *cc* or *cs* before *e* or *i,* thus: access, success.

S: The *s* sound may be spelled as *c, s,* or *sc*. Generally, the *c* or *sc* spelling occurs before *e, i, y*. The most common exceptions to this are: self, silk, system, sell, sent, site. The final *s* sound may be spelled as *s, se,* or *ce*. Although most words end in *ence* or *ance,* some (dence, sense, expense, dispense, condense, intense, nonsense, defense, pretense, immense, and recompense) end in *ense*.

Sh: The *sh* sound may be spelled as *sh* (ship), *ch* (machine), *sch* (schmo), *ce* (ocean), *s* or *ss* (issue), *ti* or *si* (mission), *sci* (conscience), and *ci* (special). The *ch* spelling occurs commonly in words of French origin, such as cache, chef, gauche, chute, chandelier, Chicago, champagne, mustache, parachute, chiffon, stanchion, and luncheon. The *sh* sound of *ci* is evident in ferocious, ancient, glacial, spacious. The *sh* sound of *s* or *ss* occurs in fissure, issue, pressure, sure, sugar, and tissue.

The pupil needs to learn the *sh* sound of *ti* and *si*. Numerous words in English are examples of this: thus, compulsion, expulsion, impulsion, propulsion, immersion, submersion, aversion, diversion, ascension, comprehension, controversial, transient, vexatious, contentious, negotiate, partial, venetian, spatial, condition, expedition, ignition, ingratiate.

T: The *t* sound is spelled commonly as *t;* in past particles, such as clapped, dipped, and dripped, it often is spelled *ed*.

Z: The *z* sound is spelled as *s, z,* and *x*. The pupil needs to become especially familiar with the suffixes *ize, lyze, ism*. Some common words in which the *z* sound is spelled as *s* are: is, his, was, has, rise, pose, wise, those, poise, these, tease, close, chose, prose, noise, cause, ease, lose, easel, use, cheese, abuse, amuse, propose, please, praise, confuse, dispose, infuse, busy, advise, advertise, exercise, surprise, blouse, accuse, rose, nose, and hose.

Zh: The *zh* sound often is spelled as *s* or *z:* thus, treasure, pleasure, collision, casual, azure, and seizure.

Multiple Spelling of Vowels

The spelling of vowel sounds presents many more difficulties for the pupil. In the first place, there are so many alternatives. However, the teacher, if not the pupil, may benefit from knowing what these alternatives are. Here is a list of the most common spellings for the long and short vowel sounds:

short a	*long a*	*long u*	ȯ
a (bat)	a (lake)	eau (beauty)	o (off)
ai (plaid)	ai (pain)	eu (feud)	ou (cough)
	au (gauge)	ew (few)	
short e	ay (day)	ewe (ewe)	ȯ *or* ȯ(ə)
a (any)	ea (break)	ieu (lieu)	o (orb)
ae (aetna)	ei (veil)	ou (you)	a (all)
ai (said)	ey (obey)	ueue (queue)	au (caught)
ay (says)	eigh (weight)	u (use)	aw (awe)
e (pet)	a-e (safe)	ue (cue)	ah (Utah)
ea (feather)		ui (suit)	as (Arkansas)
ei (heifer)	*long e*	u-e (mule)	oi (board)
eo (leopard)	ae (Caesar)		ou (court)
ie (friend)	ay (quay)	ä	oi (memoir)
u (bury)	e (be)	a (far)	
	ea (beam)	ea (hearth)	*ou*
short i	ee (feet)	e (sergeant)	ou (out)
e (pretty)	ei (deceive)	oi (memoir)	ow (cow)
ee (been)	eo (people)		
i (sit)	ey (key)	e(ə)	*oi*
ia (carriage)	i (machine)	a (care)	oi (boil)
ie (sieve)	ie (field)	e (there)	oy (oyster)
o (women)	oe (phoebe)	ea (bear)	
u (busy)	e-e (these)	ai (chair)	ə
ui (build)		ay (prayer)	u (urn)
y (hymnal)	*long i*	ei (heir)	e (fern)
	ai (aisle)	e'er (e'er)	i (bird)
short o	ay (aye)		o (work)
a (was)	ei (height)	i(ə)	ea (heard)
o (not)	ey (eye)	e (here)	ou (journal)
ou (hough)	i (ice)	ea (fear)	y (myrrh)
	ie (vie)	ei (weird)	eu (jeu)
short u	igh (high)	ee (deer)	o (können)
io (nation)	oi (choir)	ie (bier)	u̇

o (come)	uy (buy)	i (fakir)	oo
oe (does)	y (sky)		oo (foot)
oo (blood)	ye (rye)	ər	o (wolf)
ou (double)	i-e (pine)	e (ever)	ou (should)
u (sun)	y-e (type)	a (liar)	u (pull)
wo (twopence)		i (elixer)	ü
	long o	o (actor)	oo
	au (hautboy)	u (augur)	oo (food)
	e (sew)	ou (glamour)	ew (brew)
	eau (beau)	y (zephyr)	o (ado)
	eo (yeoman)		wo (two)
	o (old)	ə	oe (canoe)
	oa (roam)	a (senate)	eu (maneuver)
	oe (foe)	ai (mountain)	ue (blue)
	oh (oh)	ay (always)	u (endure)
	oo (brooch)	ei (forfeit)	ou (group)
	ou (shoulder)	eo (pigeon)	ui (fruit)
	ou (soul)	e (women)	u-e (rule)
	ow (grow)	ie (mischief)	
	o-e (home)		

APPENDIX II   *Intelligence Tests*

Before giving a list of various tests, it would seem important to say something about test interpretation.

The user of tests needs a philosophy of interpretation. In the following principles we have sought to identify at least some aspects of such a philosophy. It is hoped that when tests are utilized to diagnose pupil difficulties and to plan special help to meet the needs indicated by the tests, the following points might be kept in mind:

1. Tests are designed basically for the purpose of understanding children better. Schools at one time got along without tests, but physicians also got along without x-rays. The good teacher can understand children better by using tests. Education without testing may be target practice in the dark.

2. Teachers cannot simply believe or not believe in tests. Tests are not articles of faith. Tests should provide an objective situation for studying a sample of the child's behavior. And they are useful only if they are interpreted correctly. Testing without the ability to interpret the results is rather useless, and a test score neatly recorded in a folder that is not interpreted is a waste of time.

3. Tests do not measure something fixed and immutable that characterizes the pupil for all time. They measure rather how well the pupil performs certain tasks at a given point in time. No test score can determine with complete accuracy what the pupil can or cannot learn in the future. Any one score may be misleading. Tests do not really predict. It is more accurate to say that they estimate. They attempt to forecast a person's chances and express this chance mathematically.

4. The pupil needs to develop the attitude that tests merely offer samples on which he is to try his skill. The tests should be looked upon as a challenge rather than as an instrument that stigmatizes him.

5. The user of tests should ask four questions about any tests that he uses:

   a. *Is the test valid?* Does it measure or predict whatever it is supposed to measure or predict? No test is infallible. It is therefore highly important that the teacher utilize the results of more than one test and that he obtain the best test possible.

   b. *Is the test reliable?* Does it measure consistently whatever it is measuring? Is the score stable and trustworthy? Does the person taking the test generally maintain about the same ranking in a group of persons upon retaking the test? There is no such thing as reliable performance on an unreliable instrument. A student suffering a severe headache may not do as well as he normally does even on a well-built test. If, on the other hand, the items are ambiguous or the directions are unclear, he may not be able to perform reliably regardless how propitious his mental condition.

   c. *Is the test usable and objective?* Is it practical? Is it economical? Is the test too long? Is it too expensive? Is it easy to score?

   d. What is the norm group? Is the group, on which the instrument was standardized, representative of the group on which the instrument is to be used? In short, is the student being compared with the correct group? A boy with an IQ of 145 would be classified with the below average group if the average IQ of the group were 150. In another group, his IQ might be the highest score.

6. It is wrong to assume that a given grade norm for a test is an acceptable standard for a given pupil in a grade. If the average score for a given grade is 65, this does not mean that for a given pupil a score of 65 could be considered acceptable.

7.   When achievement scores do not measure up to ability or aptitude scores, it is not always correct to assume that the pupil is lazy or uninterested.

8.   Tests do not give answers to problems. They do not tell us what to do. They are designed to give additional information on the basis of which the teacher or pupil can come to wiser decisions. Tests are aids to judgment, not judgment itself. Test results should not be the sole determinant of the course of action which the reading specialist should follow. The remedial program should be based on other data and should be modified as the teacher works with the pupil, watches his responses, and observes his progress as a result of some activities and his failure as a result of others.

9.   Test scores frequently have a direct bearing on the self-concept of the pupil. If the test results, for example, place him in an inferior position with other members of his family or close friends, he may feel threatened by the result. If the intellectual recognition of his limitations is not accompanied by emotional acceptance, the pupil may become hostile, reject the results, and seek compensation in another area. The teacher must understand how the child evaluates himself as a reader and what reading success means to him.

10.   Test interpretations to the pupil should not be accompanied by expressions of pleasure or displeasure over the test score. The pupil will infer that the teacher likes him if the score is high and does not like him if the score is low. The teacher is on safer grounds with statements such as the following: "Does this test score fit in with what you think of yourself?" or "Is this about what you expected?"

11.   Tests should be given at the beginning of the semester rather than at the end of the school year. The test then is more likely to be interpreted as revealing something about the child rather than about the school or the teacher. To judge a school or teacher on the basis of test data only is invalid and dangerous.

12.   The individual child's performance must be interpreted in terms of the curriculum to which he has been exposed. It is reasonable to expect less evidence of ability in reading ability than in some other areas if the pupil has had substantially less acquaintance with this area.

13.   Accurate test results are possible only if the tests are carefully administered, scored accurately, and interpreted in terms of appropriate norms. Numerous errors may and often do creep into testing. Even though the test has been standardized,

we need to keep in mind the fact that the persons who administer the tests and who interpret the test data are not standardized.

Here is a list of tests of intelligence.

1. *Arthur Point Scale of Performance* [The Psychological Corporation, New York]. This test, for ages 5–15, affords a means of measuring the abilities of deaf children, those suffering from reading disabilities, those with delayed or defective speech, and the nonEnglish speaking population. The test is composed of five nonlanguage subtests which consists of the following: Knox Cube Test, Seguin Form Board, Arthur Stencil Design Test I, Healy Picture Completion Test II, and Porteus Maze Test (Arthur Modification).

2. *California Test of Mental Maturity* [California Test Bureau, Monterey, California]. In this test, Memory, Spatial Relationships, Logical Reasoning, and Verbal Concepts are measured to determine IQ. The test is available on kindergarten to adult level.

3. *Chicago Non-Verbal Examination* [The Psychological Corporation, New York]. This test is designed for students handicapped in the use of the English language such as the deaf, those with reading difficulty, and those with a foreign language background. The test has been standardized for both verbal and pantomime directions. It is usable from age 6 through adult level.

4. *Columbia Mental Maturity Scale* [Harcourt, Brace and World, Chicago, Illinois]. This test for ages 3 to 12 has one hundred items, each printed on a card 6 × 19 and each containing from three to five drawings. This is an individual scale suitable for cerebral palsy patients and others physically handicapped. No verbal response is required. The specific task in each item is to select from a series of drawings the one which does not belong.

5. *Full Range Picture Vocabulary Test* [Psychological Test Specialists, Missoula, Montana]. This is an intelligence test for ages 2 through adult level based on verbal comprehension using cartoon-like cards. No reading or writing is required of the testee, and thus the test can be given to anyone able to signal "yes" or "no" in any interpretable way. The examinee must be able to hear or read words.

6. *Gessell Development Schedules* [Psychological Corporation, New York]. These preschool-age tests provide measures of mental growth through quantitative measurements of language, motor

development, adaptive behavior, and social behavior.

7. *I. P. A. T. Culture Fair Intelligence Tests* [Institute for Personality and Ability Testing, Champaign, Illinois]. This test gives a measure of general intelligence. The IQ scores are relatively free of educational and cultural influences. It is nonverbal and nonpictorial and uses a perceptual approach. Scale I, ages 4–8 or adult defectives, requires 30 minutes. There are two other scales, ranging to superior adult level.

8. *Kahn Intelligence Tests: Experimental Form* [Psychological Test Specialists, Missoula, Montana]. This test is almost independent of differential educational and cultural learning forces. It requires no reading, writing, or verbal knowledge and includes a scale for assessment of the intelligence of blind persons plus special scales to measure ability in concept formation, recall, and motor coordination.

9. *Kuhlmann-Anderson IQ Test* [Personnel Press, Inc., Princeton, New Jersey]. There are tests at each grade level, kindergarten through grade twelve, measuring general learning ability.

10. *Kuhlmann-Finch IQ Test* [American Guidance Service, Inc., Minneapolis, Minnesota]. This test for grades one through twelve measures general mental development and provides an IQ score. The predecessor of this test was the Kuhlmann-Anderson. Nonverbal tests only are used through grade three.

11. *Lorge-Thorndike Intelligence Tests* [Houghton Mifflin Co., Boston, Massachusetts]. A verbal series of these tests is available for grades four through twelve. These tests measure scholastic aptitude through subtests of verbal reasoning ability, vocabulary, verbal classification, sentence completion, arithmetic reasoning, and verbal analogy. The nonverbal series is available for grades kindergarten through twelve. These tests measure one aspect of intelligence, namely, abstract reasoning ability, through subtests involving pictorial classification, pictorial analogy, and numerical relationships.

12. *Otis-Lennon Mental Ability Test* [Harcourt, Brace and World, Chicago, Illinois]. The first two levels (K-3) of these tests contain both pictorial and geometric items sampling the mental processes of classification, following directions, quantitative reasoning, verbal conceptualization, and reasoning by analogy. No reading is required at either level. The upper levels through grade thirteen contain both verbal and nonverbal items sampling fourteen different mental processes.

13. *Peabody Picture Vocabulary Test* [American Guidance Service, Inc., Minneapolis, Minnesota]. This is an individual wide range

picture vocabulary test utilizing a graduated series of 150 plates, each containing four pictures. The test is usable from age 2.6 through 18.

14. *Pictorial Test of Intelligence* [Houghton Mifflin Co., Boston, Massachusetts]. This is an individual test of general ability designed for administration by a trained examiner to one child at a time. It may be used with normal or handicapped individuals between the ages of three and eight. The child responds to verbal instructions of the examiner by selecting one of four drawings.

15. *Pintner General Ability Test (Verbal Series)* [Harcourt, Brace and World, Chicago, Illinois]. This is a four-battery, K-12, series measuring a variety of aspects of general mental ability.

16. *Pressey Classification and Verifying Tests* [Bobbs-Merrill Company, Indianapolis, Indiana]. This test provides a quick measure of general intelligence. The primary test (grades one through two) is composed completely of pictures. The intermediate (grades three through six) and senior (grades seven to adult) tests consist of tests of similarities and opposites, information, and practical arithmetic.

17. *Quick Test* [Psychological Test Specialists, Missoula, Montana]. This is a standardized individual intelligence test in three forms. It requires no reading, writing, or speaking by the testee. Anyone who can see the drawings, hear or read the word items, and signal yes or no can be tested. It may be used ages 2 through adult level.

18. *Slosson Intelligence Test for Children and Adults* [Slosson Educational Publications, East Aurora, New York]. This short individual test takes about 20 minutes to administer and score. It is an abbreviated form of the Stanford-Binet.

19. *S. R. A. Primary Mental Abilities Test* [Science Research Associates, Chicago, Illinois]. This test indicates grade placement for ability grouping. The areas tested include verbal meaning, perceptual speed, spatial ability, reasoning, and number sense. The primary battery requires no reading.

20. *Stanford-Binet Intelligence Scales: 1960 Revision* [Houghton Mifflin Co., Boston, Massachusetts]. This latest revision has combined *l* and *m* forms of the 1937 revision into one single form. Examiner must have special training.

21. *Wechsler Intelligence Scale for Children* (WISC) [Psychological Corporation, New York]. The WISC was standardized on twelve tests, which are divided into two subgroups identified as verbal and performance. Ordinarily only ten of these are administered to the subject, and the IQ tables are calculated on this basis.

APPENDIX III *Reading Survey Tests*

1. *American School Achievement Reading Tests* [Bobbs-Merrill Co., Indianapolis, Indiana]. This is a battery of tests for grade levels one through nine which provides information material on ability, skill, progress, and reading difficulties. The reading test measures sentence and word meaning and paragraph meaning.

2. *Botel Reading Inventory* [Follett Publishing Company, Chicago, Illinois]. This test, for grades one through twelve, measures word recognition, listening comprehension, and phonics. It is used to determine whether a pupil is reading at an instructional, frustration, or free-reading level.

3. *California Reading Test* [California Test Bureau, Monterey, California]. This is a battery divided into two major areas: reading vocabulary and comprehension. It has tests for grades one through fourteen.

4. *Developmental Reading Tests:* Primary Level [Lyons and Carnahan, Chicago, Illinois]. These tests are designed for grades 1 to 3, and provide a measure of basic vocabulary, general comprehension, and specific comprehension.

5. *Developmental Reading Tests:* Intermediate Level [Lyons and Carnahan, Chicago, Illinois]. These tests are designed for grades 4 to 6, and provide measures of basic vocabulary, factual reading, reading to organize, reading to evaluate-interpret, and reading to appreciate.

6. *The Durrell-Sullivan Reading Capacity and Achievement Tests* [Harcourt, Brace and World, Inc., New York]. The purpose of this test is to determine whether or not a pupil is reading up to his capacity. It is designed for grades 2 to 6: the primary level for grades 2.5 to 4.5; the intermediate for grades 3 through 6. It has two sections: a reading capacity section and a reading achievement section. The reading capacity section, composed entirely of pictures, has subtests on word meaning and on paragraph meaning. The reading achievement section contains a word meaning test, a paragraph meaning test, a spelling test, and written recall test. The reading capacity section requires no reading. The comprehension test (word meaning and paragraph meaning) of the reading capacity section is given orally. The reading achievement test is read by the pupil without help from the examiner.

7. *Gates-MacGinitie Reading Tests* [Bureau of Publications, Teachers College, Columbia University]. This test is available on different levels. Primary A, Grade one, and Primary B, Grade two, and Primary C, Grade three, measure vocabulary and comprehension. Primary CS, Grades two and three, measures speed and accuracy. It is only seven minutes long. Survey D, for grades four, five, and six, measures speed and accuracy, vocabulary, and comprehension. Survey E does the same for grades seven, eight, and nine.

8. *Iowa Silent Reading Test* [Harcourt, Brace and World, Chicago, Illinois]. This test is designed on two levels: grades four to eight and grades nine through thirteen. The elementary test measures rate and comprehension, directed reading to locate answers to factual questions, word meaning, paragraph comprehension, sentence meaning and location of information (alphabetizing, using guide words, and use of index). On the advanced level there are measures of rate of comprehension of connected prose, directed reading to locate answers to factual questions, poetry comprehension, word meaning in content areas, sentence meaning, paragraph comprehension, and location of information.

9. *Lee-Clark Reading Tests* (1963 Revision) [California Test Bureau, Monterey, California]. These tests, for grades K-2, measure readiness, reading achievement, and silent reading skills. The four subtests are auditory stimuli, visual stimuli, following directions, and completion.

10. *Metropolitan Achievement Tests: Reading* [Harcourt, Brace and World, Inc., New York]. This test is designed for five levels: primary I (last half of grade one), primary II (grade two), elementary (grades three and four), intermediate (grades five and six), and advanced (grades seven through nine). The primary tests measure word knowledge and word discrimination; the elementary test adds reading comprehension; and the intermediate and advanced tests measure word knowledge and reading comprehension.

11. *Monroe Revised Silent Reading Tests* [Bobbs-Merrill Co., Indianapolis, Indiana]. The tests, for grades three through twelve, consisting of exercises in which the student is asked to read seventeen short paragraphs and answer a question on each, measure both reading comprehension and reading rate.

12. *National Achievement Test* [Acorn Publishing Company, Long Island, New York]. This test measures sentence meaning, paragraph meaning, and speed. It is designed for grades four through nine.

13. *Nelson Lohmann Reading Test* [American Guidance Service, Inc.,

Minneapolis, Minnesota]. This test measures comprehension with a graduated sequence of difficulty. It is designed for grades four through eight.

14. *Nelson Reading Test* (1962 Edition) [Houghton Mifflin Company, Boston, Massachusetts]. This test, for grades three through nine, is designed to measure reading ability in terms of vocabulary and comprehension. This test replaces the Nelson Silent Reading Test.

15. *Pressey Diagnostic Reading Tests* [Bobbs, Merrill Company, Indianapolis, Indiana]. This test measures speed, vocabulary, and paragraph meaning. It is usable in grades three through nine.

16. *Primary Reading Test* [Acorn Publishing Company, Long Island, New York]. This test, for grades two through three, measures word recognition, sentence meaning, and paragraph meaning.

17. *Pupil Progress Series: Reading* [Scholastic Testing Service, Inc., Bensenville, Illinois]. This is a reading achievement test, measuring total comprehension, rate, vocabulary, and knowledge and use of sources. It is designed for grades one through eight.

18. *Sequential Tests of Educational Progress: Reading* [Educational Testing Service, Princeton, New Jersey]. This test measures five major categories of comprehension skills, abilities, and attitudes: ability to recall ideas, to translate ideas and make inferences, to analyze motivation (of the author), to analyze presentation, and ability to criticize (constructively). The test is usable grades four through fourteen.

19. *SRA Achievement Series: Reading* [Science Research Associates, Inc., Chicago, Illinois]. This test measures comprehension, vocabulary, verbal-pictorial association, and language perception. It is for grades one through nine.

20. *Stanford Achievement Test: Reading* [Harcourt, Brace and World, Inc., New York]. This test is on three levels: elementary (grades 3.0 to 4.9), intermediate (grades 5.0 to 6.9), and advanced (grades 7.0 to 9.0). It provides a paragraph meaning score, a word meaning score, and a total score.

21. *Stroud-Hieronymus Primary Reading Profiles* [Houghton Mifflin Co., Boston, Massachusetts]. This test is designed to evaluate pupil progress upon the completion of the usual first-grade reading program. Level 2 helps the teacher to determine the relative strengths and weaknesses in the pupil's ability to read by the time he has reached the end of the second year of instruction. Each level consists of a battery of five tests to be administered to the class as a group: Aptitude for Reading, Auditory Association, Word Recognition, Word Attack, and Comprehension.

APPENDIX IV   *Diagnostic Reading Tests*

1. *Bond-Clymer-Hoyt Silent Reading Diagnostic Tests* [Lyons and Carnahan, Chicago, Illinois]. This group test is designed for grades 2.5 to 6 and for retarded readers. It is made up of eleven subtests. These are: (1) recognition of words in isolation; (2) recognition of words in context; (3) recognition of reversible words in context; (4) location of parts of words useful in word recognition; (5) syllabication; (6) locating root words; (7) phonetic knowledge—general word elements; (8) recognition of beginning sounds; (9) rhyming sounds; (10) letter sounds; and (11) ability to blend visually and phonetically.

    This test is basically a test of silent reading skills. The chief weakness of the test is that it cannot be used with children who are nonreaders or who have serious reading problems.

2. *Botel Reading Inventory* [Follett Publishing Company, Chicago, Illinois]. This inventory consists of a Phonics Mastery Test, a Word Recognition Test, and a Word Opposites Test. It determines whether the pupil is reading at an instructional, frustration, or free-reading level.

3. *Diagnostic Reading Examination for Diagnosis of Special Difficulty in Reading* [C. H. Stoelting Company, Chicago, Illinois]. This test, for grades one through four, is a combination of assessment procedures consisting of Revised Stanford-Binet Scale, Gray's Standardized Oral Reading Paragraphs, Monroe's Standardized Silent Reading Tests, adaptation of Ayres Spelling Scale, arithmetic computation from Stanford Achievement Test, Iota Word Test, and eight other additional tests of special areas in reading.

4. *Diagnostic Reading Scales* [California Test Bureau, Monterey, California]. These scales, for grades one through eight, are individually administered tests designed to identify reading deficiencies that hinder pupils from reading adequately. The scale is recommended for normal and retarded readers at the elementary, junior high, and senior high levels. The test battery comprises three word recognition lists, twenty-two reading passages, and six supplementary phonics tests; consonant sounds, vowel sounds, consonant blends, common syllables, blends, and letter sounds. Three reading levels are yielded for each pupil: instruc-

tional level in oral reading, independent level in silent reading, and potential level in auditory comprehension.

5. *Diagnostic Reading Tests* [Committee on Diagnostic Reading Tests, Inc., Mountain Home, North Carolina; distributed also by Science Research Associates, Chicago]. The test has a kindergarten-fourth-grade battery, a lower level battery (grades four to eight), and an upper level battery (grades eight to thirteen). It includes tests for word recognition, comprehension, vocabulary, story reading, story comprehension, and, at the upper levels, rate of comprehension.

6. *Diagnostic Reading Test* [Scholastic Testing Service, Inc., Benseville, Illinois]. This series of tests is offered on four levels, primary level I, primary level II, elementary (grades four, five, and six), and advanced (grades seven and eight). The primary level I test measures vocabulary, rate, and comprehension and provides diagnostic subscores for word recognition, word to content relation, words in use, recalling information, locating information, and reading for descriptions. The primary level II provides subscores also for reading for meaning and following directions. The elementary and advanced levels measure rate, comprehension, and knowledge and use of sources. They provide additional subscores for functions of common sources, selection of suitable sources for a specific purpose, use of the index, and use of the table of contents.

7. *Doren Diagnostic Reading Test* [American Guidance Service, Inc., Minneapolis, Minnesota]. This group test for children in need of remedial instruction tests for beginning sounds, sight words, rhyming, whole word recognition, words within words, speech consonants, blending, vowels, ending sounds, discriminate guessing, and letter recognition.

8. *Durrell Analysis of Reading Difficulty*, New Edition [Harcourt, Brace and World, Inc., New York]. This test is designed for grades one to six and is made up of the following subtests: (1) Oral Reading Test; (2) Silent Reading Test; (3) Listening Comprehension Test; (4) Word Recognition and Word Analysis Test; (5) Naming Letters; (6) Identifying Letters Named; (7) Matching Letters; (8) Writing Letters; (9) Visual Memory of Words; (10) Hearing Sounds in Words; (11) Learning to Hear Sounds in Words; (12) Learning Rate; (13) Phonic Spelling of Words; (14) Spelling Test; and (15) Handwriting Test.

This test is generally recommended for less severe cases. The profile is not as adequate as it might be in that it makes no provision for recording tests 5 through 13. The check list of errors that accompanies the tests is probably the best of its kind.

9. *Dvorak-Van Wagenen Diagnostic Examination of Silent Reading Abilities* [Psycho-Educational Research Laboratories, Minneapolis, Minnesota]. This test is provided on three levels: four to six, seven to nine, and ten to twelve. It measures rate of comprehension, perception of relations between words, vocabulary in context, vocabulary of isolated words, range of general information, ability to grasp the central thought of a paragraph, ability to grasp an idea that is spread through several sentences, and the ability to interpret inferences from ideas in a paragraph.

10. *Gates-McKillop Reading Diagnostic Tests* [Bureau of Publications, Teachers College, Columbia University]. This battery, for grades one through eight, is for detailed diagnosis of specific deficiencies in reading performance. It is a revision of the Gates Reading Diagnostic Tests and includes a battery of individually administered tests. It tests oral reading, word perception, phrase perception, blending word parts, giving letter sounds, naming letters, recognizing visual form of sounds, auditory blending, spelling, oral vocabulary, syllabication, and auditory discrimination.

11. *McCullough Word-Analysis Tests* [Experimental Edition, Ginn and Company, Chicago, Illinois]. This test, for grades four through six, provides ten scores; initial blends and digraphs, phonetic discrimination, matching letters to vowel sounds, sounding whole words, interpreting phonetic symbols, phonetic analysis, dividing words into syllables, root words in affixed forms, structural analysis, and total score.

12. *Monroe Diagnostic Reading Test* [C. H. Stoelting Company, Chicago, Illinois]. This test offers a diagnostic profile showing specific reading retardations as well as arithmetic, spelling and mental age.

13. *Pupil Progress Diagnostic Reading Tests* [C. H. Stoelting Company, Chicago, Illinois]. This series of tests is offered on four levels: primary level I, primary level II, elementary (grades four, five, and six), and advanced (grades seven and eight). The primary level I test measures vocabulary, rate, and comprehension and provides diagnostic sub-scores for word recognition, word to content relation, words in use, recalling information, locating information, and reading for descriptions. The primary level II provides subscores also for reading for meaning and following directions. The elementary and advanced levels measure rate, comprehension, and knowledge and use of sources. They provide additional subscores for functions of common sources, selection of suitable sources for a specific purpose, use of the index, and use of the table of contents.

14. *The Roswell-Chall Diagnostic Reading Test of Word Analysis Skills* [Essay Press, New York, New York]. This is a test, for grades two through six, of word analysis skills, constructed for teachers and psychologists who need a simple test to supplement information obtained from standardized silent and oral reading tests. The basic skills measured by this test provide the teacher with a qualitative evaluation of the pupil's strengths and weaknesses in word recognition. The five parts deal with single consonants and combinations, short vowel sounds, rule of silent e, vowel combinations, and syllabication.

15. *Stanford Diagnostic Reading Test* [Harcourt, Brace and World, Chicago, Illinois]. This test, for grades 2.5–8.5, aids in the identification of specific strengths and weaknesses in reading comprehension, vocabulary, syllabication, comprehension, auditory skills, various aspects of phonetic analysis, and rate of reading. The tests are auditorily loaded.

APPENDIX V   *Oral Reading Tests*

1. *Gilmore Oral Reading Test* [Harcourt, Brace and World, Chicago, Illinois]. This individual test, for grades one through eight, consists of ten paragraphs, measuring comprehension, speed, and accuracy of comprehension. Pupil errors can be recorded: substitutions, mispronunciations, insertions, and omissions.

2. *Gray Standardized Oral Reading Check Tests* [Bobbs Merrill Co., Indianapolis, Indiana]. This test, for grades one through eight, can be used to secure measures of progress of pupils in rate and accuracy of oral reading. The information obtained will aid the teacher in determining the specific nature of problems which poor readers have and what can be done to correct difficulties.

3. *Gray Standardized Oral Reading Paragraphs Test* [Bobbs Merrill Co., Indianapolis, Indiana]. This test is designed for grades one through eight and measures rate and accuracy of oral reading. As the child reads the various passages aloud, all errors and hesitations are recorded: gross mispronunciation, partial mispronunciation, omission, insertion, repetition, substitution and inversion. Other observations include word by word reading, poor phrasing, lack of expression, monotonous tone, poor enunciation, overuse of phonics, no method of word attack, head movement, finger pointing, and loss of place. The teacher under-

lines mispronounced words, encircles omissions, writes in substitutions, and indicates any repetitions with a wavy line. This test emphasizes the process rather than the end *product* of reading. It represents a record of the errors that can be studied rather than a total score that may mean little or nothing. It is an individual test and consists of twelve paragraphs progressing from simple to more difficult material.

4. *Leavell Analytical Oral Reading Test* [American Guidance Service Inc., Minneapolis, Minnesota]. This is an oral reading test, administered individually, in which the content is a continuous story. It is designed for grades one through ten and is made up of paragraphs of increasing difficulty. The first paragraph is adapted to beginning readers and the last presents difficulty to high school students. It provides measures for comprehension, mechanical errors, and rate.

The following errors are noted: repetition of words, unknown words, oral spelling of words, inserted or miscalled words, omitted words, lines skipped, and lines reread.

5. *Slosson Oral Reading Test* [Slosson Educational Publications, East Aurora, New York]. This is an individual test for grades one through twelve and is based on the ability to pronounce words at different levels of difficulty.

Bibliography

CHAPTER 1

1. Aaron, I. E., "What Teachers and Prospective Teachers Know About Phonics Generalizations," *Journal of Educational Research*, 53 (May 1960) 323–330.

2. Austin, Mary C., Kenney, Helen J., Gutmann, Ann R., and Fraggos, Madeleine, *The Torch Lighters: Tomorrow's Teachers of Reading*, Cambridge: Harvard University Press, 1961.

3. Buswell, G. T., "An Experimental Study of the Eye-Voice Span in Reading," *Supplementary Educational Monographs*, No. 17, Chicago: University of Chicago, 1920.

4. Cook, Luella B., "Man's Reach Should Exceed His Grasp," *English Journal*, 46 (February 1957) 73–78.

5. Cribbin, James J., "The Teacher: Hercules, Tantalus or Sisyphus?" *Education*, 80 (October 1959), 100–105.

6. Durrell, Donald D., "Challenge and Experiment in Teaching Reading," *Challenge and Experiment in Reading*, International Reading Association Conference Proceedings, 7 (1962), 13–22.

7. Gates, Arthur I., *The Improvement of Reading*, New York: The Macmillan Company, 1927.

8. Hanson, Earl H., "Uses and Misuses of Criticism," *NEA Journal*, 48 (October 1959), 35–37.

9. James, William, *Talks to Teachers on Psychology*, New York: Holt, Rinehart and Winston, Inc., 1920.

10. Judd, C. H., and Buswell, G. T., "Silent Reading: A Study of the Various Types," *Supplementary Educational Monographs*, No. 23, Chicago: University of Chicago Press, 1922.

11. Kendler, Howard H., "Stimulus-Response Psychology and Audiovisual Education," *AV Communication Review*, 9 (No. 5, 1961) 33–41.

12. Ramsey, Z. Wallace, "Will Tomorrow's Teachers Know and Teach Phonics?" *The Reading Teacher*, 15 (January 1962), 241–245.

13. Rogers, Carl. *On Becoming a Person*. Houghton Mifflin Company, Boston, 1961.

14. Smith, Nila Banton, "What Have We Accomplished in Reading?—

A Review of the Past Fifty Years," *Elementary English,* 38 (March 1961) 141–150.

15. Spache, George D. and Baggett, Mary E. "What Do Teachers Know About Phonics and Syllabication?" *The Reading Teacher,* 19 (November 1965) 96–99.

16. Thorndike, E. L., "Reading as Reasoning: A Study of Mistakes in Paragraph Reading," *Journal of Educational Psychology,* 8 (June 1917) 323–332.

17. Vogel, Francis X., "The Skiles Program for Reading Improvement," *The Clearing House,* 35 (February 1961), 331–335.

18. Witty, Paul, "Reading Instruction—A Forward Look," *Elementary English,* 38 (March 1961), 151–164.

19. Young, Ross N., *Reading in the Junior and Senior High School,* Minneapolis: Educational Test Bureau, 1927.

CHAPTER 2

1. Ballantine, F. A., "Age Changes in Measures of Eye Movements in Silent Reading," *Studies in the Psychology of Reading,* pp. 67–108, Monographs in Education, No. 4, Ann Arbor: University of Michigan Press, 1951.

2. Bayle, Evalyn, "The Nature and Causes of Regressive Movements in Reading," *Journal of Experimental Education,* 11 (September 1942) 16–36.

3. Bond, Guy L., and Tinker, Miles A. *Reading Difficulties: Their Diagnosis and Correction.* Appleton-Century-Crofts, Division of Meredith Publishing Company, New York, 1967, p. 22.

4. Botel, Morton. "What Linguistics Says to the Teacher of Reading and Spelling." *The Reading Teacher,* 18 (December, 1964) 188–193.

5. Bruner, J. S., "On Perceptual Readiness," *Psychological Review,* 64 (March 1957) 123–152.

6. Burton, W. H., "The Characteristics of a Good Reading Program," *Developing Personal and Group Relations Through Reading,* Fifteenth Yearbook of the Claremont College Reading Conference, Claremont, 1950, pp. 3–15.

7. Buswell, G. T., *Fundamental Reading Habits: A Study of Their Development,* Supplementary Educational Monographs, No. 21, Chicago: University of Chicago Press, 1922.

8. Dallmann, Martha, "Reading for Meaning," *Grade Teacher,* 74 (February 1957) 34, 97.

9. Dawson, Mildred A., "The Role of Oral Reading in School and Life Activities," *Elementary English,* 35 (January 1958) 30–37.

10. Dawson, Mildred A., and Bamman, Henry A., *Fundamentals of*

Reading Instruction, Longmans, Green and Company, Inc., New York, 1959.

11. Deboer, J. J., and Dallmann, Martha. *The Teaching of Reading.* Henry Holt and Company, New York, 1960, p. 19.

12. *The Evolution and Growth of Controlled Reading Techniques,* Huntington, New York: Educational Developmental Laboratories, Inc., 1958.

13. Gates, A. I., "Character and Purposes of the Yearbook," *Reading in the Elementary School,* Forty-eighth Yearbook of the National Society for the Study of Education, Part II, pp. 1–9, Chicago: University of Chicago Press, 1949.

14. Gibson, Eleanor J. "Experimental Psychology of Learning to Read," p. 42 in *The Disabled Reader,* ed. by John Money, Johns Hopkins Press, Baltimore, 1966.

15. Goodman, Kenneth S. "A Linguistic Study of Cues and Miscues in Reading." *Elementary English,* 42 (October, 1965) 639–643.

16. Gray, W. S., "Growth in Understanding of Reading and Its Development Among Youth," *Keeping Reading Programs Abreast of the Times,* Supplementary Educational Monographs, no. 72, pp. 8–13, Chicago: University Press, 1950.

17. Harris, Albert J. *How to Increase Reading Ability.* David McKay Company, Inc., New York, 1961, p. 10.

18. Hebb, D. O., *A Textbook of Psychology,* Philadelphia: W. B. Saunders Company, 1958.

19. Hildreth, Gertrude, *Teaching Reading,* New York: Holt, Rinehart and Winston, Inc., 1958.

20. Horn, Ernest, *Methods of Instruction in the Social Studies,* New York: Charles Scribner's Sons, 1937.

21. Jan-Tausch, James, "Concrete Thinking as a Factor in Reading Comprehension," *Challenge and Experiment in Reading.* International Reading Association Conference Proceedings, 7 (1962), 161–164.

22. Langman, Muriel Potter, "The Reading Process: A Descriptive, Interdisciplinary Approach," *Genetic Psychology Monographs,* 62 (August 1960) 1–40.

23. Leverett, Hollis M., "Vision Test Performance of School Children," *American Journal of Ophthalmology,* 44 (October 1957) 508–519.

24. Liublinskaya, A. A., "The Development of Children's Speech and Thought," *Psychology in the Soviet Union,* edited by Brian Simon, pp. 197–204, Stanford, California: Stanford University Press, 1957.

25. Norberg, Kenneth, "Perception Research and Audio-Visual Education," *Readings for Educational Psychology,* ed. by W. A. Fullagar, H. G. Lewis, and C. F. Cumbee, pp. 26–36, New York: Thomas Y. Crowell Company, 1956.

26. Schmidt, Bernard. "Changing Patterns of Eye Movement." *Journal of Reading*. 9 (May, 1966) 379–385.

27. Semelmeyer, Madeline, "Can Johnny Read?" *Education,* 77 (April 1957) 505–512.

28. Shaw, Philip, "Rhetorical Guides to Reading Comprehension," *The Reading Teacher,* 11 (April 1958), 239–243.

29. Shores, J. Harlan. "Dimensions of Reading Speed and Comprehension." *Elementary English,* 45 (January 1968) 23–28, 43.

30. Smith, D. E. P., and Carrigan, Patricia. *The Nature of Reading Disability.* Harcourt, Brace and World Company, Inc., New York, 1959, p. 6.

31. Smith, Henry P., and Dechant, Emerald V., *Psychology in Teaching Reading,* Englewood Cliffs, N.J.: Prentice-Hall, Inc., 1961.

32. Spencer, L. Peter. "The Reading Process and Types of Reading." *Claremont College Reading Conference,* Eleventh Yearbook, 1946, pp. 19–20.

33. Stroud, James B., *Psychology in Education,* New York: Longmans, Green and Company, 1956.

34. Taylor, Earl A., "The Spans: Perception, Apprehension, and Recognition," *American Journal of Ophthalmology,* 44 (October 1957) 501–507.

35. Taylor, E. A., *Eyes, Visual Anomalies and the Fundamental Reading Skill,* New York: Reading and Study Skills Center, 1959.

36. Taylor, S. E., Frackenpohl, H., and Pettee, J. L., *Grade Level Norms for the Components of the Fundamental Reading Skill,* Huntington, N.Y.: Educational Developmental Laboratories, Inc., Bulletin No. 3, 1960.

37. Taylor, Stanford E. "Eye Movements in Reading: Facts and Fallacies." *American Educational Research Journal,* 2 (November, 1965) 187–202.

38. Thorndike, Edward L., "Reading as Reasoning: A Study of Mistakes in Paragraph Reading," *Journal of Educational Psychology,* 8 (June 1917) 323–332.

39. Tillson, M. M. "Changes in Eye-Movement Patterns." *Journal of Higher Education,* 27 (November, 1955) 442–445.

40. Tinker, M. A., "The Use and Limitations of Eye-Movement Measures in Reading," *Psychological Review,* 40 (July 1933) 381–87.

41. Tinker, M. A., "Time Relations for Eye-Movement Measures in Reading," *Journal of Educational Psychology,* 38 (January 1947) 1–10.

42. Tinker, M. A., "Recent Studies of Eye Movements in Reading," *Psychological Bulletin,* 55 (July 1958) 215–231.

43. Walker, R. Y., "The Eye Movements of Good Readers," *Studies in Experimental and Theoretical Psychology: Psychological Mono-*

graphs, 44 (Nov. 3, 1933) 95–117.

44. Whatmough, Joshua, *Language: A Modern Synthesis,* New York: St. Martin's Press, Inc., 1956.

45. Wilson, Robert M. "Oral Reading is Fun." *The Reading Teacher,* 19 (October, 1965) 41–43.

CHAPTER 3

1. Alexander, Duane and Money, John. "Reading Disability and the Problem of Direction Sense." *The Reading Teacher,* 20 (February, 1967) 404–409.

2. Anastasi, Anne, and Foley, John P. Jr., "A Proposed Reorientation in the Heredity-Environment Controversy," *The Child: A Book of Readings,* ed. by Jerome M. Seidman, pp. 2–15, New York: Holt, Rinehart & Winston, Inc., 1958.

3. Baller, Warren R., and Charles, Don C. *The Psychology of Human Growth and Development.* Holt, Rinehart, and Winston, New York, 1961.

4. Balow, I. H. "Lateral Dominance Characteristics and Reading Achievement in the First Grade." *Journal of Psychology,* 55 (1962) 323–328.

5. Balow, I. H., and Balow, B. "Lateral Dominance and Reading Achievement in the Second Grade." *American Educational Research Journal,* 1 (1964) 139–143.

6. Belmont, Herman S. "Psychological Influences on Learning." *Sociological and Psychological Factors in Reading.* Proceedings of the 21st Annual Reading Institute, Temple University, Philadelphia, 1964, 15–26.

7. Belmont, Lillian, and Brick, H. G. "Lateral Dominance, Lateral Awareness, and Reading Disability." *Child Development,* 36 (March, 1965) 57–71.

8. Bing, Lois B., "Vision and Reading," *The Reading Teacher,* 14 (March 1961) 241–244.

9. Bond, Guy L., and Tinker, Miles A., *Reading Difficulties: Their Diagnosis and Correction,* New York: Appleton-Century-Crofts, Inc., 1957.

10. Bond, Guy L., and Tinker, Miles A. *Reading Difficulties: Their Diagnosis and Correction.* Appleton-Century-Crofts, Inc., New York, 1967.

11. Bothwell, Hazel. "The Child with Impaired Hearing." *NEA Journal,* 56 (November, 1967) 44–46.

12. Brungardt, Joe B., and Brungardt, Mike J. "Let's Stop the Prevailing Injustices to Children," *Kansas Teacher* 73 (January, 1965) 14–15, 50.

13. Brzeinski, Joseph E. "Beginning Reading in Denver." *The Reading Teacher,* 18 (October, 1964) 16–21.

14. Brzeinski, Joseph; M. Lucile Harrison, and Paul McKee. "Should Johnny Read in Kindergarten?" A Report on the Denver Experiment." *NEA Journal,* 56 (March, 1967) 23–25.

15. Bugelski, B. R., *The Psychology of Learning Applied to Teaching,* Bobbs-Merrill Company, Inc., Indianapolis, 1964.

16. Chall, Jeanne; Roswell, Florence G.; and Blumenthal, Susan H. "Auditory Blending Ability: A Factor in Success in Beginning Reading." *The Reading Teacher,* 17 (1963) 113–118.

17. Cohen, Alice and Glass, Gerald G. "Lateral Dominance and Reading Ability." *The Reading Teacher,* 21 (January, 1968) 343–348.

18. Coleman, Howard M. "Visual Perception and Reading Dysfunction." *Journal of Learning Disabilities,* 1 (February, 1968) 26–31.

19. Davis, H., editor, *Hearing and Deafness: A Guide for Laymen,* New York: Murray Hill Books, Inc., 1947.

20. Durkin, Dolores, "Children Who Read Before Grade One," *The Reading Teacher,* 14 (January 1961) 163–166.

21. Durkin, Dolores, "Reading Instruction and the Five-Year-Old Child," *Challenge and Experiment in Reading,* International Reading Association Conference Proceedings, VII (1962), 23–27.

22. Durkin, Dolores. "The Achievement of Pre-School Readers: Two Longitudinal Studies." *Reading Research Quarterly,* 1 (Summer, 1966) 5–36.

23. Durkin, Dolores. *Children Who Read Early.* Teachers College Press, Teachers College, Columbia University, New York, 1966.

24. Dvorine, Israel, "What You Should Know About Sight—Part III—Symptoms of Abnormal Function of the Visual Process," *Education,* 79 (December 1958) 240–246.

25. Eames, Thomas H., "Visual Handicaps to Reading," *Journal of Education,* 141 (February 1959) 1–36.

26. Eames, Thomas H., "The Effect of Endocrine Disorders on Reading," *The Reading Teacher,* 12 (April 1959) 263–265.

27. Eames, Thomas H., "Some Neural and Glandular Bases of Learning," *Journal of Education,* 142 (April 1960) 1–36.

28. Eames, Thomas H., "Physical Factors in Reading," *The Reading Teacher,* 15 (May 1962) 427–432.

29. Eberl, Marguerite, "Visual Training and Reading," *Clinical Studies in Reading II,* Supplementary Educational Monographs, No. 77, pp. 141–148, Chicago: University of Chicago Press, 1953.

30. Engh, Jeri. "Are You Sure Your Child Can Hear?" *Parent's Magazine,* February, 1968.

31. Enstrom, E. A., "The Extent of the Use of the Left Hand in Hand-

writing," *Journal of Educational Research,* 55 (February 1962) 234–235.

32. Feinberg, Richard, "A Study of Some Aspects of Peripheral Visual Acuity," *American Journal of Optometry and Archives of American Academy of Optometry,* 62 (February–March 1949) 1–23.

33. Gray, George W., "The Great Ravelled Knot," *Scientific American,* 179 (October 1948) 26–39.

34. Harris, A. J., *How To Increase Reading Ability,* third edition. New York: Longmans, Green and Company, 1956.

35. Harris, A. J., "Lateral Dominance, Directional Confusion, and Reading Disability," *Journal of Psychology,* 44 (October 1957) 283–294.

36. Harris, Albert J., "Perceptual Difficulties in Reading Disability," *Changing Concepts of Reading Instruction,* International Reading Association Conference Proceedings, pp. 282–290, New York: Scholastic Magazines, 1961.

37. Harris, Albert J. *Effective Teaching of Reading.* David McKay Company, Inc., New York, 1962.

38. Henry, Jules. *Culture Against Man.* Random House, New York, 1963.

39. Hinshelwood, James, *Congenital Word-Blindness,* London: H. K. Lewis and Company, Ltd., 1917.

40. Hirsch, Katrina de, "Reading and Total Language Disability," *Changing Concepts of Reading Instruction,* International Reading Association Conference Proceedings, pp. 211–214, New York: Scholastic Magazines, 1961.

41. Holmes, Jack A., "When Should and Could Johnny Learn to Read?" *Challenge and Experiment in Reading,* International Reading Association Conference Proceedings, VII (1962), 237–240.

42. Horrworth, Gloria L. "Listening: A Facet of Oral Language." *Elementary English,* 43 (December, 1966) 856–864, 868.

43. James, William. *Talks to Teachers on Psychology,* New York: Holt, Rinehart and Winston, Inc., 1920.

44. Jensen, M. B., "Reading Deficiency as Related to Cerebral Injury and to Neurotic Behavior," *Journal of Applied Psychology,* 27 (December 1943) 535–545.

45. Karlin, Robert. "Research Results and Classroom Practices." *The Reading Teacher,* 21 (December, 1967) 211–226.

46. Ketchum, E. Gillet. "Neurological and Psychological Trends in Reading Diagnosis." *The Reading Teacher,* 17 (May, 1964) 589–593.

47. Knox, Gertrude E., "Classroom Symptoms of Visual Difficulty," *Clinical Studies in Reading:* II, Supplementary Educational Monographs, No. 77, pp. 97–101, Chicago: University of Chicago Press, 1953.

48. Kosinski, W., "Die Myopie als Variköses Syndrom der Augen," *Klinische Monatsblätter fur Augenheilkunde,* 130 (1957) 266–270, cited by Linksz, Arthur, "Optics and Visual Physiology," *A. M. A. Archives of Ophthalmology* 59 (June 1958) 901–969.

49. Labov, W. "Linguistic Research on Non-Standard English of Negro Children;" paper read at New York Society for the Experimental Study of Education, New York, 1965.

50. Lindsley, Donald B., "Bilateral Differences in Brain Potentials from the Two Cerebral Hemispheres in Relation to Laterality and Stuttering," *Journal of Experimental Psychology,* 26 (1940) 211.

51. MacGinitie, Walter H. "Auditory Perception in Reading." *Education,* 87 (May, 1967) 532–538.

52. Mason, George E., and Prater, Norma Jean. "Early Reading and Reading Instruction." *Elementary English,* 43 (May, 1966) 483–488, 527.

53. Mason, George E. and Prater, Norma J. "Social Behavioral Aspects of Teaching Reading to Kindergartners." *Journal of Educational Research,* 60 (October, 1966) 58–61.

54. McCabe, Brian F. "The Etiology of Deafness." *Volta Review,* 65 (October 1963) 471–477.

55. McCormick, Nancy. "The Countdown on Beginning Reading." *The Reading Teacher,* 20 (November, 1966) 115–120.

56. Mills, Lloyd, "The Functions of the Eyes in the Acquisition of an Education," *Journal of the American Medical Association,* 93 (September 1929) 841–845.

57. Money, J.; Alexander, D.; and Walker, H. T. Jr. *A Standardized Road-Map Test to Direction Sense.* Johns Hopkins Press, Baltimore, 1965.

58. Mood, Darlene W. "Reading in Kindergarten?" *Educational Leadership,* 24 (1967) 399–403.

59. Muehl, S. "Relation Between Word Recognition Errors and Hand-Eye Preference in Preschool Children." *Journal of Educational Psychology,* 54 (1963) 316–321.

60. National Committee for Research in Neurological Disorders, *Exploring the Brain of Man,* Minneapolis: The Medical School, University of Minnesota.

60*a*. Napoli, Joseph. "Environmental Factors and Reading Ability." *The Reading Teacher,* 21 (March, 1968), 552–557, 607.

61. Nelson, C. Donald, "Subtle Brain Damage: Its Influence on Learning and Language," *The Elementary School Journal,* 61 (March 1961) 317–321.

62. O'Connor, Clarence D., and Streng, Alice. "Teaching the Acoustically Handicapped." *The Education of Exceptional Children,* Forty-

ninth Yearbook of the National Society for the Study of Education, Part II, University of Chicago Press, Chicago, 1950, 152–176.

62a. Olson, W. D. "Child Growth and Development." *Reading,* Association for Childhood Education International (Washington, D.C., 1956), 2–5.

63. Orton, S. T., "An Impediment to Learning to Read—A Neurological Explanation of the Reading Disability," *School and Society,* 28 (September 1928) 286–290.

64. Plessas, Gus P., and Oakes, Clifton R. "Prereading Experiences of Selected Early Readers." *The Reading Teacher,* 17 (January, 1964) 241–245.

65. Rosenbloom, Alfred A. Jr., O.D., "Promoting Visual Readiness for Reading," *Changing Concepts of Reading Instruction,* International Reading Association Conference Proceedings, pp. 89–93, New York: Scholastic Magazines, 1961.

66. Schiffman, Gilbert B. "An Interdisciplinary Approach to the Identification and Remediation of Severe Reading Disabilities." *Junior College and Adult Reading Programs,* National Reading Conference, Milwaukee, 1967, pp. 14–26.

66a. Schubert, Delwyn G., and Watson, Howard N. "Effects of Induced Astimatism." *The Reading Teacher,* 21 (March, 1968), 547–551.

67. Silvaroli, Nickolas J., and Wheelock, Warren B. "An Investigation of Auditory Discrimination Training for Beginning Readers." *The Reading Teacher,* 20 (December, 1966) 247–251.

68. Silver, Archie A., and Hagin, Rosa A. "Maturation of Perceptual Functions in Children with Specific Reading Disability." *The Reading Teacher,* 19 (January, 1966) 253–259.

69. Smirnov, A. A., "Psychological Research, 1953–5," *Psychology in the Soviet Union,* ed. by Brian Simon, pp. 29–45, Stanford: Stanford University Press, 1957.

69a. Smith, D. E. P., and Carrigan, Patricia M. *The Nature of Reading Disability* (New York: Harcourt, Brace and Co., 1959).

70. Stephens, W. E.; Cunningham, E. S.; and Stigler, B. J. "Reading Readiness and Eye Hand Preference Patterns in First Grade Children." *Exceptional Children,* 33 (1967) 481–488.

71. Strang, R., and Bracken, D. K., *Making Better Readers,* Boston: D. C. Heath and Company, 1957.

72. Stroud, James B., *Psychology in Education,* New York: Longmans, Green and Company, 1956.

73. Sutton, Marjorie H. "Readiness for Reading at the Kindergarten Level." *The Reading Teacher,* 17 (January, 1964) 234–239.

74. Taylor, Stanford E., *Speed Reading Vs. Improved Reading Efficiency,* Educational Development Laboratories, New York: Huntington (April 1962).

75. Tinker, Karen J. "The Role of Laterality in Reading Disability." In J. A. Figurel (Ed.) *Reading and Inquiry.* Proceedings of the International Reading Association, 1965, 300–303.

76. Vygotsky, Lev Semenovich. *Thought and Language,* ed. and translated by Eugenia Hanfmann and Gertrude Vakar. John Wiley and Sons, Inc., New York, (c) 1952, p. 104.

77. Wepman, Joseph M., "The Interrelationship of Hearing, Speech and Reading," *The Reading Teacher,* 14 (March 1961) 245–247.

78. White, Robert W., *The Abnormal Personality,* New York: The Ronald Press Company, 1956.

79. Witty, Paul, and Kopel, D., *Reading and the Educative Process,* Boston: Ginn & Company, 1939.

80. Worley, Stinson E., and Story, William E. "Socio-Economic Status and Language Facility of Beginning First Graders." *The Reading Teacher,* 20 (February, 1967) 400–403.

CHAPTER 4

1. Barbe, Walter B., "A Study of the Reading of Gifted High-School Students," *Educational Administration and Supervision,* 38 (March 1952) 148–154.

2. Bentzen, Francis. "Sex Ratios in Learning and Behavior Disorders." *American Journal of Orthopsychiatry,* 33 (January, 1963) 92–98.

3. Bettelheim, Bruno, "The Decision to Fail," *The School Review,* 69 (Winter 1961) 377–412.

4. Brookover, W. B. "A Social Psychological Conception of Classroom Learning." *School and Society,* 87 (February, 1959) 84–87.

5. Brookover, W. B., Shailer, T., and Paterson, A. "Self Concept of Ability and School Achievement." *Sociology of Education,* 37 (Spring, 1964) 271–278.

6. Budoff, Milton and Quinlan, Donald. "Reading Progress as Related to Efficiency of Visual and Aural Learning in the Primary Grades," *Journal of Educational Psychology,* 55 (February, 1964) 247–252; Budoff, Milton, and Quinlan, Donald. "Auditory and Visual Learning in Primary Grade Children," *Child Development,* 35 (June, 1964) 583–586.

7. Chambers, D. "Let Them Read." *The Reading Teacher,* 20 (1966) 254–257.

8. Clark, W. W., "Boys and Girls—Are There Significant Ability and Achievement Differences?" *Phi Delta Kappan,* 41 (November 1959) 73–76.

9. Cummins, W. D., and Fagin, Barry, *Principles of Educational Psychology.* Ronald Press, New York, 1954.

10. Committee of the Upper Grades Study Council, "Developing the

Reading Interests of Children," *Elementary English Review*, 20 (November 1943) 279–286.

11. Davis, O. L., and Slobodian, June Jenkinson. "Teacher Behavior Toward Boys and Girls During First Grade Reading Instruction." *American Educational Research Journal*, 4 (May, 1967) 261–269.

12. Dolch, E. W., *A Manual For Remedial Reading*, second edition, Champaign: Garrard Press, 1945.

13. Duffy, Gerald G. "Developing the Reading Habit." *The Reading Teacher*, 21 (December, 1967) 253–256.

14. Durrell, Donald D., "Challenge and Experiment in Teaching Reading," *Challenge and Experiment in Reading*, International Reading Association Conference Proceedings, 7 (1962), 13–22.

15. Dykstra, Robert. "Auditory Discrimination Abilities and Beginning Reading Achievement." *Reading Research Quarterly*, 1 (Spring, 1966) 5–34.

16. Eisenberg, Leon. "Epidemiology of Reading Retardation," pp. 3–19 in *The Disabled Reader* by John Money, Johns Hopkins Press, Baltimore, 1966.

17. Eysenck, H. J. *The Structure of Human Personality*. Methuen and Company, Ltd., London, 1953.

18. Foster, Guy L., "Freshman Problem: 44% Couldn't Read Their Texts," *The Clearing House*, 29 (March 1955) 414–417.

19. Frymier, Jack R. "The Effect of Class Size Upon Reading Achievement in First Grade." *The Reading Teacher*, 18 (November, 1964) 90–93.

20. Getzels, Jacob W. "The Nature of Reading Interests: Psychological Aspects." *Developing Permanent Interest in Reading*, Supplementary Educational Monographs, No. 84, University of Chicago Press, Chicago, 1956, pp. 5–9.

21. Gray, W. S., *The Teaching of Reading and Writing*, UNESCO, Chicago: Scott, Foresman & Company, 1956.

22. Harris, A. J., "Unsolved Problems in Reading: A Symposium II," *Elementary English*, 31 (November 1954) 416–430.

23. Harris, Albert J., *How to Increase Reading Ability*, third edition. New York: David McKay Company, Inc., 1956.

24. Haywood, Danielle H. "Audio-Visual Concept Formation," *Journal of Educational Psychology*, 56 (June) 126–132.

25. Hildreth, Gertrude, "Some Misconceptions Concerning Phonics," *Elementary English*, 34 (January 1957) 26–29.

26. Holmes, J. A. "Emotional Factors and Reading Disabilities." *The Reading Teacher*, 9 (October, 1955) 11–17.

27. Hughes, Ann; Carl B. Smith; and Nellie Thomas, "Beginning Reading for Disadvantaged Children." *The Instructor*, 75 (March, 1966) 128–129, 160.

28. King, Ethel M. and Muehl, Siegmar. "Different Sensory Cues as Aids in Beginning Reading." *The Reading Teacher,* 19 (December, 1965) 163–168.

29. Jersild, Arthur T., "Emotional Development," *Manual of Child Psychology,* ed. by Leonard Carmichael, New York: John Wiley & Sons, Inc., 1954.

30. Malmquist, Eve. "Organizing Instruction to Prevent Reading Disabilities." *Reading as an Intellectual Activity,* International Reading Association Conference Proceedings, Scholastic Magazines, New York, 1963, pp. 36–39.

31. McCabe, Brian F. "The Etiology of Deafness." *Volta Review,* 65 (October, 1963) 471–477.

32. McNeil, J. D. and Keislar, E. R. "Value of the Oral Response in Beginning Reading: An Experimental Study. *British Journal of Psychology,* 33 (1963) 162–168.

33. Murphy, George E. "And Now—The Package Deal." *The Reading Teacher,* 20 (April, 1967) 615–620.

34. Nelson, Frederic, "How Well Are We Teaching Reading?—Reply," *Controversial Issues in Reading,* 1 (April 1961) 1–3; Tenth Annual Reading Conference, Lehigh University.

35. Ofman, William and Shawvitz, Morton. "Kinesthetic Method in Remedial Reading," *Journal of Experimental Education,* 31 (March, 1963) 317–319.

36. Patel, A. S. and Parlikar, R. K. "Comprehension of Learning Materials as a Function of Aural, Visual and Pictorial Presentation of Material," *Manas.* 8 (August, 1961) 15–19.

37. Preston, Ralph C., "A Comparative Study of the Reading Achievement of German and American Children," *Changing Concepts of Reading Instruction,* International Reading Association, pp. 109–112, Vol. 6, New York: Scholastic Magazines, 1961.

38. Reed, David W. "A Theory of Language, Speech and Writing." *Elementary English,* 42 (December, 1965) 845–851.

39. Ryans, David G. "Motivation in Learning." *Psychology of Learning,* Forty-first Yearbook of the National Society for the Study of Education, Part II, University of Chicago Press, Chicago, 1942.

40. Schiffman, Gilbert B. "An Interdisciplinary Approach to the Identification and Remediation of Severe Reading Disabilities." *Junior College and Adult Reading Programs.* National Reading Conference, Milwaukee, 1967, pp. 14–26.

41. Smuts, J. C., *Holism and Evolution,* New York: Viking Press, 1961.

42. Squire, James R., "The National Interest and Teaching of Reading," *Challenge and Experiment in Reading,* International Reading Association Conference Proceedings, 7 (1962), 95–98.

43. Strickland, R. G., "Children, Reading, and Creativity," *Elementary English,* 34 (April 1957) 234–241.

44. Taylor, Earl A., *Eyes, Visual Anomalies and The Fundamental Reading Skill,* New York: Reading and Study Skills Center, Inc., 1959.

45. Terman, Sibyl, and Walcutt, C. C., *Reading: Chaos and Cure,* New York: McGraw-Hill Book Company, Inc., 1958.

46. Thorpe, L. P., Meyers, C. E., and Sea, M. R., *What I Like to Do; An Inventory of Children's Interests,* Grades 4–6, Chicago: Science Research Associates, 1954.

47. Vernon, M. D., *Backwardness in Reading,* London: Cambridge University Press, 1957.

48. Walters, Richard L., and Kosowski, Irene. "Symbolic Learning and Reading Retardation," *Journal of Consulting Psychology,* 27 (February, 1963) 75–82.

48a. Weiss, M. Jerry. "More Than One Way to Develop Lifetime Readers." *Junior College and Adult Reading Programs* (Milwaukee: National Reading Conference, 1967), pp. 254–258.

49. Wepman, Joseph M. "The Interrelationship of Hearing, Speech, and Reading." *The Reading Teacher,* 14 (March, 1961) 245–247.

50. Wheat, H. G., *Foundations of School Learning,* New York: Alfred A. Knopf, Inc., 1955.

51. White, Robert W., "The Dangers of Social Adjustment," *Teachers College Record,* 62 (January 1961) 288–297.

52. Witty, Paul, *Reading in Modern Education,* Boston: D. C. Heath & Company, 1949.

53. Witty, P., Kopel, D., and Coomer, A., *The Northwestern Interest Inventory,* Psycho-educational Clinic, Northwestern University, 1949.

54. Wolfson, Bernice J., "What Do Children Say Their Reading Interests Are?" *The Reading Teacher,* 14 (November 1960) 81–82.

CHAPTER 5

1. Anshen, Ruth N. "Language as Idea." in Ruth N. Anshen (ed.), *Language: An Inquiry Into Its Meaning and Function.* Harper and Brothers, New York, 1957.

2. Artley A. Sterl, "Oral-Language Growth and Reading Ability," *Elementary School Journal,* 53 (February 1953) 321–328.

3. Barton, Allen, "Social Class and Instructional Procedures in the Process of Learning to Read," In Culbreth, Y. Melton and Ralph C.

Staiger (eds.) *Twelfth Yearbook of the National Reading Conference,* Milwaukee, 1962.

4. Berry, M. F., and Eisenson, Jon, *Speech Disorders: Principles and Practices of Therapy,* New York: Appleton-Century-Crofts, Inc., 1956.

5. Beyer, Margaret, "Unity or Division in Language Arts?" *The Reading Teacher,* 11 (April 1958) 244–248.

6. Brown, Charles T. "Three Studies of Listening of Children." Speech Monographs, 32 (June, 1965) 129–138.

7. Brown, James I., and Carlsen, G. Robert, *Brown-Carlsen Listening Comprehension Test: Manual of Directions.* New York: Harcourt, Brace & World, Inc., 1953.

8. Bruner, J. S., "On Perceptual Readiness," *Psychological Review.* 64 (March, 1957) 123–152.

9. Buckingham, B. R., "Language and Reading—A Unified Program," *Elementary English Review,* 17 (March 1940) 111–116.

10. Burns, Paul C., "Teaching Listening in Elementary Schools," *Elementary English,* 38 (January 1961) 11–14.

11. Caffrey, John, "Auding," *Review of Educational Research,* 25 (April 1955) 121–138.

12. Cassirer, Ernst, *An Essay on Man,* Garden City: Doubleday & Company, Inc., 1956.

13. Cherry, Colin, *On Human Communication,* Massachusetts Institute of Technology, 1957.

14. Clark, Ann D., and Richards, Charlotte J. "Auditory Discrimination Among Economically Disadvantaged and Nondisadvantaged Pre-school Children." *Exceptional Children,* 33 (December, 1966) 259–262.

15. Cox, Marian Monroe, "The Relationship of Speech and Reading in an Elementary School Program," *The Speech Teacher,* 8 (September 1959) 211–218.

16. Davis, Hallowell, editor, *Hearing and Deafness: A Guide For Laymen,* New York: Holt, Rinehart & Winston, Inc., 1947.

17. Davis, Irene P., "The Speech Aspects of Reading Readiness," *The National Elementary Principal,* 17 (July 1938) 282–288.

18. Dawkins, John, "Reading Theory—An Important Decision," *Elementary English,* 38 (October 1961) 389–392.

19. Dechant, Emerald. "The Philosophy and Sociology of Reading." *The Philosophical and Sociological Bases of Reading.* National Reading Conference Yearbook, Milwaukee, 1965, pp. 9–20.

20. DeLaguna, Grace. "Perception and Language." *Human Biology,* 1 (1929) 555–558.

21. Deutsch, Martin; Maliver, Alma; Brown, Bert; and Cherry, Estelle. *Communication of Information in the Elementary School Class-*

room. Institute for Developmental Studies, New York Medical College, New York, 1964.

22. Dewey, John, *Logic: The Theory of Inquiry*. New York: Henry Holt and Company, 1938.

23. Edfeldt, Ake W., *Silent Speech and Silent Reading*, Almquist and Wiksell, Stockholm, 1959, Chicago: University of Chicago Press, 1960.

24. Fawcett, Annabel E. "Training in Listening." *Elementary English*, 43 (May, 1966) 473–476.

25. Frisina, D. Robert, *Hearing: Its Interrelation with Speech*, Bulletin No. 1, Washington, D. C.: Gallaudet College, 1957.

26. Gleason, H. A. Jr., *An Introduction to Descriptive Linguistics*, New York: Holt, Rinehart & Winston, Inc., 1955.

27. Goldstein, Kurt, and Scheerer, Martin, "Abstract and Concrete Behavior: An Experiment with Special Tests," *Psychological Monographs*, 2 (1941).

28. Green, Arnold W. *An Analysis of Life in Modern Society*. McGraw-Hill Book Company, New York, 1960.

29. Guilford, J. P. "Creativity." *American Psychologist*, 5 (September, 1950) 444–454.

30. Harris, A. J., *How to Increase Reading Ability*, third edition, New York: Longmans, Green and Company, 1956.

31. Hebb, D. O., *A Textbook of Psychology*, Philadelphia: W. B. Saunders Co., 1958.

32. Hildreth, Gertrude, *Teaching Reading*, New York: Holt, Rinehart & Winston, Inc., 1958.

33. Hinman, Mary Peebles, "The Teacher and the Specialist," *NEA Journal*, 49 (November 1960) 24–25.

34. Hollingsworth, Paul M. "Can Training in Listening Improve Reading?" *The Reading Teacher*. 18 (November, 1964) 121–123, 127.

35. Horworth, Gloria L. "Listening: A Facet of Oral Language." *Elementary English*, 43 (December, 1966) 856–864, 868.

36. Jacobson, Edmund, "Electrophysiology of Mental Activities," *American Journal of Psychology*, 44 (October 1932) 677–694.

37. Kegler, Stanley B., "Techniques in Teaching Listening for Main Ideas," *English Journal*, 45 (January 1956) 30–32.

38. Keller, Helen, *The Story of My Life*, New York: Doubleday & Company, Inc., 1920.

39. Kraus, Silby, "Sputnik and the Three R's," *Education*, 78 (March 1958) 402–405.

40. Langer, Susanne K., *Philosophy in a New Key*, New York: Mentor Books, New American Library, 1948, published originally by Harvard University Press.

41. Lefevre, Carl A. *Linguistics and the Teaching of Reading.* McGraw-Hill Book Company, Inc., New York, 1964.

42. Many, Wesley A. "Is There Any Difference—Reading vs. Listening?" *The Reading Teacher,* 19 (November, 1965) 110–113.

43. Maritain, Jacques. "Language and the Theory of Sign." In Ruth N. Anshen. ed. *Language: An Inquiry Into Its Meaning and Function.* Harper and Brothers, New York, 1957.

44. Metz, F. Elizabeth. "Poverty, Early Language Deprivation, and Learning Ability." *Elementary English,* 43 (February, 1967) 129–133.

45. Nichols, Ralph G., and Stevens, Leonard A., *Are You Listening,* New York: McGraw-Hill Book Company, Inc., 1957.

46. Pei, Mario, *Language for Everybody,* New York: Pocket Books, Inc., 1958.

47. Poole, I., "Genetic Development of Articulation of Consonant Sounds in Speech," *Elementary English Review,* XI (June 1934) 159–161.

48. Pooley, Robert C., "Reading and the Language Arts." *Development in and Through Reading,* ed. by Nelson B. Henry, National Society for the Study of Education Yearbook, No. 60, pp. 35–53, Chicago: University of Chicago Press, 1961.

49. Porter, William E., "Mass Communication and Education," *The National Elementary Principal,* 37 (February 1958) 12–16.

50. Pronovost, Wilbert, *The Teaching of Speaking and Listening,* New York: David McKay Company, Inc., 1959.

51. Revesz, Geza. *The Origins and Prehistory of Language.* Philosophical Library, New York, 1956.

52. Ross, Ramon. "Teaching the Listener: Old Mistakes and A Fresh Beginning." *The Elementary School Journal,* 66 (February, 1966) 239–244.

53. Ruddell, Robert B. "The Effect of the Similarity of Oral and Written Patterns of Language Structure on Reading Comprehension." *Elementary English,* 42 (April, 1965) 403–410.

54. Ruddell, Robert B. "Oral Language and the Development of Other Language Skills." *Elementary English,* 43 (May, 1966) 489–498, 517.

55. Sapir, Edward, *Language: An Introduction to the Study of Speech,* New York: Harcourt, Brace & World, Inc., 1921.

56. Sapir, Edward. "Language," *Encyclopedia of the Social Sciences.* The Macmillan Company, New York, 1933, 155–169.

57. Simon, J., "Contribution a la Psychologie de la Lecture," *Enfance,* 5 (November–December, 1954) 431–447.

58. Smillie, David, "Language Development and Lineality," *ETC. A Review of General Semantics,* 17 (Winter 1960) 203–208.

59. Strickland, Ruth G., *The Language Arts in the Elementary School,* Boston: D. C. Heath & Company, 1951.

60. Stroud, James B., *Psychology in Education,* New York: David McKay Company, Inc., 1956.

61. Van Riper, Charles, and Butler, Katharine G., *Speech in the Elementary Classroom,* New York: Harper & Row, Publishers, 1955.

62. Van Riper, C. "The Speech Pathologist Looks at Reading." *The Reading Teacher,* 17 (April, 1964) 505–510.

63. Wagner, Guy. "Teaching Listening." *Education,* 88 (November–December, 1967) 183–188.

64. Walcott, Fred G., "Language as a Function of Doing," *English Journal,* 45 (December 1956) 532–536, 554.

65. Warfel, H. R., and Lloyd, D. J., "The Structural Approach to Reading," *School and Society,* 85 (June 1957) 199–201.

66. Warfel, Harry R., "Prolegomena to Reading Instruction," *Journal of Developmental Reading,* 1 (Spring 1958) 35–45.

67. Watson, J. B., "Is Thinking Merely the Action of Language Mechanism?" *British Journal of Psychology,* 11 (October 1920) 87–104.

68. Weintraub, Samuel. "Listening Comprehension." *The Reading Teacher,* 20 (April, 1967) 639–647.

69. Wepman, Joseph M., "Auditory Discrimination, Speech, and Reading," *Elementary School Journal,* 60 (March 1960) 325–333.

70. Whatmough, Joshua, *Language: A Modern Synthesis,* New York: Mentor Books, New American Library of World Literature, Inc., 1957.

71. Whorf, Benjamen L. "Science and Linguistics." *Technology Review,* 42 (1939–1940).

72. Winter, Clotilda. "Listening and Learning." *Elementary English,* 43 (October, 1966) 569–572.

73. Womack, Thurston, "Is English a Phonetic Language?" *Elementary English,* 34 (October 1957) 386–388.

74. Worley, Stinson E., and Story, William E. "Socioeconomic Status and Language Facility of Beginning First Graders." *The Reading Teacher,* 20 (February, 1967) 400–403.

75. Ziller, Robert C. "The Social Psychology of Reading." *The Reading Teacher,* 17 (May, 1964) 583–588, 593.

CHAPTER 6

1. Berry, Mildred F., and Eisenson, Jon, *Speech Disorders: Principles and Practices of Therapy,* New York: Appleton-Century-Crofts, Inc., 1956.

2. Brooks, Nelson, *Language and Language Learning,* pp. 238, New York: Harcourt, Brace & World, Inc., 1960.

3. Buswell, Guy T., "The Process of Reading," *The Reading Teacher,* 13 (December 1959) 108–114.

4. Carroll, John B. "Language Development." *Encyclopedia of Educational Research,* The Macmillan Company. New York, 1960, p. 748.

5. De Boer, John J., "Grammar in Language Teaching," *Elementary English,* 36 (October 1959) 413–421.

6. Eastman, Milton, "Speech Improvement Activities," *The Grade Teacher,* 70 (May 1953) 60, 95.

7. Emery, R. M., "The Classroom Teacher and Speech Correction," *Elementary School Journal,* 56 (November 1955) 110–116.

8. Ervin, Susan M. and Miller, Wick R. "Language Development," *Child Psychology.* Sixty-Second Yearbook of the National Society for the Study of Education, Part I. Chicago: The University of Chicago Press, 1963, p. 125.

9. Gleason, H. A., Jr., *An Introduction to Descriptive Linguistics,* New York: Holt, Rinehart & Winston, Inc., 1955.

10. Goodman, Kenneth S. "A Linguistic Study of Cues and Miscues in Readings." *Elementary English,* 42 (October, 1965) 639–643.

11. Hockett, Charles F., *A Course in Modern Linguistics,* New York: The Macmillan Company, 1958.

12. Ives, Sumner. "Some Notes on Syntax and Meaning." *The Reading Teacher,* 18 (December, 1964) 179–183, 222.

13. Johnson, Wendell, *Children With Speech and Hearing Impairment,* Washington, D.C.: U. S. Department of Health, Education, and Welfare, Bulletin No. 5, 1959.

14. Joos, Martin. "Language and the School Child." *Language and Learning.* Harcourt, Brace & World, Inc., New York, 1966, p. 205.

15. Karlin, Isaac W., "Speech- and Language-Handicapped Children," *Diseases of Children,* 95 (April 1958) 370–376.

16. Kasdon, L. M., "The Place of Games in the Language Arts Program," *Elementary English,* 35 (February 1958) 106–107.

17. Kean, John M., and Yamamoto, Kaoru. "Grammar Signals and Assignment of Words to Parts of Speech Among Young Children: An Exploration." *Journal of Verbal Learning and Verbal Behavior,* 4 (August, 1965) 323–326.

18. Lefevre, Carl A., "Reading Our Language Patterns: A Linguistic View—Contributions to a Theory of Reading," *Challenge and Experiment in Reading,* International Reading Association Conference Proceedings, 7 (1962) 66–70.

19. Leutenegger, Ralph R., "What We Have Learned About Stuttering in the Past Twenty-Five Years," *The Speech Teacher,* 9 (January 1960) 23–30.

20. Lindsley, D. B., "Bilateral Differences in Brain Potentials from the

Two Cerebral Hemispheres in Relation to Laterality and Stuttering," *Journal of Experimental Psychology*, 26 (February 1940) 211–225.

21. Lloyd, Donald, "Reading American English as a Native Language Process," *Challenge and Experiment in Reading*, International Reading Association Conference Proceedings, 7 (1962) 247–251.

22. Morency, Anne S., Wepman, Joseph M., and Wiener, Paul S. "Studies in Speech: Developmental Articulation Inaccuracy." *The Elementary School Journal*, 67 (March, 1967) 329–337.

23. Naylor, Rex V., "Helping the Stutterer," *NEA Journal*, 49 (November 1960) 35–36.

24. Pei, Mario, *Language for Everybody*, New York: Pocket Books, Inc., 1958.

25. Pooley, R. C., *Teaching English Usage*, National Council of Teachers of English, New York: Appleton-Century-Crofts, Inc., 1946.

26. Pooley, Robert C., "The English Teacher's Preparation in Speech," *English Journal*, 45 (April 1956) 181–187, 200.

27. Pooley, Robert C., "What is Correct English Usage," *NEA Journal*, 49 (December 1960) 17–20.

28. Pronovost, Wilbert, *The Teaching of Speaking and Listening*, New York: David McKay Co., Inc., 1959.

29. Rasmussen, Carrie, "Choral Reading," *NEA Journal*, 49 (November 1960) 26.

30. Reed, David W. "A Theory of Language, Speech, and Writing." *Elementary English*, 42 (December, 1965) 845–851.

31. Roberts, Paul, "Linguistics and English," *California Journal of Secondary Education*, 34 (March 1959) 163–168.

32. Rotter, Julian B., "The Nature and Treatment of Stuttering: A Clinical Approach," *Journal of Abnormal and Social Psychology*, 39 (April 1944) 150–173.

33. Schneiderman, Norma, "Teaching the Child with Delayed Speech," *Education*, 79 (March 1959) 419–422.

34. Sonenberg, Charlotte and Glass, Gerald G. "Reading and Speech: An Incidence and Treatment Study." *The Reading Teacher*, 19 (December, 1965) 197–201.

35. Strauss, A. A., and Kephart, N. C., *Psychopathology and Education of the Brain-Injured Child*, II, *Process in Theory and Clinic*, New York: Grune & Stratton, 1955.

36. Strickland, Ruth G., *The Language Arts in the Elementary School*, Boston: D. C. Heath & Company, 1957.

37. Tidyman, W. F., and Butterfield, M., *Teaching the Language Arts*, New York: McGraw-Hill Book Company, Inc., 1959.

38. Van Riper, Charles, and Butler, Katharine G., *Speech in the Elementary Classroom*, New York: Harper & Row, Publishers, 1955.

39. Van Riper, C. "The Speech Pathologist Looks at Reading." *The Reading Teacher,* 17 (April, 1964) 505–510.
40. Vernon, M. D., *Backwardness in Reading,* London: Cambridge University Press, 1957.
41. *Webster's Seventh New Collegiate Dictionary,* Springfield: G. & C. Merriam Company, 1963.

CHAPTER 7

1. Bagford, Jack. "Reading Readiness Scores and Success in Reading." *The Reading Teacher,* 21 (January, 1968) 324–328.
2. Barrett, T. "Visual Discrimination Tasks as Predictors of First Grade Reading Achievement." *California Journal of Educational Research,* 14 (1963) 108–117.
3. Barrett, Thomas C. "Visual Discrimination Tasks as Predictors of First Grade Reading Achievement." *The Reading Teacher,* 18 (January, 1965) 276–282.
4. Barrett, Thomas C. "Performance on Selected Prereading Tasks and First-Grade Reading Achievement." *Vistas in Reading,* International Reading Association, Newark, 1967, 461–464.
5. Beckett, Dorothy B. "Philosophical Differences in Reading Concepts." *The Reading Teacher,* 18 (October, 1964) 27–32.
6. Berry, Mildred F., and Eisenson, Jon, *Speech Disorders: Principles and Practices of Therapy,* New York: Appleton-Century-Crofts, Inc., 1956.
7. Bremer, Neville, "Do Readiness Tests Predict Success in Reading?" *The Elementary School Journal,* 59 (January 1959) 222–224.
8. Bruner, Jerome S. *On Knowing Essays for the Left Hand.* Cambridge: Harvard University Press, 1962, p. 108.
9. *Bulletin-Board Lessons for First-Graders on Important Phonetic Skills,* Chicago: Scott, Foresman & Company, No. 654, 1958.
10. Buswell, Guy T., "The Process of Reading," *The Reading Teacher,* 13 (December 1959) 108–114.
11. Cole, Luella, *The Improvement of Reading with Special Reference to Remedial Instruction,* New York: Holt, Rinehart & Winston, Inc., 1938.
12. Connell, Donna. "Auditory and Visual Discrimination in Kindergarten. *Elementary English,* 45 (January, 1968) 51–54, 66.
13. Cordts, Anna D., "And It's All Known as Phonics," *Elementary English,* 32 (October 1955) 376–378, 412.
14. Davis, Hallowell, editor, *Hearing and Deafness: A Guide for Laymen,* New York: Holt, Rinehart & Winston, Inc., 1947.
15. *The Dot-To-Dot Zoo,* Akron, Ohio: Saalfield Publishing Company.

16. Durrell, Donald D., *Improving Reading Instruction,* New York: Harcourt, Brace & World, Inc., 1956.

17. Durrell, Donald D., "First-Grade Reading Success Study: A Summary," *Journal of Education,* Boston University, 140 (February 1958) 2–6.

18. Durrell, Donald D., and Murphy, Helen A., "The Auditory Discrimination Factor in Reading Readiness and Reading Disability," *Education,* 73 (May 1953) 556–560.

19. Goins, Jean T. *Visual Perceptual Abilities and Early Reading Progress.* Supplementary Educational Monographs, No. 87. Chicago: University of Chicago Press, 1958.

20. Gould, Lawrence N. "Visual Perception Training." *The Elementary School Journal,* 67 (April, 1967) 381–389.

21. Gray, Lillian, and Reese, Dora, *Teaching Children to Read,* New York: The Ronald Press Company, 1957.

22. Harrison, M. Lucille, and Stroud, James B., *Harrison-Stroud Reading Readiness Profiles: Teacher's Manual,* Boston: Houghton Mifflin Company, 1956.

24. Huggins, M. I., "Come to School Puzzle," *The Grade Teacher,* 76 (September 1958) 51.

25. Jones, J. Kenneth. "Color as an Aid to Visual Perception in Early Reading." *The British Journal of Educational Psychology.* 35 (February, 1965) 21–27.

26. Keislar, Evan. "Conference on Perceptual and Linguistic Aspects of Reading." *The Reading Teacher,* 18 (October, 1964) 43–49.

27. Linehan, Eleanor B., "Early Instruction in Letter Names and Sounds as Related to Success in Beginning Reading," *Journal of Education,* Boston University, 140 (February 1958) 44–48.

28. McKee, Paul, and Harrison, M. L., *Getting Ready,* revised edition, Boston: Houghton Mifflin Company, 1957.

29. McKee, Paul and Harrison, M. Lucille, *Getting Ready to Read,* Boston: Houghton Mifflin Company, 1962.

30. McKibbin, Mary Adeline, "Children's Art Interests," *Education,* 80 (December 1959) 235–238.

31. Morency, Anne S., Wepman, Joseph M., and Weiner, Paul S. "Studies in Speech: Developmental Articulation Inaccuracy." *Elementary School Journal,* 67 (March, 1967) 329–337.

32. Muehl, Siegmar and King, Ethel M. "Recent Research in Visual Discrimination: Significance for Beginning Reading." *Vistas in Reading.* International Reading Association, Newark, 1967, pp. 434–439.

33. Olson, Arthur V., "Growth in Word Perception Abilities as it Relates to Success in Beginning Reading," *Journal of Education,* Boston University, 140 (February 1958) 25–36.

34. Orton, S. T., "An Impediment to Learning to Read—A Neurological Explanation of the Reading Disability," *School and Society,* 28 (September 1928) 286–290.

35. Parke, Margaret B., "Picture Dictionaries," *Elementary English,* 32 (December 1955) 524.

36. Potter, Muriel C. *Perception of Symbol Orientation and Early Reading Success.* Bureau of Publications, No. 939, Teachers College, New York, 1949.

37. Powell, M., and Parsley, K. "The Relationship Between First Grade Reading Readiness and Second Grade Reading Achievement." *Journal of Educational Research,* 54 (1961) 229–233.

38. Schoephoerster, Hugh, Barnhart, Richard, and Loomer, Walter M. "The Teaching of Prereading Skills in Kindergarten." *The Reading Teacher,* 19 (February, 1966) 352–357.

39. Shea, Carol Ann. "Visual Discrimination of Words and Reading Readiness." *The Reading Teacher,* 21 (January, 1968) 361–367.

40. Silvaroli, Nicholas J., and Wheelock, Warren H. "An Investigation of Auditory Discrimination Training for Beginning Readers." *The Reading Teacher,* 20 (December, 1966) 247–251.

41. Spache, G. D., "Factors Which Produce Defective Reading," *Corrective Reading in the Classroom and Clinic,* Supplementary Educational Monographs, No. 79, pp. 49–57, Chicago: University of Chicago Press, 1953.

42. Spache, George D. *et al.* "A Longitudinal First Grade Reading Readiness Program." *The Reading Teacher,* 19 (May, 1966) 580–584.

43. Wepman, Joseph M., "Auditory Discrimination, Speech, and Reading," *The Elementary School Journal,* 60 (March 1960) 325–333.

44. Wheelock, Warren H., and Silvaroli, Nicholas J. "Visual Discrimination Training for Beginning Readers." *The Reading Teacher,* 21 (November, 1967) 115–120.

45. Weintraub, Samuel. "Readiness Measures for Predicting Reading Achievement." *The Reading Teacher,* 20 (March, 1967) 551–558.

46. Zingle, H., and Hohol, A. E. "Predictive Validity of the Metropolitan Readiness Tests." *Alberta Journal of Educational Research,* 10 (1964) 99–104.

CHAPTER 8

1. Ames, Louise B., and Walker, Richard N. "Prediction of Later Reading Ability from Kindergarten Rorschach and I.Q. Scores." *Journal of Educational Psychology* 55 (1964) 309–313.

2. Ames, Wilbur S. "The Understanding Vocabulary of First Grade Pupils." *Elementary English,* 41 (January 1964) 64–68.

3. Anderson, I. H., and Dearborn, W. F., *The Psychology of Teaching Reading,* New York: The Ronald Press Company, 1952.
4. Ausubel, David. "Cognitive Structure: Learning to Read." *Education,* 87 (May, 1967) 544–548.
5. Betts, Emmett Albert, "How Well Are We Teaching Reading?— Reply," *Controversial Issues in Reading,* Tenth Annual Reading Conference Proceedings, Lehigh University, 1 (April 1961) 7–9.
6. Bliesmer, E., and Yarborough, Bett. "A Comparison of Ten Different Beginning Programs in First Grade." *Phi Delta Kappa,* 1965, 46, 500–504.
7. Bond, Guy L. "First-Grade Reading Studies: An Overview." *Elementary English,* 43 (May, 1966) 464–470.
8. Bond, Guy L., and Dykstra, Robert. "Final Report No. X-001, Coordinating Center for First Grade Reading Instruction Programs.
9. Bruner, J. S., "Going Beyond the Information Given," *Contemporary Approaches to Cognition,* pp. 41–49, Cambridge: Harvard University Press, 1957.
10. Brown, Roger, *Words and Things,* Glencoe, Illinois: The Free Press, 1958.
11. Carroll, J. B. "Words, Meanings, and Concepts." *Harvard Educational Review* 34 (1964) 178–202.
12. Chall, Jeanne. *Learning to Read: The Great Debate.* McGraw-Hill Book Company, New York, 1967.
13. Chall, Jeanne, and Feldman, Shirley. "First Grade Reading: An Analysis of the Interactions of Professed Methods, Teacher Implementation and Child Background." *The Reading Teacher,* 1966, 19, 569–575.
14. Cottrell, Alice B., and Brown, Grace M., "A Study of the Degree of Disability in Phonetic Analysis Among College Freshmen, and Its Relationship to Silent Reading Comprehension," A paper presented at the 1961 American Personnel and Guidance Association Convention, Denver, Colorado.
15. Daniels, J. C., and Diack, H., *Progress in Reading,* University of Nottingham, Institute of Education, 1956, Summarized in Vernon, M. D. *Backwardness in Reading,* Cambridge: 1957, 205–207.
16. Davis, O. L., and Slobodian, June Jenkinson. "Teacher Behavior Toward Boys and Girls During First Grade Reading Instruction." *American Education Research Journal* 4 (1967) 261–269.
17. Dawson, Mildred A. "Looking Ahead in Reading." *The Reading Teacher,* 21 (November, 1967) 121–125.
18. Delacato, Carl H. *The Treatment and Prevention of Reading Problems.* Charles C. Thomas, Springfield, 1959.
19. Delacato, Carl H. *Diagnosis and Treatment of Speech and Reading Problems.* Charles C. Thomas, Springfield, 1963.

20. Downing, John. "The ITA (Initial Teaching Alphabet) Reading Experiment." *The Reading Teacher,* 18 (November, 1964) 105–110.

21. Downing, J. A. *The Initial Teaching Alphabet Explained and Illustrated.* The Macmillan Company, New York, 1964.

22. Downing, J. A. *The ITA Reading Experiment.* Evans Brothers, London, 1964.

23. Downing, John. "Current Misconceptions About ITA." *Elementary English,* 42 (May, 1965) 492–501.

24. Durrell, Donald D., and Nicholson, Alice K., "Preschool and Kindergarten Experience," *Development in and Through Reading,* Sixtieth Yearbook, National Society for the Study of Education, pp. 257–269, Chicago: University of Chicago Press, 1961.

25. Elwell, C. E., "Phonics Indeed—But When?" *Changing Concepts of Reading Instruction,* ed. by J. Allen Figurel, International Reading Association Conference Proceedings, Vol. 6, pp. 127–130, New York: Scholastic Magazines, 1961.

26. Fernald, G. M., *Remedial Techniques in Basic School Subjects,* New York: McGraw-Hill Book Company, Inc., 1943.

27. Fry, Edward. "Programmed Instruction in Reading." *The Reading Teacher.* 17 (March, 1964) 453–459.

28. Fry, Edward. "A Diacritical Marking System to Aid Beginning Reading Instruction," *Elementary English,* 41 (May, 1964) 526–529, 537.

29. Fry, Edward. "I/T/A: A Look at the Research Data." *Education,* 87 (May, 1967) 549–553.

30. Garrison, Karl C., and Gray, J. Stanley, *Educational Psychology,* New York: Appleton-Century-Crofts, Inc., 1955.

31. Garrison, S. C., and Heard, Minnie T., "An Experimental Study of the Value of Phonetics," *Peabody Journal of Education,* 9 (July 1931) 9–14.

32. Gattegno, Caleb. *Words in Color: Background and Principles.* Learning Materials, Inc., of Encyclopaedia Britannica Press, 1962.

33. Gattegno, Caleb. "Teaching Reading: An Indefinitely Renewable Problem." *Spelling Progress Bulletin,* 4 (Fall, 1964) 15–17.

34. Gattegno, Caleb. "Words in Color," pp. 175–191, in *The Disabled Reader,* ed. by John Money. Johns Hopkins Press, Baltimore, 1966.

35. Goins, Jean T., "Visual and Auditory Perception in Reading," *Reading Teacher,* 13 (October 1950) 9–13.

36. Goins, Jean T., *Visual Perception Abilities and Early Reading Progress,* Supplementary Educational Monographs, No. 87 Chicago: University of Chicago Press, 1958.

37. Gray, W. S., "Current Reading Problems: A World View," *Elementary School Journal,* 56 (September 1955) 11–17.

38. Guilford, J. P., "Frontiers in Thinking That Teachers Should

Know About," *The Reading Teacher*, 13 (February 1960) 176–182.

39. Harris, Albert J., "Perceptual Difficulties in Reading Disability," *Changing Concepts of Reading Instruction*, ed. by J. Allen Figurel, International Reading Association Conference Proceedings, Vol. 6, pp. 282–290, New York: Scholastic Magazines, 1961.

40. Heilman, Arthur W., *Principles and Practices of Teaching Reading*, Columbus: Charles E. Merrill Books, Inc., 1961.

41. Hildreth, Gertrude, *Teaching Reading*, New York: Holt, Rinehart & Winston, Inc., 1958.

42. Huey, Edmund B., *The Psychology and Pedagogy of Reading*, New York: The Macmillan Company, 1912.

43. Johnson, Dorothy K. "Experimenting with the Talking Typewriter." New Directions in Reading, ed. by Ralph Staiger and David A. Sohn. Bantam Books Inc., New York, 1967, pp. 32–36.

44. Katona, G., *Organizing and Memorizing: Studies in the Psychology of Learning and Teaching*, New York: Columbia University Press, 1940.

45. Keisler, Evan. "Conference on Perceptual and Linguistic Aspects of Reading." *The Reading Teacher*, 18 (October, 1964) 43–49.

46. Knutson, Dorothy M. "I.T.A. Aids Reading Disability." *The Pointer*, 11 (Number 2, 1966) 7–12.

47. Köhler, Wolfgang, "Gestalt Psychology Today," *The American Psychologist*, 14 (December 1959) 727–734.

48. Langman, Muriel Potter, "The Reading Process: A Descriptive, Interdisciplinary Approach," *Genetic Psychology Monographs*, 62 (August 1960) 1–40.

49. Lefevre, Carl A., "Language Patterns and Their Graphic Counterparts: A Linguistic View of Reading," *Changing Concepts of Reading Instruction*, ed. by J. Allen Figurel, International Reading Association Conference Proceedings, Vol. 6, pp. 245–249, New York: Scholastic Magazines, 1961.

50. Marchbanks, G., and Levin H. "Cues by Which Children Recognize Words." *Journal of Educational Psychology*, 56 (April, 1965), 57–61.

51. Mason, George E., "The Role of Phonics in the First Grade Program," *Challenge and Experiment in Reading*, International Reading Association Conference Proceedings, 7 (1962) 27–29.

52. McKee, Paul. *Reading: A Program for the Elementary School*. Houghton Mifflin Company, Boston, 1966.

53. Miller, Melvin L. "Another Look at Reading and the Teaching of Reading." *Reading Horizons*, 7 (Summer, 1967) 157–163.

54. Mowrer, O. H., "Hearing and Speaking: An Analysis of Language Learning," *Journal of Speech and Hearing Disorders*, 23 (May 1958) 143–152.

55. Mowrer, O. Hobart, *Learning Theory and the Symbolic Processes*,

New York: John Wiley & Sons, Inc., 1960, pp. 473.

56. Muehl, Siegmar, "The Effects of Visual Discrimination Pretraining with Word and Letter Stimuli on Learning to Read a Word List on Kindergarten Children," *Journal of Educational Psychology,* 52 (August 1961) 215-221.

57. Naeslund, Jon, *Methods of Teaching Primary Reading: A Co-Twin Control Experiment,* Research Bulletin from the Institute of Education, No. 4, University of Stockholm, 1955.

58. Osgood, Charles E., "A Behavioristic Analysis of Perception and Language as Cognitive Phenomena," *Contemporary Approaches to Cognition,* pp. 75-118, Cambridge: Harvard University Press, 1957.

59. Pavlov, I. P., *Conditioned Reflexes,* London: Oxford University Press, 1927.

60. Petty, Mary C., "An Experimental Study of Certain Factors Influencin Reading Readiness," *Journal of Educational Psychology,* 30 (March 1939) 215-230.

61. Pitman, I. J. "Learning to Read: An Experiment." *Journal of the Royal Society of Arts.* 190 (February, 1961), 149-180.

62. Pooley, Robert C., "Reading and the Language Arts," *Development in and Through Reading,* Sixtieth Yearbook of the National Society for the Study of Education, pp. 35-53, Chicago: University of Chicago Press, 1961.

63. Razran, Gregory, "A Note on the Use of the Terms Conditioning and Reinforcement," *American Psychologist,* 10 (April 1955) 173-174.

64. Sartain, Harry W. *Language Arts for Beginners.* Fourteen chart activities for use in teaching kindergarten and first graders. D. C. Heath & Company, Boston.

65. Seashore, Robert H., "How Many Words Do Children Know?" *The Packet,* Service Bulletin for Elementary Teachers, Boston: D. C. Heath & Company, 2 (November 1947) 3-17.

66. Shibles, Burleigh, "How Many Words Does a First Grade Child Know?" *Elementary English,* 41 (January 1959) 42-47.

67. Smith, Henry P., and Dechant, Emerald V., *Psychology in Teaching Reading,* Englewood Cliffs, N. J.: Prentice-Hall Inc., 1961.

68. Soffiètti, James P., "Why Children Fail to Read: A Linguistic Analysis," *The Harvard Educational Review,* 25 (Spring 1955) 63-84.

69. Spearman, C. *The Nature of Intelligence and the Principles of Cognition.* The Macmillan Company, New York, 1923.

70. Squire, James R., "New Directions in Language Learning," *Elementary English,* 39 (October 1962) 535-544.

71. Stroud, James B., *Psychology in Education,* New York: David Mc-

Kay Company, Inc., 1956.

72. Tabachnick, B. Robert, "A Linguist Looks at Reading: Leonard Bloomfield and the Phonemic Criterion," *Elementary English*, 39 (October 1962) 545–548, 561.

73. Terman, Sibyl, and Walcutt, C. C., *Reading: Chaos and Cure*, New York: McGraw-Hill Book Company, Inc., 1958.

74. Tyler, Priscilla, "Sound, Pattern, and Sense," *Changing Concepts of Reading Instruction*, ed. by J. Allen Figurel, International Reading Association Conference Proceedings, Vol. 6, pp. 249–252, New York: Scholastic Magazines, 1961.

75. Vernon, Magdaley Dorothea, *Backwardness in Reading*, London: Cambridge University Press, 1957.

76. Wepman, Joseph M., "Auditory Discrimination, Speech, and Reading," *The Elementary School Journal*, 60 (March 1960) 325–333.

CHAPTER 9

1. Barbe, Walter B., "Personalized or Individualized Reading Instruction?" *Education*, 81 (May 1961) 537–539.

2. Betts, Emmett Albert, "Issues in Teaching Reading," *Controversial Issues in Reading*, Tenth Annual Reading Conference, Lehigh University, 1 (April 1961) 33–41.

3. Bloomfield, Leonard & Barnhart, Clarence L., *Let's Read*, Detroit: Wayne State University Press, 1961.

4. Bormuth, John R. "Validities of Grammatical and Semantic Classification of Cloze Test Scores." *Reading and Inquiry*, ed. by J. A. Figurel, Proceedings of the IRA Convention (1965) 283–286.

5. Bormuth, John R. "Readability: A New Approach." *Reading Research Quarterly*, 1 (Spring, 1966) 79–132.

6. Bormuth, John R. "Comparable Cloze and Multiple-choice Comprehension Test Scores." *Journal of Reading*, 10 (February, 1967) 291–299.

7. Bormuth, John R. "Designs of Readability Research." *Vistas in Reading*, ed. by J. A. Figurel, Proceedings of the IRA Convention (1967) 485–489.

8. Bormuth, J. R. and O. L. MacDonald, "Cloze Tests as a Measure of Ability to Detect Literary Style," *Reading and Inquiry*, International Reading Association Conference Proceedings, 10 (1965) 287–290.

9. Bradley, Mary A., "The Construction and Evaluation of Exercises

for Providing Meaningful Practice in Second Grade Reading," unpublished doctoral dissertation, Boston University, School of Education, 1957.

10. Calder, Clarence R., Jr. "Self-Directed Reading Materials." *The Reading Teacher,* 21 (December, 1967) 248–252.

11. Chall, Jeanne, "The Measurement of Readability," *Readability: Finding Readable Material For Children,* Tenth Annual Conference on Reading, University of Pittsburgh, 1954, pp. 26–37.

12. Dale, E., and Chall, J. S., "A Formula for Predicting Readability," *Educational Research Bulletin,* Ohio State University, 27 (January 1948) 11–20, 28.

13. Dale, E., and Chall, J. S., "The Concept of Readability," *Elementary English,* 26 (January 1949) 19–26.

14. Dawson, Mildred A. "Looking Ahead in Reading." *The Reading Teacher,* 21 (November, 1967) 121–125.

15. Dechant, Emerald, "Rate of Comprehension—Needed Research," *Changing Concepts of Reading Instruction,* ed. by J. Allen Figurel, International Reading Association Conference Proceedings, Vol. 6, pp. 223–225, New York: Scholastic Magazines, 1961.

16. EDL, *Report on Reading Instrument Usage,* EDL Newsletter, No. 19, Huntington, N. Y.: Educational Developmental Laboratories.

17. Flesch, R., "A New Readability Yardstick," *Journal of Applied Psychology,* 32 (June 1948) 221–233.

18. Fletcher, J. Eugene, "Rapid Reading Perception, and the Tachistoscope," *College of Education Record,* University of Washington, 25 (May 1959), pp. 52–55.

19. Gates, Arthur I., "Vocabulary Control in Basal Reading Material," *The Reading Teacher,* 15 (November 1961) 81–85.

20. Goldberg, Miriam *et al. The Effects of Ability Grouping.* Teachers College Press, New York, 1966.

21. Goodman, Kenneth S. "A Linguistic Study of Cues and Miscues in Reading. *Elementary English* (October, 1965) 639–643.

22. Goodman, Kenneth S. "Word Perception: Linguistic Bases." *Education* 87 (May, 1967) 539–543.

23. Grayum, Helen S., *An Analytic Description of Skimming: Its Purposes and Place as an Ability in Reading,* Studies in Education, 1952, Indiana University.

24. Hafner, Lawrence E. "Relationships of Various Measures to the Cloze." *New Concepts in College-Adult Reading.* National Reading Conference, Milwaukee, 1964, pp. 135–145.

25. Hafner, Lawrence E. "Cloze Procedure." *Journal of Reading,* 9 (May, 1966) 415–421.

26. Harris, T. L., Herrick, V. E., MacDonald, J. B., and Rarick, G. L. *Experimental Development of Variability in Reading Rate in*

Grades 4, 5, and 6. USOE Cooperative Research Project No. 1755. Madison, Wisc.: University of Wisconsin, 1965.

27. Harris, A., and Serwer, Blanche. "Comparing Reading Approaches in First Grade Teaching Disadvantaged Children." *The Reading Teacher,* 1966, 19, 631–635.

28. Hawkins, Michael. "Changes in Reading Groups." *The Reading Teacher,* 21 (October, 1967) 48–51.

29. Heilman, Arthur W., *Principles and Practices of Teaching Reading.* Columbus: Charles E. Merrill Books, Inc., 1961.

30. Herrick, Virgil E., Anderson, Dan, and Pierstorff, Lola, "Basal Instructional Materials in Reading," *Development In and Through Reading,* National Society for the Study of Education, Sixtieth Yearbook, pp. 165–188, Chicago: University of Chicago Press, 1961.

31. Hildreth, Gertrude, "New Methods for Old in Teaching Phonics," *Elementary School Journal,* 57 (May 1957) 436–441.

32. Hillson, Maurie, *et al.* "A Controlled Experiment Evaluating the Effects of a Non-Graded Organization on Pupil Achievement." *Journal of Educational Research,* 1964, 77, 548–550.

33. Hunt, Kellogg W. "Recent Measures in Syntactic Development." *Elementary English,* 43 (November, 1966) 732–739.

34. Justman, Joseph. "Reading and Class Homogeneity." *The Reading Teacher,* 21 (January, 1968) 314–316, 334.

35. Karlin, Robert. "Research Results and Classroom Practices." *The Reading Teacher,* 21 (December, 1967) 221–226.

36. Kierstead, R. "A Comparison and Evaluation of Two Methods of Organization for the Teaching of Reading." *Journal of Educational Research,* 56 (1963) 317–321.

37. King, Ethel M. and Muehl, Siegmar. "Different Sensory Cues as Aids in Beginning Reading." *The Reading Teacher,* 19 (December, 1965) 163–168.

38. Kingston, Albert J. and Weaver, Wendell W. "Recent Developments in Readability Appraisal." *Journal of Reading,* 11 (October, 1967) 44–47.

39. Klare, George R. "The Role of Word Frequency in Readability." *Elementary English,* 45 (January, 1968) 12–22.

40. Knight, Elva E., "Mobility Grouping," *Reading Bulletin* 224, Chicago: Educational Service Department, Lyons and Carnahan.

41. Lambert, P. *et al.* "A Comparison of Pupil Achievement in Team and Self-Contained Organizations." *Journal of Experimental Education,* 1965, 33, 217–224.

42. Leary, Bernice E., "Developing Word Perception Skills in Middle and Upper Grades," *Current Problems in Reading Instruction,* Seventh Annual Conference on Reading, pp. 22–27, Pittsburgh: University of Pittsburgh Press, 1951.

43. Levin, H., and Ford, B. *Studies of Oral Reading IV. Homographs vs. Non-Homographs,* 1965; also: *Studies of Oral Reading V. Homographs in Grammatical Frames,* 1965.

44. Lorge, Irving, "Predicting Readability," *Teachers College Record,* 45 (March, 1944) 404–419.

45. Louthan, V. "Some Systematic Grammatical Deletions and Their Effects on Reading Comprehension." *English Journal,* 54 (April, 1965) 295–299.

46. Luckiesh, Matthew, and Moss, Frank K., *The Science of Seeing,* New York: D. Van Nostrand Co., Inc., 1937.

47. Marita, Sister M. "Beginning Reading Achievement in Three Classroom Organizational Patterns." *The Reading Teacher,* 20 (October, 1966) 12–17.

48. MacGinitie, Walter. "Comments on Professor Coleman's Paper." *Symposium on Verbal Learning Research and the Technology of Written Instruction,* ed. by E. Z. Rothkopf. Columbia University.

49. Marks, Merle B. "Improve Reading Through Better Format." *Journal of Educational Research,* 60 (December, 1966) 147–151.

50. Maxwell, Martha J. and Mueller, Arthur C. "Relative Effectiveness of Techniques and Placebo Conditions in Changing Reading Rates." *Journal of Reading,* 11 (December, 1967) 184–191.

51. McCanne, R. "Approaches to First Grade English Reading Instruction for Children from Spanish-Speaking Homes." *The Reading Teacher,* 1966, 19, 670–675.

52. McDonald, J., Harris, T., and Mann, J. "Individualized Versus Group Instruction in First Grade Reading." *The Reading Teacher,* 1966, 19, 643–646.

53. McKee, Paul. *Reading: A Program for the Elementary School.* Houghton Mifflin Company, Boston, 1966.

54. McNamara, Walter J., Paterson, Donald G., and Tinker, Miles A., "The Influence of Size of Type on Speed of Reading in the Primary Grades," *Sight Saving Review,* 23 (Spring, 1953) 28–33.

55. Morton, J. "The Effects of Context on the Visual Duration Threshold of Words." *British Journal of Psychology,* 55 (1964) 165–180. Vol. 6, pp. 81–84, New York: Scholastic Magazines, 1961.

56. Murphy, Helen A., "Mutual Aid in Learning in the Primary Grades," *Changing Concepts of Reading Instruction,* ed. by J. Allen Figurel, International Reading Association Conference Proceedings,

57. Newport, John F. "The Joplin Plan: The Score." *The Reading Teacher,* 21 (November, 1967) 158–162.

58. Olson, Arthur V. "An Analysis of the Vocabulary of Seven Primary Reading Series." *Elementary English,* 42 (March, 1965) 261–264.

59. Olson, Willard C., and Hughes, Byron O., "The Concept of Organ-

ismic Age," *Journal of Educational Research,* 35 (March 1942) 525–527.

60. Paterson, Donald G., and Tinker, Miles A., *How to Make Type Readable,* New York: Harper & Row, Publishers, 1940.

61. Reeve, Olive R., "The Vocabulary of Seven Primary Reading Series," *Elementary English,* 35 (April 1958) 237–239.

62. Robinson, Helen M., "The Role of Auxiliary Services in the Reading Program," *The Reading Teacher,* 14 (March 1961) 226–231.

63. Ruddell, R. B. "The Effect of Oral and Written Patterns of Language Structure on Reading Comprehension," *The Reading Teacher,* 18 (January, 1965) 270–275.

64. Russell, David H., *Children Learn to Read,* Boston: Ginn & Company, 1961.

65. Shores, J. Harlan. "Dimensions of Reading Speed and Comprehension." *Elementary English,* 45 (January, 1968) 23–28, 43.

66. Smith, Helen K. "The Development of Effective, Flexible Readers." *Proceedings of the Annual Reading Conference,* University of Chicago Press, Chicago, 1965, 159–168.

67. Smith, Henry P., and Dechant, Emerald V., *Psychology in Teaching Reading,* Englewood Cliffs, N. J.: Prentice-Hall Inc., 1961.

68. Spache, George, "A New Readability Formula for Primary-Grade Reading Materials," *Elementary School Journal,* 53 (March, 1953) 410–413.

69. Spache, George D., "Classroom Reading and the Visually Handicapped Child," *Changing Concepts of Reading Instruction,* ed. by J. Allen Figurel, International Reading Association Conference Proceedings, Vol. 6, pp. 93–97, New York: Scholastic Magazines, 1961.

70. Strickland, Ruth G., "Interrelationships of Language and Reading," *Changing Concepts of Reading Instruction,* ed. by J. Allen Figurel, International Association Conference Proceedings, Vol. 6, pp. 262–265, New York: Scholastic Magazines, 1961.

71. Taylor, Stanford E., *Speed Reading . . . vs. Improved Reading Efficiency,* Huntington, N. Y.: Educational Developmental Laboratories, 1962.

72. Taylor, Stanford E., and Frackenpohl, Helen, *EDL Skimmer,* Huntington, N. Y.: Educational Developmental Laboratories, 1961.

73. Taylor, Stanford E., and Frackenpohl, Helen, *Teacher's Guide: Tach-X Flash-X.* Huntington, N. Y.: Educational Developmental Laboratories, 1960.

74. Taylor, Stanford E., and Frackenpohl, Helen, *Teacher's Guide: Controlled Reader,* Huntington, N. Y.: Educational Developmental Laboratories, 1960.

75. Taylor, W. L. *"Application of Cloze and Entropy Measures to the Study of Contextual Constraint In Samples of Continuous Prose."* Unpublished doctoral dissertation, University of Illinois, 1954.

76. Tinker, M. A., "The Effect of Illumination Intensities Upon Speed of Perception and Upon Fatigue in Reading," *Journal of Educational Psychology,* 30 (November, 1939) 561–571.

77. Tinker, M. A., "The Effect of Typographical Variations Upon Eye Movement in Reading," *Journal of Educational Research,* 49 (November, 1955) 171–184.

78. Tinker, Miles A., "Print for Children's Textbooks," *Education,* 80 (September, 1959) 37–40.

79. Tinker, Miles A. "Devices to Improve Speed of Reading." *The Reading Teacher,* 20 (April, 1967) 605–609.

80. Vite, Irene W., "Grouping Practices in Individualized Reading," *Elementary English,* 38 (February 1961) 91–98.

81. Vite, Irene W. "Individualized Reading—the Scoreboard on Control Studies." *Education.* 1961, 81, 285–290.

82. Vogel, M., and Washburne, G., "An Objective Method of Determining Grade Placement of Children's Reading Material," *The Elementary School Journal,* 28 (January, 1928) 373–381.

83. Washburne, C., and Morphett, M. V., "Grade Placement of Children's Books," *Elementary School Journal,* 38 (January, 1938) 355–364.

84. Weaver, W. W. and A. J. Kingston. "A Factor Analysis of the Cloze Procedure and Other Measures of Reading and Language Ability." *Journal of Communication,* 13 (December, 1963) 252–261.

85. Weintraub, Samuel. "The Effect of Pictures on the Comprehension of a Second Grade Basal Reader." Unpublished doctoral dissertation. University of Illinois, 1960.

86. Weintraub, Samuel. "Illustrations for Beginning Reading." *The Reading Teacher,* 20 (October, 1961) 61–67.

87. Weintraub, Samuel. "The Cloze Procedure." *The Reading Teacher,* 21 (March, 1968) 567–571, 607.

88. Williams, Wilmajean. "Academic Achievement in a Graded School and in a Non-Graded School." *The Elementary School Journal,* 67 (December, 1966) 135–139.

89. Wolfe, Josephine B., "Changing Concepts of Reading Instruction in the Development of Basic Skills," *Changing Concepts of Reading Instruction,* ed. by J. Allen Figurel, International Reading Association Conference Proceedings, Vol. 6, pp. 32–35, New York: Scholastic Magazines, 1961.

90. Yoakam, G. A. "Determining the Readability in Instructional Materials." *Current Problems of Reading Instruction,* Seventh Annual

Conference in Reading, University of Pittsburgh Press, 1951, pp. 47–53.

CHAPTER 10

1. Bailey, Mildred H. "The Utility of Phonic Generalizations in Grades One Through Six." *The Reading Teacher,* 20 (February, 1967) 413–418.

2. Bagford, Jack. *Phonics: Its Role in Teaching Reading.* Sernoll, Inc., Iowa City, 1967, pp. 47–58.

3. Barnhart, Clarence L. "A Reaction to Sister Mary Edward Dolan's Linguistics in Teaching Reading." *Reading Research Quarterly,* 2 (Spring, 1967) 117–122.

4. Bartkowiak, Deanna. "Linguistics and Reading: Four Views." *Elementary English,* 44 (April, 1967) 386–391.

5. Betts, Emmett Albert, "Issues in Teaching Reading," *Controversial Issues in Reading,* Tenth Annual Reading Conference, Lehigh University (April 1961), pp. 33–41.

6. Bloomer, Richard H., "Reading Methodology: Some Alternative Organizational Principles," *The Reading Teacher,* 14 (January 1961) 167–171.

7. Bloomfield, L. "Linguistics and Reading." *Elementary English,* 19 (1942) 125–130, 183–186.

8. Bloomfield, Leonard & Barnhart, Clarence L. *Let's Read: A Linguistic Approach.* Detroit: Wayne State University Press. 1961.

9. Botel, Morton. "Strategies for Teaching Sound—Letter Relationships." *Vistas in Reading,* International Reading Association, Newark, 1967, pp. 156–159.

10. Breen, L. C., "Vocabulary Development by Teaching Prefixes, Suffixes and Root Derivatives," *The Reading Teacher,* 14 (November 1960) 93–97.

11. Burmeister, Lou E. "Vowel Pairs." *The Reading Teacher,* 5 (February, 1968) 445–452.

12. Coleman, E. B. "Experimental Studies of Readability." *Elementary English,* 45 (February, 1968) 166–178.

13. Daniels, J. C., and Diack, H. *Royal Road Readers.* Chatto and Windus, London, 1954.

14. Daniels, J. C., and Diack, H. "The Phonic Word Method." *Reading Teacher,* 13 (1959) 14–21.

15. Daniels, J. C., and Diack, Hunter. *Progress in Reading in the Infant School.* Institute of Education, University of Nottingham, 1960.

16. Davis, Irene P., "The Speech Aspects of Reading Readiness," *The National Elementary Principal,* 17 (July 1938) 282–288.

17. Edwards, Thomas J. "Teaching Reading: A Critique," pp. 349–362 in Money, John, *ed. The Disabled Reader.* Johns Hopkins Press, Baltimore, 1966.

18. Emans, Robert. "When Two Vowels Go Walking and Other Such Things." *The Reading Teacher,* 21 (December, 1967) 262–269.

19. Fries, Charles C. *Linguistics and Reading.* Holt, Rinehart & Winston, New York, 1963.

20. Gibson, E. J., Bishop, C. H., Schiff, W., and Smith, J., "Comparisons of Meaningfulness and Pronuncability as Grouping Principles in the Perception and Retention of Verbal Material," *Journal of Experimental Psychology,* 67 (1964), pp. 173–182.

21. Gibson, E. J., Osser, H., and Pick, A., "A Study of the Development of Grapheme-Phoneme Correspondence," *Journal of Verbal Learning and Verbal Behavior,* 2 (1963), pp. 142–146.

22. Gibson, E. J., Pick, A., Osser, H., and Hammond, M., "The Role of Grapheme-Phoneme Correspondence in the Perception of Words," *American Journal of Psychology,* 75 (1962), pp. 554–570.

23. Hanna, R. R., and Moore, T. Jr. "Spelling—From Spoken Word to Written Symbol." *Elementary School Journal,* 53 (1953) 329–337.

24. Hanson, Irene W. "First Grade Children Work With Variant Word Endings." *The Reading Teacher,* 19 (April, 1966) 505–507, 511.

25. Harris, Albert J., *How to Increase Reading Ability,* New York: David McKay Co., Inc., 1956.

26. Hay, Julie, and Wingo, Charles E., *Reading with Phonics,* Chicago: J. B. Lippincott Co., 1954.

27. Hildreth, Gertrude, *Teaching Reading,* New York: Holt, Rinehart & Winston, Inc., 1958.

28. Herr, Selma E. *Learning Activities for Reading.* Wm. C. Brown, Publishers, Dubuque, 1961, p. 88.

29. Ives, Sumner. "Some Notes on Syntax and Meaning." *The Reading Teacher,* 18 (December, 1964) 179–183, 222.

30. Joos, Loyal W. "Linguistics for the Dyslexic," pp. 83–92, in *The Disabled Reader, ed.* by John Money, Johns Hopkins Press, Baltimore, 1966.

31. Keislar, Evan. "Conference on Perceptual and Linguistic Aspects of Reading." *The Reading Teacher,* 18 (October, 1964) 43–49.

32. Lefevre, Carl A. "A Comprehensive Linguistic Approach to Reading." *Elementary English,* 43 (October, 1956) 561–659.

33. Lefevre, Carl A. "Reading Our Language Patterns: A Linguistic View—Contributions to a Theory of Reading," *Challenge and Experiment in Reading,* International Reading Association Conference Proceedings, 7 (1962) 66–70.

34. Lefevre, Carl A. *Linguistics and the Teaching of Reading.* McGraw-Hill Book Company, New York, 1964.
35. Levin, Harry. "Reading Research: What, Why, and for Whom." *Elementary English,* 43 (February, 1966) 138–147.
36. Levin, H., and Watson, J., "The Learning of Variable Grapheme-to-Phoneme Correspondences," in Levin, H. *et al. A Basic Research Program on Reading.* Final Report, Coop. Res. Project No. 639.
37. McKee, Paul. *Reading: A Program for the Elementary School.* Houghton Mifflin Company, Boston, 1966.
38. Newburg, Judson E. *Linguistics and the School Curriculum.* Science Research Associates, Inc. Chicago.
39. Poole, Irene, "Genetic Development of Articulation of Consonant Sounds in Speech," *The Elementary English Review,* 11 (June 1934) 159–161.
40. Pooley, Robert C. "Introduction," p. 6 in Bloomfield, Leonard and Barnhart, Clarence L. *Let's Read.* Wayne State University Press, Detroit, 1961.
41. Popp, Helen M. "Visual Discrimination of Alphabet Letters." *The Reading Teacher,* 17 (January, 1964) 221–225.
42. Soffietti, J. P. "Why Children Fail to Read: A Linguistic Analysis." *The Harvard Educational Review,* 25 (Spring, 1955) 63–84.
43. Stauffer, R. G., "A Study of Prefixes in the Thorndike List to Establish a List of Prefixes That Should Be Taught in the Elementary School," *Journal of Educational Research,* 35 (February 1942) 453–458.
44. Stone, David R. "A Sound-Symbol Frequency Count." *The Reading Teacher,* 19 (April, 1966) 498–504.
45. Van Riper, Charles, and Butler, Katherine G., *Speech in the Elementary Classroom,* New York: Harper & Row, Publishers, 1955.
46. Weber, R. *A Linguistic Analysis of First Grade Reading Errors,* 1966, mimeo., reported in: Williams, Joanna P., and Levin, Harry. "Word Perception: Psychological Bases." *Education,* 87 (May, 1967) 515–518.

CHAPTER 11

1. Bagford, Jack. *Phonics: Its Role in Teaching Reading.* Sernoll, Inc., Iowa City, 1967.
2. Bailey, Mildred Hart. "The Utility of Phonic Generalizations in Grades One Through Six." *The Reading Teacher,* 20 (February, 1967) 413–418.
3. Burmeister, Lou E. "Usefulness of Phonic Generalizations." *The Reading Teacher,* 21 (January, 1968) 349–360.

4. Burmeister, Lou E. "Vowel Pairs." *Reading Teacher* 5 (February, 1968) 445–452.
5. DeBoer, John J., and Dallmann, Martha. *The Teaching of Reading.* (New York: Holt, Rinehart and Winston, Inc., 1960), p. 105.
6. Emans, Robert. "When Two Vowels Go Walking and Other Such Things." *The Reading Teacher,* 21 (December, 1967) 262–269.
7. Fry, Edward. "A Frequency Approach to Phonics." *Elementary English,* 51 (November, 1964) 759–765.
8. Glass, Gerald G. "The Strange World of Syllabication." *The Elementary School Journal* (May, 1967) 403–405.
9. Rudd, Josephine. *Word Attack Manual.* (Cambridge, Massachusetts: Educators Publishing Service, 1961) p. 119.
10. Sabaroff, Rose. "Breaking the Code: What Method? Introducing an Integrated Linguistic Approach to Beginning Reading." *The Elementary School Journal,* 67 (November, 1966) 95–102.
11. Schell, Leo M. "Teaching Structural Analysis." *The Reading Teacher,* 21 (November, 1967) 133–137.

CHAPTER 12

1. Bruner, Jerome S. "Going Beyond the Information Given." *Contemporary Approaches to Cognition.* Harvard University Press, Cambridge, 1957.
2. Bugelski, B. R. *The Psychology of Learning Applied to Teaching.* Bobbs-Merrill Company, Inc., Indianapolis, 1964.
3. Bulletin of the National Association of Secondary-School Principals, "Teaching Essential Reading Skills," Part II of "Improving Reading Instruction in the Secondary School," 34 (February 1950) 39–130.
4. Carroll, John B. "Words, Meanings and Concepts." *Harvard Educational Review,* 34 (Spring, 1964) 178–202.
5. Cassirer, E., *The Philosophy of Symbolic Forms,* New Haven: Yale University Press, Vol. III, 1957.
6. Cook, Luella B., "Language Factors Involved in Interpretation," *The Reading Teacher,* 12 (February 1959) 152–157.
7. Dawson, M. A., and Bamman, Henry A., *Fundamentals of Basic Reading Instruction,* New York: David McKay Company, Inc., 1959.
8. Durrell, Donald D., *Improving Reading Instruction,* New York: Harcourt, Brace & World, Inc., 1956.
8a. Durrell, Donald D., Murphy, Helen A., Spencer, Doris U., and Catterson, Jane H. *Word-Analysis Practice* (New York: Harcourt, Brace & World, Inc., 1961).
9. Embler, Weller, "Metaphor in Everyday Speech," *ETC.: A Review of General Semantics,* 16 (Spring 1959) 323–342.

10. Eson, Morris E. *Psychological Foundations of Education.* Holt, Rinehart & Winston, Inc., New York, 1964.

11. Furness, Edna Lue, "Pupils, Pedagogues, and Punctuation," *Elementary English,* 37 (March 1960) 184–189.

12. Groesbeck, Hulda Gwendolyn, "The Comprehension of Figurative Language By Elementary Children: A Study in Transfer," Unpublished Doctoral Dissertation, University of Oklahoma, Norman, Oklahoma, 1961.

13. Hanfmann, Eugenia, Rickers-Ovsiankina, Maria, and Goldstein, Kurt. "Case Lanuti: Extreme Concretization of Behavior Due to Damage of the Brain's Cortex." *Psychological Monographs,* Volume 57, No. 264, 1944.

14. Horn, T. D., "What's New in Words These Days?" *Education,* 79 (December 1958) 203–205.

15. Karlin, Robert. "Research Results and Classroom Practices." *The Reading Teacher,* 21 (December, 1967) 211–226.

16. McCullough, C. M., "Context Aids in Reading," *The Reading Teacher,* 11 (April 1958) 225–229.

17. McDonald, Frederick J., *Educational Psychology,* San Francisco: Wadsworth Publishing Company, Inc., 1959.

18. McKee, Paul, *The Teaching of Reading in the Elementary School,* Boston: Houghton Mifflin Company, 1948.

19. Radke, Frieda, *Living Words,* New York: The Odyssey Press, 1940.

20. Sawrey, James M., and Telford, Charles W. *Educational Psychology,* Allyn and Bacon, Inc., Boston, 1964.

21. Scheerer, Martin, "Cognitive Theory," *Handbook of Social Psychology,* Vol. I, ed. by Gardner Lindzey, Cambridge: Addison-Wesley Publishing Company, 1954, pp. 91–142.

22. Scheerer, Martin, "Spheres of Meaning: An Analysis of Stages from Perception to Abstract Thinking," *Journal of Individual Psychology,* 15 (May 1959) 50–61.

23. Severson, Eileen. "The Teaching of Reading-Study Skills in Biology." *American Biology Teacher,* 25 (1963) 203–204.

24. Shaw, Philip, "Rhetorical Guides to Reading Comprehension," *The Reading Teacher,* 11 (April 1958) 239–243.

25. Travers, John F. "A Return to Sanity in Learning Theory." *Catholic Educational Review,* 61 (January, 1963) 16–25.

26. Travers, John F. *Learning: Analysis and Application.* David McKay Company, Inc., New York, 1965.

27. Vanderlinde, L. "Does the Study of Quantitative Vocabulary Improve Problem Solving?" *Elementary School Journal,* 65 (1964) 143–152.

28. Warren, James E., Jr., "The Heart of Language," *Education,* 80 (January 1960) 259–263.

CHAPTER 13

1. Anderson, Lorena; Dechant, Emerald; Gullion, Floyd Thomas; and Taylor, Stanford E., *Listen & Read* (Workbook), Huntington, N. Y.: Educational Developmental Laboratories, 1961.
2. Artley, A. S. "Implementing a Critical Reading Program on the Primary Level." *Reading and Inquiry.* International Reading Association Proceedings, 10 (1965), 111.
3. Berg, Paul C., and Rentel, Victor M. "Improving Study Skills." *Journal of Reading,* 9 (April, 1966) 343–348.
4. Bond, Guy L., and Tinker, Miles A., *Reading Difficulties: Their Diagnosis and Correction,* New York: Appleton-Century-Crofts, Inc., 1957.
5. Bond, G. L., and Wagner, E. B., *Teaching the Child to Read,* revised edition, New York: The Macmillan Company, 1950.
6. Call, R. J., and Wiggin, N. A. "Reading and Mathematics." *The Mathematics Teacher,* 59 (1966) 149–157.
7. Davis, F. B., "Fundamental Factors of Comprehension in Reading," *Psychometrika,* 9 (September 1944) 185–197.
8. Davis, F. B., "The Teaching of Comprehension in Reading in the Secondary School," *Education,* 76 (May 1956) 541–544.
9. Dawson, Mildred A., and Bamman, Henry A., *Fundamentals of Basic Reading Instruction,* New York: David McKay Company, 1959.
10. DeBoer, John J., and Dallmann, Martha, *The Teaching of Reading,* New York: Holt, Rinehart & Winston, Inc., 1960.
11. Deighton, Lee C., "Developing Vocabulary: Another Look at the Problem," *The English Journal,* 49 (February 1960) 82–88.
12. Donald, Sister M. "The SQ3R Method in Grade Seven." *Journal of Reading,* 11 (October, 1967) 33–35, 43.
13. Eisner, Sigmund and Rohde, Kermit, "Note Making During or After the Lecture," *Journal of Educational Psychology,* 50 (December 1959) 301–304.
14. Eller, William and Wolf, Judith G. "Developing Critical Reading Abilities." *Journal of Reading* (December, 1966).
15. Gray, W. S., "Is Your Reading Program a Good One?" University of Kansas Conference of Reading, International Reading Association (October 12, 1957).
16. Gray, Lillian, and Reese, Dora, *Teaching Children to Read,* New York: The Ronald Press Company, 1957.
17. Guszak, Frank J. "Teacher Questioning and Reading." *The Reading Teacher,* 21 (December, 1967) 227–234.
18. Harvison, Alan R. "Critical Reading for Elementary Pupils." *The Reading Teacher,* 21 (December, 1967) 244–247, 252.

19. Huelsman, Charles B. Jr., "Promoting Growth in Ability to Interpret When Reading Critically: In Grades Seven to Ten," *Promoting Growth Toward Maturity in Interpreting What Is Read,* Supplementary Educational Monographs, No. 74, pp. 149–153, Chicago: University of Chicago Press, 1951.

20. Jenkinson, Marion D. "Laying the Foundation for a Critical Reading Program in the Primary Grades." *Reading and Inquiry.* International Reading Association Proceedings, 1965, 10, p. 112.

21. Johnson, Harry W. "Another Study Method." *Journal of Developmental Reading,* 7 (Summer, 1964) 269–282.

22. Kingston, Albert J. Jr., "A Conceptual Model of Reading Comprehension." *Phases of College & Other Adult Reading Programs,* Tenth Yearbook of the National Reading Conference, 1961, pp. 100–107.

23. Kottmeyer, William, "Classroom Activities in Critical Reading," *School Review,* 52 (November 1944) 557–564.

24. Mahoney, Sally. "Basic Study Skills and Tools." *Elementary English,* 42 (December, 1965) 905–915.

25. Maloney, Martin, "The Writer's Itch (III): How to Write Obvious Lies," *Etc. A Review of General Semantics,* 17 (Winter 1959–60) 209–216.

26. Olson, Arthur V. "Teaching Critical Reading Skills." *Reading Improvement,* 4 (Fall, 1966) 1–4, 19.

27. Pauk, Walter. "On Scholarship: Advice to High School Students." *The Reading Teacher,* 7 (November, 1963) 73–78.

28. Perry, William G. Jr., and Whitlock, Charles P., "The Right to Read Rapidly," *Atlantic Monthly,* 190 (November 1952) 88–96.

29. Petitt, Dorothy. "Reading Literature: An Act of Creation." *Vistas in Reading.* International Reading Association, Newark, 1967, pp. 176–181.

30. Popp, Helen M., and Porter, Douglas, "Programming Verbal Skills for Primary Grades," *Audio-Visual Communication Review,* 8 (July–August 1960) 165–175.

31. Robinson, Alan, "A Cluster of Skills: Especially for Junior High School," *Reading Teacher,* 15 (September 1961) 25–28.

32. Robinson, Francis P., *Effective Study,* New York: Harper & Row, Publishers, 1946.

33. Robinson, Francis P., *Effective Study: Revised Edition,* New York: Harper & Row, Publishers, 1961.

34. Rushdoony, Haig A. "Achievement in Map Reading: An Experimental Study." *Elementary School Journal* (November, 1963).

35. Russell, D. H. "Research on the Process of Thinking with Some Implications to Reading." *Elementary English,* 42 (1965) 375.

36. Sartain, Harry W., "How Children and Youth Learn to Study," *Educational Leadership,* 16 (December 1958) 155–160.

37. Seashore, Robert H., "How Many Words Do Children Know?" *The Packet,* Service Bulletin for Elementary Teachers, Boston: D. C. Heath & Company, 2 (November 1947) 3–17.

38. Shibles, Burleigh, "How Many Words Does a First Grade Child Know?" *Elementary English,* 41 (January 1959) 42–47.

39. Smith, Madorah E., "An Investigation of the Development of the Sentence and the Extent of Vocabulary in Young Children," *University of Iowa Studies in Child Welfare,* 3 (No. 5, 1926) 1–92.

40. Smith, Nila B. "Patterns of Writing in Different Subject Areas: Part I." *Journal of Reading,* 8 (1964) 31–37; Part II, *Journal of Reading,* 8 (1964) 97–102.

41. Smith, Nila B. "Reading for Depth." *Reading and Inquiry.* International Reading Association Proceedings, 1965, 10, p. 118.

42. Spache, G. D., and Berg, P. C., *Better Reading for College Students,* New York: The Macmillan Company, 1955.

43. Stauffer, R. G. "A Vocabulary Study Comparing Reading, Arithmetic, Health, and Science Tests." *The Reading Teacher,* 20 (1966) 141–147.

44. Stone, D. R., "Teaching Three Functions of Study-Reading," *Journal of Developmental Reading,* 3 (Winter 1960) 137–141.

45. Strang, R., and Bracken, D. K., *Making Better Readers,* Boston: D. C. Heath & Company, 1957.

46. Strang, Ruth, McCullough, Constance M., and Traxler, Arthur E., *The Improvement of Reading,* New York: McGraw-Hill Book Company, Inc., 1961.

47. Thompson, A. Gary. "Map Skills Development." *Catholic School Journal,* 68 (January, 1968) 46–48.

48. Tremonti, Joseph B., and Algero, Celestine. "Reading and Study Habits in Content Areas." *Reading Improvement,* 4 (Spring, 1967) 54–57.

49. Vineyard, Edwin E., and Massey, Harold W., "The Interrelationship of Certain Linguistic Skills and Their Relationship with Scholastic Achievement When Intelligence is Ruled Constant," *Journal of Educational Psychology,* 48 (May 1957) 279–286.

50. Weintraub, Samuel. "Reading Graphs, Charts and Diagrams." *The Reading Teacher,* 20 (January, 1967) 345–349.

CHAPTER 14

1. Baldwin, Maurine. "Effective Reading as Springboard for a High School Reading Program." *Developing the Mature Reader,* 1966 Proceedings, Portland Oregon Council of International Reading Association, 1966.

2. Balow, Bruce. "The Long-Term Effect of Remedial Reading Instruction," *The Reading Teacher*, 18 (April, 1965) 581–586.

3. Bannatyne, Alex D. "The Color Phonics System," pp. 193–214 in Money, John, ed. *The Disabled Readers*. Johns Hopkins Press, Baltimore, 1966.

4. Barbe, Walter B. "Differentiated Guidance for the Gifted." *Education*, 74 (January, 1954) 306–311.

5. Barbe, Walter. "Identification of Gifted Children." *Education*, 88 (September–October, 1967) 11–14.

6. Betts, Emmett A. *Foundations of Reading Instruction*. American Book Company, New York, 1957.

7. Black, Millard H. "Characteristics of the Culturally Disadvantaged Child," *The Reading Teacher*, 18 (March, 1965) 465–470.

7a. Boder, Elena. "Development Dyslexia: A Diagnostic Screening Procedure Based on Three Characteristic Patterns of Reading and Spelling," *Claremont Reading Conference*, 1968, pp. 173–187.

8. Bond, Guy L. and Tinker, Miles A. *Reading Difficulties: Their Diagnosis and Correction*. Appleton-Century-Crofts, New York, 1967.

9. Brownell, W. A. "The Evaluation of Learning Under Dissimilar Systems of Instruction. *California Journal of Educational Research*, 17 (March, 1966), 80–90.

10. Bruecker, Leo J. "Introduction," *Educational Diagnosis*. Thirty-fourth Yearbook of the National Society for the Study of Education, Public School Publishing Company, Bloomington, 1935, pp. 1–14.

11. Bryant, N. Dale. "Learning Disabilities in Reading," *Reading as Intellectual Activity*. International Reading Association Conference Proceedings, Scholastic Magazines, New York, 1963, pp. 142–146.

12. Bryant, N. Dale. "Some Principles of Remedial Instruction for Dyslexia." *The Reading Teacher*, 18 (April, 1965) 567–572.

13. Buerger, Theodore A. "A Follow-Up of Remedial Reading Instruction." *The Reading Teacher*, 21 (January, 1968) 329–334.

14. Burt, Cyril. "Critical Notice: *Creativity and Intelligence* by J. W. Getzels and P. W. Jackson," *British Journal of Educational Psychology*, 32 (November, 1962).

15. Chall, Jeanne. "How They Learn and Why They Fail." *Improvement of Reading Through Classroom Practice*. International Reading Association Conference Proceedings, Newark, 1964, pp. 147–148.

16. Cohen, S. Allen. "Some Conclusions About Teaching Reading to Disadvantaged Children." *The Reading Teacher*, 20 (February, 1967) 433–435.

16a. Critchley, Macdonald. *Developmental Dyslexia*. William Heinemen Medical Books, Ltd., White Friars Press, London, pp. 81–89.

17. Cronbach, Lee J. "The Counselor's Problems from the Perspective

of Communication Theory," *New Perspectives in Counseling,* University of Minnesota Press, 1955.

18. Dechant, Emerald. *Diagnosis and Remediation of Reading Disability.* Parker Publishing Company, West Nyack, New York, 1968.

19. Dolch, E. W. "School Research in Reading." *Elementary English,* 33 (February, 1956) pp. 76–80.

20. Durrell, Donald D. *The Improvement of Basic Reading Abilities.* World Book Company, Yonkers, New York, 1940.

21. Durrell, Donald D. *Improving Reading Instruction.* World Book Company, New York, 1956.

22. Eisenberg, Leon. "Epidemiology of Reading Retardation," p. 19, in *The Disabled Reader,* ed. by John Money, Johns Hopkins Press, Baltimore, 1966.

23. Elder, R. "Behavioral Criteria and Pupil Achievement." *Michigan Educational Journal,* 40 (1963) 502, 536.

24. Ekwall, E. E. "The Use of WISC Subtest Profiles in the Diagnosis of Reading Difficulties." Unpublished Doctoral Dissertation, University of Arizona, 1966.

25. Ellingson, C. C. "The Obsolescent Child." *Journal of Learning Disabilities,* 1 (February, 1968) 34–37.

26. Emans, Robert. "Teacher Evaluations of Reading Skills and Individualized Reading." *Elementary English,* 42 (March, 1965) 258–260.

27. Fernald, Grace M. *Remedial Techniques in Basic School Subjects.* McGraw-Hill Book Company, Inc., New York, 1966.

28. Frierson, Edward C. "The Governor's Honors Program at Georgia." *The Gifted Child Quarterly,* 9 (No. 2) 77–78.

29. Frostig, Marianne. "Corrective Reading in the Classroom." *The Reading Teacher,* 18 (April, 1965) 573–580.

30. Guilford, J. P. "Creativity." *American Psychologist,* 5 (September, 1950) 444–454.

31. Harris, Albert J. *How to Increase Reading Ability.* 3rd Edition, David McKay Company, Inc., New York, 1961.

32. Hegge, T.; Kirk, Samuel; and Kirk, Winifred. *Remedial Reading Drills.* George Wahr, Publisher, Ann Arbor, 1955.

33. Heilman, Arthur W. "Moving Faster Toward Outstanding Instructional Programs." *Vistas in Reading,* Proceedings of the Eleventh Annual Convention, International Reading Association, Newark, 1967, pp. 273–276.

34. Hildreth, Gertrude. *Introduction to the Gifted.* McGraw-Hill Book Company, New York, 1966.

34a. Johnson, Marjorie S., and Kress, Roy A. (eds.), *Corrective Reading in the Elementary Classroom.* International Reading Association, Newark, N.J., 1967.

35. Keough, Jack, *Practical Programs for the Gifted.* Science Research Associates, Chicago, 1960.
36. Kincaid, Gerald L. "A Title I Short Course for Reading Teachers." *The Reading Teacher,* 20 (January, 1967) pp. 307–312.
37. King, Fred M. "Student Attitudes Toward Acceleration." *Education,* 88 (September–October, 1967) 73–77.
38. Kirk, Samuel A. "Characteristics of Slow Learners and Needed Adjustments in Reading," *Classroom Techniques in Improving Reading,* Supplementary Educational Monographs, No. 69, University of Chicago Press, Chicago, 1949, pp. 172–176.
39. Klausner, Dorothy C. "Screening and Development of the Remedial Reading Teacher." *Journal of Reading,* 10 (May, 1967) 552–559.
40. Krippner, Stanley. "Characteristics of Gifted Children." *Education,* 88 (September–October, 1967) 15–21.
41. Kuhn, Virginice, Sr. M. "A Comparative Study of Teacher Judgment and the Metropolitan Reading Readiness Test in Predicting Success in First Grade Reading." *Research Abstracts.* Cardinal Stritch College, Milwaukee, Vol. 8, 1966.
42. Mackintosh, Helen K.; Gore, Lillian; Lewis, Gertrude M. *Educating Disadvantaged Children in the Primary Grades.* U. S. Department of Health, Education, and Welfare. U. S. Office of Education, 1965.
43. McGee, Robert T., and McClintic, Jean M. "Early Instruction in Readiness: Who Speaks for the Children?" *The Reading Teacher,* 20 (November, 1966) 122–124.
44. McLeod, John. "Reading Expectancy from Disabled Learners." *Journal of Learning Disabilities,* 1 (February, 1968) 7–15.
45. Money, John, ed. *Reading Disability.* Johns Hopkins Press, Baltimore, 1962.
46. Monroe, Marion. *Children Who Cannot Read.* University of Chicago Press, Chicago, 1932.
47. National Education Association. *Schools for the 60's.* McGraw-Hill Book Company, New York, 1963.
48. Neville, Donald. "Learning Characteristics of Poor Readers as Revealed by Results of Individually Administered Intelligence Tests." *Vistas in Reading,* Proceedings of the Eleventh Annual Convention, International Reading Association, Newark, 1967, pp. 554–559.
49. Olson, Arthur V. "Teaching Culturally Disadvantaged Children" *Education,* 87 (March, 1967) 423–425.
50. Otto, Wayne and McMenemy, Richard A. *Corrective and Remedial Teaching of Reading.* Houghton Mifflin Company, Boston, 1966.
51. Plowman, Paul D. "Encouraging the Development of the Talented —In Academic Areas." *Education,* 88 (September–October, 1967) 35–42.
51a. Quadfassel, F. A., and Goodglass, H. "Specific Reading Disability

and Other Specific Disabilities," *Journal of Learning Disabilities,* 1 (October, 1968), pp. 590–600.

52. Rankin, Earl F. Jr., and Tracy, Robert J. "Residual Gain as a Measure of Individual Differences in Reading Improvement," *Journal of Reading,* 8 (March, 1965) pp. 224–233.

53. Tracy, Robert J., and Rankin, Earl F. Jr., "Methods of Computing and Evaluating Residual Gain Scores in the Reading Program," *Journal of Reading,* 10 (March, 1967) pp. 363–371.

54. Rauch, Sidney J. "Ten Guidelines for Teaching the Disadvantaged." *Journal of Reading,* 10 (May, 1967) 536–541.

55. Reich, Riva R. "More Than Remedial Reading." *Elementary English,* 39 (March, 1962) 216.

56. Reid, William R., and Schoer, Lowell A. "Reading Achievement, Social Class and Subtest Pattern on the WISC." *Journal of Educational Research,* 59 (July–August, 1966) 469–472.

57. Riessman, Frank. *The Culturally Deprived Child.* Harper and Row, New York, 1962.

58. Rogers, Carl R. "The Place of the Person in the New World of the Behavioral Sciences." *Personnel and Guidance Journal,* 39 (February, 1961) 442–451.

59. Roswell, Florence. "Psychotherapeutic Principles Applied to Remedial Reading." *Improvement of Reading Through Classroom Practice,* International Reading Association Conference Proceedings, Newark, 1964, pp. 145–47.

60. Sawyer, Rita I. "Does the Wechsler Intelligence Scale for Children Discriminate Between Mildly Disabled and Severely Disabled Readers?" *The Elementary School Journal,* 66 (November, 1965) 97–103.

61. Schiffman, Gilbert. "Early Identification of Reading Disabilities: The Responsibility of the Public School." *Bulletin of the Orton Society,* 14 (1964) 42–44.

62. Sipay, E. A. "A Comparison of Standardized Reading Scores and Functional Reading Levels." *The Reading Teacher,* 17 (January, 1964) 265–268.

63. Smith, D. E. P., and Carrigan, Patricia M. *The Nature of Reading Disability.* Harcourt, Brace and Company, Inc., New York, 1959.

64. Sommerfield, Roy E. "Some Recent Research in College Reading." *Techniques and Procedures in College and Adult Reading Programs,* Sixth Yearbook of the Southwest Reading Conference, Texas Christian University Press, Forth Worth, 1957, p. 24.

65. Strang, Ruth. "Teaching Reading to the Culturally Disadvantaged in Secondary Schools." *Journal of Reading,* 10 (May, 1967) 527–535.

66. Tiegs, Ernest W. "Educational Diagnosis." *Educational Bulletin,* No. 18, California Test Bureau, a Division of McGraw-Hill Book Company.

67. Thorndike, Robert L. "The Measurement of Creativity." *Teachers College Record,* 44 (February, 1963).

68. Warner, Dolores. "The Divided-Day Plan for Reading Organization." *The Reading Teacher,* 20 (February, 1967) 397–399.

69. Whipple, Gertrude and Black, Millard H. *Reading for Children Without—Our Disadvantaged Youth.* International Reading Association, 1966.

70. Wilson, Robert M. *Diagnostic and Remedial Reading.* Charles E. Merrill Books, Inc., Columbus, 1967.

71. Witty, Paul A. "Twenty Years in Education of the Gifted." *Education,* 88 (September–October, 1967) 4–10.

72. Yamamota, K. "Creativity and Intellect." Mimeo. A paper delivered at Minnesota Psychological Association Meeting, 1961.

73. Young, Robert A. "Case Studies in Reading Disability." *American Journal of Orthopsychiatry,* 8 (April, 1938) pp. 230–254.

CHAPTER 15

1. Ausubel, David P., "A New Look at Classroom Discipline," *Phi Delta Kappan,* 43 (October 1961) 25–30.

2. Barton, Allen H., "The Sociology of Reading Research," *Teachers College Record,* 63 (November 1961) 94–101.

3. Bayles, Ernest F. "The Idea of Learning as Development of Insight," *Educational Theory,* 2 (April, 1952) 65–71.

4. Blair, G. M., Jones, R. S., and Simpson, R. H. *Educational Psychology.* The Macmillan Company, New York, 1962.

5. Brunswik, Egon, "Scope and Aspects of the Cognitive Problem," *Contemporary Approaches to Cognition,* pp. 5–31, Cambridge: Harvard University Press, 1957.

6. Bugelski, B. R. *The Psychology of Learning Applied to Teaching.* Bobbs-Merrill Company, Inc., Indianapolis, 1964.

7. Cannon, W. P., *The Wisdom of the Body,* New York: W. W. Norton & Company, 1939.

8. Chall, Jeanne S., "The Influence of Previous Knowledge on Reading Ability," *Educational Research Bulletin,* Ohio State University, 26 (December 10, 1947) 225–230.

9. Combs, Arthur W., and Snygg, Donald, *Individual Behavior,* Revised edition. New York: Harper & Row, Publishers, 1959.

10. Downey, Lawrence W., "Direction Amid Change," *Phi Delta Kappan,* 42 (February 1961) 186–191.

11. Dunlap, K., *Habits: Their Making and Unmaking,* New York: Liveright, 1932.

12. Ellis, W. D. (Ed.) *A Source Book of Gestalt Psychology*. Harcourt, Brace, New York, 1938.

13. Festinger, Leon. "Cognitive Dissonance." *Scientific American,* 207 (1962) 93–102.

14. Festinger, Leon. "The Relation Between Behavior and Cognition." *Contemporary Approaches to Cognition*. Harvard University Press, Cambridge, 1957, pp. 127–150.

15. Goldstein, Kurt, *The Organism,* p. 532ff., New York: American Book Company, 1939.

16. Guthrie, Edwin R. *The Psychology of Learning*. Harper and Brothers, New York, 1952.

17. Hebb, Donald Olding, *A Textbook of Psychology,* p. 276ff., Philadelphia: W. B. Saunders Co., 1958.

18. Hebb, Donald Olding, "The American Revolution," *American Psychologist,* 15 (1960) 735–745.

19. Hilgard, Ernest R., *Theories of Learning,* Second edition, New York: Appleton-Century-Crofts, Inc., 1956.

20. Hilgard, Ernest R. "The Place of Gestalt Psychology and Field Theories in Contemporary Learning Theory." *Theories of Learning and Instruction*. Sixty-third Yearbook of the National Society of the Study of Education. University of Chicago Press, 1964, pp. 54–77.

21. Hunt, J. McV., "Experience and the Development of Motivation: Some Reinterpretations," *Child Development,* 31 (September 1960) 489–504.

22. Immergluck, Ludwig, "Determinism—Freedom in Contemporary Psychology," *American Psychologist,* 19 (April, 1964) 270–281.

23. James, William, *Principles of Psychology,* New York: Holt, Rinehart & Winston, Inc., 1890.

24. Kingsley, Howard L., and Garry, Ralph, *The Nature and Conditions of Learning,* Englewood Cliffs, N. J.: Prentice-Hall Inc., 1957.

25. Koehler, W. *Gestalt Psychology: An Introduction to New Concepts in Modern Psychology*. Liveright Publishing Company, New York, 1947.

26. Koffka, Kurt, *Principles of Gestalt Psychology,* New York: Harcourt, Brace & World, Inc., 1935.

27. Lange, K., *Apperception: A Monograph on Psychology and Pedagogy,* ed. by Charles De Garma, Boston: D. C. Heath & Company, 1902.

28. Langman, Muriel Potter, "The Reading Process: A Descriptive, Interdisciplinary Approach," *Genetic Psychology Monographs,* 62 (August 1960) 1–40.

29. Lashley, K. S., "Persistent Problems in the Evolution of Mind," *Quarterly Review of Biology,* 24 (1949) 28–42.

30. Lindsley, Donald B. "Psychophysiology and Motivation." *Nebraska*

Symposium on Motivation, ed. by Marshall R. Jones. University of Minnesota Press, Lincoln, 1957, 44–105.

31. Logan, Frank A. "Micromolar Behavior Theory and Performance Speed in Education." *Harvard Educational Review,* 33 (Spring, 1963) 178–185.

32. McClelland, David C. "The Psychology of Mental Content Reconsidered." *Psychological Review,* 62 (July, 1955) 297–302.

33. McDonald, Frederick J. *Educational Psychology.* Wadsworth Publishing Company, San Francisco, 1959.

34. Nemoitin, Bernard O. "Relation between Interest and Achievement." *Journal of Applied Psychology,* 16 (no. 1, 1932) 59–73.

35. Nissen, Henry W. "The Nature of the Drive as Innate Determinant of Behavioral Organization." *Nebraska Symposium on Motivation,* ed. by Marshall R. Jones. University of Nebraska Press, Lincoln, 1954, pp. 281–321.

36. Olds, James. "Self-stimulation of the Brain." *Science,* 127 (February 14, 1958) 315–324.

37. Otto, Wayne. "Inhibitory Potential in Good and Poor Achievers." *Journal of Educational Psychology,* 56 (August, 1965) 200–207.

38. Otto, W., and Fredericks, R. C. "Relationship of Reactive Inhibition to Reading Skill Attainment." *Journal of Educational Psychology,* 54 (August, 1963) 227–230.

39. Otto, Wayne. "Reactive Inhibition (The Hullian Construct) and Achievement in Reading." *New Frontiers in College—Adult Reading.* National Reading Conference, Inc., Milwaukee, 1966.

40. Pavlov, I. P. *Conditioned Reflexes.* Oxford University Press, London, 1927.

41. Richter, C. P., and Eckert, J. F., "Mineral Appetite of Parathyroidectomized Rats," *American Journal of the Medical Sciences,* 198 (July 1939) 9–16.

42. Rogers, Carl, *Client Centered Therapy,* New York: Houghton Mifflin Company, 1951.

43. Rogers, Carl R. "Toward a Science of the Person," in *Behaviorism and Phenomenology,* ed. by T. W. Wann, University of Chicago Press, Chicago, 1964, pp. 109–149.

44. Scheerer, Martin, "Cognitive Theory." *Handbook of Social Psychology,* Vol. I, ed. by Gardner Lindzey, pp. 91–142, Cambridge: Addison-Wesley Publishing Company, 1954.

45. Sells, S. B. "An Interactionist Looks At the Environment," *American Psychologist.* 18 (November, 1963) 696–702.

46. Sinnott, Edmund W., *Matter, Mind, and Man,* New York: Harper & Row, Publishers, 1957.

47. Skinner, B. F. "Reinforcement Today." *The American Psychologist,* 13 (March, 1958) 94–99.

48. Smith, Henry P. *Psychology in Teaching*. Prentice-Hall, Inc., Englewood Cliffs, 1954.

49. Smith, B. Othanel, "A Concept of Teaching." *Teachers College Record*, 61 (February 1960) 229–241.

50. Snow, Robert H., "Education Is a Slippery Word," *The Clearing House*, 34 (March 1960) 398–400.

51. Solley, Charles M., and Gardner Murphy, *Development of the Perceptual World*, New York: Basic Books Inc., 1960.

52. Spence, Kenneth W. "Cognitive Versus Stimulus-Response Theories of Learning," *Psychological Review*, 57 (January, 1950) 159–172.

53. Stroud, James B., *Psychology in Education*, New York: David McKay Company, Inc., 1956.

54. Thorndike, E. L. *Animal Intelligence*. The Macmillan Company, New York, 1911.

55. Thorndike, E. L. *Educational Psychology*, Vol. I, *The Original Nature of Man*, Teachers College, Columbia University, 1913.

56. Thorndike, E. L. *Educational Psychology*, Vol. II, *Psychology of Learning*. Teachers College, Columbia University, 1913.

57. Thorndike, Edward L. *Educational Psychology*, Teachers College, Columbia University, 1932.

58. Thorndike, E. L. *Man and His Works*. Harvard University Press, Cambridge, 1943.

59. Tolman, E. C. "A Stimulus-Expectancy Need-Cathexis Psychology," *Science*, 101 (1945) 16–166.

60. Travers, John F. *Learning: Analysis and Application*. David McKay Company, Inc., New York, 1965.

60a. Watson, John B. "Psychology as the Behaviorist Views It." *Psychological Review*, 20 (1913), 158–177.

61. Wheat, H. G., *Foundations of School Learning*, New York: Alfred A. Knopf, Inc., 1955.

62. White, Robert W., *The Abnormal Personality*, New York: The Ronald Press Company, 1956.

63. Williamson, E. G., "The Fusion of Discipline and Counseling in the Educative Process," *Personnel and Guidance Journal*, 34 (October 1955) 74–79.

64. Woodruff, Asahel D., *Basic Concepts of Teaching*, San Francisco: Chandler Publishing Company, 1961.

65. Woodworth, R. S. *Psychology*. Copyright 1921, Henry Holt & Company, New York.

Index

Biological-environmental controversy, preferred to hereditary-environmental, 47
Biology and intellectual development, 45
Bloomer, Richard H., 327
Bloomfield, Leonard, 293, 294, 296
Bond, Guy L., 16, 53, 69, 238, 471–472, 480
Books:
    Benjamin Franklin on reading, 15
    surveying, 423–424
Boston University, 185
Botel, Morton, 33
Botel Reading Inventory, 464
Bradley, Mary A., 258
Braille, 19
Brain:
    agnosia, 508
    association areas of, 72
    cerebral dominance, 77–79, 232–234, 474
    damage of, 46–47, 74–76, 476
    description and operation of, 71–72
    diagram of, 73
    injury to, 45–46, 73, 75–76 (*see also* Aphasia)
    neural adequacy and reading, 71–80
    neurological disorders, 74
    reading and, 53, 74
    wordblindness and, 74–77
Bremer, Neville, 197
Brick, H. G., 79
Brown, Roger, 212
Brueckner, Leo J., 452
Bruner, Jerome S., 217–218, 371
Brunswik, Egon, 553
Brzeinski, Joseph E., 51
Buerger, Theodore A., 511
Bugelski, B. R., 371, 541, 574, 575
"Building" readiness, 163
Burmeister, Lou E., 339, 347
Bush, Bernice, 96
Buswell, Guy T., 4, 19, 21, 147
Butler, Katherine G., 121, 133, 153, 300

Call, R. J., 446
Cannon, Walter P., 533
Capital letters, 304
Carhart (researcher), 123–124
Carrigan, Patricia, 30, 459, 479
Carroll, John B., 147, 364
Cassirer, Ernst, 114
Categorizing, 370–371, 375
Cattell, R. B., 212
CBS, 8
Cerebral dominance (*see* Brain—cerebral dominance)
Cerebral palsied speech, 159
Chall, Jeanne S., 245, 278–279, 486, 553
Charles, Don C., 43
Chicago Institute, 231
Children (*see also* Development of children):
    culturally deprived, 42
        reading readiness and, 42
    with foreign-language background, 42, 152
    individual differences in, 16, 521–522

less privileged, 41–42
master consonant sounds, 132–133
mechanics of grammar and, 147
reaction to symbols and, 27
reading interests of, 92–94
six-year olds' articulatory errors, 300
speech development of (*see* Speech)
speech difficulties of, 133
their nature as readers, 37–107
Children's differences and teaching methods, 236
Child's behavior:
    experimental methods applied to analysis of, 5
    statistical methods applied to analysis of, 5
Choral reading, 29
City College of San Francisco, 224
Claremont Reading Conference, 15
Clark, Ann D., 124
Clark, W. W., 100
Classical conditioning, 205–206
Classroom grouping, 255–260
    ability grouping, 255
    group vs. individualized instruction, 255–260
    individualized reading, 255–256
    Joplin interclass ability grouping plan, 258–259
    mobile groups, 258
    team grouping, 256–257
Classroom organization, eclecticism in, 256–260
Classroom Reading Inventory, 464–465
Clauses, 295
Cleft lip, 158–159
Cleft palate, 158–159
Cluttering, 158
Coding system for learning to read, 203, 222
Cognition, 46, 551, 554 (*see also* Thinking)
Cohen, Alice, 49, 79
Cohen, S. Allen, 496–497
Coleman, E. B., 301
Coleman, Howard M., 57
College students:
    phonic ability of, 224
    rate of reading and, 275
Color and contrast in printing, 285–286
Color and words, 227, 290, 292
Color Phonics System, 507
Comb, Arthur W., 554
Common words for beginning reader, 248
Communication, 111, 123
    nature of, 112–113
    oral, emphasis today on, 125
    reading and, 16, 111, 117
    reading as, 2, 28, 115, 122–123
Compound words (*see* Words—compound)
Comprehension skills, 400–448
    basic reading skills, 262–263
    charts, reading of, 427–428, 439–440
    conceptualization and, 364
    context reading (*see* Context)
    details, reading for, 408–409
    diagram reading, 440
    evaluation, reading for (critical reading), 418–422